THE HORSEMAN'S MANUAL

The Horseman's Manual

Lt-Col. C. E. G. Hope

CHARLES SCRIBNER'S SONS

NEW YORK

1 3 5 7 9 11 13 15 17 19 C/P 20 18 16 14 12 10 8 6 4 2
1 3 5 7 9 11 13 15 17 19 C/C 20 18 16 14 12 10 8 6 4 2

Printed in the United States of America
Library of Congress Catalog Card Number 73-9303
ISBN 0-648-13622-8 (cloth)
ISBN 0-684-14612-6 (paper)

To
The Gentleman of the Party – the Horse

Contents

Illustrations

Preface by William Luscombe

(Managing Director, Pelham Books)

We all called him 'Charles'.

As the co-founder and Editor of the magazines *Light Horse* and *Pony*, he was known and loved by followers of the equestrian scene everywhere. Always cheerful, whatever the pressures, and ready to give advice, patiently and with enthusiasm, Charles Hope observed and reported on equestrian events for over thirty years and was still the active Editor of his two magazines at the time of his death.

He finished *The Horseman's Manual* a few weeks before he went into hospital. His last letter to me said, modestly, that this, his seventeenth book, was, he felt, the best he had ever written.

In my view, his claim was entirely true.

The Horseman's Manual is the culmination of many instructional books by Charles Hope. It aims at being a comprehensive textbook on riding theory and practice today, based on personal experience and on the wisdom of the many masters of the subject all of whom were personal friends of the author.

The book starts with an introductory section containing a survey of the development of horsemanship through the ages to the present day. There are chapters on the 'Points of the Horse', conformation, psychology and equipment. Then the training of the rider and the training of the horse are treated in separate sections, with step-by-step instruction in each case for the complete novice up to high school. Other sections include the practical application of teaching to equestrian sports on driving. Here, then, is the complete book for all horselovers.

Charles Hope will be sadly missed.

He will never be forgotten.

THE HORSEMAN'S MANUAL

ONE

Setting the Scene

1 The Development of Horsemanship

It has been suggested that early man rode other, easier animals before he got round to mounting a horse – the ox, perhaps, or, as a child, goats and sheep. As a universal carrier the ass certainly precedes the horse, and, most likely, the camel. The ancient inhabitants of Arabia are known to have ridden the latter long before the horse.

There is a clay figurine, found at Susa in southern Iraq and dated about 3000 B.C., which shows a just recognisable human astride an unrecognisable quadruped. It could be an ass. That gives a visible starting point in time for equitation of a sort, but the idea could well have been borrowed from the wilder lands to the north, the steppes of Central Asia, the plains of Mongolia, which were the cradle of the horse in the Eurasian continent after the Behring contact with America was broken. A combination of unlimited numbers of wild horses and the nomad herdsman with his flocks of domesticated cattle makes horsemanship inevitable.

The moment anybody, at any time, first sits on the back of a horse he has problems. Today there is an instructor at hand to help him solve them, to show him how to sit, how to hold his hands, how to use his legs; and there are all sorts of equipment available. It is hard to imagine a situation in which these problems had to be solved for the first time, but it is not fanciful to suggest that prehistoric man, who was no fool, began to think about them and, within the limitations of his means and requirements, to solve them. A reasonable parallel from more recent times is the case of the American Indian, who had never seen a horse until the Spaniards brought it to America in the sixteenth century. By various means the Indians quickly acquired horses of their own and learned to ride them with no equipment to begin with but a rope.

The earliest document on the breaking in and backing of a horse is a frieze on a Kumis jug, dated the fourth century B.C. at Chertomlyk found in the Ukraine in the last century. It shows a group of men with ropes stalking wild horses on the steppe, shepherding them into a *cul de sac* in the hills, lassoing a horse,

17

playing it on the long rein, mounting it and belting it on at a gallop over the boundless plain, free forward movement. Later the exhausted horse is brought back, the rider dismounts, and with his assistants makes much of the horse, handling its whole body and legs, picking up its feet; then the horse is quietly thrown. Finally a pad is put on its back. A not unfamiliar process today, and one which must have been repeated many times before it was so realistically depicted.

Kikkuli's famous book, *The Training of Horses*, written in the fourteenth century B.C., presumably for the Hittite monarch, Suppliluliumas, to whom it is dedicated, precedes the Chertomlyk jug by 1,000 years, but the horses to be trained to the chariot were probably broken in, in the same way. The programme is a progressive, and tough course of 148 days, which includes selection, conditioning, and work at the walk, amble and gallop over increasing distances. Stable management and feeding is included. The object of the work was the training of chariot horses, but there is no reason to suppose that the horses were not ridden also, although we do not see documentary evidence of a mounted man until the Assyrian records of the ninth century B.C.

It is interesting to note the riding positions and accountrements of these first cavalry men as portrayed on the reliefs from the bronze gates of Shalmaneser III of Assyria (859–824 B.C.). They ride bareback, of course, sometimes with a square cloth, sitting well back on the horses' croups, knees up and legs wrapped round the flanks, heels tucked in just in front of the stifle joints, which is in fact the most comfortable and secure way to ride when you have neither saddle nor stirrups.

The soldiers are either archers or spearmen. The archer is fully occupied handling his composite type bow, so he has a half-section who carries a small shield and handles the reins of both horses. The spearman has a small round shield on his left arm, holding the reins with the left hand, spear wielded in the right hand rather like a hoghunter's stabbing spear. While the archers ride on saddle cloths, the lancers are completely bareback. Their bits are snaffles, with all kinds of murderous devices in the mouthpiece, studs, discs, and spikes on the outside. They have long, sometimes rectangular cheekpieces, attached to divided straps from the bridle cheekpieces, with or without a noseband. The bits were jointed, and the effect of the rein action was to close the cheekpieces, with all their spikes and protuberances on to the sides of the mouth. Equitation was not

18

of a high order: go and stop, and turns and circles were probably the limit of it, with perhaps some rearing and prancing to show off. Two hundred years later, in the reign of Ashurbanipal, the bitting is much the same, but the riders are sitting forward, just behind the withers, with straighter legs. This style of riding continues to the time of Xenophon, and after.

Hippike, Xenophon's book on horsemanship is a high water mark in the study of the art, after which the tide ebbs away to very low levels until the work was rediscovered in the Renaissance. Like the work of his predecessor, Kikkuli, his book is so finished and detailed, that it must be the culmination of a considerable body of thought and discussion and writing. We know of one such author, Simon of Athens, who seems to have flourished round the turn of the fifth and fourth centuries B.C. He was obviously known to Xenophon, who refers to and quotes him with respect in *Hippike*, which was probably written about 360 B.C.

'It is true,' he says, 'that a book on horsemanship has already been written by Simon . . . who dedicated the bronze horse at the Eleusinion in Athens with his own exploits in relief on the pedestal. Still, I shall not strike out of my work all the points in which I chance to agree with him, but shall take much greater pleasure in passing them on to my friends, believing that I speak with the more authority because a famous horseman, such as he, has thought as I do.' In Chapter XI, he cites Simon in support of his remark that 'what the horse does under compulsion is done without understanding'. It is a pity that, apart from a few isolated references such as these, nothing remains of Simon's book but a brief description of the points of the horse.

Xenophon was a man of parts, soldier of fortune, horseman and writer. His most famous work is, of course, the *Anabasis*, the story of how he conducted the Greek mercenaries of Cyrus back to the Black Sea after the latter's defeat and death in the battle of Cunaxa in 401 B.C. As he was only a supernumerary staff officer when he took over command, his feat is all the more remarkable. Exiled by Athens for serving against Artaxerxes, he took service with the Spartans and settled at Scillus in Elis, about 387 B.C., where he wrote several books. Before that he was almost certainly a member of the equestrian *corps d'elite* of the Athenians, and, obviously had considerable experience of horses and cavalry work, as well as the ability to write freely and lucidly. His book on the Cavalry Commander (*Hipparchikos*) was written about 362 B.C. before the Battle of

Mantinea where one of his sons was killed, and *Hippike* shortly after.

This book of twelve short chapters, admirably clear and concise, sets the pattern for all the many books on equitation that have succeeded it. First there is a description of the horse so that one may 'escape being cheated in buying a horse'. Xenophon is not aware of the anatomy of the fore limbs, nor of the shock-absorbing function of the frog, but he insists on good bone and well-muscled upper limbs, broad chest, cresty neck, and small, clean-cut head with large eyes and wide nostrils. He likes high withers and a 'double back', i.e. one broad and well covered with flesh on either side of the spine, a great comfort to a bareback rider. The horse he describes would be well coupled with a short back and strong hindquarters.

The breaking-in of young horses he leaves to the professional trainers, who must have been fairly plentiful, for he considers the cavalryman, for whom he is primarily writing, should not waste his time over a routine job. 'For states lay the duty of cavalry service upon those who are best provided with money and who play the major part in politics, and a young man should see to his own health and horsemanship, or, if he is already a good rider, should practise riding. And a grown man, rather than breaking-in horses had far better pass his time in looking after his estate and friends and political and military affairs.' But he should make it quite clear to the horsebreaker in writing exactly what he is to teach the colt.

However, before being sent to the horsebreaker the colt should be well gentled and taught to associate everything good and pleasant with man and to seek his company. He must also be got used to crowds and strange sights and noises, again rough treatment is to be avoided. It is astounding how all Xenophon's words and thought about the horse ring with sympathy and understanding far ahead of his time, and are combined with shrewd common sense.

When buying a made horse he likes him to be about five years old, not having lost his milk teeth; he must be easily bridled and be a quiet ride; he must be willing to pass or to leave other horses, and must not be nappy or one-sided. The test for this is to try them on turns to right and left; he must be good across country; and above all he must have courage.

There then follow instructions in stable management with emphasis on routine, mounting – without stirrups of course – then riding. Xenophon's riding position is well-known, not sitting as if on a chair but 'like a man standing upright with his legs apart',

an instruction not to be repeated until Piero Santini's interpreta-
tion of the ideas of Caprilli twenty-three centuries later. Actually
such a position is extremely rare, if one is to judge by the art of
the period. Nothing could be sounder, however, than his recom-
mendation that the upper part of the body should be as supple
as possible, or that, once mounted, the horse should be taught
to stand still while the rider adjusts his dress. The Greeks rode
usually in the normal skirted tunic (*chiton*) or in nothing at all.
If dressed for battle he wore a helmet (Xenophon recommends
the Boeotian pattern), cuirasses, a kilt of tassets (overlapping
flaps attached to the waist of the cuirasse), greaves and boots.
Xenophon also recommends that the cloth on which the warrior
sits should be padded; a first step surely towards a saddle, and
it is a wonder that the highly intelligent Greeks never pursued
the matter.

Xenophon talks about signals for movement but unfortunately
never describes them in detail. As he deprecated violent methods
with the whip, it may be safe to assume that he means leg and
voice aids. The aid for the gallop (canter) on the left lead is to
be given when the right foot is in the air. Turns and figures
of eight are used extensively in the training, equally on both
reins. The horse should be checked on the turns, and the rider
should keep upright; after the turn the horse is urged forward
again at greater speed. Turning here means a half-turn of 180
degrees, 'for in active service one turns either in order to pursue
or to retreat'. Practice is also given in direct halts from the
gallop, and turns; in fact the well-trained Greek horse must
have been almost as handy and supple as a polo pony. Of course
we do not know how long it took to bring the horse to a stop
in full gallop. All this was done in a snaffle bit; not unlike a
modern jointed snaffle but a good deal more severe. The mouthpiece was covered with prickles or small spikes, rounded or
pointed according to the degree of severity required. For a
highly-couraged, excitable horse Xenophon recommends a
smooth bit, and the opposite for a slug; but he also adds that
a rough bit must be used with 'lightness of hand'. He deprecates
showy, meretricious performances obtained by misuse of the bit,
whip and spurs. The Greek spur was a small goad without
rowels strapped to the heel.

Jumping lessons for the horse start by leading in hand over
obstacles, with a man behind with a whip to be used only if
he refuses. One such treatment is deemed to be enough. When
the horse leads freely over jumps, mounted work begins, first
over small ones and gradually progressing, using the spur at the

take-off. The rider leans forward when the horse goes forward, back when he stops; in jumping or going uphill the rider should hold on to the mane. Going down a steep slope 'you must lean backwards yourself and hold the horse with the bit, so that neither horse nor rider may be carried headlong down the slope'. Throughout calmness is the watchword, avoiding unnecessary hurt to the horse, and all training is progressive. Reward and punishment, especially the former, is emphasised, and, it is interesting to note, in connection with the handling of the reins that 'you must pull on the horse's mouth, neither too roughly, so that he throws up his head to evade the bit, nor too gently, so that he does not feel it. And when the action of the bit makes him raise his neck, give rein at once.' And, 'when he curvets (or rears?) beautifully you should at once dismount and unbridle him. If you do this, you must know well that he will come to curvet of his own free will.'

There has been great debate as to whether Xenophon taught, or performed, anything approaching modern high school airs. Probably not, but he certainly liked a showy, prancing horse, with his hocks well under him. Not every horse, however, was suitable. 'If you want,' he says, 'to train a horse for parade, for high school, it is certainly not every horse that can develop the necessary qualities.' He suggests one 'naturally endowed with greatheartedness of spirit and strength of body ... with loins supple and short and strong (meaning not the part under the tail, but that between the ribs and the haunches, along the flank) ... able to bring his hindlegs further forward under him'. And he goes on to describe the movement: 'When he has gathered them well in, if you take him up with the bit, he falls back on his hocks and raises his forehand so that his belly and sheath can be seen from the front.' He adds, 'You must give him the bit when he does this, and it will look to the spectators as if he were doing all of his own accord.' What else can this movement be but a levade? There is a monument in Athens to an Athenian knight, Dexileus, who fell in battle near Corinth in 394 B.C., which shows his horse doing just this over a prostrate foeman. And the action of the horses of the famous Parthenon frieze shows a close approximation of it.

No other movements are mentioned, but it might be possible to discern the rudiments of piaffe and passage in the following excerpt: 'If you teach your horse to go with a light hand on the bit, and yet to hold his head well up and to arch his neck, you will be making him do just what the animal himself glories and delights in. A proof that he really delights in it is that when a horse is turned loose and runs off to join the other horses, and especially towards mares, then he holds his head up as high as he can, arches his neck in the most spirited style, lifts his legs with a free action, and raises his tail.'

One must not exaggerate Xenophon's influence on horsemanship. He was a man of his time, working with the means and techniques that were available to him and limited by them. It is not suggested that the strutting and prancing and rearing that he describes to be compared with the ordered, disciplined and methodical airs produced by the training of the Spanish Riding School of Vienna. Lateral movement appears to have been unknown to him; he would surely have mentioned it otherwise. Both he and his contemporaries were primarily interested in producing efficient officers' chargers and troop horses. But he has laid down in lapidary sentences the foundations of horse management and schooling, teaching a psychological approach and humane methods, which are not always followed, even now. For this reason his name comes first in the long line of equestrian writers, and towers above many of them.

Xenophon died in about 355 B.C. at the age of about ninety. His works disappeared, and it was some eighteen centuries before anything constructive on equitation was written again.

2 The Development of Horsemanship — Renaissance to Modern Times

The study of horsemanship flashes into the equestrian scene like a comet, makes its brilliant appearance, in the form of Xenophon's book, then vanishes into the outer darkness suddenly to reappear nearly two thousand years later in Renaissance Italy. Then the analogy breaks down; instead of a mighty flash there starts a gentle stream which quickly expands to a torrent, quickly swollen to a spate which never seems to lessen.

There was no lack of interest in the horse in the intervening centuries, but it centred on the animal's appearance and stable management rather than upon the art of riding. When classical authors like Virgil wrote on rustic or agricultural matters they could not fail to mention the horse. The Romans do not seem to have been great horsemen; when the army wanted cavalry it had to fall back on auxiliaries furnished by the barbarian horsemen. Chariot racing was the great sport of the age. Trick riding was popular in Rome, as it must have been at all times, and we still have the term 'Roman riding' to describe that kind of display.

The Middle Ages produced some works on stable management, veterinary care, and equipment, with only a few scattered references to actual horsemanship. The best known of these medieval writers was Rusius (Lorenzo Rusio), who wrote on the care of the horse and equipment (*Hippiatrica Sive Marescalia*). He died in 1350, but the book, first in manuscript then in print (1486), was current until the seventeenth century.

Thought about equipment and saddlery was slow in application. One must avoid the temptation, enticing though it is, to turn this study into a history of horse equipment, but the accoutrements of the horse do have a bearing on the development of horsemanship so a summary of the important events is relevant. The only instrument which has had a full and detailed treatment from the beginning of recorded history is the bit. The two main concerns of the early horsemen were to make their mounts go, and then to stop them – they still are.

The bit has been coeval with the tamed horse; as soon as there was metal available the bit appeared, in the Bronze Age, say 2000 to 1400 B.C. according to the area. There is a Yorkshire Bronze Age double-jointed snaffle in the British Museum, most modern in appearance and mild, compared with eastern contraptions of about the same period which stopped the horse by pressing spikes and knobs into the sides of the horse's mouth. The true curb bit, with its lever action on a curb chain fitting into the chin groove, was a long time coming. In Europe it seems to appear during the age of chivalry, from about the ninth century A.D. From being long and murderous, with mouthpieces filled with painful ironmongery it gradually reduced in size and severity as ideas about horsemanship grew more sophisticated. In this case it was not the bit that made horsemanship but the reverse.

A true landmark in the development of riding is the saddle. Until a proper bearing surface to protect the back from direct contact with the weight of the rider, in other words a tree, was devised it was impossible for the horse to carry efficiently the increasing burden of warrior and his armour. This development took place in the East, and came to the West via Byzantium in late Roman times. The Column of Marius in Rome of the second century A.D. shows a saddle with a pommel and cantle. These became more exaggerated during the Middle Ages, when the principle military action was the charge with couched lance, to keep the jousting knight in his saddle, and subsequently were reduced with the demise of the armoured knight and the beginnings of equitation for its own sake in the seventeenth century. But it is doubtful whether the age of chivalry, which rested on the power of the mounted man in armour with lance and sword, mace or battle axe, would ever have happened but for the stirrup.

The introduction of the stirrup into the West was the real turning point of equitation, and, it is said, of the feudal system. By giving his followers lands filched from the Church, Charles Martel was able, in the eighth century, to put a strong cavalry force into the field, his followers then being rich enough to buy and maintain the costly horses. But it was the stirrup which made this cavalry efficient, because at last the mounted soldier was secure in the saddle.

Historical and archaeological opinion places the origin of the true stirrup in China in perhaps the sixth century A.D. It spread westwards through Central Asia, Persia and the Middle East and Russia, reaching the Francs sometime in the eighth century.

The idea of supporting the foot of the rider had of course occurred to people earlier than that. Sculptures in India of the second century B.C. show a rider supporting himself with his big toe in a loop from the girth, all right so far as it went, but no good for a cold climate. A Kushan engraved gem of 100 A.D. shows a rider apparently booted, resting his foot on a sort of hook hanging from the saddle. But the real metal stirrup with its platform for the sole of the foot did not appear for another 400 years. The way was then prepared for real equitation, once the English longbow and the cannon and the musket had driven the armoured knight from the battlefield.

The process was a slow one, and European thought, even in the enlightened Renaissance, was a long way from Xenophon when Rusius, already mentioned, could write:

'The nappy horse should be kept locked in a stable for forty days, thereupon to be mounted wearing large spurs and a strong whip; or else the rider will carry an iron bar, three or four feet long and ending in three well-sharpened hooks and if the horse refuses to go forward he will dig one of these hooks into the horse's quarters and draw him forward; alternatively an assistant may apply a heated iron bar under the horse's tail, while the rider drives the spur in with all available strength.'

The book in which this was written only stopped being current in the sixteenth century when Federico Grisone was founding a new school of riding, which was to start an equestrian revolution. His book, *Ordini di Cavalcare*, published in 1550 was the first serious approach to systematic training of the horse since Xenophon, but there the resemblance to the Greek work ends.

Grisone was a pioneer in teaching the use of combined aids, leg and hand, getting a horse on the bit, obtaining collection, reining back, lateral movement, and so on. The methods of obtaining these results had none of the humanity and gentleness of Xenophon. The aim was the complete subjugation of the horse by violent and painful means. For a horse that refused to be mounted Grisone recommended that 'you will hit with a stick between the ears (but be careful of the eyes) and on all parts of the body where it seem best to you, and also threatening him with a rude and terrible voice...' until he gives in through fear, when 'you must also pat and caress him'. The time-honoured principles of punishment and reward are there.

A most potent instrument of coercion and punishment was the bit, still of medieval proportions. A drawing of one of

Grisone's bits shows cheekpieces nearly as long as the medieval ones, with an absolute mouthful of iron. Spurs were still pretty murderous. Extreme collection was certainly achieved, and high school movements were performed, including rearing and the capriole. Whether these latter, as often suggested, were of any use for military purposes is debatable. Grisone and his successors may have thought so, but the execution of them in the hurly-burly of combat must have been extremely difficult. Even with the highly trained horses of the Spanish Riding School of Vienna quite a lengthy process of preparation and winding up is necessary to get a horse into the air for a courbette or capriole and a rearing horse would be extremely vulnerable to a bold pikeman on foot. Indeed, cavalry at any time have never been consistently successful against infantry.

However that may be, Grisone and other Italian riding masters like Cesar Fiaschi of Ferrara and Jean-Baptiste Pignatelli, who was the instructor of the Frenchman, de la Broue, started a vogue of sophisticated, elegant riding in the grand manner, which was immediately followed by the horsemen of the rest of Europe, particularly France. As Vladimir Littauer says, 'The sixteenth century's cultivated approach to horsemanship originated in Italy as a part of that refinement of material living that accompanied the Renaissance.' (*Horseman's Progress.*)

The Baroque age seemed just made for showy but deliberate form of riding, with its high stepping Andalusian stallions, the pirouettes, the levades and all the rest, all performed by wealthy men of rank, superbly dressed and their horses clad in most ornamental accoutrements. Such arts were not for the common man, who had to be content with his ambling palfrey or even mule. One doubts if they ever thought much of riding as an art, though probably their mounts were far happier than the horses of the manège.

At the end of the sixteenth century the focus on horsemanship switched to France. There were writers in England, such as Thomas Blundeville, Gervaise Markham, and John Astley, but the authority from now on is French. The first of these writers and the direct link with the Italian school was Salomon de la Broue whose book, *Le Cavalerie François* appeared in 1594. More than a hundred years later de la Guérinière, deploring the decadence of horsemanship in his day, wrote: '...we can only seek the truth in the principles of those who have left us in writing the fruits of their work and inspiration. Among a large number of authors we have only two, by the unanimous consent of all connoisseurs, whose works are worth considering, those of M. de la Broue and the Duke of Newcastle.' Praise indeed from such a weighty authority.

De la Broue was the first to advocate the use of the snaffle in the preliminary stages of training, and developed the use of direct flexions and of the legs (and/or spurs) to bring the horse to hand. His contemporary, Antoine de Pluvinel, also a pupil of Pignatelli, followed him with his book, *Instruction du Roi*, in 1623. He took an important step forward to the more humane and understanding approach to the training of the horse, insisting on an appeal to the intelligence and goodwill of the horse instead of the use of brute force, and seeking to find the reasons for resistances and evasions, which, he said, came not usually from malice but from misapprehension. And the prevailing severity of bits and spurs was greatly softened.

The second of de la Guérinière's recommendations, William Cavendish, Duke of Newcastle, published his book, *A General System of Horsemanship* in 1657 in French, while he was a refugee on the Continent from the Cromwell government. Not being concerned with mere money, he only had fifty copies printed which he distributed free to sundry noblemen, and then broke up the plates. The work was later printed again in English and translated into French.

The Duke understood the use of the snaffle for softening the mouth and the suppling of the shoulders, which he sought to obtain by work on the circle, a practice opposed by de la Guérinière, who substituted the shoulder-in and kindred movements. He divided the body of the rider into mobile and immobile parts: the former comprised the upper part of the body down to the waist, and the legs from the knees downwards; the latter being the part in between. He objected to the pillars, for the invention of which de la Guérinière credits de Pluvinel, because 'on them one unnecessarily overburdens and torments a horse in order to make him lift his forehand, hoping thereby to put him on his hocks'. De la Guérinière defends them, however, when used to obtain the piaffe.

The real turning point in the study and teaching of equitation comes with François Robichon de la Guérinière, who opened his riding academy in Paris in 1715 and published his great work, *Ecole de Cavalerie*, in, 1733. This book is probably the most complete manual of the horse ever written. It begins with a comprehensive section on the points of the horse, ageing, colours, different breeds, the bridle, bits, bitting, shoeing, saddlery; the second part deals with the training of the horse, and its use in outdoor sports as well as in the manège; a third part covers anatomy (skeleton), veterinary details and breeding.

He castigates the practical horseman – still with us – who dismisses theory as unnecessary. 'Without theory practice is always uncertain . . . theory teaches us to work on sound principles, which instead of opposing nature should be a means of perfecting nature with the help of art. Practice gives us the ability to put into execution what theory teaches us. And to acquire this ability one must *love the horse, be strong and bold, and have great patience*. These are the principal qualities which go to make a true horseman.' (The italics are mine.) And he defends work in the manège because its 'object is to make a horse supple, gentle and obedient and to come back on its haunches'.

He then spends considerable time on the psychology of the horse, describing its physical and mental characteristics and seeking causes for its so-called vices and resistances. He finds them in the varied characters of horses, lack of courage, sluggishness, impetuosity, bad temper, not all of which, he admits are necessarily inherent in the creature but the 'fault of those who have broken them in badly' or 'punished them excessively', or asking of them 'things of which they are not capable'. Another interesting reason, very pertinent in this age, he gives for the various faults he finds in horses is 'riding them too young. It makes them weak in the loins and hocks, and sickens them permanently of the whole process.' The right age, in his view, to start training a horse is six, seven or eight years, 'according to the climate of the place of his birth'.

Contrary to present dressage practice the reins were for the most part held in the left hand only, the right holding the whip. 'One uses separated reins with horses that are not yet accustomed to obey the bridle hand; or with horses that resist and refuse to turn on one hand.' A good hand must be 'light, soft and firm'. The light hand has no contact, the soft hand very light contact, and the firm hand full contact; and de la Guérinière describes very clearly the process of give and take in the handling of the reins, also the combined action of hands and legs. It must be remembered that the basis of all the work described is extreme collection, the horse still controlled by a severe curb bit, an instrument of torture in the wrong hands, of which there are always many in every age. The only slight relaxation is that allowed in hunting.

The short chapter on hunting insists that the manège training is the foundation of the preparation of the hunter, but he is allowed more galloping in a less elevated manner, with the angle of the head in front of the perpendicular. De la Guérinière, by the way, much admired the English hunter. The progressive training for the gallop, however, is well on modern lines. Jumping receives scant attention, but the short paragraph, based directly on de la Broue, is very well in line with modern principles and practice. 'Take a hurdle, about three to four feet wide and ten to twelve feet long; first of all lay it flat on the ground and take the horse over it at the walk and trot and then at the gallop; if it steps on it instead of clearing it, punish him with whip and spur. Then raise the hurdle about a foot, and, as the horse jumps freely, raise it its full height, embellishing it with branches and leaves. This method, which he (de la Broue) says he has often practised, certainly teaches a horse to extend and stretch itself for jumping hedges and ditches; but this lesson, necessary for a war horse and a hunter, should not be used until he turns obediently to either hand, nor until his head is set and his mouth accepts the bit.'

Ecole de Cavalerie sets the tone for all future manège riding and what we now call dressage until the present time, and is acknowledged to be the fountainhead of the riding at the two remaining great high school riding establishments of Europe – Vienna and Saumur (now removed to Fontainebleau). But in the eighteenth century another school of thought (if you can call it that, for its proponents were not much given to thought of that kind), takes the field with that peculiarly English sport of hunting.

The pursuit of game is common to all nations, but the equable climate and open countryside of England, together with a plentiful supply of deer and foxes, were ideally suited for hunting on horseback with packs of hounds; and the squires of England were admirably placed financially and temperamentally to exploit them to the full. They were not concerned with the niceties of the manège; all they wanted of their horses was that they should carry them safely and fast across country. They were in their way superb horsemen and had something to teach the Continentals, but it was a long time before the lessons went home, by which time their descendants had realised that the manège had a meaning for them too.

Side by side with hunting went racing, requiring still greater speed and lighter saddlery. The English took their horses and their riding habits to North America, mingled with the descendants of the Spanish horses, to produce the range rider of the pioneer West and the whole school of Western riding. It was a case, as always, of adapting methods to needs and circumstances.

The development of military tactics also had its effect on the Continental ideas of horsemanship. Until the age of mechanisation the ultimate object of all equitation was to produce a cavalryman. As the cavalries of Europe assumed the function of shock assault in orderly formed bodies, it was felt that the prolonged and sophisticated training of the manège, of establishments like the School of Versailles, and the Spanish Court Riding School of Vienna (founded in 1580) was no longer necessary. Frederick the Great in Germany and the Earl of Pembroke in England were chiefly responsible for this changed approach. Pembroke published his book, *A Method of Breaking Horses and Teaching Soldiers to Ride*, in 1762, which was followed in France in 1776 by *Traité sur la Cavalerie* by a French soldier of Scottish descent, Count Drummond de Melfort. Both were an attack on the conventional manège riding as out of date for practical people and in need of modification. All that a trooper needed to know in their opinion was 'to make his horse go forward, to make it stop when he wishes, to make it back, turn to the right and the left, walk, trot and gallop'. For jumping they still relied on de la Broue. The School of Versailles, on which the Spanish Riding School is based, continued, but a School of Instruction for Cavalry Officers was opened at Saumur in 1771. Closed during the revolutionary and Napoleonic period, they re-opened afterwards, Saumur to continue into the twentieth century, Versailles to close finally in 1830.

The nineteenth century saw the refinement of military riding and the expansion of cross-country riding, the *campagne* school. The English foxhunters carried on more or less regardless of these developments. The two great figures of the first half of the century were Viscount d'Aure, who came to Saumur from Versailles, and François Baucher. Both were outstanding horsemen, both in direct opposition. The former a soldier and riding master stood for sporting riding, in the freedom of the horse to co-operate with the rider rather than to be coerced into obedience; the latter, a circus rider, went back to the classical school in requiring complete submission of the horse to the will of the rider, principally by extreme collection at the halt followed by forward movement. The one represented the outdoor school of riding, the other the indoor – Fillis said that he never saw Baucher ride outside the school – and never the twain should meet. Their controversy made headlines in the 1840s, and was, of course, never resolved. But d'Aure won in the end, his ideas and methods helped to produce much of the riding of today, and foreshadowed perhaps the doctrine of Caprilli, the inventor of forward riding. Baucher's tricks and innovations mostly remained where they started, in the circus.

This is not to decry the circus. Much brilliant riding is seen there, even if the effects are not always obtained by classical means, and it is observable that the lighter horses used in circus equitation perform airs above the ground with a great deal more apparent freedom and lack of obvious effort than the classically trained ones. James Fillis (1834–1913), who studied high school under a pupil of Baucher and ended by disagreeing flatly with the latter's methods, spent his early career in the circus, until he became chief instructor at the Officers' Cavalry School in St Petersburg. Fillis was a very great high school rider and his influence on equitation at the end of the nineteenth and even in the present century has never been fairly acknowledged.

Equitation in the Continental armies had become very artificial and entirely unsuited for jumping when in 1892 at the Italian Cavalry School of Tor Di Quinto a young officer, Federico Caprilli, began to develop his ideas on the natural schooling and riding of the horse which gave birth to the last great revolution in horsemanship, the forward seat. He left very little in writing himself; he died too young in 1907; but was fortunate in having as his interpreter, the late Piero Santini, who died in 1960.

Before his time the English foxhunters and steeplechasers sat well back over fences; the latter mostly still do. The military riders taught that one should lean forward at the take-off and lean back on landing. Although even after World War I there were archaic cavalry officers like a major in my regiment who instructed his young officers thus: 'Take a firm hold of the reins, lean well back, and let him *pull* you over.' At that time Caprilli was not so well known in British cavalry circles, but Colonel M. F. McTaggart, of the 5th Royal Irish Lancers, invented an exaggerated form of forward seat of his own which aroused so much heated controversy that, in India, an Army Order was issued banning all discussion of the subject in Messes.

So, at the beginning of the twentieth century there were four main streams of horsemanship: the classical school, which still continued, revived by the introduction of Grand Prix dressage in the Olympic Games of 1912; the new forward riding school of Caprilli; the untutored 'practical' horsemanship of the English squires; and the 'Western' riding of the cowboys of the Americas. The soldiers developed a compromise between de la Guérinière and Caprilli, which the latter would never have have countenanced. 'Manège and cross-country equitation,' he said, 'are, in my opinion, antagonistic: one excludes and destroys the other.' (This and other statements by Caprilli are taken from *The Caprilli Papers*.)

He maintained that 'we must strive to leave a horse as nature fashioned him, with his balance and attitude of head un-altered', which eliminated collection from the training of the military or outdoor horse. He described the riding position based on the knee grip, shortened leathers and pressure on the stirrup irons, buttocks off the saddle except at rest – the forward seat. 'The hands must be held naturally on either side of the withers, always low and ready to advance towards the horse's mouth. The lightest possible contact must, however, always be preserved between the horse's mouth and the rider's hands. A horse has never fallen because of galloping on the wrong lead. I therefore consider it useless to trouble a pupil regarding the lead his horse may happen to be galloping on.'

The Caprilli Papers take up less than forty pages, but the teaching of Caprilli, interpreted and expanded by Piero Santini in his three key books, *Riding Reflections, The Forward Impulse,* and *The Riding Instructor,* spread all over the world. The proof of the pudding' was in the Italian show jumping successes in the early 1900s, and all the countries of Europe took it up. Inevitably the purity of 'Il Sistema' has been adulterated by compromise, but the foundations remain. All the cavalry equita-tion schools had their version of it, but the most thoughtful and practical exposition of its modifications are those of Captain Vladimir Littauer, a Russian cavalry officer who became a successful riding master in New York between the wars, especially in his books, *Be a Better Horseman* and *Common-sense Horsemanship.*

School riding, now called 'dressage', long neglected in England, also had a revival between the wars, thanks to the efforts of Colonel and Mrs V. D. S. Williams, Henry Wynmalen and Mr E. Schmit-Jensen, and with the establishment of the three-day event at Badminton in 1949 there occurred, amazingly, a sort of marriage between the hunting man and the dressage rider. The former wanted to compete in a galloping cross-country event, but had to perform a dressage test in order to do so. Coming to scoff, he stayed to practise.

So, at long last, two opposing schools of thought have come together. The extremes in either direction, represented by racing and high school, still remain on their own, just to show that rigidity in horsemanship, whether of mind or body, is a negation of the art.

3 The Points of the Horse — Anatomy

The horse is a vertebrate mammal of the order of hoofed animals; that is to say it has an internal bony framework – the skeleton – built round a more or less rigid series of bones down the back (we shall qualify the term 'rigid' later on), covered with muscles and hair.

The beauty of any living vertebrate depends, so say the artists, on the bone structure, which is the chassis, as it were, setting the external proportions which we see when we look superficially at a horse, or any other animal. The effect of the bones, combined with the muscles, is also functional. 'When we speak of the conformation of a horse, we refer to the adaptability of his body for general or special work.' (Hayes, *The Points of the Horse*.) And the proportions of the bones and muscles of any animal are appropriate to that work. Generally speaking a very strong, slow-moving animal, adapted for carrying or pulling heavy weights, will have short legs in proportion to the length of the body; while a creature built for speed will have long legs in relation to the body. One has only to compare a racehorse with a heavy draught horse.

The purpose of all living things is to move, so, to quote Hayes again, 'The chief duties of bones in the act of progression are: 1. To bear weight; 2. To resist in combination with the ligaments the effects of concussion; 3. To act as levers. Capability for performing (1) and (2) is dependent on conditions of texture ("quality"), size ("substance") and arrangement.' Hence the preoccupation of all horsemen with 'bone' and its quality, especially below the knees and hocks.

Bone is composed partly of animal matter (fibrous tissue) and partly of earthy matter (phosphate and salts of lime). The latter give rigidity and hardness to the bone, the former bind it together. The denser the composition of these parts, the stronger the bone, and so the greater endurance and soundness of the horse. And one can see the importance of good, dry limestone soil for the breeding and keeping of horses. In the main dry climates and hard food make for tougher animals.

The picture (Fig. 1) shows the outline of the skeleton and lists

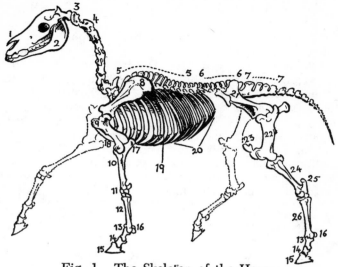

Fig. 1.   The Skeleton of the Horse

1. *Nasal Bone*   2. *Lower Jaw*   3. *Atlas*   4. *Axis*   5. *Back (Dorsal Vertebrae)*   6. *Loins (Lumbar Vertebrae)*   7. *Croup (Sacral Vertebrae)* 8. *Shoulder Blade (Scapula)*   9. *Upper Arm (Humerus)*   10. *Forearm (Radius)*   11. *'Knee' Bones*   12. *Cannon Bone (Metacarpal)* · 13. *Long Pastern Bone*   14. *Short Pastern Bone*   15. *Pedal Bone*   16. *Sesamoid* 17. *Point of Elbow (Ulna)*   18. *Breast Bone (Sternum)*   19. *True Ribs* 20. *False Ribs*   21. *Pelvis*   22. *Thigh Bone (Femur)*   23. *Stifle (Patella, true knee)*   24. *Tibia (Shin)*   25. *Point of Hock*   26. *Cannon Bone (Metatarsal)*

the bones in order. It should be realised that the forelegs of a horse are the equivalent of the human arm and hand. So the term 'knee' given to the bony structure above the cannon bone is only a conventional, and convenient, way of describing that part. It is in fact the carpus or wrist. From the fetlock joint downwards the formation corresponds to the human finger, except that the long process of evolution has reduced it all to one, the same of course in the hindquarters, so the horse walks literally on finger and toe.

The skeleton sustains and protects the vital organs of the body, the heart and lungs, in the rib-cage, and to the rear of them, separated by a sheet of muscle known as the diaphragm, the stomach, bowels, liver, kidneys, bladder, spleen and glands. These work involuntarily and continuously all through life, without having to be actuated by nerves carrying instructions from the brain, e.g. the heart, which pumps blood over the whole body.

The main axis of the body is the backbone, the vertebra, which runs from the head to the tail. It is divided into sections: the neck or cervical vertebrae, the back or dorsal vertebrae, the loins or lumbar vertebrae, the croup or sacral vertebrae, and the tail or coccygeal vertebrae. From the base of the neck to the loins there are eighteen vertebrae, from which spring eighteen pairs of ribs. The first eight pairs are anchored to the breastbone (sternum) and are known as true ribs, constituting the rib-cage; the remaining ten pairs grow out of each other in a steadily diminishing scale and are the false ribs.

There is great variety of mobility in the various parts of the backbone. The neck bones have considerable power of move-

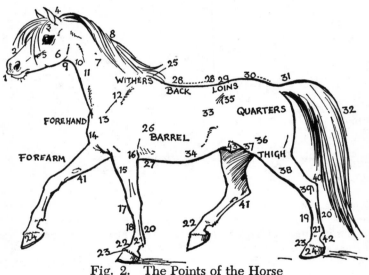

Fig. 2.   The Points of the Horse

1. *Mouth (nostril, muzzle, lips)* 2. *Face* 3. *Forehead* 4. *Poll* 5. *Cheekbone* 6. *Cheek* 7. *Neck* 8. *Crest* 9. *Throat* 10. *Windpipe* 11. *Jugular Groove* 12. *Shoulder* 13. *Point of Shoulder* 14. *Breast* 15. *Forearm* 16. *Elbow* 17. *Knee* 18. *Cannon* 19. *Shannon (hindleg)* 20. *Back Tendons* 21. *Fetlock Joint* 22. *Pastern* 23. *Coronet* 24. *Hoof* 25. *Withers* 26. *Chest* 27. *Girth* 28. *Back* 29. *Loins* 30. *Croup* 31. *Dock* 32. *Tail* 33. *Flank* 34. *Belly* 35. *Hip* 36. *Thigh* 37. *Stifle (True Knee)* 38. *Gaskin (Second Thigh)* 39. *Hock* 40. *Points of Hock* 41. *Chestnuts* 42. *Ergot* 43. *Sheath*

ment, a horse's neck can be too mobile at times. The loins have fair flexibility but not much power of lateral movement; there is little movement in the croup, but the tail is extremely flexible. Lateral movement is possible where the neck joins the dorsal vertebrae (the withers), and behind the lumbar vertebrae, but although the articulation of the bones of the back is flexible, having a play of about one eighth of an inch only very slight lateral curvature is possible, and that only in a highly trained horse. Nor is there much upward (arching) movement; though the whole backbone will sag in old age. The belief that a buck-jumper arches its back when making its bid to remove its rider is not borne out by countless photographs which show the back absolutely straight, the effect being obtained by the devastating upward drive of all four legs together and the lowering of the head and hindquarters. The ribs, having moveable joints with the vertebrae, can expand, the more so towards the rear.

The other bones of the body are mostly joined together with either ball and socket or hinge joints. The shoulder and hip joints are ball and socket, which give them a wide range of movement. The elbow is a hinge joint, which can be bent and extended. The whole system of the fore limbs, however, is attached through the shoulder blades to the backbone at the base of the neck by a very strong fan-shaped muscle (serratus magnus). The horse, by the way, has no collar bone.

The main bones of the forehand, below the shoulder blade are the humerus (upper arm), which slopes back from the shoulder blade to meet the radius (forearm), which goes straight down from the elbow to the 'knee', below which are the cannon bone, the long and short pasterns, sesamoid bones, and, inside the hoof, the pedal or coffin bone and the navicular bone.

In the hindquarters the thigh bone joins the pelvis at the hip joint, sloping forwards to meet the tibia (shin) and the patella (knee cap or true knee), the latter being held in a groove firmly at the top of the tibia by three vertical ligaments and two laterals. The tibia, sloping backwards to the hock joint and point of the hock, is known as the gaskin or second thigh. The bones below the hock joint are the same as those below the 'knee' in the foreleg.

The bones of a joint are held together by ligaments, which can be either cords or flat bands, and between the bones is a pad of hard cartilage to reduce concussion. A joint is covered with a sheet-like membrane – the joint capsule – which is composed of two layers, the outer being thick to support the joint, the inner containing cells which secrete the joint oil, synovia, which lubricates the joint. Damage to these ligaments and membranes causes much of the lameness that occurs in working horses.

The whole skeleton is covered with muscles, which go to make up what we call flesh, the red edible meat. There are voluntary muscles for every part of the body, which means that they act on the commands of the brain, received via the nerves, which also cover the whole body. Muscles are attached to bones – and also to cartilages by tendons. These are tough inelastic ropes, composed of many threads, and like ligaments rounded or flat, which enable the elastic muscles to do their work without damage. The sprain of any joint is usually due to the tendon giving way, not the muscle.

The muscles move the body by acting on the bones. One set of muscles will bend or flex a joint (flexors), and another will straighten the joint out (extensors). There are an enormous number of muscles in the body with varied functions, too complicated to be detailed here, but some of the more important ones should be noted.

An important muscle is the panniculus, a broad sheet of muscle which lies immediately underneath the skin covering the neck, sides of the chest and abdomen, being attached by sheets of fibrous tissue. This is the muscle that makes the skin twitch when a fly lights on it, caused by its contraction and relaxation, and it is a great blessing to horses.

Running from behind the ear to the shoulder is the brachiocephalicus, which is one of the muscles for moving the head and neck. The principal muscle connecting the fore limbs with the trunk is the serratus magnus, a powerful fan-shaped muscle; another is the trapezuis, a triangular muscle covering roughly the area before and behind the withers. The most powerful muscle in the body is the longissimus dorsi, which runs roughly from the croup to the neck, attached to the pelvis, sacrum, all the loin and dorsal vertebrae, the last four bones of the neck, and to the ribs.

All locomotion, preferably forward, with which we are most concerned in a horse, is brought about by displacement of the centre of gravity, in other words loss of balance. A man standing at attention is in balance; if he leans forward so that his centre of gravity is in front of his base of support, he loses his balance, and will fall forward unless he takes a step forward to adjust his centre of gravity; and so on. It is the same with a horse, when he starts from the walk into a halt: '...by the straightening of one or both hindlegs he brings the centre of gravity of his body beyond the toe of the most advanced forefoot, with the result that the other foreleg has to be carried forward in order to restore the equilibrium. In doing this, the first foot to quit the ground will usually be a fore one.' (Hayes, *The Points of the Horse.*)

The same authority describes the movements of the limbs as follows. Fore limb: 'The shoulder blade (scapula) is rotated, chiefly by its upper end being pulled downwards by the posterior portion of the serratus magnus, and by its lower end being drawn upwards by the levator humeri, which also draws the entire limb to the front; the flexor muscles of the forearm bend the knee and the points of the fetlock and pastern, so as to enable the foot to clear the ground; the flexor brachii assists in straightening the shoulder joint and raises the knee; and the extensor muscles of the forearm finally straighten the knee and all the joints below it. When full extension of the fore limb takes place all the bones of the leg (from the shoulder blade to the pedal bone) are straightened as far as possible. It is evident that the less upright (more sloping) the shoulder blade is, the more can the foot and knee be advanced and raised.' The reason why, of course, horsemen look for a sloping shoulder in a riding horse.

Hind limb: Propulsion by the hind limb of the horse takes place through the hip joint and pelvis. When a horse moves at any speed, there is a tendency to displace the centre of gravity first to one side and then the other, which gives a rocking effect. The wider the limbs are apart the more pronounced the rocking will be. The muscular effort needed to counteract it reduces that available for forward movement, and consequently for speed. So in schooling a principal object is to train the horse to go straight. It is a fault in conformation if either the forelegs or the hindlegs are too far apart. Being too close together is also a fault and leads to brushing, which is the knocking of the inside of the fetlock joint with the opposite hoof; more common in the forelegs than the hind.

Over the muscles is the outer covering of the body, the skin, consisting of two layers: the top one being the epidermis, of cellular material having in its turn two layers; the lower layer is the dermis or true skin, composed of fibrous tissue and elastic fibres. Out of the skin grows the hair, which in the horse is regularly shed and replaced twice a year, spring and autumn. In the skin are two kinds of glands, sweat glands, and sebaceous glands, the latter producing an oily secretion to lubricate the hair, and give the coat its much prized glossy sleekness. The hoof is an extension of the skin, which, instead of growing hairs, produces a collection of closely connected tubular horn fibres, cemented together and forming the horn. The chief functions of the skin are to protect the muscles underneath, and to regulate the body temperature.

COLOURING AND MARKINGS

The hairs of the horse grow in different colours, with variations on the body which constitute various markings. In 1954 the Royal College of Veterinary Surgeons issued a pamphlet on colours and markings of the horse for the benefit of veterinary surgeons giving descriptions of animals so that there should be consistent uniformity of nomenclature. The descriptions below follow that pamphlet.

The four main whole colours are black, brown, bay and chestnut.

Black is wholly black, including the muzzle and eyelids, apart from white markings as described below.

Black-brown is predominantly black but with brown muzzle and sometimes brown or tan flanks.

Brown is a mixture of black and brown pigment, with black limbs, mane and tail.

Bay-brown has brown as the predominant colour, black limbs (black points), mane and tail, bay muzzle.

Bay is usually a reddish brown colour like a ripe horse chestnut, but it can vary towards brown and chestnut, but always accompanied by black limbs, mane and tail.

Chestnut has variations of yellow colouring, distinguished as light, dark, liver. 'A 'true' chestnut has a chestnut mane and tail, which may be lighter or darker than the body colour. Light chestnuts, verging on palomino, may have flaxen manes and tails.

Other colours are dun, cream (Palomino), grey, roan, piebald, skewbald, odd-coloured, spotted (Appaloosa).

Blue dun is diluted black in colour, evenly distributed, with black mane and tail and black skin. There can be a dorsal stripe or withers stripe.

Yellow dun has a widely diffuse yellow pigment in the hair, with or without dorsal and withers stripes and bars on the legs. The striping usually goes with black on the head and limbs. The skin is black.

Cream: The body is of a light cream colour with unpigmented skin. The eyes often have a pinkish or bluish appearance.

Palomino is officially described as a pure gold colour, as in a 'newly-minted gold coin' if such is available for comparison. Varying shades from light to dark are permissible. Mane and tail are pure white, varying from silver to flaxen, eyes dark. The skin is dark with no sign of albinism.

Grey: The body coat is 'a varying mosaic of black and white hairs, with the skin black. With increasing age the coat grows lighter in colour'. There is no such thing officially as a white horse. Grey horses are born almost black.

Flea-bitten grey is when the white is mixed with one or more of the other colours.

Roans vary according to the basic whole colours.

Blue Roan: The body colour is black or black-brown with a sprinkling of white hair which gives the coat its bluish tinge. Black hairs usually predominate on the lower limbs, but there can be white markings.

Bay or Red roan: The same as above except that the body colour is bay or bay-brown, with the white hairs giving a reddish tinge to the coat.

Strawberry, or chestnut, roan: The body colour is chestnut with an admixture of white hairs.

Piebald: Large irregular patches of black and white over the body, with usually clearly defined lines of demarcation between them.

Skewbald: Large irregular patches of white and any other colour but black on the body.

Odd coloured: Large irregular patches of more than two colours, which may merge into each other on the dividing lines.

Whole coloured is used where there are no hairs of any other colour on the body, head or limbs.

Spotted, or Appaloosa: Spots of various sizes and patterns on white, or white on other colours. This does not include piebald, skewbald, or dappled grey. The following markings are recognised by the societies in England and the U.S.A. governing the breeding of these types. *Leopard:* Spots of any colour on a white or light coloured background. *Blanket:* Animals having a white rump or back on which are spots of any colour. *Snowflake:* White spots on a foundation of any colour. Special characteristics of this type are: white scelera round the eye (like the white round the human eye); hooves striped, yellowish-white and black or brown in vertical stripes; bare skin is mottled; manes and tails are often very sparse.

The many and various markings superimposed on these colours are described as follows.

Head

Star: White mark on the head, of varying size, described as large, small, faint, triangular, round, etc. If there are only a few white hairs, they should be so described. *Stripe:* A narrow white strip down the face, with or without a star, not wider than the surface of the nasal bones. If separated from a star, it is called an 'interrupted stripe starting from . . .' It can be distinguished as broad, narrow, inclined to right or left, etc. *Blaze:* White marking covering almost the whole of the forehead between the eyes and extending beyond the width of the nasal bones and usually to the muzzle. *White face:* The white covers the forehead and front of the face, and extending on either side to the mouth, or one side only.   *Snip:* An isolated white mark independent of those already named, usually found between or near the nostrils. *Lip markings:* Spots or marks round about the lips, which should be described as observed. *White muzzle:* White on both lips and up to the nostrils. *Wall-eye:* Caused by lack of pigment, partial or total, in the iris, giving a pinkish-white or bluish-white tinge to the eye. *Showing the white of the eye:* Where some part of the white sclerotic of the eye shows between the eyelids. *Whorls:* Irregular setting of the coat hairs, like little eddies or whirlpools.

Body

Grey ticked: White hairs sparsely distributed through the coat also called white hairs on coat. *Flecked:* Small collections of white hairs appearing irregularly in any part of the body. May be heavily or lightly flecked. *Black marks:* Small areas of black hairs among white or any other colour. *Spots:* Small, more or less circular collections of hairs differing from the general body colour, distributed in various parts of the body. (See also *Spotted.*) *Patch:* A term to describe any larger irregular area of differing colour not covered by previous definitions. *Zebra marks:* Stripes on the limbs, neck, withers or quarters. *Mane and tail:* If different in colour from the rest of the body, it should be stated in any description of the animal. *Whorls: See* under *Head,* above.

Limbs

Hoofs: Any variation in colour should be noted. *White markings:* These used to be described as 'stocking' or 'sock', but it is recommended that this be discontinued in official descriptions, the actual markings and their extent being exactly stated, e.g. 'white to half pastern', 'white to below the fetlock', etc. *Black points:* The name commonly used to describe the black legs of a bay horse below the knee.

General

Mixed: To describe a white marking which contains varying amounts of hairs of the general body colour. *Bordered:* To describe a marking that is surrounded by a mixed border, e.g. 'bordered star', 'bordered stripe'. *Flesh marks:* Patches where the pigment of the skin is absent. *Acquired marks:* Such as saddle marks, girth marks, brands, tattoo marks, docking, which have been acquired through human agency.

THE FOOT

It is superfluous to dwell on the importance of the foot to the horse and its rider and the work that it has to do. At every stride the weight of the horse – and rider – falls on each hoof in turn; at about forty strides to the minute and a weight of 1,000 lb. there is quite an accumulation of weight on each foot.

Contained within the hoof are three bones: the lower part of the short pastern bone, the navicular bone and the pedal or coffin bone (Fig. 3). The last-named, situated inside the actual

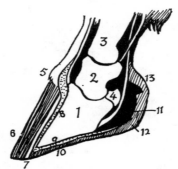

Fig. 3.   The Formation of the Foot

1. *Coffin or Pedal Bone*   2. *Short Pastern Bone*   3. *Long Pastern Bone*   4. *Navicular Bone*   5. *Coronary Band*   6. *Wall of Hoof*   7. *White Line*   8. *Fleshy leaves or Laminae*   9. *Fleshy Sole*   10. *Horny Sole*   11. *Fleshy Frog*   12. *Horny Frog*   13. *Plantar Cushion*

hoof, is a roughly semi-circular wedge, cut away at the back. Surrounding the top of this bone are the lateral cartilages, which can be felt at the bulges of the heel as 'springy' tissue. They act by helping to suspend the pedal bone. Above is the coronary band, which surrounds the hoof at the upper border and is made up of horn-producing cells from which the horn of the hoof is supplied; and at the rear of the foot the cushion of the heel or the plantar cushion. Behind the pedal bone, and protected by the plantar cushion is the navicular bone, a small boat-shaped bone, which acts as a pulley or roller for the deep flex or tendon (perforans) attached to the pedal bone. Resting in the socket at the top of the pedal bone is the lower end of the short pastern bone, to which is attached the superficial flexor tendon (perforatus). Anatomically the pedal bone is the third phalanx or finger tip. The short pastern bone and the long pastern above it correspond to the second and first phalanges of the human finger, or on the hindlegs to the toe. The horse, it will be realised, moves on its toes and finger tips.

The hoof proper consists exteriorly of the horny wall, a hard, black, insensitive horny substance which grows out of the coron-

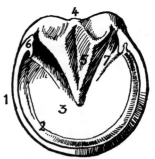

Fig. 4. The Sole of the Foot

1. *Wall of the Hoof* 2. *White Line* 3. *Horny Sole* 4. *Cleft of the Frog*
5. *Frog* 6. *Angle of the Heels* 7. *Bars*

ary band. This horn grows downwards continually during life, its length having to be regulated either by natural means of wear and tear, or by rasping back with a file in the case of domesticated animals whether shod or unshod. The inside of this hard shelter dovetails into an enormous number of fleshy leaves or laminae, which are attached to the pedal bone and completely fill the interior of the foot. These laminae are copiously supplied with blood vessels, so that the foot inside literally floats in blood. If these parts are pricked in shoeing by a wrongly-directed nail, they bleed freely. They are extremely sensitive and subject to compression and expansion every time the foot strikes and leaves the ground. If these laminae become excessively filled with blood, through over-rich food or too much concussion, they expand against the hard casing of the wall and get inflamed, producing the troublesome and painful disease of laminitis or fever in the feet, which is very common amongst English ponies.

The horn of the wall grows out of the front of the coronary band at an angle of about 50 degrees in the case of the fore foot and at a steeper angle, about 30 degrees, in the hind foot. The hoof is rounded at the front, but straightens up somewhat on the inside and is also more upright; the outside curves and slopes more markedly, so that the foot presents a broad round surface to the ground. The hind foot is altogether steeper, narrower and more elongated.

At the back of the foot, on both sides, the wall curves sharply forwards, this part being known as the bars, to form a wedge-shaped area to accommodate the frog. This is a thick, wedge-shaped piece of rubbery horn, with a cleft in the middle, set point forward in the space between the bars. This exterior part, which shows, is extremely tough and resilient, and, with an unshod horse, was the first part of the shock-absorbing system which reaches up the leg via the pasterns, to the shoulders in the forehand and the pelvis in the hindquarters, touching the ground at every stride.

It grows out of an inner, fleshy frog which is closely connected with the interior bones and cartilages. Like the wall of the hoof it constantly replaces itself by growth. The under surface of the foot is occupied by the sole, a hard, insensitive substance on the outside, roughly crescent-shaped, with a soft laminated fleshy sensitive sole behind it. This sole, which is slightly concave, is part of the bearing surface of the foot, and it joins the horny wall, a white line marking the division between the hard and fleshy laminae. The appearance of this white line is a sign to the farrier that the wall of the hoof has been rasped back far enough. It is a guide also for the direction of the nails when putting on a shoe, which should never go inside it. The inner fleshy sole at the angle of the wall of the hoof and the bars is susceptible to bruising, through pressure and concussion brought about by excessive work on hard surfaces, picking up stones, lack of regular shoeing, showing as a red mark. This is a corn, and the area is known as the seat of corn.

4 The Points of the Horse — Conformation

When one judges a horse from the outside one of the first considerations will be the work it is expected to do. If speed is required, sloping shoulders and good length above the knees and hocks are desirable; for a harness horse a straight shoulder and longish back are acceptable; a heavy draft horse will have short, strong legs; a cutting horse will be found to have a powerful forehand and well-developed forearm muscles. But there are basic factors of conformation which are common to all equines.

Looked at from the side a well-shaped horse should give the general impression of proportion and symmetry. If the back looks too long, or the head appears overlarge for the rest of the body, or the body seems too far away from the ground, 'showing too much daylight', or the feet are too ponderous, then the proportions are wrong. For the purpose of judging and description, the horse is usually divided into three parts, forehand, middlepiece, hindquarters. The forehand takes in the head, neck, forelegs, shoulders and withers; the middlepiece all parts between the withers and the croup; the hindquarters, or quarters, comprise all the rear part of the body from the pelvis, exteriorly the hip, down to the feet. A horse must be judged, of course, from the front and rear as well from the side, but first impressions are always received from the side view. After first impressions one must assess each part individually from front to rear.

Head

A head can be too small for the body as well as too large, and a good guide estimating the right proportion is the fact that the length of the head from the poll to the nostrils should be about equal to the distance from behind the withers to the hip; and also to the depth of the girth taken from a point behind the withers. Other equal distances to the head are from the croup to the stifle, and from the point of the hock to the ground.

46

The length of the body of a well-proportioned horse from the point of the shoulder to the point of the buttock is roughly three times the length of the head.

The head itself should have a bony, rather ascetic, appearance, with a good straight or slightly concave profile, more pronounced in some breeds, e.g. the Arab, than in others. Heavy, cold-blooded horses, such as the Shire and some German breeds, will tend to have Roman noses. A horse with a pronounced lump between the eyes is widely considered to be unreliable in temperament. There should be a good deep jaw bone, and no thickness where the head joins the neck, so that the horse can bend its head easily downwards and backwards when called upon to do so by the action of the bit. This facilitates the very necessary process of flexion, without which there is no real control of the horse.

The eyes should be large, nearly horizontal, and generous in expression. A horse with small or shifty eyes, tending to show too much white, will usually have a mean disposition. The horse breathes through its nostrils, so they must be wide and fine and sensitive. The ears should be in proportion to the head, firm but mobile, continually switching backwards and forwards, displaying interest in all that is going on. A rider should always watch the movements of his horse's ears; they will tell him whether the horse is really *listening* to him or not. 'One must never,' said Willi Schultheis, the great German dressage rider and trainer, 'underrate the importance of the ears.' A horse that continually lays its ears flat back is one to be avoided. In any case it is a danger signal.

Neck

The neck should be long, graceful and muscular. A fair proportion is that, measured from withers to poll, it should be a little less than one and a half times the length of the head. Seen from the side it should appear light and slender, but when felt by the fingers along the crest it should be tough and full of muscle. A slack or stringy neck means weakness and unfitness. The muscles of the neck play a great part in movement, especially in jumping. When seen from above by a rider the crest should appear quite thick and broad.

The crest should start straight from the withers for the first half of its length, and then describe a slightly convex curve towards the head. The lower side of the neck takes the gullet and windpipe and goes straight into the space between the jaw bones, which is another reason for there having to be plenty of room at the join. When the neck starts from the withers with a concave curve the result is known as a ewe neck and it is a serious fault in conformation. It often appears in young horses that are unfit and under-fed, when it can sometimes be eradicated, or improved, by proper training and conditioning. A swan neck is when this concavity is more accentuated and the horse carries its head high, with a tendency to star gaze. A short, thick neck is ugly and usually goes with thickening and stiffness at the jowl, which makes the horse virtually unmanageable. The withers, which are formed by a group of bony processes growing out of the vertebrae, should be fairly high and narrow and well covered with muscle. Flat withers below the level of croup tend to give a downhill ride, and also allow a saddle to move forward, with the danger of rubbing and galling. Flat withers are often found with straight and loaded shoulders.

Fore limbs

The shoulders should be long, narrow and muscular, with a good slope forwards to the point of the shoulder, from which the upper arm or humerus slopes back and downwards to the point of elbow (ulna). The shoulder slope is made by the shoulder blade or scapula, which should be flat and merge into the withers and quite close to the opposite bone. When the shoulder blades are wide apart they cause a lumpy, 'loaded' shoulder. They are attached to the ribs by powerful muscles, which give the body a kind of elastic suspension, and are the top link in the shock-absorbing chain of the forelegs. A good shoulder should slope forwards at approximately an angle of 45 degrees, and the upper arm roughly at right angles to it.

The forelegs should be vertical from the point of the elbow to the fetlock joint. From the elbow to the 'knee' is forearm or radius, and it should be long in proportion to the rest of the leg, straight and broad and well covered with muscle. The knee (corresponding to the human wrist) should appear deep from front to rear, large and flat from the front view. Below this is the cannon bone, which it is desirable to have short in comparison with the forearm, and thick when seen from the side. Tendons and ligaments run down the rear edge of this bone, and the outer circumference of this part is measured to assess the amount of bone which a horse is said to have. This measurement is taken immediately below the knee, and in an average horse can be eight to nine inches. A horse with narrow 'bone' is not likely to be a weight carrier, but of equal importance to the dimensions is the quality of the bone itself which is gauged by the density of its composition. This, of course, is something you cannot discover until the horse is dead; but as a general rule the better the breeding the better the quality of the bone. Pure-bred Arab horses do not show a great deal of bone but they are renowned for their endurance and weight carrying over long distances. The circumference of an Arab horse's head may not appear as large as that of an Irish hunter, but because the Arab is capable of assimilating more from a given diet, its bone is denser and stronger.

The fetlock joint should be large, and below it the pasterns slope forward at an angle of about 45 degrees to the hoof, which they join at the coronet. Behind and between the two pastern bones are the small sesamoid bones, over which run the tendons and ligaments. Inflammation of this bone through excessive concussion or strain causes the condition known as sesamoiditis. The slope of the pasterns gives springiness, and they are another vital link in the shock-absorbing system. Too straight a pastern will subject the legs to considerable wear and tear; this and the opposite over-flat pastern are sources of weakness to be avoided. The foot has already been described, so we will now consider the rest of the body.

Middlepiece

The principal parts are the chest, back, barrel, flank and loins. The previous study of the skeleton shows that the ribs enclose most of the vital organs of the body. In front – the chest – are the heart and lungs; to the rear, separated by the diaphragm, are the digestive and other organs, which are partially protected by the false ribs and by strong abdominal muscles. There is an unprotected gap in the lumbar region, the loins, where lie part of the liver and kidneys. This gap should be as small as possible, thus making for a short back, regarded as a very great virtue in a horse. However, the requirements of this part vary with the type of horse and the work it has to do. A weight-carrying animal, such as a heavyweight hunter or polo pony, needs to have a short back, but in a hack, where a comfortable and smooth ride is essential, judges usually look for a rather longer back. Longer backs, and straight shoulders, are also favoured for harness horses of all kinds. Too short a back gives an uncomfortable ride, shortening the stride, and so sometimes, but not invariably, reducing speed. Very fast sprinters are likely to be very short in the back with accompanying well-developed largissimus dolsi, which enables them to muster an enormous effort. To the contrary, a long back means that the animal is standing over a larger area so that at each stride more ground is covered, which will tell over a staying distance.

The saddle-bearing surface of the back, behind the withers, should be well covered with flesh to protect the spine and the bony processes which project upwards from it. The barrel and chest should be well rounded, and there should be no slackness of the flanks, which occupy the sides of the horse between the ribs and the hindquarters. Excessive hollowness here, herring-gutted, shows weakness and difficulty in keeping in condition. The girth, which is the area round the chest from just behind the withers, where the saddle girth goes in fact, should be deep, providing more room for the vital heart and lungs.

Hindquarters

The true thigh of the horse slopes forward from the pelvis to the patella (stifle), and outwardly this area, which extends from the point of the hip to the buttocks, should be well rounded and muscular. From the stifle to the point of the hock runs the gaskin or second thigh (tibia or shin bone), which, like the fore-arm in front, should be long and thick and well muscled up, this being part of the propelling mechanism of the horse. The hock, which is composed of several bones, should be large, and the cannon (sometimes called shannon) bone, below, short in proportion to the gaskin. The lower parts, fetlock, pasterns, etc., are the same as in front and similar criteria apply, except that the hind pasterns, which do not have to endure the same sustained shocks as the front ones, have a straighter angle to the ground.

The sum and arrangement of all these various parts adds up to the qualities that one wants to see in a good riding horse. Looked at first from the side, the first impression, as has been said above, should be of symmetry and proportion: head not too large and heavy, or too small, or too coarse, well set on the neck and showing plenty of room at the union with it; the neck elegant but strong, about the same length as the head, rising out of moderately high and fairly narrow withers; shoulder should slope forward at an angle of about 45° and show clean but muscular lines; forelegs straight, with muscular forearm, short cannon, showing good bone, sloping pasterns, hoof well rounded with a moderate slope to the ground and good quality horn without cracks or flaking or horizontal lines indicating a laminitis condition; knees should not be bent forward (over at the knees), or sag back behind the vertical (back at the knees).

A good foot should always be proportionate to the size of the horse, neither too broad and heavy nor narrow and boxy with a steep angle to the ground. Heels should be wide to give room for a healthy frog. The two fore feet and hind feet should each make an exact pair, and the toes should point straight to front, neither turned in (pigeon toed) nor turned out (splay footed). The front pair are placed level and squarely on the ground, neither foot in advance of the other (pointing, and a sign of lameness). The hind pair, when the horse is standing alertly and to attention, are together, but when relaxed either hind foot can be raised on its toes (resting). When, however, a horse is being photographed all four legs must appear separately in the picture, otherwise there is the unsightly effect of the horse appearing to have only two legs; so the foreleg on the side furthest from the photographer is drawn back and the hindleg placed forward.

The chest should be broad, but not excessively wide, which will give the horse a rather waddling action. The back should be short, with no slackness between the barrel, which should be well rounded, and the quarters; the girth deep. The back should be straight, or rising slightly from behind the withers towards the croup. When the top line of the back is convex the horse is said to be roach-backed; the opposite condition of hollow back is usually a sign of old age, the ligaments which bind the vertebrae together becoming relaxed. The croup should be convex and high at the tail; a drooping croup, giving a lowly-placed tail (goose rump), is unsightly and a sign of weakness. The hips should be rounded; often prominent, pointed hips are a sign of poor condition.

The hindlegs should be placed directly under the quarters, and a line drawn down from the point of the buttocks should touch the point of the hock and the rear edge of the cannon bone and the back of the fetlock. The tail should be set high and carried gaily.

Two small parts not yet mentioned are chestnut and ergot. They are horny callosities found on the limbs, the chestnuts on the insides of the forearms and of the hind legs just below the hock joints, the ergots at the backs of the fetlock joints. They are skin growths, and are thought to be vestigial remains of extra foot pads or toes long since vanished.

Viewed from the front, the legs should appear straight and

clean, vertical from the point of the shoulder; chest neither too broad nor too narrow (legs coming out of the same hole), a sign of weakness and cause of brushing. The legs should not be bowed outwards nor knock-kneed. Similarly,. from the rear, the quarters should show straight lines, with no turning in or out of the hocks, and again neither too broad (going wide behind) nor too narrow. When the hocks are turned in and the toes turned out the horse is said to be cow-hocked. Sickle hocks are those which show an ill-defined angle at the point permanently bent, hence the greater strain and predisposition to curbs – giving the impression of couching. Hocks set behind the buttocks is also a bad fault.

In all the foregoing the horse has been stationary; but a horse fulfils its being in movement. Again, the action of the horse in motion must be observed from the side and from each end. The walk stride should be long and energetic, the rear foot making an imprint well up to or in advance of that of the forefoot. It is generally reckoned that a good walker will make a good galloper. The trot should be active and well marked, feet picked up, with no dragging of the toes. Seen from the ends, the action should be straight, without throwing the feet outwards (dishing) or crossing one foot over the other (plaiting).

Obviously absolute perfection of form is rarely found in any horse, and one usually has to be content with the next best thing. It is true, also, that conformation and performance do not necessarily go together. Many great show jumpers and three-day eventers would find themselves in the back row of a show class; but they would be found, nevertheless to possess the basic attributes of good limbs, sound feet, plenty of bone, and good fronts. The art of assessing the conformation of the horse, expressed in the phrase 'having an eye for a horse', lies in the balancing of the good points against the bad.

However beautiful a horse may be, it is useless if it is not sound. We have already seen that a horse lame in his fore feet will tend to 'point' the affected foot, especially in the case of navicular disease but lameness shows more clearly when the horse is seen trotting, preferably on level and fairly hard ground. Pronounced lameness in front will reveal itself by an uneven action, the horse coming down more heavily on the sound foot and more lightly (favouring) on the lame foot, accompanied by a nodding of the head on the lame side. Detecting lameness in the hind limbs is more difficult, but a general guide is to watch the hips of the horse trotting away; if they tend to rise and fall alternately, the rising one will indicate the lame side.

So far we have considered the physical make-up of the horse, but equally important for both rider and trainer is an understanding of his mind.

5 The Mind of the Horse

Human appreciation of equine intelligence usually depends on the extent and quality of the horse's responses to the instructions given him, by various signals, which in its turn depends on the efficiency and clarity of those signals. This tells us as much about the limitations of the rider or instructor as it does about the understanding of the horse. Nevertheless the consensus of experienced opinion confirms that, whatever the capabilities of the trainer, the horse is *willing* to try to understand and to do what he is told. In spite of his great strength – and few riders really appreciate the truly enormous power of the horse – the horse seldom resists or rebels, not for long anyway. His is essentially docile and gentle, even a stallion, if he is intelligently treated.

Docility is the keynote of the horse's character, on which, combined with his excellent memory, all training is based. In a sense he is like a computer, which requires to be correctly programmed to produce the right answer. Only of course he is not just a computer; he is a creature of sense and sensibility, subject to aberrations and off days; which makes everything to do with riding and training horses at once frustrating and fascinating, and in the end supremely rewarding.

This willingness to co-operate helps to overcome the limitations of his intelligence, though we must be careful of our terms. If we measure his intelligence by his relations with the human race, it is of course negligible, in order of precedence below that of the primates and the dog, but above in some people's opinion that of the elephant. If we measure it in terms of survival, this particular quadruped had developed, improved and maintained itself for some sixty million years before man appeared on the scene, and since then has adapted itself to man's exacting requirements in a remarkable way. It should be a sobering thought.

One should pause, too, to consider how the horse learns to do all that it is asked to do by man, to solve all the conundrums that are put to it by exacting trainers. It has no common language; it cannot understand a word *qua* word. It has to translate in that small brain of his a series of external signs – movements of the body on its back, pressures of leg and spur and whip, tugs and vibrations on its mouth, movements of the hand or whip of a dismounted man – into actions, some simple, some very complicated and difficult, in the circus ring, in the Grand Prix dressage arena, playing polo, or just quietly hacking. And by and large, it does it so well that the achievement is taken for granted. Clever Hans was so responsive to the almost invisible signals of his master that many people credited him with human calculating powers. Perhaps, when a horse fails to translate the human sign language correctly, it may be conceded that he is not just a bloody fool but has not been given the signals correctly. Like the computer when it is given the wrong programme, it becomes confused, which makes it frightened and obstinate, and finally violent. Of course, there are horses which will not co-operate, deliberately resist, and appear to hate the human race, or will only tolerate it in certain ways. The Arabian mare, Nichab, bred by Lady Hester Stanhope in 1818 and later sold to France for breeding lived for twenty-eight years without once allowing a rider to stay on her back. Apart from this she had the sweetest of temperaments. Erika Schiele in *The Arab Horse in Europe* tells the story of how on her birth Turkish astrologers cast the filly's horoscope and prophesied that Nichab should never carry any common rider, unless she had first been ridden by the mightiest warrior on earth. The only candidate was Napoleon, who was by then not available.

Docility is a quality produced by domestication, but there is in the horse a conflicting characteristic inherited from millions of years of wildness, fear. For the most part docility and the regular routine imposed upon it overcomes fear, but it is still there in the horse, and cannot be ignored. It manifests itself in shying or spooking at unfamiliar objects or, sometimes, at nothing in particular, starting at sudden movements or noises, taking fright in traffic, bolting. For all his size and strength and apparent confidence the horse is a timid creature. His age-old instinct when confronted with anything potentially dangerous is to shy away and run.

Another characteristic of the horse is his gregariousness. He has always been used to going about in small, fairly close-knit communities, with a well-established leader. Several horses in a field will usually get on well together, and they quickly establish an hierarchy under a boss. Sometimes the members of a group will take a dislike to one of them, and make his life a hell; but this does not often happen. Normally mares and geldings get on well together. Domesticity has interfered with this natural order of things; horses in stables live a life of solitary confinement for twenty or more hours a day, only coming out for exercise. In the old-fashioned stables of the horse era they were usually in semi-darkness as well. No wonder the vices of crib-biting, wind-sucking, weaving and kicking of stable doors are so prevalent among the horses of civilised countries. I do not ever remember a troop horse kept in open horse lines becoming addicted to any of them. Modern stables are better, letting horses look out on some kind of living activity, and they are all the better for it. The bad temper of many thoroughbred stallions must have been mainly due to their lonely and boring lives. A much more enlightened treatment of that noble creature has had the most remarkable results.

Everybody knows that the horse has a good memory, and all his training depends on it; but it is an odd sort of memory. He certainly is able to connect effect with cause, provided the sequence is quick enough. If he is not corrected or rewarded at the very instant of his doing wrong or right, it will be too late; he will have forgotten why he is being punished or praised. That is why it is so futile to whip a horse after he has refused. It is not much use patting him either when he has got over the fence, unless it is done in the air. This is not to say that reward and punishment are not effective; they are essential, but their use has to be carefully thought out and very quickly applied.

On the other hand a horse will remember lessons he has learnt through constant repetition, and places where things have happened. A dressage horse will often learn the test as well as his rider, and anticipate the movements; while a milk horse will regularly stop his cart at the same places in the street every day. Horses obviously recognise places, such as their stables, for they will find their way to them unaided. I had a buggy horse in India who very well knew his way from the club to his stables, but he developed a habit of cutting his corners. Whether he would have done this from greater distances or after a lapse of time, I do not know. Many vast claims have been made for the horse in this way, but the evidence is not conclusive. Bernhard Grzimek, director of the Frankfurt Zoo, made some experiments with Arabs to test their homing instinct, with negative results. Perhaps the answer is that some horses have better memories than others.

Many people claim that their horses recognise them by sight, but here again the evidence is inconclusive. It is more likely that they identify people and things by their sense of smell, which is much more acute than their eyesight. I was told once of a pony which was very much attached to its young owner but could not stand her mother. I suggested that the mother should approach the pony wearing a coat belonging to her daughter. She did this and the pony accepted her quite readily, and then gradually got used to her. Ewart Evans in *The Horse and the Furrow* has suggested that the secret of the Horseman's Word which gave some Suffolk horsemen such power over their horses was the cunning application of the horse's sense of smell. This may have been the power behind the old Horse Whisperers but, as practitioners of this kind of horse control are few and far between, there must be something more to it than that. The practice described by Barbara Woodhouse of breathing into a horse's nostrils done by South American gauchos must be of the same *genre*. And horses, in common with most other animals, say how-do-you-do to each other by sniffing.

The horse's hearing is generally very acute, more so in finely bred, hot-blooded ones than in the coarser, cold-blooded types. Breed tells. Horses will often pick up distant sounds inaudible to the human ear, and they seem to distinguish between friendly and, to them, hostile sounds. The cry of hounds, however far away, will strike a responsive chord in any horse, but another sound will frighten him. Perhaps this hearing of odd sounds may explain otherwise inexplicable shying or bolting; a sudden echo of his prehistoric past. There are few horsemen who have not been bolted with and it is a terrifying experience; but usually the horse stops or slows down, presumably when he thinks he has got far enough away from the unseen danger. It is necessary of course to have plenty of space ahead when a horse does bolt with you. Many years ago I was riding a small pony mare, and we turned into the drive of the house where I was living which was off the road halfway up a steep hill. There may have been something coming, either up or down that hill, but it was certainly not in sight. Suddenly, without warning, she put her ears back and bolted along the drive, and I mean *bolted*. She seemed to be impelled by sheer ungovernable panic, and nothing on earth could stop her. The drive was about 200 yards long, and I had time to wonder in quite a detached way what would happen when we got to a bend at the end of it, when equally suddenly she stopped, and walked calmly back to the stables. I never told anybody about it for fear I would not be allowed to ride her any more. Up to then she had been a hundred per cent safety ride, and she was again after it.

Apart from that, horses seem to understand the nuances of the human voice, and obey words of command according to the way in which they are given. 'Whoah' is the universal sound for stopping, *à propos* of which I have always enjoyed this story. An old farmer, who had ploughed with horses for some forty years, at last gave in to modernism and bought a tractor. The first day he took it out he got to the end of the furrow and shouted 'Whoa!' and went on through the hedge.

But the human voice has a great effect on a horse, conveying as it does appreciation or anger; so to make it more difficult the regulations for dressage competitions ban the use of the voice, along with whip, martingales, blinkers and other extraneous aids. But, in private, riders talk a lot to their horses; show jumpers, for whom there are no restrictions, chatter regularly to their horses as they go along.

The eyesight of the horse is naturally very important; and it is regulated by its anatomy. With eyes at the sides of the head, not frontally placed, it can see well enough ahead at a distance, but has difficulty at close quarters; which is why, if you approach a horse from the front and hold out your hand to pat his nose, he will generally throw his head up as if to take avoiding action. Come up from the side, and he can see you quite well. He has good lateral and rearward vision.

When a horse comes up to a jump with his head in the normal position, he will be able to see the top of the jump but not the base line. To look at the latter he must lower his head, which is what all horses do before a fence, if they are allowed to. Then he is able to calculate the distance away, when he should take off, and how he should leap to get over it; and he does this instantaneously, usually making his decision before the rider gets round to it. This was the basis of Caprilli's thinking when he developed forward riding.

How far can a horse see? It is a moot point. Go to the gate of a field with horses in it at the far end from the gate, say 200 yards away. The chances are that they will notice you, whether you call out or not. A horse can probably see a good deal further than that; after all, in his wild incarnation he had to, for the plains on which he lived were wide open, the horizon a long way off. But it is probable that his vision was not very clear, or he would not be frightened of quite simple objects.

Can he see colours? It was long considered that the horse was colour blind, seeing everything in black and white. Grzimek, already mentioned, carried out a number of experiments on a group of horses and came to the conclusion that they could recognise the four primary colours, yellow, green, blue and red, the first two more clearly than the last two. (*Such Agreeable Friends.*) There are also authentic instances of a horse recognising a red-painted van. So it is not to be wondered at if horses introduced suddenly to red and white or blue and white poles on a fence are apt to take exception to them.

The sense of touch plays a major part in the training of the equine. The sensitivity varies with the breeding, but all will react to the human touch in some degree or other. There is the feel of the body in the saddle, of the legs, on the sides of the horse, of the bit in its mouth, of the whip and the spur. He is able to endure great pain, but is also extremely sensitive to it, witness immediate signs of lameness, and flinching when sore points are touched. Most horses seem to like being patted and stroked; gently pulling the ears is soothing for some, though quite a few horses are very chary of having them touched, due sometimes, no doubt, to ill-treatment. They have their special ticklish places, under the belly, inside the stifle and it is as well to respect them, but handling those parts delicately and gradually will usually eradicate most phobias of this kind. The horse will get used to practically anything, if you set about it gradually and with continual repetition.

A horse is an emotional being, and he usually shows his feelings very clearly, most often when he is disturbed. A swishing tail, rolling eyes, flat back ears, and restive feet betoken loss of temper or discomfort. Horses in a dressage test will often swish their tails, a sure sign of their disgust at the whole proceedings. However, a horse which goes along with his ears permanently pricked is not paying any attention to his rider. An attentive, intelligent horse will usually go along with ears flicking back and forwards alternatively. When both ears go back together, it is time for the rider to pay attention. On the other hand a horse at full gallop has both ears back. Not many horses have won the Derby with their ears pricked forward. A horse which lays its ears absolutely flat back and starts shaking its head is usually planning some devilment, so be prepared.

It is universally agreed, I think, that horses are very sensitive to atmosphere and to the state of mind of their human masters. A horse, more especially a pony, will try to 'old soldier' a nervous or weak rider. If the rider is frightened of an obstacle ahead – and who isn't some time or other? – the horse will know it at once and get frightened too. The courage of a horse is often a measure of the courage and determination of the rider and of the horse's trust in him.

This does not contradict the statement that the horse is a timid animal but underlines the courage that he shows in overcoming fears at the behest of the rider. Here also his docility and willingness to co-operate come into play. Such a horse will face any hazard and go on to the limit of his powers of endurance. Horse literature and tradition abounds in tales of the endurance of horses, which make Grand Nationals and three-day events look like child's play. Of course there are horses, as there are people, who are slugs and craven at heart, because while horses generally conform to a set pattern of rules and principles they are individuals too, widely differing in character and physical power.

The horse seems able, immediately, to detect and assess human character and reactions. He is also, I believe, affected by the wider atmosphere of group or environment, and has a sense of occasion. I had two polo ponies once, who were accustomed to playing first-class polo, not always ridden by me; their names were Sam and Santu; an Australian of good breeding and an Indian country-bred. Before a tournament match Sam would stand at the side of the ground trembling all over literally like a jelly; it was quite alarming to watch if you did not know him. The moment he was mounted and in the game the trembling ceased and he was ready for anything. Santu regarded station polo and practice games as waste of time; neither whip nor spur would get him to go faster than an unwilling slow gallop. In a tournament I carried neither, and he used to go like the wind. On the other hand, I had a charger, also a Waler, who was such a comfortable ride that he was known as Thunderbox; he was a most beautiful jumper – in private. Hopefully I entered him for show jumping competitions, but we never got beyond the second or third fences. No power on earth would make him jump in public. All horsemen will have similar experiences.

So we have this great, strong four-legged friend and servant of ours; a bundle of nerves, timid and fearful of the unexpected; sensitive to atmosphere, liable to suffer from nerves and to have off days; docile and obedient by nature, always in need of a leader and master; receptive to affection; I am sure that human love, if it is really given unstintingly and continuously, influences a horse very strongly indeed; and if the evidence of many people is true he can and does, respond to it in his own way. Relationships of this kind are rare, however; there are horses which are quite impervious to all signs of affection, unaffected by reward or punishment, I have known them too. For the most part horses are honest, down-to-earth creatures, who thrive on hard work and the right food, not playthings but servants and companions, who will always repay study. The better you understand the horse you ride the happier will be your riding.

6 Equipment and Accoutrements

The basic items are bridle; bit or bits; reins; saddle.

The bridle is the leather equipment on the horse's head for holding the bit and the reins. The principle part is the headpiece, a broadish strap which goes over the head behind the ears and merges into the narrower strap on either side of the head, called the cheekpiece, to which the bit is attached. The headpiece is kept in position by the front or browband, which goes horizontally round the forehead below the ears, and has a loop at each end through which passes the broad part of the headpiece. This bifurcates just below the browband into the cheekpieces, already mentioned, and a narrow strap which passes under the jaw, helping to keep the bridle in place. This is called the throat latch, always pronounced 'lash'. This should always be kept fairly loose, allowing two fingers to be inserted between it and the throat.

At the end of the cheekpiece is the bit in the horse's mouth, to which is attached the rein or reins, depending on the type of bridle and bit. Each rein is a single strap from three-quarters to one inch wide, attached to the bit either by sewing, buckles or studs. The cheekpieces are also attached to the bit in the same way, usually by buckles; few people have a bridle for each horse nowadays. The cheekpieces are divided into two with buckles for adjustment according to the size of the horse's head; and the throat latch has a buckle on the near side for the same purpose.

The simplest form of bridle is the snaffle bridle with only one bit attached to it and no noseband. This is a broad strap with a buckle for adjustment at the rear, and a head strap of its own, which also goes through the loops on the browband. The front strap should lie on the nasal bone a little below a point midway between the eyes and the nostrils. Its main use is for the attachment of martingales and other gadgets. It is commonly known as a cavesson noseband, but that is, strictly, the name given to a training noseband, which will be described later.

There is a variety of utility nosebands which have definite

purposes of their own for controlling the horse, usually for stopping it: drop noseband, flash, grakle, kineton, sheepskin, which are described below.

The snaffle bridle can also be used for a Pelham bit, which combines curb and snaffle effects in one. When two bits – bridoon (snaffle) and curb are used, another headstrap and

Fig. 5.   Snaffle Bridle with drop noseband

cheekpiece are added to carry the extra bit, and you have the double bridle. The reins of a double bridle are usually rather narrower than the single one of a snaffle, for ease of holding. Once reins were always made of leather, either plain straight-forward straps, or, in the case of snaffle reins, for better grip plaited, partially covered with rubber, or made of a mixture of rubber and leather to make them more elastic; nowadays they are also made of webbing or nylon and similar materials. Some-times reins are made in two pieces, buckled at the ends. In Western tack they are not joined at all, so that they can immedi-ately be dropped to the ground when the rider dismounts, the American cow pony being trained to stay put when the reins hang like this. British and European horses never seem to be taught this useful trick.

It is convenient at this point to consider the bits. 'There is a bit for every horse,' is a common saying in the horse world, but I am not sure if it is not wishful thinking. The number of varieties of bit invented over the centuries is uncountable, and still horses pull and run away. It is always the hand at the other end of the rein that counts. But all these different bits have only been variations on two original themes, the snaffle and the curb.

The snaffle or bridoon, which is the 5,000-year-old proto-type of all bits, simply consists of a mouthpiece and two rings. The most commonly used type is the jointed snaffle, which has the mouthpiece divided into two parts linked by welded rings in the middle. The two pieces broaden towards the ends, which are pierced to take the side rings. When the snaffle is used on its own, the side rings are large, often with a thick oval-shaped union to make it less likely to cut the horse's lips; it is known then from its appearance as an egg butt snaffle. Another variety with the same object is cut in the shape of the letter D, and called naturally a Dee snaffle. The mouthpiece of a single snaffle is thick, again to lessen the chance of cutting the tongue or the bars of the mouth. This is the part of the jaw between the horse's incisors or front teeth and molars or back teeth. When the bit is used in combination with a curb bit, it is much smaller and lighter, there being not so much direct pressure from it, and also it has to fit inside the mouth. The mouthpieces of a jointed snaffle are usually plain rounded smooth steel or stainless steel bars, do not use nickel or any other kind of metal for bits or stirrups, but occasionally the metal is twisted to make grooves and ridges, which can be very severe. This is known as a twisted snaffle. Other varieties of snaffle have straight bars, curved (halfmoon) mouthpieces, bars with ports (an arch in the middle of varying height), or chain mouthpieces – very severe and not to be used. For horses with very sensitive mouths, or for restraining, rubber or vulcanite mouthpieces are occasionally used.

The snaffle acts directly on the corners of the mouth with the object of raising the head. The jointed snaffle also has a nutcracker action on the mouth, which can be quite severe.

The curb bit is younger than the snaffle; the earliest of its kind known is a Celtic bit of the third century B.C. It was in general use in the Middle Ages in the days of the armoured knight. The mouthpiece is a single bar, usually with a port in the centre of it, with holes at each end through which go arms, short above the mouthpiece, longer below it. These are called cheekpieces, not to be confused with the leather straps of the bridle, upper and lower. The upper cheekpiece has a loop for attachment to the bridle and an open hook which takes the curb chain. The lower cheekpiece, which tapers nearly to a point, has a ring attached to take the rein. The proportions of the upper and lower cheekpieces determine the power of the

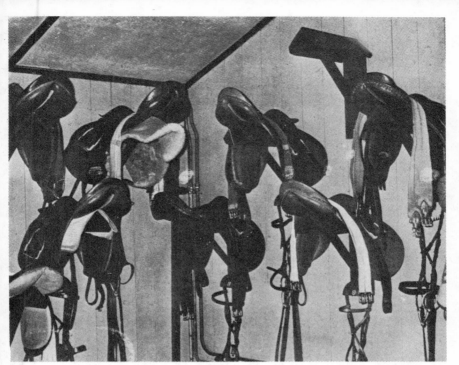

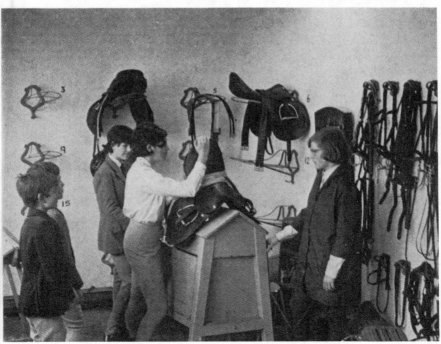

Two orderly and well-kept tack rooms (*Light Horse*)

GROOMING. The basic items of equipment for grooming a pony are as follows: *Top row (left to right).* Dandy brush (tail and mane), sweat scraper, curry-comb, body brush. *Bottom row.* Water brush, sponges (one for dock and sheath, and one for eyes and nose), hoof pick, wisp (made of straw) and below a comb. All these are laid out on a stable rubber, of which you should have a plentiful supply. A rubber curry-comb is a useful extra to use on thick and

action of the bit. The upper is, nowadays, more or less constant at about an inch; the lower can be anything from three

Fig. 6.   Double Bridle

1. *Browband*   2. *Cheekpieces*   3. *Throat Latch (pronounced 'lash')*   4.
Cavesson Noseband   5. *Reins*   6. *Curb Chain*   7. *Lip Strap*   8. *Snaffle*
9. *Curb Bit*

inches upwards; the old medieval bits used to be twelve inches or more. In the case of a modern Weymouth or Ward Union bit used in a double bridle the length will not be less than three inches or more than five. Mouthpieces can also be plain straight bars, or curved (halfmoon), or made of vulcanite or rubber. To make it milder in the mouth the steel bar can be covered with leather.

The curb chain is made of a series of closely meshed steel links, about three-quarters of an inch broad and about eight inches long. The broad link exerts a more or less level pressure on the soft hollow behind the lower jaw known as the chin groove. It is put on by hooking one end over the off side hook, laying the links right-handed so that they are flat in the chin groove, and hooking the other end over the near side hook, Then the required length is found by taking up the requisite number of links, and looping the last one over the hook. Sometimes the chain can be covered with leather, or made of leather altogether, or elastic.

The curb has a lever action. The effect of a pull of the rein on the end of the lower cheekpiece is to pivot the mouthpiece in the horse's mouth and to move the top of the upper cheekpiece forward, which takes the curb chain with it and causes it to press on the chin groove. The effect of this is to induce the horse to open (flex) its lower jaw a little and bend its head from the poll: always provided that the training has been correctly done from the outset and the horse's conformation allows it.

Fig. 7.   Normal Curb Bit with moveable mouthpiece

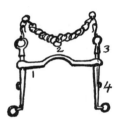

Fig. 8.   A Halfmoon Pelham Bit

1. *Mouthpiece*   2. *Port*   3. *Upper cheekpiece*   4. *Lower cheekpiece*

A horse with a thick neck and no play where the jowl and the throat meet is unable to flex properly and so is very difficult to control. So in the double bridle there are two different actions, the flexing and slight lowering of the head by the curb, and its raising by the snaffle, so that the carriage of the head is maintained at a normal level.

The mouthpiece of the curb bit can be either moveable (up and down) or fixed. In the normal double bridle, which only concerns us here, the bit with a moveable mouthpiece was known as the Ward Union, and with a fixed mouthpiece it is usually called a Weymouth. In dressage competitions the Weymouth bit with a fixed mouthpiece is *de rigueur*.

The Pelham bit is a curb bit which contrives to combine the functions of snaffle and curb in one bit. Rings at the ends of the lower cheekpieces take the curb rein, while side rings attached to the mouthpiece take the bridoon or snaffle rein. It is a compromise which does not quite come off; nevertheless it is a useful bit for many occasions, and it must on the whole be more comfortable for the horse to have only one bit in its mouth instead of two. Horses always seemed to go well in the Army bit, which is a variety of Pelham. It can be used either with one rein or two, but should never, repeat never, be used with a single double-ended rein, which has a completely deadening effect on the mouth.

The correct fitting of bit and bridle is of the utmost importance to all riding, so here are the points to look for when inspecting a horse before mounting.

The browband should be well clear of the ears and above the bony ridge which runs from the eye socket (orbit).

The leather cheekpieces should be the same length on either side of the head.

The noseband is two fingers' depth below the cheek bones, and loose enough to allow two fingers' breadth between it and the face of the horse.

The throat latch should allow at least two or three fingers' breadth between it and the back of the jaw.

The bit. (a) Snaffle. This should be high enough just to wrinkle the soft corners of the lips and no more. (b) Pelham. This is also a single bit, and it must be so placed that when the curb reins are pulled, and the upper cheekpiece goes forward, the curb chain should act on the chin groove and not above it on the bony jaw. (c) Double bridle. The snaffle must lie above the curb, fitting, as above, into the corners of the lips; the curb bit must be below it, resting on the bars of the mouth, again so placed that the curb chain acts in the correct place. The curb chain itself must not be too tight, and all the links must lie in the same direction.

All leather work must be clean, soft and pliable, all metal work bright and clean.

As a matter of interest, here are some of the different styles of bit most generally in use. Snaffle gag: There are holes in the rings of the snaffle, which are fairly large, and through them pass the reins, which with the headpiece make a single length of leather. When the reins are pulled they exert pressure on the poll at the same time as on the corners of the mouth, which is very effective with a puller. Many polo players, not to say show jumpers, use this bit. A variation is the Hitchcock gag, in which the cheekpiece (leather) goes from the bit to a ring on the head-piece, down again to a ring on the bit, and then to the reins, giving an extremely strong lifting effect. The Fulmer or Austra-lian snaffle has a straight bar between the loose side ring and mouthpiece. In a ball-cheek snaffle the sidebar and ring are one rigid piece of metal. These sidebars or cheeks prevent the bit being drawn through the mouth, avoid pinching the lips, and by pressing against one side or other of the mouth help lateral movement, and so make good training bits. The loose ring type is to be preferred, because it allows movement of the bit in the mouth, promoting saliva, and encouraging the horse to play with the bit, which is an aid to obtaining a soft and yielding mouth. The cheeks can be kept in one posi-tion, if required, by a keeper attached to the leather cheekpiece.

The egg butt or Dee family of snaffles achieve the same ob-jects, and are generally the most popular bit. Sometimes the rings of the egg butt snaffle have slots in them to maintain one position. A very popular snaffle is the German, which has a large hollow mouthpiece, making it very light in the mouth. It can be had either with a plain ring or an egg butt one.

The basic curb bit is the Weymouth fixed mouth or sliding mouth with a port. The variations on this theme are endless, mostly in the direction of longer cheekpieces and more com-plicated mouthpieces, all with the object of making the bit more severe and so giving it more stopping power. The cheek-pieces are either straight or curved (swan-cheek). Mostly the mouthpieces and cheeks move together, but in the Banbury, which has a straight-bar mouthpiece slightly tapering from each end to the centre, the cheekpieces can revolve round the mouthpiece and also independently of each other. The move-ment facilitates mouthing, and the bit can be useful with very hard-mouthed or dry-mouthed animals. The Chifney, whose invention is attributed to the jockey, Sam Chifney, is a very powerful bit, but, in the right hands, effective and humane. The lower cheek pivots round the mouthpiece, while the upper cheekpiece is fixed, which helps to keep the curb chain in the correct position in the chin groove. A bit much in use at one time by polo players, but never seen now, is the Ninth Lancer, which had a straight mouthpiece and flat short lower cheek-pieces, with two slots for reins, so that the strength of the action could be varied. The Western bit is an ordinary curb with curved cheekpieces and a variety of mouthpieces.

The Pelham bit most often seen is the halfmoon Pelham. The

military bit, the port-mouth universal, reversible, is an Angle-cheek Pelham; the snaffle rings are so made that the lower cheekpieces extend down not directly below the upper cheek-piece but a little way behind it. This tends to give quicker action of the curb chain; the lower cheek is provided with two slots, as in the Ninth Lancer, to give a wide range of curb effect. The mouthpiece has a port in it, and one side of it is smooth, the other serrated so that the bit can be reversed to use either way.

Other types of Pelham are: Globe cheek, in which all parts are fixed and the lower rings are part of the actual cheekpieces. Hanoverian, a high-port mouthpiece with rollers round the two arms on either side of the port. It is in effect a jointed bit, which with a high port can be very severe. This also was much used by polo players. A tendency of the normal Pelham to chafe the corners of the mouth is countered by the Scamperdale, popularised by Sam Marsh between the wars, in which the mouth-piece is angled forward so that the snaffle rings miss the corners. A similar result is obtained by the Rugby Pelham with a fixed cheekpiece but an independent linked snaffle ring. The Three-in-One (Swales) has the snaffle rings fixed to the mouthpiece independently of the cheekpieces and inside them. The bridle and bridoon reins are attached to this and not to the upper cheek-piece, so there is no displacement of the mouthpiece or the upper cheek before the curb chain begins to act, which is an

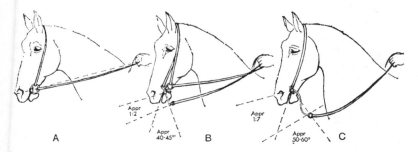

Fig. 9. Three different types of bits and their actions

a. *Modern Snaffle Bit.* No lifting, no pressing effects, only that in the corner of the mouth. The mildest possible effects.
b. *Modern Double Bridle.* Curb bit with straight lower cheek. Medium effects.
c. *Middle Age Curb Bit á la Guérinière.* Long 'S' shaped lower cheek with no bridoon. The possible strongest effects.

advantage; on the other hand the inside rings squeeze the mouth.

Included in the Pelham family is the Kimblewick, which was devised by the saddler, F. E. Gibson of Newmarket for Phil Oliver from a Spanish jumping bit, and so called from the village in Buckinghamshire where he lives. The essence of this is a short cheekpiece with a rather more than semi-circular ring which goes from the lower end of the cheekpiece to the upper cheek above the mouthpiece. The rein can move up and down the ring, so that when the hands are held low the rein slips down and the action is that of a mild curb; when the hand is held high, there is a snaffle effect. This bit has been popular with show jumpers, but needs skilful use.

Nosebands play an important part in the control of the horse, and the most widely used of them all, certainly since the war, is the drop noseband, a German invention for use with horses that throw their heads about and get their tongues over the bit. It consists of a front strap, which goes over the lower part of the nose, and a rear strap joined to it by a ring, which hangs nearly at right angles to it just in front of the rings of the snaffle. The front strap is adjustable so that it can be tightened round the nose, and it can also be placed up and down. The correct position is about two-thirds of the way down the face and clear of the nostrils. Used as a brake it is placed low down and used with a standing martingale, so that when pressure is exerted by the reins and by the horse trying to raise its head the nostrils are constricted and the breathing interfered with. In 1962 the British Show Jumping Association at last put an end to this unpleasant practice by banning the use of the standing martingale with a dropped noseband. Used with a running martingale the effect is less severe.

Other types of noseband are: Flash, an ordinary noseband with two straps attached to it which cross below it over the nose and are buckled at the rear. The object is to obtain something approximate to the effect of the drop noseband while having a standing martingale attached to the normal one. Grakle, named after the winner of the 1931 Grand National, consists of two straps crossing over the nose, one passing over the bit and one under it, and connected at the rear. The pressure on the nose is concentrated at the point of intersection, and it is a powerful instrument against a confirmed puller or a horse which crosses its jaws. The Kineton is a severe type of noseband, invented by Mr Puckle of Kineton, Warwickshire, which comprises a front piece of metal covered with leather, with adjustable buckles at each end attached to two open metal loops in contact with the bit. The action of the reins causes direct pressure on the nose. The sheepskin noseband is a bit of mystery, but people who use it must think that it does some good. It might be pleasant for a horse with very sensitive skin. It could act as a kind of blinker, preventing the horse from looking down at the ground and seeing sudden shadows or movement which might make him shy. The most practical suggestion that I have heard is that it makes a stargazer keep his head down. Raising his head up, he becomes temporarily blinded by the ridge of the sheepskin, and so has to lower his head to see where he is going.

Martingales: This word, of uncertain derivation, describes a small family of leather attachments between the girth of the saddle and the bridle for the purpose of correcting the horse's head carriage. The standing martingale is a direct connection between the girth, between the forelegs, by a loop, to the back of the noseband by a loop or buckle. It can also be made from a broad piece of cloth, adjusted by knotting, which has the advantage of being more resilient than leather. In the running martingale the strap is divided about a foot from the bridle end into two parts, each with a ring at the end through which the reins are passed. With a double bridle it is usually used with the curb rein. The bib martingale is a running martingale with flat piece of leather joining the two separate straps. The Cheshire martingale has the divided ends attached to the rings of the snaffle bit, and is best not used at all. A martingale with a very flexible sort of action, especially for lateral movement, is the pulley martingale. The strap, instead of being divided, ends with a ring, through which passes a cord with rings at each end, these taking the reins. A combined martingale incorporates the features of both the standing and running martingale, with the action of both. The Irish martingale, naturally, is not a martingale at all, but a short strap, six to eight inches, with a ring at each end through which the reins, the object being to keep them together.

Two special training martingales are the Market Harborough and the French Chambon. They both work on the principle of self-inflicted, and self-relieved, discomfort and pain. The first works through two strips of rawhide or rounded leather attached to rings on the main strap of the martingale, passing through the rings of the bit and then attached to the reins. If the horse throws its head up extreme pressure is brought to bear on the mouth, instantly relieved when the head is lowered into its right position. The Chambon, used for dismounted work, has the martingale straps going through the rings of a strap over the poll and down to the bit. Resistance in the form of head raising exerts pressure on the poll.

The present form of the saddle has been set for nearly 1,000 years, and is not likely to change in the foreseeable future, except possibly as regards materials. The rigid inner framework of the tree consists of two waisted strips of wood, usually beechwood, united in front by a curved arch called the head or pommel, reinforced by a steel gullet plate. Below the arch two wings project downwards to fit on either side of

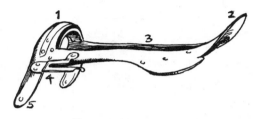

Fig. 10 Conventional Saddle Tree
1. *Head* 2. *Cantle* 3. *Panels* 4. *Stirrup leather bar* 5. *Point*

the withers, called points. The two waisted panels spread out to the rear to form a wide flattish arch called the back arch or cantle. Attached to the points on either side, just below the gullet, two slotted metal plates project backwards, the bars, which take the stirrup leathers. The slots are open at the rear but can be closed by a moveable catch (gate), a safety device to allow the stirrup leather to come away from the saddle in an emergency.

This type of tree has been replaced for specialist riding; show jumping, dressage, eventing; by a spring tree, the pommel of

Fig. 11. A Spring tree made of laminated sheets of wood

which is shaped more forward. The actual 'spring' is obtained from two pieces of light steel, one on either side, which connect the widest part of the panels to the waist. This gives resilience to the saddle seat, and so to the action of the rider in the saddle. The head of a spring tree is always set back at an angle of about 45 degrees. The panels are now often made of laminated sheets of wood, or of fibre glass.

The covering of the saddle is still made of leather-pigskin or cowhide, stretched on to the tree over a tightly strained webbing base. This is the seat. Welted on to the narrow part of the seat are the skirts, small flaps to cover the bars and protect the legs from the buckles of the stirrup leathers. Attached to the tree underneath the skirt is the flap, a large shaped piece of leather against which the knees and thighs of the rider are pressed when riding. The flap can be cut in various ways, from straight down in a showing saddle to well forward over the shoulders with knee rolls for jumping saddles. Fixed to the tree underneath the flaps are the girth straps.

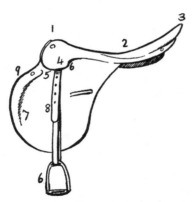

Fig. 12. A modern Spring tree saddle
1. *Head or Pommel* 2. *Seat* 3. *Cantle or Back Arch* 4. *Skirt* 5. *Stirrup leather Bar (under skirt)* 6. *Stirrup iron* 7. *Flap, with knee roll* 8. *Stirrup leather* 9. *Panel, inside flap*

The under side of the saddle is covered with well stuffed panels lined with linen, serge or leather. These panels rest on the back on either side of the spine, leaving a central space well clear of it. The best lining is perhaps linen over serge. Leather is the strongest material, of course, but needs constant care to keep it soft and pliable. The panels are stuffed with wool or thick felt. Underneath the outer flap is a subsidiary, thin piece of leather (sweat flap), the same shape as the outer one, slotted to receive the points of the tree. To the rear of the outer flap is a slot to take the surcingle, a broad leather strap which fits tightly over and round the saddle as a reinforcement to the girths, for greater security in sports like racing, show jumping and eventing. The pommel and cantle of the saddle can have D-rings either side for attaching personal equipment, raincoats, rugs, etc. Rings on the forward edges of the flaps are for use with draw reins or other gadgets. There are always three girth straps on either side, two in use one in reserve.

Attached to the saddle are girths and stirrup leathers, and, on occasion, breast plate or crupper. Girths have two straps and buckles at each end, and come in sizes from about thirty-six inches to fifty-four inches and from three and a half to five inches wide. The main varieties of girth are plain web or nylon, used two together; Balding, double straps crossing over each other at the middle so as to give plenty of clearance at the elbows and to avoid chafing; Atherstone, which tapers to the centre with the same object as the Balding; T-fold, a strip of leather folded into three, with usually a piece of serge within the fold so that the leather can be kept greased. I have always found that this girth, if the leather is properly looked after, is the best and strongest of them all and the least likely to cause girth galls. Webbing and nylon girths must be kept scrupulously clean and dry, and brushed carefully to remove dust and all foreign bodies.

Stirrup leathers are thickish straps, five-eighths to one and one-eighth inches wide, and from four to four feet six inches long with a buckle at one end, made of cowhide, rawhide or buffalo hide (red leathers), the latter being the toughest and also the most expensive. Leathers go in pairs and are punched with holes for adjustment. These start equal, but the leather stretches unequally, so constant adjustment is necessary. Leathers are like motor tyres; 'they should be changed the moment they show signs of wear. Stirrup irons should be of steel of stainless steel, heavy enough to hang down freely, and wide enough to take the broad welt of the rider's boot easily, leaving a clearance either side, but not so wide as to let the foot slip right through and get caught. There are various patterns of stirrup iron on the market, but the best is the conventional bell-shaped design, with a good broad, serrated footplate. A 'safety' stirrup is made with one side open and connected with a piece of elastic. Very useful for young children is the box stirrup, which has a leather outer boot into which the toe of the rider's boot is inserted, automatically coming out if the rider falls off.

Breast plate and crupper speak for themselves. The former is fitted in front of the saddle to prevent it from slipping backwards on a high-withered horse; the latter has a rounded loop to go over the tail, and, attached to the rear of the saddle, it prevents it from going forward on a low-withered horse or, more usually, pony.

TWO

The Training of the Rider

7 Mounting, Dismounting and Position

The first act of riding is, naturally, to get on to the back of the horse, and there are various ways of doing it. Before mounting, however, one routine should never be omitted, the checking of the horse's tack, for its condition as well as its correct fitting. The correct fitting of the bridle has already been described on page 62. The parts of the saddle to be checked are all the straps and buckles of the girth (and to see that it is tight enough and that the skin lies flat underneath it) and the stirrup leathers. The approximate correct length for the rider is the length of his arm. Now you can proceed to mount.

The easiest way is from a mounting block. The horse is led alongside a platform on which the rider is standing. He takes the reins in his left hand and rests it on the pommel; puts his left foot in the stirrup, steps quietly over and settles gently into the saddle, finding the outside stirrup with his right foot.

The normal way of mounting is from the ground with stirrups. In the case of a beginner the horse should be held for him. The Army, which knows a lot about teaching, always does things by numbers, so we will follow suit.

1. Approach the horse from the near side and give him a pat.
2. Take the reins from the horseholder, and bring them over the horse's head.
3. Separate the reins for riding in the left hand. The beginner will always work with a snaffle bridle and a single rein, so the separation of the reins is as follows: Left rein outside the little finger; right rein between the first and second fingers, with the slack of the rein across the palm and between the first finger and thumb. Alternatively, the right rein can be held between the first finger and thumb; in which case the end of the right rein passes downwards across the palm and under the little finger, and the end of the left rein in the opposite direction and between the first finger and thumb. This method seems to give more flexible control when riding with one hand, playing polo or in gymkhana events, with less chance of the reins slipping.
4. Place the left hand on the horse's neck in front of the withers, or on the pommel, and turn your body so that it is level with

the horse's shoulder and facing partly to the rear. Rein contact should be enough to prevent the horse from moving forward, and even; unless the horse is fidgety, in which case have the near rein (left) slightly shorter than the off (right), so that if the horse does move about, it will turn inwards towards you and not away from you, which can be awkward.

5. Take the stirrup in the right hand and place the left foot in the stirrup, with the toe pointing well down so that it does not stick into the horse's side and make him move away.

6. Take hold of the waist or cantle of the saddle with the right hand.

7. Press the left knee into the saddle flap, and spring up from the right foot, still taking care to keep the left toe pointing downwards.

8. Pull and push the body up with hands and feet, until you are upright against the side of the horse, supported by the hands on the pommel and cantle of the saddle, mainly, and by the left foot in the stirrup. Pause momentarily here.

9. Bend the body forward and to the left, i.e. towards the horse's head, swing the right leg well over the back of the saddle, keeping the foot clear of the horse's croup, and shift the right hand from the cantle to the pommel.

10. As your right leg comes down the other side of the horse, support yourself on the left stirrup and with your hands on the pommel, and lower yourself *gently* into the saddle.

11. Sit quietly in the saddle and find the right stirrup with the toe of your right foot; if necessary hold the stirrup leather with the right hand. Make sure that both leathers are flat against the legs and not twisted.

12. Separate the reins with your hands, by slipping the little finger of the right hand inside the right rein and drawing the reins apart, securing the respective ends between the first finger and thumb of each hand. Some people prefer to have the reins between the third and little fingers. Hold the reins with enough contact to prevent the horse from moving forward (in this case there will be an assistant at the horse's head to do that, but it is a good habit to get into from the start).

The instructor should make the beginner practise this operation several times until he does it smoothly in one flowing movement. Then he should practise it from the opposite side, reversing the above instructions. Mounting can, in fact, be used as a valuable gymnastic exercise for the rider. The whole thing can be practised on a dummy horse. If the rider is small and the horse large, lower the stirrup leather by several holes on the mounting side, to be re-adjusted when mounted.

This leads to mounting without stirrups, another good physical exercise. Except with very small ponies, children should not be asked to do this.

1. With the reins in the left hand, face the horse opposite the saddle.

2. Place the left hand on the pommel, the right hand on the cantle.

3. Bend the knees and spring up smartly off both feet, and pull up with the arms until the body is straight, as in mounting with stirrups, but this time supported only by both arms.

4. Swing the right leg over the pommel and carry on as from No. 9 above.

A fourth method mounting is the leg-up.

1. The rider stands facing the saddle, reins in left hand, both hands on the pommel, or the right hand can be on the waist.

2. The assistant stands directly behind and close to the rider.

3. The rider lifts his left leg so that it is horizontal from the knee downwards.

4. The assistant cups the knee with his left hand and holds the ankle with his right.

5. When the rider says he is ready, the assistant gives a controlled hoist, smoothly and without violence, high enough to enable the rider's right leg to clear the horse's croup. The rider assists by springing lightly off the right foot. Then he carries on as before.

The beginner should practise this on both sides of the horse, and should also learn to take the part of the hoister. There is a happy medium about this procedure which takes a little learning. I have seen a rider thrown over the horse to the other side by a too-energetic hoister; and it has been known for a rider to lift the wrong leg.

The last method of getting on to the back of a horse is vaulting. This is really a gymnastic exercise, and also a prelude to circus riding. It is a recognised sport for young riders in Germany, for which there is an annual championship; and it has been taken up in the U.S.A. as well, in recent years.

From the halt: Stand beside the horse, level with his shoulder, both hands on the pommel. Swing the right leg forwards, then sharply back, and with the forearms and back muscles swing the body backwards and up over the saddle.

This exercise is of course much easier when done on the move. Run with the horse, holding the saddle pommel, or hand grips on either side of the withers, body facing forward and level with the shoulders. Jump *forward* so that you land with both feet on the ground *ahead* of the shoulders and forelegs, and make the spring from there. The momentum will help the spring, and the forward position will land you correctly into the saddle or on to the horse's back. If you do not get far enough forward for the spring, you will get left behind.

This exercise must be done with a quiet horse and under supervision, but it is a really good bit of equestrian gymnastics and helps to strengthen and supple the body and gives confidence to the rider.

Dismounting

The horse knows several ways of getting rid of you, but the quickest and safest way is to take the feet out of the stirrups, and quickly swing the right leg over the horse's back, again avoiding banging the croup, and land facing the horse with both feet on the ground together. *Don't* let go of the reins.

Position

'The normal position', wrote Gustav Steinbrecht in his *Das Gymnasium des Pferdes*, 'does not exist.' He qualified it by adding, 'if one means by that one single attitude which will suit the majority of occasions'. He goes on to explain how the position of the rider in the saddle depends on the movements of the horse and the shifting location of its centre of gravity, to which the rider must conform if he is to stay in balance with his mount.

Ideas about the normality of the seat have varied with the ages and with the tack available. In the days of no saddle or stirrups, the riders sat well back on their buttocks (ischia); the knight of the Middle Ages restricted by his armour rode straightlegged on his crutch, as did the early American cowboys; de la Guérinière, with a more suitable saddle, brought the rider back on to his buttocks in the precursor of the modern balanced seat; Caprilli insisted that the rider's buttocks should never 'come into brusque contact with the saddle'. The English hunting man and the Australian stockrider, defying all rules, sat well back on the broad part of the saddle seat, and the balanced brigade seldom saw anything but their heels.

Now there is no seat for all seasons; it entirely depends on what you are doing. Gregor de Romaszkan distinguishes four different kinds of seat: the full seat; the upper part of the body forward; the half-seat; the racing seat. The prime requirement of any position in the saddle is security, which is obtained principally from correct balance, combined with the gripping of the legs assisted by the design of the saddle and the support of the stirrups.

The ancient riders had no security except that which came from balance. The belted knight was kept in the saddle by its high pommel and cantle and, of course, the stirrups. The hunting man sat on a small flat saddle with superb suppleness and balance that seem to defy the laws of gravity and anything else. The cavalry soldier from the eighteenth century onwards has had the benefit of a deep saddle, hemmed in with kit front and back, and his seat at its best was approximately that of the balanced seat of de la Guérinière.* The show jumper follows the injunctions of Caprilli and tends to keep his seat off the saddle, resting on stirrup and knees tucked into supporting knee rolls.

The position of the soldier deteriorated in the nineteenth century into a stiff, backward straphanging, which is what caused Caprilli to rebel and reject it altogether. But with the teaching of Steinbrecht and others there came a return at the end of the century to the basic principles and to the recognition of the necessity for suppleness and adaptability. Now, apart from racing, there are two kinds of position, which we can call the balanced seat and the forward seat, though the latter is balanced too.

The forward seat was designed for outdoor riding – the *campagne* school – for going at speed over any kind of terrain and over fences on the way; Caprilli wanted the Italian cavalry to be able to go freely and straight across country, without interfering with their horses' mouths or putting any weight on their quarters. He limited the aids to their simplest form: forward movement of the hand and leg pressure to go forward. ('The leg,' he said, 'should never be brought into play without a corresponding forward movement of the hands.'); for turning, a pull on the direct rein and a corresponding relaxation of the opposite hand; it was immaterial to him which was the leading leg at the canter, arguing that 'a horse has never fallen because of galloping on the wrong lead'.

The position in the saddle he required was that the knees should be kept against the forward flaps of the saddle, stirrups short enough for the feet to press well down on the stirrup, toes pointing up and heels down; grip would be with the lower

---

*But Waldemar Zeunig (*Horsemanship*) says that the inventor of this seat was a German, Pinter von der Au, in his *Horse Treasury*, published in Frankfurt in 1688.

part of the thigh and the knee, the calves and heels never touching the horse except for good reason; the upper part of the body had to lean slightly forward, the seat just off the saddle. The trot is always a rising one. To achieve this a special saddle was necessary, with a low pommel, flaps cut well forward and with knee rolls, and a high pommel, which would tend to throw the body forward and into the lowest part of the saddle. The hand is held low, and bit, reins, hands, wrists and forearms make a straight line. This, with individual variations, is the position which was adopted all over Europe during the present century for show jumping and cross-country riding.

Piero Santini, Caprilli's pupil, has described it in detail in his two books, *Riding Reflections* and *The Forward Impulse*. Paul Rodzianko took it to Russia, and Vladimir Littauer took it from there to the New World – *Commonsense Horsemanship* and *Be a Better Horseman*. With it has come the new development in saddle making, already touched on above, which has spread not only to the outdoor school but to the indoor manège and dressage riding; the saddle has been adapted to place the rider in the correct position without effort, which could never be done by the old-fashioned flat saddle.

The forward seat has its limitations. It will not take the rider beyond the school of the open air, the cross-country course and the show jumping arena; but that is all its advocates required of it. The rider who is not content with this, who wants to penetrate the uttermost secrets of the control of the horse, must take a rather different standpoint. For Caprilli there was no meeting point for his system of forward riding and manège riding; collection and the curb were dirty words to him. Yet nowadays many riders combine the two in horse trials, the one-day and three-day events, where dressage riding and its skills always precedes the outdoor forward riding and its special requirements. They seem to make the transition without difficulty, as does the horse, and both seem all the better for the combination.

In the full, balanced seat, the rider rests on his seat bones in the lowest and narrowest part of the saddle, at least a hand's breadth in front of the cantle. Any modern type of saddle will help him into this position. The hips should be equally placed on either side, not one lower than the other, which is riding with a dropped hip and destroys balance and flexibility. The body should be upright, shoulders square and level, but no hollowing of the back. Neck and head should be erect, eyes looking to the front over and beyond the horse's ears. The head, shoulders, hips, and the heels should be in one vertical plane.

Below the hips, the thighs should slope gently forward in contact with the saddle, so that the insides of the knees are tucked into the flaps of the saddle. The lower leg is placed slightly behind the vertical (behind the girth), ball of the foot resting on the stirrup, toes pointing upwards and very slightly outwards, but never turned in. Heels are pressed down to keep the foot firm on the plate of the stirrup, with rather more pressure on the inside. Calves are in light contact with the sides of the horse.

The arms hang down naturally to the elbow, and the forearm, wrists, hands and reins to the bit should be in one straight line. The reins held in both hands as already described (page 79, 80), fingers turned inwards and the backs of the hands turned outwards.

Hands and wrists must be absolutely supple and relaxed. It is really the fingers which hold the reins and control the horse. In this there is no disagreement among any of the schools of thought. 'Nothing is quicker and stronger if properly applied than the fingers...' (Piero Santini – *Riding Reflections*.) 'The hand... must never turn into a cramped fist even when strong action is employed, which requires a fixed hand with firmly closed fingers. The fist makes the rider lose his "feel" for the horse's mouth and kills the "feel" in the horse's mouth.' (Waldemar Zeunig – *Horsemanship*.) The sensitive play of the fingers on the reins will make the horse in its turn 'play' with the bit, chew it and champ at it, and flex and unflex its jaw. To obtain these effects the reins must be lightly held, very slightly sagging rather than taut and tense. 'Lightness', 'softness', 'suppleness', are words used by every distinguished writer on equitation, and in the official manuals of the F.E.I., yet seldom are they seen in any dressage arena. All the more reason to cultivate these attributes at the outset.

Some lucky people are supposed to have been born with good hands, and this is often true. We have all met those people who, without any apparent effort, or even knowledge, on their part, have the most sensitive contact with any horse's mouth and seem able to control animals that would run away with riders of more common clay. But I have noticed that people with 'good hands' usually have perfect balance and security in the saddle, and I think that this is the key to lightness of control; the hand – fingers – must have behind them the support of a strong position in the saddle. 'The hand can be steady,'

Zeunig again, 'only if it finds support in the small of the back, which is flexed more or less for this purpose. But the small of the back can provide support at all times only if the seat is firm and independent. This is also a prerequisite for a soft hand, which promotes mouth activity and follows motion elastically.'

A term often found in instructional books is the 'fixed hand', which is death to all lightness. 'The completely closed hand used when the reins are tightened must never become hard and fixed.' For most of the time when riding the hands, and fingers, should always be in slight movement, following the motion, as Zeunig says above, of the mouth as it plays with the bit, and the nodding and stretching of the head. There are times, when changing to a slower gait or beginning collection, when the hand must be still, steady but not fixed or rigid.

Alas! The prerequisite for all this is a well-trained horse with a perfectly soft mouth. Too often the rider will find himself on a horse with a mouth that is dead or callous, which tries to support itself on the rider by leaning on the bit. The principle, however, remains the same, only the movements of the hand and the rein effects will have to be exaggerated. If a rider perseveres long enough with the soft movements of the hand and fingers, he will find it having an effect, even if slight, on the horse.

To return to the back, the muscles of the small of the back play a considerable part in all physical activity, and they are particularly important in riding. By bracing the small of the back, the rider's pelvis and hips are pressed forward and his seat bones forward and down into the saddle. This, combined with the pressure of the legs, pushes the horse forward up to his bit, so that it 'comes to hand'. 'Bracing the back' does not mean stiffness. If practised properly it should make the rider more supple, and becomes virtually an unconscious, reflex, action. The theory and practice of the braced back has been described in detail by Wilhelm Müseler in *Riding Logic*.

The lower part of the body – thighs and calves – remain in easy contact with the body, without any deliberate hard gripping. The leg from the knee downwards should normally be still, without flapping or niggling at the horse's sides, which only helps to blur the effect when leg aids are actually applied. Firm contact resides with the knees against the saddle, and the feet against the stirrup plates. These, with the seat bones, are the three main points of support of the rider, which should be maintained so far as possible in all circumstances. So far as possible, once movement begins and the pace quickens, adjustments forward, always forward, have to be made, so that the body always goes with the movement of the horse, which means harder contact with knees and feet and less with the seat, until at fast speeds it will be off the saddle altogether.

8 Riding on the Lunge

If the possession, or acquisition, of a firm position in the saddle, well balanced and independent of the reins, is the foundation of good riding, then the chief method of so acquiring it is that of riding without stirrups on a horse that is being lunged – riding on the lunge.

Caprilli was opposed to preliminary riding without stirrups, mainly because of the prevalent military practice of putting all cavalry recruits on stirrupless blankets and bumping them round the riding school for an hour or so a day for several weeks. They had their reins, however, and the net result was to produce a great many straphangers. Mainly for that reason, he did not permit the sitting trot in his curriculum, only the rising trot or posting; though he did allow periods of trotting without stirrups for gymnastic exercises 'to cause them (the pupils) to relax and prevent rigidity'.

Riding on the lunge as taught and practised by the Spanish Riding School of Vienna is very different from all this. It takes the form of a series of systematic and controlled exercises by the pupil sitting in the saddle on the back of a horse without stirrups or reins, while the horse is being driven on the lunge rein in a circle at varying speeds.

Properly carried out this kind of work makes great demands on both pupil and instructor; it is tiring and, at first, not a little frightening. The pupil must have courage, or at least trust in his instructor and the horse he is riding; above all he must have a genuine desire to ride well. He should set his sights high, even if he has no apparent hope of hitting the target. At whatever level of equitation he finally reaches he will be all the better for having ridden on the lunge. It is important, too, that he should be a willing pupil; the decision to take lessons on the lunge must be his and his alone. Civilian riding schools of the present day cannot force their pupils into difficult work as could a military riding master with all the authority of *King's* or *Queen's Regulations* behind him. So riding on the lunge must be voluntary.

On the other hand it is not essential, and no detriment, to

have ridden before; nor, within limits, is age any bar. I would not recommend children to start riding on the lunge before they are ten or eleven, but bareback riding before then on small ponies or donkeys is an excellent preparation for it. The danger that they will become too dependent on the reins can be overcome by insisting on the use of a neckstrap. Indeed the neckstrap should be an essential part of riding training equipment for young and old.

The most important person in this set-up is the horse. In the first place he must be quiet and thoroughly accustomed to this sort of work. He must be well trained and obedient to the correct aids. He must go forward freely and steadily without constant encouragement. His gaits must be level and comfortable, so as not to throw the rider up and down too violently in the saddle. He must be suitable in size for the rider, about 15 hands to 15.2 hands for an adult, and smaller, of course, for a child; narrow withers are an advantage.

The instructor must be competent with a lungeing rein so that he will not be busy handling that when he should be watching the rider. He must of course know his business as a teacher, with a clear idea of what he wants to achieve in the immediate lesson being given and as an ultimate objective. He must be able to assess the limitations and possibilities of the pupil and set his target accordingly. He must be quick at spotting faults and able to correct them, but he must also be able to distinguish the basic ones to be corrected from superficial bad habits which can be eradicated in time, so that the pupil is not under a continuous bombardment of corrections and commands. He must be able to inspire absolute confidence and trust in his pupil.

In all lunge work progress must be voluntary, so that a pupil should not be forced into any new position or exercise until he feels ready for it. No exercise should be carried on too long, and every exercise, indeed all work, should be done on both reins equally. Changing the rein gives a chance for a short rest. If the pupil appears to be tiring unduly the lesson should be stopped immediately, and some ordinary lessons with stirrups given instead. Sometimes lunge-riding is done with stirrups, but this loses the whole point of the exercise, which is to get the rider *down* in the saddle. If it is required to give some confidence and balance, a spell of normal lessons can be given, either individually or in a ride. The essence is to be flexible and adaptable, to be able to gear the work and the instruction to the capabilities of the pupil.

The work should be done in a quiet place away from distractions. A covered school is usually the first choice, but it is not at all necessary: an open manège will do just as well. In fact, I would recommend as much riding school work to be done in the open air as possible. The cult of the covered school is a little overdone, and sometimes I wonder whether there are not some riders who never emerge from its twilight security. It is of course useful in bad weather, for very novice riders and nervous young horses; but after all they must all come into the open sooner or later, so why not sooner? So, perhaps, a few sessions in the school for the beginner lunge rider and then out into the fresh air.

The equipment required is simple. For the horse: Snaffle bridle, with a cavesson lungeing noseband over it; the reins are knotted short enough to prevent them flapping or interfering with the horse's mouth; they are not necessary, but their presence gives confidence from the feeling that they are available in an emergency; neckstrap, also for the benefit of the rider; side reins, lightly adjusted so as to keep the horse evenly bent on the circle and restrained from going too fast; saddle; lungeing rein and whip.

The lungeing rein is attached to the front ring of the cavesson. One sees lungeing reins attached to sundry parts of the bit and bridle, a practice which should be avoided. The saddle, of course, must be a modern one, with a deep waist, high cantle and moderate pommel, forward-cut flaps and knee rolls, all to help the rider into the correct position.

For the rider: Breeches and riding boots, the latter giving better support and grip to the rider. Alternatively, jodhpurs or trousers with leather strappings and seat. Riding jacket, pullover, shirtsleeves, or whatever according to the weather. Riding cap or bowler. Jeans are better avoided for this work.

We now have the time, the place and horse and rider all together, so work can begin. An essential preliminary is for the instructor to ride the horse on the lunge himself for a few minutes on each rein, with an assistant holding the lunge rein, in the presence of the pupil. The objects of this are first to ride the horse in before the pupil mounts him; and secondly to show the pupil what it is all about and that it is really quite easy and safe. The instructor can demonstrate the various exercises. If the lunge horse is a pony, a lightweight assistant can do the demonstrating under orders from the instructor. Finally, on the ground before mounting the instructor will explain to the pupil the objects and scope of lunge riding. He will emphasise that the pupil will not be asked to do anything for which he does not feel quite ready, and that he should say when he is getting tired.

For most adult beginners the first lessons should not last longer than about twenty minutes, ten minutes on each rein, not counting short rest periods. As the muscles of the legs and back become attuned to the work the time can be increased to thirty minutes and then to a maximum of forty-five minutes. The longer the time that can be spent comfortably and without tiring the better, but the pupil must be the judge, although the instructor should be able soon to size up his ability to go on. There is no point, however, in going on if overtired, for there will be no value in the exercises.

With children the initial period should not be more than ten minutes, five minutes on each rein, and that can seem an age to a young mind. I recall a delightful book by Josephine Pullein-Thompson about children who, for various good reasons, ran their pony club themselves. They decided to do work on the lunge, and one of them was trotted round. After a few circles she asked how long she'd been doing it. 'One minute,' said the girl on the lunge. 'Only one minute!' screamed the other. 'It seems like *hours*.'

The rate of increase of riding time in ordinary civilian conditions will depend inevitably on the amount of time the pupil can give to riding, every day, two or three days a week, once a week or even less. The ideal of course is daily lessons.

First lessons on the lunge are at the halt. The instructor gives the pupil a leg-up on to the horse, which is being held by an assistant, and allows him to settle into a natural position, telling him to relax completely, letting his legs hang straight down naturally and loosely, with no attempt at gripping, hands resting on the thighs away from the saddle, body normally upright but unbraced. This is the moment to impress on the pupil that intensive gripping is not necessary for staying in the saddle; indeed that it will tend to push him out of the saddle instead of deep into it. The working of the muscles of the small of the back can be explained now, and the pupil can use them himself and feel the effect.

Then the instructor can start building up the riding position which has been described in the last chapter. Allowing the hands to hang loosely down on each side, the pupil will gradually straighten his back and square his shoulders, holding his head up and eyes to the front. If he really feels it necessary to keep his balance, he can touch the pommel of the saddle with the finger tips of one hand, not holding on to it tightly, nor leaning forward: but he should be encouraged to do without that support for the present.

Then a squeezing of the knees forwards, with accompanying pressure of the inside thigh muscles, will bring the knees forward into their more or less normal position behind the knee rolls. Pressure should be just firm enough to hold them there, but not excessive. The lower leg will now hang vertically below the knee.

The heels are pressed down, and the toes raised, which will bring the toes in a line with the knees, and the heels in the same vertical plane as the hips and shoulders.

When the pupil is comfortable in his position, he can raise his hands as if holding the reins: elbows lightly to the sides, forearms nearly horizontal, wrists in a line with them and supple, backs of the hands outwards, fingers flexed, hands four or five inches apart. The interval between the hands is of course variable, depending on the movements of the horse and needs of the rider.

Having been, as it were, fitted into this position, the pupil should fall back into his original relaxed position and start the process over again. Doing this several times is a useful exercise in itself. The pupil should be encouraged to ask questions and to record his impressions and sensations during this and other stages of the lessons.

The main faults to look for are: tenseness and excessive gripping with knees and calves; stiffness of the joints – ankles, knees, wrists and elbows, and of the back and neck; a tendency to crouch forward with rounded shoulders and to get a perched position in the saddle; not sitting level, with one hip lower than the other; looking down; lower leg too far back, or too far forward; body leaning back; a tendency to let the toes droop; turning the toes out, or in; all signs of stiffness and tension.

When the rider's position at the halt is fairly stable, the assistant leads the horse round in a circle at the walk, and the positioning exercises are repeated while the horse is circling. The pupil can make use of a hand on the pommel to preserve his balance, but should try to manage without it. As a preliminary exercise, the rider, holding the pommel with one hand, is asked to 'push' his seat and weight down into the saddle. After a few turns, the horse is halted, and the instructor explains the various suppling and muscle-building exercises.

These are ordinary physical training exercises, and they can be divided into basic and advanced.

The basic ones are: Hands on hips; arms stretching sideways; arms swinging; body turning sideways; legs swinging forwards and backwards.

The advanced ones are: Arms stretching upwards; head turning; touching the toes; bending forwards and backwards.

The difference between the basic and advanced exercises is that the former do not interfere with the position of the rider in the saddle, while the latter tend to raise the seat, which has to be counteracted, so these are really tests of the stability of the rider's position.

The exercises are self-explanatory, and should be done in a regular sequence:

Hands on hips: Palms over and round the hip bones, thumbs to the rear, bracing the loins, elbows out and in the same plane as the body. There should be a strong downward pressure. This exercise helps to straighten the shoulders and encourage an upright position. On the command 'hands down' the hands are dropped smartly to the sides. This can be repeated several times.

Arms stretching sideways: The arms are raised slowly outwards from the hands down position until they are level with the shoulders, where they are held for a few seconds then lowered slowly to the sides. This is an aid to balance, and enables the instructor to check the pupil's position in the saddle. This exercise can be varied by raising the arms forward and stretching them in front of the body. It is important that the shoulders should remain braced and not follow the arms forward. A variation of this is to start with the hands touching in front of the chest, arms held horizontal, then fling the hands outwards briskly so that the arms end stretched to right and left as before. This is good for chest expansion and suppling of the shoulders.

Arms swinging: First swing the right arm round and round, keeping the other arm hanging down to the side. Repeat with the left arm. Then swing both arms together the same way, first of all forwards, then backwards; then swing them in opposite directions. There must be no shifting of the position of the rest of the body while this is being done. Done smoothly and rhythmically these exercises improve balance, increase suppleness and strengthen the body position. Faults to avoid are moving the head and neck, swinging the body out of the saddle with the movement of the arms, swinging the legs and letting the toes drop, and moving the body sideways with the arms.

Body turning sideways: This can be done from the hips firm position and with the arms stretched. The body is turned from the waist, first to the left then to the right. The whole of the upper part of the body – shoulders, neck and head – turn, but the hips and the lower part of the body should remain facing to the front in the same plane as the shoulders of the horse. This strengthens and supples the muscles of the waist and back. The rider should not be allowed to overdo the turning, i.e. too much movement of the shoulders and too little of the waist; the whole upper part of the body must move together and in the same plane. As in all these exercises, a little movement correctly done is worth all the excessive but incorrect movement.

The above exercises tend either to help the body downwards into a deep central position in the saddle or to maintain it there. The following advanced exercises should not be asked for until the instructor is satisfied that the rider's position has been well established. They are really tests of the rider's ability to stay in the saddle in spite of the contrary influences.

Arms stretching upwards: Carried out in the same way as the other stretching exercises, helps to straighten the back and correct crouching.

Head turning: The body remains facing to the front as the head is turned slowly from side to side, first to the left then to the right, keeping erect without any bending forwards or sideways. At first the head should stop between turns in each direction, but with practice the full turn from left to right can be made in one movement. The hands can be in the riding position, on the hips, down to the sides, or stretched sideways. The objects are to loosen and supple the neck muscles and improve balance. This is a difficult exercise and three or four turns at a time are ample. More than six are liable to cause dizziness. It should not be performed on the move until the rider has done a good deal of lunge riding and really established his position.

Touching the toes, body bending forwards and backwards, body turning in the saddle, legs swinging forwards and backwards from the knees are more in the nature of test exercises and games in the saddle to show the rider's control over himself and his position in the saddle. They should never form part of elementary exercises, whether on the lunge or during ordinary riding lessons. Too often they are recommended in books at this stage or given to young novice riders long before they are ready for them.

When the pupil has learnt the basic exercises and done them

at the halt, regular work on the move can be started. These preliminaries take a long time to describe, but they can be got through quite easily in the first lesson.

The pupil can, if he wishes, balance himself to begin with by his hand lightly on the pommel, quickly reducing to a mere finger touch, but he should be encouraged to do it without keeping the hands in the riding position and letting the muscles of the small of the back and the thighs get to work.

The first tendencies will be either to crouch forward with excessive grip with the consequent raising of the knees, or to get left behind with the legs going forward. Halt and correct these faults, repeating as often as necessary. Another tendency will be for the legs to start swinging with the movement of the horse, especially at the trot, and a lowering of the toes. The movement being on a circle the inner leg may stretch downwards and the body lean inwards, causing a collapsing of the hip. These are initial faults which must be corrected at the outset, otherwise a good deal of the time on the lunge will be wasted.

The exercises should be done first at the walk, but with intervals of trotting to get the rider used to the faster pace. At first there should be frequent pauses for rest and relaxation, which should become fewer and fewer as progress is made and all the riding muscles are strengthened. Not all the exercises will be carried out in a single lesson, but two or three at a time, with a short revision at the beginning of each new session.

At the trot, and later, the canter, another reaction of the rider by putting more weight on his outside leg and buttock and leaning outwards. Often it will be found that this and other tendencies will be more pronounced to one side than the other, which is the reason why all work, whether with riders or horses, should be done more or less equally on each rein.

In the early stages the same horse should be used all the time, but as progress is made a change of mount is a good thing to prevent the rider's reactions from becoming stereotyped.

Progress in these lessons depends on the skill and understanding of the instructor and the determination of the pupil. Their duration depends on circumstances. For the riders of the Spanish Riding School, riding on the lunge goes on for about a year, and does not entirely stop even then; as a concert pianist continually does scales to keep his fingers in trim so must the horseman continually exercise himself in this basic way. The actual lunge-riding session is about forty-five minutes daily. Few civilian riders can afford the time or money for such concentrated basic equitation, but the more they can do of it the better. Even the rider who does not aspire to the higher flights of advanced riding but only to jump and have fun across country in the hunting field and in hunter trials will benefit from it, and it will certainly not interfere with forward riding. If he wants to excel in horse trials, where a dressage test is part of the exercise, he will find this experience all the more helpful.

The reason for all this labour is of course perfection. 'Perfect self-control is the stipulation for every rider; he must have not only his body in hand but must be able to control his own temperament at any moment, because only then will he be able to subordinate the other living creature, and help it to develop the talents given to it by nature.' (Colonel Alois Podhajsky in *The Spanish Riding School*.)

Above (and overleaf): a variety of exercises in indoor riding establishments
(*Light Horse*)

9 The Language of Riding

A sensitive and skilled horseman communicates with his mount by all the means at his disposal; his mind, his voice, his whole body, but principally his legs and hands. This, so far as the horse is concerned, is the language of riding; commonly called the *aids*. The term is not wholly accurate, because in general they do not actually help the horse but tell it what to do.

It will have been noticed that all through the work on the lunge described in the previous chapter the rider has been completely passive in his relations with the horse, which has just been a vehicle to carry him round while he worked his own body into a fit state to be able to talk to the horse accurately and intelligibly on all occasions. That is where riding on the lunge contrasts with the old military habit of bumming around on a blanket, hanging on with the reins and trying to apply leg aids at the same time.

If lunge-riding cannot be carried out, owing perhaps to there being a lack of time or facilities for individual tuition of this kind, a ride of say three or four pupils can be led by a mounted assistant round the manège while they carry out as near as possible the same procedure without reins and stirrups for a preliminary period in each lesson. The time that be given even to this will not be wasted.

As soon as the pupil is on a free horse, reins in his hands, feet in the stirrups, he will start using 'aids', however elementary. He must use his legs to keep an old soldier of a school horse in his proper place in the line, or restrain him with the reins to prevent him closing up on the horse in front of him; he must stop him, make him go on or faster, and change direction. He will be asked to feel the reins with one hand while relaxing with the other – to make a turn or a circle – and to support it with more pressure from one leg than from the other; and more often than not the school horse will know the answers before the rider. These will be simple signals, but the prelude to a whole gamut of effects which will vary with every individual horse and with the skill and sensitivity of the rider, who at this early stage will discover that the aids, that is to say

97

the means by which the signals are given, have three different ways of making themselves felt by the horse. They can *act*; they can *resist;* they can *yield.*

The hands, through the reins, act when they increase the tension of the reins. Extreme cases of this are when the reins are pulled sharply backwards to stop a galloping horse, as in polo, or when one rein is used to make a jibber turn smartly round and round.

The legs act when they are used decisively against the horse's flanks to stimulate movement, forward, lateral or back.

The hands resist when they are used passively, held steady, to keep the horse's head in position.

The legs resist when they too act passively but firmly to prevent unauthorised movements – swinging of quarters – of the horse's body.

The hands yield when, after acting or resisting, they relax the tension on the reins, as when a horse has halted in obedience to the signals. The immediate giving of the rein is an immediate sign to the horse that he has done correctly, and usually a sufficient reward. A single hand can yield, while the other hand is acting or resisting, as in the case of a turn.

The legs yield in the same way by relaxing pressure as soon as the horse has obeyed the signal.

The body, by altering the position of the seat, supports the actions of the reins. A shifting of the weight to one side or the other will have the effect of pinning down one hindleg while releasing the other. Normally, shifting the weight forward will make the horse lengthen its stride; shifting it back towards the quarters will shorten it. But in the case of an extended trot, for example, the 'pushing' of the seat will induce the horse to lengthen its stride.

It is an axiom that all movement starts from the hindquarters, and that the signals to the horse begin with the leg aids. These are simple enough to apply, and usually go in stages according to the sensitiveness and submissiveness of the horse. They begin with a squeeze of the legs against the flaps, a drawing back of the lower leg and the direct contact of the calf with the flanks of the horse, a stronger action with the heels, and finally the added support of spur and whip. Books are very keen on soft, subtle aids, but not every horse is responsive to such refinements, as every horseman well knows. Too often the imperceptible squeeze is replaced by a succession of banging heels before the required result can be obtained. The principle is the same, but the performance is less elegant. Particularly is this the case with children, who seldom have the strength to make any impression on their thick-skinned little ponies. The same condition applies to the hands and reins. The steady and yielding hands, the supple fingers, have very little effect on mouths which have become deadened from a long succession of strap-hanging riders and owners. The action must be sharp not to say violent. However, even this must never be sustained, but intermittent, conforming to the principle of take and give which is at the heart of all riding at whatever level.

Still, we must have our ideals, and all instruction in this book will aim at perfection and presuppose a reasonable horse, while remembering that different circumstances and problems require different, or rather variations of the same, solutions.

The progress of the horse is conducted by a series of transitions. Dressage test jargon has given this word a somewhat esoteric significance, but it is, quite simply, a change from one gait, including the halt, to another. Thus, we can have a transition from the halt to the walk, trot or canter, and to the rein back; from the walk to the trot or canter, and to the halt; from the trot to the canter, and back to the walk and halt; from the canter to the gallop, and back to the trot and halt; from the gallop to the canter and halt; from the trot to the walk or halt; from the walk to the halt. Transitions from a slow to a faster gait are upward, and from a fast to a slower gait downward. There are other transitions, too, from forward to lateral movement, which will be considered in their proper place.

The object of applied aids is to translate the will of the rider into a language that a horse can understand and obey, and so carry out these various transitions and movements as instantly and as smoothly as possible. It is not fair to take the horse by surprise with a sudden command; he should be physically and mentally prepared for any change from his present state.

So, you are at the halt, relaxed, standing easy as it were. You warn the horse of impending action by an easy closing of the legs with steady contact of the reins and a slight vibration of the fingers. This alerts the horse and brings him to attention. To go forward, the leg pressure is increased firmly but moderately, the hands still steady, so that the horse starts to stretch his head forward as he starts to move. The hands must not lose contact but must go forward with the movement of the head, while at the same time restraining that movement from becoming excessive. The moment the horse walks steadily forward the action of the legs is reduced to normal contact with the sides, and the hands remain steady. The legs first of all acted, then yielded; the hands have yielded slightly and then remained passive.

The horse should walk briskly with a long, level stride, which will be described in more detail in Part III. If he tends to slow down or to get unbalanced, by one pair of diagonals coming closer together than the other pair, leg pressure must be applied to correct it, the legs signalling actively, the hands remaining steady, resisting. To halt, still holding the hands steady press the horse up to the bit with the legs. If the horse does not respond, the hands must act more decisively, first by a backward vibration of the fingers, then, more drastically, by short sharp pull, instantly relaxed. Once halted the horse should stand evenly balanced on all four feet, placed foursquare underneath him. Any taking up of tension by the hands should be relaxed, so that there is the lightest possible contact with the mouth, the head held up so that the poll should be about level with the rider's chest, the head at an angle of 45 degrees to the ground.

To digress slightly, every horseman and horse owner likes to be photographed on a horse or to have his horse photographed, but the halt position described is no good for photography, as the resultant picture will make it appear that the horse has only two legs, one in front one behind. So the horse has to get used to standing with the legs furthest from the camera slightly inside the nearer pair, the outer foreleg *behind* the inner one, the outer hindleg *in front* of the inner one. It takes a great deal of adjustment and experience to get this position just right, but the trouble is worth taking in order to get a really pleasing picture.

Returning to the riding lesson, the pupil may now try a reinback. This movement is not taught at this early stage to a young horse, but the rider is, or should be, on a fully trained horse. As before prepare the horse for a movement by alerting him with the legs and hands. Then, as with all movement, apply the legs smoothly and firmly to push him forward up to the bit, which is in firm contact with steady hands. The horse will understand that some movement is required of him; it is obviously not remaining at the halt, and the hands prevent him from going forward, so the only alternative is to go back. Once more, it will often be necessary to support the leg action with more positive action of the hands. The horse should step back diagonally – near fore, off hind, off fore, near hind, or the opposite pairs. One or two strides are sufficient, then stop the horse

The Language of Riding

by yielding with the hands, and go forward at once. (See page 98)

Now move forward at the walk, and prepare the horse for the trot. The signal for the change of pace is the same as for the halt to the walk. Preliminary work on the lunge or in a ride should have accustomed the rider to sitting easily at the trot. If the rider is relaxed and supple at the sitting trot, he should have no difficulty in rising at the trot, or posting, as the Continentals first called it from seeing English postillion riders using it.

The horse trots in two-time by using his diagonal pairs of legs alternately, off fore, near hind, near fore, off hind. In fact the pairs of feet do not come to the ground exactly together, but in succession, though so close together that only high-speed photography can detect it; for practical riding purposes the movement of the diagonals can be regarded as instantaneous. There is a moment of suspension between each diagonal when all four feet are in the air. The ancient Egyptians depicted this several thousand years ago, but they were not believed until Muybridge's photography again revealed it in 1882. When the horse moves with lateral instead of diagonal pairs – off fore, off hind, near fore, near hind – he is said to be pacing or ambling, a gait which does not concern us here.

To rise at the trot, the rider must raise his seat, using his back and thigh muscles while keeping his knees and legs against the saddle, for one diagonal and lower it back on to the saddle for the next, and so on. A common tendency is to rise up too high and to make a jerky movement of it, coming down into the saddle with a bump. Rise up just enough to clear the waist of the saddle, and sink down easily and quietly without bumping. Knees should be pressed against the saddle and the lower legs in sufficient contact with the sides of the horse to keep them still. The legs should neither flap outwards nor move forwards and backwards. The hands remain independent of the up-and-down movement of the body, and the body from the waist upwards should keep with the forward movement of the horse, that is the weight of the body should be placed slightly more forward than at the halt and the walk.

The hands should be in light and sensitive contact all the time with the mouth, the fingers playing with the reins to make the horse in its turn play with the bit, chewing it, nodding its head and yielding its jaw, while keeping a steady, regular speed of about eight to ten miles an hour. The legs maintain the speed, and make the horse use his hindlegs and engage them underneath the quarters, not letting them drag behind; while the hands regulate the speed.

The description of the diagonal is determined by the foreleg; thus off fore and near hind make a right diagonal, near fore and off hind the left. When riding in a manège it is more convenient at all times to speak of outside (the side nearest to the wall or outer edge of the school) and inside (the side nearest to the centre of the school). These diagonals should be changed regularly whether in the school or in the open. It is easy to tell when this has not been done, for a horse that has become used to being ridden on the same diagonal all the time will not readily take to a change, throwing back to the accustomed one a rider who tries to make a change. Riding on the right diagonal (when the rider's weight is on the saddle) tends to overburden the horse's near hind, and *vice versa*.

When riding the rising trot in a manège or on a circle, which diagonal should one choose? There are two schools of thought about this. The first, and majority opinion says the rider should post on the outside diagonal, i.e. if on the right rein, the near (left) fore and off (right) hindleg. Thus the weight of the rider burdens the inside (off) hind, and, it is claimed, achieves 'an increased and energetic engagement of the inside hock by the driving aids of the rider'. (Richard L. Wätjen, *Dressage Riding*.)

The opposite opinion is that the rider should go on the inside diagonal, i.e. (again on the right rein) the off (right) fore and near (left) hindleg. The object again is the full engagement of the inside hindleg to support the weight of horse and rider and to maintain equilibrium. It is maintained, however, that the horse can better do this by having this inside leg free and not overburdened, because of the increased flexion caused by the weight, which it will try to counteract by reducing the engagement of that hindleg. It is maintained that it will be much easier for the driving aids to encourage the movement of the inside hindleg under the horse, if it is in the air to start with and not on the ground. However, in competitions the rider can use whichever diagonal he prefers, provided that he is consistent throughout the movement. Of course the diagonal must be changed with the changing of the rein, as smoothly as possible and without interfering with the cadence of the trot. The diagonal is changed by simply sitting down in the saddle for one stride, reducing the bump to a minimum.

The transitions up to the trot and down to the halt and the rein-back should be practised frequently in the first lessons, until the signals are given smoothly and precisely. The response of the horse will be the best guide to progress.

So far we have been theoretically on a straight line, but, the manège not being limitless, it regularly becomes necessary to change direction, to turn at the corners and to change the rein diagonally across the school, which brings into action the lateral aids. The simplest signal is the rein acting on one side of the mouth to make the horse turn his head in the required direction. If this action is continued alone, the horse may follow the indication of the rein and move round in the direction of the aid, to right or left, but the unsupported hindquarters will tend to swing out in the opposite direction. Or the horse may just bend his head round and continue going forward. So supporting action is necessary with the legs, combined aids. If the turn is to be to the right, the right leg will remain passive, merely assisting forward movement while the left leg increases pressure behind the girth to keep the quarters from swinging to the left and to urge the horse to move to the right, using his hindquarters as the pivot. The signal is the same for both turns and circles. When the movement is completed the hand and leg are relaxed to go forward again.

This action, like every other phrase in the language of horsemanship, can have many variations, nuances of meaning, according to the state of training of both horse and rider. Assuming that we are on the right rein, the hand can be moved away from the side of the horse outwards to the right, called by Blacque Belair (*Cavalry Horsemanship*) the direct opening rein. First the head bends to the right, then the neck, and the shoulders follow the neck. This would be used on a very green horse in its first lessons, or to intensify the normal direct lateral signal. The hand can be drawn straight back, when it has an opposing effect on the shoulders and quarters, moving the latter to the left. This has been called the direct rein of opposition.

A further action of the same rein will be across to the left. This will turn the head to the right but shifts the weight of the neck on to the left shoulder. More movement of the hand to the left will make the horse turn in that direction. This is an indirect rein, and it will be used in lateral movement on two tracks, and in neck reining. The effect is varied by moving the hands in front of and behind the withers. To turn to the right the right direct and left indirect reins are used, combined with the right leg regulating the movement forward and the left leg supporting the movement to the right.

A final refinement of these signals is not to activate the right direct rein, i.e. to move it back, but to hold it steady and at

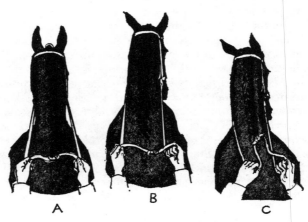

Fig. 13. *The Actions of the Reins*

A. Direct: reins acting equally on either side. B. Lateral: for simple turns to left or right. C. Indirect: the opposite rein is used to support the other for turns or other movements sideways. This is also called neck reining.

the same time yield with the left rein by moving the left hand forward. The relaxation of contact on the left side of the mouth will intensify the contact on the right side, and, supported again by the legs, will indicate to the horse that a movement to the right is required. Further emphasis can be given by the shifting weight of the body, and, in the last resort, by spur and whip, and the voice.

This is the simple grammar of the language of riding. It will be interpreted by the horse according to the context in which it is given, i.e. its gait, pace and direction, and by the standard of its training. Its transmission to the horse by the rider must also be adapted to circumstances, and again to the individual horse and its level of education. If a horse holds its head too low, it is corrected by extra drive of the legs combined with a light upward action of the hands. Excessive raising of the head is a definite resistance. To counter this, first of all slow down the pace by applying the normal aids; then with the driving action of the legs and a yielding of the hands encourage the horse to lengthen its stride, to do which he will have to lower his neck and head. Repeat the action as often as is necessary, but do not try to hold the horse's head down by lowering the hands, which will only increase the resistance. Whatever the position of the horse's head, the rider's hands must still be in a straight line from the elbow to the horse's mouth. It is the art of equitation to understand the horse you are riding, its individual idiosyncrasies and limitations, and to be able to apply the signals in harmony, clearly, and sufficient for the purpose required.

Learning to ride is the practising of this application so that it becomes instinctive. Regular work in the manège is like doing scales in music. An obvious proviso here is that the 'scales' must be done correctly. It is not *what* is done that matters but *how*. As William Steinkraus, horseman and musician, says, 'There is nothing beneficial at all in the mechanical repetition of wrong movements, no matter how interminably prolonged. A bad scale becomes a good one not by repeating it, but by correcting the causes of its badness.'

10 Balance, Impulsion, Flexion and Collection

Balance

Basically there is no mystery about balance. Any object at rest is in balance so long as it is able to stay at rest without altering its position. A table on four legs is in balance; so is a horse on four legs, so long as it remains in that position. The difference between the two is that the horse is alive, has muscles, and is seldom, if ever, really motionless.

A horse on its own may stay with his weight evenly distributed on all four feet for a short time, but before long he will shift his position, take the weight off (rest) one hindleg, which will entail a muscular adjustment of his whole body by taking more weight on the other three legs in order to remain in balance. The point is that he will see to it that he remains in a comfortable balanced position whatever the distribution of the weight. Of course, with each change of position there is a slight shifting of the centre of gravity, which has to remain within the base of support, inside the oblong made by the four feet on the ground. In riding, all movement results from a loss and recovery of balance.

Whether at rest or on the move a horse on its own has little trouble about balance. Anybody who has watched riderless horses in a steeplechase will note that they jump much better than their still burdened colleagues. A horse galloping normally will extend himself, his centre of gravity well forward. When a horse is excited, or suspicious, he will collect himself, raise his neck and do something like a passage or a piaffe, his centre of gravity shifted to the rear.

In turns and circles, the horse naturally places more weight on the inside legs, principally in front, and the centre of gravity shifts accordingly. To counteract centrifugal forces, he tends to lean inwards. This is slight at slow paces, but when done at a gallop, as when playing polo, or in the case of a hunter going all out round a show ring, or a cutting horse baulking a steer, the inward list is extreme, perhaps at an angle of 50 degrees to the ground. The horse is then strictly not in balance, because his centre of gravity could be outside the base of support – the four feet; the only things which keep him from falling are the grip of the ground and his own power to resist the centripetal forces. It is not a problem which arises in *haute école*, but a very real one in hunting and outdoor riding of all kinds.

The presence of a rider on his back naturally makes things harder for the horse; a great deal depends on the tact and skill of the rider, but more on the strength and natural balance of the horse. The problem for the rider is to make his own centre of gravity coincide with that of the horse. The value of the central seat is manifest as a starting point for all sorts of movement.

At a normal halt position, with the rider upright in the lowest part of the saddle, the two will be in perfect balance. If the rider is sitting nearer the cantle, or leaning back, his centre of gravity will be behind that of the horse, and the balance will not be perfect. The centre of gravity of the combined weight will be somewhere between those two points, and as a result of this shifting of the weight to the rear the horse will have to make a greater effort to move forward than before.

A man on a horse galloping must lean forward in order to keep his centre of gravity with that of the horse; if he leans back, he is not in harmony with the movement and the true balance is disturbed, again requiring unnecessary effort on the part of the horse. On the other hand, if the rider collects a horse at the walk or trot and maintains his correct position, the horse will adjust his weight to the rear to conform with the lowering of the hocks and the redistribution of the rider's own weight. In one case the extension of the horse requires the rider to adapt his posture to the horse's equilibrium; in the other the shortening of the horse requires the horse to adapt its equilibrium to the burdening of the rider (de Romaszkan, *Horse and Rider in Equilibrium*).

The same kind of adjustments have to be made in lateral movements and in jumping. The situation is entirely fluid; every instant horse and rider have to make adjustments of weight (of the rider's position) in order to preserve true balance. Part of equestrian tact is the rider's feeling for the movement and balance of the horse, so that he conforms to it or controls it as the case may be. These are the feels of riding, which can only come from experience and knowledge and the riding of many horses.

The balance of the rider has already been achieved by his

work on the lunge, with which he should refresh himself and re-practise himself as often as possible. The natural balance of the horse can also be improved, first by his initial training on the lunge, and then by balancing exercises in the school, consisting of turns, circles, halts, half-halts, which constitute the ordinary riding school exercises. (See Part III)

Impulsion

Very few of the great equestrian writers mention impulsion; it is something that seems to be taken for granted. Yet it is the essence of that forward movement which is the basis of all training and all horsemanship. Here are three definitions:

'A forward urge manifested by the energetic use of the hocks.' (*Summerhays' Encyclopaedia for Horsemen.*)

'Impulsion is forward movement made use of under the exact discipline of the aids, in accordance with the end desired. It is the basis of training. Its seat is in the hindquarters, which push the weight forward, or at any rate ought always to be ready to do so.' (Blacque Belair, *Cavalry Horsemanship.*)

'Impulsion varies greatly in individuals, and primarily relates to *the manner in which the horse moves.* Excellent natural impulsion is characterised by that ample, supple and springy action of the joints which gives an appearance of great momentum generated with but little effort.' (Harry D. Chamberlain, *Training Hunters, Jumpers and Hacks.*)

Impulsion has no connection with speed. A galloping horse may well lack impulsion, as is often manifest when he comes up against an obstacle. On the other hand a horse at an alert halt may be full of it; like a compressed spring full of latent power. Impulsion comes from the hocks and is controlled by the reins, and is one of the results of the correct gymnastic training of the horse.

Flexion

The yielding of the jaw and the bending of the head from the poll are the prerequisites of collection and control. Flexion begins with the lower jaw of the horse giving to the action of the curb bit and curb chain. The bending of the head from the poll follows after that, and can be distinguished from the incorrect bending of the head from the neck by the fact that from the latter the head is lowered and drawn back beyond the perpendicular, so that the horse becomes behind the bit. For the beginner rider to experience the effects of flexion he must use a double bridle.

Successful flexion depends, apart from the skill of the rider and trainer, on the horse's conformation (pages 46–53). A horse with a short thick neck and a too-closely coupled lower jaw, giving no room for play backwards, will never be able to flex easily, if at all. Even if he has a good neck, he will not be able to flex unless there is room between the jaw and the top of the neck. Many ponies suffer from this fault of conformation, and so are very difficult for children to control.

Collection

The collection and proper head carriage of a well-trained riding horse cannot be mechanically determined, but must always be adapted to the conformation and individuality of the horse.' (Richard L. Wätjen, *Dressage Riding*.)

In English, 'collection' is a portmanteau word covering a wide range of effects, for which French and German have different names. The term is apt, however, because one does really collect, or unite the horse, bringing together its forehand and quarters, so that the forehand is lightened (the centre of gravity shifts back) and the hocks are engaged underneath the quarters, with a flexing of the hip, stifle and hock joints. The horse has the appearance of being shortened (*raccourci*).

The first degree of collection is merely being at attention, in fact the positioning or preparation of the horse for other movements (pages 84–7). There should be slight engagement of the quarters, and the head should be raised so that the muzzle is about level with the rider's knees, the angle of the head in front of the vertical, at an angle of about 30 degrees to the ground. The action for collection of any kind is first the legs and a bracing of the back, then the restraining action of the hands. The horse is thus collected from rear to front and receives an urge to go forward.

More complete collection is produced by the engagement of the quarters followed by more active action of the hands to flex the head from the poll, so that it comes nearer the vertical (*ramener*). As collection becomes more extreme the head will be vertical, but it should never be allowed to go behind the vertical. Total collection for high school airs is *rassembler.*

Collected movements must be energetic and full of impulsion, rather more elevated than ordinary gaits. The official dressage definition makes it clear. At the collected trot 'the neck is raised, thus enabling the shoulders to move with greater ease in all directions, the hocks being well engaged and maintaining energetic impulsion, notwithstanding the slower movement. The horse's steps are shorter but he is lighter and more mobile.' (F.E.I. *Rules for Dressage Competitions*, Section 404.) The actual rate of progression is slow, not from any slackness of movement but from the shorter steps, whether at walk, trot or canter.

For ordinary riding school and outdoor work (the *campagne* school), only elementary collection is necessary. Collected movements were taken out of one-day and some three-day event dressage tests some years ago. But some collection is necessary for all forms of riding.

One thing leads to another, and the novice rider may want to move beyond just galloping across country and jumping, to taste the fascination of a highly trained and responsive horse, a rare thing. The one thing to remember is that collection should never be forced. The horse must really lead the way, responding to the tentative suggestions of the rider through his legs and hands; and the rider must know enough about his horse to appreciate when he has gone far enough.

Here are the official (F.E.I.) descriptions of the collected walk and canter.

> *Walk.* The horse moves resolutely forward, with his neck raised and arched. The head approaches the vertical position, the light contact with the mouth being maintained. The hindlegs are engaged with good hock action. The pace should remain marching and vigorous, the legs being placed in regular sequence. Each step covers less ground and is higher than at the ordinary walk because all the joints bend more markedly. The hind feet touch the ground behind the footprints of the forefeet. In order not to become hurried or irregular the collected walk is slightly shorter than the ordinary walk, although showing greater mobility. (*Rules for Dressage Competitions*, Section 403 (b).)
>
> *Canter.* At the collected canter, the shoulders are supple, free and mobile and the quarters very active. The horse's mobility is increased without any loss of impulsion. (*Rules for Dressage Competitions*, Section 405 (b).)

The word 'cadence', usually applied to high school work, means the rhythmical succession of measured beats of the feet in movement; four at a walk, two at a trot, three at a canter, and every rider, whatever his standard, should try to ensure that his horse moves with an even, level cadence, particularly marked, of course, in collected movements.

11 The Canter and Gallop, Turns and Lateral Work

The Canter and Gallop

The canter, as we have already observed, is a three-time gait, which differs from the trot through the breaking of the beat of one of the diagonal pairs of legs, so that the leading foreleg and following hindleg will be on the same side during one complete canter stride. Both the canter and the gallop are springing gaits, with an obvious moment of complete suspension, and the taking of the weight by one (leading) foreleg. One hindleg also carries the weight for an instant during a stride.

Canter is an English word and usually indicates variations of speed up to about twelve miles an hour, after which it is considered to merge into the gallop, which can be any speed up to and over thirty miles an hour. A very slow canter can become a four-time gait, with little or no suspension. In America this is called a *lope*, and it is an exceedingly comfortable pace for both horse and rider, which can be maintained for long periods without tiring. It is, of course, not a school gait, and regarded as faulty in the dressage arena, where the three-beat movement must be clearly marked. This three-time gait is also known as a *hand-gallop*.

In the gallop the horse reaches out his leading foreleg and takes a much longer stride than at the canter, and it really seems to leap from the hindlegs to the forelegs, as the old artists portrayed it before rapid photography and slow motion cinematography revealed the true situation. The length of stride of the ordinary canter is about ten to twelve feet, and of the gallop from fifteen to twenty-four feet. The school gaits are assessed at eight feet for ordinary canter, five feet for collected, and twelve feet for extended canter.

The riding pupil will have experienced the canter during work on the lunge, or at an early stage in the riding school, when it is a welcome change from the trot. At this stage the horse will act on the command of the instructor; the use of the aids and the correctness or otherwise of the canter will be

immaterial. Turning the corners at the canter will help to give balance and confidence. Mistakes of the horse in cantering are:
1. Going on the right rein with the left leg leading and *vice versa* (false canter). But this can be done deliberately as a school movement (counter canter).
2. The leading leg followed by the opposite hindleg (disunited).

The school canter is ridden with the seat in the saddle, activated downwards by the muscles of the small of the back. The rider should strive to go smoothly with the movement without being rocked up and down and swaying the upper part of his body backwards and forwards, or going up and down in the saddle. The ideal is a smooth flowing motion forwards in harmony with the advance of the horse.

For outdoor riding, jumping, cross-country, hunting, the body should lean moderately forwards, the seat out of the saddle, hands going forward to release the head, and body going easily with the movement. In the first case the horse will adjust its balance to the position and movement of the rider; in the latter the pace and extension of the horse will dictate the forward position to the rider.

The faster the movement, up to a full gallop, the more forward will be the rider's position – and the stirrup leathers will be shortened according to the purpose of the outing until the extreme position of the jockey on a racehorse is reached.

There are several ways of obtaining the canter, according to the state of training of the horse, amounting really to a 'convention between horse and rider' (Jean Froissard, 'The Departure at the Canter', *Light Horse*, July, 1969); but the pupil rider will only be concerned with a trained horse. So the transition from the trot to the canter is produced by the application of the same principles as for the walk and trot. In a canter to the right the horse leads with his off fore, and to the left with his near fore, and he will tend to bend his head in the direction of the canter. An untrained horse will tend to go crooked, almost on two separate tracks of the fore and hind feet; a trained horse will go straight, but in the preparation for the transition his spine will be flexed longitudinally from front to rear.

The first intimation of a change will be a half-halt, after which the sequence for a canter to the right (off fore leading) will be as follows: feel the right rein to move the horse's head slightly to the right, and support with the left rein to keep him going straight on the track; left leg behind the girth to stimulate the near hindleg which will start the movement; right against the girth to maintain straightness and impulsion; shift of the body weight to the left to free the off hindleg. The hands must continue to act directly to control the pace, so that the horse will not try to make the canter by increasing its trotting rate or extending its trot stride. If a horse (ponies are more prone to it, however) persists in doing this, halt and start again. As in all leaping movements, the horse will want to stretch his neck and head forward, and the moment he does this after receiving the signal, the hands should yield accordingly. During the canter, the right hand should continue to act gently to keep the bend of the head to the right; and the right leg should act to keep the horse straight and prevent the hindquarters from moving inwards off the track. (See pages 117–20.)

The signal for the gallop is simply strong pressure of the legs, with a forward bending of the body and steady hands, which will yield to the natural extension of the head and neck. Contact must normally be maintained, and with most horses it is likely to be pretty strong. Some riders like their horses to take a good hold at the gallop, but the idea sometimes expressed that a horse will fall down if the contact is relaxed at the gallop is entirely disproved by the polo pony, the ideal for which is a full gallop ('sixteen annas' as they used to say) on a loose rein. And, as a matter of fact, Gordon Richards used to ride many of his finishes on a light or loose rein. In the long run it all depends on the horse.

At this point it is as well to stress the value of riding with one hand. Every horseman should be able to ride confidently with the reins in either the left (usually) or the right hand, leaving the other free. For the soldier it was a necessity, and still is for the polo player, hunt staff, or gymkhana rider; it used to be *de rigueur* in hack classes. Now the influence of the dressage arena is making it almost a lost art. A concomitant of this of course is that the horse or pony must be bridle wise. I have seen courageous riders with the arms in slings in the jumping phase of a three-day event struggling round with most bewildered though willing horses who could not understand what was happening to them. Ted Edgar, the show jumper, once performed a *tour de force* by completing the Hickstead jumping 'Derby' course in just this way. So in all instruction periods and at all paces there should be spells of riding with one hand.

Turns

Turns at the Halt: Simple turns are changes of direction on the move, either at right angles or diagonally (French *la conversion,* German *die Wendung*). The volte and half-volte are small circles or half circles, usually at the corners of the manège. Circle (*cercle; Zirkel*) is a larger round with the short side of the manège as diameter. Turns on the quarters and forehand, apart from their practical applications, are training exercises for both rider and horse, teaching the one how to apply aids correctly and the other to understand and obey them. A turn on the quarters on the move is a pirouette, half (180 degrees) or complete (360 degrees). Turns at the halt usually begin with a quarter-turn (90 degrees), and progress to half and complete turns. The same applies to the turn on the forehand.

Turn on the forehand: With the main weight of his body in front a horse usually finds it all too easy to turn on its forehand, although it requires precise aids to perform it as a schooling exercise. For this reason it should be practised sparingly whether by rider or horse. It has a practical value for the opening of gates, or when a quick change of direction is required.

In this case the horse pivots on its foreleg, the off one in the case of a right turn, when the quarters go to the left but the horse ends up facing to the right. The rider's body weight is concentrated on the off shoulder. The right rein turns the head slightly to the right, left rein supporting as before. The right leg behind the girth moves the quarters over to the left and round the pivot of the off fore, while the left leg maintains impulsion and prevents the quarters from swinging outwards. (See pages 106–10.)

Turn on the quarters at the halt: Let us assume that the turn is to the right. Reverse the aids for the left turn. Halt about midway on one or other of the long sides of the manège, going on the right rein. Steady the horse by slight collection. With the right (direct) rein invite the horse to move his head to the right. At the same time the left leg applied behind the girth encourages the body to follow the direction of the head and neck. The left rein yields slightly and acts on the neck, making the horse step to the right with the off fore. The right leg on the girth holds the quarters in position and maintains impulsion. The weight of the body to the right rear pins the off hind-leg and foot to the ground to make that the pivot of the movement. With continued impulses from the reins and legs the horse takes the next step with the near fore and hind, which should go in front of the off fore and off hind respectively. And so the movement proceeds, step by step. The end of a half-turn places the horse facing the way he originally advanced, thus changing the rein. For a beginner a quarter-turn will be

114

enough, and then he can practise the reverse turn to the left, using the opposite aids.

Except to shift his weight the rider should not change his normal position throughout the movement; and he should endeavour to make the turn as rhythmical and cadenced as possible. To make a good turn the horse must be light in hand and on his hocks, with the head perhaps raised a little during the movement.

In both cases, the movement is made a step at a time, pausing after each step. In both cases also, movement forwards or backwards must be avoided as far as possible.

Turning on the quarters on the move is really a school movement and comes into more advanced training of the rider. The essence of it is that the same aids are used but there is no preliminary halt, the horse, at the walk, going straight into the movement. At the trot and canter it becomes a pirouette, half and full, which will be considered later. (Pages 176–82.)

Changing the leading leg at the canter: It is noticeable that even a very young and untrained horse will change his leading legs at the canter smoothly and effortlessly, and without change of gait, the flying change in fact, for which so much thought and preparation will be given later on when he is mounted. A normally trained horse will also do it automatically to keep its balance when changing direction suddenly, for example during a show jumping round. Neither then, nor at polo, has the rider time to give carefully prepared aids. Caprilli did not care which leg was leading when his pupils' horses started to gallop, remarking that 'a horse has never fallen because of galloping on the wrong lead'.

For practical purposes, however, in the riding school, the horse should always be asked to lead with the inside leg, or the same as the rein on which he is going, i.e. off fore for right rein, near fore for left rein. In advanced riding making a horse canter with the opposite lead, or counter-canter, is a demonstration of its training and obedience. Otherwise, at every change of rein the lead must also be changed, and it is a good thing for a pupil to learn fairly early both the simple change of leg and the flying change. These exercises are best done on a circle to start with.

For a simple change of leg, the rider is, say, on a right-handed circle of half the manège, cantering with the off fore leading. On approaching the centre of the school, he will slow down to a trot, straighten up and prepare the horse for a change of movement, then give the aids for the canter on the near fore leading, and turn into the left circle in the other half of the school. Ultimately only two or three intermediate steps will be necessary. In due course the pupil, whether on his own or in a ride, will do the same on the straight on the long sides of the manège. Going into the canter and also the simple change should be done from the halt as well as from the trot. Indeed, for a horse that is impetuous at the trot, starting from the walk will be beneficial.

The flying change done under command is most satisfying for the rider. Once a rider has become well accustomed to the rhythm of the canter, and can obtain the leading leg at will on the straight, and perform simple changes smoothly and correctly, and can feel which leg his horse is leading with without looking down, there is no reason why he should not start learning the flying change.

The actual change from one pair of leading legs to the other must obviously happen when the horse is in a state of suspension with all four legs in the air. So the rider's signal must be given just before that instant, when the leading foreleg is about to strike the ground, having previously prepared the horse with a half-halt. The signal for a change from off fore to near fore will be the same as for a strike off on the near fore, left rein, right leg. If the signal has been correctly timed, the near hind and forelegs will be felt to move forward in a new rhythm. Of course the aids must be given as smoothly as possible.

Turns, voltes and circles are preliminaries to lateral work, and a word about riding them is appropriate here. When a horse makes a turn of any kind, the main force which acts on him is centrifugal, pulling him outwards, to counteract which he tends to place more weight on his inside legs and to lean inwards, to the right, if on a right rein and *vice versa*. At slow paces, walk and trot, this is hardly noticeable, but becomes very obvious when circling at the gallop. In a circular movement, also, the inner legs have a shorter distance to cover at each stride than the outer legs; though the difference is virtually imperceptible. A horse going on a circle is rather like a four-wheeled railway coach with fixed wheels, only of course the body and spine are far more flexible than the chassis of the coach.

The position of the rider in a turn or circle should remain upright in the same plane as the body of the horse, i.e. at walk and trot it should be as near upright as makes no difference, and his chest and shoulders should be square to the front of the horse all the way through the movement. As with the horse, the rider will find an outward pull which has the effect of lowering his outside leg, which he will adjust by an extra pressure of the inside foot on the stirrup iron. If the pace is faster – canter or gallop – or the turn sharper, volte, he must adjust his position accordingly, so that the above conditions are fulfilled.

When turning, the horse's head will, of course, be flexed slightly in the direction of the movement, the spine also bending as much as it can, which is slight, in the same direction. The inside leg on the girth will control the body and keep it moving forward, while the outside leg will keep the quarters from swinging outwards; and the horse will keep on a single track, the hind feet stepping in the same line as the tracks of the fore feet.

Lateral work

Practising turns at the halt and in turns and circles will have prepared the rider for moving sideways. There are two kinds of lateral movements. 1. Those in which the head is flexed (bent) opposite to the direction of movement. 2. Those in which the horse bends his head in the same direction as the movement.

The first is a training and suppling exercise in the school known as the shoulder-in. This exercise was invented by the French master, François de la Guérinière, and he regarded it as the 'first and last of all the lessons we can give the horse in order to obtain complete suppleness and perfect freedom in all parts of his body . . .', and it has remained a basic exercise in all equestrian schools ever since. 'The object of this movement,' wrote Richard Wätjen, 'is to increase the lightness and suppleness of the horse, and to obtain a higher degree of obedience. These exercises improve the activity of the hindlegs, and the horse becomes more responsive to the rider's leg and rein aids.' (*Dressage Riding*.)

The shoulder-in is usually performed or practised on the tracks on the long side of the manège, so that there is a wall or guiding line to keep the direction straight; but of course it can be done on any straight line anywhere. In this exercise the horse continues to go forward in its original direction, it is positioned at an angle made by the shifting of the forehand off the track, the fore feet making their own separate track parallel to the original one, on which the hindquarters are still moving. So it is an exercise on two tracks.

The head is flexed slightly inwards, as in every turn or sideways motion, that is away from the direction of movement. The body is at an angle of about 30 degrees to 45 degrees to the main track, the horse goes forward with a side-stepping movement, inside fore and hind feet crossing in front of the outside ones. So, on the right rein, in a right shoulder-in, the horse's head is flexed to the right, the horse moves forward, and the right fore and hind feet cross in front of the left (outside) ones.

A preliminary lesson for the rider is the wall to the wall movement. On the right rein: the rider changes direction to the right, with right rein and left leg, at an angle of about 30 degrees, continuing the movement until the horse is just clear of the track, then straightening up for three or four strides, then bearing left on to the track. As the horse departs from the track it is in position for the shoulder-in.

After a little practise at this, the rider can ask the horse for the shoulder-in. The right rein, left rein supporting, flex the head to the right, and the left leg turns the forehand just off the track to the right. The trained horse can carry on the movement for the length of the school, but normally a few steps at a time are sufficient. Then the horse is straightened up by the outside rein and inside leg bringing the forehand on to the track again. A yielding of the aids for a few steps forward brings relief and is a reward for carrying out the movement.

The opposite position to the shoulder-in is the quarters-in, known also as head to the wall or travers. On the right rein, the left leg will move the quarters off the track to the right, while the reins, with a slightly increased action of the right rein, will keep the forehand on the track, and the head flexed to the right. So, in this case, the bend of the horse is in the direction of movement not against it as in the shoulder-in. The horse will continue to move forward, on two tracks, the outside (left) fore and hindlegs crossing in front of the inside (right) fore and hind.

The exact opposite to the travers is the renvers, also called quarters-out, or tail to the wall. The hindquarters remain on the track, while the forehand is moved off it, but this time the bend of the head is to the left, *with* the direction of movement. The outside leg (left when on the right rein) and the outside indirect rein move the forehand inwards while keeping the head flexed outwards or forwards.

The shoulder-in and its variations are not asked for in dressage tests; they are solely training exercises for the horse, and also for the rider in improving his aid application and general at-homeness in the saddle. The aids should be applied on the principle of minimum force, smoothly and, in time, imperceptibly, or as much so as the training of the horse will allow.

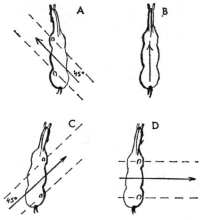

Fig. 14.   Lateral Movements

(a) Half-pass (left) or left half-pass (b) Straight position for one length of horse before changing the flexion to the left (c) Half-pass (right) or right half-pass (d) Full pass (right) or right full pass

The second type of lateral movement is when the horse moves sideways with his body straight and head flexed in the direction of the movement. The movement can be straight across at right angles to the original direction, full pass, or diagonally at an angle to the original direction, half-pass.

The full pass has disappeared from the normal school curriculum, and is never asked for in a dressage test, but in moderation it is a most useful movement and an excellent training exercise for rider and horse. I remember once seeing a line of about twenty mounted policemen formed up at the old Richmond Show to receive their awards after a competition. The stewards decided they were in the wrong place and asked them to move over several yards to the right. An ordinary group of present-day riders would have had to do a great deal of manoeuvring, going forward and turning, or going back and turning, and there would have been a good deal of milling around before they got safely into the new position. The policemen merely did a full pass to the right, moving altogether with amazing precision, and were in position in a few seconds. It was a most impressive sight. The danger to be avoided is a tendency to get behind the bit.

There are many occasions out hunting when a change of position can be most quickly effected by doing a full pass.

So the ability to obtain, or perform, a full pass smoothly and without fuss is a most practical accomplishment for any outdoor rider and horse, and I would strongly recommend its practice in the school.

First of all, however, we will consider the half-pass. The horse moves diagonally across the school at an angle of 45 degrees to the side track, keeping its body as near parallel to it as possible. The head is flexed in the direction it is going, and the outer legs cross over the inner legs, in a half-pass to the right the head is flexed to the right, and the left fore and hindleg cross over their right opposite numbers. The horse makes progress sideways and forwards across the school.

This, like the shoulder-in, is always a collected movement, and the horse must be prepared beforehand by being collected, with a preliminary half-halt and lengthways flexing of the body. The degree of collection need not be very great, but sufficient to give it an energetic and slightly elevated gait. The half-pass must be a well cadenced movement, the feet stepping in a lively manner, with lots of impulsion.

The active aids are the inside rein and outside leg. For a half-pass to the right, the right rein, kept close to the neck, flexes the horse lightly to the right, so that he merely looks in the required direction, and the left leg on the girth moves the body to the right. The right leg maintains impulsion and forward movement, while the left rein supports the forward impulse of the legs.

To begin with half a dozen or so diagonal steps will be enough, the rider then going forward about the same distance and then making the movement across in the opposite direction back to the track. Eventually the rider will cross to the centre of the school, which is the limit of the movement in any one direction in dressage tests. Finally the half-pass can be done right across to the other side of the school, when the rider will straighten up, go round the short side of the school and on the other long side repeat the exercise across the school in the opposite direction.

An advanced two-track exercise is the *zig-zag*, in which the horse is asked to change direction without stopping the two-track movement, i.e. direct from right half-pass to left half-pass and *vice versa*. In dressage terms this is the counter-change of hand. The action of the rider in half-pass is called *tenir les hanches,* holding the quarters, in German *das Pferd stellen.*

All these exercises are done at the walk, trot and canter, and are always collected movements.

12 Riding Exercises and Games

There is always a debate whether it is better to learn to ride solo or in a class. The horsemen of my generation mostly began their riding solo with a groom or other mentor running on foot beside them, and I always admired the fitness and willingness of these not so young men, or taking them mounted on a leading rein. The classical schools of the past, so far as we know, gave their instruction solo. In the army numbers enforced training by classes, and most of the great military riders must have been through this mill. Today the bulk of instruction is given by civilian riding schools in classes; if you want individual attention, you pay extra.

There is a place, I think for both in the training of a horseman. The pupil in this book began solo on the lunge, and I am confident that, if it can be achieved, that is the best of all foundations for whatever progress in horsemanship the pupil wishes to make. Every rider has his ceiling, but the grounding given by that work on the lunge will probably make that ceiling higher and increase his proficiency at whatever level he finally reaches.

After that, riding in a class has many advantages: companionship and a spirit of emulation and competition; practice in considering and adjusting to the horses and riders in front of and behind you; experience in riding other horses in the class, for changing horses should be a regular exercise in a riding lesson. If riding on the lunge has been impracticable, then I would advocate beginning work in a class, if it is not too big, four for absolute beginners, with a maximum of eight after further progress. Solo instruction can be given periodically at later stages, perhaps to correct bad habits that may creep in unchecked in a class, or to bring the pupil on to more advanced work. When the pupil has mastered the simple aid applications sufficiently, he can be allowed spells of completely solo work on a programme provided by the instructor, say for more practice at canter transitions or lateral work, which cannot be conveniently done in a ride.

Class instruction takes the form of various permutations and

121

combinations of the regular school movements, transitions, turns, voltes, circles, walk, trot, canter, rein back, and lateral work. The whole object of these for the rider, is to practise him in applying the aids for the various occasions, to give him balance, flexibility of control, experience of the reactions of his horse to aids, especially when wrongly given, knowledge of different horses, and generally the acquisition of a whole range of experiences which we call the feels of riding. Keeping one horse length behind the rider in front is in itself a constant exercise in the interplay of driving and restraining aids.

The first exercise of all is the turn at the corners of the school. This is, of course, inevitable, and the horses know it; so they try to cut the corner. The pupil should make every effort to keep the horse going forward right up to the actual corner, then apply the aids for the turn.

The next exercise is the change of rein, when the horse is moved off the track just after the turn on to one long side of the school and directed on a diagonal path to the opposite corner. The pupil learns to modulate his aids for the exact limits of the change of direction, to keep the horse straight along the diagonal path, and to bring it exactly to the same spot relatively on the other side of the school as the one he has left.

The change of rein is also effected by turning inwards at any point on the long side, going straight across, and making the opposite turn on the other long side. In all these descriptions we will assume that the ride starts on the right rein, so the above mentioned turns will be right and then left. The class can first of all follow the leader in single file, and the essence of the exercise is for the followers to turn exactly at the point taken by the leader. When the class turns together, the riders must endeavour to keep their horses in perfect alignment.

There can be a great many variations of these simple movements. The ride divides itself into two by going down the centre, then odd numbers turning to the right, even numbers to the left, turning in the same direction at the long sides, and so passing each other – always right hand to right hand – in opposite directions. They can unite by turning down the centre in pairs – half sections. They can also change the rein at opposite corners and cross on the diagonal at the centre of the school. And it will be noticed that these and other movements can all figure in the evolutions of a quadrille or musical ride. Piped music is a mixed blessing, but it can be used with advantage in a riding school; most horses seem to go better under its influence, and it gives rhythm to all the work.

Circles should begin in single file using the width of the school as diameter. The ride can then make circles together of half the width diameter. Here again the benefits of the exercise spring from aid applications to maintain impulsion, keep alignment all through the circle, and to preserve balance.

Voltes, and half-voltes are carried individually, starting at the corners with a maximum diameter of six and a half yards, which can be gradually reduced until it is almost a pirouette.

The serpentine is a first-class exercise for practising aid application and preservation of balance, which is good for the horse as well as the rider, as of course all these exercises are. Usually three loops are made, the first starting at the centre of one short side, the third ending at the centre of the opposite short side. The loops should be sharp so that the horse goes straight across the school at the end of each loop.

A useful and entertaining variation of the circle exercises is reducing and enlarging the circle. Starting from a circle of half the school, the class in single file gradually reduces the radius of the circle until the leader reaches the very centre, when he starts to enlarge again. It can be a preparation for the pirouette, and of course is a spectacular item in any musical ride.

For the ladies chain the ride must separate to intervals of eight to ten yards. The leader circles about, a tight half-volte – and zig-zags between the rider from front to rear, passing on the right and left hands alternately. At the end he turns again and takes position at the rear of the ride, and the next rider follows suit, and the others in succession. All this will be done at the same pace. In the same movement from rear to front, the overtaking rider must move at the next faster pace to the rest of the ride.

Other exercises teaching independent action are the leading rider trotting or cantering ahead to join the rear of the ride, and leaving the ranks singly when lined up in the centre of the school, both by going forward and reining back.

Games on horseback all help to produce suppleness, balance and muscular strength, gaining as it were complete freedom of the horse. Examples are vaulting, changing horses on the move, bending, and jumping exercises without reins or stirrups. For the latter, a series of three or four cavalletti are laid on the long sides of the school. First of all the riders become proficient at going down simply without reins or stirrups. Then they try other concurrent actions such as taking off their jackets; then taking them off and putting them on again; then ungirthing and removing the saddles from underneath them as they go down.

All these performances vary the monotony of learning, keep riders and horses mentally and physically alert and supple; they make riding fun.

There is a tendency now to do too much work in the covered school, which nearly every up-to-date riding school now possesses. Of course it has great advantages, especially in bad weather, and enabling instruction to be given after normal working hours at night. But there is no substitute for riding out of doors.

So outdoor manèges should be used as much as possible, the school work combined with riding across country, not necessarily over a lot of jumps at the start, but over uneven and unexpected terrain. Practice should be given at opening and shutting gates. The horseman of today may never have to open and shut a gate but the operation exercises all his aid-applying powers, as well as the steadiness of the horse. I remember once watching a girl groom at Cowdray Park, before polo, riding one horse and leading three others, come up to a gate, open it, get all four horses through, and shut it, without the slightest hitch or fuss. In its way it was a perfect piece of horsemanship.

Jumping has not been mentioned yet, as it is more convenient to deal with it in a separate chapter, but of course it will be part of all the training just described.

13 Jumping

Like nearly everything that we try to teach the horse, he can, on his own, jump just as well as after months of effort trying to teach him, if he wants to. A case in point is an Australian remount at the Indian Army Equitation School, Saugor, in the Central Provinces. A thoroughly unwilling horse, he had only been in training a week or two, and certainly had never jumped, when he was admitted to the veterinary hospital for some reason or other. He stayed there a few days, then one day his stable was found empty. It was the usual Indian type with bars across the opening, the top one being about five feet three inches high, with a gap of three feet to the top.

He had taken a very skilful and accurate standing jump without any apparent trouble at all. That was the last to be seen of him until about a year later he was discovered in the jungle not very far from Saugor, woolly as a bear, fat as butter, having maintained himself successfully against every predator in the jungle. So a horse is not a bad jumper at any time; it is the man on his back who complicates matters.

In the 'Thirties in New York, Captain Vladimir Littauer and Captain S. Kournakoff carried out a series of photographic experiments to show how a horse jumped and how its movement was affected by the way people rode. The object then was to prove the advantage, to the horse, of the forward seat, which the results did do very conclusively. The whole experiment was described in *The Defense of the Forward Seat,* a book which is now out of print; but a summary is given in Vladimir Littauer's *Commonsense Horsemanship.* Nobody denies the value of the forward seat for jumping now, but the photographs taken of the movement of light bulbs attached to various parts of the body, such as the withers and the croup, showed that under the best conditions – of horsemanship, the path of the two spots coincided in a fairly shallow parabola, while the whole body of the horse altered its position continually during the leap. These pictures have been confirmed recently by more sophisticated photography, published and described in *The Kingdom of the Horse* by Hans-Heinrich Isenbart and Emil Martin Buhrer.

However, the idea often expressed that a horse 'arches' its back over a jump is not correct. I have taken many photographs of horses in every phase of the leap (See *Riding Technique in Pictures*, by C. E. G. Hope and Charles Harris), and they show a number of interesting things. In the approach, the horse carries his head normally high, but gradually lowers it in the last three strides. Then at the last stride it flexes its hocks and, practically simultaneously, raised its forehand – the skeleton drawing on page 35 shows this conclusively. The hindlegs straighten out to give the push forward and upwards, so that the forehand is raised enough to clear the jump. The hindquarters follow the forehand up until the whole body is over the obstacle at its highest point and roughly parallel with the ground. This is the instant when horse and, sometimes, rider look their best while jumping, and is much favoured by photographers. In this fraction of a second also the movement is at its slowest.

But the motion of the leap is continuous, of course, and immediately the forehand of the horse begins to descend, while the hindquarters continue the upward movement, following the arc made by the withers. The forelegs, which have been curled up over the top of the fence, stretch forward and down to meet the ground. The head and neck are raised to adjust the balance. The hindlegs are flexed upwards to avoid the top of the fence.

The fore feet meet the ground, with a terrific flattening of the pasterns to take the shock, the leading foot of the take-off being still in the lead. The hind feet come to the ground almost on the same spot as the fore feet, the hocks are flexed again to propel the horse forward.

It will be seen from this that the body of the horse has swung upwards, and then downwards like a see-saw, which is exactly how the French describe it, *bascule*. If the bascule is correct and smooth, then the leap will be good.

Of course, all sorts of things can happen to spoil the regular flow of this action. The horse can get too close, when he will either go through the fence, jump like a cat off all four legs – demonstrating once again the extraordinary strength and agility of the creature – or refuse. He can take off too far away from the fence, in which case he will either hit it with his fore feet, or drag his hindquarters into it. A very powerful horse will sometimes be able to make an extra effort at the last minute to make the extra spread necessary to clear the obstacle; clever, agile horses will discover a fifth leg in an amazing way to get themselves and their riders out of trouble. Never forget that the rider can get himself and his horse into trouble, only the horse can get them out of it.

It follows from all this that the rider must do as much as he possibly can to help the horse during a leap, which means doing as *little* as possible. Once the horse has started to take off the rider can do nothing more about it; the horse is in charge and generally, like an airline, will look after him. So the rider should first of all keep his weight off the horse's hind-quarters until he lands, which he does by leaning forward and keeping his seat in the air and off the saddle throughout the leap. He should keep his hands forward to give the greatest possible freedom to the horse's head and neck. His position should be such as to keep his weight concentrated behind the withers, which is the point of oscillation of the bascule. The rider will grip, without excessive tension, from the lower part of his thighs downwards to the calf, and keep as still as possible without changing position throughout the leap.

There is probably, in the whole range of horsemanship, no thrill like that of a big leap on a good horse performed in complete harmony. Certainly, at the present time, there are more people riding who find this to be so than those who gain their peak thrill from some other activity, dressage, polo, racing or whatever. There are more people, too, who enjoy watching it, witness the millions of television viewers. The great thing is to achieve this harmony from the outset.

The rider's jumping training can begin as soon as he has acquired reasonable security in the saddle and maintain his position at all paces. It is desirable that the horse should be a willing jumper, going forward freely and smoothly.

The first jump will be over a low bar or *cavalletto*. This last piece of equipment, usually referred to in the plural – *cavalletti* – is an Italian word for trestle, and it is a pole attached at each end of an X-shaped support, which enables the pole to be placed at three levels – close to the ground, about six inches high, and twelve inches high. The use of this equipment for jumping training was invented by Captain Ubertalli – later to become a General – of the Italian Army between the wars, and has been adopted by schools of instruction all over the world.

So the ride is formed up in the centre of the school, the trestle is laid across the track at its lowest level, and each rider goes over it in turn at the trot. The horses' reactions will vary; some just stepping over, others making a great fuss to clear it, another will hesitate and inspect the fearsome object most closely, and yet another will rush at it. The rider's task is to remain steady in the saddle, pivot slightly forward from the knees to raise the seat just off it, and let his hands go forward with the movement. If desired he can put one hand on the pommel or hold the neckstrap. An assistant should give a lead to the first horse over. It should not be necessary to shorten stirrup leathers at this stage.

Progress to higher obstacles should be quite quick. The cavalletti can be used successively at their next two heights, up to twelve inches. The emphasis all through should be on the rider's position and timing over the fence, so that he learns to go with the horse and to adjust his position forward as much as is necessary. The final practice at this point should be going over the jump without holding on to the reins; the arms folded in front.

Special points to note are: smoothness of body movement, no sudden flopping on to the horse's neck, or crouching with rounded shoulders; no resting of the hands on the neck or making a bridge of the reins; stillness of the legs; no slipping or leaning backwards; seat off the saddle.

The next stage is practise over two or more fences. Go back to the lowest level of jump, this time with two placed two strides apart. The jumps can be raised progressively up to twelve inches, and the interval reduced to five feet. From there the instruction moves on to cavalletti in series of three, following the same procedure as above.

Higher jumps up to two feet can then be tackled. Two cavalletti, one on top of the other, will provide the height, or a post and rails with adjustable heights can be used. The stirrup leathers should be shortened by one or two holes.

If possible, there should now follow work in a jumping lane. A jumping lane is really a most essential item of equipment for training both horse and rider. In fact there should be two; one a straightforward series of obstacles, mainly post-and-rails type, on the flat; the other a cross-country type over uneven ground.

The first type can be either in a straight line, or circular, or, better, oval. The former requires more staff to operate it, and considerable mobility on the part of the instructor. The latter facilitates control, can be worked singlehanded, and is more economical.

The late Colonel Jack Talbot-Ponsonby, three times winner of the King George V Cup, was a strong advocate of the jump-

Exercising over the cavalletti in an indoor arena (*Light Horse*)

Exercising over the cavalletti in a jumping lane at Porlock Vale Riding School (*Light Horse*)

Dressage

A perfectly turned-out horse and rider (*Light Horse*)

ing lane, and describes one in his book, *Harmony in Horsemanship*. The dimensions he gives are seventy-two feet long
by thirty-five feet wide, with a track nine feet wide, the length
of the straight on either side being forty-nine feet, with a semi-
circle at each end. The jumping track is enclosed with open
timber fencing, and the centre area is free for the instructor.
The basic fences are four, one on each side, one at each end
on the curve. There is room on the straight sides for a combination (double), and, of course, spread fences. A screen of hurdles
or close fencing on the outside is a desirable refinement, shutting out possible distractions, but not absolutely essential. The
fences in the lane must be adjustable upwards from one foot
to four foot six inches, and for the provision of spreads (parallels) up to five feet. All obstacles in a lane should be fixed, and
jumpable in both directions, the ideal being a pole that cannot be knocked down but which has a slight play horizontally.
This can be achieved by fixing the poles between two pairs of
uprights. Additional variations can be introduced by the use
of brush fences, cavalletti, and so on.

Usually the entrance and exit to the lane are at the same
point on the curve at one end; but there is a case for having
them separate, which anyway would happen if the lane were a
straight one. The chief point is that the horse must always
receive a reward of some corn or other tit-bit at the end of the
circuit, and he will grow to appreciate this fact and so be all the
more eager to get to the other end.

Another point about the lane is that it should be used sparingly, especially for the horse. For the rider it is first of all a
safe introduction to higher obstacles than those first encountered
in the school, practice in negotiating a series of jumps, under
direct and close observation and control of the instructor, and,
later on, a challenge when the jumps are four feet and over.

Before work in the lane, the rider can be practised in various
combinations of cavalletti and twelve-inch jumps, one, two, then
three cavalletti preceding the higher fence; and in spread jumps,
two twelve-inch cavalletti placed one foot, then two feet, apart.

The fences are then raised, eighteen inches, two feet, two
and a half feet, taken singly, and then in various combinations
as before. The rider can practise 'doubles', the fences being
placed first about twenty-two feet apart to allow one full non-
jumping stride in between, then closed to half that distance for a
definite in-and-out. Hitherto all work has been at the trot, but
now it can be done over the higher fences at the canter.

Whenever convenient at this stage the lane can be tackled.

The ride goes out into the open field and makes a large circle close to the lane at a walk, continuing to do this all through the lesson. As a preliminary, the horses should be sent down the lane free. Each rider in turn dismounts, tucks the stirrup irons to the top of the leathers, knots the reins, leads the horse into the lane and sends it on its way, being ready to meet it at the exit with a handful of corn. The riders then mount and go in one by one.

For this first run, the fences are at their lowest – one foot – and the riders leave the reins knotted and go round holding the neckstrap or pommel. The second time they go round without holding on to anything, arms folded in front of them. The instructor in the centre keeps the horses moving by a show of the lungeing whip, and watches the positions of the riders, who should also use their legs to maintain impulsion if their horses show any hesitation. The circular ends test their balance and grip. In due course they will go round with reins in their hands.

Up to now the approach and placing before the jump has been left to the horse, but for higher fences and jumping in the open the rider will start to take control to some extent. This does not mean interference but a greater control of pace and stride before the jump is reached.

To interfere or not to interfere used to be the subject of furious debate, which seems to have died down of late. There were the 'let the horse do it' school, *à la* Caprilli, and the 'give him the office' brigade, signally exemplified by the Mexicans and Spaniards after World War II. The latter enforced strict control right up to the final pre-jump stride, often finishing off with a jerk upwards of the reins to 'raise' the horse. As the horse must have made his own arrangements long before that instant, I very much doubt if it affected the issue in any way, but there is no doubt that this method achieved many successes. However, as Littauer has pointed out (*Commonsense Horsemanship*) the exponents of this method were highly specialised and expert riders on highly trained horses in a particularly exacting sport, show jumping. For the open air rider, hunting, racing, horse trials, far less exact not to say risky control is needed. Even in show jumping the tendency is much more for freedom of movement all through, with only such steadying and control of stride as may be necessary in special situations. This inevitably involves a good deal of yanking about, but it does not alter the principle.

The great problem, whatever the method of jumping, is timing – the timing of the approach to the fence and of the take-off. For the timing to be right, the rider must first of all acquire a feeling for pace and stride, which is one of the objects of the preliminary lessons; then he must be able to judge quickly the distance in front of the fence known as the take-off zone.

It is universally recognised that a horse is likely to be in difficulty if he takes off closer to the fence than the horizontal distance equal to the height of the jump, i.e. for a fence four feet high the closest take-off point is four feet away from the base of the fence. In front of this point there is an interval, varying in depth, within which an optimum jump can be obtained. It is hard to be exact about this, for every horse's stride and power varies to some extent, but roughly it is the length of a normal stride over a fence less twice its height. Taking the scope of a leap over a four-foot fence as about eleven feet, the extent of the take-off zone will be eleven feet minus eight feet equals three feet. The optimum take-off point would then be about halfway between the inner and outer limits of the take-off zone. For lower fences the take-off zone is extended, and for higher ones it is reduced. These measurements refer to upright fences, which are always the most difficult to jump accurately.

Spread fences present different problems, but on the whole, until they become really big, they are less difficult to negotiate cleanly. So far the pupil has only been dealing with small upright fences, but henceforward he will be tackling a greater variety of obstacles, including the spreads. These fall into four categories: parallel, staircase, pyramid (this is the nomenclature of the late Jack Talbot-Ponsonby) and water.

The true parallel has two upright fences of the same height at a given distance apart, which can be anything up to five feet. Most parallels, however, have the first element slightly lower than the rear one, which makes it easier. The horse has to jump both high and wide, and so the take-off point will be further away than for an upright.

The staircase is one of three elements which rise up in steps, best known as a triple bar. The spread from the lowest to the highest pole can be anything up to six feet, and, the highest being the furthest away, the take-off point will be close to the first and lowest element, which acts as a guide to both horse and rider. In fact, it is one of the easiest of fences.

The pyramid has its highest point in the middle with a lower element on either side, again at varying spreads. It can take many forms, the most usual being the double oxer. The rules about take-off are the same as for an upright, and this again

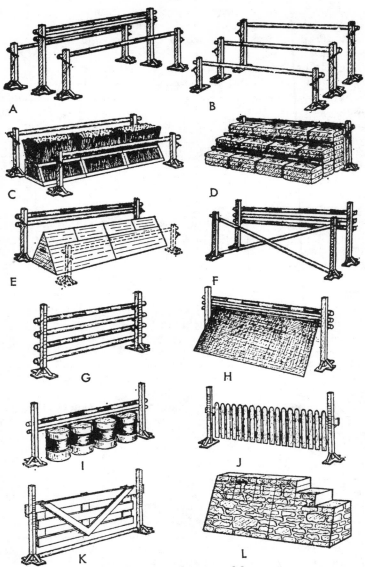

Fig. 15. A selection of fences

(a) Hog Back (b) Triple Bar (c) Double Oxer (d) Triple Bar with Straw Bales (e) Oxer with Chicken Coop (f) Rails with crossed poles (g) Plain rails (h) Rails with Panel (i) Rails over Oil Drums (j) Picket Fence (k) Gate (l) Stone Wall

in its straightforward form is a comparatively easy fence to jump.

Water always seems to present the most difficulties, horses and riders often making a great fuss over it. The width of water can be from ten to sixteen feet, and it is usually presented with a small brush fence on the take-off side, which acts as a sort of ground line. The timing here is to make the take-off just in front of the brush fence, or the edge of the water if there isn't one. Judging by performance, not even the world's champions are quite decided on how best to tackle it, whether at speed or steadily and well collected. Whatever else is lacking, there must be maximum impulsion, and perfect timing. What is nearly always useless is a furious uncontrolled gallop. A horse can often be encouraged to jump water by placing a rail across the middle of it, but it should not be more than eighteen inches high, otherwise it will make the horse jump too high and lose length. A lot depends on the horse; one will soar over it, another go very flat. The rider's own part in the affair is, as always, to keep still with the body forward and seat off the saddle, to give the hindquarters every chance to clear the far edge of the jump.

Once the basic work has been done, the rest of the rider's training will be to ride over as many different kinds of obstacle as possible, with steadily increasing heights up to four feet, and to practise the timing of the approach. It can be begun in the school over, say, three-foot fences. The horse should be steadied five strides from the jump, and for the last three the instructor should count out loud: 'One – two – three – squeeze,' (or 'up' or 'off'). The rider will already be using his legs during the three strides but will give a final pressure (squeeze) for the take-off. In time he should do the counting for himself. Only practice can make perfect.

A useful training aid is to have a low cavalletti placed in front of the main jump at the five stride point. This steadies an impetuous horse, and should ensure the correct timing of the approach. The legs should act progressively more strongly with every stride up to the last so as to produce the maximum impulsion in the horse. The main fence can be raised up to four feet, and it can be varied, an upright to begin with, then a triple bar, a pyramid, and a parallel.

Some instructors insist that the rider should sit down in the saddle for the approach, only leaving it to go forward at the take-off. The Caprilli school is opposed to this, requiring that the horse's quarters should be free all the time. There is no certainty as to which is the more effective. The followers of Caprilli achieved some wonderful jumping feats with their method; so have the 'sit-down' school. It is really a matter of individual choice, governed as much by the horse you are riding as by any other consideration. The essence is correct timing and not being left behind during the approach.

The next stage is work in the open paddock with a laid-out course of jumps of various kinds. They should all be numbered, and the instructor will name the numbers of the fences to be jumped in succession. At first two fences in a straight line, then the second fence coming after a circle, or one set diagonally to the first one. Then the rider will be required to take three and later four in one run, involving change of direction and of the leading leg. This practises him in control and approach, and in thinking, and looking, ahead to the next fence. Finally the complete course can be jumped. If the rider is 75 per cent sure of his timing and can maintain his position consistently, he will be doing very well.

A further exercise is riding against time. This involves taking fences at a faster speed than normal, and also taking them at an angle. All competition jumping, except puissance or nations cup types, is either wholly or in part against the clock. Time is saved by greater speed and by shortening the distance to be covered, by sharp turns – for which you need a very handy horse – and by jumping obliquely. Some horses can go a consistently fast speed over the whole course, others need to be steadied before each fence, and will often be presented at a big fence from barely two strides away. In the last resort everything depends on the horse, who will do his best and often achieve the impossible. Apart from guiding him, the only help the rider can give is to keep his own point of balance well forward and to give the horse impulsion through his legs. This of course goes back to the preliminary training of the rider for the acquisition of a firm and independent seat and the strength and ability to apply the aids.

Practice in this particular art is simple. Go back to the cavalletto, and approach it first on a fairly wide circle, gradually shortening it until it is just a sharp turn in front of the fence. Another exercise is to ride towards the cavalletto on a parallel line, first three or four strides from the fence and gradually reducing the distance, then turn sharply towards it when it comes opposite. In the same way practise jumping obliquely, first at an angle of about 30 degrees off the straight, increasing to 45 degrees. Do this, of course, to right and left, and both ways over the fence. The jumps are raised progressively, and their type varied. Finally, practise a double combination, taking the first part at one edge of it, crossing over in the interval to take the second part over the opposite edge. All this will be done slowly at first but with increasing speed.

Concurrently with this work on a flat surface, the pupil rider should be practised in going across country, over uneven, undulating ground and odd unsuspected obstacles such as ditches, logs, brush fences and so on. The work should be done at a steady canter, following the instructor as leader, and the forward position, seat off the saddle, should be maintained all the time. If the means and land are available, a cross-country jumping course with a circuit of half to three-quarters of a mile should be built. This should contain twelve to fifteen cross-country type fences, with adjustable heights or alternate fences, of the kind likely to be met out hunting, in hunter trials or in horse trials (one-day and three-day events). Used with circumspection, say a run over it once a week or once a fortnight, this kind of course is the finest instruction for both horse and rider in cross-country riding, in particular accustoming the horse to meet strange fences and to ride alone, which is the essence of this particular sport. The late Stewart Goodfellow, an enthusiastic and dedicated supporter of the horse trials sport, was the originator of this kind of lane, building it on his own land near Wokingham, Berkshire, and making it available free to any rider who wished to use it. Many leading riders did with great advantage to their horses.

Again, if means permit, it is useful to have a couple of steeplechase fences in a big field which can be taken at real speed. They need not be full-scale obstacles but approximate to them. Once again the work must be progressive, starting with a twelve to fifteen mile-an-hour gallop, finishing at twenty to twenty-five m.p.h. The rider's position before the fence will be that of a normal racing seat, short stirrups, body and hands well forward, seat high off the saddle. The horse will be allowed to make his own arrangements about the take-off; trying to steady him or position him when going at speed only unbalances him. So leave it to the horse and concentrate on going with him. Once in the air we part company with principles and allow nature to take its course. It is not impossible to maintain the forward seat throughout the leap, but improbable. The best steeplechase jockeys in the world will be seen invariably sitting, even lying, well back on the landing side of a fence, especially at top speed and over big ones. What they do not do, however, is to interfere with the horse's mouth; they allow the reins to slip through their fingers, if necessary to the fullest extent. That is really the essence of steeplechasing – non-interference. At slower paces the beginner should try to ride forward from take-off to landing, but as the speed increases it is a matter for his own judgement and dynamics.

The word 'style' has not been mentioned so far, although in fact we have been talking about nothing else. Style in any sport is the correct placing of the performer to enable him to get the best results. Obviously there is a position of feet, body, eyes in all ball games which will ensure the most efficient use of whatever implement is used. The result of correct style also happens to be pleasing to the eye. True, all sorts of other factors operate all the time, and players, when they reach a certain level, develop their own individual styles and methods; but every good player has been taught the basics first. The same applies to riding.

Good style in riding stems from the position and techniques of the use of hands and legs that have been taught from the outset, based on the principle of always being in balance with the horse. So the signs of good style will be recognisable: straight head, neck, shoulders and trunk, upright or leaning forward according to the gait and nature of the exercise; knees and thighs to the saddle, lower legs close to the girth, slightly to the rear, heels down and toes up, hands in light contact with the horse's mouth, making a straight line with wrist and forearm: the whole effect elegant and firm. The rider who moves on to higher things in top-class show jumping or eventing may adapt his style to circumstances, but he will always benefit from the discipline of the basic training, and will always show it.

There are two kinds of obstacle which a rider will seldom encounter except in competitions, banks (and in Ireland of course) and drop fences or slides.

A bank is a solid earthwork, grass covered, usually four to five feet high, and of varying width. A training bank will be about three to three and a half feet high, and five to six feet wide. The approach and take-off is the same as for an upright jump, but there is no descent; the horse lands on the platform, takes a stride, or not, according to the width of the platform, and then jumps down. A variation is to have a post-and-rails on the far side of the bank to make the horse jump big and wide. The most famous of show jumping banks proper is the big double bank at Dublin; and there used to be a tremendous bank at Aachen. The Jumping Derby bank of Hamburg, Hickstead and other places, is not so much a bank as a long steep slide after a gradual climb up by steps.

This brings us to the slide or steep descent, about which there are different ideas. The final verdict of Caprilli and his followers was that the rider should adopt the forward seat all the way down, on the theory that this released the quarters and also took the weight off the forehand. The climax of this teaching was the descent by Colonel Francesco Forquet, Commandant of the slide of the Tor di Quinto Cavalry School of Italy between the wars, without reins and leaning forward. Lesser mortals may prefer to lean back. It is doubtful whether the horse is materially affected by either method. Perhaps for short distances a forward position is all right. The nastiest slide that I ever met personally was the one at the Indian Army Equitation School, Saugor, from which all the earth and dust had long since been rubbed off leaving very literally a slide of almost virgin rock, of about ten feet. It was taken sitting forward, and I never heard of anybody coming to grief on it. The most dangerous and impressive slide is the famous *Cortoduras* at the Madrid Cavalry School, which is a cliff some forty to fifty feet high, the first part of it being almost vertical; but it is all soft sand, which helps. This is invariably negotiated leaning back.

The essence of tackling both banks and slides is strong impulsion, and, for the slide, keeping absolutely straight all the way down. Deviation from the straight and narrow leads most truly to perdition. Considerable control of the position and strength of leg is necessary to keep the right contact or even to give the horse's mouth complete freedom while negotiating these obstacles. The pupil should not take on these jumps until his seat is well stabilised and he is able to jump four-foot fences of all kinds successfully.

This brings us to the parting of the ways, the end of what can be called the intermediate stage of horsemanship. The rider should be ready to make his choice for the future: high school riding; show jumping; outdoor riding, which includes horse trials and hunter trials. (I do not include hunting in this, because it is more than likely that, whenever possible, hunting will have been added to the formal part of the training.) All these advances will involve competition, for there are few people who are content with art for its own sake, at least in the horse world, so they will be considered in a later part of this book.

It may be realised by now that the basic test and criterion of horsemanship at any stage is the ability to give the right signals to the horse at the right time; in other words a full understanding of the language of horsemanship. It sounds easy, but only constant practice aided by the muscular power that comes from riding exercises can produce results. In thinking on this I was reminded by Mrs Lorna Johnstone of the story told by the great French horseman, General L'Hotte, in his *Souvenirs*.

A great nobleman of France took his son to the most celebrated riding master of his time, Monsieur Duplessis, and said: ' "I am not bringing my son to you to make him an *ecuyer*. All I ask is that you will be so good as to teach him to co-ordinate his legs and his hands with the thought of what he wishes his horse to do."

"Monseigneur," replied Duplessis, "that is the height of my own ambition, and what I have been striving to achieve myself for about sixty years." '

THREE

The Training of the Horse

14 Kindergarten

The education of a horse begins at birth. Or it should. Horses that have been allowed to run wild can be difficult to break in when they come to three or four years old. This was particularly the case with Australian remounts, who mostly did not take kindly to that sort of thing at all. Bad education of a foal is even worse in its effects, because the horse will have acquired a built-in hatred or fear of the human race; or, in cases where he has been weakly handled and surfeited with tit-bits, he has developed into a bully.

This happens especially to children, whose well-meaning parents have allowed them to buy foals with the idea of their 'growing up together', in fact the height of folly. It is most disturbing to see advertisements, not in horsy papers, of yearlings for sale for that purpose and declared to be quiet to ride.

However, it is everybody's dream to breed, break in and train a young horse and win glittering prizes on him in the jumping ring, dressage arena or whatever. There is no harm in dreaming. Yet, if the conditions are right, proper facilities of land, stabling and equipment, time, and experienced advice, the training of a foal, even if not of your own breeding, can be a very satisfying experience.

Every foal is an individual with its own special characteristics, its own virtues and vices; but in common with every other young animal, it is particularly a compound of curiosity and timidity. If you have the foal from birth, its curiosity can be stimulated and its timidity overcome by growing familiar with its surroundings and its confidence in man. This confidence, once won, is a priceless asset in the future education of the foal.

First impressions are all important. Right handling at the beginning makes the foal appreciate human contacts and also impresses it with the power of human authority. 'I teach my foals,' said the late Henry Wynmalen (*Horse Breeding and Stud Management*), 'to lead from the first time they go out ... it is the easiest thing in the world, and quite an enchanting pastime, to teach a little foal to lead; if left till later, it becomes a much more difficult matter and the results are hardly ever quite so good.'

So, at the very first opportunity, in the box, with somebody holding the mare, put your arms round the foal, one round his breast, the other round the quarters. Stay passive while he struggles, but do not let go. At this stage, for the first and only time in his life, you are stronger than he is and he will recognise the fact remarkably quickly; so the first battle has been won without it being fought. It will take a lot of bad treatment to make him forget this lesson.

After that a soft halter can be put on, and the foal is led about with the mare, from and back to the loose box for the first few days, and afterwards every day in the field. These leading lessons should not be long, but they must be regular and systematic. At the same time the foal should become accustomed to being handled all over, to having its feet picked up, its hoofs cleaned out, and to the presence of the farrier and his tools. It is common sense that all the things that will be happening to him in the future should, as far as possible, be made to appear perfectly normal to him in these early days. It is wise, too, that the foal should become used to being handled and led by as many different people as possible. It is very gratifying to the human ego to think that you are the only person who can do anything with a foal, but very bad for those who will have to follow you. The properly trained horse is one which will obey anybody who gives the correct signals.

All this is very ideal, however. Most acquire a young horse for training at a much later stage, after weaning at the earliest, preferably as a yearling, more probably at two or three. You are no longer dealing with a blank page, but one on which all sorts of marks have been made, good and bad, and in invisible ink. You will try to discover from the previous owner as much as you can about the treatment and character of the foal to date, but no one is going to tell you if he has made mistakes or beaten up the youngster or whatever. You have got to get your information, as far as you can, from the foal itself.

Whatever its background and short past may be, the mere fact of being uprooted from its birthplace and familiar surroundings will be a traumatic experience in itself. Once again its first impressions will affect his future outlook on man. Quietness should be the keynote of the reception, produced by preparedness and the absence of fuss. A loose box well bedded down should be ready for the new arrival, with water and hay available. Arrange for the youngster to arrive at the end of the day, and lead him straightaway from the horse box to the stable and let it loose. Chat to it, and, if it is not too obviously nervous, give it a pat. If it looks nervous, one can always tell, and keeps its distance from you, do not attempt to touch it. Talk to it for a minute or two in reassuring tones, then leave it for the night.

In the morning a good test of its reactions will be whether it has eaten its hay or not. It may be friendly but wary, or it may still view the whole human race with deep suspicion; whichever it may be do not force yourself upon it. Carry on with the routine chores of mucking out, spreading fresh bedding, filling up the water bucket, which should be fixed to the wall, and so on; make everything appear as normal as possible. Leave it again and go to breakfast.

After breakfast, come back with a chair and a book. Put some corn mixed with some sliced carrots and chaff in the manger, but on no account offer it tit-bits in the hand. Put the chair in the middle of the box and sit down with your book, apparently ignoring the creature altogether, but keeping an eye on it all the same. It had better be an interesting book and a comfortable chair, for the treatment may take a little while. It may be an hour, perhaps less, or it may take several sessions before the youngster settles down. But sooner or later he will settle down, curiosity will overcome fear and distrust, and true confidence will be born. Don't react to the first tentative sniff; stay quiet, then get up and leave him for a spell. When you come back he may even be pleased to see you.

Before long he will allow himself to be patted gently and stroked on the neck and back; but leave his head and ears and legs to the last. Some people will reward him with a piece of sugar or something when he allows himself to be handled, but it is much better not to do so. The foal can become very greedy for such tit-bits, will expect them every time he sees you, and get quite angry if nothing is forthcoming, nipping and kicking with his fore feet. The young horse can easily grow into a bully, and I have known of inexperienced people being terrorised by one small foal. Start as you mean to go on: quietly, gently, but firmly.

The next stage is to slip a halter on to his head, and once he is used to that, lead him out of doors. If he hangs back, get someone to push him from behind. Once in the field let him go and leave him to explore and play on his own. If no other horses are available for company, get a donkey or a goat; the great thing is a companion of some kind.

All this may seem an unnecessarily complicated procedure, a superfluity of fuss and caution, but it is worth it in the end, if only for gaining the full trust of the youngster from the outset. Why have unnecessary battles in the future, if a little present patience will avoid them?

Home-bred foals which have been born in a loose box should be accustomed gradually to being out of doors, until in a few weeks they can stay out altogether with their dams, if necessary coming in at night. Although left free to play and enjoy their foalhood, there is no reason why their education should not continue quietly, with regular contacts with people, leading, and handling, particularly of the feet. Nothing is so maddening as a horse or pony which will not allow its feet to be picked up; and care of the feet is also all important. The foal should be regularly visited by the blacksmith to have his hooves rasped and kept in good condition, which will prepare him for shoeing later on. The object of all training is to produce a well-mannered, well-schooled and obedient horse, and at this stage manners and obedience are paramount.

Another valuable lesson which can be taught during this first year of the foal's life is to enter a horse box or trailer without fuss or resistance. The obvious way is to leave a horse box, ramp down and all partitions removed, in the field or stable yard, and put the foal's food and water inside it. If he can be persuaded to go in on his own, and associates it inevitably with food, there should be no more trouble in the future. If this is not feasible, he can be practised at leading up the ramp and into the box, enticed by food at frequent intervals. It is all simple common sense plus a little forethought.

Soon you have a yearling: either one that you have brought up or one that you may have bought. In the case of a colt, unless it is to be kept especially for stud purposes, gelding will be necessary. This can be done in his second spring, i.e. while still a yearling, or you can wait until he is two years old, but not much longer than that. Choose a mild spell in the spring, if possible without an east wind, to avoid the risk of chill.

More serious leading lessons can now begin. If you intend showing the yearling, and even if you do not, it is essential that the youngster should learn to walk freely forward and straight. The basis of all horse training is free forward movement, and like so much else it can begin now.

All the equipment required is a head-collar on the horse, a long leading rein attached to it, and a long switch. Show him the latter, scratch his neck and tickle his nose with it, so that he has no fear of it. It is not, and should never be during training, an instrument of punishment, but the first aid, a substitute for the future leg aids, and a stimulator of impulsion. If you are dealing with the home-bred product, there should be no trouble at all. The newly-purchased animal may make a fuss, dancing away from you. Let him go to the end of the leading rein and have his fling, playing him quietly like a fish; gradually he will come back to you, perhaps all the better for the demonstration.

Take up the leading rein leaving three or four feet slack, and start walking forward beside the pupil, encouraging him to go forward with the command 'Walk,' and clicking with the tongue. If he hangs back, flick him on the quarters with the switch, held in the left hand. In difficult cases it may be necessary to have someone behind to shoo him on; but it is better, if possible, to work quietly on your own.

After a short walk, give the command 'Whoa', and bring him to a halt. In this way he soon learns the meaning of the different sounds. After one or two halts practise standing him up correctly as if before a judge. Directly he has stopped step round in front of him, hold the head-collar with a hand on either side, and manoeuvre him quietly into position, square on all four legs, head up and alert. Some horses will show lively energy at the halt, others contrive to look like dead ducks; a bit of sugar in your hands will often work the miracle.

After the walk, the trot, when he should trot freely forward at the end of the lead rein three feet or so from the leader running beside him. Remember to repeat the lessons on the off side as well as the near; the more the young horse becomes used to working from both sides the better. As well as the display halt, there is also, as already mentioned above (page 100) the photographic stance, which it is worth while teaching the horse also. If you win a class at a show, someone will want to take a picture, or you will want a good photograph for your own record or for selling purposes. The object is to get one pair of legs showing inside the other, the inside ones being those furthest away from the photographer. The technique is to make the horse step backwards diagonally, starting from the pair nearest the photographer in the hope that the outside legs will then fall into place. Sometimes they will, but usually a good deal of manoeuvring forwards and backwards has to be done before the horse gets into the right position. As in the display position the feet must be placed directly under the horse, not splayed out or crossing one in front of the other; the body must be quite straight, there being sometimes a tendency for the quarters to be out of alignment with the forehand.

In the actual photography there is a lot more to it than that: the head must be placed right, ears pricked and alert, not the hangdog expression that many horses and ponies seem to take delight in assuming, mainly, I suppose, through boredom. The ears of even the most stubborn horse can be made to prick forward, if the operation is carefully planned. Usually the act of bending down to pick up a handful of grass will interest the subject, but it must be done at the right moment. An assistant should stand a little way from the pony slightly to one side of the holder and on the same side as the photographer, so that the horse's attention will be focused in that direction. When the camera-man is ready, and not before, the assistant starts to pick up the grass. If this fails, the same assistant, again under orders from the photographer, walks in front of the subject at right angles to his position and carrying a rug or coat or something large. As he crosses the line of vision of the horse he throws the rug up into the air, and there are very few case-hardened characters which can resist that. At the same time the other end of the model, the tail, must be right, not tucked in between the legs or swishing about. Always face the horse into the wind if possible when having a picture taken.

It can be objected that teaching two ways of standing will be confusing for the youngster. Perhaps so, but provided the basic display position is taught first, I have never known the other exercise worry them overmuch. Yearlings, foals even, are photographed at every show during the season, as well as privately, and one exercise does not seem to affect the other. The ones presenting the greatest difficulty are hackneys, Welsh mountain ponies, Welsh cobs, and heavy horses, who are trained to place their feet so that they cover the maximum amount of ground.

Is all this unnecessary waste of time? I do not think so. Photography is part of the modern equestrian scene, and preparation for it is all part of the training and discipline of the horse. One thing it will do is to introduce the young horse to the rein back, which can save a lot of time and trouble later on when one comes to do it mounted.

From leading at the walk and trot it is quite simple to proceed to the next stage, lungeing. All this, it must be emphasised again is quiet preliminary training and nothing to do with the serious work to follow later on, but a valuable and lasting preparation for it. You already have the leading rein attached to the head-collar, under the chin, and the switch or lungeing whip with which the horse will already be familiar. From the straight line forward gradually change to a circle, wide at first and gradually narrowing to the diameter of the leading or lungeing rein. The leader then moves away from the horse, progressively lengthening the rein, until the horse is on its own. Holding the rein in the left hand, the trainer will show the pupil the lungeing whip, flicking it along the ground behind it. This should be enough to get the horse moving round after some preliminary hesitation; if not, touch his hocks lightly with the whip to stimulate him to go forward. A few circles will be enough, then repeat the lesson on the opposite rein. All that is required at this stage is for the horse to go round quietly and freely and stop at the word of command.

None of these lessons should last more than twenty minutes, and need only be continued until the horse has acquired the necessary confidence, obedience and free forward action. After that, except for regular contact and occasional refreshers, the youngster can be left until the time comes for serious training and backing.

15 Lungeing and Backing

Finance rather than science dictates the age at which a horse should be backed and put to work. The Derby and other classic races are for three-year-olds, which means that thoroughbreds are raced as two-year-olds and broken in and backed as yearlings. How many of them remain sound?

The horse is a big and enormously strong animal and is backed by lightweight riders, by contrast with ponies who are asked at equally early ages to carry proportionately heavier weights and suffer more in consequence. The fact is that backing and working a yearling or two-year-old is like making five-year-old children work in the mines, and all veterinary opinion that I know of is against it. But horses and ponies are expensive to keep and owners and breeders want to see their money back as soon as possible; so it goes on.

However, these breeders and owners might reflect that a sound horse at four or five years is worth more than one already gone in the legs at three. The prospect too of a longer working life might encourage buyers to go for the older horse. Moreover, we are not concerned here with breaking in racehorses but training good riding horses to be hunters, hacks, show jumpers, event horses and high school performers. For them the programme should start not earlier than three years old, with lungeing and backing, and then no serious riding until the age of four years, coming into full work at five.

Henry Wynmalen preferred to wait a year longer than that: 'As a rule, I break them as four-year-olds, and get them to ride nicely and quietly, mostly at the walk, with a little trotting and cantering later on. But I do no strenuous work with them. At five years old, I take them into regular hacking exercise, I may send them to a few shows, and I may take them cub hunting; but I still give them no real hard work, no long days, no big jumping, and no heavy going. Then at six they are ready for anything. . . . We may well be lucky with a four-year-old in hard work, but the chances of unsoundness occurring in such a youngster are at least ten times greater than in the mature horse.' (*Horse Breeding and Stud Management*.) The Lipizzaners

148

come into training at four years and the process lasts for three years. De la Guérinière preferred to wait until six years at the earliest.

People have invented all sorts of short cuts for the breaking and training of horses. The Red Indians used to do the job in an hour or so by first tying the captured mustang so that it could not resist. As Chenevix Trench makes clear in *A History of Horsemanship* the horses were under-sized ponies of about thirteen hands, so it was really no problem. The Argentine gauchos throw the unbroken horse with a *bola* (three ropes joined starwise with a small heavy ball at the each free end) or with a lariat, tie it to a strong post and leave it to exhaust itself, then fit a rawhide thing (*bocado*) round the lower jaw and wait until it gets used to that; finally a saddle is put on and the horse is ridden. Another method suggested to us in India, as Argentinian and humane for dealing with a stubborn remount, is to tie one foreleg up and lunge the horse round on soft going until it collapses from exhaustion. Then you sit on it, gentle it all over, and generally try to make friends with it. We tried it out on a very unwilling, not to say malicious, Australian remount of about five years, with negative results.

Another wild Waler, which I was supposed to train at Saugor, went through the preliminary lungeing lessons quietly enough, though with a marked lack of enthusiasm, but there was no joy when it came to backing. I spent several back-jerking days riding his prodigious bucks in an Australian buck-jumping saddle, while he was only prevented from rubbing me off on the walls of the covered school where the operation took place by the equally prodigious power of Regimental Sergeant Major Hefferman of the 17/21 Lancers hanging on to the lungeing rein. The horse settled down eventually but he never really gave up the fight and was never safe. The last day of the Saugor course he threw himself over backwards, and I watched him gallop back to the horse lines with no regret.

The course of horse breaking does not necessarily run smooth, but a good deal of trouble, if not all of it, can be avoided by careful and humane preliminary training of the very young horse. And the long way is the surest and quickest in the end. Whether you go the short cut or the long way round, the basic task is to con the horse into thinking he has not the power to disobey, and then to keep on until obedience is a habit. If this can be achieved without a fight, so much the better. Another theory is that you should provoke a fight at an early stage and win it. To make victory certain the French use the Chambon tackle already described (pages 71–2). However, the great majority of English and European horses have the habit of obedience ingrained in them by generations of domesticity, and they respond well to the process to be described.

Choosing three years as the earliest to start serious training, the preliminary work will be to introduce the pupil to the bit, and practise him in being led in a straight line. If he has been with you since he was a yearling or earlier, there should be no problem. If he comes fresh as a three-year-old, then time will have to be spent on this preliminary stage, gaining confidence, and so on.

Bridling and bitting should be done with care. The bit will be a light jointed snaffle attached to a simple bridle without a noseband. Warm the bit beforehand, and rub it over with sugar. Let the horse have a sniff and lick at it, so that he will almost welcome it into his mouth, making a pleasant fuss of him at the same time. He will already be used to wearing a head-collar, so he will not mind the bridle being put over his head and ears, and then a pressure on the corners of his lips will make him open his mouth and accept the bit. The pleasant taste will occupy his attention while the bridle is adjusted and the throat latch is buckled up. Walk him about for about ten minutes with the bit in his mouth, then take it out; and be as careful taking it out as when putting it in. Frequent short lessons like this will soon get him used to the bit in his mouth, and the sweet taste will induce him to play with it and chew it. Let him have it in his mouth for one of his daily feeds.

Later on he can be left alone with the bit in his mouth for about an hour at a time, without side reins. Henry Wynmalen had little use for side reins at any time, and he is a good guide. If used they should be long enough not to interfere with the natural head carriage of the horse. Some people advocate special mouthing bits, and they do no harm if used in the manner prescribed above. It is the sensitive handling of the reins which really do the mouthing in time to come.

This is a good time also to introduce the horse to a body-roller and surcingle and pads, as a foretaste of the saddle. Place the pads quietly on the horse's back, and loosely do up the strap, talking to him the while. An assistant is useful here to hold his head and keep his attention fixed on a bowl of corn. Gradually over a couple of days the girthing can be tightened, until he is quite used to the process.

Lungeing

Side by side with this goes lungeing. This time a proper caves-son noseband is put on over the snaffle bridle, and the lunge-ing rein is clipped or buckled to the ring in the centre of the front of the noseband. An assistant is useful now, but if none is available it must just be done singlehanded.

The trainer gets into the leading position, holding the rein about three feet from the horse; the assistant takes the rest of the rein and stands in the centre of a circle of twenty-five feet radius. Assuming the movement is left-handed, he will hold the rein in the left hand with the remaining slack in the right, coiled up. If the horse should play up and try to get away, there is then some play in the rein to break the force of the pull, and the horse should be allowed to move away, trainer and assistant following him, until he subsides. The effect of the rein on the cavesson ring will tend to turn the horse's head inward facing the humans.

At first the trainer will lead the horse forward as usual, the assistant keeping pace with him; then almost imperceptibly the horse is led on to a circle, and kept going on it for a round or two, with halts and walks-on. Then the trainer gradually moves away from the horse, until he is about halfway between him and the assistant. Stay there for a while, walking round with the horse. If the latter tries to turn inwards to follow him, show him the whip, pointing it at his nose or his flanks. Then a flick of the whip on the ground behind his hindquarters should make him move on. If the horse still turns inward, take a firm step towards him – never move back – speak the word of command to 'walk on', and touch his hocks. There is no idea of punishment in this, nor should it ever enter into the training period, but an aid or signal to be obeyed. This half-way position of the trainer gives him close control of the pupil while it is at the same time on the full length of the lungeing rein.

Working by himself, the trainer must combine both functions, holding the lungeing rein coiled in his left hand, and the whip in the right. When working on the opposite rein the positions are of course reversed. As before, start on a straight line, then merge it into a circle, and start moving away from the horse, pointing the whip at its shoulder if the horse tries to follow. If the horse tries to get away, let the rein run out until nearly its full length then take the strain with the right hand, holding the whip across as in driving, the slack still in the left hand. When the horse has settled down, shorten the rein to the required length of about twenty-five feet and show him the whip behind his quarters to start him moving on the circle again. However often the horse may play up, quietly repeat the process with a kind of inexorable firmness which will have its effect in the end.

Opinions are divided about the method of attachment of the lungeing rein. Some prefer it attached to the ring behind the jaw instead of the front ring on the nose. Others lunge off the snaffle bit direct; others with the rein attached to the far ring and running through the near ring. It is said that the rein on the front ring causes discomfort and pain to the sensitive nose; but with a well-padded noseband it should not be too upsetting, and there is the important element of better control. With the rein on the bit or to the rear of the jaw, if the horse wants to get away, he will only have to gallop on and pull you along, unless you are exceptionally strong. I only knew one man who could hold an unwilling horse this way – the aforementioned R.S.M. Hefferman.

What is the point of lungeing? It has, in fact, a number of advantages. First, it exercises the horse helping to make it fit and to tone up the muscles, it is basic gymnastics for the horse. Next, it inculcates the habit of obedience. It teaches free forward movement, and it improves the action at all gaits. It helps to supple the spine on the circle and to balance the horse. It is also a sure method of retraining a badly made horse or one that has got into bad habits.

The venue of this lungeing work has to be considered. Whenever possible trainers use a covered school, for obvious reasons; but it is not absolutely necessary. In fact there is a lot to be said for doing as much work as possible out of doors. There is a growing tendency nowadays to confine the horse, and rider for that matter, cosily in a somewhat twilight covered building far from the madding crowd, which seems unnatural. The horse is an outdoor creature, and he can learn just as well in the open as indoors. Of course his 'schoolroom' needs to be quiet and undisturbed, to start with at any rate; but even this can be overdone. The horse is a gregarious creature and loves company, and anyway he has got to do most of his work in later years in public, so why not get him used to it at an early date. Sheila Willcox used to school all her horses at one time in a manège situated next door to the entrance to the Clitheroe Golf Club, and nothing ever shook their self-possession in the dressage arena. Police horses learn very soon to cope with crowds and noises. Anyway, not every private owner and trainer has a covered school.

Lungeing and Backing

A nicely prepared manège, sixty yards by forty yards, is a nice thing to have, but a fenced off corner of a field will do equally well, provided it is level, quiet and not too far from the stables, where the young horse will be tacked up for the great adventure. One must always adapt methods to the means available; on the other hand no one should attempt the training of a horse without adequate facilities and assistance ready to hand and without experience. For instance, do not start wielding a lungeing whip without first practising with it in private, so that you learn to handle it moderately and with maximum control.

Once the horse settles down and begins to move freely forward on the circle, the words of command which he should have already learnt in the leading sessions can be given: 'Walk', 'Trot on', 'Halt' or 'Whoa', and so on. Commands for movement or increase of pace will be given in a sharper more high-pitched tone, for slowing down and stopping at a lower pitch and more drawn out. If the horse does not respond immediately to a retarding order, repeat, and vibrate the lungeing rein slightly.

The rein should be changed frequently, and this is an opportunity to teach the horse to come to the centre of the circle on the word of command. Draw him in with the lungeing rein, and at the same time trail the lungeing whip along the ground in front of him, so that he associates it with the inward movement. Make much of him and give him a small reward, then – at first – lead him to the circumference of the circle facing the other way. In time he will go there himself on being turned round to face outwards and given a touch on the quarters with the lungeing whip.

During all the work on the lunge the trainer must bear in mind the principle objects, namely to improve action and stabilise the gaits, to produce balance and correct head carriage, and to make the horse supple and his back flexible. He cannot bend his rib-cage, that is the body between the withers and the lumbar vertebrae, but the bones of the spine can become flexible and enable him to move freely on a circle and balance himself with greater ease. So the trainer should plan each lesson beforehand, so that no time is wasted in the horse aimlessly bumming round and round. After one or two steadying circles, changes of pace, stop and go, change of rein, should happen in regular succession, equally on either rein, so that the horse is always kept on the alert. Of course things will not always go according to plan, so the trainer must be flexible in his handling of situations, modifying the programme if necessary, but always returning to it as closely as possible. Lessons for the first week or so should not last longer than fifteen to twenty minutes.

When the horse is steady and obedient at the walk and trot, he can be asked to take-off at the canter. Have the horse going at a smart, energetic trot; with the lunge rein turning him slightly inwards, then yield immediately so that he turns outward again on to the original circle and at the same time give the command 'Canter' and apply the whip aid. This is described by Waldemar Zeunig as 'the most favourable position for a gallop depart'. Repeat the aids until he complies. If on the other hand he dashes off into an uncontrolled gallop – usually from sheer exuberance – signal down to a trot again, helped by a vibration of the lunge rein, taking your time about it, and start again. You may have to do this several times before he finally gets the message. Do the same thing if he should strike off with the outer leg leading.

The trainer must watch the action of the horse all the time, and check any tendency to sloppy movement in any of the gaits. There will be no collection, but the trainer can bear in mind the F.E.I. definitions of the ordinary gaits (*Rules for Dressage Competitions*, Sections 403, 404, 405).

> '*Walk.* A free, regular and unconstrained walk of moderate extension. The horse should walk energetically but calmly, with even and determined step, distinctly marking four equally spaced beats.'

The longer the walk stride the better, and the hind feet should be well into the prints of the fore feet. A horse with a short, tipputy walk stride will seldom be a good galloper, and frustrating to ride.

> '*Trot.* The horse goes forward freely and straight, engaging his hindlegs with good hock action . . . his position being balanced and unconstrained. The steps should be as even as possible. The hind feet touch the ground in the footprints of the fore feet.'

Dragging the hind feet is a common fault in many horses. The horse may hang his head on account of the weight of the lunge rein, in which case raise it at the centre, and stimulate the quarters with the lungeing whip. Use the whip whenever necessary to maintain the energy of the movement and regularity of cadence.

> '*Canter.* The horse . . . moves freely, with a natural balance. The strides are long, even, and the pace well cadenced. The quarters develop an increasing impulsion.'

With a normal eager horse the problem will be always to restrain him from going too fast, and so swinging his quarters outwards on the circle. Try to reduce the inward drag on the head to the centre by walking round on a small inner circle and giving a bit with the rein. Slow him down with retarding sounds and a vibration of the rein, at the same time showing the whip to maintain the gait. A slug will have to be pushed forward with the whip on the hocks.

Backing

Before these lessons the horse will have become accustomed to a body-roller and girth, as already described (page 150); during them he can be introduced to the saddle. Begin with a light numnah pad, which can be kept on with a surcingle. Put it on before taking him to wherever the lungeing lessons are taking place, and he will soon get used to being lunged with this on his back. Repeat this process with the saddle. The first time have an assistant at his head with the usual bowl of corn, and there should be no trouble. Make sure from the outset that the saddle is put on gently and correctly, a little in front of the withers and then slid quietly back into place so that the hairs of his coat are smoothed down with the grain and not against it.

The horse can be backed any time the trainer chooses, after he has got used to being lunged with a saddle on his back, and to having it girthed up. No one can predict with certainty how a spirited young horse of three years old and upwards will react to having a man on his back for the first time. He may accept it quietly, or he may explode. In the latter case the battle is on, and it must be won by the rider. To make certain of this I would recommend the use of an Australian buck-jumping saddle, which has a deep seat, wide cantle and two knee flaps in front. To sit it correctly the rider must depart from the accepted canons of modern horsemanship and sit well back in the saddle, with his legs forward and his knees under the flaps. Every movement of the horse will then press the knees more firmly and safely up to the flaps. There are not many horses who will dislodge you. This would ensure victory in the shortest time. Failing this, use a show-jumping saddle with good knee rolls and hope for the best.

Helpers are needed for this backing business: somebody at the horse's head with the corn bowl; the backer; and somebody to lift him up. The sudden appearance of these auxiliaries on the lungeing scene could make the horse suspicious and nervous, thinking, rightly, that something must be up. Let the extras appear a few times before the backing is to begin, perhaps checking the saddle and making much of him in the intervals of lungeing. All this will help to reassure him and calm him on the day.

Do not fix a definite day in your mind – such decisions cause a slight anxiety, which has a way of communicating itself to the horse – but choose the right moment during a lesson, perhaps at a change of rein and the horse has been brought into the centre, when everything has gone well, and horse and trainer are calm and happy. If either is hot and bothered postpone the operation to a more propitious moment.

The horseholder takes the lungeing rein, coils it up in one hand so that it can easily be let out if necessary, and interests the horse in the bowl of oats. The horseholder must keep his mind concentrated on the horse, not letting his attention wander by watching the proceedings behind the withers. Without any delay the trainer will give the backer a leg up far enough for him to lay the upper part of his body across the saddle. He stays there a moment, then slips back to the ground, and the holder makes much of the horse. Repeat this several times, and that may be enough for one lesson. It all depends on the attitude of the horse and the insight of the trainer. However, it is always better to proceed slowly rather than hurrying things.

The next day the backer can stay across the saddle for a longer time, patting and stroking the opposite flanks of the horse while he does so. If he gets fidgety, slip off his back before he can think of taking more violent action, and start again. If all has gone well, the backer puts his right leg over the saddle and actually sits astride on the horse's back. The holder should make the horse keep his head up, which will lessen the chance of his trying to buck or plunge about; few English or European horses really buck, at least not with the technical skill of the Australian or the mustang. Reward at this stage should be lavish; much patting and gentling and plentiful oats. After a few minutes in the saddle, the backer dismounts, and the ordinary lunge lesson is carried on, or the horse is led back to its stable, according to when the backing took place.

Finally, stirrups are put on the saddle and the backer mounts carefully with them, but he will not handle the reins at this stage. A few steps forward can be taken, and in a few days it should be possible to do a few circles on the lunge with the rider in the saddle, and then to walk about independently.

There should be a short backing lesson like this every day,

but this should be the limit of the ridden work for several months, until the horse is rising four at the earliest.

The length of the lungeing period is a variable one, depending on the receptivity and aptitude of the pupil, bearing in mind always the principle of never rushing the horse but letting it assimilate the lessons slowly but surely. Three months is about the average, and the trainer should plan his work ahead on that basis, always keeping his mind flexible and ready to modify the plan according to circumstances. The following suggested programme is taken from *Riding Technique in Pictures*, by C. E. G. Hope and Charles Harris:

First month. Exercise approximately fifteen to twenty minutes. First fortnight. (Commence with left rein.) Twice on each rein at walk and trot for about two to three minutes – mainly trot. During the first two days, horse should be led at the beginning of each rein change. *Second fortnight.* (Commence with the right rein.) Twice on each rein for about two to three minutes at walk and trot – mainly trot.

Second month. Exercise approximately thirty minutes. Third fortnight. (Commence with left rein.) Twice on each rein for about four to five minutes with walk and trot variations during each period. *Fourth fortnight.* (Commence with right rein.) Twice on each rein for about four to five minutes with walk and trot variations during each period. If the horse breaks into a canter during any part of these lessons do not immediately suppress the gait.

Third month. Exercise approximately forty-five minutes. Fifth fortnight. (Commence with left rein.) About four five minutes each rein. First time both reins: walk-trot variations; second time both reins: canter trot variations; third time both reins: walk-trot variations. At the end of the daily school during the fifth fortnight - mounting and dismounting at the halt. *Sixth fortnight.* (Commence with right rein.) Same work as above. During the third, and last, rein period in the sixth fortnight rider mounted (being led first time round on each rein).

16 Forward Movement and Balance

After all this going round in circles we come back to straight lines. The young horse has learnt certain signals given by the voice and by the whip and indirectly on the mouth by the leader when going in hand. Now he must translate them into the language of leg and hand, assisted by the body. These aids and their application has already been described previously in Chapter 8 and need not be repeated. Then we were considering a beginner rider in charge of an experienced horse; now we have the young horse in the hands of a skilled and understanding horseman.

The youngster will have been ridden for a few lessons while on the lunge; now, with the trainer on his back he should be led up and down in straight lines, making fairly wide turns at each end of the manège. The verbal orders to walk on, halt, and the touching with the whip will be accompanied by the appropriate leg and hand actions, very gently applied at first, but quite definitely. In a very short time the horse should be interpreting the simple aids correctly, but this initial instruction must continue until he does thoroughly understand the new language. There is no need for this work to be confined to a manège or indoor school. Take the young horse into an open field, so that he does not get the idea that there is a special place for lessons. It does not matter if the ground is uneven in places or on a slope; the pupil will have already spent three months, perhaps more on a level surface, now the occasional variation will alert him mentally, make him pick his feet up, and start the process of muscling him up and opening his lungs.

As soon as the horse has assimilated this new lesson, the leader's job is done and the youngster is finally out of leading strings. He is now alone with his rider to be made – or marred. If all this apparently pernickety preliminary work has been carefully and patiently done, there should be no question of marring. The horse will be well prepared mentally and physically for all that is to follow; what he needs from the trainer is skill combined with patience and perseverance: the skill to know what is wrong and to apply the remedies; the patience to keep calm on all occasions; and the perseverance to go on and on until the right answer is obtained. It always will be obtained up to the limits of any particular horse's understanding and capability. Every horse, like every man, has his ceiling of intelligence and ability to learn and perform and the trainer must be able to recognise when this top limit has been reached.

The first job is to go forward freely in straight lines, and to move straight. Use the wall of a school, a fence or hedge, or a spitlocked line in the open field. At first, with the new weight on his back, the horse may be unbalanced; he may take uneven strides, which can be corrected by a slight check of the pace and then firmly pushing the horse forward into a long easy stride on a free rein.

The primary task of the rider of a young horse doing mounted work for the first time is to gain contact with the horse's mouth. The bit used is of course a snaffle, with a good thick mouthpiece and large rings of the egg butt type. Reins are held in both hands, which should be more widely separated than normal so as to give more lightness and flexibility to the handling of the reins. A long switch should be carried to supplement the leg aids when necessary; spurs need not be worn at first, but should be added later when the horse is going freely and quietly. They should be used very lightly at first but always definitely. With a free-going eager horse they should not be necessary, but with an unresponsive, sluggish animal they will have to be used sharply. Only the trainer can decide on their use.

The search for contact is slow and gradual. Let the horse walk forward on its own, pushed forward by the legs. Hold the reins loosely, then carefully increase the tension so that there is a feel on the mouth, then instantly relax. Driven by the legs the horse will tend to reach forward with his head and neck until he makes contact of his own accord. A gentle vibration of the reins will make the bit move in his mouth and encourage him to play with it and chew it. After a few steps make much of him, relax the reins and let him go on a loose rein, which he will appreciate as freedom after the slight constraint.

Remember always at this stage to have the reins relaxed when the legs signal him to go forward. Halting the horse should be carried out from a position of contact; the legs act to make the horse go forward, accompanied by the downward action of the back muscles, and the hands then pull back slightly. When the horse comes to a halt make much of him and relax the reins.

The transitions from walk to halt, halt to walk and back again are an excellent and necessary preliminary suppling exercise, and help to achieve the correct head carriage. At first the tendency is to hold the head low, with the neck stretched out; but gradually the increase of the soft – always soft – contact will raise the head and flex the neck. When the horse comes to the end of the school, outdoor manège or field, he can be turned with a simple direct rein aid to right or left, quietly assisted by the outer leg. There will be, of course, no deliberate attempt at flexion or collection, but the horse will achieve a sort of natural collection as he responds to the gentle actions of the hands on the bit, and as he learns to engage his quarters and thrust forward from obeying the actions of the legs.

These lessons should be short, fifteen to twenty minutes, only at the walk. It will take several sessions to achieve true soft contact, and the process should on no account be hurried, no matter how willing the horse may appear to be. To have a horse with a soft mouth is the ambition, perhaps only a dream, of every horseman, so it is worth taking time at the beginning to increase the chances of achieving it.

Once the horse is going freely, not fast, on a light contact he can be encouraged to lengthen his stride into what will eventually become an extended walk. 'A horseman should make continuous effort throughout the career of his horse to develop and maintain a long, low-striding walk.' (Harry D. Chamberlain, *Training Hunters, Jumpers and Hacks.*) To this end he practises obtaining extension.

Begin this work in a manège or covered school, and continue it in the open. The rider should have a slightly forward position, and will use his legs and hands alternately to combine with the natural roll of the horse. The left leg is applied and the left hand goes forward to follow the movement of the horse's head, when the horse is swinging leftwards, and with the next stride the right leg and hand act in the same way. The hands must of course be well separated. The horse is allowed to extend his head and neck as much as he likes, and the stride of the hindleg is gradually lengthened. Three or four strides at a time are ample, but the exercise can be practised several times in a lesson.

The actual requirements of an extended walk under the F.E.I.

Negotiating a Derby Bank; notice the rider
leaning well back (*Light Horse*)

Mrs L. Bates' John Blandon ridden over a fence at Wylye by Lorna
Sutherland

The approach to the jump at a trot. The rider is sitting down in the saddle, quite relaxed, keeping the horse lightly in hand but pushing forward with the legs

The take-off. The rider has pivoted forward slightly from her knees and lowered her hands in order to give complete freedom to the horse's head and neck, keeping the weight of her body over the forehand. This has freed the quarters to do the work of propelling the horse over the jump. Compare the steady position of the legs with those in the above picture

A later stage of the take-off over a higher obstacle. The body is rather more forward than in the centre picture, but the basic position is exactly the same note again the easing forward of the hands and the firm position of the legs from the knee downwards

Forward Movement and Balance

Rules for Dressage Competitions, Section 403 (c) are as follow:

> The horse should cover as much ground as possible, without haste and without losing the regularity of his steps. The hind feet touch the ground clearly beyond the footprints of the fore feet. The rider lets the horse stretch out his head and neck without, however, losing contact, the head being carried in front of the vertical.

The formal lessons can be varied by walks across country in company with a quiet trained horse as auxiliary instructor. Practice can also be given in getting the young horse used to traffic.

This can well begin at an early age within the confines of the training area. The horse should become accustomed to the sight of as many different sorts of vehicles as possible, a man riding a bicycle to begin with. Let somebody lead a bicycle beside the trainer and his horse on some of their leading rein lessons; then let him meet the horse and pass him. Progress from there to a mounted cyclist; at some stage the horse should allow a mounted cyclist to lead him.

Let him then become inured to the appearance of a scooter and motorcycle and to the sound of the engine running. Do not suddenly start the engine up behind him, but let him hear it from a distance at first and then gradually approaching. Common sense will dictate the kind and progress of instruction from then on. The principle is quiet progression from one thing to another. By the same token use should be made of music in the riding school, because it undoubtedly has a soothing effect and promotes good rhythm.

The horse can be got used to flags waving, clothes hanging on a line, people moving about. Once the preliminary lessons are over, the more company he has the better. He can work in the school with another horse, either a pupil the same as himself or a trained horse. After he has got used to sights and sounds on his home ground, he can be taken for walks, dismounted at first, on roads, progressing from quiet to busy. When doing this put on knee caps in case of accidents. Great care must be taken all the time to avoid these, and the trainer must be alert to give clear signals to traffic, and be prepared to have them disregarded. If there is a response, do not let your preoccupation with the horse prevent you from acknowledging it with a smile, a wave or some sign of gratitude. Some other horseman on the road will benefit from it somewhere sometime. As for the horse, the voice, the petting, the material reward, and above all the quiet confidence of the trainer whom he knows, will increase his present trust in him and encourage him to accept the unknown.

After two or three weeks of walking exercise trotting can start, still on straight lines. The signals for the trot (already described in Chapter 8) are given during an ordinary walk with rein contact. The experts are silent on whether the first mounted trotting lessons should be given sitting or posting, but I would suggest a sitting trot to begin with, for the main reason that it is easier to restrain the horse from trotting too fast. The object is a lively energetic gait, rather slower than normal. If the horse persists in trying to go faster than you wish, halt him, and start again. Repetition is the answer to nearly all resistances.

Ring the changes of transitions – walk, halt; walk, trot; trot, walk, halt – and so on, so that the horse becomes continually more alert and supple, mentally as well as physically. There is no reason why you should not try a rein back at this stage; the horse already having learnt something about it during his dismounted training (pages 148–57). It is all part of forward movement, for the horse is given the leg signals to go forward, the impetus being transmitted to the rear by the reins.

The first lessons are best done on the ground, thus avoiding any danger of rough handling of the horse's mouth. Stand the horse alongside a hedge or wall, hold the reins close to the bit on either side of the mouth and quietly manoeuvre the horse to stand up to attention, squarely balanced on all four feet. Gently move the hands forward (backward from the point of view of the horse), saying 'Back'. Holding the reins in one hand and tapping the horse on the breast with the butt of the whip, will help to make it understand what is required. If the horse is reluctant to lift a foot, tap it with the toe of your boot below the fetlock joint while using the reins and voice aids, and it will usually comply. The moment one foot has moved backwards, relax and make much of the horse, then move him forward a step. Gradually progress from this to one full step, then two, making sure that he moves diagonally, the opposite hindleg moving with the foreleg. After that carry on with the work mounted.

Begin the first lessons in front of a school wall, or a hedge or fence, to impress on him that he cannot go forward. Press the horse forward into the bit, holding it steady but gently vibrating backwards to make quite clear what is wanted. The rider's body should be just a little forward so as to free the hindquarters. One foreleg will go back first, followed by the opposite hindleg and that will be enough for the first lesson. Make much of him and let him go forward on a light rein. Some equines, ponies more than horses, can be very obstinate about going backwards. One reason is that they are not ready for it, not supple enough; so do not make an issue of it at this stage. When you do try again, have an assistant to stand at his head and tap one of his forelegs to make him lift it up. But if the early training has been done correctly there should be no trouble.

The most important element of all this preliminary stage is the handling of the reins and the establishment of the right relations between hand and mouth. The rider's hands must follow the movements of the horse's head, allowing him to stretch his neck, and by constant give and take encourage him to play with the bit in his mouth, to chew it. 'Letting the horse chew the bit is an indispensable aid of training, for it makes the horse's trusting contact with the bit while stretching its back and neck as comfortably as possible for the horse and turns it into a habit.' So says Waldemar Zeunig (*Horsemanship*); and he adds, 'It is also an infallible indication of correct dressage of riding horses, besides being very important in evaluating previous training.'

The position of the hands can be flexible, not rigidly fixed in one posture. They should be fairly wide apart, ready to be adapted to the requirements of the situation. If the horse tends to be too strong to one side, the opposite hand will remain low and firm, while the hand on the same side can be light and yielding and placed rather higher. Constant opening and closing of the fingers will give a vibratory action on the bit via the reins, without any pulling back or tightening of the reins. It is impossible to translate these reactions into words, but the experienced trainer, with his firmly acquired seat independent of the reins will *feel* it, so that there is a continuous back and forth flow of dialogue between horse and man along the reins and from the legs and body of the rider – which is *equestrian tact*.

The sitting trot can be alternated with the rising, and the horse accustomed to the regular change of diagonal, and soon he will be ready for balancing exercises. These are turns and circles on the move and at the halt; they have already been described in relation to the pupil rider (Chapters 10 and 11). The young horse has already worked on a circle when on the lunge; now he has a rider on his back, and so has to use himself to adjust his position and centre of gravity. The axis of all this effort is the spine which must be kept straight along the line of movement and made supple by the effort of conforming to the circular movements. The spine can only bend, slightly, in front of and behind the rib-cage, but the vertebrae which compose it can become flexible with exercise and have a small play in them, preventing complete stiffness and ramrod rigidity.

In a turn or a circle the horse has to resist the inward, centripetal, pull of gravity, and the outward centrifugal, force, which tends to throw a circling body outwards. In this he is helped by the rider, who will first prepare him for the turn or circle by flexing him longitudinally with a half-halt, and then by giving him the right aids and by his, the rider's, weight adjustment.

The half-halt is a very subtle instrument in the education of the horse. It is a momentary checking of forward movement, to alert him for a change of plan and to loosen the muscles of his neck and shoulders. It is obtained by a closing of the legs and a quick acting and immediate yielding of the hands, so that the horse will flex his head slightly and engage his hindquarters. This, as it were, *positions* the horse for whatever is to come. The half-halt can begin to be taught during the straight line period, and its use continues all through the horse's career. It is the basic means of retraining and resuppling horses which have become stiff and of curing hard mouths.

The first turns have already been performed, on a widish circle and with simple aids. Now the pupil goes back to the manège or riding school. Do not push him into the corners yet, but let him take a wide turn, using the inside rein and action of both legs to maintain impulsion, with additional pressure of the outside leg to impart extra energy to the horse's outside legs, which have just a little bit further to go than the inner ones and must not be allowed to lag behind. The left hand yields and at the same time the indirect rein on the neck, but not brought across the withers, supports the turning movement.

About now a useful exercise for teaching the aids to a horse and gaining quick response to them, especially making him obedient to the leg, is the turn on the forehand at the halt.

Halt the horse somewhere on the long side of the manège, alert it with a half-halt, and proceed as follows for a right turn, which is accomplished by moving the hindquarters to the left, the horse being on the left rein.

Keep the horse steady and facing straight to its front by light and even contact with the reins. Apply extra pressure with the right leg, and shift the weight of the body to the left, which will start the hindquarters moving to the left, by the raising of the right hindleg and its shifting to the left in front of the left hindleg. The rider's left leg is close to the girth to maintain impulsion and prevent a step backwards. In this movement the horse should pivot on his left fore foot, moving neither forwards nor backwards.

After one step relax the aids and make much of the horse. Continue step by step until one eighth of a full turn (45 degrees) has been made, which will be enough for the first lesson. This can be repeated later on in the same session, but no more for that day. As I have said already, most horses find that this is an easy movement to make, so that their co-operation is more or less assured, which makes it a valuable educational exercise. A few lessons will enable the lesson to be completed in full, and it can be repeated occasionally as a refresher, but it should not be overdone. It is not recognised by the F.E.I. as a test movement, though it was once included in the B.H.S. novice tests, but fortunately abandoned some years ago.

Balancing exercises, which also supple the spine and forehand of the horse, preparing it for collection and advanced work, can be carried on concurrently with the above lessons. The are simply a variety of circles of progressively diminishing radius, from half the width of the school, say ten yards, to three yards or less.

The essential thing is to vary the work as much as possible. Alternate circles with straight lines, frequent transitions, and also changes of tempo in each gait. Intersperse half-halts at walk and trot, on the straight as well as on the circle. Make sure the action in each gait is regular and evenly cadenced. Count the beats out loud and see that the horse conforms to them. Suitable music is conducive to rhythmic movement, and a tape player is very much part of the modern training equipment. A cine-camera is not quite a luxury these days; better if it has an ultra-fast speed so that the resulting films can be shown in slow motion. Better than nothing is a robot-type camera. The great thing is to be able to see yourself as the camera sees you, so that you can check the errors.

Change the rein frequently, sometimes by going diagonally across the school, or going straight across, or by a large figure of eight. Progress to smaller circles, and serpentines, and lateral changes of direction, from the wall to the wall; and by half circles in the corners of the school, returning diagonally back to the track in the opposite direction.

Gradually the head carriage will become stabilised, the horse's poll being about level with the rider's chest, and the head at an angle of 30 degrees to 45 degrees to the vertical. **Frequent** relaxations for free-going walks and trots will reward the horse for his labours and prevent him from stiffening up.

This work done over some three to six months will prepare the horse for more exciting things – the canter and the gallop. As explained in Chapter 11, only the English have separate words for the different speeds of the gallop gait, and the canter or hand gallop is the first gait that is now asked of the horse. He will have cantered already under orders while on the lunge, and, of course, freely whenever let out on his own; the youngest of horses can change quite effortlessly from trot to canter, but with a rider they have the problems of weight and balance to overcome. The task now is to teach the young horse to move into the canter from the trot, and later from the walk and halt, at command and on the required leg.

The generally accepted method is to start from the trot, at a corner of the school or on a circle, preferably on the less favoured side, all horses tending to be one-sided, to the left more usually, or to the right. Assuming that our horse is biased to the left, let us consider the canter depart with the off fore leading.

The main phases of the canter on the right, off fore leading, are: suspension (all four legs in the air); near hind on the ground; off hind, near hind, near fore; off hind, near fore (diagonal); off hind, near fore, off fore, off fore (leading leg); suspension.

Start in the manège or covered school, towards the end of a normal schooling session, when everything has gone well, the horse quiet and relaxed. Get into a slightly collected but energetic trot, ridden sitting on the right rein. On the long side of the school, approaching the corner, position the horse with a half-halt, and then, as the horse enters the corner, and when he is on the left diagonal (off hind, near fore), feel the right rein lightly, supporting with the left to control the speed, and at the same time apply both legs, the right against the girth, the left (outer leg) more strongly behind the girth, and shift the body weight slightly to the left.

The legs activate the hindlegs and push him up to the bit. The hands restrain the movement, preventing the horse from trying to go into a fast trot, and bend the horse's head gently to the right. The activated near hind will be accompanied by the leading of the off fore, followed by the off hind, thus breaking the rhythm of the trot and starting the canter.

Do not allow the horse to try to make the canter depart by

speeding up his trot, which many are inclined to do. At the first sign of that relax the aids, bring him quietly back to a walk and halt. Calm him down with a few walk-trot, trot-walk transitions, then start again. An increase of speed *at the start* of the canter is permissible for a few strides, after which steady him down.

A few departures at the corners should be sufficient to get the idea into his head, when you can practise on a large circle (half the manège), following with lessons on the straight. When the horse is confirmed on the off fore leading, repeat the whole process for the near fore leading. At a later stage, he can be practised in the canter depart from the walk, and then from the halt.

The aids described above are diagonal ones. Many instructors start by using lateral aids, that is right rein and strong right leg (for off fore leading), and change to diagonal aids later on. It would appear to be less confusing to the horse, and possibly for the rider, to start as you mean to go on, using diagonal aids from the outset, which was the opinion of the late Henry Wynmalen (*Equitation*).

Once the horse is thoroughly obedient to these aids in the manège, he can be taken out into the open, and cantered and galloped over all sorts of country: up and down hill, over ploughland, if it is the right time of year. There is nothing like it for conditioning the horse, strengthening his muscles, and perfecting his balance. Also give the horse variety. 'After a time,' says Lyndon Bolton (*Training the Horse*), 'I shall rarely go twice running to the same place to school. I like change, and so does my horse.' And he too emphasises the value of getting a horse used to all sorts of distractions, which will never happen in the seclusion of the covered school.

At the walk and canter, the horse nods his head as he steps along, oscillating it backwards and forwards, which is why it has already been said that the hands must follow the movement of the horse's head and neck. They should go backwards and forwards, keeping always a light play on the bit through the reins. At the trot the horse holds his head steady, and the same should happen to the hands, subject to the delicate nuances of contact through the fingers. The horse has become used to going free on a loose rein at the walk and trot, and he should also do so at the canter.

It is true that 'on the bit' is the watchword of the horseman, but too often it is interpreted as a steady hard pull on the reins. Watch any dressage test. The horse, provided he has been properly schooled from the start, can be on the bit through the weight of the reins alone. The skilled cutting horse can be effectively on the bit without one in its mouth at all.

A simple change of leading leg at the canter can be taught quite simply. The mechanics have been described already in Chapter 11. The best way is to make a large figure of eight, making the change at the trot at the intersection point of the figure. Half a dozen strides at first can be reduced to three and two. Then the change is practised on the straight. Finally the horse should be well able to do the flying change. Great care must be taken to apply the aid, which is simply that for the opposite canter lead, at the correct time, so that the signal is felt when the horse is in the state of suspension between strides. Start the sign – diagonal aids – when the present leading forefoot is just about to strike the ground.

The balancing exercises already described will be carried on at the canter as well as at the trot, and, towards the end of this period, the preliminaries to advanced work, flexion and collection, can begin.

17 Flexion, Collection and Suppling

Flexion

If the training up to now has been successfully carried out, the horse should already have begun to flex his lower jaw, and to some extent to collect himself. The suppling work, especially the half-halt and the changes of tempo, will have prepared him for greater collection, as described in Chapter 10.

There are all kinds of flexions, of the spine, flexing the hind-legs, as well as of the mouth, head and neck, but specifically the term applies to the direct flexion of the head and lateral flexion of the neck.

Direct flexion is when the horse yields his lower jaw to the action of the bit and bends his head downwards from the poll, thus straightening somewhat the angle of the head to the vertical. Incorrect flexion is when the horse bends his head from the crest of the neck, which accentuates the straightening of the head, causes stiffness and over-bending, and puts the horse behind the bit.

Lateral flexion is the bending of the neck to the right or left.

Elementary flexion and collection can be obtained with a snaffle bit, but for the serious work which must now begin the change to a double bridle must be made. If the horse has become well mouthed, used to playing with and chewing his bit, he should accept the double bit without any difficulty. As when the horse was introduced to the snaffle bit for the first time, extreme care should be taken over this new introduction. Insert the two bits gently into the mouth, and let them hang loosely in the mouth before making the adjustments. The sizes of the bits must be just right for the horse's mouth, and the adjustment of fitting must be carefully made and must be exact. It is not easy to do, and the perfectly fitted double bridle with the curb chain acting in the right place is a rare sight in my experience.

The snaffle bit (bridoon) goes above the curb bit, set just high enough to wrinkle the corners of the lips. The curb bit rests just below the bridoon on the tongue and the bars of the mouth. When it hangs straight down as an extension of the bridle cheekpiece, the curb chain should lie slack just below the chin groove, and it should be turned so that all the links lie flat. While dismounted, hold the snaffle reins above the bits with the left hand, and gently pull the curb reins with the right so that the arm of the curb moves backwards and raises the curb chain into the chin groove. The horse should just begin to yield his lower jaw a little in response to the concentrated action on it of the curb and the chain. The upward pull of the bridoon reins prevents the horse from lowering his head, but allows him to bend it slightly towards the vertical – but nowhere near it – from the poll. Once the response is made, relax and make much of him.

Both direct and lateral flexion can be taught from the ground. James Fillis and Baucher were great artists at this, achieving most extreme flexion, especially lateral, in this way; but modern riders seem to prefer to practise it mounted and can be equally successful. In any case the kind of lateral flexion obtained by Fillis of the horse looking practically at right angles to his proper direction is not required of a modern horse, even in the most advanced dressage. The preliminary exercise described above is really connected with the fitting of the double bit, and thereafter the work can be done mounted.

Start at the halt, holding the bridoon reins in the left hand and the curb reins in the right. The bridoon hand will be held higher than the curb hand, not so much to raise the head as to keep it in position and prevent it from being lowered by the action of the curb bit. As always there should not be a direct pull, but a light fingering action. The snaffle is a simple bit with a straightforward action, so it can be used more frequently and more firmly when necessary than the curb bit.

The curb hand has to make the action of the bit as sensitive and subtle as possible, actuating straight backwards on the bars and against the jaw, so that it will yield slightly, the head nodding from the poll. The legs should act to keep the horse in position at the halt, resisting a possible tendency to rein back. The instant the horse yields his jaw for the first time, relax and make much of him, and let him go forward on light normal contact on the snaffle, the curb rein loose. Repeat this a few times at the halt, which will be sufficient for the first session.

Lateral flexion of the neck can be practised at the same time, still at the halt, by using a direct rein to bend the head slightly to the left, while keeping the horse steady in the halt position with the legs and opposite rein, which yields enough to allow the head to turn but avoids indirect effects on the withers. Bend alternately to right and left a few times, being content with only just noticeable results at first, relaxing the reins between each flexion. There is no need for excessive flexion of the neck, but enough to make the horse obedient to the aids and to supple his neck and jaw muscles.

Once the horse responds easily and gently to these exercises, flexion can be practised on the move; walk and trot at first, later the canter, on turns and circles and serpentine as well as on a straight line. It is a good exercise in finesse to ride with a loose bridoon rein, and the lightest of contact with the curb, so that the horse will respond to the slightest restraining action of it. Obtain halts this way; the transition must be gradual at first, especially at trot or canter, but, according to the way the horse has responded to training, they can become quick. Yield the hand immediately after each response.

A useful flexing and suppling exercise, which was recommended by Harry Chamberlain (*Training Hunters, Jumpers and Hacks*) is the half-turn and half-turn in reverse. For the half-turn, assuming you are on the left rein, and going straight along the side of the manège, or in the open for that matter, at the corner of the manège, or a selected point in the open, make a half circle to the left, using the left opening rein and the right indirect rein (Chapter 8), and the right leg, the left (inside) leg acting to control the quarters. The head is flexed to the left. Proceed diagonally at an angle of about 45 degrees back to the original line of march, but in the opposite direction.

The half-turn in reverse is done in the opposite circle. From the original line of march on the left rein, veer off from the straight at an angle of about 45 degrees, using the left direct opening rein, the right indirect rein and the right leg. Proceed in that direction five to ten yards, then turn right on a half circle back to the side of the manège or the original line of march, but of course going in the opposite direction and now on the right rein. In this case the right opening rein is used with the left rein supporting, the left (outside) leg asking for the turn to the right, the right leg keeping the haunches under control. This teaches obedience to the reins, activates and lightens the quarters, helps to put the horse on the bit, and promotes the flexing of the jaw and the neck, supples the spine, and begins the flexing of the poll; it is also a preliminary to the shoulder-in exercise to come. These exercises are best done at a slow trot sitting.

The horse's head carriage should be stabilised now in the position described on page 170. The bridoon and curb reins can be separated in each hand as before, or the curb rein can be held outside the little fingers of each hand, the bridoon inside. This rein then holds the head in position, while flexing and vibration of the fingers actuate the curb bit, impulsion being increased by leg action. The horse should yield his jaw completely, which will be accompanied by a nodding of the head from the poll. Immediately yield the hands to give the horse the reward of instant relief for his obedience. The head should go forward into the normal position and the mouth close. A horse which keeps its mouth continually open shows that this flexion has been overdone and that contact has become too harsh. Revert to the snaffle and a free rein. In obtaining flexion of the poll the hands should, if anything, be held a little higher than usual; holding them too low will make the horse lower his head and arch his neck from the axis instead of from the highest point of the head, which is totally incorrect.

As has already been said (pages 170–1) successful flexion depends very considerably on the conformation of the horse's head and neck. It is a waste of time to attempt any more than the most elementary flexion, if that, with a horse that has a short thick neck and a coarse tied-in jaw. On the other hand difficulties will also arise from a horse with a long slender neck, which will tend to become rubber and overflexible, encouraging the horse to successful evasions. In this case approach flexion very cautiously, and practise it at a trot, at which pace the head and neck are held more stiffly by the horse than at the walk and canter.

During this period it is well worth teaching the horse to go freely with one hand only holding the reins, in other words to become bridlewise. The influence of formal dressage competition has almost destroyed this art amongst modern riders, except polo players and mounted soldiers, who have to use one hand for other purposes, but I hold that no horse is fully trained (or horseman for that matter) until he can be controlled as easily with one hand as by two, and go nearly as well. A horse which in the course of this basic training has come to accept the effects of the indirect rein will quite easily and willingly become bridlewise, and be an even greater pleasure to ride because of it.

Collection

Collection follows flexion; and here we come to a parting of the ways of the outdoor (*campagne*) school of riding and what is now particularised as dressage riding. Collection has been defined on pages 109–10. It is generally accepted now that some kind of collection is necessary for an outdoor horse, even if you call it engagement of the quarters, but also that it can be kept to a minimum. The tests for the dressage phase of a three-day event do require collection, but as the use of a snaffle is optional, it need be of only very low degree. For novice and intermediate grade one-day events in England no collection is asked for.

The preliminary to collection is the *ramener*, the correct placing of the head in preparation for the signals that will ask for engagement of the quarters and lightening of the forehand. This is in fact the flexion of the poll, which has already been obtained. In the first degree of collection the head should be in the normal position between 45 degrees and 30 degrees to the vertical, jaw slightly flexed. For greater collection the head will be nearer to the vertical, *but never behind it.* It should be emphasised that flexion and collection can only be obtained at slow speeds. On the other hand there must be no loss of impulsion in collected gaits (see the definitions given on pages 108 and 110). What happens is that instead of the legs moving extended horizontally they move just as actively but more vertically and with more elevated steps. In the extreme case you have the *passage*.

The horse learns natural collection all through his early mounted training in the constant repetition of transitions of all kinds, already described in Chapter 16. The method is the close and subtle relation of the hand and leg aids; the legs provide the driving force, while the hands restrain and, as it were, canalise the energy produced upwards instead of forwards – *without, however, losing forward impulsion* – compressing the horse like a steel spring.

It cannot be repeated too often that these exercises should be carried out for short periods only, alternating with plenty of relaxed movement with free extension of head and neck. Even if the horse proves to be an apt pupil and appears to enjoy doing collected work, the rider should strictly limit the amount.

Suppling
All this work, properly done, should have a continuous softening and suppling effect on the horse's muscles, especially those of the neck and shoulders and back, at the same time as they are being developed and strengthened by the gymnastic exercises, which is what in fact they are. But the supreme suppling

instruments are the half-halt and the shoulder-in. Both of these have been described on pages 164 and 117 to 120. They should be used regularly in training and school work, and, more intensively, for remaking pullers and spoiled horses. The use of the half-halt for suppling has been meticulously described by A. d'Endrody in *Give Your Horse a Chance*. The process was regularly used for the training of polo ponies. It can also help show jumpers to achieve the speed and handiness which is demanded of them nowadays.

The method is the application of repeated half-halts on a wide circle (school diameter) at the trot and canter, mostly the latter, using a snaffle bit. The work can be direct or lateral, this in the case of horses that are one-sided naturally, or have been allowed to become so by excessive work on one rein. As a preliminary do two or three circles at the walk with a half-halt every few steps, then carry on at the trot first and then at the canter, alternating half-halts with full halts, and turns across the circle to change the rein. Using this as a refresher for a trained horse, there will also be turns (pirouettes), on the haunches, of 180 degrees. The frequency should be about two movements per circle, and the length of the lesson for one horse should be about fifteen minutes.

For one-sided animals work at first at the walk on a straight line, alternating the aids – left rein left leg, right rein right leg – in a series of half-halts. Then work on a circle, using the lateral aids according to which rein you are on. Stiff horses are inclined to carry their heads low and to be on their forehands, so that there must be an upward action of the reins. If the horse tends to throw his head up, apply the treatment described on page 169.

The second suppling exercise, the *shoulder-in*, can run concurrently. The wall to the wall routine is a good preliminary exercise for the shoulder-in, but the best way to move into it is by way of a turn at the corner of the manège or a half-turn as described on page 114. In the first case the horse is not asked to straighten up along the side of the school when the turn is completed but allowed to continue the movement until his forelegs are off the track. Taken at the walk on the right rein, the horse's head will be bent slightly to the right, and he will be checked from going any further on the turn by the left (outside) rein, and the right (inside leg) will act to move him along the side of the school, stepping sideways with his hindlegs on the track and his forelegs just off it, at angle of about 45 degrees to the track. The right rein will act to keep his head flexed to

174

the right (inwards). Before the movement the horse will be positioned on the long side of the school with a half-halt and moderately collected. The right (inside) feet must cross over the left (outside) ones. Two or three steps will be enough to start with. Then the exercise is repeated on the opposite rein.

Using the half-turn, the shoulder-in will begin as the horse is about to take the diagonal direction back to the side of the school, making the way back with a shoulder-in instead of on a straight line. Two or three times per session will be enough for a few days, after which the number of steps can be increased, and the lesson varied with the travers (quarters in), and renvers (quarters out). Gradually progress to exercises at the trot and canter.

18 Turning at the Halt, Lateral Work, and Pirouettes

Turning on the forehand at the halt has already been practised, as an instruction in aid application and recognition (described earlier), and the horse should now be balanced and light on the forehand, and so ready for the half-turn on the haunches, which is the prelude to turns on the move or pirouettes, which come within the range of advanced equitation.

Notes on Dressage, issued by the British Horse Society after World War II, described the movement as follows: 'In the turn on the haunches, the horse's forehand is moved in even, quiet and regular steps round the horse's inner leg. The inner hindleg, acting as a pivot, should remain as nearly as possible on the same spot.'

The turn can be quarter (90 degrees), half (180 degrees), three-quarter (270 degrees), or full (360 degrees). With a still novice horse, an eighth (45 degrees) or less is sufficient. For a turn to the right, halt the horse in a collected manner after a collected walk, on a long side of the manège. Pause to make sure that the horse is standing correctly balanced, hindquarters engaged and burdened, the forehand light, rider's body upright, seat well in the saddle.

With a light action of the right direct rein invite the horse to turn his head to the right. At the same time the legs stimulate movement, but with greater strength from the left leg behind the girth. This accompanied by the action of the left indirect rein on the neck, and yielding forwards. The rider braces the muscles of the small of the back, and shifts his weight slightly to the right to pin down the right (inside) hindleg. The shifting of balance will cause the horse to move his right foreleg to adjust it. Then increased pressure of the left leg and action of the left indirect rein will cause the left foreleg to follow it, moving across and in front of the right. The continued action of the right rein and left leg will move the right foreleg across behind the left foreleg, to resume the normal halt position. Once this first step is accomplished, relax the aids and make much of the horse. It may not happen the first time, but patience and quiet application of the aids will achieve it.

As always it is the first step which counts. Call the horse to attention again and invite him in the same way to take the next step. Three steps will be enough for one lesson; next repeat it on the other rein to the left. As the horse moves round his left (outer) hindleg should move round the right (inside) hindleg, which will move as little as possible. A little forward movement is permissible in the early stages, but not backward. At whatever stage you stop the turn move the horse forward in the new direction, bringing him back on to the track with a circle. Every movement in the school should be a piece of planned gymnastic.

The combined centre of gravity will be shifted rearwards, and the head can be a little higher than normal, further to lighten the forehand. The steps should be taken at a regular, cadenced beat. The moment there is a break in the rhythm stop and start again. Gradually the horse will accomplish the quarter, the half – the most frequently used – and the full turn, which requires a considerable sustained effort.

This too is a balancing and suppling exercise, and prepares the horse for turns on the move (pirouettes). The school pirouette, which will be discussed later (page 238 *et seq*), is a slow highly cadenced movement, requiring considerable muscular control on the part of the horse, and skilful guidance by the rider. It is not the same as that performed by, say, a polo pony, whose 180 degrees turn will be one at top speed, in response to violent and sudden aids from the rider, but the principle is the same. So although the pirouette comes into the realms of high school, it is also necessary for a well-trained outdoor horse albeit in a rough and ready form. Apart from polo and gymkhana events, it is a great asset to a show jumper in the modern style of show jumping where speed is the ultimate governing factor.

After the shoulder-in sequence of movements, the next important exercise in lateral movement is the half-pass (two tracks). The details of this have been described in Chapter 11. The essence is that the horse moves diagonally with his body as straight as possible, his head bent slightly to the direction in which he is going. At first this will be across the manège, but later on it should be done out of doors. The outside feet cross over in front of the inside: if going to the right, left over right; if to the left, right over left. This is a collected movement, and the horse should be prepared for it in the usual way. Aids (to the right): left leg, acting well behind the girth, and the right rein softly leads the horse's head to the right; right leg maintains the movement forward, and the left indirect rein on the neck supports the movement to the right. The horse moves sideways and forwards, body nearly straight, at an angle of about 45 degrees to the original line of direction.

Here is the official description:

'The horse moves on two tracks, the head, neck and shoulders always slightly in advance of the quarters. A slight bend permitting the horse to look to the direction of the movement adds to his grace and gives more freedom of movement to the outside shoulder. The outside legs pass and cross in front of the inside legs. No slowing down of the pace can be tolerated.'

F.E.I. *Rules for Dressage Competitions*, Sec. 411 (d). The French term for this movement is *tenir les hanches*.

The original pace and cadence must be maintained throughout the movement. As usual, two or three correct steps are enough for one lesson, and normally only the distance from the side wall to the centre-line of the manège is enough; but for practice, as the horse progresses in performance, the whole distance can be covered.

After working in this way in both directions, the more sophisticated exercise of the *counter-change of hand,* which means changing direction from one side to the other in a zig-zag movement. At first, starting to the right, move to the centre-line of the manège, straighten and change the bend of the head, then change direction, reversing the aids, timing them to coincide with the inside (right) foreleg reaching the ground, so that it immediately becomes the outside leg, passing across and in front of the left (formerly the outside now the inside leg). Gradually the distance can be reduced until the horse can zig-zag alternate steps.

Practise at the walk first, then trot, and finally at the canter; but the canter zig-zag should not be done until the horse is proficient at the flying change. The value of the half-pass is that it is able to 'Develop muscular control. Increase flexibility of the spine. Promote co-ordinated limb action. Improve limb flexibility. Improve balance by lateral variations of the flow of the centre of gravity *in* the direction of movement. Strengthen abdominal muscles.' (*Riding Technique in Pictures* – C. E. G. Hope and Charles Harris.) When accomplished correctly the single alternate step zig-zag is a wonderful suppling exercise, but the horse must be well advanced in his work before it is attempted.

The full pass has been discussed on page 119, and although it is not a school movement it is well worth practising as a gymnastic exercise in obedience and muscular control. Both reins must keep the horse in position, the inside direct rein bending the head in the direction of the movement, the outside indirect rein and outside leg pushing the point of balance in the same direction, and both legs keeping up the impulsion. As always, the outside legs must step in front of the inside ones, but care must be taken to see that the steps are level. Often there is a tendency to overstep or leap to one side, followed by a short and rather scrambling step, the result of inexperience and not being properly balanced, or possibly the signal being given too sharply. If this happens, stop the movement and go forward a few steps, then start again; a procedure which of course applies to all lateral lessons.

As the horse's muscles become strengthened and toned up by all these exercises and his collected work is sufficiently up to the standard required at this stage, i.e. moderate, extended work can begin. The horse will already have achieved some extension at the walk in the preliminary lessons (page 160), but he will not have attempted extended trot or canter.

Going back to the F.E.I. *Rules for Dressage Competitions* the requirements are:

> '*Extended trot.* The horse covers as much ground as possible. He lengthens his stride, remaining on the bit with light contact. The neck is extended and, as a result of great impulsion from the quarters, the horse uses his shoulders covering more ground at each step without his action becoming much higher'. (Section 404 (c).)

In a test the extended trot can be executed either sitting or rising according to instructions, but for the trainee horse a rising trot is best to begin with.

> '*Extended canter.* The horse extends his neck; the tip of the nose points more or less forward, the horse lengthens his stride without losing any of his calmness and lightness.' (Section 405 (c).)

The object of extended work is to teach the horse to use himself with the greatest efficiency by the strengthening and toning of the muscles, especially those of the neck, back and hindquarters (see pages 160–2), by the lengthening of his stride

179

and by stimulating forward movement. Extension should only be asked for on a straight line. It is better begun in a manège, but can be carried on out of doors.

The essence of extension is that it begins from the back end of the horse with the active and energetic engagement of the quarters. The daisy-cutting pointing of the toes without any hock action, which is so often seen and which appears to bamboozle the judges, is not extension. It is the hocks which must literally *drive* the forelegs forward.

Prepare for the exercise with a short period of collected work, then a transition to an ordinary gait, which leg action will keep energetic and lively; at the walk the hands will follow the movement of the head, but just softly restrain it from being extended too much; at the trot the hands will be steady, keeping the head in a normal position, with possibly a slight restraint backwards. Go down one long side of the manège and across the short side in this way, then start the diagonal across the school, slightly increasing the pace to stimulate as much energy and impulsion and eagerness to go forward as possible. Before the halfway point apply the legs forcefully and at the same time yield a little with the hands to allow the horse to extend his head as he extends his forelegs. The rider should be able to feel the increased drive of the hocks and see the lengthened movement of the shoulders. One, or at the most two, long strides like this will be enough. Then relax the aids and let the horse calm down, going into an ordinary gait and then to a collected gait, before repeating the lesson.

Do not expect a long extension at first; in any case it is the energy of the movement which counts. Strive to have the horse going forwards with his head slightly extended beyond the normal, which requires very sensitive and accurate actions of the hands. Too often a horse is seen doing an extended trot with his head tucked in to his chest to a taut rein. The rein tension has to be firmer than normal, but the hands must be further forward. They can also be held lower down, if desired, to allow the horse to lower his head as he extends it. It is most desirable to have an observer for this movement, if not for any others, to check on its quality, and, if possible, to take moving pictures of it for study at leisure. Finally the horse should be able to start to build up the extension a stride or two after turning on to the diagonal, bring it to its peak in the last two or three strides before the centre, hold it the same distance afterwards, then gradually contract again.

The extended canter needs more space than is usually available in any normal manège; in competitions the minimum is the long side of the arena, sixty metres (65.6 yards); so it is best practised out of doors. The same procedures apply, the extension being obtained from the ordinary school canter. This is a fairly high action, but as the horse's steps extend they will become flatter and also faster. The extended trot, it must be emphasised, is not a *campagne* school movement but purely a training exercise and test performance. Out of doors any increase of speed above the ordinary trot is made by going into the canter and gallop. This, of course, does not apply to high speed trotters and hackneys, whether ridden or driven, who are specialists.

The turn on the haunches while moving, or pirouette, is conventionally a high school movement, but it is also a highly practical, indeed necessary, accomplishment for any outdoor horse (see page 238), so it properly comes in here at the end of basic training.

As usual let us base the work on the official requirements of the F.E.I. *Rules for Dressage Competitions.*

> '*Half-pirouette.* This is the half-turn on the haunches. The forehand commences the half-turn tracing a half circle round the haunches, without pausing, at the moment the inside hindleg ceases its forward movement. The horse moves forward again, without a pause, upon completion of the half turn.
> During this movement the horse should maintain his impulsion and should never in the slightest move backwards or deviate sideways. It is necessary that the inside hindleg, while forming the pivot, should return to the same spot each time it leaves the ground.' (Section 413 (a).)

This half-turn (180 degrees) is sufficient for all practical purposes, and can be carried out at walk, trot and canter, gallop.

The first lessons are of course at the walk, starting from a collected walk. Towards the end of a lesson, choosing a time when everything has gone smoothly and horse and rider are mentally calm, practise the halted half-turn on the haunches on both reins. Then go into a collected walk on the long side of the manège and at the corner make a sharp turn and continue it round so that the horse goes back parallel to the track and in the opposite direction. Repeat this at the other end, when the turn will be on the opposite rein to the first one. Then gradually shorten the circle until the hindquarters become the centre of the circle, which has the length of the horse as radius. Do not halt, but with the inside direct rein, fully supported by the outside indirect rein and outside leg, lead the forehand round the quarters, the rider's legs keeping up the impulsion and the movements of the hindlegs, particularly the inside one, which should step up and down in the rhythm of the collected gait. There must be no pause when the turn is complete, the horse moving forward at once.

The movement can also be developed from the renvers or quarters out (page 118). Once again start with a collected walk up the long side of the manège; about halfway make a normal turn which will merge into the renvers position, heading back the way you have come, but well off the track. Do the renvers back to the corner, and then make the moving turn from there. The horse will already be in the right position for it, head bent in the required direction, body flexed longitudinally, and the outer feet stepping across the inner.

Assuming that the horse is destined for outdoor activities, great precision is not required, the important thing being instant obedience and smoothness of movement. I would recommend also the increasing use of the indirect rein to make the horse bridlewise, and, ultimately, schooling with one hand. After being practised at the walk and canter, the half-pirouette can be used in the suppling exercises already described (pages 173–5).

With the exception of jumping, which has the next chapter to itself, this brings us to the end of basic training. The horse should now understand the aids and be obedient to them. It should be supple and strong, and able to move straight. It should be well balanced and light in hand. It should be capable of moderate collection. It should be quiet in traffic, and a comfortable and pleasant ride across country. It will have done some preliminary jumping.

This process will have taken anything from six to twelve months, and the horse should be four to four and half years old. It will still be green, very much a novice, but it will have been allowed to muscle up gradually and grow into its adult strength, and be ready for serious work and long spells of riding. It should be possible to recognise by now its potential, whether it has the aptitude for further advances in training and in what direction. These possibilities and the higher training involved will be discussed in Part IV.

19 Jumping

The general process of jumping has already been described above (Chapter 13), and, as we have seen, the horse is on the whole quite willing and able to jump, if he can see any immediate advantage to himself. It is the job of the trainer to make use of this characteristic and direct it to his advantage.

Mounted jumping should not begin until the horse is at least four years old. If the horse has been with the trainer since foalhood or from two to three years old, he can be given a little gentle encouragement by placing a small obstacle on the way to his water supply, or to the gate where his food will come from. If the lay-out of the fields will allow it, this is a good way of getting the young horse to enjoy jumping without doing himself any harm.

Apart from that he should do no jumping until he has progressed somewhat in the lunge work. Then, at the end of the lesson, he can be led over a pole on the ground. Always leave the jumping lesson to the end of the session, when the horse has been 'worked in' and settled down, so that there is less chance of excitement and resistance. The pupil should be encouraged to step over rather than jump it, literally take it in his stride. The idea is primarily to accustom him to an obstacle across his path. When he walks quietly over the pole in both directions, introduce the cavalletti, set first at the lowest and then at the higher position.

This procedure can then be repeated on the lunge. This requires considerable expertise, and everything should be carefully prepared beforehand. Do not stop the proceedings to fix up a jump in front of the horse, but have one in position (the usual pole at first) somewhere near the lungeing area. At the right time, towards the end of the lesson, manoeuvre the lunge circuit gradually towards the jump, at the same time making it more of an oval than a circle, until the horse sees the pole on the ground in front of him, crossing his path. As he will have already got used to this in the leading lessons, it should not cause him any alarm, despondency or even excitement. Let us hope that he will take it quietly in his stride as he did when led. The reason for the oval track is so that the horse will approach and take the obstacle on a straight line and not on a curve. Two or three turns over the pole will be enough for one lesson.

It is very desirable that every obstacle shown to the horse after this should be heavy and solid and fixed. Peg the cavalletti into the ground for these lessons, and, later on, have the higher fences as solid as possible. The young horse must definitely know when he has hit it, and so be all the more inclined to miss it the next time. It will be useful to have an assistant waiting beyond the jump to give the horse an immediate reward, before he continues on the lunge circuit. The reward should not be given if he hits the obstacle. So deterrent and reward will combine towards the desired end. The great thing is to face the horse with obstacles that are well within his capacity at any given stage, not to over-face him at the start. If the horse runs out, circle him round again to approach the jump and assist him at the last moment with the lungeing whip above his hocks. If he persists in refusing, lower the jump and make him take it at a faster pace. A tendency to rush at a fence should be checked at once, by moving back with the lunge rein and guiding the horse past the jump. Then circle him a few times to steady him down, and approach the jump again at a walk.

Jumping on the lunge can continue progressively but slowly until the horse will go calmly over heights of up to three feet, by which time he should be ready for jumping with a rider on his back. Always put on a neckstrap when ridden jumping work is to be done, and use it when necessary, to avoid any risk of interfering with the mouth at this early stage.

Begin again at the beginning, over a pole on the ground at the end of a normal lesson. A few times over it at the walk and trot should be sufficient, after which the cavalletti can be brought into use progressively at the three heights. Schooling on the flat is the essential preparation for jumping. The pre-jumping lesson should be steady work at the walk and trot, with circles, halts and half-halts, and rein-backs, so that the horse is stepping out well and light in hand.

If you have an assistant, at a given signal from you he will place the cavalletto, at its lowest height first, across the track. If you are on your own, then you will have to dismount and do it yourself, or arrange to have it put in position beforehand in a separate manège. If you have had to do it yourself at the time, circle round one end of the school once or twice, then go

large and approach the jump at an energetic trot, the legs acting to make the horse use his hocks. In spite of the fact of
having seen this thing many times before when on the lunge,
the presence of a rider on his back may change everything, and
he will try to have a look at it, or get fussed and lose his cadence,
not being able to make up his mind actually to jump or step
over it. At this stage you want him to stride over it, so hold
him fairly firmly between hand and leg and push him forward
without any alteration of your position. Repeat until he goes
over smoothly without losing cadence. Make much of him
once he is over.

When he is thoroughly practised at all three heights of the
single cavalletto, introduce a second one; both should be at the
lowest height and three or four yards apart. Once again approach them at walk and then trot, and then at the middle
height, six to eight inches. Then close them up, once again back
at the lowest height, to one step apart, four to five feet (this
distance depends on the size and normal stride of the horse).
The horse should step over the two quietly without interrupt-
ing its stride. This is really a gymnastic exercise, to make
the horse use his hocks, balance himself, and pick his feet
up. Once he does this well at the middle height at walk
and trot, repeat it over three and then four cavalletti in
series.

The horse should then be ready for higher jumps, for which
a post-and-rails will be more suitable. The bar, heavy and solid,
should start at eighteen inches, and should be placed in front
of the uprights, not behind them, making it more difficult to
dislodge, and the uprights should be pegged into the ground.

Warm the horse up over a twelve-inch cavalletto and carry
straight on to the post-and-rails at a steady trot. Squeeze with
the legs three strides before the jump, lean forward and say
'Up!' Pat him once he is over, but do not pull up, or else he
will get the idea of always stopping after a leap, which could
be ludicrous as well as annoying. Pay great attention to making
the horse go straight at the jump, not wandering off to one side
or the other, which might be an incipient refusal. Wings can be
useful, but, if the poles are reasonably long, at least eight feet,
it should be possible to dispense with them, unless the horse
continually runs out. But the more likely tendency will be
to get excited and rush at the jump. Two or three cavalletti
in series about ten feet from the jump will have a steadying
effect. The horse should be exercised in taking the jump from
both directions; but alter the pole so that it is more or less

fixed. Don't forget to have a pole on the ground underneath the upper rail to act as a ground line.

If the horse knocks this low jump, it is probably due to a badly timed take-off and slack movement. Place a pole about two feet in front of the jump, and use the legs more strongly at the approach to increase impulsion. If he persists, lunge him over higher fences than the ones for mounted work, and exercise him over a series of cavalletti as before.

When the horse takes the first low jump calmly and smoothly, without hitting it, raise the pole to two feet. After that point is reached, free jumping practice in a lane can be introduced. An oval lane, as described in Chapter 13, page 128 *et seq* is the best, partly because of greater facility of control and partly because the corners prevent rushing and improve balance.

Push up the stirrup irons to the bars, knot the reins, and lead the horse into the lane; point the horse at the first fence and run with him towards it, then get into the centre of the lane with a lungeing whip. Hesitation on the part of the horse will probably be the least likely trouble; but if he does stop, use the lungeing whip on his hocks. If the horse seems nervous, put a trained horse in beside him and let them go down together. If an assistant is available, the task is made so much easier, the trainer remaining in command of the operation in the centre of the lane, the assistant leading the horse in and greeting him with a bowl of corn at the exit, and leading him quietly in a circle for a few minutes.

One circuit of the lane a day is sufficient. The fences will be upright at first, but gradually they can be varied by the introduction of spread fences, and double combinations or in-and-outs. The lane jumps will always be higher than the ridden jumps. Ridden work can now follow the pattern of the liberty work in the lane but always at a lower height.

To introduce a spread jump when ridden, start with two cavalletti at the top height of twelve inches close together, and gradually separate them to two feet. In the lane the horse will be jumping a spread of three feet, two feet high. After the cavalletti, two post-and-rails up to eighteen inches high and two and a half feet apart will be introduced. The dimensions in the school will increase proportionately to those in the lane up to a limit of about four feet.

This, of course, will take time, first of all because the amount of jumping each day should be strictly limited in the beginning. It is possible to proceed more quickly, many people do; but the horse is still young and comparatively immature, even at four years, however strong he may be, and there is always the danger of strain on the legs and of the horse getting sour and fed up with it, instead of enjoying the jumping as he should.

The above plan of work does not have to be rigidly adhered to. The important thing is the notion of progressive advancement, and of making no step forward until the previous position has been completely consolidated. 'No advance without security,' as one's bank manager says, and sometimes not even then. Every horse is different and will progress at different speeds; the trainer must keep the principles in mind and adjust their application to his special circumstances and the means available. If a separate jumping lane is not feasible, it should be possible to rig up a temporary one in a covered school, or even in an outdoor manège.

A tendency to drop the hind feet over a jump and hit the pole may well be due to weakness or laziness, and consequent lack of engagement of the hindquarters. More oats and more intensive schooling on the flat could be the answer. A thin iron bar or tube placed on top of the pole can often help; it is not harmful or damaging, provided it is passively used, but the different feel of it and noise will surprise the horse, who will try to avoid it in future. Exercises over cavalletti in series will also strengthen the hindleg action and make it more elevated.

Rushing can be dealt with in various ways. If the horse's intention is noticed in time, some distance from the fence, nip it in the bud with a quick halt, then proceed at a collected trot to within three strides of it. The introduction of two or three cavalletti about ten strides in front of the jump will also have a restraining effect. If the rushing starts at the last minute, turn the horse away from it, circle once or twice, then start again. None of these remedies will probably be effective the first time; it is calm and patient repetition which does the trick.

In the lane the horse will almost certainly go at a canter, but in ridden work up to a height of two feet six inches all the work should be at a trot. Most of it can be out of doors, and the jumps varied a bit – oil drums, hurdles with a pole on top, a wall – and they will generally be upright. With the jumps still at two feet six inches, start cantering up to them. Trot to within ten strides, then break into a canter. Use the legs and hands to create enough impulsion without increasing the pace, and give the horse absolute freedom at the take-off, holding on the neck strap. If he has not had the benefit of the lane to prepare him, practise him jumping at the canter on the lunge.

From now on the obstacles can be progressively raised in

height and varied in shape and spread. As has already been mentioned (page 128) timing is all important, and the great difficulty lies in judging one's position at some distance from the obstacle so that one can arrive precisely at the critical point, three strides in front of the take-off point. By trial and error on a trained horse that point can be fixed for every fence in the field, with an allowance for the extent of the take-off zone, and that point can be marked with a stone or flag or something. This will greatly help the trainer to place the horse at, say, ten strides from the fence so that he will come correctly at the end.

More practice can be given now over spread jumps. Begin with the triple bar – the staircase type of fence – which is actually the easiest of all big fences. Start with a simple post-and-rail construction. If the highest pole is two feet six inches, the lowest pole can be a ground line, the middle one eighteen inches, and the total spread three feet six inches; dimensions will increase in roughly these proportions.

For the more difficult parallel bar type, start with a false parallel, i.e. with the front pole lower than the rear one, so that the horse can see both poles clearly. Making the highest pole three feet, the near one should be two feet six inches, and the distance between them three feet six inches. Have a low cavalletto just in front of the front pole to make a ground line and encourage the horse to spread himself. In the true parallel bars, both elements of the fence will be the same height.

Another variation is the open ditch, which is in fact a triple bar with the middle element removed. The pyramid type again starts as a triple bar, but with the lowest element removed, and with a pole behind the centre element the same height as the one in front; also known as a double oxer, from the old type of country fences designed to keep cattle in, having a centre post-and-rails (or wire) fence with a hedge on one side only (oxer) or on both sides (double oxer). The spread will be the same as for a triple bar but distributed equally on either side of the centre element. There will of course be a ground line. The elements can be varied almost infinitely so far as training and competition jumping are concerned: a centre wall with brush fences; a centre brush fence with rails or walls; the rounded 'pig pen' seen in American competitions and at the team Olympic jumping at Stockholm in 1956; plain rustic poles, and so on. In training, always put a pole on top of, or just behind, a brush fence, so that the horse will not be tempted to take a chance with it.

188

Have plenty of colour. Paint the poles red and white, blue and white, green and white. The horse is now known to be sensitive to primary colours (page 59), so the more he can be accustomed to the different colours that will face him in all future competitive activities the better.

One of the great, if not the greatest, jumping problem is water. It is not all that difficult to find natural water obstacles in the English countryside, but somehow horses never seem to like them. As in every other field of equine education, getting horses used to jumping flat ditches on the ground is a matter of progressive training. It should be possible to provide three ditches in the jumping paddock – two feet, five feet, and ten feet wide. Existing ditches in a field can often be adapted for the purpose.

A water jump is a spread jump, and the horse's first introduction to it can be in the manège over two poles or low cavalletti placed two feet apart. Approach with plenty of impulsion so that he will take it in his stride. Widen the gap gradually to four feet, and raise the near cavalletto to six inches. Next, widen the gap to six feet and put a twelve-inch cavalletto in the middle, which will encourage the horse to jump a little high as well as wide. The approach to this sort of obstacle should be a collected canter with the maximum of impulsion; the horse should be accelerating as he takes off. Three strides should be measured back from the lip of the jump and a mark placed there to guide the take-off. More than anything else jumping water successfully is a matter of exact timing.

The real thing can then be tackled in the open. As in the manège, line each edge of the ditch with a pole, so that it will appear familiar to the horse. There need not be water in the small ditch, but there should be in the two wider ones, showing a proper expanse of water not just a shallow puddle. If the horse persists in putting his foot in the water, or in refusing, put a post-and-rails, up to about two feet high in the middle. The jumpable width of the ditch can be increased by setting back the take-off fence a foot at a time up to three feet; but the horse should also be practised in jumping without any guide fence. The wider the fence the faster, within reason, the speed of approach, but there must always be something in hand to accelerate at the last three strides. The one thing to avoid is to come at the jump at a flat-out gallop, almost inevitably slowing up for the take-off.

The last type of obstacle the horse should get to know is the bank. This obstacle is more often found out hunting or on cross-country courses than in the show-jumping ring, except at a few permanent grounds like Dublin, Hickstead or Lucerne. I do not count the 'Derby' bank, which is not a bank in the ordinary jumping sense of the word. A training bank could be about three feet six inches high, with a small ditch on either side. Banking is a good education for the horse, even if he is not likely to see many of them in his career. As Paul Rodzianko said, 'it teaches the horse not to jump wildly but to think'. (*Modern Horsemanship.*) To take a bank well, the horse must stand back from it, which the ditch encourages him to do, leap well up so that he lands comfortably on the top, collect himself, change legs and spring out and down to the other side. A post and rails on the far side (the pole free to fall) will encourage him to do this. The trainer must take great care not to interfere with the mouth when banking, moving his position well forward and using the neckstrap.

The combination of two or three fences in a single series of jumps (double or treble) is a difficult problem for both horse and rider, and the former must be thoroughly fit and well muscled before these are attempted at any height. As always the beginning is with cavalletti at twelve inches high, set at first far enough apart for three jumping (canter) strides. The rough and ready method of calculating the distance between the two fences, from ground line to ground line is to add the height of each fence to the length of the number of jumping strides required. The latter is a variable, according to the size of the horse and its speed, but an approximate length for most purposes is about eight to nine feet. In the case of the cavalletti the minimum distance would be three strides eighteen feet plus two feet for the heights of the two obstacles, total twenty feet. This can be adjusted in the light of experience. There should be no sort of difficulty over this, and the gap can be narrowed to two and then one jumping stride. After that the fences are raised, the interval opened out again, and so on as the horse gains in experience. Then a third fence can be added to make the treble. At first let the distances be equal, but in time they can be varied – two and three jumping strides; three and two; one and two; one and three, and so on. So far use only upright types of fence, but finally the types can be varied – a spread and then an upright, two spreads, one upright and a spread; it all helps to increase the strength and agility of the horse.

In jumping combinations, the rider must help the horse as much as possible, first by keeping resolutely with the movement, and then by really *driving* the horse forward with his legs to work up the maximum impulsion and acceleration for the last part of the combination. At the same time he must not let the horse over-jump the first fence, or he will come wrong at the second, finding himself say one and half strides away, instead of two. An experienced horse will get the team out of trouble by putting in a short one, but one wants to avoid this in the early stages of training.

In the final stages of training the jumping will be all in the open, and the horse can be practised in getting away quickly after the landing. The rider must be ready, when the hindlegs come to the ground to lean forward with his weight off the quarters, and apply strong leg pressure so that the horse goes forward without losing either its balance or impulsion. In this way it is ready within three or four strides to face another jump or change direction; there is no loss of concentration.

In the jumping paddock there should be jumps in a straight line, in pairs if there is no room for more, at distances of five to ten strides apart, and fences at each end which have to be approached after turning a corner, and some at different angles in the centre of this framework. At first jump only two at a time, first in straight line, then changing direction. Gradually increase the number of fences jumped, until eventually all the jumps are taken as a specific course. In this practice keep the jumps low, three feet to three feet six inches, although you may have got up to four feet over single jumps. The risk of over-facing is a very real one at all times during training; once you *know* that the horse can easily jump higher if required, do not ask it of him too often.

In all this work the horse has always come straight to the fence, if possible to the centre of it. Now jumping at an angle can be practised, and the procedure is the same as when practising a rider (page 127 *et seq*), going back to cavalletti, singly then placed as double and treble combinations.

Give the horse a change from these artificial fences on the flat by taking him for an occasional run across country over as natural jumps as can be found or made up. Take him with an old hand to keep him company and, at first, to give him a lead and confidence. There is nothing like this in all stages of jumping training, provided you have a reliable horse 'tutor' to the novice.

If the horse starts knocking the fences, or refusing, he is probably being over-faced and having too much of it. Go back to lower fences and less jumping. It is impossible to say how much jumping should be done, but the trainer should err on the side of discretion. At the very early stages two or three jumps per session are sufficient, increasing at the low heights to perhaps a dozen jumps; but when the jumps get higher, reduce the number again, say half a dozen at the end of the normal schooling period.

The time spent on jumping training should be at least six months, and the horse should be rising five, if not older. He should show clearly by then what his true *métier* will be – show jumping, cross-country and eventing, high school. He may have reached his ceiling as a good hack, hunter, or one-day-event horse, and you can call it a day and not force him any higher, remembering the twenty-five centuries-old advice of Xenophon: 'What a horse does under compulsion he does blindly.'

It is time, anyway, to apply all the school work to practical affairs.

The excitement of polo

The speed of polo

The skill of polo

FOUR

Applications

20 Show Jumping

Modern show jumping is a highly specialised professional sport. Except in the Foxhunter competitions there is no room for amateur part-time performers, horses or humans. The horses as much as the riders are professionals. The old idea that show jumping is the image of hunting has died long ago; I doubt if any top show jumper ever sees a hound. It would do him good if he did, but he simply has not the time, with the spread of the indoor competition making show jumping an all the year round sport.

It is ruled in this country by the British Show Jumping Association as firmly and almost as autocratically as racing is by the Jockey Club. Gone are the happy-go-lucky days when show jumpers, mostly soldiers, and judges could make their own rules as they went along. The British Show Jumping Association came into being about 1921, but its writ did not run very far. In India in the 'twenties there used to be a lot of talk about B.S.J.A. Rules, but very few people, if any, knew what they were. Before World War I there used to be a picturesque custom, whether universal or not I do not know, of the winner of a jumping competition doing his 'lap of honour' actually over the jumping course. I recall at the Bath and West Show about 1913 when a rider was placed first and second and third in the big competition, whatever it was, and he rode one horse and led the other two faultless over the course. The rider was Harry Buckland, father of Mrs Betty Skelton, famous in the post World War II years as a producer of show ponies. Which goes to show that the modern show jumper has no monopoly of horsemanship or showmanship.

Apart from the greater sophistication of the fences and courses, which of themselves make the problems of today's riders and horses so much harder, the great difference between now and then is speed. In the old days there were no time limits; riders could, and did, take their time over a jump, not having to jump unless they felt everything was right. The whole thing was much more deliberate and precise, slats – the thin, easily detachable laths of wood placed on the tops of jumps

– putting a premium on accuracy, right up to the first years after World War II. The jumps were on the whole no lower than they are now.

Now the clock rules all. In any ordinary competition there is a time limit for the first round, and sometimes the second, but a race against the clock for the final jump-off. Some competitions are judged on time from the start. This has altered the whole pattern of show jumping, requiring new techniques and attitudes of mind from the participants. For a number of years it afflicted the horses with a pile-up of tack on their unfortunate heads – drop nosebands, gags, martingales, check reins – you name it they had it, all with the object of stopping the horse quickly. The drop noseband, a training device for correcting faults of head carriage and head shaking, became an instrument of torture by being lowered to the nostrils and tightened almost to the point of suffocation. The breathing of the horse so maltreated could be heard all round the ground. Happily, it began gradually to be realised that more and better training on the flat could be more effective in the long run than these gadgets. The B.S.J.A. also banned the use of a standing martingale with a dropped noseband.

For both the novice rider and the novice horse the last preparatory work for the show ring follows the same lines: practise in jumping with and against the clock, and over higher fences, up to four feet six inches. The latter lessons will be progressive, needless to say, and the top height jumped very sparingly.

For the former, the jumping field should be laid out as a jumping course with its distance measured. Start with the fences at three feet six inches, and, with the aid of an assistant with a stop watch, time yourself at different speeds. The minimum speeds, that is with the maximum time allowed for the round are laid down for all types of competition, both national and international. The B.S.J.A. Rules cover national competitions, the F.E.I. Rules international ones. Both codes provide for two types of competition, designated Table A and Table S under the former and Table A and Tables B and C under the latter. Would-be show jumpers must of course make themselves familiar with these rules, and they are summarised below.

B.S.J.A.

Table A1 In the event of equality of faults for first place in the second jump-off the prize money will be divided.

Table A2 In the event of equality of faults for first place in the second jump-off time will decide, i.e. the final jump-off will be against the clock.

Table A3 In the event of equality of faults for first place in the jump-off time will decide.

Table A4 In the event of equality of faults for any award in the first round of the competition time will decide. In the event of equality of faults and time for first place there may be a jump-off at the discretion of the judge.

Table A1 is used when there is no automatic timing, or unless otherwise stated. Table A2 is used in Foxhunter competitions and in B.S.J.A. championships, unless otherwise stated. Table A3 is used in Area International Trials. Table A4 is only used in special types of competition which do not concern us here.

Table S covers all speed competitions, and penalties are measured in seconds. Every time a fence is knocked down eight seconds are added to the total time taken on the round. Refusals penalise themselves by loss of time, except that the third refusal, as in every type of competition, eliminates.

The time ratings for Table A competitions vary according to the standard, and are based on the speed of yards per minute: 300, 328, 350, 382, 436 yards. The time allowed without loss of time penalties is calculated by the distance to be covered in a round; for a 600-yard course at 300 yards per minute the time allowed will be two minutes, and the time limit, after which a rider is eliminated, is twice that or four minutes in this example. At the top speed of 436 yards per minute the distance to be covered in two minutes is 872 yards.

In Table S competitions the speed is always 436 yards per minute for adults and 350 yards per minute for juniors. The penalty for being over the time allowed in every case is one-quarter fault for every second over.

Under F.E.I. Rules (*Rules for Jumping Competitions,* Chapter VIII), the normal speed for international competitions is 350 metres (382 yards) per minute. In speed competitions it is the same, and for nations cup competitions it is 400 metres (436 yards) per minute. For a puissance competition the first round speed is 300 metres (327 yards) per minute, with no timing thereafter.

Both the B.S.J.A. and the F.E.I. obligingly supply tables of times, distances and penalties in their Rules.

Another necessary piece of information is the minimum heights for fences. Under B.S.J.A. Rules (Para. 20), the the lowest height is three feet six inches for the first three fences and three feet nine inches thereafter (all these figures are for first rounds only); the maximum starting height for Grade C is four feet; for Grades B and C is four feet three inches; for young riders and Grade B four feet six inches. For ponies the Grade J.C. height is three feet nine inches and for Grade J.A. four feet three inches. In international competitions the heights of fences start from 1.30 metres. (Four feet three inches.)

The inside distances for combinations vary under both rules from twenty-three feet (seven metres) to thirty-nine feet five inches (twelve metres). The distance between the starting line of a course and the first fence varies under B.S.J.A. Rules from seven yards to twenty-seven yards, and under F.E.I. Rules twenty-five metres (eighty-two feet) and six metres (twenty feet); and the distance from the last fence to the finishing line is seventeen to twenty-seven yards and fifteen metres (forty-nine feet two inches) and twenty-five metres respectively.

Incidentally, the actual rate of progress at 300 yards per minute is 10.3 miles an hour, and at 436 yards per minute it is just under 16.5 miles an hour. Obviously the horse will be travelling a good deal faster than that at certain periods during the round; and jump-off speeds against the clock will be greater still.

Another point to be considered is the distance between non-combination fences, for the modern course builder, following the lead of the late Jack Talbot-Ponsonby, will vary these distances with quite diabolical cunning. Apart from combinations, successive fences can be unrelated and treated quite separately by the rider, or related and considered together as one problem. The key distance given by Talbot-Ponsonby ('Testing by Distance', *Light Horse*, May, June, July, 1962) is eighty feet, and simple distances were fifty-five, sixty-five and seventy-five feet. Problems are created by shortening these distances, for example to fifty-one, sixty-two and sixty-nine feet respectively. These are slightly less than six, eight and nine strides, and the rider has to make adjustments accordingly. In a competition the rider is able to walk the course, during which he must check all such distances carefully, without which knowledge he cannot make a coherent jumping plan.

Another problem arises from the siting of successive fences. They can be in a straight line and reasonably straightforward, or they can be set just off the line, requiring a change of direction. The basic shape of a jumping course is oblong or elliptical with a figure-of-eight design. Fences placed on the short sides or on the centre diagonal can be placed so that the rider can go straight on after the previous jump and make a normal turn or circle, or, by slightly altering the angle or moving nearer the longer line of jumps, they can demand a deviation by the rider, which has got to be planned for in advance.

These and similar problems can be prepared in the practice course and worked on first at lower heights and slower speeds, until the horse and rider become really proficient. It would be wise for the rider to practise walking the course on his home ground, for, other things being equal, the correct assessment of distances beforehand is at least half the battle in jumping competitions. The rider will have already learnt in his preliminary training how to estimate speeds at various gaits, and, if a sand track is available, he can work out on the ground the actual stride lengths of the horse, or horses, he is dealing with. This will enable him to deal with the distance, problems already posed above, and all sorts of other ones.

The solution, of course, is to vary the length of the stride between the obstacles so that the horse will reach the further one correctly placed for the take-off. The usual way is to shorten the stride, making seven, nine and ten in the above instance. Shortening makes things rather easier for the horse than lengthening, the action of the driving leg aids and retarding rein aids causing strong engagement of the hocks and so producing greater propelling power. Take care that there is no reduction in speed; this is not quite the same as an exercise in collection, although the previous training in collection will certainly facilitate the operation.

Sometimes, in a speed competition or if the horse has overjumped, lengthening the stride may offer better chances of success, so it as well to practise it too over these same lower fences. Here the aids are as for the school extension: driving action of the legs, and yielding forward of the hands slightly, then steadying. Very often a horse, particularly in a combination, will lengthen his stride of his own accord.

Bearing these methods in mind will give a new significance to practice in walking the course, even if you happen to have laid it out yourself. Watching the methods of top show jumpers will also be a fruitful exercise. Get used to making your own walking strides an exact yard in length, and always pace out the course on the route that you propose to take, so that you can translate it into strides of the horse. All of this requires great concentration, but the standard of modern show jumping is such that any kind of success is impossible without *preparation* and *concentration* all the way.

There is no need to spend too much time on the ring work; the real training comes with experience in actual competition, and I cannot repeat too often the necessity to avoid over-jumping or over-facing the horse, making him bored or sour. Take him out hunting as a recreation. The company of large numbers of other horses and people will prepare him for the excitements of the collecting ring and the general atmosphere of competition. The thrill of a hunt, which undoubtedly is felt by horses, can well liven up a too placid temperament. In the summer a few one-day events in novice classes or with riding clubs can also be a useful preparation. A few horses graduate to show jumping from this sport, a notable example being, of course, Merely-a-Monarch.

The education of rider and horse does not end with the first show-jumping competition; in a sense it is only beginning. Competition, especially with the speed element, makes tremendous demands on both. The good style of the rider, easy enough to maintain in the quiet conditions of the manège and jumping field, may well go to the winds from the stress and strain of it all. All professional show jumpers – and, let us face it, irrespective of money rewards, show jumping is a professional sport – develop their own characteristic styles, because the taking of big jumps at speed and odd angles requires unusual efforts, not to say contortions, of the body; but correct basic training will always show itself. And two things will always be noticeable: the freedom of the horse's head, and keeping of the body weight well off the quarters.

Choose for the first formal debut a small local show, one if possible where the opposition is not likely to be too strong, not worrying about the prize money, which anyway will be small. Make the first class a Foxhunter or Grade C, or both if they are available. If you and the horse have been able to gain experience in riding club events so much the better. Nowadays riders go quickly into high grade competition, perhaps using the various young rider competitions as stepping stones; many come up through the junior classes. With an experienced horse the more competitions you can go in for, and so the more experience you can gain, the better; there is really no limit except your purse and the stamina of the horse. The novice horse, however, should be taken on quietly in his first season, no matter how much promise he shows. Hold him back the first year, then he will really go places the next.

A lot has to happen before the first adventure in the ring. Check all equipment very carefully at home beforehand, make sure that nothing vital is left behind; and always take spare parts, especially girths, stirrup leathers and irons, bits, reins, straps. Prepare everything the day before you actually start for the show, leave early, and don't forget to send your entry before the closing date. There should always be a vet and a farrier available at any show, but take your own first aid kit all the same.

The routine before a class is well established: exercise, warming-up, studying the plan of the course, weighing in, walking the course, waiting in the collecting ring, and then into the ring, and out again two minutes later.

The plan of the course has to be posted conveniently to the collecting ring, and the first task is to study it carefully, noting the various distances between jumps and their positions and make a preliminary plan of campaign, subject to the final inspection of the actual course.

The time spent warming-up depends on what exercise has been done before that. If the class is a very early one – as Foxhunter and Grade C classes usually are – the two can be combined.

Warming-up is the process of loosening up the horse, and suppling and exercising the muscles to be used in jumping. Begin with fifteen to twenty minute walk and trot on a loose rein; then about the same time doing suppling exercises on a circle; half-halts, turns, rein-backs, all with the purpose of making him obedient to the aids, and getting him alert and on his hocks; finally about ten minutes of jumping practice.

Shows provide practice jumps of the post-and-rail variety, officially placed in the exercising area, which often coincides with the collecting ring, where there is always a milling crowd of show jumpers in various stages of exercising and warming-up. Most of them seem to jump incessantly, but with a novice horse it is better to do three or four jumps, lower than those he will meet in the ring, perfectly and leave it at that.

All this work should be timed to end about fifteen minutes before the class is due to start, and the riders pour into the ring to walk the course. This process has already been explained, and practised, and there is not much to add except to stress the need to concentrate on the distances and angles to each other of related fences, including doubles, noting especially the positions of jumps following the end of one line. You have to plan your line one or even two jumps ahead, so that the horse will make an easy circle and come straight at the next jump; as you go over a jump you will always be looking in the direction of the next fence, wherever it may be. During this inspection time you can also take note of possible short cuts in the expectation – or pious hope – of getting into the jump-off. This is the last chance of a close inspection of the course, so make the most of it.

If you are high up in the jumping order, on your return to the collecting ring, weigh in, have a final check of the tack, mount, and walk the horse round quietly until your number is called. If you are low down in the starting order, you may have an hour or more to wait. In this case your warming-up plan can be modified, carrying it out after you have walked the course instead of before.

It is customary on entering the ring for your round to salute the judges, or the V.I.P. watching, if there is one, not likely at 9.00 in the morning. Then canter round quietly until the signal to start is given, taking this opportunity to see how your plan made on the ground matches up with the different look of things from the saddle. Have a good look at the fences, in case a pole is not properly down in its cup, or a gate has not been adjusted after the previous round, which could tell against you in your own round if not corrected beforehand. You have the right to tell the jump stewards and have it put right.

The tension of being in the ring and eagerness to get on with the business may tempt you to pass through the starting lights before the signal to start is given, when of course you will be eliminated. Not to worry. Better riders than you have done that in bigger competitions. It is just one of those things. Sometimes, however, with all the competing noises outside the ring, it is difficult to hear the signal, and and you may not be sure whether it has been sounded or not. If in doubt, ask.

Once the 'go' signal has been given, you are finally on your own to put all the long period of training to the proof. The horse does the jumping; the rider's part is to guide and restrain it whenever necessary, so that its movements between the fences and coming up to them conform as closely as possible with the plan you have made. Things of course do not always go according to plan, and may not do so the first time; so be prepared to be opportunist and adjust your own actions to the changed situation.

The great thing is to try to keep the horse in regular rhythm, especially before and after the approaches, and to steady him if he has knocked down a pole, or even rapped it hard, which always excites a horse for a few seconds and throws it out of balance. The clatter of a rapped pole has an ominous sound, but resist the temptation to look back; it takes away from concentration on the next jump, at the least. Even if the pole has come down and you are out of the hunt for that competition, in the interests of the horse help him to recover and regain his balance, so that in spite of that one unfortunate mistake he jumps a good smooth round. At this time maintaining regularity and preserving the confidence of the horse are more important than a clear round, though of course it will be nice to do one.

Once over the last fence accelerate as much as possible up to the finishing line. You are being timed in this first round, though not actually racing against the clock, and you do not want to risk losing time faults. Once past the automatic timing lamps, slow down gradually, circling the arena if necessary, calming the horse with the voice and giving him a congratulatory pat, and leave the ring at a quiet trot. If you have no further interest in the competition, walk quietly back to the horse lines, off-saddle, inspect legs and mouth for any bumps or cuts, put a rug on, give him a drink, and have him walked round and let him have a quiet graze. Then put him in his box with a feed, and go back to watch the rest of the jumping. There is always something to be learned from other people's performances and mistakes.

On the other hand you may have had a clear round. In this case, on leaving the ring, dismount, loosen the girths, put a rug on, and have the horse walked round quietly, while you take stock of the situation. Supposing there are forty starters – as there can easily be in Foxhunter or Grade C classes – and you went twentieth, there are twenty more to go, which means about an hour to wait for the jump-off. There may be fifteen clear rounds, which could mean another twenty-five minutes if you were the last in the draw. Assuming you have the full time to wait, rest the horse for about twenty minutes, then spend forty minutes warming-up, on an outside exercising area if possible, concentrating on quick starts and halts, and achieving good acceleration for short gallops, and turns and small circles. Then take him three or four times quickly over practice jumps. For the last twenty minutes before you go in have him walked round briskly while you look at the course. It is not allowed to walk the course for the jump-off, but you can inspect it from the ringside, noting the fences that have been removed, and the new circles and turns that have been introduced as a result; if you are not early in the draw, you can watch those who are and see how they go, noting what sort of times are achieved and the speed required to do it.

If you went very early in the first round, say among the first ten, you can take the horse back to the box for an hour and let him relax completely. If you went last, there is no time for anything but one or two sharp gallops to work up speed. You have to be entirely flexible and adjust your plans to the situation; but the great thing in show jumping is that it is as nearly precise in timing as it is possible to be, and you can tell almost to the minute when you will be required. The order of starting is always drawn for in a timed jump-off, and naturally the best place from every point of view is the last. The first rider in a jump-off rarely wins. Sometimes the course is left as it is, but more often it is shortened by cutting out some of the fences, most of the remainder being raised in height.

With a novice horse do not attempt to push him too much or cut corners too sharply; you do not want to over-face him with impossible jumps and consequently dishearten him. Be content with only a slightly faster speed than normal, and try to gain it by a lengthening of stride thus covering more ground at the same speed. At the same time he will need more impulsion for the higher fences. Steady him before the fences, and take generous circles at the corners, concentrating on a clear round before anything else; it can usually bring you into the money.

A novice rider on a trained horse can take more chances – though remember that a Grade C horse is bound to be inexperienced too. But he should also take things steadily; it is not flat-out galloping that wins jumps-off against the clock, but handiness and balance. A mad gallop at a big fence can end in disaster, for the horse will come at it unbalanced and out of control, liable either to refuse or to take it by the roots. Quick starting, stopping, turning and accelerating again, so that you cover the shortest possible distances, taking fences at angles with short approaches, are what brings success. A speed round well ridden is very exhilarating for the rider and spectacular for the onlooker.

When all is over there should be a post mortem. Every rider, in his early days at all events, should have a trainer or mentor with him to watch his performance and comment on it as mercilessly as he likes. It is only by intelligent and fair criticism that one gains experience and improves. Did you lose impulsion at this jump? Or push him too close at that one? Did you turn him too sharply and face him too suddenly at a fence in the jump-off? Did you get left behind during the double? If photographs were taken, they can be studied later to see how they confirm, or otherwise, the observations of the day. How did the horse go at each fence? Which ones did he find difficult? All this deep self-questioning can help to iron out weaknesses in both horse and rider.

Things will not always go as easily, according to plan, as described here. The horse is not a machine, but a thinking, sensitive creature. He will have his own ideas about what is possible or impossible; if he has been well trained he will often valiantly attempt the impossible, or he will decide definitely that he has been presented wrongly or unfairly at a jump and refuse it. Recriminations are pointless; he must be circled out of the way and re-presented, and nine times out of ten he will take it without difficulty. Other times a horse can feel out of sorts, his legs may be tender, he may have a touch of colic without you knowing it, or anything, and he will decide that he has had enough and refuse point-blank to jump. It is impossible to fathom all the motives of a horse, however well trained he may be, however courageous. Bow to the inevitable and take him out; but you are allowed to jump another fence after being eliminated so that you and the horse can end on a good note. Choose an easy one in the direction of the exit.

Bad crashes can occur, especially over spread jumps. If the horse has decanted you, no great harm has been done; but if the horse has fallen, perhaps entangled with poles, then trot him out quickly before remounting, and if he shows any sign of lameness, retire. It may only be a momentary tenderness, but it could be something worse. Give him the benefit of the doubt.

All this and other idiosyncrasies of the horse in the ring can be madly irritating, but nothing is worse than showing it, either publicly in the ring or outside it. Do not, as I have seen people do, flog your horse in fury out of the ring, or dismount and thrash him in the collecting ring or at the horse box, or pull his mouth about. In the first place, such 'punishment' has no effect, because it has no direct relationship to the offence, if it was an offence. Experienced riders can sometimes correct a horse sharply after a refusal, or give him two or three cuts with the whip because they think he has become sluggish; it may be effective, but it never looks well. In any case the jumping ring is not the place for correction, schooling or punishment, so the rider bent on making show jumping his career should school himself to the discipline of patience and complete control of his feelings.

Charges of cruelty have often been made against show jumpers, sometimes well founded, sometimes not. The demands and the high standards of modern show jumping, the rewards that can now be won, and indeed the dedication of riders to the sport, have resulted in all sorts of questionable methods being used in all countries at some time or other – rapping, the use of spiked poles, the deliberate bringing down of a horse over a fence, turpentine on the legs – and they have all been condemned by both national federations and the F.E.I. The B.S.J.A. and the F.E.I. Rules are very clear, and both these organisations have now stipendiary stewards to enforce them at national and international events. There is no doubt that the effect of both official action and public opinion has been salutary.

Meanwhile the novice rider and the novice horse have before them the choice of pursuing the path of show jumping fame and achievement to its ultimate limits by becoming dedicated professional devotees, giving their whole lives to a most demanding sport, or of simply enjoying themselves at the lower levels with limited appearances, as not a few do. The latter has the advantage of not being restricted to one sport; he can dabble in one-day events, hunter trials, and even dressage and combined training competitions and have a great deal of fun. The former must specialise, and every event he goes in for from now on will add to his experience and skills, provided he has the firm foundation of basic training.

21 The Outdoor Horse — Cross-Country

The simplest application of the training of an outdoor horse is hunting. The training requirements for a hunter were, and often still are, considered to be modest in the extreme – good manners, willingness to gallop, ability to jump, and reasonable stoppability. But under the influence of dressage training, particularly in horse trials, it has been realised that a hunter is all the better for a good degree of basic training, such as has been described. From another point of view, hunting is part of that basic training; most horses who take part in competitive outdoor sports, except perhaps polo and flat racing, start their career as hunters.

As far as the rider is concerned, the more training he has had and the more secure seat he has established, the happier he, and his horse, will be in any of these pursuits. It will be especially valuable for him, if he plans to go in for riding and producing show horses, whether hunters, cobs or hacks.

Showing hunters and cobs looks a rough and ready sort of business, but a considerable amount of work and skill goes into it. The horse has to be amenable and move well at normal paces, walk, trot and canter, and to be unmoved by crowds and noises. He also has to gallop full out in a comparatively restricted area, for even the biggest show ring is not exactly a wide open space, and the horse must be well balanced and controlled to get round the corners. In addition he has to stand up well when being inspected for conformation, and to trot freely in hand. Finally, he must stand quiet to be mounted by a stranger, the judge, and then go well for him; though it is noticeable that many horses go better for the judge than for their own riders, the former being usually very fine horsemen. All this is nothing but basic training applied to special circumstances.

The hack is an outdoor horse, indeed all the best hacking used to be done in the country, while the elegant social riding in the Row or the Bois was near-dressage. The hack was the horse on which farmers rode round their farms, or which carried hunting men to the meet while grooms walked the hunters well in advance, a practice which was commemorated in the old show category of 'covert hack'. This was a rougher, sturdier type than the other category, the 'park hack', which had to have the elegance and élan to show off its rider to his girl friend in the carriage and pair, and stand still while he flirted with her under the eyes of the chaperon.

The modern hack is rarely seen outside a show ring – or a dressage arena, and is mostly ridden by girls anyway. The training of a hack used to be very advanced indeed, two-track movements and flying changes being included in the repertoire, and in the past they were nearly always ridden with one hand. To watch men like Jack Hance or Horace Smith or Sam Marsh or Robert Orrsich showing off hacks was both a pleasure and an education. For lightness and handiness, as well as steadiness, a well-trained hack was hard to beat. Polo ponies, as I recall, made excellent, quiet hacks, though not usually show ring animals; perhaps it was, as Brigadier Lyndon Bolton has suggested (*Training the Horse*), because of the galloping they had to do. Owners of restive dressage horses might take note of this.

Modern show hack riders, under the influence of competitive dressage, ride firmly with two hands, and the old lightness and elegance is sadly lacking in most cases.

All this is by way of an introduction to the real present-day career of an outdoor horse (excluding show jumping), which is competitive cross-country riding. The basic, and oldest, form of this is *hunter trials*. With this one might include drag-hunting and paper-chasing, which are means of having good gallops over unseen country without undue waste of time and without the disappointments of blank days. They, in fact, can be an excellent way of preparing a horse for the more complicated competitions of hunter trials and *horse trials*, which is the general English term for the sport of the three-day and one-day event, known variously abroad, where they really started as the *Military*, because it was originally a competition for soldiers only and for troop horses and officers' chargers, the *concours du cheval complet d'equitation, Vielseitigkeits-prufung,* and so on according to the language of the country.

Hunter trials have all the image of horse trials without their complications. They are galloping competitions over prepared courses of varying distances up to three or four miles and up to thirty fences of various types, which aim at being as natural as possible. Most of the fences are solid, but a certain number have top poles which can be knocked down for the usual penalties. There can be half a dozen or so classes in a meeting for different types of horses, for riders going singly, in pairs, or in teams of three or four, in which case they are also judged on the style with which they approach fences together. All competitions are timed. A high degree of training is not required, but the more carefully a horse has been trained to jump, especially out of doors, the better. A horse that can gallop on and achieve a paddock jumping height of four feet or so should have no trouble.

Hunter trials can be used as a preparation for horse trials, or they can be competed in concurrently, or used as a relaxation from the more rigorous discipline of the latter with its triple aspect of formal dressage, cross-country and endurance, and formal jumping. As with all these far-flung events, hunter trials require careful organisation and good intercommunication, and a fair army of devoted voluntary helpers as judges, stewards, etc., which does not concern us here. They are exceedingly popular, with hundreds of events every year, mostly organised by hunts, riding clubs, Pony Club branches riding schools, and for the rider whose ambitions or purse will not carry him further they can provide enormous fun.

The horse trial is a sterner test altogether. It is, really, the apotheosis of all training, the comprehensive exercising of horse and rider in three contrasting, yet complementary, modes of horsemanship to produce a truly all-round horse and horseman. The horse must be able first of all to be calm and steady and obedient in a fairly circumscribed arena and able to show that purity of gait and regularity of rhythm at whatever stage the particular test requires up to moderate collection; at the same time he must be able on the second day, or an hour or two later in the case of a one-day event, to gallop at speed and with boldness over a cross-country course, with or without a steeplechase course, of varying length and severity; finally he must be capable of turning out fit after these exertions to behave as a Grade B show jumper.

The training, process described in Parts II and III should have taken both rider and horse well up to the level of training in each department, indeed beyond it. The horse should be up to the standard of medium dressage tests, though he will of course start in the novice grade; he should be ready for Grade C show jumping; and he should be well practised in cross-country work. The job is to weld these accomplishments into one all-round horse.

The decision to enter a horse for horse trials may well have been taken very early in his training, but it is as well, before actually embarking him on this career, to consider the essential qualities for success in this sport. First of all the horse must be bold and eager, and he must be fast. As in show jumping the old enemy is Time. Throughout a horse trials competition the clock is ticking against you. There is a time limit for the dressage test, and you lose marks if you exceed it; the time allowance is liberal enough, but it is still there as a factor to be reckoned with. In the second phase, called the 'speed and endurance test' or the 'épreuve de fond', there is a time set for covering several miles of field and woodland ('roads and tracks') at a normal exercising pace, and so you have to watch that. On the steeple-chase course (about two and a half miles) a fast speed is required, something over twenty m.p.h., and over the cross-country course (four and a half miles) the speed is rather less, a bit over fifteen m.p.h., both circuits full of hazards which can delay one, and many marks can be lost. In the third show jumping phase there is quite a stringent time factor too; so you are virtually against the clock from start to finish. To keep up with it the horse must go at a good racing pace for an appreciable part of the time.

Then, to cope successfully with the dressage part of the test, and not jump out of the arena as some horses have been known to do, he must have a calm temperament. Finally, he must be sound and fit. The latter quality is the business of the rider, and will be considered later in Part V. If a horse has all these qualities in good measure, he should go far.

It is not a bad idea, in his fifth year to try the horse out in a few point-to-points. It will encourage a sluggish horse to gallop, get him used to taking fences at speed, and will give a very good idea of his maximum capability. By the same token point-to-point riding is an excellent preparation for the event rider. Besides giving him the necessary experience of jumping biggish fences at racing speed, it enables him to estimate distances before fences and judge his actual speed, which will stand him in good stead when riding against the clock on steeplechase and cross-country courses. Most successful event riders have ridden in point-to-points and/or hunter chases, and many more nowadays are taking it up both for preliminary practice and as a continuing kindred sport.

For the horse, however, this racing practice should not be overdone, there being a fundamental difference between the two skills of racing and eventing. The former – and hunting for that matter – is done in company with other horses, whose presence round our novice both stimulates and reassures, conforming to the inherent gregariousness of his nature. The latter is done alone.

The difference is not so marked in a one-day event, when the various phases are quickly got through, the longest being the six minutes or so of the dressage test, and there are always intervals between that and the cross-country and jumping. In the three-day event the second, speed and endurance phase, consists of about ninety minutes of solitary riding, over fourteen and twenty miles, partly plodding along, partly hurtling over a steeplechase course and over a tricky cross-country course. It is quite a psychological challenge to the horse to ask it to do all this on its own, to move about in an isolated arena (the habit of relegating the usually sparse audience to a line twenty yards or more from the arena accentuates the isolation) and to face strange and often alarming obstacles by himself. All this has to be taken into consideration in the training of an event horse.

As always the preparation should be gradual and progressive. Begin at the riding club or Pony Club level with, separately, dressage competitions (preliminary and novice tests), and jumping competitions; then link them up with combined training tests, which are dressage with jumping. The great value of competition at this level is that it is usually light-hearted and so without the nervous strain of serious events.

However, the preliminaries for all these competitions must be taken seriously, and they should be carried out more or less as prescribed for show jumping (page 200 *et seq*), i.e. preparation and checking of tack, timing of arrival, preliminary exercise and warming-up, limited and adapted, of course, to the end in view. The great thing to remember about warming-up procedures before any kind of event is that they are exactly that – warming-up and suppling-up – not last minute attempts to school the horse. But the performance of your horse in these elementary tests will give you a clear guide as to his potentialities, and to strong and weak points, which can be improved upon or corrected.

The next step, obviously, is the one-day event. There were over fifty official ones organised under the auspices of the British Horse Society in 1971, and the number seems to be steadily growing. There are also several hundred slightly lower grade events during the summer organised by the Pony Club and riding clubs, which form the primary school of the sport.

The order of action of the one-day event is that it starts with the dressage test, which will be one of those prescribed by the

British Horse Society for that standard of event, preliminary, novice or elementary, copies of all the tests being available from the Society. One of the first actions of the aspiring eventer should be to join the Combined Training Group within the British Horse Society, which controls and co-ordinates all activities of this kind. After the dressage test there follow the cross-country and jumping phases, but not always in that order. Sometimes the jumping phase comes first and the cross-country phase last.

There has always been a division of opinion about this, but the consensus seems to be in favour of the latter order, although it is not strictly according to the general intention of the horse trials competition. The reason given, and it is a valid one, is that if the cross-country phase is run first, horses may have a long time to wait before their jumping turn arrives, in which chills can be caught, horses stiffen up, and general inconvenience caused. The jumping, being a lesser effort, does not cause such difficulties. The answer lies in proper horsemastership, but you must be prepared for either arrangement.

As in the case of show jumping, a great deal depends on your place in the starting order, and you should be told this before the competition starts. Unless you live close to the venue of the event, and are in the second half of the starting order, it is best to come the day before, and as early as possible on that day, so that you can follow the preparation procedure adequately. Sometimes, because of the number of entries, the dressage tests begin on the day before the actual competition, in which case you may have to come a day earlier anyway. Another problem caused by the popularity of this sport is that the event may not be able to accommodate all the entries and you may be balloted out of it altogether for one or more events. This makes it even more important to gain as much experience in riding club and other events.

The amount of time you give to warming-up depends on the individual horse, but it should not be less than hour, and should be timed to finish about fifteen minutes before you are due to go into the arena. Always begin the warming-up with some relaxed riding on a loose rein, to calm the horse down. But the whole process should be done as calmly and smoothly as possible; do not try to teach the horse something at the last moment, or get involved in any kind of argument with him. Let the atmosphere be as peaceful as possible.

Many, if not all, of the problems of the dressage test and the preparation for it, spring from a surfeit of oats unrelated to the work done. Stuffing a horse with oats is not necessarily making him fit; it fills him with energy, it is true, but to the point of intoxication, so that he is almost literally 'jumping out of his skin', as they say, and has to be worked for hours in order to calm him down sufficiently to get him into the arena at all. A balanced conditioning process is described in Part V.

After the warming-up process go into the collecting ring and walk round on a loose rein, with a rug on if it is chilly, until it is your turn. You are usually allowed to walk round the arena before actually going in, and those few minutes can be spent doing a few quiet suppling exercises and transitions. When you get the signal to go into the arena, do not rush it. Take your time to adjust the horse from whatever he was doing to the pace and attitude of mind appropriate to the entry. Take a wide circle at the far end of the arena so that you can come straight to the entrance from a good distance with the horse settled down at the appropriate pace, usually a trot. If you feel the rhythm is wrong, go round the arena again.

Once inside concentrate on the horse. 'Ride the "horse" during the performance and not the "test",' says Colonel d'Endrody most aptly (*Give Your Horse a Chance*). You will have memorised the actual test and practised all the movements with your horse, separately as well as combined in the test, which should not be done too often, as it tends to make the horse too familiar with the routine and bored. Now, with the order of movements fixed in the background of your mind, aim to present the horse to the judges in as brilliant and accurate performance as possible.

The official novice test is a very simple one, consisting of the basic gaits; walk, trot, canter; transitions and large twenty-metre circles and half circles three to five metres – in reverse, and of course the halt at the beginning and end of the test. The entry is at the trot. In the Pony Club championship the serpentine has been introduced into the test with excellent results. The aids for these movements are simple, straightforward ones, but they must be given very definitely and clearly, a stride before the point in the arena at which the change is required, so that the transition can be smooth.

After the entry there is the halt at the centre of the school. Start slowing down two or three strides in front of it so that the horse flows easily into the halt without a sudden jerk. The moment he stops yield the hands very slightly, so as not to be obvious to the judges, to tell the horse he has done rightly and to prevent fidgeting. If you feel him start to rest a hind foot, shift your weight and press with that heel and spur. Transfer the reins to the left hand and with the right hand remove your cap or hat with a generous sweeping movement, carry it down to the side, pause an instant, then replace it in the same way. If you are a lady, lower the right hand to the side, and bow from the hips. If you are a soldier, drop the right hand to the side smartly, hold it for a second, then raise it in a correct salute, lowering the hand briskly to the side directly after it. Then, in every case, take the reins in both hands again with a precise unhurried movement, pause a second, then move off. You are now being timed until the final salute. First impressions are very important, so spend time in training on the entry, halt and salute, and on the final movement and salute. It can gain you valuable marks.

Try to ride as relaxed as possible. Any tension of the rider will convey itself quickly to the horse. Keep the head erect but not fixed with a stiff neck. Other points of stiffness are the wrists and ankles; keep the hands and fingers always slightly in play, encouraging the horse to chew at the bit as he goes along, instead of having his mouth wide open through being pulled against. A little faster tempo than required, provided it is regular, will give an impression of eagerness and élan. If you have to make corrections or adjustments, try to do them with the hands and legs on the far side from the judges, and, if possible, at the more distant end of the arena from them.

The time from the end of the test to the start of the next phase will be short, so loosen girths, put on a rug and walk the horse round, changing tack if necessary. If the jumping comes next the same formal clothes are worn as for the dressage test; if it is the cross-country, the jacket is exchanged for a pullover, or some such, with the large back and front number flaps put on over it, and a proper crash cap.

Somehow or other time must be found to walk the courses. If the jumping comes after the dressage, there is time to walk that course then and there, and the procedure for show jumping applies (page 200 *et seq*). Walking the cross-country course takes longer and is more important. Its inspection is best done at leisure on the day before the event; on the day, if there is a long enough interval between the phases.

The length of the course will be between one mile and one and three-quarters, with sixteen to twenty obstacles, with a maximum height of three feet six inches and a maximum spread of nine feet. They are all fixed, and should be solidly built. The minimum speed for a novice course is 575 yards per minute, or just over nineteen and a half m.p.h. No marks are gained by exceeding this speed, but penalties at the rate of one per three seconds are incurred for going slower. For the Advanced and Intermediate classes the distance is two to two and a half miles, the heights and spreads of fences are – Advanced to three feet eleven inches and twelve feet, Intermediate three feet nine inches and twelve feet, and the speed is 656 yards per minute or just under twenty-three m.p.h. The number of fences will be between twenty and thirty.

There are two main problems here. First, how to approach and deal with the various fences; second, how to get the best speed over the course as a whole. The first problem is in fact the easiest to solve. Most of the obstacles will be straightforward, even if they look big, and it is comforting to remember that an obstacle is always more terrifying to the man on the ground than to the horse with his loftier viewpoint, which is why the observer is so often wrong in his diagnosis of the possible effects of various obstacles. The chief points to be decided are the angle of approach and the speed, and, in the case of alternative presentations of a composite obstacle, whether to choose the more difficult and quicker route or the safer but slower one. With a young and untried horse choose the latter. Each fence on the course must be considered in detail in this way.

The other problem is a time and motion one. In order not to lose time faults you have got to average nineteen and a half m.p.h. You will advisedly consider this too fast for a completely novice horse; so accept the fact of penalties, and settle for an average speed of eighteen m.p.h. Take for example the novice course of the Crookham Horse Trials at Tweseldown in 1968: 2,750 yards long, with a minimum time of four minutes forty-seven seconds. At fifteen m.p.h. this would take six minutes fifteen seconds, which would give thirty time penalties; fair enough for the first go.

Now look at the map of the course, which will show you that between some jumps there is quite a considerable distance, some of it, actually, at Tweseldown, on the racecourse itself, and that other fences come in groups of two or three, others at more or less regular intervals. There will be some sharpish turns and also some good wide circles. Obviously on certain parts of the course you will be able to go at a good gallop, sufficiently faster than fifteen m.p.h. to make up for the parts where you will have to go slow, a case of the swings and the roundabouts. Then with a rough idea of your riding plan in your head you set out to walk the course.

You will find, of course, what the map does not show, that

the course is hilly, sometimes short sharp climbs, sometimes a long hard pull up with several fences, some downhill going, and a few nice long spells on the flat. By pacing out the course and noting the distances of various parts of it, and the intervals between fences, you should get a fair idea of the variations of speed that will be more or less forced on you, where you must go slow, where you can make up time. Perhaps there will be 1,000 yards of fast galloping country, 1,000 yards of moderate speed, and 750 yards where you will have to go slow, for instance between closely related fences, up steep ascents, round sharp corners and so on. As in the case of a show jumping course, you may be able to note fences which you can take at an angle to save distance.

With these facts, and your own knowledge of your horse's speed and length of stride, you should be able to work out a riding plan for the whole course with reasonable accuracy. This can be a pre-determined average of fifteen m.p.h., you would have to aim at speeds of twenty, fifteen, and ten m.p.h. respectively. Whether you can achieve this time will show, and it will be extremely instructive to see how close you can get to the time for which you have planned.

The point of all this careful preparation is that by studying the ground closely in this way, you will acquire a very accurate knowledge of it, the type of going and the variations of contour. This will enable you to anticipate the various changes before you come to them, so that you can change gear, as it were, with the minimum delay, saving yourself the possibility of overshooting a fence by coming at it too fast and having to haul the horse back on to the line, or of not being ready to accelerate directly you come to a fast galloping section. You will also be able to go the shortest way. All this will save many seconds on the round – and every three seconds saved is one penalty the less and reduce unnecessary wear and tear on the horse.

Your riding plan will tell you where you ought to be at certain times, so wear a wrist watch when you start out on the course and time yourself. It is always possible to save a few seconds by speeding up, but it is no use trying to make up large amounts of time lost by refusals or falls. You will always hope to have none, but the unforeseen always happens in this game, and you just have to accept them. Write off the lost time and carry on according to your riding plan.

This system of preparation applies to every level of event up to championship and international three-day events. It is described in considerable detail, together with many other aspects of horse training by Lieutenant-Colonel A. L. d'Endrody in his book, *Give Your Horse a Chance.*

The routine for a three-day event is more complicated than for a single day; the effort required of a horse is immeasurably greater. If possible get to the venue two nights before the event starts, so that the horse can have one full day of normal exercise to get over the effects of the journey, especially if it has been a long one. This is not so necessary for short journeys of up to half a day, but it is as well not to ignore the effects of travelling on horses, and to work on the principle that the more time a horse has to recover after a journey the better.

On arrival, give the horse half a pound or so of glucose in his drinking water, which will help him to overcome the stress of travelling; otherwise treat as usual. Also give normal feeding and exercise the next day. On the first day of the event, make sure that any feed is given at least two hours before competing. This may be very early in the morning on the dressage day, depending on your place in the starting order. Reduce the amount of hay to not more than ten pounds daily during the event.

The amount of work done to 'ride him in' before the dressage test depends entirely on the individual horse and on your method of training, but it is best for it to be plain simple exercises as already described, rather than any schooling with a risk of conflict, when harmony is essential.

The three-day event test is longer and more complex than for the one-day event, but not really more demanding, if the horse has been carefully schooled up to that level. The present F.E.I. test generally in use was introduced in 1963 and is still current at the time of writing. There are nineteen separate movements and the time allowed is seven and a half minutes. The more advanced movements required are two tracks (half-pass at the trot), rein-back (six steps), counter-canter, and some moderate collection. The use of snaffle or double bridle is optional. The practice riding of the full test should be done as much as possible on a horse other than the competition one, who should only do the full test a comparatively few times during the preparation period.

Many riders opt for the snaffle, and, unless the horse is exceptional, usually put up very dull performances without true lightness, for, as already pointed out, (page 108), proper collection cannot be obtained with a snaffle. I would always recommend that this test be ridden in a double bridle. In a test it is always better to make the movements slightly larger than life.

Smooth and easy transitions from one gait to another are essential, but also there should be a sharp distinction between them; between, say, an ordinary trot and an extended trot, and an ordinary trot and a collected one. The effect of the curb lightly used, and with a great deal less effort, will make the collected movement much more of a contrast from the ordinary one, and will so catch the judges' eyes. Before an extension, very light and imperceptible aids can produce a slight slowing up of the ordinary trot before going into the extended trot, again highlighting the contrast. Aim at achieving maximum extension towards the second half of the diagonal across the school; it is better to have three or four strides of full extension than double that amount of an insufficient movement.

After the test, a short gallop as a pipe opener is desirable, followed by a walk to cool off, a rub down, then bed him down and feed. Allow the horse a good two hours rest, then groom thoroughly, water and feed, and leave him alone, except for a check up of feet and shoeing, until the last night feed. This is a good time to check all saddlery, especially stirrup leathers and girths before the endurance phase.

On the second day, give a short feed and water at least two hours before the time of starting, but no hay or chaff. To avoid risk of his eating his bedding the horse should be racked up after his first feed.

You will have inspected the course the day before, and the procedure for planning the cross-country ride has already been described, but this will naturally be a bigger and more complicated business, with a four and a half mile circuit and over thirty fences to cater for. There is also the steeplechase course to be treated in the same way. Aim at completing the two rounds in exactly the time needed to gain a maximum bonus *and no more*. This means that you have to plan the ride as carefully as you have done for the cross-country. You do not want to extract one ounce more energy from your horse than is absolutely necessary, for he still has a long way to go. Mad, uncontrolled galloping can lead to disaster later on.

The two roads and tracks sections are easy to plan, but they *must be* planned. The first section will be between three and three-quarter and four and a half miles, the second between four and six miles. Divide up your time between walk, trot and canter, so that you start and end with a walk. As a sample, take the 1970 Badminton figures, and assume that you know that your horse walks at four m.p.h., trots at ten m.p.h., and canters quietly at fifteen m.p.h.

The first roads and tracks were three miles 484 yards, total 5,764 yards (5,280 metres), and the time allowed was twenty-two minutes, an average speed of just under nine m.p.h. You gain nothing by being under the time allowed but lose one fault for every second over, so you cannot afford to dawdle.

At the above speeds your riding plan could be something like this:

Walk 220 yds at 4 m.p.h.	1¾ min.
Trot 2,640 yds (1½ m.) at 10 m.p.h.	9 min.
Walk 220 yds at 4 m.p.h.	1¾ min.
Canter 1,760 yds (1 m.) at 15 m.p.h.	4 min.
Trot 800 yds at 10 m.p.h.	2¾ min.
Walk 124 yds at 4 m.p.h.	1 min.
Total 5,764 yds	20¼ min.

You have one and three-quarter minutes in hand, and you will probably need it. This sort of timing can be practised during training.

Make a similar riding plan for the second roads and tracks, and, of course, the plans for the steeplechase and cross-country sections. Another reason for going to all this trouble is that it is illegal to rely on having friends and relations posted at strategic intervals to signal information about how you are doing. The F.E.I. Rules are clear and explicit on this point. Among other prohibitions it is forbidden 'To be followed, preceded or accompanied, on any part of the course, by any vehicle, bicycle, pedestrian, or horseman not in the competition.' And, 'To post friends at certain points to call directions or make signals in passing.' (Rule 336.)

In the stables give a final check to everything, then hack or lead the horse to the Box – the starting, finishing and intermediate halting point, about ten minutes before you are due to start. Weigh in, then saddle up, make sure the girths and surcingle are tight and correctly adjusted, mount and give the horse a little short pipe opener to get him on his toes for the start, which is a standing one. Then walk round until your turn comes.

After the first roads and tracks you should have time for a quick check of girths, etc., before starting round the steeplechase course. Work out your second roads and tracks plan so that you have about two extra minutes in the Box for the veterinary inspection. There should be a well-rehearsed routine for the ten minutes' inspection and rest in the Box, so that not one second is wasted.

The moment you have passed the time keeper, dismount, and while the inspecting panel is looking at the horse, off-saddle the horse. As soon as you have passed the panel, take the horse to one side where the groom will be waiting. Stand the horse facing into the wind, while the groom sponges out his mouth, swabs down the face, neck, flanks and between the thighs, then scrapes the water off with a sweat scraper. Dry him thoroughly after that, with a vigorous hand rubbing, to tone him up. Examine the legs and feet thoroughly for any wounds, cuts, bruises, and to check that the shoes are all right. Saddle up with the girths loose, lead the horse around quietly for the remaining minutes to let him relax. Three minutes before the 'off' girth up, two minutes before mount, one minute before move up to the starting point. You may find lots of people willing to come and help you in the Box, but allow nobody near the horse who has not been well drilled in this procedure.

Ride the cross-country course according to your plan, and let us hope that all will go according to it. If it does not, it is just one of those things. As in the case of show jumping, have a careful post mortem the same evening, while everything is fresh in your mind, to find out what went wrong, or rather what you did wrong. You may not have assistants on the course, but there is nothing against having observers, who can tell you afterwards how things looked to them as you passed, how the horse took difficult fences, and so on.

After the last fence gallop as fast as you can to the finishing line, decelerate gradually after that and return to the collecting ring. Off-saddle, and weigh out while the groom puts on a rug. After weighing out, replace the saddle, put on the light rug again, and, if it is a fine day, walk about for fifteen to twenty minutes to allow him to cool off, then take him back to the stable. If it is wet, get back to the stable as soon as possible.

There give the horse two mouthfuls of cold water to encourage him to stale, then give him a bucket of water with the chill off and with half to three-quarters of a pound of glucose in it. Give him a hay net to nibble at, while you massage the body and legs with straw until dry. Pick out his feet, dry his body thoroughly and remove the worst of the mud from the legs, then wrap them with gamgee and woollen bandages, rug up, and give a light feed of warm bran and oats to which a little cold linseed tea has been added, and leave the horse to rest in peace.

Two or three hours later, take the horse out and walk him about to remove stiffness and to check for lameness; carefully examine for any cuts or bruises, any thorns picked up, shoes loose, or any strain of tendon or ligament. If there is the slightest fear of bruised tendons, apply a cooling pack, such as the following: white wine vinegar and whiting made into a paste and smeared on to a piece of lint to a thickness of half an inch, applied to the legs and covered with the bandages. Then a short period of grazing will help him to relax and freshen up, and act as an appetiser for his last meal.

On the third day there is a veterinary inspection in the morning, so have your own inspection at least two hours before it, and warm him up before the official one. Apart from this revert to normal routine.

The last part of this contest, the jumping phase, takes place in the afternoon. The pre-jumping arrangements will be the same as for show jumping (Chapter 20). In Britain your order of starting will be changed from that of the previous two days. In 1966 I suggested that, to give the final phase more tension and excitement, riders should go in the reverse order of their positions at the end of the second day, literally the last should be first and the first last. This was tried out at Badminton in 1967, and has remained in force in this country, but not yet abroad. Perhaps one day it will be adopted by the F.E.I. for international use. There is always a parade of all those who have got through to this last test before the jumping starts.

All this procedure should be practised constantly before the event, and all grooms and helpers should know exactly what their job is at any given time, so that there is no last minute rush or panic, which is bound to have an adverse effect on the horse. *Always allow plenty of time before the start of the event or any part of it.*

Obviously the whole preparation of horse and rider for a three-day event is a long, arduous and exacting task, requiring in good measure the qualities of patience, perseverance and technical know-how, together with the necessary material factors of space and equipment. In modern conditions it is beyond the reach of many horse owners, but those who do make the effort can, and do, gain success.

22 The Outdoor Horse — Polo

The modern version of the ancient game of polo (the present name derives from the Tibetan word, *pulu*, a root, from which the ball was made, usually willow) is possibly the most difficult ball game in the world. In addition to the usual three elements of a ball striking game, the ball, instrument, and the striker, a fourth, often unpredictable one, is added, the horse, always known as a 'pony' whatever his height. Another element, common to all ball games, the playing surface, is an extra complication, for the polo ground is no billard table, 'The ball no question makes of Ayes and Noes, but Here or There as strikes the Player goes . . .'

Curiously enough, experience has shown that good horsemanship is not an absolute condition for reaching the top levels of polo, although naturally it is a very great asset. More important, however, is that combination of wrist, hand and vision which makes 'a good eye', what polo players call 'a stick-and-ball eye'. But superlative training of the vehicle, the polo pony, is the prime essential. Opinions of the relative values of horse power vary from 75 to 90 per cent. So let us begin with the pony, and we will continue to call him such, although he has risen in height from thirteen hands (which was about the height of the immortal Maltese Cat and his colleagues (*The Day's Work*, by Rudyard Kipling)) to sixteen hands and over (but modern players after experimenting with failed racehorses up to 15.2 hands, have found the optimum height to be 14.2 to fifteen hands, and the best ponies to be Argentinians).

The making of a polo pony is largely empirical, once he has acquired the basic training of Part III. The final answer is the test of the game itself. Everything he does has to be at speed, two-tracks when he rides off another pony, flying changes whenever required, deceleration from thirty m.p.h. to nothing in a few strides, pirouettes in one motion, leaping from a standstill to full gallop. On top of that he has to be smooth-going for ball hitting and staunch to face oncoming ponies and riders. Until you take him into a game you do not know how he will fare.

So all the movements that the horse has learnt in the school must be progressively quickened up. He must become bridle-wise, to be ridden with one hand. Nearly all the work must be done on a loose rein; and most of the schooling and suppling in a snaffle. I would reserve the curb bit for the actual play itself. After preliminary suppling exercises, the pace for the later stages of schooling should be an easy moderately collected canter. If the horse tends to poke its nose – which many polo ponies do – change to a mild double bridle, and work mainly on the curb. An equal tendency is for the head to be raised extra high when stopping and turning, and the only remedy for that in a game is a standing martingale. Instead of leather, a broad strip of muslin-type cloth (in India, where this kind of martingale originated, it was pagri cloth as used for the winding of turbans) has a slightly elastic 'give' in it, which cushions the violence of the effect of the sudden retarding aids applied at full speed.

The quick stop and the 180 degrees turn are the key to polo tactics, and it has to be faced that in the full heat of a game half measures are useless. The aids of leg and hand must be applied strongly and violently and the hand equally suddenly released. The halt obtained, the turn follows without a pause, usually right-handed: neck reining with the left indirect rein, strong left leg, and the weight of the body helping to swing the pony round on its haunches in one uninterrupted movement; then strong driving aids with both legs, the body forward, to make the pony strike off immediately at the gallop. On hard grounds with little topsoil, this method of stopping and turning is the only one to be used. On English grounds, where there is good holding turf, it is equally effective to swing the pony round in a very small circle. In this case there is no stopping, only a slight check, half-halt, to steady the pony and give him a chance to change legs, if necessary, then using the outside leg and neck rein and body weight guide him round at an accelerating speed in as close a circle as possible.

There is considerable unavoidable wear and tear on the pony's mouth during a game, which must be counteracted as much as possible by slow loose rein schooling and suppling in a snaffle or a bitless bridle. There is no little strain on the legs too, so supporting bandages should be worn by the pony for all schooling.

This is all basic schooling applied to a special purpose; but it is all to no purpose if the pony will not accept the polo stick in the rider's right hand and the ball in front of it. One pre-

liminary practice recommended was to hang a few polo sticks
up in the green pony's loose box, so that he could get used to
the look of them and, occasionally, the feel of them. Whether
this was effective I do not know.

The normal way is to start riding the pony about with the
stick held in the right hand, at first held upright as a sword
at the carry, and then dangling vertically to the ground. Next,
hold it out in front of you past the pony's face so that he can
see the head of the stick (mallet) in front of him. Then swing
it quietly backwards and forwards. Having done this on the
off side with the right hand, change hands and repeat on the near
side. The pony may shy away from it at first, but most seem
to get used to it very quickly. The final stage is to introduce the
ball. Place it on the ground in the field, and have the pony
walk up to it, while the stick is hanging down, the head practically trailing along the ground, so that it will hit the ball as
the pony passes by. The slight click of ball on mallet may make
the pony start, but carry on forwards after the ball, which will
have travelled a little way, and let the mallet hit it again.
Progress from there to combining a swinging of the mallet with
the striking of the ball, until, eventually, you can take a full
swing at the ball without the pony flinching. If the pony is
going to be permanently ball-shy, it will show the symptoms
early on; but the majority seem to accept the situation. The
difficult practices are the shots on the near side, whether forwards (near side forehander, although it is actually a backhand
stroke) or backwards (near side backhander, although it is actually a forehand stroke, but directed to the rear), and shots
under the pony's neck, whether from the off or the near sides.
Always use a loose rein when practising these shots and hold
on to the neck rein, which every polo pony should wear, whether
it has a standing martingale or not. Needless to say you practise
all these shots at the walk first, then at the canter. The trot does
not come into the polo pony's vocabulary.

Riding off is a lively exercise in two-track work. Begin by
getting the pony used to half-passing to the left and right at
the canter and then at the gallop. The angle of the diagonal
movement should be fairly flat, for there are stringent rules
about coming in at too sharp an angle, but the pony should be
thoroughly used to obeying the aids. After that, you must have
another (trained) horse and rider. First of all at the walk ride
close together side by side and gradually ease the pony inwards
against the other pony, so that they definitely jostle each other
as they go along. If the pony shows willing, separate to a yard

The increasingly popular style of Western
riding is demonstrated here

The elegance and control of dressage riding, note that there is no bridle
used

Two fine examples of the revived interest in driving

or so apart and then half-pass him into the other pony, still at the walk, letting them meet with quite a bump. Progress from there to canter and gallop.

When doing this, aim your pony's shoulder just a bit ahead of that of the other pony, so that your knee makes contact in front of the knee of the other rider and just in front of the saddle. This enables your pony to head the other off from the line of the ball. Most ponies seem to enjoy this rough and tumble, but some will not take to it at all.

Another necessary exercise is to pass another pony at a gallop, and to stand to face an oncoming pony. As before, work with a trained pony, passing first at a canter, then at a gallop, the riders swinging their polo sticks as they do so. When the pony is used to this, make him stand still while the other pony gallops up to and past him. Make sure that the pony is absolutely straight for this. Ponies are seldom, if ever, absolutely still during a game of polo, but often in defence a player must turn to meet the ball and the attacking player following it up, a manoeuvre requiring a good deal of nerve and steadiness at first.

The pony's education then continues in slow chukkars, an essential practice for both mount and man, when everything is done in slow motion, as it were, galloping being frowned on if not specifically forbidden. It used to be a term of abuse among polo playing soldiers to say of somebody that he was the sort of man who would gallop in a slow chukkar. Again, however apt the pupil may be, it is best not to hurry things, and even in fast practice chukkars to take him quietly. But, if a pony is going to be any good at all, he will soon show it; and, starting in slow chukkars at the beginning of the season, he should be ready for tournament polo by the end of it.

As for the rider, the more basic schooling he has had the better. It is true that moderate, even indifferent, riders have excelled at polo, by virtue of courage, balance, skill at other ball games, particularly rackets, but the aspirant to polo who has not had much riding training would be well advised to go back to school and acquire a firm independent seat and mastery over the application of the aids. (Part II)

Special training for polo consists in learning to hit the ball from all angles, at all speeds and in all directions. First of all, the implement. The *polo stick* (called *mallet* in U.S.A.) is in fact a mallet, a cylindrical or cigar-shaped piece of wood, sycamore, ash or bamboo, the latter being sometimes covered with vellum, eight and a half to nine and a half inches long, one and five-eighths to one and thirteen-sixteenths inches diameter, and weighing six to seven and half ounces, attached to a springy cane with a racket grip at the other end, fifty to fifty-four inches long. The cane is either Malacca or Moonah, or a combination of the two spliced together. The whippiness of the cane shaft can vary considerably, from quite stiff to extreme flexibility. The type used is very much a matter of personal choice, but it is a fair generalisation that somebody with a strong forearm, who relies on muscular strength to get length from his strokes, and also perhaps has a slightly slower eye than the next man, will tend to use stiffer canes, while the player with supple wrists and quick eye, will rely on swing and perfect timing to achieve a long shot, with as whippy a cane as possible. The length of the shaft will also depend on several factors: the length of the player's arm, his manner of riding, the height of the pony, and his position on the field, a back, having to hit more backhanders than anything else, will usually prefer a longer stick than forward; but the general principle is that the polo stick should be as short as reasonably possible, so that the player has to get down closer to the ball for his shots.

The normal grip is flat, broadening towards the head, which has a raised rim designed to prevent the handle from slipping through the hand when the full palm grip was used. This very comfortable grip has largely been superseded by the finger grip, in which the little finger goes over the rim, its great advantage being that it facilitates the keeping of arm, wrist and stick in one line at the moment of impact with the ball. A modern grip, known as the *Parada*, has a kind of pistol grip, which gives added security. Two types of normal grip are the O.H.K. or Rugby and the Lloyd or Racquet. Every grip has a sling attached to it, to enable you to retain possession of the stick if it is hooked by an opponent.

The head presents a great variety, but the basic are the cylinder and the cigar. The ball, be it understood, is struck with the long face of the head not with either end as in croquet. The cigar head has its weight and bearing surface concentrated at the centre where it joins the shaft and where the head should hit the ball. The cylinder has the weight and hitting surface evenly distributed, so, although it is not so concentrated at the critical point, it can nevertheless have some effect even if perfect accuracy is not achieved. Both types can have a slice taken off the heel (the inner end, nearest the pony) to make a reaching-out shot from the off side of the pony, or under his neck and tail, easier, or one each taken off both heel and toe (the outer end, furthest from the pony) to simplify close-in shots.

The great debate used to be on the values of the large head (greater diameter) and the small head. The large head was stronger, with more driving power, but the small head had the valuable lofting power through getting more underneath the ball. This was resolved in the 'thirties by the invention by the Royal Naval Polo Association of the elliptical head, which combined both effects very successively, without adding or sacrificing weight. It is known as the R.N.P.A. Head.

Marco (now known to be Earl Mountbatten) in his book, *An Introduction to Polo* sets out league tables of the various qualities of the different parts of the polo stick. Top of the shaft league is the spliced Malacca and Moonah; the best head for drive is sycamore, but it is low down on the durability rating. The vellum-covered bamboo gets ten for durability but is low on drive, although I did not find this to be the case on Indian polo grounds. Moreover, it has one slight advantage: if the head breaks, the vellum cover keeps the thing together until you can change sticks. This book was, and brought up to date in 1950, still is, the last word in instruction for modern polo.

Having chosen your weapon, you start to practise hitting the ball. The accepted training instrument is the wooden horse at the centre of a sort of crater with sloping sides and a netting screen all round. The diameter of the base circle, where the wooden horse is placed, can be about ten feet, and of the top of the crater anything from twenty to thirty feet, depending on the space available. The wire netting screen should be divided into panels about six feet wide, numbered consecutively from the front panel directly in the way of a straight forehand drive from the horse. The horse itself can be entirely rudimentary, provided it is firmly based and can take a saddle. Reins are not necessary, because the beginner should learn to make all his shots without recourse to the reins, but a neck strap can be used if necessary in the early stages.

The late John Board in his *Polo* which has an added value for his graphic and inimitable illustrations, recommended a preliminary to the polo horse and pit in the shape of a packing case 'standing about two feet six inches off the ground and of substantial construction'. The pupil stands on this in braced position, feet about two feet apart, knees bent, and practises swinging the stick, forwards and backwards, timing the swing so that the head of the stick reaches the ground in front of him, about where the pony's fore foot would be when it reaches the ground in that phase of the canter stride, off or near depending on which side you are swinging. When the straight swing has been acquired, the ball can be introduced. The packing case, or a firmly fixed low table, can be an economical substitute for a wooden horse; but a properly made polo pit is essential.

Hitting the ball at polo is like boxing the compass. There are four cardinal points or shots: off side forehand, off side backhand, near side 'forehand' (in fact a backhand shot forwards) near side backhand (a forward shot backwards); then, on either side, there is every direction of the compass, for each of which a special approach and swing is required. In every case the ball should be struck by the centre of the head.

For the straight forward and backward shots the head of the stick must be at right angles to the line of movement. For a cut shot to the right it must be at a wide angle to that line, i.e. more than 90 degrees. For a shot across the line of movement, the angle of the head to the line must be less than 90 degrees.

As in all ball hitting games the body must be correctly placed for the shot, and it must be on a secure base. On a pony this is obtained from the stirrups and a firm grip of calves and knees. At one time polo players tended to ride long and sitting down in their saddles; because of this they needed longer sticks and were inclined to hit the ball from behind the saddle, relying more on brute force than timing. The Indian players of Patiala, Jodhpur and Jaipur were not guilty of this; relying on a well-timed swing with flexible wrists and unerring eye, they achieved equal length with much less effort. A book called *As To Polo*, by an American, William Cameron Forbes, emphasised the value of the forward seat in polo, and players shortened their stirrups several holes, with excellent results. Firmly based on their stirrups, they were able to lean forward and down, getting much nearer to the ball – with shorter sticks – and hitting it well in front of the saddle, thus obtaining both momentum and accuracy. The same downward movement paid off for backhand shots, and the difficult near side strokes were made that much easier by the greater flexibility of the upper part of the body.

Practice with a polo ball should begin in the pit with a standing ball. Make sure the stirrups are correctly adjusted for your height and for the length of the polo stick, fifty-two inches say to start with. Place the ball alongside on the off just about level with the front 'legs' of the 'horse'. Sit upright, the left hand in the position of holding the reins, the right hand holding the stick vertically upright in the normal 'rest' or 'carry' position, which is where you keep it during a game when you are not actually using it to hit the ball or to hook an opponent's stick. Now make your swing for a forehand drive.

The first, and last, lesson of all ball games is *'Keep your eye on the ball'*. So, bend your body a little forward, eyes looking down at the ball. Tighten your grip on the handle of the stick, so that you have the correct, strong finger grip, thumb round the handle. Simultaneously bring the left shoulder forward, so that the body bends over the plane of the ball, sloping the stick slightly forwards, and raise and straighten the right arm backwards and upwards, taking the stick with it, until the hand is as far back as possible and above the shoulder, the stick making a direct extension of arm and hand. Then swing downwards – slowly in the initial practising – so that the head follows the stick and hand in a large and ever-accelerating circle, which should be at its peak of speed when it hits the ball. Four things impart length to the ensuing shot: flexibility of the wrist, resilience of the cane, both giving that extra flick at the last instant, correct moment of impact, and the speed of the pony. Practise this swing many times before putting a ball there to be hit. Your own body and head will bend forward and down so as to give your hand the correct distance from the ball, which is the length of the shaft.

For an off side backhander, you have to shift your grip, so that the thumb is along the rear side of the handle. Bring the right shoulder to the left as you raise the right arm upwards and backwards over the left shoulder, bending your body over to the right and downwards, again looking down and at the ball. At the start of the swing the elbow will be bent, but straighten it about halfway down. The head of the stick should come to the ground just about level with the stirrups. As before, bend the body down as far as is necessary. In every case after a swing, follow through until the stick is held out horizontally in front of or behind you as the case may be. Many players, especially Indian and Pakistani ones, make a double backhand swing at the ball, which can be very effective in imparting greater length to the stroke; but there is also more chance of the stick being hooked during the swing. It is worth while practising this double swing, so as to be able to use either according to the situation.

On the near side, the action is more or less reversed. For the 'forward' stroke, take the reverse grip, as for the off side backhand, lean the right shoulder well over to the left, so that it is over the line of the ball, head looking down, body braced, as

before, on stirrups, calves, knees and thighs, and leaning forward and down as far as necessary. Extend the right arm,
with the stick, backwards over the left shoulder, and bring it
down straight in the same plane as the ball. This, with its
variants, is the most difficult shot of all and requires a good deal
of practise.

For the 'backhand' stroke, keep the forward grip, raise the
right hand as high as possible above the right shoulder, the stick
swinging slightly off the vertical; then rotate the shoulders, so
that your right shoulder is over the ball, and swing down towards it. In every case, at the moment of impact shoulder,
arm, hand, stick and head should be in one vertical line.

If you have hit the ball correctly, it should go straight as a
bullet into the netting panel immediately opposite you, or behind you, as the case may be. You will *feel* if your timing has
been right.

Concentrate first on the off side strokes, getting the forehand
drive as perfect as possible with a stationary ball before changing
to the backhand. Then the near side forehand stroke, which is a
great deal more tiring to execute than the off side shots; so
avoid overtiring yourself by too much repetition at a time.
Practise when your arm and wrist are tired can only do harm.
After a few near side shots, change over to the off side for a
rest. Remember that, if the ball at any of these shots goes off
to one side or the other, instead of straight into the target area,
you have it wrong. You may not have hit the ball true with the
centre of the head, but with one side or the other, causing the
ball to go to the right or to the left. You may have sliced it,
by hitting it with the head not at right angles to the line of the
ball but turned outwards; or pulled it by the head being turned
inwards.

Other faults are topping the ball, caused by not getting
down far enough and by raising your eyes off the ball; or hitting
the ground in front of it, the result of a faulty swing and pressing by relying on strength not swing and timing to hit the ball
correctly. It is always best to have an instructor to point out
these faults to you, but in default of that these indications
will tell you when, and where, you are going wrong.

When you are reasonably sure of accuracy at these four
strokes at a sitting ball, progress to a moving one. Whenever you
have hit the ball up into the netting surround of the polo pit
the force of gravity will bring it back to you, more or less
straight, if you have hit it straight in the first place. In this
case, make your swing, timing it to meet the ball as it arrives

in front of you; if you have mishit and the ball is coming down at you from an angle, stop it and take another standing shot correctly, we will hope. Only when you are able to hit the straight moving ball straight back again into the target area, should you tackle the ball coming from angle.

This should happen when you have practised angle shots, into panels of the netting screen to the right and then to the left of the centre one. To the right they will be cut shots, to the left pulls. To make this change of direction, the stick must be brought down so that the head is facing in the required direction, still at right angles to the line of the ball. To do this successfully, the ball must be struck further out from the side of the pony than was necessary for the straight forehand drive; the same applies for the backhand stroke on the near side. The wider the angle of the cut the further out the ball has to be, and more to the front in the case of the forehand shot, and to the rear for the backhand; and the same on the near side.

The whole secret of success at polo is accurate and reliable stroke play, and the only way to achieve it is by constant practise, remembering two instructions:

1. Keep your eye on the ball.
2. Aim every shot at a mark.

A third point to remember is not to keep on hitting at the ball when tired.

Mounted practice follows the same course as in the pit on a wooden horse. Practise your swings on both sides, first of all without a ball, then with it. Variations can be introduced; half swings, tapping the ball along, which makes one at ease with the stick and strengthens the wrists; and the ability to control the length of one's shot is of great importance.

The following form of mounted practice is of great value in acquiring accuracy of timing and direction. In a field, set up a pair of flags, four yards apart or half the normal width of the goal. Get as many polo balls as you can up to a dozen, and lay them in line from right to left about sixty yards from the goal, five or six feet apart. Canter round in a circle on the right rein, so that you come up to the first of the balls opposite the goal. Aim to get it through the goal with a slow easy swing. Then move the circle so as to approach the next ball, and so on. Do not attempt to hit the ball into the next county, let the swing, your wrist and the momentum of the pony do the work for you; the great thing is to get all those balls through or into the goal mouth.

Then re-align the balls from left to right so that the right-hand one is directly opposite the goal, and you come at it, still on a right-handed circle, on the near side. Arrange your circle so that you are always on a straight line when you come up to the ball. In due course you turn about and take backhand shots. Steady practice in this way entails no unnecessary wear and tear on the horse.

This is the time also to practise special shots, for which the tapping exercise will have prepared you. But do not make a habit of this tapping – or dribbling – in a game; you will never get very far if you do; though the occasional single tap to position the ball or to get it out of the way of an oncoming opponent can be very effective. A useful shot is the low push (Marco calls it a 'jab shot' in his *An Introduction to Polo.*). If you and your opponent are about to meet each other, off side to off side, you may find that you are going to do so fractionally later than him in getting to the ball. Bend right down as low as you can, run the head of the stick along the ground with your right hand as far in front of you as you can get, so that the under side of the head hits the ball and pushes it under the opponent's swing.

Many a goal has been scored by tapping the ball under the pony's belly between his legs. The chance usually comes in front of goal when the pony is moving comparatively slowly, and you have no time or opportunity to turn or take a shot under the neck. A quick half-halt will help to position the pony's legs, and you make a swing at right angles to the line of the pony, aiming to hit the ground just before you hit the ball, which will help you to stop the follow through and the possibility of the stick and the pony's legs becoming entangled. Another trick, if you notice that the man behind you is contemplating hooking your stick, is to entice him to bring his stick forward with a dummy shot, break off your swing and beat down the stick, and then make a quick half swing so as to make your getaway. All these things happen very quickly, so very quick reflexes are required.

If you have the pony power, you must have the occasional galloping stick-and-ball practice, before you venture on an actual slow chukkar. Henceforward the difficulty will be to restrain your ardour, but try to do so for a while before really getting into the fast game, which you will find exceedingly bewildering at first, with the other members of both teams shouting at you at once. The beginner is invariably placed at No. 1, the leading forward position, and the one instruction given him will be to mark the opposing back (No. 4) and forget about the ball.

Indeed some military martinets were alleged to have sent their tyros into action without polo sticks at all.

Once you have learned how to hit the ball, you can only learn polo from playing it. To the uninitiated it looks like a mad gallop up and down the ground by people swearing at each other and trying to stop their ponies. One shrewd observer once noted that polo was always played on the opposite side of the ground to the spectator. However, there is a definite pattern in good polo which soon becomes clear.

It is first and foremost a team game. The brilliant individualist looks spectacular, but he ruins the game for the others. I am talking about sides whose players are fairly level; a good player in a team of rabbits has to be a bit of an individualist. The four players of a team are numbered 1, 2 (forwards), 3 (centre-half), and 4 (full back). The back defends, passing the ball up to No. 3 (the pivot of the side), who sets an offensive in motion, either taking the ball up the ground himself or, if he is being interfered with, passing it up to the No. 2 forward, who should be given a clear run by the No. 1 forward marking the back, so as to prevent him from backhanding the ball away from his territory. That is the pattern that both sides aim at, and which both sides aim to disrupt, so the game takes fascinating turns all over the ground, riders placing themselves to receive passes in directions unexpected by the enemy; the anticipation of good players who know each other's ways and capabilities is uncanny, one of the things that makes a high handicap player.

And all the time you have to watch that you do not cross the line of the man who has possession of the ball or right of way. The Rules provide very clearly the various ways in which you can infringe the rights of the man in possession, and prescribe severe penalties for infringement. The would-be player should get a copy of the Rules at the very beginning of his career and read and re-read them.

Polo is a very expensive game. To play four chukkars in station polo or in a match, you must have at least three ponies. A pony can normally play two chukkars, but there must be a reserve. This is why, in any country, only a comparative handful of people can afford to play polo with any regularity or hope of success As in the old mounted cavalry days the cost for impecunious but enthusiastic officers was mitigated by the regimental framework and the use of troop horses, many of which were superlatively good, so at the present time the club organisation, which is pretty universal, enables many young players to enjoy some sort of polo, and, sometimes, to acquire the skill which will get them into a team.

In Britain there are twenty-four polo clubs, and the number of players on the 1970 handicap list was 367, to which can be added eighty-two in the Rhine Army. Many, if not all, clubs have a reservoir of club ponies, which they can hire for a fee of £2 per chukkar upwards (£5 for tournaments.). A limited number of young players come up through the Pony Club. Sex equality is established in theory, but in practice very few girls play polo. The governing body of polo in this country is the Hurlingham Polo Association, though it no longer has any connection with the Hurlingham Club.

The leading polo playing countries of the world are the Argentine and U.S.A., with Australia, Mexico and other South American countries not far behind. Great Britain is unable to take on any of them on level terms. Polo is also played in Eire, India and Pakistan, New Zealand, France, Germany and Italy, Rhodesia and South Africa, Kenya, Nigeria, Ghana, Malaysia, and Jamaica.

23 High School
and Grand Prix de Dressage

By the end of the basic training period (Part III) the horse's potentiality should be fairly clearly discernible: whether for the technically lower, but thoroughly rewarding and skilled, fields of show jumping, horse trials and polo, or for the rarefied heights of *haute école*, which has its highest expression in the performances of the Cadre Noir of Saumur and the Spanish Riding School of Vienna, and, competitively, in the Grand Prix de Dressage.

The four movements, or airs, which mark the change from basic and medium to advanced equitation are the named flying changes of leg at the canter, the pirouettes, the piaffe and the passage. The rears and leaps, levade, courbette, capriole are outside the scope of the ordinary private horseman. The overall requirement for high school is extreme collection (*rasembler*) and, above all, the horse must be *willing*.

There must come a time in the training when the horse will not so much obey blindly the aids but seem to *lead* the way, to want to execute more difficult airs of his own volition. After all, they arise out of work already done, in response to aids already learnt, so that they are part of an exciting dialogue between horse and rider, on much more equal terms than it has been hitherto. The sensitive horseman will recognise this thrilling moment, take the horse on as high as he wants to go, re-train him tactfully from overdoing it, encourage his generosity and at the same time maintain the discipline necessary to add accuracy and precision to natural freedom and brilliance which combine to make the perfect performance. The movements of a horse which is *forced* into them will always appear dead and laboured, unsatisfying to both rider and spectator.

Flying change. The horse should already be able to execute a smooth flying change (pages 115–16), and it should not be difficult to train him to do it as often as required at given points: at every third and second stride, then at every stride, as required in the test of the Grand Prix de Dressage. It is interesting to recall that flying changes now reserved for the highest riding test of all, were once part of the manège test for officers' chargers at the Indian Army School of Equitation, Saugor, in the 'twenties. Only three changes were asked for on the straight, but they had to be done consecutively, and I never knew any horse to make any difficulty over it. I trained a polo pony to make the single stride change by changing the lead of the canter half-pass (counter-change of hand on two tracks), first every three strides and reducing to one. I say 'trained', but he took to it quite naturally once he saw what was required, and seemed to enjoy doing it.

The flying change was reached at the end of Chapter 16 (page 168), but, if it is known by then that the horse will be going forward to advanced equitation, it is advisable not to overdo those lessons until the horse has achieved good collection (Chapter 17). It must be thoroughly supple before being asked to do named changes.

The horse makes the change during the period of suspension, but as the phases of the canter stride follow each other so quickly, the preparation for it must begin well before. First there is the positioning with the half-halt, and the collecting of the horse to the right degree, i.e. so that the horse is well balanced fore and aft, without excessive movement of the centre of gravity to the rear.

The first requirement of a flying change is straightness, the horse not swinging his quarters to the left or right and going on two tracks while doing it, which is of course much easier for him. So begin work in the manège on straight lines, using for a few lessons the tracks on the long sides. Only a *few* times like this, then revert to straight lines down the centre of the school, along the diagonals, or across from one side to the other, 'so that the rider can clearly see how much of the horse's straightness is attributable to its obedience to the controls and be sure that the horse is kept from growing accustomed to securing moral support from the wall'. (Zeunig, *Horsemanship.*)

Start by making a few transitions from trot to canter, followed by a few simple changes, then prepare it as above for the final effort. Assuming a change from the left lead to the right canter on the right rein; position the horse as soon as possible after turning the corner from the short side; when you feel the horse is going smoothly and quietly and is ready for the change apply the aids for the canter with the right lead before the left leading leg comes to the ground, when the horse will be on the diagonal; near hind, off fore. This will give time for the change to take place during the ensuing moment of suspension. Apply the left leg behind the girth, while activating the horse with the right leg, the weight of the body shifted to the left by a movement of the seat bones, the right rein meanwhile asking for a slight bend to the right, supported by a slight yielding of the left rein. The moment the change has been made, relax the aids, slow down to walk and make much of the horse.

If the horse fails to make the change, or gets into a disunited canter, do not attempt to force it into the movement. Relax back to a trot, and try it on the other rein. If you are successful on that rein, try again from the original direction. If there are still difficulties, try working on a figure of eight. Consider whether you have been too rough and abrupt with the aids, applying them too late, making it impossible for the horse to obey, however willing he may be. It is worth recalling another piece of advice from Waldemar Zeunig: 'Lymphatic and plump horses should be spared all instruction in the flying change for they should not be tormented with the demands of higher dressage, since they lack the required congenital verve.'

It may take two or three sessions to obtain correct – smooth and straight, flying changes, or they may be achieved the first time. In any case do not overdo them, but gradually bring the horse to an easy freedom in, and even liking for, the movement, before beginning changes at named positions and in given rhythms of strides.

In the high school tests the flying changes are done on the diagonals across the arena, so make your practice along them, not necessarily all the time, but certainly to begin with, so that they will not come as a surprise to the horse when he eventually meets them both in preliminary schooling for and in the actual tests. Place a couple of marks at odd distances on each diagonal, which can remain there during ordinary schooling sessions, so that the horse will get used to their presence. When next you have a flying change practice, make up your mind at which mark you will make the first change, position the horse for it, and apply your aids so that the change will be made exactly at that spot. Knowledge of the horse's stride already acquired will help to obtain accuracy.

Having done the change correctly on one diagonal, change the rein and execute it at a chosen mark on the opposite diagonal. Then call it a day. For the next three or four lessons make the changes at the same spots, but the next time ride the full lengths of the diagonals without asking for any change, just to prevent it from becoming a habit on that one spot. Following that, ring the changes for the chosen positions, still making only one flying change on each diagonal. In due course obtain two changes on one straight line, say six strides apart; and from there progress to a change every five, four, three and two strides.

Vary the flying changes with transitions from canter to walk, and from halt to canter, and of course plenty of relaxed periods as a rest and reward. If a horse can go directly to a walk after five canter strides, he should be able to make a flying change smoothly after six strides (Zeunig), and so on downwards. At the same time the aids should become more subtle, the rider's seat more immovable – or apparently so to onlookers and judges – especially judges. Once the horse has got the idea – and some will get it very quickly, the lightest combination of the aids will be sufficient to achieve the final gymnastic effort of the flying change at every stride.

If any trouble should arise, from boredom or for any other reason, restart from an earlier stage and work up again. On the other hand, the horse may take to it so well that his changes will get out of hand, so care must be taken to keep him always to the exact number and kind of changes required. Profit to the full from his willingness but always retain the ultimate command.

The *pirouette* is the hardest of all the high school movements to do well. Here is the official definition.

> This movement is a small circle on two tracks, with a radius equal to the length of the horse, the forehand moving round the haunches. At whatever pace the pirouette is executed, the horse should turn smoothly, maintaining the exact cadence and sequence of legs at that pace.
>
> At the pirouette, as at the half-pirouette, the forelegs and the outside hindleg move round the inside hindleg, which forms the pivot and should return to the same spot each time it leaves the ground. If, at the canter, this leg is not raised and returned in the same way as the other hindleg, the pace is no longer regular.
>
> In executing the pirouette, the rider should maintain perfect lightness while accentuating the collection and engagement of the quarters. (F.E.I. *Rules for Dressage Competitions*, Sec. 413.)

The method of teaching the pirouette has been described above (pages 181, 182), and starting from the renvers position is the most practical way of setting about it, for the horse is in the right position for the movement before it begins. As I have said, it can be accomplished by a moderately trained horse in a rough and ready way, as for polo, but for a school horse, the approach must be more gradual. In the first place, the horse must be able to canter quietly, but with a lively high action, in perfect collection. He should be supple, able to halt and strike off at the lightest aids, which is a necessary preparation for the movement. He should be responsive to the lightest aids, so that the rider can sit as still as possible, without trying to make use of his weight or using too heavy rein aids. The less the rider moves the easier it is for the horse.

In the first lessons from the renvers position the turn in the corner should be a very small volte, the essential thing being to maintain the cadence all through. Apply firm driving aids before going into the turn to keep up impulsion, and restrain the horse with the inside leg from trying to make the turn too fast. After one turn, go straight and reduce to a walk. Two turns are enough for one lesson at this stage. If the horse makes any resistance, go back to larger turns, then very gradually shorten them.

The operative word is *gradually*. Four turns, two each way, should be the maximum for a session, and not at every session – say four times a week. 'It takes quite a long time and diligent, systematic work before the horse is in a position to execute correct and cadenced pirouettes.' (Richard L. Wätjen, *Dressage Riding*.)

The *piaffe* and the *passage* are usually associated together as the acme of the training of a high school horse, and for perfection the latter should proceed from the former. As usual let us start with the official descriptions.

> The *piaffe* is a movement resembling the very collected trot on the spot. The horse's back is supple and vibrating. The haunches with active hocks are well engaged giving great freedom and lightness to the action of the shoulders and forelegs.
>
> The neck is raised, the poll supple, the head perpendicular, the mouth maintaining light contact on a taut rein. The alternate diagonals are raised with even, supple, cadenced and graceful movement, the moment of suspension being prolonged. In principle, the height of the toe of the raised foreleg should be level with the middle of the cannon bone of the other foreleg. The toe of the raised hindleg should be slightly lower, reaching just above the fetlock joint of the other hindleg.
>
> The body of the horse should move up and down with a supple and harmonious movement without any

swinging of either the forehand or the quarters from one side to the other.

The piaffe, although being executed strictly on the spot and with perfect balance, must always be animated by an energetic compulsion which is displayed in the horse's constant desire to move forward as soon as the aids calling for the piaffe are discontinued. (F.E.I. *Rules for Dressage Competitions,* Sec. 415.)

One definite mark of a good piaffe is apparent effortlessness. Another is the lowering of the croup, which means that the hocks are well flexed. Laboured, unequal steps, with swinging quarters and swishing tale are marks that the horse has not been correctly prepared.

The piaffe should not begin to be taught until the horse has acquired a perfect trot at all paces, and perfect collection. The use of cavalletti in the early stages of training help to produce an habitual reasonably elevated trot, which can facilitate to some extent the ultimate achievement of the piaffe and passage, but the use of cavalletti at the last moment, as it were, is no substitute for proper and methodical preparation.

Preparatory exercise should be aimed at increasing suppleness, engagement of the quarters and flexing of the hocks, and strong impulsion. They can include the usual half-halts; transitions from trot to walk; collected walk; transitions in the following sequence: (a) halt – trot – halt; (b) trot – halt – trot. (General de Carpentry, *Piaffer and Passage.*) The number of trot steps in (a) may be a dozen or more at first but progressively reduced; and the halt pause in (b) will be several seconds at first, and also gradually diminishing. The trot should be slow but well cadenced, and the halt and depart absolutely straight. Take care in these exercises not to use the hand and leg aids together, but separately and reciprocally, i.e. hand action should be accompanied by passivity or yielding of the legs, leg action by a yielding or steady hand.

The direct depart from halt to trot may not come easily at first, hence the need for several trot steps and for a good period of immobility after the halt, and the very gradual reduction of the trot steps and the halting time. There should be no loss of balance or scrambling in the trot depart. After repeating the sequences five or six times the lesson should end with a longer trot, a longer halt, and then complete relaxation of the reins.

The piaffe and the passage are closely related and they should not be taught or practised in isolation. One proceeds from the other, and they are both included together in the Grand Prix de Dressage test. It is possible, but not really profitable to start with the passage, and most authorities teach the piaffe first. And three good reasons are given for it by Lieut.-Col. G. von Kazslinszky: '1. The piaffe is the foundation of "high school"; 2. With the piaffe one is better able to establish control of the easily evasive hindquarters; 3. The horse which has learnt the passage without previously achieving the piaffe will drag his quarters.' (*Light Horse*, January, 1967.)

The piaffe can be taught direct in the mounted position, but it seems logical to begin on the ground, which is indeed the way adopted by the Spanish Riding School of Vienna, who begin with work on the short reins, followed by the pillars, before executing the piaffe mounted. Not everyone has pillars at his command, or is sufficiently skilled with the long (short) reins to obtain the best results. The method recommended by Richard Wätjen (*op. cit.*) is to start with a leading (lunge) rein, using it as a substitute for the hand-held reins, and a whip as substitute for the leg aids. Side reins, and a cavesson noseband should be worn. An advantage is that the horse, 'without being burdened by the weight of a rider ... learns more easily to engage and bend the hocks and bring the hindlegs well forward.'

Starting on the left rein, place the horse beside one wall of the manège. The side reins must be adjusted to keep the head in the position of maximum collection, a little in front of the vertical. The leading rein, attached to the cavesson, is held short; the whip is in the right hand. The gentle action of the whip on the hocks encourages the horse to move forward, but the restraint of the leading rein in the left hand holds him back. The horse will start to lift his feet, to mark time as it were. Go on repeating this exercise until the horse starts to make more elevated and quicker movements of his feet which will amount to a trotting action. It is permissible to let the horse go a little forward at the beginning of these lessons, but he must not be allowed to move his quarters off the straight line. If he does so, let him go forward at the trot, and start the exercise again. One or two steps are enough to begin with, and the lesson should not exceed about five minutes at a time. Unauthorised attempts to go forward can be restrained by quick halts with the leading rein. After a few steps done well, relax and reward the horse, and give him some normal uncollected work.

Very gradual progress is essential, and it is best to concentrate on getting the movement perfected on one rein before changing to the other side. The movement must always be on the trot diagonal, and the back should be kept as supple as possible, which is best achieved by not overdoing the lessons to the point of boredom, irritation and resistance. The whip aid should be intermittent, not applied continuously during the movement. Once got into the rhythm of the piaffe the horse should be allowed to free-wheel, as it were, without constant application of the aids. When the whip (or the legs when mounted) acts, the hand should be steady. Over-collection is to be avoided, and care must be taken to see that the horse keeps on the bit, not getting behind it. If the horse tries to rear, he should be driven forward immediately. The probable cause is too much of the exercise at a time, making the horse sick of it. It must be remembered that the piaffe is a most strenous gymnastic exercise, for which the horse must be carefully and progressively prepared.

If this preliminary ground work has been thoroughly carried out, it should be possible to proceed direct to mounted work. Repeat the preparatory exercises and include rein-backs after halts.

The essence of it is a series of alternating back and forth movements controlled by alternating aids. Apply the hand aids without the leg aids, and directly the horse obeys yield the hand and act with the leg, using the whip at first, as on the ground, and gradually supported and supplanted by the legs. Never let the horse become completely immobile. After two or three alternations of this kind relax the horse by going forward at the trot for a few strides then halting. The cadence of the diagonal trot movement must be maintained throughout. The forehand must be raised slightly, the croup lowered. The reins should be taut but light, which can be detected by the position of the curb bit; this should be at a very narrow angle to the vertical. If the cheeks of the bit are drawn back to an angle of 45 degrees or more the rein tension will be too great and there will be stiffness of the back.

The raising of the foreleg is obtained by shifting the weight so that one foreleg is pinned down momentarily while the other is released. Do this by the action of one rein on the neck, so that the weight shifts to the shoulder on that side, e.g. action of the right rein will tend to burden the right shoulder and release the left. This should be done when that leg is on the ground, and to balance itself the horse will raise the opposite (left) leg. The horse must bend his neck willingly to the aid, and must remain quite straight. If any resistances occur, either insufficient bend or too much, break off the movement, trot forward, halt and start again. When the horse responds well to one side, repeat the exercise on the other.

The rider should be able to *feel* the movements of the legs under him, all this being part of the feels of riding without which it is not possible to gain full success at this art. The rein aid should be little more than a closing of the fingers as the leg comes to the ground. The action must be very delicate, so that the forelegs are not raised too high, which is as bad a fault as not being raised enough. Once more the gradualness of the progress must be stressed, and the imperative need not to overdo any part of the training. One perfect, or near perfect, step is enough to begin with. There is no saying how long the process will take; it entirely depends on each individual horse.

The passage can proceed from the piaffe, or it can be developed from the collected school trot. As usual let us start with the official description.

> This a measured, very collected, very elevated and very cadenced trot. It is characterised by a pronounced engagement of the quarters, a more accentuated flexion of the knees and hocks and the graceful elasticity of the movement. Each diagonal pair of legs is raised and put to the ground alternately, gaining little ground and with an even cadence and a prolonged suspension. In principle the height of the toe of the raised foreleg should be level with the middle of the cannon bone of the other foreleg. The toe of the raised hindleg should be slightly above the fetlock joint of the other hindleg.
>
> The neck should be raised and gracefully arched with the poll as the highest point and the head close to the perpendicular. The horse should remain light on the bit and be able to go smoothly from the passage into the piaffe and *vice versa*, without apparent effort and without altering the cadence, the impulsion being always active and pronounced. (F.E.I. *Rules for Dressage Competitions*, Sec. 414.)

It is the rhythm and the slight dwelling in the air and pointing of the toes of the raised diagonal which are the charm and delight of this movement at its best. The sideways swinging of the quarters, seen in circus displays, can be impressive but is a fault in classical high school riding.

If a good effortless piaffe has been achieved, use firm driving aids to make the horse step forward, but maintain the elevation with the hands, so that only a little forward ground will be made but more upward movement. Two steps like this are ample for a start. Relax into an ordinary trot and halt. The same can be done from a good collected school trot by elevating aids with the hands, which must be as light as possible but definite, followed by driving action with the legs. Again the angle of the curb bit is a good guide to the correctness of the aids. If horse and rider have become accustomed in the preliminary training to the delicate control by finger action, rather than by rigid movement of wrist and forearm, the progress to these elevated gaits will be greatly facilitated.

The piaffe and the passage can be taught on the long reins, or the short hand reins as is practised and displayed by the *reiters* of the Spanish Riding School of Vienna, the whip acting as the leg aid. The procedure is a gradual slowing down of the trot until the horse is trotting on the spot, though a slight advance is permissible, to avoid constricting the horse and stiffening its back. The piaffe is then perfect in the pillars.

The principle of this is clear enough, the horse, wearing side reins, being restrained by reins from the pillars attached to the cavesson noseband, so that he is prevented from going forward or back and is encouraged to elevate his steps at the driving aid of the whip. The application is not so easy, requiring very great care, first in introducing the horse to the pillars, then the application of the aids and the maintenance of straightness. The help of a trained assistant is essential. The horse may get excited or frightened at the restraint of the pillar reins and the trainer must wait patiently, soothing him with voice and hand, until he settles down before applying the driving aid of the whip, and then only very softly.

It can take a year or more before a sufficient piaffe and passage have been obtained to warrant entering for high level competitions; but of course the horse can gain experience by progressing through the lower levels of competition.

Riders should try to gain experience by riding older horses that have already been trained in the high school movements, so that they can get the feel of them before trying to impart them to a novice horse. This is easier to come by in Germany and elsewhere on the Continent, where there are more trained horses about and also high school instructors. In England really expert high school horses are few by comparison. However, a start was made in this direction by the introduction, at the Henley Horse Show in 1969, on the initiative of Mrs Julia Wynmalen, of a special class for novice riders on horses trained up to the level of the higher tests short of Grand Prix. This innovation proved very popular and seems already to have the effect of bringing young riders on and so swelling the ranks of those capable of producing high school horses.

The other problem is the horse. The plan of this book has tried to show a young horse developing from foalhood onwards to the highest levels of equitation, but I hope it has also been made clear that the process is not an inevitable one. The truth is that, whatever the branch of equitation, the top horse is exceptional; he is usually found by accident, especially so in the case of the dressage and high school horse. The skill of the horseman often lies in recognising the latent ability of any horse to begin with, as well as in exploiting it.

As the Rule says, all horses are different and individual, and their training programme must take that fact into consideration all the time, 'the same passage cannot be of all horses . . . some horses have a more rounded and longer action, others a more lively shorter action'.

Heredity may have something to do with the production of a high school horse. It must certainly be born and bred into the very bone and spirit of the Lipizzaner; but even in his case there are many rejects. The German Hanoverians, Holsteins and Trakehners seem to have an inbred docility which makes them good material for the high school rider. On the other hand, James Fillis preferred Thoroughbreds to all others; perhaps, in the right hands, they can be brought to great heights of elegance, power and brilliance. One thing is certain, they cannot be forced into it.

The horse learns from his trainer; the horseman learns from every horse he rides, and there is no end to it.

FIVE

Additional Considerations

24 Racing and Western Riding

Racing

There are sundry equestrian activities, of considerable importance and world wide, which are outside the main streams of
orthodox teaching described so far, and which, indeed, appear
to be contradictory to them. For instance, while orthodoxy
emphasises the role of the rider's body weight, the action of the
muscles of the small of the back, and the function of the 'driving
seat' to produce and preserve impulsion, we find the fastest
horse on earth – the racehorse – being driven forward from start
to finish without the rider ever touching the saddle with his
posterior. And there is no doubt that, ever since British jockeys
abandoned the long-legged seat *on* the saddle in favour of
Sloan's forward position, racehorses have galloped faster and
faster.

This was also the essence of the Caprilli revolution some
seventy years ago, and it certainly produced startling results
within his limited range of requirements for outdoor riding.
Even now, when the then widely separated ideas have coalesced
to a great extent there are two schools of show jumping thought
and practice, as to whether one should sit down in the saddle
for the approach to a fence or keep the seat off it. Both seem
to show equal dividends.

Similarly, there is an apparent contradiction in the riding of
the Western range horse, and in particular the cutting horse
and the riding and schooling of any horse under classical
European principles: on the one hand no, or minimal, contact,
on the other full contact.

Such contradictions may be more apparent than real. Every
horse, whatever his future role, experiences the full force of
the driving seat in his early training; every horse must accept
the bit and contact with the rider's hand before he can learn
to do without it. Every rider learns to use his back muscles
and seat and weight in obtaining impulsion, and in fact continues to use the small of his back even in the extreme forward
position. It is surely the sensible application of Steinbrecht's

dictum with which we started (page 82), 'The normal position does not exist.'

It is also a vindication of equestrian orthodoxy, if such is needed, that both the racing fraternity and the western world have recognised the value of, indeed necessity for, basic training of both horse and man to make more efficient their special skills and performance.

For the first time in the history of equitation a small book has been produced on horsemanship for jockeys, written by John Hislop and originally serialised in *The British Racehorse* during 1970.

The task of the racehorse is a straightforward one: to gallop overall faster than the other horses in the race and to conserve his energy so as to be able to exert his full power and pace at the critical moment. He achieves this through the skill of his trainer in bringing him to the starting gate or stalls exactly fit for that particular task, and under the direction of his rider.

So jockeyship, as John Hislop says, 'is the art of race riding – judgement of pace, tactics, sizing up the way a race is being run and acting accordingly, quickness from the start, riding a finish, determination and gamesmanship –' but, 'if the highest skill in flat race riding is to be attained, it is essential to master the art of horsemanship before attempting to be a jockey'. And this, perhaps, applies equally, if not more so, to riding over fences, whether under National Hunt Rules or point-to-pointing. For them all the education of a jockey 'comes in two stages. The first is learning to be a horseman, the second learning to be a jockey.'

Jockeys start their careers young, as apprentices, and many of them now, thanks to the Pony Club and the improving commercial riding schools, start with some basic training. Perhaps in time it will become a compulsory qualification for apprenticeship to hold a Pony Club or similar certificate.

Apart from the tactical handling of a horse in a race, there is a great deal more in racing horsemanship than meets the eye. It is not a question of riding with very short stirrups, perched up above the saddle and holding the horse hard by the reins. There is a right and wrong length of stirrup leather, depending on the individual horse and the work to be done, and the necessity of all horsemen to be in balance with the horse. For a slow cantering exercise the leathers will be longer than for a fast gallop; they are better short for a sprint race, and long for a distance one. Long reins and short stirrups may be more effective with a horse that pulls than the other way about.

There is also the use of the whip to be learnt and practised. The jockey must be able to transfer the whip from one hand to the other without disturbing the balance or rhythm of the horse at full stretch, and to use it equally well with both hands. He must of course know when to use a whip, and then not to overdo it, or merely for show.

The jockey's position on the horse at rest is not intrinsically different from the normal balanced seat, except that he has a most inadequate saddle to sit on. He must sit as near as possible to the lowest part of the saddle, back straight and supple, knees into the saddle, lower legs hanging naturally, feet resting on the irons on the inside edge of the footplate, toes to the front, hands in light contact with the horse's mouth. He will be using the muscles of the small of the back and the driving seat constantly for small slow actions, like manoeuvring into position at the starting gate, or urging the horse into the starting stall. The more supple and secure he is in the saddle, the better can he concentrate on handling the horse in the race.

For racing over fences both horse and rider should have basic jumping training. It is surprising how badly many steeplechasers jump; and how many races have been lost, I wonder, by bad approaches and unbalanced leaps? Admitted there is not much time to make conscious preparation as in show jumping, but patient preliminary training can make these actions instinctive.

Apropos race riding in general, John Hislop makes an interesting statement regarding the introduction of starting stalls in England, that it was 'necessitated by foreign influence and a lower standard of horsemastership among trainers and riding on the training ground and on the racecourse, than was the case before the 1939–45 war'.

Western Riding

Everybody is familiar with the cowboy and his horse. Ever since Tom Mix they have become the folk heroes of eastern youth – and the not so very young either, as the audiences to television 'Westerns' bear witness. Uninformed orthodox horsemen have tended to look down on the apparently rough and ready methods and odd clothes and tack, but at its best the horsemanship of the range was the direct descendant, adapted for special purposes, of all that was best in the Spanish and eastern styles of riding which were brought to the New World by Cortes in 1519.

In recent years there has been a growth of practical interest in Western riding in England, concentrated mainly in the New Forest, with some shows staging Western riding classes, which justifies the inclusion of it in this book.

The tack used in Western riding is a good deal more simple than that for normal Eastern and European riding. The centre piece is the saddle, which although modified in the course of the centuries is basically the direct descendant of the saddle of the later Middle Ages in Europe, when the steel-encased rider was kept in position by a high pommel and cantle and rode with a straight leg. The present-day saddle embodies these features and requires that kind of riding, the seat tending to be located more to the rear end of the horse, above the perpendicular vertebrae (Deering Davis, *The American Cow Pony*). The rider does not invariably sit so straight-legged as his predecessors, but on the whole tends to do so.

The saddle tree is of hardwood with high cantle and pommel, covered with a double thickness of rawhide. Firmly fixed to the pommel is the horn, made of steel covered with leather, over which the rope (*lariat, reata*) is tied or dallied (looped round several times) when stopping and holding a roped animal. The pommel and horn combined have a height of up to thirteen inches, and the cantle is up to four inches. The saddle is lined with sheep's wool, and placed on the horse's back over a saddle blanket. Fitting the saddle to different sizes of horse is accomplished by using more blankets. The saddle is kept in place by the cinch (girth), usually made of soft mohair cords woven together. There are no buckles; on the side of the saddle are cinch rings (rigging, single, centre or double), to which are attached long soft straps (*latigo*), which go through the cinch ring and are wound several times to brace it tight. For security a double rig with two cinches is often used. The cinch has to be strong and secure because in a working outfit it had to take the strain of the rider and saddle weight – 200 lb. or so – and of several hundred pounds of live and protesting beef at the end of the lariat.

The stirrup leathers are wide, with broad sweat flaps (*fender sudadero*), and are attached to the tree. The stirrups are large and heavy, usually made of curved oak, metal bound, the footplates leather covered. There are various local variations, the box type (tapaderos) being general in South America. The object of them all is to give protection to the foot when in the saddle and to give quick release in the event of a fall. Cowboy boots always have high heels to avoid any entanglement. The weight of a saddle can vary from thirty-five to sixty pounds, depending on the amount of metal used in decorating it, which is sometimes considerable and quite a work of art. This substantial weight is distributed by its wide skirts over some eight square feet of the horse's back, instead of being concentrated into the two or three square feet of an English hunting or show jumping saddle, which makes it much less of a burden for the horse than one might expect. Add to that the fact that the shape of the saddle helps to keep the rider still, and one can understand the tremendous distances covered by stock horses without undue damage.

The bridle or headstall is as simple as can be, headpiece, cheekpieces, brow band, throat latch, and sometimes dispensing with both the last named, the headstall kept on by passing one ear through a loop in it, hence called the slit-ear headstall. The Argentine *gauchos* used nosebands, and they are occasionally put on for decoration. The material is rawhide or latigo (soft oil-tanned pliable leather). A halter is sometimes worn over the bridle for tethering purposes. The reins are always single, attached to the curb bit and separated, so that, if dropped, they hang loose to the ground from the bit, all cow ponies being trained to remain halted when they are in that position.

The bit is a straightforward curb, of varying degrees of severity, usually with curved and sometimes highly ornamented cheekpieces. The most severe bit is the spade bit, whose mouthpiece has a broad metal plate to press against the roof of the mouth and down on the tongue, unless the horse holds his head correctly. In theory these bits are not severe because with the Western method of loose rein riding and neck reining the full power of the bit is only exerted very rarely and quickly; in practice not every Western cowboy was a heaven-sent horseman, but could straphang with the best of them.

The training bridle for the Western horse is the hackamore, a bitless bridle, whose name, deriving from the Spanish *jaquima* (pronounced 'ha-kee-mah'), and ultimately from the Arabic *hakma* reveals its ancient lineage. It consists of a head and cheekpieces combined in one strap, attached to a noseband (bosal). This is the operative part of the equipment. It is made of about eight strings of braided rawhide wound round a core of twisted rawhide, steel cable, or braided rope, the former being the most flexible yet giving solidity. It has a thickening in front where it contacts the nasal bone (nose button), and two side grooves to take the cheek and head strap. The ends are joined at the rear in a heavy heel knot, which keeps them in position away from the jaw. The side pieces of the bosal are called shanks.

With the hackamore goes a long rope, called the mecate, made of horse hair or mohair, about twenty-two feet long, half an inch thick, and usually made in two colours, black and white, red and white, sorrel or brown and white. At one end is a smart-looking tassel (*la mota*), which hangs down just in front of the heel knot, adding a decorative touch to the equipment. The other end is wrapped round one of the shanks, then up over the pony's neck and withers and back again to the heel knot to form a rein, knotted in various ways; the remaining twelve or fourteen feet of the mecate acts as a lead rope, coiled up and attached to the saddle strings in the case of a trained pony or retained by the rider if it is unbroken.

The bosal has a threefold action: 1. On the nose and nostrils, by pressure of the nose button, on the nasal bone or on the nostrils if it is fixed lower down; 2. On the jaw by the pressure of the shanks; 3. Behind the jaw, when the heel knot is pulled upwards.

Allowing for difference in equipment, the modern method of training cow ponies is based on the same principles as those already described in Part III: a very far cry from the old rough and ready method of back and buck. Ponies are not left to grow up more or less wild, but handled and gentled from foalhood. They are bitted with a snaffle, but the later training is done with the bosal before the curb bit is introduced.

Ponies are saddled and backed at a year, then left until they are two and half to three years old before beginning ridden schooling. The work is progressive, the preliminary work at the walk doing circles, turns and figures of eight; then at the trot; and finally they are asked to break into a canter from a walk. Nearly all the work is on a loose rein, and the pony is taught to be bridlewise from the beginning. The aim is to make the pony obedient to the simple aids, quiet and good mannered, yet able to look after itself. The rider uses his body weight constantly to guide the horse and prepare him for turns and changes of direction.

Spins or turn-about (pirouettes in fact) are taught by going round in a very small circle, giving aids with spurs and whip, or with two whips, one in each hand, which is preferable (Deering Davis, *The American Cow Pony*, Van Nostrand, 1962), gradually reducing the size of the circle until it is a definite swing round on the haunches. Modern western thought favours the taking of a great deal more time over training than used to be the case; Deering Davis, already quoted, declares that 'if possible a horse should have no gruelling or exhaustive work until he is at least six or even better seven'. Many trainers, led by John Richard Young (*The Schooling of the Western Horse*) have gone over to complete European methods.

Riding a Western horse in a Western saddle, although the basic teaching of riding on the lunge and the securing of a deep, independent seat is an aid to it, requires an almost complete reversal of method. To begin with, anything like a forward seat is impossible in a Western saddle; and the particular Western activities – cattle roping, rodeo riding, cattle cutting – can only be efficiently carried out from a backward position.

On getting into the saddle for the first time, the rider lets his legs hang loose, and the stirrup leather is adjusted until the footplate hangs one or two inches below the ankle bone, which is the general all round length of stirrup leather for normal work. In competition work it may be advisable to raise them by a hole or two. The rider then sits towards the cantle of the saddle, so that his seat bones are over that part of the horse's back where the upper bony processes of the vertebrae are perpendicular – approximately the eleventh or twelfth vertebra. The knees are slightly bent, heels down, upper part of the body erect, reins held loosely in the left hand (usually), which is carried high, several inches above the horn of the saddle.

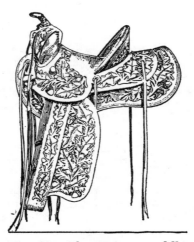

Fig. 16.   The Western saddle

From this basic well-balanced position the rider can adapt himself to circumstances, standing up in his stirrups for roping, leaning back for crash halting, and shifting his weight for turning. The rear-placed burden is not so far back as to affect the loins, and in any case the wider bearing surface of the saddle reduces the concentration of weight. This position also gives the forehand and fore limbs greater freedom of manoeuvre, which is what the range pony needs for its work, especially, for example, the cutting horse, who does nearly all his work on the forehand. It will be observed that the muscles of his forearms are highly developed and immensely powerful. From his backward position the rider can conform much more easily to the rapid movements of the cutting horse facing the reluctant steer; or he has a slightly, better chance of staying in the saddle of a professional rodeo buckjumper. An adaptation of this backward seat can be seen in the riding of gaited horses, the rider sitting almost straight-legged and almost on the loins.

Cutting horses are trained in various ways: some start straight away practising on calves as three-year-olds, so that they learn balance and obedience to the rein and body aids as they go; other trainers start with basic training, neck reining, halting and lateral work, before introducing them to their living opponent.

Cattle cutting is unique both as a labour as well as a sport in that the horse, once the preliminary training is over and the rider's controls are established, truly takes charge and works on his own. It seems true, too, that the top-class cutting horse is born not made, witness the case of Sandhill Charlie, World Champion Cutting Horse gelding in 1961, 1962, 1963, who won his first competition as a novice against the professional best. A very 'ornery critter' indeed ('Sandhill Charlie', by Loy Ann Trent in *Light Horse*, January, 1971), he was only amenable to any form of discipline when in front of a cow. Heredity must come into it as well, because the same family lines appear in the pedigrees of many famous cutting horses.

The object of cutting (called cattle draughting in Australia, where it is also a big money sport) is to prevent a selected young heifer from getting back to the rest of the herd, and it will use every sort of trick to rejoin its fellows. The technique of the horse is to keep head to head, anticipating its movements at every step. This requires real power and gymnastic agility and what amounts to an uncanny sense of anticipation. The control exercised by the rider is minimal; his main task is to stay with the pony in all its movements, difficult at all times but impossible in any but a western saddle.

The Western rider's clothes are too well known to warrant long comment. The basic garment is the denim jeans, which first entered the cowboy's life in the 1860s. The point to make is that for comfort and efficiency it must be close but easy fitting, not the skintight tubes that are fashionable in youthful circles today. It should be loose enough to be worn over riding boots, to prevent dust and foreign bodies getting into the boot tops, and to preserve the leather from sweat and other damage. In the open plains of the Argentine the gauchos wear baggy cotton pantaloons (*bombacha*), which are both cool and comfortable. The ends are fastened at the bottom so that they cannot ride up.

Chaps (Mexican *chaparreras*) are over-trousers, made of leather or sheepskin, worn to protect the rider's legs from thorn and cactus. The spreading batwing variety which is universal today was first seen in western America about 1895. Between the wars they were much favoured wear in some polo circles on both sides of the Atlantic.

Western riding boots are rather like Wellington boots, but with high heels, which were introduced in 1875. The object of the high heel is of course to prevent the foot being caught in the stirrup. The heights of boots vary from about ten inches to sixteen inches, and there is a medium size of twelve inches. Nowadays heels are lower than they used to be. The spur has been the badge of knighthood as well as a goad, and the Western variety is no exception, being usually highly chased and decorated.

25 Driving

Driving has been an amateur sport for about 200 years. Horse-drawn transport has been with us since the dawn of history and racing in chariots is practically coeval with it, but the development of driving for pleasure and of the art of handling the ribbons started when the macadamised roads made it possible. At first it was all coach driving, then smaller, more easily handled vehicles were invented, the phaeton, the cabriolet, and so on.

Among the Holy Week parade of some eighteen hundred carriages taken by Society to the Longchamp convent in the Bois de Boulogne on March 26th, 1785, called by one Sophie la Roche who recorded the event 'The pilgrimage of the coaches,' were 'white cabriolets of some of the younger gentlemen . . . bordered with painted garlands of roses and forget-me-nots'. (László Tarr – *The History of the Carriage*.) A. B. Shone, the historian of amateur driving, mentions a satirical eighteenth century print (c. 1760) which shows a 'New Fashioned Phaeton', a high perch vehicle of adjustable height with its elegant driver making love to a lady on a first floor balcony (*A Century and a Half of Amateur Driving*). *Vive le sport!* In India in the early part of this century, up to the 'twenties, many young officers used to pursue their love affairs in the cosy cabriolet with its conveniently screening hood.

This is not the place for a history of the carriage and its uses, fascinating though it may be. It is enough to point out that sporting driving grew up with the commercial use of the horsed vehicle at the end of the eighteenth century, and in fact survived it. The present flourishing existence of the British Driving Society, which was founded in 1957, is evidence enough of that.

It is a highly traditional sport too. The vehicles themselves are survivals from the past, lovingly resurrected and restored to their pristine elegance, and the accoutrements of the equipage and the principles and conventions of driving have not changed at all.

The details are of the harness as follows:

Single. The basis of traction is the collar, the most generally used being the neck collar, which is a roughly pear-shaped loop of thickly padded leather, which lies at the base of the horse's neck in front of the wither and approximately at the same angle as the shoulder. It is reinforced by the hames (from the Dutch *haam*), curved pieces of metal which in grooves on both arms of the collar, linked at the top and bottom by straps; both can be of leather, but the bottom connection is sometimes a chain. About a third of the way up the hame from the bottom is a metal projection with a ring at the end of it, to which is attached the trace on either side of the collar. A third of the way down from the top on either side is a *terret* (Old French *toret*), a swivel ring through which the reins pass.

The collar is put over the horse's head upside down, then turned so that the narrow end is at the top. To be correctly fitted the collar must lie flat on the horse's shoulders, with enough room for the fingers to be inserted between it and the sides of the neck, and for the flat of the hand at the lowest part. It should not be loose enough to rock about, a fruitful cause of galling.

An alternative equipment for light traction where there are no hills is the breast collar, which is a broad padded leather strap fitted across the horse's chest, and held in place by a narrower strap over the neck in front of the withers. The breast strap should be fitted above the point of the shoulder.

The pad is a small saddle set where a normal saddle goes, whose function is to support the pair of terrets through which the reins pass finally before going on to the hands of the driver, and to hold the shaft tugs on either side through which go the shafts. If there are no shafts, it holds the loops for the traces. The pad should be well padded to keep it off the spine, and part of the equipment is of course the girth.

The backband is part of the saddle pad, the strap to which the tug is attached, and going over it with holes for adjusting the height of the tug. It joins the bellyband, which goes outside the traces and over the girth, never tighter than it and usually slightly looser, depending usually on the type of tugs used, particularly Tilbury tugs used on a four-wheeled cart.

From the pad the backstrap runs along the spine to the crupper, a padded loop through which the tail goes. Its function is to prevent the saddle pad working forward. The backstrap also passes through the loin straps which hold up the breeching. The breeching is a broad strap which should hang horizontally between twelve and fourteen inches below the root of the dock,

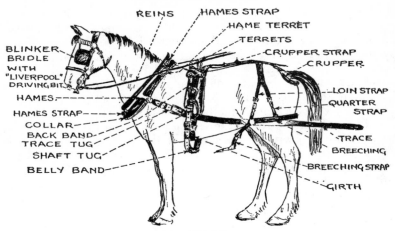

REINS HAMES STRAP
HAME TERRET
TERRETS
BLINKER CRUPPER STRAP
BRIDLE CRUPPER
WITH
"LIVERPOOL"
DRIVING BIT
HAMES LOIN STRAP
QUARTER
HAMES STRAP STRAP
COLLAR
BACK BAND
TRACE TUG TRACE
SHAFT TUG BREECHING
BELLY BAND BREECHING STRAP
GIRTH

Fig. 17. 'Gig' harness

adjusted to avoid interference with the movement of the horse's quarters. It should be so attached to the shafts that the horse, when brought back against it, should be about a foot away from the cart itself. With light vehicles, unless there is a lot of hill work, the breeching is not essential. The most widely used form of breeching is attached to slots on the shafts between the stops and the front of the cart. Another type is attached to the tugs. When used in double harness, which is not often, the breeching is supported by a strap over the loins and attached to the trace buckles.

The crupper should be tight enough to keep the pad in position, loose enough to allow a hand's breadth between it and the croup. All hairs of the tail should be passed through the tailpiece, which must be kept soft and clean. The traces should be long enough to keep the horse as close as possible to the trace hooks on the vehicle, while leaving the quarters well clear of the footboard or dashboard.

The bridle consists of headpiece, browband, cheekpieces, noseband and throat latch. On the headpiece are attachments for the bearing rein, and blinkers are attached to the cheekpieces. The ordinary canons of bridle fitting apply. The most general driving bit is the Liverpool, which is a kind of Pelham, with four different actions: plain snaffle action on the ring, slight curb action when the rein is attached to the centre bar within the ring, and more severe curb action in the two slots on the cheekpiece below the ring. The mouthpiece can vary as in other bits (pages 63–71). A useful alternative bit to the Liverpool is a double ring broken snaffle, especially for horses with light mouths or of excitable temperaments. A further decorative addition to the browband is a face drop. Made of fancy leather, it is attached to the centre of the headpiece and goes underneath the browband.

The bearing rein has suffered in reputation from frequent abuse, but it is a useful, indeed necessary, counter to a horse that bores and keeps its head low, and commits the crime of getting behind the bit. The driver has no legs to push him forward. However, it needs careful adjusting, so that it is never too tight, and should be completely loosened going up a steep hill. The driving reins should be as soft and supple as possible, thin, and not more than one inch in width, less for small hands and fingers.

Harnessing

There is a regular sequence of harnessing or putting-to. First of all, all the separate items of the assembly must be ready and handy: the harness, the horse in his loose box, the cart outside in the yard – if it is a two-wheeled vehicle, the shafts horizontal, resting on a stand; if a four-wheeler the shafts are in an upright position.

The collar goes on first. Take off the hames and give it a stretch, then, placing the wide end uppermost, manoeuvre it carefully over the horse's head, avoiding any rough contact with the eyes and ears. Replace the hames, buckle up the hame strap, then turn the collar into its right position, the narrow part on top, rotating it with the lie of the mane. The collar should lie closely, but not tightly, along the shoulder; there should be two fingers' space on either side, and a whole hand space between the bottom of the collar and the horse's windpipe. The traces are attached to the harness and looped up loosely in a figure of eight.

Next, the saddle pad with backstrap, crupper, and breeching. Place the pad lightly on the back, behind the correct position, so that the crupper can be fixed; then lift the pad up, move it in front of the normal position and slide it backwards in the same way as putting on a riding saddle. If a martingale or breastplate is to be used, do not forget to pass the girth through their loops before hitching it up. Now take the reins and thread them through the terrets, the buckle end on the near side. Make a loop of them and let them hang over on the off side.

The bridle is then put on with the same care as in the case of a riding bridle. As well as the throat latch, the noseband is usually unbuckled, and of course the curb chain hangs loose. The cheekpieces are parallel with the horse's cheek bones and behind them. The noseband is two fingers' breadth below the cheek bones and should have two fingers' play between the front of it and the nose. The blinkers are fixed to cover the eyes and block any backward view, and are kept in position by two straps to the headpiece. The throat latch is adjusted to four fingers' breadth. The horse's forelock can either go under the browband or over it. Once the bridle and bit are fitted, the reins are then buckled on to the latter, and the horse is ready to be led outside to be put-to.

The vision of a horse with blinkers is very much restricted, so lead him out very carefully and quietly and see that he does not knock himself against the sides of the doors, which should be thrown back wide open.

Place the horse in front of the cart, and run the traces between the belly band and the girth in the case of a two-wheeler, and outside the belly band if Tilbury tugs are used for a four-wheeler, and cross them over the horse's back.

Two-wheeler: Draw the cart, shafts raised high, up to the horse, until the points of the shafts when lowered will be level with the tugs. Pass the shafts through the tugs and forward until the tugs come up against the stops on the shafts. This should allow sufficient clearance between the hindquarters and the front of the cart. The balance of the cart depends on the height of the shafts, which is regulated by the lowering or raising of the tugs. The shafts should be neither too low, nor too high.

Hook the traces on to the cart as soon as the shafts are in position, and make adjustments to the breeching, and kicking strap is there is one. Then buckle up the belly band sufficient to leave a little play of the shafts.

Four-wheeler: The shafts being already raised, the horse is backed into position in front of and underneath them, and they are then lowered on to the tugs. Tilbury tugs, if used, have metal half-loops covered with leather, on which the shafts rest, being secured by straps and buckles round them. The putting-to follows the same procedure as for a two-wheeler, except that, with a Tilbury tug, the belly band is pulled tight.

Personal equipment

It is *de rigueur* to wear gloves, carry a whip, and sport an apron. Dog skin, or as an alternative doe skin, is the recommended material for driving gloves, but woollen or string gloves are better for wet weather, and should always be carried in reserve. The important thing is that the gloves are fairly thick and roomy with nearly an inch to spare in the lengths of the fingers when new.

The whip, usually made of holly wood, sometimes of cherry, is light and well balanced, with a thong, leather pointed, about half the length of the stick. When not in use, do not stand it on its butt in a corner, hand it up on a round or semi-circular block.

A box cloth rug with a V-shaped slit at the top makes a comfortable covering for the knees of driver and passenger, if there is one, in cold or wet weather, and is definitely part of the uniform of the driving 'fancy'. It also protects the clothes. In summer a light linen rug can be used.

Neatness and smartness of the whole turn-out is a must. Harness must be polished, soft and of good quality, all straps well in their keepers, and none of them too long, no strap hanging loose underneath the belly, all brass work shining, and don't forget the carriage lamps. The driver's own dress should be in keeping with the equipage.

Double harness

For driving in pairs, side by side, the individual harness is the same, except for the coupling reins. Each rein is divided at the end into two ends: the draught rein on the outside, which goes direct from the driver's hands to the outside ring of the bit, and the coupling rein, which bifurcates from the main rein, passes through the terrets and is attached to the inside bit ring of the opposite horse. This enables both horses of a pair to be turned to the right or left by the action of a single rein; and it is most important that the coupling reins should be most accurately fitted, so that when in movement the horses' shoulders are level and their heads and necks straight to the front and parallel. The first requirement for correct fitting is that the traces are absolutely level, making a basis for the adjustment of the coupling reins according to the lengths of the horses' necks, which, of course, for pair driving should be as near as possible equal. Reins and traces need to have ample holes for adjustment.

There being a centre pole instead of shafts, the cart is placed in position in the yard, and the horses, already harnessed up as before, are moved alongside, brought forward from the rear, and the coupling pole chains, to keep the horses together, are linked from a ring at the head of the pole to rings on the collars. Then the traces are attached to the roller bolts, the outside one first in each case, then the inside one as quickly as possible.

Other methods of yoking the horses are with the curricle bar, and the Cape cart harness.

'The classical two-wheeled pair horse carriage is the curricle. At its most perfect it belongs to mid-nineteenth century London and, because of the exacting requirements of perfectly matched and stylish horses, with an expensive carriage and harness, it was the perfect medium for a display of ostentation without violating the conventional good taste.' (Tom Ryder, *On the Box Seat.*) The curricle bear is a strong steel bar, with a centre slit, and removable stop nuts at each end. It requires a special strong saddle pad on each horse, with roller bolts securely built in. The bar is inserted between the rollers and rest on them, and so is able to move freely from side to side in conformity with the movements of the two horses. The rollers can be raised or lowered an inch or two according to the heights of the horses. Through the centre slit goes a strong leather brace to the centre pole, to which it is fastened over a spring, to give it resilience. To prevent the pole from tipping up when the back of the cart is overweighted, a strap can be passed under the two horses from trace buckle to trace buckle and over the centre pole.

I cannot think of the curricle and the curricle bar without recalling that delightful poem of Rudyard Kipling's, in which the impecunious young soldier, driving by tonga to Simla on leave, meditates on his chances with the girl he met last season to the beat of the jingling tonga (curricle) bar – with satisfactory results: 'Try your luck – you can't do better!' twanged the loosened tonga-bar. ('As the Bell Clinks,' *Departmental Ditties.*)

Cape Cart: The feature of this is a yoke, a bar of wood, sometimes called a *bugle*, which supports the centre pole, being slung in front of it on a strap from the withers. At the centre of the bar is a leather loop which goes over the pole, giving plenty of play both longitudinal and lateral. Only breast collars are used with this harness, which became popular in England in the 'eighties of the last century.

Tandem: The most spectacular two-horse equipage is undoubtedly the tandem – and driving it is certainly a sporting pastime, not entirely without risk. The harness for the wheeler, the horse nearest to the cart, is the same as for a single turn-out. The driver holds two pairs of reins, the leader's reins passing through the terrets on the wheeler's pad and through rings at the top of his bridle. The leader's traces can either be attached to those of the wheeler or to a swingletree (usually a double one) between the wheeler and the leader.

Four-in-hand

This is basically two sets of double harness but with modifications. The wheel pads have centre terrets for the lead reins, and there are rings for the leaders' reins on either side of the wheelers' bridles. The leaders' traces are attached to swingletrees, and they should not be too long.

The four-in-hand is the ultimate in driving in the British Isles, and a coach and four is still the most impressive vehicular turn-out on the public highway. To sit on the box of a smart coach, or even a brake, with the reins in your hands, a lively-stepping well-matched team below you, is surely the greatest thrill that the horse can offer. You are literally on top of the world, and the power that surges up the reins into your hands, and heart, is awesome. It is something no one can experience at second-hand. Unfortunately very few can enjoy this privilege.

Driving

The art of driving, even a single horse, simple though it may look, is by no means easy. After all that has been said about hand and leg, collection, light contact and so on, the driver finds himself sitting on a box seat instead of a saddle, his sole contact with the horse being the bit in its mouth about twelve feet away, his only other aids the whip in his hand and the tongue in his head. The clicking of the tongue encourages the horse to go on; 'Steady!' does in fact help to restrain an excited horse; and the human voice does seem to have an influence on the horse. Another point about driving a horse-drawn vehicle is that, like a car, it must be done on a public highway; so, like the 'L' driver, the learner whip should learn his driving from a teacher sitting beside him and showing him exactly what to do with the reins, so that he learns correct handling from the start. There are a few riding schools who also teach driving, and the British Driving Society can also help in this respect.

However, the theory of the art can be learnt from books, of which there are several good modern ones, and practice in handling the reins can be gained in private by rigging up a simple system of pulleys over which the reins, with a weight at one end, go to the hands of the learner sitting in a chair a few feet away. For a single horse practice there will be two reins, each with a four to five pound weight on one end, which will give the hands about the same tension as a trotting horse. For four-in-hand practice there will of course be four reins, each with a four pound weight. The reins are always held in the left hand, and the whip should be in the right as part of the practice. One point of this home-training method is that the left hand and wrist get accustomed to the weight placed upon them when driving; in the case of a four-in-hand it is quite considerable after a while.

Let us now suppose that the single horse is harnessed to its gig, chaise, dog cart, or whatever, and you are about to take charge.

First, make an inspection to make sure that the harness is correctly fitted and buckled up. Then, standing on the off side of the trap, take the reins in the right hand, near rein under the forefinger, off rein under the third finger. Get into the trap, sit down and adjust the rug or apron round the knees, and transfer the reins to the left hand. The whip will be in its socket on the off side wing of the trap.

Position of the reins: Near rein over the forefinger, the off rein between the second and third fingers. The ends of the rein are gripped by the third and fourth fingers. The thumb points to the right, and is not pressed down on to the reins. The forefinger points to the right rear, so that the rein is close to the knuckle, and the horse can be guided by the movement of the hand: turning it upwards to go to the left, downwards to go to the right.

Elbows should be close to the sides, the points almost touching the hips. Sit straight upright, leaning neither forward nor back, feet and knees close together. Wrists should be rounded and flexible; left forearm horizontal; back of the hand to the front and three to four inches from the body.

The whip, which should always be carried when driving, is held in the right hand, grasped lightly at the point of balance with the thumb and last three fingers, the forefinger being extended. The hand is placed at the same level as the left hand an inch or two from it, in front of the body, and the whip is pointing half left across the body. The purpose of the free forefinger is to enable it to grasp the reins whenever necessary to shorten reins or make a loop, without altering the position of the whip.

The whip is there to help control the horse, to give it the office to go forward, to keep it up to the bit, and to support the turning aids of the reins, especially when driving a pair. Even with a single horse great dexterity, and also tact, are needed in handling the whip. As a driving aid, the lash should be applied lightly between the collar and the pad, drawn across from either direction in a sort of stroking movement, the wrist and forearm being kept straight. Except for punishment or as a last resort the whip should not be applied to the flanks or quarters. Greater skill and accuracy is required to wield the whip on a tandem or four-in-hand, so that the lash hits the right place on the leader, and the beginner should not attempt it without a good deal of private practice, aiming at a mark.

Now you are on the road. To start the horse feel the mouth lightly and speak or click to him, or, if necessary touch him lightly with the whip. Yield the hand slightly the moment he starts. The reins should always be held in the left hand, and the off rein should never be taken in the right hand (except in hackney competition driving, and in certain types of driving competition, and if the horse bolts); and at all times the reins should be of equal length. Watch with the fore and aft rig-four-in-hand, tandem, etc., that the leaders' reins do not act before the wheelers. It happened to me once when learning to drive a four-in-hand, and I should have known better. The leaders halted, the wheelers and the vehicle ploughed on, and in a second there was a writhing plunging mass of horses on the ground, hooves flying, and an ominous crack. With great skill the grooms separated the horses and all was calm; by some sort of miracle not a single horse was even scratched. The only casualty was the centre pole of the brake.

With a hard-mouthed horse, or one that begins to take a hold, the left hand can be reinforced by placing the right hand on the reins in front of it, off rein under the little finger and near rein between the second and third fingers. To shorten reins, take the reins in the right hand above the left at the required distance, and slide the left hand up to the right; or it can be done the other way, the right hand taking the reins behind the left hand, which is then moved up as required.

When turning a corner, give the correct signal with the whip in good time. The usual method now is to point the whip to the right or left; or else use ordinary hand signals, temporarily shifting the whip into the left hand. It used to be customary for the driver not to take off his hat to anybody except royalty, but to salute with the whip, held horizontally level with the chin. Nowadays the whip is raised vertically until the hand is level with the brim of the hat; in America drivers transfer the whip to the left hand and raise their hats to ladies.

Continuing with turning, after giving the signal, check the pace, and keep to the near side of the road when turning to the right, and *vice versa.* Slight bends or curves of the road can be dealt with by turning the hand as explained above (page 267). For proper turns, use the right hand to shorten the required rein temporarily by placing it in front of the left hand with the appropriate rein under the little finger, pulling it steadily and without jerking. Release the rein directly the turn is completed. Drive generally with a steady firm contact, not letting the reins sag, and keep a steady consistent pace.

Looping the rein is the process of shortening one rein for a turn and leaving it still in the left hand, so that the right is free to use the whip or to check the horse, especially a green one or one that is inclined to rush or cut its corners. The normal procedure in driving a tandem or four-in-hand or similar equipage of horses in series not side by side, it is not necessary in single horse driving, except for practice.

To take up a loop, shorten the required rein as already described for a turn; then pull extra length back over the forefinger and hold it in place with the left thumb; the right hand is then free for any necessary action.

Always give yourself plenty of time to make any change of direction or before stopping; watch the traffic well ahead, learn to anticipate developments. The slow-moving vehicle will appear to leave you time in hand, but the rapid motor traffic will not. Avoid changes of pace unless they are absolutely necessary. Never jab the horse in the mouth except as a definite punishment.

Go slowly downhill, setting the pace from the top and continuing at a steady even pace. Passengers should shift their weight rearwards if they can. Four-wheel vehicles usually have brakes, but there is no need to apply them until you see the pole chains (of a pair) taking the strain. Release the moment they begin to slacken at the bottom of the hill. The brake, incidentally, should always be on when the vehicle is stationary, and while you are mounting. Up hill, give the horse his head, and get the weight forward if possible. On really steep or long hills get out and walk.

To take off on return to the stable. 1. The groom goes to the horse's head. 2. Put the whip in its socket, and descend from the cart holding the reins in the right hand. 3. Coil the spare end of the reins through the off side terret, so that they lie in front of the shaft stop. 4. Unbuckle the breeching from the slots on the shafts. 5. Unbuckle the bellyband, unhook the traces, knotting them again in a loose figure of eight. 6. Lead the horse forward from between the shafts.

Four-in-hand: The same procedure for harnessing, as with a pair, is followed with the necessary modifications. The coachman will have two pairs of reins to hold, one for the wheelers, one for the leaders, both in the left hand. The positions are: near lead rein over the first finger; off lead rein under the first finger; near wheel rein between the first and second fingers; off wheel rein between the second and third fingers. The ends of the rein are secured by the second, third and fourth fingers, and alterations to the positions of the reins are made with the right hand. The positions of the forefinger and thumb are the same as with a single pair of reins. The technique of turning is to make the leaders make as wide a circle as possible, starting well away from the direction of the turn, i.e. for a right turn, the leaders will keep well to the left and start turning when they are nearly level with the left-hand kerb of the new road. While the leaders are turned in the direction required, the wheelers are first turned towards the opposite direction, so that they do not follow the leaders too closely or quickly and make too sharp a lock.

Begin making a point or loop of the required rein, see that the leaders start to make their turn; at the same time make a loop of the opposite wheel rein, to lead the wheelers away slightly from the direction of the turn. The wheelers should in fact make their proper turn at about the same spot as the leaders made theirs. When turning to the left the leaders should start the movement when they are about level with the centre line of the new road, and the vehicle should move on to the left side of the road as soon as possible. When the leaders have made their turn, the lead loop is released to get them going straight and the wheel loop is reversed, so that the wheelers now follow the leaders round.

Reins are shortened in the same manner as for a single pair, but particular care must be taken not to shorten the lead reins without the wheel reins. The effect is to stop the leaders while the wheelers go on, which can cause the chaos described above.

The whip should be held loosely between the thumb and fingers of the right hand, the thong folded so that a fairly long loop hangs down from a point just below the junction of the stick and the binding of the quill, the remainder of the lash wound round the stick, the end secured by the hand.

To fold the whip, let the thong hang down in a large loop, the end held by the hand; then with a flick of the wrist make the point describe a backward figure of eight, so that the loop folds itself round the whip. Easier said than done! The expert coachman makes it look simple, but only long practice with a teacher can bring the required perfection and consistency in this operation.

The correct handling of the whip is the basis of good coach driving, and no one should attempt to take a four-in-hand on to the roads until he has completely mastered the art of whip control. The general principle is that the wheelers should only be hit in front of the pad, to avoid the chance of them kicking, and the leaders on their hocks under the bars, below the line of the trace.

To hit the wheelers draw the double thong across from the left with a stiff wrist and forearm; or the off wheeler can be hit from the right-hand side. The leaders' reins should not be too long when hitting the wheelers, so that both leaders and wheelers will string off together.

To hit the off leader, move the top of the whip over to the off side of the coach, swing the stick round to shake open the thong, holding the end down with the left thumb. Then swing the stick back to the right until the wrist is about level with the right shoulder, releasing the end of the lash. Swing the stick round to the front with a quick action of the wrist aiming a little in front of the spot you want to hit. To hit the near leader, make the swing of the stick so that the lash flies round on the near side, well above the heads of the passengers, then drop the point slightly so that the lash will swing towards the near leader, while missing the near wheeler's head.

To recover the thong after hitting the off leader, swing the stick up and to the right, then lay it across the left arm pointing to the left, when the thong can be caught by the right hand or under the arm, and then secured by the left thumb, by moving the right hand across to the left. Then it can be transferred to the right hand under the right thumb, and the whip can be folded again. After hitting the near leader, swing the stick to the left in a circular motion and then to the right, when the thong can be caught as before.

The best practice is to sit on the box seat of an unharnessed coach or training brake, with the centre pole in position to guide direction length, and practise swinging, folding and flighting the whip until accuracy is obtained. It is always best to have a definite mark to aim at, which can be contrived by setting poles or stools at about the position of the horse's quarters, and placing ping-pong or similar balls on them. When you can knock a ball down every time, you are doing well.

Competitive driving

The modern amateur coachman mainly drives for pleasure, but the competitive urge is strong, and of course it helps to improve driving skills. The basic competition in Britain is the 'Marathon' (six to eight miles for coaching; four to six miles for private driving), in which the competitors are first examined for condition and turn-out, go out for a country drive on the public highway, and on return the horses are again examined for condition to see how they have stood up to the test.

In 1960 a driving competition was introduced to the programme of the Royal International Horse Show at White City, and has continued at that show (now at Wembley) ever since. It took the form of a race over a set course, which included such hazards as nursemaids at zebra crossings, backing and turning, and driving through markers, and over small jumps.

On the Continent driving competitions are taken very seriously, and are held for every kind of vehicle and equipage, and can be very gruelling tests. A famous one is held at Aachen every year as part of the big equestrian show in early July. In 1970 an official international driving three-day event championship was instituted under the auspices of the F.E.I., in which the competition was divided into three phases, roughly 'dressage' or driving skill, turn-out and endurance. This has now become an annual event.

Competitive hackney driving is a close-knit professional world of its own, derived from the days of the fast-trotting Norfolk roadsters and keeping up the high-stepping tradition. The object is to present a perfectly balanced trotter, with a high knee action in front and strong active hock action behind, yet covering a lot of ground at each stride. The animals are bred to the game, assisted by special heavy shoeing and growing the hooves long; and most of great whips have been born into to it too.

It has of course a technique all its own, the basic difference between it and ordinary driving being that the reins are held in two hands separated. The light, four-wheeled show wagon has a single seat, and is mounted from the near side. The reins are taken in the left hand, the left rein over the first finger, the right between the second and third fingers, the two reins then grasped in the palm of the hand. The driver should sit leaning slightly forwards, the feet firmly braced against the foot bar. The reins are separated, one being held by each hand, the right rein under the little finger of the right hand, which also holds the whip, and a passing upwards to be secured by the palm of the hand. Both hands are held level, slightly elevated, fairly close together, wrists turned inwards, elbows at right angles to the forearms. The whip slopes forward and to the left. The strain of. keeping up the high action is very great, and usually the effort is concentrated on the few strides in front of the judges.

Training a horse to harness

Most horses that have had good basic training can be broken to harness, and horses destined for draught only should have basic training. Work with long reins is a very good preparation.

First of all accustom the horse to the harness, by putting it on carefully every day for a week or so, then leading him about in it, and then long-reining him. Progress should be careful, depending to some extent on the horse's receptivity. Temperament plays quite a big part in harness work.

Next, harness the horse to a wooden sledge, with traces long enough to have it out of kicking distance, stand on the sledge and drive the horse about, pulling the sledge behind him, holding the reins and using the whip in the same way as in a cart.

The third stage is the breaking cart, which is an ordinary fairly substantial gig, with extra long shafts, again so that the driver is out of kicking distance. Use a kicking strap then, and when the horse is put to a conventional vehicle. Go quietly at this stage, letting the horse stand still and be made much of when he is between the shafts, then leading him about, so that he gets used to the noise, weight and movement behind him. Finally drive him round the field until he goes quietly and steadily. The strongest resistance will probably come at the putting-to stage, and it should not be attempted singlehanded: the trainer at the reins, and two assistants at the shafts are necessary. Morley Knight wanted the early driving lessons to be in traffic, 'for he will go much better if he sees other things moving about, as they will distract his attention, and keep him from playing tricks on the driver'. (Capt. C. Morley Knight, *Hints on Driving*.) But that was in 1884!

No one can say how long the breaking to harness process will take, but it must be both gradual and continuous, and perfect the first stage before proceeding to the next. That seems to be the abiding lesson which we must have learnt in this book and in all our association with the horse: *festina lente!*

26 Condition and Stable Management

The foundation for all the the work and activities that have been described so far is the physical and psychological fitness of the horse. If the actual education of the young horse has been sympathetically and successfully carried out, he should be mentally prepared for anything, provided his physical training and well-being have marched along with it.

The emphasis in all the training described has been on gradualness; the word over-facing has been used in connection with jumping as something to be avoided. So it is in the physical training: at all times the work given the horse, at whatever stage he may have reached, must be well within his capacity at that time, so that he is never over-faced, but proceeds steadily from strength to strength, as it were.

It is well known that the basics of physical fitness are food, fresh air and exercise. As the horse has a delicate and complicated digestive system, it is well to start with food. I will preface this by stressing the importance of regularity and routine. Feeding and stable work should, as far as is humanly possible, conform to a rigid timetable, which should generate an atmosphere of unhurried calm about a stable, which will in its turn communicate itself to the horse and, amongst other things, aid his digestion and so the regular performance of his normal functions. Few things are so important to efficiency, equine or human, as 'inner cleanliness', as the advertisements say.

The principles of feeding should not have to be enlarged upon. The horse's basic food is grass, which man has adapted, when he requires special efforts from the horse, by converting it into 'concentrates'– oats, barley, maize, bran and other grains and pulses. In recent years this concentration has been further developed by the production of special mixtures of all these ingredients compressed into nuts and cubes.

The main constituents of these grains, or of any food for that matter, are water, nitrogenous matter (of which the muscle-building and energy-producing elements are the proteins), carbohydrates (starch and sugar, which produce energy but also fat, some horses having to watch their calories as carefully as humans), fats, woody fibre (an aid to digestion by promoting mastication) and ash. Over the years, and proved by results, oats has been universally recognised as the best balanced food for horses, containing in good measure the muscle-building and energy-producing constituents.

However, at the present time, some veterinary surgeons think that an excessive amount of oats in a diet can become indigestible and cause liver trouble. Attacks of azoturia which keep cropping up in event horses suggests that too much oats and not enough steady exercise could be the cause. It is well known, also, that oats can have a very intoxicating effect on small ponies, especially of the Mountain and Moorland breeds. Racehorses are fed exclusively on oats, but any harmful effects are absorbed in the sustained exercise they undergo and the great speeds which they have to produce on the racecourse. For ordinary horses, a top limit of fifteen pounds should normally be enough, the balance of food being made up with barley, bran, and possibly flaked maize.

The claims of barley as a primary food for horses are being more and more considered. In many parts of the East it is a staple diet; Indian cavalry horses had it combined with gram, and did very well on it. It is considered also to contain more calcium producing elements, and therefore particularly good for young, growing horses. Specimen diets for various ages of a horse, such as the one whose education we have been describing, based on a balance of grains, will be given below.

A horse must have bulk, of course, which in natural conditions he takes in by constant, unremitting grazing. Under domesticated conditions he must have hay, in quantities of anything up to fifteen pounds, and the quality of this must be a serious consideration. All hay fed must have been cut in early June, when the protein value present in the leaf and seed is at its greatest. In July and August the seed has fallen from the grass, and hay made from it, being deficient in protein, has insufficient food value. Needless to say, all the hay and corn given must be of the best quality.

The concentrated nuts and cubes already mentioned are excellent, and certainly do save labour, but they must not be regarded as a substitute for the hay bulk, which must always be added, or for the best natural grains, if they can be obtained. If nuts are used, they must be introduced gradually, like everything to do with horses, a few at a time mixed with ordinary feeds and gradually increasing. Some horses thrive on them, others do not take to them, and some again get tired of them.

Being a concentrated mixture of the best quality ingredients, they can be too rich for some horses. Feeding is always a matter of trial and error and constant watchfulness.

Nowadays, when for various reasons the natural products of the soil are lacking in mineral and vital content, the disappearance of hedgerows and the nutritious herbs (weeds) that grew there is a great loss to good horse husbandry, the use of additives becomes necessary to put back the vital elements which have been taken out. There are any number of tonics and pepping-up preparations and pills on the market now (even the horse is becoming a pill-addict), and they probably all have some value. Every owner will have his pet energiser which he swears by, but only the horse can give the final verdict.

One valuable additive, however, which must be mentioned is seaweed, which contains many necessary minerals and trace elements, which used to be found in the herbs and plants of the aforesaid hedgerows. It can be obtained in powdered form, and should be a regular addition to any diet, fed in small quantities, say a teaspoonful mixed with every feed. Cod liver oil is another important extra, but see always that the full vitamin content is declared on the label.

Two pressing problems which face horse owners and trainers in the 'seventies are possible shortages of hay, the increasing cost of it and the pollution of nearly all the food that the horse eats, with already unpleasant consequences to young-stock, the cause of which is perhaps not clearly recognised.

In the winter of 1970–71 there was an alarming shortage of hay in some parts of the country, and substitutes were being looked for. One such is sugar beet pulp, which, if fully soaked, can be fed in quite large quantities to a working horse, supplemented with wheat and oat straw, desperate remedies, perhaps, but effective.

The problem of pollution from weed killers, widespread spraying of chemicals, whose total effects are not sufficiently known, as well as industrial pollution, is more serious than many people realise. What was called the 'unprecedented number of deformed foals' in 1970 could well be due to the poisons now present in our fields. Owners of the foals are reluctant to advertise these 'failures' in their breeding, but such reticence does no service to the cause that they must have at heart, the well-being and health of their horses and ponies. And all this toxic avalanche must surely have a bad effect on the performance of the modern sporting horse.

A long-term answer to this problem, as well as to the shortage of hay, is the hydroponic process of growing grass. The word is derived from the Greek *hydor* (water) and *ponos* (toil), and it means 'water-working' by contrast with geoponics (agriculture). It is a method of raising plants without any soil, nourished instead by solutions of water and fertiliser. The first great advantages of the system are its high yield, quality and quick production: 'from the start of the operation to maturity of forage takes only six days'. (J. Sholto Douglas, 'Stable-grown Fresh Forage', *Light Horse*, February, 1969.) The other present asset is that the grower knows where his forage is coming from and can guarantee the quality. The food value is high. Tests on oats conducted by the Wisconsin Research Foundation, U.S.A., have shown that the hydroponically grown green grass had a protein content of 21.99 per cent compared with 15 per cent for dry grain. On a long-term basis the cost can be less than that of conventionally grown forage. This may be a plan for the future, but a future that is not all that distant.

The routine of feeding needs little elaboration: 'little and often' is the watchword, though it need not be overdone, like a cavalry squadron commander I once knew, who tried to take it literally and took handfuls of corn to his own horses every half hour. The optimum number of feeds a day is four, the normal three, and, if circumstances compel it, it can be less. Harry Faudel-Phillips once described how, when running his famous riding school at Temple House, Theobalds Park, near Waltham Cross, Hertfordshire, between the wars, he fed his school horses once a day, a big meal after the morning's work, followed by two hours of absolute quiet for digestion. This last was, of course, the key to it: the horse must have time to digest his meal, whatever its size may be.

The feeding plan, whatever it is, should be based on a six-day working week, with one rest day. This should be a completely corn-free day, on which the horse should have bran mashes to which linseed jelly or Epsom salt, or both, has been added, and some green food like lucerne as well as the normal hay.

One more point about the digestion concerns the teeth. Digestion depends on proper mastication of the food, and efficient mastication depends on the teeth. So watch the teeth at all times. Because of the side-to-side movement of the molars during mastication, the outer edges of the upper and inner edges of the lower row become very pointed, and these rough edges can cause minute wounds to the tongue and cheek muscles, this problem can be prevented by inspection directly any abnormality of digestion is suspected and by the timely application of the file, very lightly up and down each edge; a few movements only will suffice. A great deal of subsequent trouble can be avoided by this small but timely attention to detail.

Feeding plans

The actual amounts of each ingredient at each stage of the horse's growth or training must be as carefully worked out as possible, so as to provide at all times a sufficient and balanced diet. There are no scientific rules for this that I know of; it is a matter of trial and error, based on the size and type of the horse, the work it is expected to do, its present condition, and its own individual metabolism and temperament and the owner's personal knowledge and understanding of the horse.

In the old horse-drawn days, a London omnibus horse pulled one and a half tons for twelve and a half miles at a speed of five m.p.h. six days a week. (W. J. Gordon, *The Horse World of London, 1893.*) He did this on a total daily food weight of thirty-one pounds made up of maize, sixteen pounds; oats, one and a half pounds; peas, one and a half pounds; hay chop, twelve pounds, these figures being supplied by Captain M. H. Hayes in *Stable Management and Exercise.* And the horse lasted for five years.

Few horses do work of the intensity these days, and the bulk of the food given is oats and/or barley. The following specimen diet sheets are offered with the proviso that they are *specimen* only, to be regarded as a starting point, to be modified up or down according to individual experience and the reactions of the horse.

Horses. 15–16 h.h. and over. *Weanlings.* Barley (bruised) 2–4 lb. Bran ½ lb. Hay *ad lib.*

Yearlings. Barley (bruised) 3–5 lb. Bran 1 lb. Hay *ad lib.* Increase the barley up to 4–6 lb. by the time he is three years old.

3–4 years (lunge and preliminary training). Oats 2–3 lb. Barley 3–4 lb. Bran 1–2 lb. Hay 10–12 lb.

At maturity, in full work (up to 4 hours daily). *15 h.h.* Oats 8–10 lb., barley 2 lb., bran 2 lb., hay 12 lb.

15–16 h.h. Oats 10 lb., barley 4 lb., bran 2 lb., hay 12–14 lb.

Over EP *h.h.* Oats 12–14 lb., barley 5 lb., bran 2 lb., hay 14 lb.

Additions to this food, as tonic and to give it variety and palatability would be sliced carrots, turnips, potatoes, apples, the outsides of green vegetables; and a teaspoonful of seaweed powder to each feed. To make further variety, flaked maize can be substituted for part of the barley; or the oats can be decreased and the barley increased. This is for the working week of six days.

Ponies of mixed breed need a good deal less corn. Assuming that they are exercised every day for at least two hours, the following could be a starting diet.

14.2 h.h. Oats 2–3 lb., barley 3 lb., bran 1 lb., hay 12lb.

13.2 h.h. Oats 2 lb., barley 3 lb., bran 1 lb., hay 10 lb.

12.2 h.h. Oats and barley 2 lb., bran 1 lb., hay 10 lb.

For ponies working only at week-ends a daily feed should be maintained in preference to stuffing them at the week-end, the above amounts being reduced by half, and the bran to half a pound. The hay ration remains the same. Give the same extras as to the horses.

Mountain and moorland ponies, unless doing fast work; hunting, gymkhanas, or long hours trekking or showing, are best kept to hay and coarse grazing. The lush green pastures of civilisation are bad for them, making them over-fat and causing laminitis, and probably aggravating the allergy affliction of sweet itch.

If the work is likely to be heavy, then they might be given two to three pounds barley, half a pound bran, ten pounds hay daily.

Concentrates in the form of nuts and cubes have the paramount advantage for modern owner-grooms of being easy to feed. The main problem is what is the equivalent. The makers vary in their proportions. The average ratio is about one-third more cubes than the corn ration, e.g. eight pounds of cubes for six pounds of oats. In spite of claims to include the bulk element, hay should always be added. Police horses, doing a daily stint of three and a half hours, carrying sixteen stone and covering twelve miles, receive fifteen pounds of Spiller cubes with seven pounds of hay.

Feeds should always be measured in exact weights, not scoops or handfuls, which can never be guaranteed to furnish the same amount each day. The easiest thing is to have the different ingredients weighed in distributing receptacles such as mugs or small jugs, so that you have a known weight to work from.

Watering

Everyone knows that a horse should be watered before feeding, but there is more to it than that, especially when the time comes to prepare a horse for great exertions.

Cold water given directly on return from hard work when the horse is hot can very easily upset its sensitive bowel. If, as is usually the case, only tap water is available, it should not be given straight from the tap before it has had a chance to become aerated and to rise in temperature. If possible, the water should be drawn about an hour before return from work; or draw it before going out to work.

There is one variation to this treatment. As it is essential for the horse to stale directly on his return to the stable from work, he can be encouraged to do so by being given a mouthful or two of cold water, which will produce minor shock and cause most horses to stale at once. Then the chilled water can be given. If it has been a strenuous day during special training, powdered glucose should be added to the water. You will probably have to break him gently to the glucose; give an occasional small quantity of it in the water to get him used to the taste but not enough to make it a habit; then, after hard galloping exercise put half to three-quarters of a pound into the drink. The glucose so administered acts as a pre-digested food which will quickly restore normal tone to the nervous system upset by the strenuous exercise and the horse will turn out much better for it the next day.

Grooming

It should not be necessary to emphasise the contribution of good grooming to the fitness of a stable-kept horse. (On the other hand, a horse kept out of doors with his full coat, should be groomed very sparingly, so that the essential oils which help to keep him warm are retained.) Apart from the polishing of the coat and toning up of the muscles, grooming keeps the pores of the skin free of scurf and sebaceous material, so that toxins which come into the body with the normal food can be excreted by the sweat. Most of these toxic substances are eliminated from the body by the bowel and kidneys, but the skin is also an important outlet. So grooming must always be vigorous, a good three-quarters of an hour's work, accompanied by the hard wisping which increases the circulation, thereby providing more muscle-building material.

Psychology

The horse, it cannot be said too often, is not a machine, and he is as capable of being bored as his master or mistress. A working horse is kept in a stable, and, if he does three hours work a day, he spends the remaining twenty-one hours in prison, as it were, often in semi-darkness, and virtually alone. No wonder crib-biting, weaving, wind-sucking, stable kicking are endemic vices of the present-day domesticated horse.

He should be visited as often as possible outside feeding hours; taken for a short walk on a leading rein in the afternoon for half an hour to nibble at some grass and to see a little life. It would be better still, if his box could open out on to a small paddock which he could use at will. The physical value of mental interest and contentment cannot be measured, but it must surely be very high indeed.

Bringing up from grass

It is traditional at the end of an active season, whether it be hunting in the winter or eventing in the summer, to turn horses out to grass and give them a rest. Horses are supposed to enjoy it, but it is debatable whether they do or not, or whether it is really good for them. It is of course a great saving of forage, and also of time for an owner-groom. In the old days many grooms in private hunting stables used to be sacked in the summer.

However that may be, the practice still goes on, and the problem arises of getting horses fit again after a good many weeks of grass diet. Fix the date of the first event, whatever it may be, when the horse must be in peak condition for it; ten weeks before that will be D-day for starting training.

Normally the change from the grass to the hard diet is effected with the aid of a powerful purgative, but the best way is to prepare the horse gradually for the change by giving him two pounds of corn – half oats, half barley – daily for six weeks before the training period is to begin. The last four days of this preparation time give him bran mashes, and he will be able to come on to a progressively increased corn ration without any digestive upset or filled legs, and without the administering of the old-fashioned physic dose. This procedure can also be followed if the horse has been out of work for any period during his training. After the mashes, with the corn can be given a tablespoonful of the following powder once daily for ten days: bicarbonate of soda four ounces, potassium nitrate one ounce, powdered glucose eight ounces, Epsom salt one pound.

The normal method of training is a progressive increase of work and food on a week by week basis. The first week should be one hour's walking exercise, with, say, four pounds of oats, one pound of bran, twelve pounds of hay; working up thereafter to the full ration and anything up to three hours' exercise including schooling sessions, which must continue throughout the conditioning period.

The importance of the feet and legs can never be stressed too much, and a good deal of tendon trouble and bruised soles can be avoided if a careful hardening up process is carried out from the beginning. Plenty of road work is essential, progressively increasing periods of long walks with occasional trotting over country roads. After three weeks of this part of the work can be over any uneven surfaces and stony ground that can be found, including walking and trotting over plough, that 'ridge and furrow' work which has already been mentioned above. During this time progressively include up and down hill work, first at the walk for two or three weeks, then at the trot, and finally, at the end of the training, at the canter.

After about five weeks, spells of steady cantering (twelve to fifteen m.p.h.) for varying distances can be introduced two days a week. Start with half-mile stints, working up to a mile and a mile and a half, increasing in the latter half of the programme to three or four two-mile canters. In the last four weeks the speed can be stepped up three-quarter speed gallops at distances varying from half a mile to one and a half miles, and occasional two and three-furlong full-speed sprints. Always have a rest period after each cantering or galloping stint, which will usually be steady walking. This 'rest' period will be long at first, perhaps ten minutes, but will be reduced as the horse gets fitter and is able to recover more quickly from the energy lost through the greater exertion. There should be a certain rhythm of this 'expenditure and income' as it were.

All this is based on the traditional, empirical methods of training, which have stood the test of time; especially successful when they conform most closely to the physical reactions of the horse's body to the expenditure of energy. During great physical exertion the body uses up oxygen faster than the heart and lungs can replace it in the blood stream and carry away the excess of carbonic acid produced by the oxidisation of glucose in the muscles. The accumulation of this acid is what causes fatigue, making the muscles ache and lose their elasticity.

Given time, the heart and lungs can return to normal functioning so that the lost oxygen is replaced. The quicker the rate of recovery the fitter the horse, or man, will be. So, modern scientific training of human athletes is based on a series of strenuous efforts followed by intervals of rest, known as Interval Training. It is not so easy to apply this system to horses as it is to men and women, and perhaps not so necessary, but it has been done, and, for those who are interested, is fully described by G. N. Jackson in *Effective Horsemanship*. However, there is no reason why you should not apply this method in a rough and ready way, which will probably teach you something else about your horse that you do not know already.

The method is based on the observations of the temperature, pulse and respiration rates of the horse before, during and after work (T.P.R.). The first thing to do is to get accustomed to taking these observations on your horse at different phases of his progress, so that you know fairly accurately what is the norm for him.

Then apply it in a simple way to the training programme. For example, the normal pulse of the horse in the stable at rest is forty to the minute; after a period of trot and canter a check will show that it has increased to sixty-five; and after a short sharp gallop it may rise to 100. Halt, and check the time it takes for the pulse to recover to sixty-five, possibly about two minutes. If it takes longer, it would be as well to look into the horse's condition more closely and modify the training programme. The same procedure applies to temperature and respiration; they both rise with exertion, and they should come down with relaxation from it at approximately the same rate.

In 1964–65, the Russians carried out extensive tests of the effect of exercise on horses, and came up with, among other things, the following figures:

Clinical characteristics of sports horses of different training.

Training	Pulse	Respiration	Temperature (C.)
	At rest		
Well-trained horses	22–34	6–12	37.2–38.3
Undertrained horses	34–44	10–18	37.5–38.3
After proportioned load			
Well-trained horses	54–76	22–32	38.5–39.0
Undertrained horses	66–88	32–48	38.8–39.4
After competitions			
Well-trained horses	108–122	72–104	40.0–41.5
Undertrained horses	96–142	62–100	40.5–42.0

The conclusions drawn from this are that fit horses are more relaxed at rest than undertrained ones; have less variation of T.P.R. after moderate work; and do better under the maximum load, than the others. It was also found that the recovery period was shorter for the well-trained horse. (From a Report to the F.E.I., by Professor I. Bobylev, Moscow Veterinary

Academy, *F.E.I. Bulletin* No. 60, and *Light Horse,* November, 1965.)

All this is still in its infancy, though it is a signpost to the future; and the well-tried traditional methods still pay off, but not invariably. In every race or endurance test of any kind there are some horses who show peak condition at the right moment, and they reach the top; but there are as many whose training has not worked out just right, and they fail.

The horseman, who has got thus far in the making of a top-class riding horse, should seek more and more precise methods of ensuring that his companion and servant is as fit as possible in every way for whatever task he may be set. That, after all, is horsemanship.

Postscript

It is as hard to end a book as to begin it. The last sentence is as elusive as the opening one. Well, they have been found, and the book is ended. About what lies between them I have nothing to add but the hope that the persevering learner and the practical rider, the serious student of horsemanship in all its aspects, to whom it is offered, will find something of interest, something of help, and something of encouragement; and that the principal beneficiary of all the work that is entailed in becoming a horseman will be the horse. Without him there would be no books to be written – or read! Terrible thought! So let us echo one of the last thoughts of John Board, a great horselover, before he died in 1965: 'Thank God for the horse!'

It now only remains to thank all those who have helped in some way to the making of this book. First of all riders, great and not so great, whose performances in their varied fields have both inspired and instructed. Next, the great equestrian writers, whether orthodox or innovators, who have set out the principles and illuminated the practice of horsemanship for the benefit of lesser mortals. You cannot read too much about horsemanship; there is always something more to be learned. I have quoted from them in the text, and they and others are listed below.

More specifically, I would like to thank—

Captain Edy Goldman, of the Cheshire Equestrian Centre, for reading and checking Part II of the book, 'The Training of the Rider'.

Colonel W. S. Codrington, T.D., M.R.C.V.S., for advising on Chapters 3, 4 and 5, on the Anatomy, Conformation and Mind of the Horse.

Mrs Julia Wynmalen for patiently coping with Part III, 'The Training of the Horse', and making most pertinent and valuable suggestions.

Sanders and Biddy Watney for checking Chapter 25 on 'Driving'.

Needless to say that none of these is to be held responsible for any errors or omissions.

Postscript

The F.E.I. for permission to quote from their *Rules for Dressage Competitions.*

Bill Luscombe, of Pelham Books, for egging me on to tackle this book and for finding it worth publishing, and incidentally for the great encouragement that he gives to the horse world and to equestrian sports by producing so many excellent and varied books on the subject.

Finally, I thank my wife for reading not only the manuscript but the proofs as well with such care, and for invariably asking the right questions.

And of course I thank the reader for having got this far – if he has.

C. E. G. Hope

Earls Court
June 1970 – January 1971.

Appendix

RIDING SIDE-SADDLE

The general practice of side-saddle riding for women has had a comparatively brief reign in history: say a matter of 250 years, roughly, from about the middle of the sixteenth century to the end of World War I. There was an earlier transition period, and the beginnings of the side-saddle appeared in the fourteenth century, but, generally, women, when they did ride in the Middle Ages, rode astride.

Now the girls have come back to it in modern times, and although side-saddle riding has had a revival in the show ring in children's classes, and the traditional ladies' hunter and ladies' hack classes are still with us, and a few women still ride that way out hunting, one cannot avoid the feeling that it is an elegant irrelevance.

This does not mean that women who ride side-saddle are in any way inferior to their cross-saddle sisters; far from it. They can, or could, achieve equally high standards in many fields. In hunting certainly; they have show-jumped with success in the past; the side-saddle *haute ecole* riding of Elizabeth Schumann in the circus is quite a spectacle.

There is great security in a side-saddle, but to ride in it correctly requires as much skill and practice as, if not more than, ordinary riding astride. The horse, too, has to be specially trained to be responsive to the whip aids on the off side.

The saddle in its modern form is larger and heavier than an astride one, weighing about twenty pounds, but, like the Western saddle, the weight is well distributed. It has a long and broad and flat seat, with no raised cantle. In front are two pommels or leg rests, one sloping upwards, which takes the right leg, the other sloping downwards, giving support to the left knee. The saddle needs to be very securely fixed to the horse, and there is usually an auxiliary strap from the rear of the seat to girth to hold it steady.

The same principles of riding apply, especially the necessity for a completely upright and square position. Balance is a problem, because with two legs on one side the extra load on the near side has to be compensated for.

Mounting

The most popular way is the leg-up, which is not the same as for a cross-saddle (page 79). The difference is that the rider stands facing the horse's head, reins and whip in the right hand, which with the left is holding the pommel. Then she bends her left knee and the assistant takes the left foot in both hands. When ready, the lady moves first, springing off the left foot and straightening her leg; the assistant must hold his hands firm and not lift her until her leg is fully straight. As she is lifted she turns her body to the left, and sits sideways on the saddle behind the pommels. Finally, she swings her right leg over the pommels and turns her body to the right to get into the correct position facing the horse's head. Then she will adjust the skirt, and the assistant will fix the elastic loop at the bottom of the latter under the left foot, to hold it in position; the left foot will be put into the stirrup and the leather adjusted if necessary.

To mount independently, 1. Stand with your back to the horse's head, reins and whip in the left hand, which holds the lower pommel. 2. Take the stirrup with the right hand. 3. Move the left hand to the top pommel and hold the leaping-head with the right. 4. Spring up until the left leg is straight, knee against the saddle, back still to the horse's head. 5. Move the right hand to the back of the saddle, to help the lifting, at the same time press the left knee well into the saddle to lever the foot and stirrup away from the saddle, so that it becomes the pivot of the turn round to the left to face the horse's head. 6. Shift the right hand back to the pommel, move the right leg over the saddle and sit astride. 7. Then, using the pommels as a brace, bring the right leg up over the withers into position. 8. Adjust the elastic loop of the skirt over the right foot.

Dismount

Take off the elastic, pull back the skirt, transfer reins and whip to the right hand, bring the right leg over the pommels, so that you are sitting sideways on the saddle. Take the left foot out of the stirrup and slide down to the ground, taking care not to catch any part of the habit on the pommels.

The seat

On a side-saddle the seat must be upright, with the body

absolutely square to the front. The right knee is crooked over the upper pommel, so that the thigh is as near horizontal as possible, and the lower leg hangs vertically downwards. The left thigh should normally not be pressed against the leaping-head, but leave a clearance of the thickness of the hand. The left leg hangs down in the normal way, foot pressed home in the stirrup and facing slightly outwards, heel down. When extra grip is required, the left thigh is pressed up against the leaping-head.

The rider's hips and shoulders should be in one plane, and at right angles to the line of movement. The posterior should be firmly placed on the saddle, so that the rider's spine is exactly above the backbone of the horse. This relationship must be maintained at all times, whatever the position of the body when in movement, i.e. leaning forwards or back, or rising in the stirrup for the posting trot. The whip is held in the right hand, and it takes the place of the missing right leg aid.

The right thigh, which takes most of the rider's weight, crosses the horse's backbone just behind the withers, and the concentration of the load should be felt at that point. At the same time, in order to counteract the increased burden of the legs on the near side, the rider must work to place more weight on the right seat bone, than on the left; an even balance there will result in an imbalance to the left.

The chief faults of a side-saddle position are: leaning to the right, with the right shoulder dropped and the whole body off the vertical; trying to make an adjustment by leaning the hips to the right but keeping the shoulders straight, which causes an uncomfortable distortion; weight too much on the near side; sitting with the seat bones and buttocks too much to the right; leaning forward with rounded shoulder, or crouching. In fact, any deviation from the position described above is a fault.

To maintain the correct position entails considerable muscular effort and concentration, and it should be practised regularly on a dummy horse, or anyway a very quiet horse. There is no reason why side-saddle riding on the lunge should not be carried out, not without the stirrup, however, for the purchase given by that is an essential part of the position.

Circling and turning conform to the same principles as for riding astride: the body should always remain in the same plane as the horse. The forward seat can be maintained over fences as well as with a cross-saddle; the body moving forward at the approach and the seat leaving the saddle during the jump. The work here is done by the right thigh pressing down on the pommel and the left thigh against the leaping-head, and the brace of the left foot in the stirrup.

The aids act in the same way with hands, leg (spur) and whip, as with hands and legs. A horse that has been trained at the outset to understand the whip aids should be able to come back to the whip aid without difficulty, with careful progressive training, so that he gets used to the unusual combination of leg on one side and whip on the other. The left leg should always have a spur, as extreme leg pressure is not attainable in the same way as when riding astride.

When riding side-saddle the rider's dress and equipment should always be impeccable. Riding habits are simple affairs now of jackets and aprons, but they must still look like skirts when the rider is in the saddle, the right leg covered up by it. The hair should be done up tidily with a bun or hair net, and a top-hat and veil, or bowler hat, with or without veil; whatever hat is worn should be on straight or tilted slightly forward, *never* back.

Whether irrelevant or not, side-saddle riding still remains the peak of equestrian elegance.

Bibliography

There being over 20,000 titles in the English language alone of books dealing with the horse and horsemanship, there is no attempt here even to begin to be exhaustive. It would be pointless anyway, because no one would ever read them. Here, however, is a list of the books that have been quoted or mentioned in the text and some of others of general or special interest which are still available.

THE PRECURSORS
The Training of Horses, by Kikkuli (14th century B.C.)
Hippike, by Xenophon 350 B.C. English translation by M. H. Morgan (J. A. Allen, 1962)
Hippiatrica Sive Marescalia, by Laurentius Rusius, c. 1350
Ordini di Cavalcare, by Federico Grisone, c. 1550
Le Cavalerie François, by Salomon de la Broue, 1594
Instruction du Roi, by Antoine de Pluvinel, 1623
A General System of Horsemanship, by the Duke of Newcastle, 1657
Ecole de Cavalerie, by François Robichon de la Guérinière, 1733
A Method of Breaking Horses and Teaching Soldiers to Ride, by the Earl of Pembroke, 1762
Trait ésur la Cavalerie, by Count Drummond de Melfort, 1776

MODERN
Accoutrements of the Riding Horse, by Cecil G. Trew, Seeley Service, 1951
American Cow Pony, The, by Deering Davis, Van Nostrand, 1962
Ancient Greek Horsemanship, by J. K. Anderson, University of California Press, 1960
Arab Horse in Europe, The, by Erika Schiele, Harrap, 1970
As To Polo, by William Cameron Forbes, Manila Polo Club, 1919

Be a Better Horseman, by Vladimir Littauer, Hurst & Blackett, 1953

Bit by Bit, by Diana Tuke, W. H. Allen, 1965

Breaking and Riding, by James Fillis, Hurst and Blackett, 1902. Reprinted by J. A. Allen, 1969

Caprilli Papers, The, Ed. by Piero Santini from notes of Federico Caprilli, first published in *Light Horse* in 1951, in serial form, and in book form by J. A. Allen, 1967

Cavalletti, by Reiner Klimke tr. Daphne Machin Goodall, J. A. Allen, 1969

Cavalry Horsemanship, by Lieut-Col. Blacque Belair, tr. J. Swire, Vinton, 1919

Century and a Half of Amateur Driving, A, by A. B. Shone, J. A. Allen, 1955

Colours and Markings of Horses, Royal College of Veterinary Surgeons, London, 1954

Commonsense Horsemanship, by Vladimir Littauer, Macmillan, 1954

Das Gymnasium des Pferdes, by Gustav Steinbrecht, 1885

Defense of the Forward Seat, The, by Vladimir Littauer and S. Kournakoff

Dressage, by Henry Wynmalen, *Country Life*, 1953

Dressage Riding, by Richard L. Wätjen, tr. Dr V. Saloschin, J. A. Allen, 1958

Driving and Harness, by Colonel R. S. Timmis, D.S.O., J. A. Allen, 1965

Driving Book, The, by Maj. H. Faudel-Phillips, 1943, J. A. Allen, 1965

Effective Horsemanship, by G. N. Jackson, David Rendel Ltd, 1967

Equitation, by Henry Wynmalen, *Country Life*, 1938

F.E.I. Rules, Brussels, 1967

Forward Impulse, The, by Piero Santini, *Country Life*, 1937

Fundamentals of Private Driving, by Sally Walrond, British Driving Society, 1969

Fundamentals of Riding, by Gregor de Romaszkan, tr. M. A. Stoneridge, Pelham Books, 1965

Give Your Horse a Chance, by Colonel A. L. d'Endrody, J. A. Allen, 1959

Harmony in Horsemanship, by Colonel J. A. Talbot-Ponsonby D.S.O., *Country Life*, 1964

High Steppers, The, by Tom Ryder, J. A. Allen, 1961

Hints on Driving, by Capt. C. Morley Knight, first published 1884, reprinted by J. A. Allen, 1969

Bibliography

History of Horsemanship, A, by Charles Chenevix Trench, Longmans, 1970

History of the Carriage, The, by László Tarr, Vision Press, 1969

Horse and Rider in Equilibrium, by Gregor de Romaszkan, tr. M. A. Stoneridge, Pelham Books, 1967

Horse and the Furrow, The, by Ewart Evans, Faber & Faber, 1960

Horse Breeding and Stud Management, by Henry Wynmalen, *Country Life,* 1950

Horsemanship, by Waldemar Zeunig, tr. Leonard Mins, Doubleday, U.S.A. 1956, Robert Hale, G.B., 1958

Horsemanship for Jockeys, by John Hislop, *The British Racehorse,* 1970

Horseman's Progress, by Vladimir Littauer, Van Nostrand, 1962

Horse Psychology, by Moira Williams, Methuen, 1956

Horse World of London, 1893, The, by W. J. Gordon, Religious Tract, Society, 1933/J. A. Allen, 1971

Horses in Action, by R. H. Smythe, *Country Life,* 1963

Introduction to Polo, An, by Marco, *Country Life,* 1931/1950

Kingdom of the Horse, The, by Hans-Heinrich Isenbart and Emil Martin Buhrer, Collins, 1970

Know Your Horse, by Lieut.-Col. W. S. Codrington, T.D., M.R.C.V.S., J. A. Allen, 1963

Learn to Ride, by Lieut.-Col. C. E. G. Hope, Pelham Books, 1965

Le Gymnase du Cheval, by Gustav Steinbrecht, published in Germany, 1885, French tr. Comdt. Dupont, Epiac, 1963

Manual of Horsemastership, etc., War Office, 1937

Medieval Technology and Social Change, by Lynn White Jnr, Oxford University Press, 1962 (For the development and influence of the Stirrup)

Mind of the Horse, The, by R. H. Smythe, *Country Life,* 1965

Modern Horsemanship, by Paul Rodzianko, Seeley Service, 1933

Notes on Dressage, British Horse Society, 1947

Obstacle Conduit et Style, by Gudin de Vallerin, Henri Neveu, Paris, 1950

Olympic Dressage Test in Pictures, The, by Gregor de Romaszkan, Pelham Books, 1968

On the Box Seat, by Tom Ryder, Horse Drawn Carriages Ltd, 1969

Piaffer and Passage, by General de Carpentry, tr. Patricia Galvin, Van Nostrand, 1961

Points of the Horse, The, by Capt. M. H. Hayes, Hurst & Blackett, 1893/Stanley Paul, 1969

Polo, by John Board, Faber & Faber, 1956

Pony Owner's Encyclopaedia, The, by C. E. G. Hope, Pelham Books, 1965

Psychologie du Cheval, by Maurice Hontang, Payot, Paris, 1954

Riding, by Benjamin Lewis, J. A. Allen, 1966

Riding and Jumping, by William Steinkraus, rev. edit. Pelham Books, 1971

Riding Instructor, The, by Piero Santini, *Country Life,* 1953

Riding Logic, by Wilhelm Müseler, tr. F. W. Schiller, Methuen, 1937

Riding Reflections, by Piero Santini, *Country Life,* 1933

Riding Technique in Pictures, by C. E. G. Hope and Charles Harris, F.I.H., F.B.H.S., Hulton Press 1956/J. A. Allen, 1968

Saddle of Queens, The, by Leida Fleitmann Bloodgood, J. A. Allen, 1959

Saddlery, by E. Hartley Edwards, *Country Life,* 1963

Saddlery and Harness Making, ed. Paul N. Hasluck, Cassell, 1904/J. A. Allen, 1962

Schooling of the Western Horse, The, by John Richard Young, University of Oklahoma Press, 1954

Side-Saddle, by Doreen Archer-Houblon, *Country Life,* 1938/1961

Souvenirs, by General L'Hottt

Spanish Riding School, The, by Col. Alois Podhajsky, Vienna, 1948

Stable Management and Exercise, by Capt. M. H. Hayes, Hurst and Blackett, 1900/1968

Stable Management for the Owner Groom, by George Wheatley, Cassell, 1966

Stitch by Stitch, by Diana Tuke, J. A. Allen, 1970 (Saddles and Saddle Making)

Such Agreeable Friends, by Bernhard Grzimek, André Deutsch, 1964 (For Horse Psychology)

Summerhays' Encyclopaedia for Horsemen, by R. S. Summerhays, Frederick Warne, 1970

Tackle Riding This Way, by Lieut.-Col. C. E. G. Hope, Stanley Paul, 1959/1969

Training Hunters, Jumpers and Hacks, by Harry D. Chamberlain, Hurst & Blackett, 1938, Van Nostrand, 1969

Training the Horse, by Lyndon Bolton, Pelham Books, 1964

Index

italic numbers refer to figs

Index

Index

MURDER MOST ROYAL

Due to illness, Jean Plaidy was unable to go to school regularly and so taught herself to read. Very early on, she developed a passion for the 'past'. After doing a shorthand and typing course, she spent a couple of years doing various jobs, including sorting gems in Hatton Garden and translating for foreigners in a City café. She began writing in earnest following marriage and now has a large number of historical novels to her name. Inspiration for her books is drawn from odd sources – a picture gallery, a line from a book, Shakespeare's inconsistencies. She lives in London, and loves music, secondhand book shops and ancient buildings. Jean Plaidy also writes under the pseudonym of Victoria Holt.

Also by Jean Plaidy in Pan Books

The Tudor Series

MURDER
MOST ROYAL
Jean Plaidy

Pan Books London and Sydney

First published 1949 by Robert Hale and Company
This edition published 1966 by Pan Books Ltd,
Cavaye Place, London SW10 9PG
12th printing 1977
Copyright Jean Plaidy 1949
ISBN 0 330 20154 9
Printed in Great Britain by
Hazell Watson & Viney Ltd, Aylesbury, Bucks

Defiled is my name, full sore
    Through cruel spite and false report,
That I may say for evermore,
    Farewell to joy, adieu comfort.

For wrongfully ye judge of me;
    Unto my fame a mortal wound,
Say what ye list, it may not be,
    Ye seek for that shall not be found.

Written by Anne Boleyn in the Tower of London

Contents

THE KING'S PLEASURE

IN THE SEWING-ROOM at Hever, Simonette bent over her work and, as she sat there, her back to the mullioned window through which streamed the hot afternoon sunshine – for it was the month of August and the sewing-room was in the front of the castle, overlooking the moat – a little girl of some seven years peeped round the door, smiled and advanced towards her. This was a very lovely little girl, tall for her age, beautifully proportioned and slender; her hair was dark, long and silky smooth, her skin warm and olive, her most arresting feature her large, long-lashed eyes. She was a precocious little girl, the most brilliant little girl it had ever been Simonette's good fortune to teach; she spoke Simonette's language almost as well as Simonette herself; she sang prettily and played most excellently those musical instruments which her father would have her taught.

Perhaps, Simonette had often thought, on first consideration it might appear that there was something altogether too perfect about this child. But no, no! There was never one less perfect than little Anne. See her stamp her foot when she wanted something really badly and was determined at all costs to get it; see her playing shuttlecock with the little Wyatt girl! She would play to win; she would have her will. Quick to anger, she was ever ready to speak her mind, reckless of punishment; she was strong-willed as a boy, adventurous as a boy, as ready to explore those dark dungeons that lay below the castle as her brother George or young Tom Wyatt. No, no one could say she was perfect; she was just herself, and of all the Boleyn children Simonette loved her best.

From whom, Simonette wondered, do these little Boleyns acquire their charm? From Sir Thomas, their father, who with the inheritance from his merchant ancestors had bought Blickling in Norfolk and Hever in Kent, as well as an aristocratic wife to go with them? But no! One could not say it came from Sir Thomas; for he was a mean man, a grasping man, a man who was determined to make a place for himself no matter at what cost to others. There was no warmth in his heart, and these young Boleyns were what Simonette would call warm little people. Reckless they might be; ambitious one could well believe they would be; but every one of them – Mary, George and Anne – were loving people; one could touch their hearts easily; they gave love, and so received it. And that, thought Simonette, is perhaps the secret of charm. Perhaps then from their lady mother? Well . . . perhaps a little. Though her lady-ship had been a very pretty woman her charm was a fragile thing compared with that of her three children. Mary, the eldest, was very pretty, but one as French as Simonette must tremble more for Mary than for George and Anne. Mary at eleven was a woman already; vivacious and shallow as a pleasant little brook that babbled incessantly because it liked people to pause and say: 'How pretty!' Unwise and lightsome, that was Mary. One trembled to think of the little baggage already installed in a foreign court where the morals – if one could believe all one heard – left much to be desired by a prim French governess. And handsome George, who had always a clever retort on his lips, and wrote amusing poetry about himself and his sisters – and doubtless rude poetry about Simonette – he had his share of the Boleyn charm. Brilliant were the two youngest; they recognized each other's brilliance and loved each other well. How often had Simonette seen them, both here at Hever and at Blickling, heads close together, whispering, sharing a secret! And their cousins, the Wyatt children, were often with them, for the Wyatts were neighbours here in Kent as they were in Norfolk. Thomas, George and Anne; they were the three friends. Margaret and Mary Wyatt with Mary Boleyn were outside that friendship; not that they cared greatly, Mary Boleyn at any rate, for she could always amuse herself planning what she would do when she was old enough to go to court.

Anne came forward now and stood before her governess,

her demure pose – hands behind her back – belying the sparkle in her lovely eyes. The pose was graceful as well as demure, for grace was as natural to Anne as breathing. She was unconsciously graceful, and this habit of standing thus had grown out of a desire to hide her hands, for on the little finger of her left one there grew the beginning of a sixth nail. It was not unsightly; it would scarcely be noticed if the glance were cursory; but she was a dainty child, and this difference in her – it could hardly be called a deformity – was most distasteful to her. Being herself, she had infused into this habit a charm which was apparent when she stood with others of her age; one thought then how awkwardly they stood, their hands hanging at their sides.

'Simonette,' she said in Simonette's native French, 'I have wonderful news! It is a letter from my father. I am to go to France.'

The sewing-room seemed suddenly unbearably quiet to Simonette; outside she heard the breeze stir the willows that dripped into the moat; the tapestry slipped from her fingers. Anne picked it up and put it on the governess's lap. Sensitive and imaginative, she knew that she had broken the news too rashly; she was at once contrite, and flung her arms round Simonette's brown neck.

'Simonette! Simonette! To leave you will be the one thing to spoil this news for me.'

There were real tears in her eyes, but they were for the hurt she had given Simonette, not for the inevitable parting; for she could not hide the excitement shining through her tears. Hever was dull without George and Thomas who were both away continuing their education. Simonette was a darling; Mother was a darling; but it is possible for people to be darlings and at the same time be very, very dull; and Anne could not endure dullness.

'Simonette!' she said. 'Perhaps it will be for a very short time.' She added, as though this should prove some consolation to the stricken Simonette: 'I am to go with the King's sister!'

Seven is so young! Even a precocious seven. This little

one at the court of France! Sir Thomas was indeed an ambitious man. What did he care for these tender young things who, because they were of an unusual brilliance, needed special care! This is the end, thought Simonette. Ah, well! And who am I to undertake the education of Sir Thomas Boleyn's daughter for more than the very early years of her life!

'My father has written, Simonette. . . . He said I must prepare at once . . .'

How her eyes sparkled! She who had always loved the stories of kings and queens was now to take part in one herself; a very small part, it was true, for surely the youngest attendant of the princess *must* be a very small part; Simonette did not doubt that she would play it with zest. No longer would she come to Simonette with her eager questions, no longer listen to the story of the King's romance with the Spanish princess. Simonette had told that story often enough. 'She came over to England, the poor little princess, and she married Prince Arthur and he died, and she married his brother, Prince Henry . . . King Henry.' 'Simonette, have you ever seen the King?' 'I saw him at the time of his marriage. Ah, there was a time! Big and handsome, and fair of skin, rosy like a girl, red of hair and red of beard; the handsomest prince you could find if you searched the whole world.' 'And the Spanish princess, Simonette?' Simonette would wrinkle her brows; as a good Frenchwoman she did not love the Spaniards. 'She was well enough. She sat in a litter of cloth of gold, borne by two white horses. Her hair fell almost to her feet.' Simonette added grudgingly: 'It was beautiful hair. But he was a boy prince; she was six years older.' Simonette's mouth would come close to Anne's ear: 'There are those who say it is not well that a man should marry the wife of his brother.' 'But this is not a man, Simonette. This is a king!'

Two years ago George and Thomas would sit in the window seats and talk like men about the war with France. Simonette did not speak of it; greatly she had feared that she, for the sins of her country, might be turned from the castle. And the following year there had been more war, this time with the treacherous Scots; of this Anne loved to talk, for at the battle of Flodden Field it was her grandfather the Duke of Norfolk and her two uncles, Thomas and Edmund, who had saved England for the King. The two wars were now satisfactorily concluded, but wars have reverberating consequences; they shake even the lives of those who believe themselves remote. The echoes extended from Paris and Greenwich to the quiet of a Kentish castle.

'I am to go in the train of the King's sister who is to marry the King of France, Simonette. They say he is very, very old and . . .' Anne shivered. 'I should not care to marry a very old man.'

'Nonsense!' said Simonette, rising and throwing aside her tapestry. 'If he is an old man, he is also a king. Think of that!'

Anne thought of it, her eyes glistening, her hands clasped behind her back. What a mistake it is, thought Simonette, if one is a governess, to love too well those who come within one's care.

'Come now,' she said. 'We must write a letter to your father. We must express our pleasure in this great honour.'

Anne was running towards the door in her eagerness to speed up events, to bring about more quickly the exciting journey. Then she thought sadly once more of Simonette . . . dear, good, kind, but so dull Simonette. So she halted and went back and slipped one hand into that of her governess.

* * *

In their apartments at Dover Castle the maids of honour giggled and whispered together. The youngest of them, whom they patronized shamefully – more because of her youth than because she lacked their noble lineage – listened eagerly to everything that was said.

How gorgeous they were, these young ladies, and how different in their own apartments from the sedate creatures they became when they attended state functions! Anne had thought them too lovely to be real, when she had stood with them at the formal solemnization of the royal marriage at Greenwich, where the Duke of Longueville had acted as proxy for the King of France. Then her feet had grown weary with so much standing, and her eyes had ached with the dazzle, and in spite of all the excitement she had thought longingly of Simonette's strong arms picking her up and carrying her to bed. Here in the apartment the ladies threw aside their brilliant clothes and walked about without any, discussing each other and the lords and esquires with a frankness astonishing – but at the same time very interesting – to a little girl of seven.

The King was at Dover, for he had accompanied his favourite sister to the coast; and here in the castle they had tarried a whole month, for outside the waves rose high against the cliffs, and the wind shrieked about the castle walls, rattling its windows and doors and bellowing down the great chimneys as if it mocked the plans of kings. Challengingly the wind and the waves tossed up the broken parts of ships along that coast, to show what happened to those who would ignore the sea's angry mood. There was nothing to be done but wait; and in the castle the time was whiled away with masques, balls and banquets, for the King must be amused.

Anne had had several glimpses of him – a mountain of a man with fair, glowing skin and bright hair; when he spoke, his voice, which matched his frame, bellowed forth, and his laughter shook him; his jewel-trimmed clothes were part of his dazzling personality; men went in fear of him, for his anger came sudden as his laughter; and his little mouth, ready enough to smile at a jest which pleased him, could as readily become the most cruel in the world.

Here in the apartment the ladies talked constantly of the King, of his Queen, and – to them all just now the most fascinating of the royal family group – of Mary Tudor, whom they were accompanying across the Channel to Louis of France.

'Would it not be strange,' said Lady Anne Grey, 'if my lady ran off with Suffolk!'

'Strange indeed!' answered her sister Elizabeth. 'I would

14

not care to be in her shoes, nor in my Lord Suffolk's, if she were to do that. Imagine the King's anger!'

Little Anne shivered, imagining it. She might be young, but she was old enough to sense the uneasy atmosphere that filled the castle. The waiting had been too long, and Mary Tudor – the loveliest creature, thought Anne, she had ever set eyes on – was wild as the storm that raged outside, and about as dependable as the English climate. Eighteen she was, and greatly loved by the King; she possessed the same auburn coloured hair, fair skin, blue eyes; the same zest for living. The resemblance between them was remarkable, and the King, it was said, was moved to great tenderness by her. Wilful and passionate, there were two ingredients in her nature which mixed together to make an inflammable brew; one was her ambition, which made her eager to share the throne of France; the other was her passionate love for handsome Charles Brandon; and as her moods were as inconstant as April weather, there was danger in the air. To be queen to a senile king, or duchess to a handsome duke? Mary could not make up her mind which she wanted, and with her maids she discussed her feelings with passion, fretful uncertainty and Tudor frankness.

'It is well,' she had said to little Anne, for the child's grace and precocity amused her, 'that I do not have to make up my mind myself, for I trow I should not know which way to turn.' And she would deck herself with a gift of jewels from the King of France and demand that Anne should admire her radiant beauty. 'Shall I not make a beautiful Queen of France, little Boleyn?' Then she would wipe her eyes. 'You cannot know . . . how could you, how handsome he is, my Charles! You are but a child; you know nothing of the love of men. Oh, that I had him here beside me! I swear I would force him to take me here and now, and then perhaps the old King of France would not be so eager for me, eh, Anne?' She wept and laughed alternately; a difficult mistress.

How different the castle of Dover from that of Hever! How one realized, listening to this talk, of which one understood but half, that one was a child in worldly matters. What matter if one did speak French as well as the Ladies Anne and Elizabeth Grey! What was a knowledge of French when one was in almost complete ignorance of the ways of the world? One must learn by listening.

'The King, my dear, was mightily affected by the lady in scarlet. Did you not see?'

'And who was she?'

Lady Elizabeth put her fingers to her lips and laughed cunningly.

'What of the Queen?' asked little Anne Boleyn; which set the ladies laughing.

'The Queen, my child, is an old woman. She is twenty-nine years old.'

'Twenty-nine!' cried Anne, and tried to picture herself at that great age, but she found this impossible. 'She is indeed an old woman.'

'And looks older than she is.'

'The King – he too is old,' said Anne.

'You are very young, Anne Boleyn, and you know nothing . . . nothing at all. The King is twenty-three years old, and that is a very good age for a man to be.'

'It seems a very great age,' said little Anne, and set them mocking her. She hated to be mocked, and reproved herself for not holding her tongue; she must be silent and listen; that was the way to learn. The ladies twittered together, whispering secrets which Anne must not hear. 'Hush! She is but a child! She knows nothing . . .' But after awhile they grew tired of whispering.

'They say he has long since grown tired of her . . .'

'No son yet . . . no child of the marriage!'

'I have heard it whispered that she, having been the wife of his brother . . .'

'Hush! Do you want your head off your shoulders?'

It was interesting, every minute of it. The little girl was silent, missing nothing.

As she lay in her bed, sleeping quietly, a figure bent over

her, shaking her roughly. She opened startled eyes to find Lady Elizabeth Grey bending over her.

'Wake up, Anne Boleyn! Wake up!'

Anne fought away sleep which was reluctant to leave her.

'The weather has changed,' said Lady Elizabeth, her teeth chattering with cold and excitement. 'The weather has changed; we are leaving for France at once.'

* * *

It had been comforting to know her father was with her. Her grandfather was there also – her mother's father, that was, the Duke of Norfolk – and with them sailed too her uncle, Surrey.

It was just getting light when they set off, being not quite four o'clock in the morning. The sea was calmer than Anne had seen it since her arrival at Dover. Mary was gay, fresh from the fond farewell kiss of her brother.

'I will have the little Boleyn to sit near me,' she had said. 'Her quaintness amuses me.'

The boat rocked, and Anne shivered and thought, my father is sailing with us . . . and my uncle and my grandfather. But she was glad she was with Mary Tudor and not with any of these men, for she knew them little, and what time would such important people have to bestow on a seven-year-old girl, the least important in the entire retinue!

'How would you feel, Anne,' asked Mary, 'if you were setting out to a husband you had never seen in the flesh?'

'I think I should be very frightened,' said Anne, 'but I should like to be a queen.'

'Marry and you would! You are a bright little girl, are you not? You would like to be a queen! Do you think the old man will dote on me?'

'I think he will not be able to help himself.'

Mary kissed her.

'They say the French ladies are very beautiful. We shall see. Oh, Charles, Charles, if you were only King of France! But what am I, little Anne? Nothing but a clause in a treaty, a pawn in the game which His Grace, my brother, and the French King, my husband, play together. . . . How the boat rocks!'

'The wind is rising again,' said Anne.

'My faith! You are right, and I like it not.'

Anne was frightened. Never had she known the like of this. The ship rocked and rolled as though it was out of control; the waves broke over it and crashed down on it. Anne lay below, wrapped in a cloak, fearing death and longing for it.

But when the sickness passed a little, and the sea still roared and it seemed that this inadequate craft would be overturned and all its crew and passengers sucked down to the bottom of the ocean, Anne began to cry because she now no longer wished to die. It is sad to die when one is but seven and the world is proving to be a colourful pageant in which one is destined to play a part, however insignificant. She thought longingly of the quiet of Hever, of the great avenues at Blickling, murmuring: 'I shall never see them again. My poor mother will be filled with sorrow . . . George too; my father perhaps . . . if he survives, and Mary will hear of this and cry for me. Poor Simonette will weep for me and be even more unhappy than she was when she said goodbye.' Then Anne was afraid for her wickedness. 'I lied to Simonette about the piece of tapestry. It did not hurt anyone that I should lie? But it was a lie, and I did not confess it. It was wrong to pull up the trap-door in the ballroom and show Margaret the dungeons, for Margaret was frightened; it was wrong to take her there and pretend to leave her. . . . Oh, dear, if I need not die now, I will be so good. I fear I have been very wicked and shall burn in hell.'

Death was certain; she heard voices whispering that they had lost the rest of the convoy. Oh, to be so young, to be so full of sin, and to die!

But later, when the sickness had passed completely, her spirits revived, for she was by nature adventurous. It was something to have lived through this; even when the boat was run aground in Boulogne harbour, and Anne and the

18

ladies were taken off into small waiting boats, her exhilaration persisted. The wind caught at her long black hair and flung it round her face, as though it were angry that the sea had not taken her and kept her for ever; the salt spray dashed against her cheeks. She was exhausted and weary.

But a few days later, dressed in crimson velvet, she rode in the procession, on a white palfrey, towards Abbeville. 'How crimson becomes the little Boleyn!' whispered the ladies one to another; and were faintly jealous even though she were but a child.

* * *

When Anne came to the French court, it had not yet become the most scintillating and the gayest court in Europe; which reputation it was to acquire under François. Louis, the reigning king, was noted for his meanness; he would rather be called mean, he had said, than burden his people with taxes. He indulged in few excesses; he drank in moderation; he ate in moderation; he had a quiet and unimaginative mind; there was nothing brilliant about Louis; he was the essence of mediocrity. His motto was France first and France above all. His court still retained a good deal of that austerity, so alien to the temperament of its people, which had been forced on it during the life of his late queen; and his daughters, the little crippled Claude and young Renée were like their mother. It was small wonder that the court was all eagerness to fall under the spell of gorgeous François, the heir-apparent. François traced his descent to the Duke of Orleans as did Louis, and though François was in the direct line of succession, he would only attain the throne if Louis had no son to follow him; and with his mother and sister, François impatiently and with exasperation awaited the death of the King who, in their opinion, had lived too long. Imagine their consternation at this marriage with a young girl! Their impatience turned to anger, their exasperation to fear.

Louise of Savoy, the mother of François, was a dark,

swarthy woman, energetic in her ambition for her son – her Caesar, as she called him – passionate in her devotion to his interests. They were a strange family, this mother and her son and daughter; their devotion to each other had something of a frenzy in it; they stood together, a trinity of passionate devotion. Louise consulted the stars, seeking good omens for her son; Marguerite, Duchess of Alençon, one of the most intellectual women of her day, trembled at the threat to her brother's accession to the throne; François himself, the youngest of the trio, twenty years old, swarthy of skin with his hooked nose and sensuous mouth, already a rake, taking, as it was said, his sex as he took his meals, was as devoted a member of the trinity as the other two. At fifteen years of age he had begun his amorous adventures; he was lavishly generous, of ready wit, a poet of some ability, an intellectual, and never a hypocrite. With him one love affair followed another, and he liked to see those around him indulging in similar pleasures. *'Toujours l'amour!'* cried François. 'Hands off love!' Only fools were not happy, and what happiness was there to compare with the delight of satisfied love? Only the foolish did not use this gift which the kindliest gods had bestowed on mankind. Only blockheads prided themselves on their virtue. Another name for virginity was stupidity!

Louise looked on with admiration at her Caesar; Marguerite of Alençon said of her stupid husband: 'Oh, why is he not like my brother!' And the court of France, tired of the niggardly Louis and the influence of the Queen whom they had called 'the vestal', awaited eagerly that day when François should ascend the throne.

And now the old King had married a young wife who looked as if she could bear many children; Louise of Savoy raged against the Kings of France and England. Marguerite grew pale, fearing that her beloved brother would be cheated of his inheritance. François said: 'Oh, but how she is charming, this little Mary Tudor!' and he looked with distaste on his affianced bride, the little limping Claude.

Anne Boleyn was very sorry for Claude. How sad it was to be ill-favoured, to look on while he who was to be your husband flitted from one beautiful lady to another like a gorgeous dragonfly in a garden of flowers! How important it was to be beautiful! She went on learning, by listening, her eyes wide to miss nothing.

Mary, the new French Queen, was wild as a young colt, and much more beautiful. Indiscreetly she talked to her attendants, mostly French now, for almost her entire retinue of English ladies had been sent home. The King had dismissed them; they made a fence about her, he said, and if she wanted advice, to whom should she go but to her husband? She had kept little Anne Boleyn, though. The King had turned his sallow face, on which death was already beginning to set its cold fingers, towards the little girl and shrugged his shoulders. A little girl of such tender years could not worry him. So Anne had stayed.

'He is old,' Mary murmured, 'and he is all impatience for me. Oh, it can be amusing . . . he can scarcely wait. . . .' And she went off into peals of laughter, reconstructing with actions her own coy reluctance and the King's impatience.

'Look at the little Boleyn! What long ears she has! Wait till you are grown up, my child . . . then you will not have to learn by listening when you think you are not observed. I trow those beautiful black eyes will gain for you an opportunity to experience the strange ways of men for yourself.'

And Anne asked herself: 'Will it happen so? Shall I be affianced and married?' And she was a little afraid, and then glad to be only seven, for when you are seven marriage is a long way off.

'*Monsieur mon beau-fils,* he is very handsome, is he not?' demanded Mary. And she laughed, with secrets in her eyes.

Yes, indeed, thought Anne, François was handsome. He was elegant and charming, and he quoted poetry to the ladies as he walked in the gardens of the palace. Once he met Anne herself in the gardens, and he stopped her and she was afraid; and he, besides being elegant and charming, was very clever, so that he understood her fear which, she was wise enough to see, amused him vastly. He picked her up and held her close to him, so that she could see the dark, coarse hair on his face and the bags already visible beneath his dark, flashing eyes; and she trembled for fear he should do to her that which it was whispered he would do to any who pleased him for a passing moment.

He laughed his deep and tender laugh, and as he laughed the young Queen came along the path, and François put Anne down that he might bow to the Queen.

'*Monsieur mon beau-fils . . .*' she said, laughing.

'*Madame . . . la reine . . .*'

Their eyes flashed sparks of merriment one to the other; and little Anne Boleyn, having no part in this sport that amused them so deeply, could slip away.

I am indeed fortunate to learn so much, thought Anne. She had grown a long way from that child who had played at Hever and stitched at a piece of tapestry with Simonette. She knew much; she learned to interpret the smiles of people, to understand what they meant, not so much from the words they used as from their inflection. She knew that Mary was trying to force François into a love affair with her, and that François, realizing the folly of this, was yet unable to resist it. Mary was a particularly enticing flower full of golden pollen, but around her was a great spider's web, and he hovered, longing for her, yet fearing to be caught. Louise and her daughter watched Mary for the dreaded signs of pregnancy, which for them would mean the death of hope for Caesar.

'Ah, little Boleyn,' said Mary, 'if I could but have a child! If I could come to you and say "I am *enceinte*", I would dance for joy; I would snap my fingers at that grim old Louise, I would laugh in the face of that clever Marguerite. But what is the good! That old man, what can he do for me! He tries though . . . he tries very hard . . . and so do I!'

She laughed at the thought of their efforts. There was

always laughter round Mary Tudor. All around the court those words were whispered – '*Enceinte*! Is the Queen *enceinte*? If only . . . the Queen is *enceinte*!'

Louise questioned the ladies around the Queen; she even questioned little Anne. The angry, frustrated woman buried her head in her hands and raged; she visited her astrologer; she studied her charts. 'The stars have said my son will sit on the throne of France. That old man . . . he is too old, and too cold . . .'

'He behaves like a young and hot one,' said Marguerite.

'He is a dying fire . . .'

'A dying fire has its last flicker of warmth, my mother!'

Mary loved to tease them, feigning sickness. 'I declare I cannot get up this morning. I do not know what it can be, except that I may have eaten too heartily last evening . . .' Her wicked eyes sparkling; her sensuous lips pouting.

'The Queen is sick this morning . . . she looked blooming last night. Can it be . . .?'

Mary threw off her clothes and pranced before her mirror.

'Anne, tell me, am I not fattening? Here . . . and here. Anne, I shall slap you unless you say I am!' And she would laugh hysterically and then cry a little. 'Anne Boleyn, did you never see my Lord of Suffolk? How my body yearns for that man!' Ambition was strong in Mary. 'I would be mother to a king of France, Anne. Ah, if only my beautiful *beau-fils* were King of France! Do you doubt, little Boleyn, that he would have had me with child ere this? What do I want from life? I do not know, Ann . . . . Now, if I had never known Charles . . .' And she grew soft, thinking of Charles Brandon, and the King would come and see her softness, and it would amuse her maliciously to pretend the softness was for him. The poor old King was completely infatuated by the giddy creature; he would give her presents, beautiful jewels one at a time, so that she could express her gratitude for each one. The court tittered, laughing at the old man. 'That one will have his money's worth!' It was a situation to set a French court,

23

coming faster and faster under the influence of François, rocking with laughter.

Wildly, Mary coquetted with the willing François. If she cannot get a child from the King, whispered the court, why not from François? She would not lose from such a bargain; only poor François would do that. What satisfaction could there be in seeing yourself robbed of a throne by your own offspring? Very little, for the child could not be acknowledged as his. Oh, it was very amusing, and the French were fond of those who amused them. And that it should be Mary Tudor from that gloomy island across the Channel, made it more amusing still. Ah, these English, they were unaccountable. Imagine it! An English princess to give them the best farce in history! François was cautious; François was reckless. His ardour cooled; his passion flared. There was none, he was sure, whom he could enjoy as heartily as thè saucy, hot-blooded little Tudor. There were those who felt it their duty to warn him. 'Do you not see the web stretched out to catch you?' François saw, and reluctantly gave up the chase.

On the first day of January, as Anne was coming from the Queen's apartment, she met Louise – a distraught Louise, her black hair disordered, her eyes wild.

Anne hesitated, and was roughly thrust aside.

'Out of my way, child! Have you not heard the news? The King is dead.'

Now the excitement of the court was tuned to a lower key, though it had increased rather than abated. Louise and her daughter were overjoyed at the death of the King, but their happiness in the event was overshadowed by their fear. What of the Queen's condition? They could scarcely wait to know; they trembled; they were suspicious. What did this one know? What had that one overheard? Intrigue . . . and, at the heart of it, mischievous Mary Tudor.

The period of mourning set in, and the Queen's young body was seen to broaden with the passing of the days. Louise endured agonies; François lost his gaiety. Only the Queen, demure and seductive, enjoyed herself. In her apartments Louise pored over charts; more and more men,

24

learned in the study of the stars, came to her. Is the Queen *enceinte*? She begged, she implored to be told this was not so, for how could she bear it if it were! During those days of suspense she brooded on the past; her brief married life, her widowhood; the birth of her clever Marguerite, and then that day at Cognac nearly twenty-one years ago when she had come straight from the agony of childbirth to find her Caesar in her arms. She thought of her husband, the profligate philanderer who had died when François was not quite two years old, and whom she had mourned wholeheartedly and then had given over her life to her children, superintending the education of both of them herself, delighting in their capacity for learning, their intellectual powers which surely set them apart from all others; they were both of them so worthy of greatness – a brilliant pair, her world, or at least Caesar was; and where that king of men was concerned, was not Marguerite in complete accord with her mother? He should be King of France, for he was meant to be King of France since there was never one who deserved the honour more than he, the most handsome, the most courteous, the most virile, the most learned François. And now this fear! This cheating of her beautiful son by a baggage from England! A Tudor! Who were the Tudors? They did not care to look far back into their history, one supposed!

'My Caesar *shall* be King!' determined Louise. And, unable to bear the suspense any longer, she went along to the Queen's apartments and, making many artful enquiries as to her health, she perceived that Her Majesty was not quite as large about the middle as she had been yesterday. So she – for, after all, she was Louise of Savoy, a power in France even in the days of her old enemy and rival, Anne of Brittany – shook the naughty Queen until the padding fell from the creature's clothes. And . . . oh, joy! Oh, blessed astrologers who had assured her that her son would have the throne! There was the wicked girl as straight and slender as a virgin.

So Mary left the court of France, and in Paris, secretly and in great haste, she married her Charles Brandon; and the court of France tittered indulgently until it began to laugh immoderately, for it was whispered that Brandon, not daring to tell his King of his unsanctioned marriage with the Queen of France and the sister of the King of England, had written his apologia to Wolsey, begging the great Cardinal to break the news gently to the King.

François triumphantly mounted the throne and married Claude, while Louise basked in the exquisite pleasure of ambition fulfilled; she was now Madame of the French court.

Little Anne stayed on to serve with Claude. The Duchesse d'Alençon had taken quite a fancy to the child, for her beauty and grace and for her intelligence; she was not yet eight years old, but she had much worldly wisdom; she knew that crippled Claude was submissive, ignored by her husband, and that it was the King's sister who was virtually Queen of France. Anne would see brother and sister wandering in the palace grounds, their arms about each other, talking of affairs of state; for Marguerite was outstanding in a court where intellect was given the respect it deserved, and she could advise and help her brother; or Marguerite would read her latest writing to the King, and the King would show a poem he had written; he called her his pet, his darling, *ma mignonne*. She wanted nothing but to be his slave; she had declared she would be willing to follow her brother as his washerwoman, and for him she would cast to the wind her ashes and her bones.

The shadow of Anne of Brittany was banished from the court, and the King amused himself, and the court grew truly Gallic, and gayer than any in Europe. It was elegant; it was distinctive; its gallantry was of the highest order; its wit flowed readily. It was the most scintillating of courts, the most intellectual of courts, and Marguerite of Alençon, the passionately devoted slave and sister to the King, was queen of it.

It was in this court that Anne Boleyn cast off her childishness and came to premature womanhood, and with the passing of the years and the nourishing of that

26

friendship which she enjoyed with the strange and fascinating Marguerite, she herself became one of the brightest of its brilliant lights.

* * *

Between the towns of Guisnes and Ardres was laid a brilliant pageant. A warm June sun showed the palace of Guisnes in all its glittering glory. A fairy-tale castle this, though a temporary one; and one on which many men had worked since February, to the great expense of the English people. It was meant to symbolize the power and riches of Henry of England. At its gates and windows had been set up sham men-at-arms, their faces made formidable enough to terrify those who looked too close; *they* represented the armed might of the little island across the Channel, not perhaps particularly significant in the eyes of Europe until the crafty statesman, that wily Wolsey, had got his hands on the helm of its ship of state. The hangings of cloth of gold, the gold images, the chairs decorated with pommels of gold, all the furnishings and hangings ornamented wherever possible with the crimson Tudor rose – these represented the wealth of England. The great fountain in the courtyard, from which flowed wine – claret, white wine, red wine – and over which presided the great stone Bacchus round whose head was written in Tudor gold *'Faictes bonne chere qui vouldra'* – this was to signify Tudor hospitality.

The people of England, who would never see this lavish display and who had contributed quite a large amount of money towards it, might murmur; those lords who had been commanded by their King to set out on this most opulent and most expensive expedition in history might think uneasily of return to their estates, impoverished by the need to pay for their participation in it; but the King thought of none of these things. He was going to meet his rival, Francis; he was going to prove to Francis that he was the better king, which was a matter of opinion; he was going to show himself to be a better man, which some might think doubtful; he was going to show he was a richer

27

king, which, thanks to his cautious father, was a fact; and that he was a power in Europe, of which there could no longer be a doubt. He could smile expansively at this glittering palace which he had erected as fitting to be the temporary resting place of his august self; he could smile complacently because in spite of its size it could not accommodate his entire retinue, so that all around the palace were the brightly coloured tents of his less noble followers. He could congratulate himself that Francis's lodging at Ardres was less magnificent than his; and these matters filled the King of England with a satisfaction which was immense.

In the pavilion which was the French King's lodging, Queen Claude prepared herself for her meeting with Queen Katharine. Her ladies, too, prepared themselves; and among these was one whose beauty set her aside from all others. She was now in her fourteenth year, a lovely, slender girl who wore her dark hair in silken ringlets, and on whose head was an aureole made of plaited gauze, the colour of gold. The blue of her garments was wonderfully becoming to her dark beauty; her vest was of blue velvet spattered with silver stars; her surcoat of watered silk was lined with miniver and the sleeves of the surcoat were of her own designing; they were wide and long, and hung below her hands, hiding them, for she was more sensitive about her hands than she had been at Blickling and Hever. Over this costume she wore a blue velvet cape trimmed with points, and from the end of each of these points hung little golden bells; her shoes were covered in the same blue velvet as her vest, and diamond stars twinkled on her insteps. She was one of the very fashionable ladies in the smart court of France, and even now the ladies of the court were striving to copy those long hanging sleeves, so that what had been a ruse to hide a deformity was becoming a fashion. She was the gayest of the young ladies. Who would not be gay, sought after as she was? She was quick of speech, ready of wit; in the dance she excelled all others; her voice was a delight; she played the virginals competently; she composed a little. She was worldly wise, and yet there was about her a certain youthful innocence.

François himself had cast covetous eyes upon her, but Anne was no fool. She laughed scornfully at those women who were content to hold the King's attention for a day. Marguerite was her friend, and Marguerite had imbued her with a new, advanced way of thinking, the kernel of which was equality of the sexes. 'We are equal with men,' Marguerite had said, 'when we allow ourselves to be.' And Anne determined to allow herself to be. So cleverly and with astonishing diplomacy she held off François, and he, amused and without a trace of malice, gracefully accepted defeat.

Now Anne was in her element; there was nothing she enjoyed more than a round of gaiety, and here was gaiety such as even she had never encountered before. She was proud of her English birth, and eagerly she drank in the news of English splendour. 'My lord Cardinal seemed as a king,' she heard, and there followed an account of his retinue, the gorgeousness of his apparel, the display of his wealth. 'And he is but the servant of his master! The splendour of the King of England it would be difficult to describe.' Anne saw him now and then – the great red King; he had changed a good deal since she had last seen him, at Dover. He was more corpulent, coarser; perhaps without his dazzling garments he would not be such a handsome man. His face was ruddier, his cheeks more pouchy; his voice, though, bellowed as before. What a contrast he presented with the dark and subtle François! And Anne was not the only one who guessed that these two had little love for each other in spite of the gushing outward displays of affection.

During the days that followed the meeting of the Kings, Anne danced and ate and flirted with the rest. Today the French court were guests of the English; pageants, sports, jousting, a masked ball and a banquet. Tomorrow the French court would entertain the English. Everything must be lavish; the French court must outshine the English, and then again the English must be grander still. Never mind the cost to nations groaning under taxations; never mind if the two Kings, beneath the show of jovial good fellowship, are sworn enemies! Never mind! This is the most brilliant and lavish display in history; and if it is also the most vulgar, the most recklessly stupid, what of that! The Kings must amuse themselves.

*   *   *

Mary Boleyn had come to attend Queen Katharine at Guisnes. She was eighteen then – a pretty, plumpish voluptuous creature. It was years since she had seen her young sister, and it was therefore interesting to meet her in the pavilion at Ardres. Mary had returned to England from the Continent with her reputation in shreds; and her face, her manner, her eager little body suggested that rumour had not been without some foundation. She looked what she was – a lightly loving little animal, full of desire, sensuous, ready for adventure, helpless to avert it, saying with her eyes 'This is good; why fret about tomorrow?'

Anne read these things in her sister's face, and was disturbed by them, for it hurt Anne's dignity to have to acknowledge this wanton as her sister. The Boleyns were no noble family; they were not a particularly wealthy family. Anne was half French in outlook; impulsive, by nature she was also practical. The sisters were as unlike as two sisters could be. Anne set a high price upon herself; Mary, no price at all. The French court opened one's eyes to worldly matters when one was very young; the French shrugged philosophical shoulders; *l'amour* was charming – indeed what was there more charming? But the French court taught one elegance and dignity too. And here was Mary, Anne's sister, with her dress cut too low and her bosom pressed upwards provocatively; and in her open mouth and her soft doe's eyes there was the plea of the female animal, begging to be taken. Mary was pretty; Anne was beautiful. Anne was clever, and Mary was a fool.

How she fluttered about the ladies' apartments, examining her sister's belongings, her little blue velvet brodiquins, her clothes! Those wonderful sleeves! Trust Anne to turn a disadvantage into an asset! I will have those sleeves on my new gown, thought Mary; they give an added grace to the figure – but is that because grace comes naturally to her? Mary could not but admire her. Simple Anne Boleyn looked elegant as a duchess, proud as a queen.

'I should not have known you!' cried Mary.

'Nor I you.'

Anne was avid for news of England.

'Tell me of the court of England.'

Mary grimaced. 'The Queen . . . oh, the Queen is very dull. You are indeed fortunate not to be with Queen Katharine. We must sit and stitch, and there is mass eight times a day. We kneel so much, I declare my knees are worn out with it!'

'Is the King so devoted to virtue?'

'Not as the Queen, the saints be praised! He is devoted to other matters. But for the King, I would rather be home at Hever than be at court; but where the King is there is always good sport. He is heartily sick of her, and deeply enamoured of Elizabeth Blount; there was a son born to them some little while since. The King is delighted . . . and furious.'

'Delighted with the son and furious with the Queen because it is not hers?' inquired Anne.

'That is surely the case. One daughter has the Queen to show for all those years of marriage; and when he gets a son, it is from Elizabeth Blount. The Queen is disappointed; she turns more and more to her devotions. Pity us . . . who are not so devoted and must pray with her and listen to the most mournful music that was ever made. The King is such a beautiful prince, and she such a plain princess.'

Anne thought of Claude then – submissive and uncomplaining – not a young woman enjoying being alive, but just a machine for turning out children. I would not be Claude, she thought, even for the throne of France. I would not be Katharine, ugly and unwanted Katharine of the many miscarriages. No! I would be as myself . . . or Marguerite.

31

'What news of our family?' asked Anne.

'Little but what you must surely know. Life is not unpleasant for us. I heard a sorry story, though, of our uncle, Edmund Howard, who is very, very poor and is having a family very rapidly; all he has is his house at Lambeth, and in that he breeds children to go hungry with him and his lady.'

'His reward for helping to save England at Flodden!' said Anne.

'There is talk that he would wish to go on a voyage of discovery, and so doing earn a little money for his family.'

'Is it not depressing to hear such news of members of our family!'

Mary looked askance at her sister; the haughtiness had given place to compassion; anger filled the dark eyes because of the ingratitude of a king and a country towards a hero of Flodden Field.

'You hold your head like a queen,' said Mary. 'Grand ideas have been put into your head since you have been living at the French court.'

'I would rather carry it like a queen than a harlot!' flashed Anne.

'Marry and you would! But who said you should carry it like a harlot?'

'No one says it. It is I who say I would prefer not to.'

'The Queen,' said Mary, 'is against this pageantry. She does not love the French. She remonstrated with the King; I wonder she dared, knowing his temper.'

Mary prattled lightly; she took to examining the apartment still further, testing the material of her sister's gown; she asked questions about the French court, but did not listen to the answers. It was late when she left her sister. She would be reprimanded perhaps; it would not be the first time Mary had been reprimanded for staying out late.

But for a sister! thought Mary, amused by her recollections.

*   *   *

In a corridor of the gorgeous palace at Guisnes, Mary came suddenly upon a most brilliantly clad personage, and hurrying as she was, she had almost run full tilt into him before she could pull herself up. She saw the coat of russet velvet trimmed with triangles of pearls; the buttons of the coat were diamonds. Mary's eyes opened wide in dismay as confusedly she dropped onto her knee.

He paused to look at her. His small bright eyes peered out from the puffy red flesh around them.

'How now! How now!' he said, and then 'Get up!' His voice was coarse and deep, and it was that perhaps and his brusque manner of speech which had earned him the adjective 'bluff'.

The little eyes travelled hastily all over Mary Boleyn, then rested on the provocative bosom, exposed rather more than fashion demanded, on the parted lips and the soft, sweet eyes.

'I have seen you at Greenwich . . . Boleyn's girl! Is that so?'

'Yes . . . if it please Your Grace.'

'It pleases me,' he said. The girl was trembling. He liked his subjects to tremble, and if her lips were a little dumb, her eyes paid him the homage he liked best to receive from pretty subjects in quiet corridors where, for once in a while, he found himself unattended.

'You're a pretty wench,' he said.

'Your Majesty is gracious . . .'

'Ah!' he said, laughing and rumbling beneath the russet velvet. 'And ready to be more gracious still when it's a pretty wench like yourself.'

There was no delicacy about Henry; if anything he was less elegant, more coarse, during this stay in France. Was he going to ape these prancing French gallants! He thought not. He liked a girl, and a girl liked him; no finesse necessary. He put a fat hand, sparkling with rings, on her shoulder. Any reluctance Mary might have felt – but, being Mary, she would of course have felt little – melted at his touch. Her admiration for him was in her eyes; her face had the strained set look of a desire that is rising

33

and will overwhelm all else. To her he was the perfect man, because, being the King, he possessed the strongest ingredient of sexual domination – Power. He was the most powerful man in England, perhaps the most powerful in France as well. He was the most handsome prince in Christendom, or perhaps his clothes were more handsome than those worn by any others, and Mary's lust for him, as his for her, was too potent and too obvious to be veiled.

Henry said 'Why, girl . . .' And his voice slurred and faded out as he kissed her, and his hands touched the soft bosom which so clearly asked to be touched. Mary's lips clung to his flesh, and her hands clung to his russet velvet. Henry kissed her neck and her breasts, and his hands felt her thighs beneath the velvet of her gown. This attraction, instantaneous and mutual, was honey-sweet to them both. A king such as he was could take when and where he would in the ordinary course of events; but this coarse, crude man was a complex man, a man who did not fully know himself; a deeply sentimental man. He had great power, but because of this power of his which he loved to wield, he wanted constant reassurance. When a man's head can be taken off his shoulders for a whim, and when a woman's life can hang on one's word, one has to accept the uncertainty that goes with this power; one is surrounded by sycophants and those who feign love because they dare show nothing else. And in the life of a king such as Henry there could only be rare moments when he might feel himself a man first, a king second; he treasured such moments. There was that in Mary Boleyn which told him she desired him – Henry the man, divested of his diamond-spattered clothes; and that man she wanted urgently. He had seen her often enough sitting with his pious Queen, her eyes downcast, stitching away at some woman's work. He had liked her mildly; she was a pretty piece enough; he had let his eyes dwell lightly on her and thought of her, naked in bed, as he thought of them all; nothing more than that. He liked her family; Thomas was a good servant; George a bright boy; and Mary . . . well, Mary was just what he needed at this moment.

Yesterday the King of France had thrown him in a wrestling match, being more skilled than he in a game which demanded quickness of action rather than bullock strength such as his. He had smarted from the indignity. And again, while he had breakfasted, the King of France had walked unheralded into his apartment and sat awhile informally; they had laughed and joked together, and Francis had called him Brother, and something else besides. Even now while the sex call sounded insistently in his ears, it rankled sorely, for Francis had called him 'My prisoner!' It was meant to be a term of friendship, a little joke between two good friends. And so taken aback had Henry been that he had no answer ready; the more he thought of it, the more ominous it sounded; it was no remark for one king to make to another, when they both knew that under their displays of friendship they were enemies. He needed homage after that; he always got it when he wanted it; but this which Mary Boleyn offered him was different; homage to himself, not to his crown. Francis disconcerted him and he wanted to assure himself that he was as good a man as the French King. Francis shocked him; Francis had no shame; he glorified love, worshipped it shamelessly. Henry's affairs were never entirely blatant; he regarded them as sins to be confessed and forgiven; he was a pious man. He shied away from the thought of confession; one did not think of it before the act. And here was little Mary Boleyn ready to tell him that he was the perfect man as well as the perfect king. She was as pretty a girl as he would find in the two courts. French women! Prancing, tittering, elegant ladies! Not for him! Give him a good English bedfellow! And here was one ready enough. She was weak at the knees for him; her little hands fluttering for him, pretending to hold him off, while what they meant really was 'Please ... now ... no waiting.'

He bit her ear, and whispered into it: 'You like me then, sweetheart?'

She was pale with desire now. She was what he wanted.

In an excess of pleasure, the King slapped her buttocks jovially and drew her towards his privy chamber.

This was the way, the way to wash the taste of this scented French gallantry out of his mouth! There was a couch in this chamber. Here! Now! No matter the hour, no matter the place.

She opened her eyes, stared at the couch in feigned surprise, tried to simulate fear; which made him slap his thigh with mirth. They all wanted to be forced . . . every one of them. Well, let them; it was a feminine trait that didn't displease him. She murmured: 'If it please Your Grace, I am late and . . .'

'It does please Our Grace. It pleases us mightily. Come hither to me, little Mary. I would know if the rest of you tastes as sweet as your lips.'

She was laughing and eager, no longer feigning feminine modesty when she could not be anything but natural. The King was amused and delighted; not since he had set foot on this hated soil had he been so delighted.

He laughed and was refreshed and eased of his humiliation. He'd take this girl the English way – no French fripperies for him! He would say what he meant, and she could too.

He said: 'Why, Mary, you're sweet all over. And where did you hide yourself, Mary? I'm not sure you have not earned a punishment, Mary, for keeping this from your King so long; we might say it was treason, that we might!'

He laughed, mightily pleased, as he always was, with his own pleasantries; and she was overawed and passive, then responsive and pretending to be afraid she had been over-presumptuous to have so enjoyed the King. This was what he wanted, and he was grateful enough to those of his subjects who pleased him. In an exuberance of good spirits he slapped her buttocks — no velvet to cover them now — and she laughed, and her saucy eyes promised much for other times to come.

'You please me, Mary,' he said, and in a rush of crude tenderness added: 'You shall not suffer for this day.'

When he left her and when she was scrambling into her

clothes, she still trembled from the violence of the experience.

In the Queen's apartment she was scolded for her lateness; demurely, with eyes cast down, she accepted the reprimand.

*　　*　　*

Coming from Mary Boleyn, the King met the Cardinal.

Ah, thought the Cardinal, noting the flushed face of his royal master, and guessing something of what had happened, who now?

The King laid his hand on the Cardinal's shoulder, and they walked together along the corridor, talking of the entertainment they would give the French tonight, for matters of state could not be discussed in the palace of Guisnes; these affairs must wait for Greenwich or York House; impossible to talk of important matters, surrounded by enemies.

This exuberance, thought the Cardinal, means one thing – success in sport. And as sport the Cardinal would include the gratification of the royal senses. Good! said the Cardinal to himself; this has put that disastrous matter of the wrestling from his thoughts.

The Cardinal was on the whole a contented man – as contented, that is, as a man of ambition can ever be. He was proud of his sumptuous houses, his rich possessions; it was a good deal to be, next the King, the richest man in England. But that which he loved more than riches, he also had; and to those who have known obscurity, power is a more intoxicating draught than riches. Men might secretly call him 'Butcher's cur', but they trembled before his might, for he was greater than the King. He led the King, and if he managed this only because the King did not know he was led, that was of little account. Very pleasant it was to reflect that his genius for statecraft, his diplomacy, had put the kingdom into the exalted position it held today. This King was a good king, because the goodness of a king depends upon his choice of ministers.

There could be no doubt that Henry was a good king, for he had chosen Thomas Wolsey.

It pleased the statesman therefore to see the King happy with a woman, doubtless about to launch himself on yet another absorbing love affair, for then the fat, bejewelled hands, occupied in caressing a woman's body, could be kept from seeking a place on the helm of the ship of state. The King must be amused; the King must be humoured; when he would organize this most ridiculous pageant, this greatest farce in history, there was none that dare deny him his pleasures. Buckingham, the fool, had tried; and Buckingham should tread carefully, for, being so closely related to the King, his head were scarcely safe on his shoulders, be he the most docile of subjects. Francis was not to be trusted. He would make treaties one week, and discard them the next. But how could one snatch the helm from those podgy hands, once the King had decided they must have a place on it? How indeed! Diplomacy for ever! thought the Cardinal. Keep the King amused. It was good to see the King finding pleasure in a woman, for well the Cardinal knew that Elizabeth Blount, who had served her purpose most excellently, was beginning to tire His Majesty.

They parted affectionately at the King's apartments, both smiling, well pleased with life and with each other.

* * *

The Queen was retiring. She had dismissed her women when the King came in. Her still beautiful auburn hair hung about her shoulders; her face was pale, thin and much lined, and there were deep shadows under her eyes.

The King looked at her distastefully. With Mary Boleyn still in his thoughts, he recalled the cold submissiveness to duty of this Spanish woman through the years of their marriage. She had been a good wife, people would say; but she would have been as good a wife to his brother Arthur had he lived. Being a good wife was just another of the virtues that irritated him. And what had his marriage with her been but years of hope that never brought him his desires? The Queen is with child; prepare to sing a Te Deum. Prepare to let the bells of London ring. And then . . . miscarriage after miscarriage; five of them in four years. A stillborn daughter, a son who lived but two months, a stillborn son, one who died at birth and another prematurely born. And then . . . a daughter!

He had begun to be afraid. Rumours spread quickly through a country, and it is not always possible to prevent their reaching the kingly ear. Why cannot the King have a son? murmured his people. The King grew fearful. I am a very religious man, he thought. The fault cannot be mine. Six times I hear mass each day, and in times of pestilence or war or bad harvest, eight times a day. I confess my sins with regularity; the fault cannot be mine.

But he was superstitious. He had married his brother's widow. It had been sworn that the marriage had never been consummated. Had it though? The fault could not be his. How could God deny the dearest wish of such a religious man as Henry VIII of England! The King looked round for a scapegoat, and because her body was shapeless with much fruitless child-bearing, and because he never had liked her pious Spanish ways for more than a week or two, because he was beginning to dislike her heartily, he blamed the Queen. Resentfully he thought of those nights when he had lain with her. When he prayed for male issue he reminded his God of this. There were women in his court who had beckoned him with their charms, who had aroused his ready desire; and for duty's sake he had lain with the Queen, and only during her pregnancies had he gone where he would. What virtue . . . to go unrewarded! God was just; therefore there was some reason why he had been denied a son. There it was . . . in that woman on whom he had squandered his manhood without reward.

He knew, when Elizabeth Blount bore his son, that the fault could not lie with him. He had been in an ecstasy of delight when that boy had been born. His virility vindicated, the guilt of Katharine assured, his dislike had become tinged with hatred on that day.

But on this evening his dislike for the Queen was mellowed by the pleasure he had had in Mary Boleyn; he smiled that remote smile which long experience had taught the Queen was born of satisfied lust. His gorgeous clothing was just a little disarranged; the veins stood out more than usual on the great forehead.

He had thrown himself into a chair, and was sitting, his knees wide apart, the glazed smile on his face, making plans which included Mary Boleyn.

The Queen would say a special prayer for him tonight. Meanwhile she asked herself that question which had been in the Cardinal's mind – 'Who now?'

* * *

'Venus était blonde, l'on m'a dit.
L'on voit bien qu'elle est brunette.'

So sang François to the lady who excited him most in his wife's retinue of ladies. Unfortunately for François, she was the cleverest as well as the most desirable.

'Ah!' said François. 'You are the wise one, *Mademoiselle* Bouillain. You have learned that the fruit which hangs just out of reach is the most desired.'

'Your Majesty well knows my mind,' explained Anne. 'What should I be? A king's mistress. The days of glory for such are very short; we have evidence of that all around us.'

'Might it not depend on the mistress, *Mademoiselle* Bouillain?'

She shrugged her shoulders in the way which was so much more charming than the gesture of the French ladies, because it was only half French.

'I do not care to take the risk,' she said.

Then he laughed and sang to her, and asked that she should sing to him. This she did gladly, for her voice was good and she was susceptible to admiration and eager to draw it to herself at every opportunity. Contact with the Duchesse d'Alençon had made her value herself highly, and though she was as fond of amorous adventures as any, she knew exactly at what moment to retire. She was

40

enjoying every moment of her life at the court of France. There was so much to amuse her that life could never be dull. Light-hearted flirtations, listening to the scandal of the court, reading with Marguerite, and getting a glimmer of the new religion that had begun to spring up in Europe, since a German monk named Martin Luther had nailed a set of theses on a church door at Wittenberg. Yes, life was colourful and amusing, stimulating mind and body. Though the news that came from England was not so good; disaster had set in after the return from the palace of Guisnes. Poverty had swept over the country; the harvest was bad, and people were dying of the plague in the streets of London. The King was less popular than he had been before his love of vulgar show and pageantry had led him to that folly which men in England now called 'The Field of the Cloth of Gold.'

There was not very exhilarating news from her family. Uncle Edmund Howard had yet another child, and that a daughter. Catherine, they called her. Anne's ready sympathy went out to poor little Catherine Howard, born into the poverty of that rambling old house at Lambeth. Then Mary had married – hardly brilliantly – a certain William Carey. Anne would have liked to hear of a better match for her sister; but both she and George, right from Hever days, had known Mary was a fool.

And now war clouds were looming up afresh, and this time there was fear of a conflict between France and England. At the same time there was talk of a marriage for Anne which was being arranged in England to settle some dispute one branch of her family was having with another.

So Anne left France most reluctantly, and sailed for England. At home they said she was most Frenchified; she was imperious, witty, lovely to look at, and her clothes caused comment from all who beheld them.

She was just sixteen years old.

* * *

Anne's grandfather, the old Duke of Norfolk, was not at home when Anne, in the company of her mother, visited the Norfolk's house at Lambeth. The Duchess was a somewhat lazy, empty-headed woman who enjoyed listening to the ambitious adventures of the younger members of her family, and she had learned that her granddaughter, Anne, had returned from France, a charming creature. Nothing therefore would satisfy the Duchess but that this visit should be paid, and during it she found an especial delight in sitting in the grounds of her lovely home on the river's edge, dozing and indulging in light conversation with the girl whom she herself would now be ready to admit was the most interesting member of the family. And, thought the vain old lady, the chit has a look of me about her; moreover, I declare at her age I looked very like her. What honours, she wondered, were in store for Anne Boleyn, for the marriage with the Butlers was not being brought at any great speed to a satisfactory conclusion; and how sad if this bright child must bury herself in the wilds of that dreary, troublesome, uncivilized Ireland! But – and the Duchess sighed deeply – what were women but petty counters to be bartered by men in the settlement of their problems? Thomas Boleyn was too ambitious. Marry! An the girl were mine, to court she should go, and a plague on the Butlers.

She watched Anne feeding the peacocks; a figure of grace in scarlet and grey, she was not one whit less gorgeous than those arrogant, elegant birds. She's Howard, mused the Duchess with pride. *All* Howard! Not a trace of Boleyn there.

'Come and sit beside me, my dear,' she said. 'I would talk to you.'

Anne came and sat on the wooden seat which overlooked the river; she gazed along its bank at the stately gabled houses whose beautiful gardens sloped down to the water, placing their owners within comfortable distance of the quickest and least dangerous means of transport. Her gaze went quickly towards those domes and spires that seemed to pierce the blue and smokeless sky. She could see the heavy arches of London Bridge and the ramparts of the Tower of London – that great, impressive fortress whose towers, strong and formidable, stood like sentinels guarding the city.

Agnes, Duchess of Norfolk, saw the girl's eager expression, and guessed her thoughts. She tapped her arm.

'Tell me of the court of France, my child. I'll warrant you found much to amuse you there.'

As Anne talked, the Duchess lay back, listening, now and then stifling a yawn, for she had eaten a big dinner and, interested as she was, she was overcome by drowsiness.

'Why, bless us!' she said. 'When you went away, your father was of little import; now you return to find him a gentleman of much consequence – Treasurer of the Household now, if you please!'

'It does please,' laughed Anne.

'They tell me,' said Agnes, 'that the office is worth a thousand pounds a year! And what else? Steward of Tonbridge. . . .' She began enumerating the titles on her fingers. 'Master of the Hunt. Constable of the Castle. Chamberlain of Tonbridge. Receiver and Bailiff of Bradsted, and the Keeper of the Manor of Penshurst. And now it is whispered that he is to be appointed Keeper of the Parks at Thundersley, to say nothing of Essex and Westwood. Never was so much honour done a man in so short a time!'

'My father,' said Anne, 'is a man of much ability.'

'And good fortune,' said Agnes slyly, eyeing the girl mischievously, thinking – Can it be that she does not know why these honours are heaped on her father, and she fresh from the wicked court of France? 'And your father is lucky in his children,' commented Agnes mischievously.

The girl turned puzzled eyes on her grandmother. The old lady chuckled, thinking – She makes a pretty pose of ignorance, I'll swear!

Anne said, her expression changing: 'I would it were as well with every member of our family.' And her eyes went towards a house less than half a mile away along the river's bank.

'Ah!' sighed the Duchess. '*There* is a man who served his country well, and yet . . . She shrugged her shoulders. '*His* children are too young to be of any use to him.'

'I hear there is a new baby,' said Anne. 'Do they not visit you?'

'My dear, Lord Edmund is afraid to leave his house for fear he should be arrested. He has many debts, poor man, and he's as proud as Lucifer. Ah, yes . . . a new baby. Why, little Catherine is but a baby yet.'

'Grandmother, I should like to see the baby.'

The Duchess yawned. It had ever been her habit to push unpleasant thoughts aside, and the branch of her family which they were now discussing distressed her. What she enjoyed hearing was of the success of Sir Thomas and the adventures of his flighty daughter. She could nod over them, simper over them, remember her own youth and relive it as she drowsed in her pleasant seat overlooking the river. Still, she would like the Edmund Howards to see this lovely girl in her pretty clothes. The Duchess had a mischievous turn of mind. The little Howards had a distinguished soldier for a father, and they might starve; the Boleyn children had a father who might be a clever enough diplomatist, but, having descended from merchants, was no proud Howard; still, he had a most attractive daughter. There were never two men less alike than Lord Edmund Howard and Sir Thomas Boleyn. And to His Majesty, thought the Duchess, smiling into a lace handkerchief, a sword grown rusty is of less use than a lovely, willing girl.

'Run to the house and get cloaks,' she said. 'We will step along to see them. A walk will do me good and mayhap throw off this flatulence which, I declare, attacks me after every meal these days.'

'You eat too heartily, Grandmother.'

'Off with you, impudent child!'

Anne ran off. It does me good to look at her, thought her grandmother. And what when the King claps eyes on *her*, eh, Thomas Boleyn? Though it occurs to me that she might not be to his taste. I declare were I a man I'd want to spank the haughtiness out of her before I took her to bed. And the King would not be one to brook such ways. Ah, if you go to court, Anne Boleyn, you will have to lose your French dignity – if you hope to do as well as your saucy sister.

Though you'll not go to court; you'll go to Ireland. The Ormond title and the Ormond wealth must be kept in the family to satisfy grasping Thomas, and he was ever a man to throw his family to the wolves.

The Duchess rose, and Anne, who had come running up, put a cloak about her shoulders; they walked slowly through the gardens and along the river's edge.

The Lambeth house of the Edmund Howards was a roomy place, cold and draughty. Lady Edmund was a delicate creature on whom too frequent child-bearing and her husband's poverty were having a dire effect. She and her husband received their visitors in the great panelled hall, and wine was brought for them to drink. Lord Edmund's dignity was great, and it touched Anne deeply to see his efforts to hide his poverty.

'My dear Jocosa,' said the Duchess to her daughter-in-law, 'I have brought my granddaughter along to see you. She has recently returned from France, as you know. Tell your aunt and uncle all about it, child.'

'Uncle Edmund would doubtless find my adventuring tame telling,' said Anne.

'Ah!' said Lord Edmund. 'I remember you well, niece. Dover Castle, eh? And the crossing! Marry, I thought I should never see your face again when your ship was missed by the rest of us. I remember saying to Surrey: "Why, our niece is there, and she but a baby!"'

Anne sipped her wine, chatting awhile with Lord Edmund of the court of France, of old Louis, of gay François, and of Mary Tudor who had longed to be Queen of France and Duchess of Suffolk, and had achieved both ambitions.

The old Duchess tapped her stick imperiously, not caring to be left to Jocosa and her domesticity. 'Anne was interested in the children,' she said. 'I trow she will be disappointed if she is not allowed to catch a glimpse of them.'

'You must come to the nursery,' said Jocosa. 'Though I doubt that the older ones will be there at this hour. The babies love visitors.'

In the nursery at the top of the house, there was more evidence of the poverty of this branch of the Howard family. Little Catherine was shabbily dressed; Mary, the baby, was wrapped in a piece of darned flannel. There was an old nurse who, Anne guessed, doubtless worked without her wages for very love of the family. Her face shone with pride in the children, with affection for her mistress; but she was inclined to be resentful towards Anne and her grandmother. Had I known, thought Anne, I could have put on a simpler gown.

'Here is the new baby, Madam,' said the nurse, and put the flannel bundle into Anne's arms. Its little face was puckered and red; a very ugly little baby, but it was amusing and affecting to see the nurse hovering over it as though it were very, very precious.

A little hand was stroking the silk of Anne's surcoat. Anne looked down and saw a large-eyed, very pretty little girl who could not have been very much more than a year old.

'This is the next youngest,' said Jocosa.

'Little Catherine!' said the Duchess, and stooping picked her up. 'Now, Catherine Howard, what have you to say to Anne Boleyn?'

Catherine could say nothing; she could only stare at the lovely lady in the gorgeous, bright clothes. The jewels at her throat and on her fingers dazzled Catherine. She wriggled in the Duchess's arms in an effort to get closer to Anne, who, always susceptible to admiration, even from babies, handed the flannel bundle back to the nurse.

'Would you like me to hold you, cousin Catherine?' she asked, and Catherine smiled delightedly.

'She does not speak,' said the Duchess.

'I fear she is not as advanced as the others,' said Catherine's mother.

'Indeed not!' said the Duchess severely. 'I remember well this girl here as a baby. I never knew one so bright – except perhaps her brother George. Now, Mary . . . she was more like Catherine here.'

At the mention of Mary's name Jocosa stiffened, but the

46

old Duchess went on, her eyes sparkling: 'Mary was a taking little creature, though she might be backward with her talk. She knew though how to ask for what she wanted, without words . . . and I'll warrant she still does!'

Anne and Catherine smiled at each other.

'There!' said the Duchess. 'She is wishing she had a child of her own. Confess it, Anne!'

'One such as this, yes!' laughed Anne.

Catherine tried to pluck out the beautiful eyes.

'She admires you vastly!' said Jocosa.

Anne went to a chair and sat down, holding Catherine on her lap, while her grandmother drew Jocosa into a corner and chatted with her of the proposed match for Anne, of the advancement of Sir Thomas and George Boleyn, of Mary and the King.

Catherine's little hands explored the lovely dress, the glittering jewels; and the child laughed happily as she did so.

'They make a pretty picture,' said the Duchess. 'I think I am proud of my granddaughters, Anne Boleyn and Catherine Howard. They are such pretty creatures, both of them.'

Catherine's fingers had curled about a jewelled tablet which hung by a silken cord from Anne's waist; it was a valuable trinket.

'Would you like to have it for your own, little Catherine?' whispered Anne, and detached it. They can doubtless sell it, she thought. It is not much, but it is something. I can see it would be useless to offer help openly to Uncle Edmund.

When they said farewell, Catherine shed tears.

'Why, look what the child has!' cried the Duchess. 'It is yours, is it not, Anne? Catherine Howard, Catherine Howard, are you a little thief then?'

'It is a gift,' said Anne hastily. 'She liked it, and I have another.'

*   *   *

It was pleasant to be back at Hever after such a long absence. How quiet were the Kentish woods, how solitary the green meadows! She had hoped to see the Wyatts, but they were not in residence at Allington Castle just now; and it was a quiet life she led, reading, sewing, playing and singing with her mother. She was content to enjoy these lazy days, for she had little desire to marry the young man whom it had been ordained she should. She accepted the marriage as a matter of course, as she had known from childhood that when she reached a certain age a match would be made for her. This was it; but how pleasant to pass these days at quiet Hever, wandering through the grounds which she would always love because of those childhood memories they held for her.

Mary paid a visit to Hever; splendidly dressed – Anne considered her over-dressed – she was very gay and lively. Her laughter rang through the castle, shattering its peace. Mary admired her sister, and was too good-natured not to admit it wholeheartedly. 'You should do well at court, sister Anne,' she told her. 'You would create much excitement, I trow. And those clothes! I have never seen the like; and who but you could wear them with effect!'

They lay under the old apple trees in the orchard together; Mary, lazy and plump, carefully placing a kerchief over her bosom to prevent the sun from spoiling its whiteness.

'I think now and then,' said Mary, 'of my visit to you ... Do you remember Ardres?'

'Yes,' said Anne, 'I remember perfectly.'

'And how you disapproved of me then? Did you not? Confess it.'

'Did I show it then?'

'Indeed you did, Madam! You looked down your haughty nose at me and disapproved right heartily. You cannot say you disapprove now, I trow.'

'I think you have changed very little,' said Anne.

Mary giggled. '*You* may have disapproved that night, Anne, but there was one who did not!'

'The tastes of all are naturally not alike.'

'There was one who approved most heartily – and he of no small import either!'

48

'I perceive,' said Anne, laughing, 'that you yearn to tell me of your love affairs.'

'And you are not interested?'

'Not very. I am sure you have had many, and that they are all monotonously similar.'

'Indeed! And what if I were to tell His Majesty of that!'

'Do you then pour your girlish confidences into the royal ear?'

'I do now and then, Anne, when I think they may amuse His Grace.'

'What is this?' said Anne, raising herself to look more closely at her sister.

'I was about to tell you. Did I not say that though you might disapprove of me, there was one who does not? Listen, sister. The night I left you to return to the Guisnes Palace I met him; he spoke to me, and we found we liked each other.'

Anne's face flushed, then paled; she was understanding many things – the chatter of her grandmother, the glances of her Aunt Jocosa, the nurse's rather self-righteous indignation. One of the heroes of Flodden may starve, but the family of Boleyn shall flourish, for the King likes well one of its daughters.

'How long?' asked Anne shortly.

'From then to now. He is eager for me still. There never was such a man! Anne, I could tell you . . .'

'I beg that you will not.'

Mary shrugged her shoulders and rolled over on the grass like an amorous cat.

'And William, your husband?' said Anne.

'Poor William! I am very fond of him.'

'I understand. The marriage was arranged, and he was given a place at court so that you might be always there awaiting the King's pleasure, and to place a very flimsy cover of propriety over your immorality.'

Mary was almost choked with laughter.

'Your expressions amuse me, Anne. I declare, I shall tell the King; he will be vastly amused. And you fresh from the court of France!'

'I am beginning to wish I were still there. And our father...'

'Is mightily pleased with the arrangements. A fool he would be otherwise, and none could say our father is a fool.'

'So all these honours that have been heaped upon him...'

'... are due to the fact that your wicked sister has pleased the King!'

'It makes me sick.'

'You have a poor stomach, sister. But you are indeed young, for all your air of worldly wisdom and for all your elegance and grace. Why, bless you, Anne, life is not all the wearing of fine clothes.'

'No? Indeed it would seem that for you it is more a matter of putting them off!'

'You have a witty tongue, Anne. I cannot compete with it. You would do well at court, would you but put aside your prudery. Prudery the King cannot endure; he has enough of that from his Queen.'

'She knows of you and...'

'It is impossible to keep secrets at court, Anne.'

'Poor lady!'

'But were it not I, 'twould be another, the King being as he is.'

'The King being a lecher!' said Anne fiercely.

'That is treason!' cried Mary in mock horror. 'Ah! It is easy for you to talk. As for me, I could never say no to such a man."

'You could never say no to any man!'

'Despise me if you will. The King does not, and our father is mightily pleased with his daughter Mary.'

Now the secret was out; now she understood the sly glances of servants, her father's looks of approbation as his eyes rested on his elder daughter. There was no one to whom Anne could speak of her perturbation until George came home.

He was eighteen years old, a delight to the eye, very like Anne in appearance, full of exuberant animal spirits; a poet and coming diplomat, and he already had the air of both. His eyes burned with his enthusiasm for life; and Anne was happy when he took her hands, for she had been afraid that the years of separation might divide them and that she would lose for ever the beloved brother of her childhood. But in a few short hours those fears were set aside; he was the same George, she the same Anne. Their friendship, she knew, could not lose from the years, only gain from them. Their minds were of similar calibre; alert, intellectual, they were quick to be amused, quick to anger, reckless of themselves. They had therefore a perfect understanding of each other, and, being troubled, it was natural that she should go to him.

She said as they walked together through the Kentish lanes, for she had felt the need to leave the castle so that she might have no fear of being overheard: 'I have learned of Mary and the King.'

'That does not surprise me,' said George. 'It is common knowledge.'

'It shocked me deeply, George.'

He smiled at her. 'It should not.'

'But *our* sister! It is degrading.'

'She would degrade herself sooner or later, so why should it not be in that quarter from which the greatest advantages may accrue?'

'Our father delights in this situation, George, and our mother is complaisant.'

'My sweet sister, you are but sixteen. Ah, you look wonderfully worldly wise, but you are not yet grown up. You are very like the little girl who sat in the window seats at Blickling, and dreamed of knightly deeds. Life is not romantic, Anne, and men are not frequently honourable knights. Life is a battle or a game which each of us fights or plays with all the skill at his command. Do not condemn Mary because her way would not be yours.'

'The King will tire of her.'

'Assuredly.'

'And cast her off!'

'It is Mary's nature to be happy, Anne. Do not fear. She will find other lovers when she is ejected from the royal bed.

She has poor Will Carey, and she has been in favour for the best part of three years and her family have not suffered for it yet. Know, my sweet sister, that to be mistress of the King is an honour; it is only the mistress of a poor man who degrades herself.'

His handsome face was momentarily set in melancholy lines, but almost immediately he was laughing merrily.

'George,' she said, 'I cannot like it.'

'What! Not like to see your father become a power in the land! Not like to see your brother make his way at court!'

'I would rather they had done these things by their own considerable abilities.'

'Bless you!' said George. 'There are more favours won this way than by the sweat of the brow. Dismiss the matter from your mind. The Boleyns' fortunes are in the ascendant. Who knows whither the King's favour may lead – and all due to our own plump little Mary! Who would have believed it possible!'

'I like it not,' she repeated.

Then he took her hands and kissed them lightly, wishing to soothe her troubled mind.

'Fear not, little sister.'

Now he had her smiling with him – laughing at the incongruity of this situation. Mary – the one who was not as bright as the rest – was leading the Boleyns to fame and fortune.

*   *   *

It seemed almost unbearably quiet after Mary and George had gone. Anne could not speak of Mary's relationship with the King to her mother, and it irked her frank nature perpetually to have to steer the conversation away from a delicate topic. She was glad when her father returned to the court, for his obvious delight in his good fortune angered Anne. Her father thought her a sullen girl, for she was not one, feeling displeased, to care about hiding her displeasure. Mary was his favourite daughter; Mary was a sensible girl; and Anne could not help feeling that he would be relieved when the arrangements for the

Butler marriage were completed. She spent the days with her mother, or wandered often alone in the lanes and gardens.

Sir Thomas returned to Hever in a frenzy of excitement. The King would be passing through Kent, and it was probable that he would spend a night at Hever. Sir Thomas very quickly roused the household to his pitch of excitement. He went to the kitchen and gave orders himself; he had flowers set in the ballroom and replaced by fresh ones twice a day; he grumbled incessantly about the inconvenience of an old castle like Hever, and wished fervently that he had a modern house in which to entertain the King.

'The house is surely of little importance,' said Anne caustically, 'as long as Mary remains attractive to the King!'

'Be silent, girl!' thundered Sir Thomas. 'Do you realize that this is the greatest of honours?'

'Surely not the greatest!' murmured Anne, and was silenced by a pleading look from her mother who greatly feared discord; and, loving her mother while deploring her attitude in the case of Mary and the King, Anne desisted.

The King's having given no date for his visit, Sir Thomas fumed and fretted for several days, scarcely leaving the castle for fear he should not be on the spot to welcome his royal master.

One afternoon Anne took a basket to the rose garden that she might cut some of the best blooms for her mother. It was a hot afternoon, and she was informally dressed in her favourite scarlet; as the day was so warm she had taken off the caul from her head and shaken out her long, silky ringlets. She had sat on a seat in the rose garden for an hour or more, half dozing, when she decided it was time she gathered the flowers and returned to the house; and as she stood by a tree of red roses she was aware of a footfall close by, and turning saw what she immediately thought of as 'a Personage' coming through the gap in the conifers which was the entrance to this garden. She felt the blood rush to her face, for she knew him at once. The jewels in his clothes were caught and held by the sun, so that it seemed as if he were on fire; his face was ruddy, his beard seemed golden, and his presence seemed to fill the garden. She could not but think of Mary's meeting with him in the palace of Guisnes, and her resentment towards him flared up within her, even as she realized it would be sheer folly to show him that resentment. She sought therefore to compose her features and, with admirable calm – for she had decided now that her safest plan was to feign ignorance of his identity – she went on snipping the roses.

Henry was close. She turned as though in surprise to find herself not alone, gave him the conventional bow of acknowledgment which she would have given to one of her father's ordinary acquaintances, and said boldly: 'Good day, sir.'

The King was taken aback. Then inwardly he chuckled, thinking – She has no notion who I am! He studied her with the utmost appreciation. Her informal dress was more becoming, he thought, than those elaborate creations worn by some ladies at a court function. Her beautiful hair was like a black silk cloak about her shoulders. He took in each detail of her appearance and thought that he had never seen one whose beauty delighted him more.

She turned her head and snipped off a rose.

'My father is expecting the King to ride this way. I presume you to be one of his gentlemen!'

Masquerade had ever greatly appealed to Henry. There was nothing he enjoyed as much as to appear disguised at some ball or banquet, and after much badinage with his subjects and at exactly the appropriate moment, to make the dramatic announcement – 'I am your King!' And how could this game be more delightfully played out than in a rose garden on a summer's afternoon with, surely, the loveliest maiden in his kingdom!

He took a step closer to her.

'Had I known,' he said, 'that I should come face to face with such beauty, depend upon it, I should have whipped up my horse.'

'Would you not have had to await the King's pleasure?'

'Aye!' He slapped his gorgeous thigh. 'That I should!'

She, who knew so well how to play the coquette, now did so with a will, for in this rôle she could appease that resentment in herself which threatened to make her very angry as she contemplated this lover of her sister Mary. Let him come close, and she – in assumed ignorance of his rank – would freeze him with a look. She snipped off a rose and gave it to him.

'You may have it if you care to.'

He said: 'I do care. I shall keep it for ever.'

'Bah!' she answered him contemptuously. 'Mere court gallantry!'

'You like not our court gallants?'

Her mocking eyes swept his padded, jewelled figure.

'They are somewhat clumsy when compared with those of the French court.'

'You are lately come from France?'

'I am. A match has been arranged for me with my cousin.'

'Would to God I were the cousin! Tell me . . .' He came yet closer, noting the smooth skin, the silky lashes, the proud tilt of the head and its graceful carriage on the tiny neck. 'Was that less clumsy?'

'Nay!' she said, showing white teeth. 'Not so! It was completely without subtlety; I saw it coming.'

Henry found that, somewhat disconcerting as this was, he was enjoying it. The girl had a merry wit, and he liked it; she was stimulating as a glass of champagne. And I swear I never clapped eyes on a lovelier wench! he told himself. The airs she gives herself! It would seem I were the subject – she the Queen!

She said: 'The garden is pretty, is it not? To me this is one of the most pleasant spots at Hever.'

They walked around it; she showed him the flowers, picked a branch of lavender and held it to her nose; then she rolled it in her hands and smelt its pleasant fragrance there.

Henry said: 'You tell me you have recently come from the court of France. How did you like it there?'

'It was indeed pleasant.'

'And you are sorry to return?'

55

'I think that may be, for so long have I been there that is seems as home to me.'

'I like not to hear that.'

She shrugged her shoulders. 'They say I am as French as I am English.'

'The French,' he said, the red of his face suddenly tinged with purple that matched his coat, 'are a perfidious set of rascals.'

'Sir!' she said reproachfully and, drawing her skirts about her, she walked from him and sat on the wooden seat near the pond. She looked at him coldly as he hurried towards her.

'How now!' he said, thinking he had had enough of the game.

He sat down beside her, pressing his thigh against hers, which caused her immediate withdrawal from him. 'Perfidious!' she said slowly. 'Rascals! And when I have said I am half French!'

'Ah!' he said. 'I should not use such words to you. You have the face of an angel!'

She was off the seat, as though distrusting his proximity. She threw herself onto the grass near the pond and looked into still waters at her own reflection, a graceful feminine Narcissus, her hair touching the water.

'No!' she said imperiously, as he would have risen: 'You stay there, and mayhap I will tarry awhile and talk to you.'

He did not understand himself. The joke should have been done with ere this. It was time to explain, to have her on her knees craving forgiveness for her forwardness. He would raise her and say: 'We cannot forgive such disrespectful treatment of your sovereign. We demand a kiss in payment for your sins!' But he was unsure; there was that in her which he had never before discovered in a woman. She looked haughty enough to refuse a kiss to a king. No, no! he thought. Play this little game awhile.

She said: 'The French are an interesting people. I was fortunate there. My friend was *Madame la Duchesse*

D'Alençon, and I count myself indeed happy to have such a friend.'

'I have heard tales of her,' he said.

'Her fame travels. Tell me, have you read Boccaccio?'

The King leaned forward. Had he read Boccaccio! Indeed he had, and vastly had the fellow's writing pleased him.

'And you?' he asked.

She nodded, and they smiled at each other in the understanding of a pleasure shared.

'We would read it together, the Duchess and I. Tell me, which of the stories did you prefer?'

Finding himself plunged deep into a discussion of the literature of his day, Henry forgot he was a king, and an amorous king at that. There was in this man, in addition to the coarse, crude, insatiable sensualist, a scholar of some attainment. Usually the sensualist was the stronger, ever ready to stifle the other, but there was about this girl sitting by the pond a purity that commanded his respect, and he found he could sit back in his seat and delight in her as he would in a beautiful picture or piece of statuary, while he could marvel at her unwomanly intellect. Literature, music and art could have held a strong position in his life, had he not in his youth been such a healthy animal. Had he but let his enthusiasm for them grow in proportion to that which he bestowed on tennis, on jousting, on the hunting of game and of women, his mind would assuredly have developed as nobly as his body. An elastic mind would have served him better than his strong muscles; but the jungle animal in him had been strong, and urgent desires tempered by a narrow religious outlook had done much to suppress the finer man, and from the mating of the animal and the zealot was born that monster of cruelty, his conscience. But that was to come; the monster was as yet in its infancy, and pleasant it was to talk of things of the mind with an enchanting companion. She was full of wit, and Marguerite of Alençon talked through her young lips. She had been allowed to peep into the *Heptameron* –

that odd book which, under the influence of Boccaccio, Marguerite was writing.

From literature she passed to the pastimes of the French court. She told of the masques, less splendid perhaps than those he indulged in with such pleasure, but more subtle and amusing. Wit was to the French court what bright colours and sparkling jewels were to the English. She told of a play which she had helped Marguerite to write, quoting lines from it which set him laughing with appreciative merriment. He was moved to tell her of his own compositions, reciting some verses of his. She listened, her head on one side, critical.

She shook her head: 'The last line is not so good. Now this would have been better . . .' And so would it! Momentarily he was angered, for those at court had declared there never were such verses written as those penned by his hand. From long practice he could pretend, even to himself, that his anger came from a different cause than that from which it really sprang. Now it grew – he assured himself – not from her slighting remarks on his poetry, but from the righteous indignation he must feel when he considered that this girl, though scarcely out of her childhood, had been exposed to the wickedness of the French court. Where he himself was concerned he had no sense of the ridiculous; he could, in all seriousness, put aside the knowledge that even at this moment he was planning her seduction, and burn with indignation that others – rakes and libertines with fancy French manners – might have had similar intentions. Such a girl, he told himself, smarting under the slights which she, reared in that foreign court, had been able to deliver so aptly, should never have been sent to France.

He said with dignity: 'It grieves me to think of the dangers to which you have been exposed at that licentious court presided over by a monarch who . . .' His voice failed him, for he pictured a dark, clever face, a sly smile and lips which had referred to him as 'My prisoner.'

She laughed lightly. 'The King of France is truly of an amorous nature, but never would I be a king's mistress!'

It seemed to him that this clever girl then answered a question which he had yet to ask. He felt worsted, and angry to be so.

He said severely: 'There are some who would not think it an indignity to be a king's mistress, but an honour.'

'Doubtless there are those who sell themselves cheaply.'

'Cheaply!' he all but roared. 'Come! It is not kingly to be niggardly with those that please.'

'I do not mean in worldly goods. To sell one's dignity and honour for momentary power and perhaps riches – that is to sell cheaply those things which are beyond price. Now I must go into the house.' She stood up, throwing back her hair. He stood too, feeling deflated and unkingly.

Silently he walked with her from the rose garden. Now was the time to disclose his identity, for it could not much longer be kept secret.

'You have not asked my name,' he said.

'Nor you mine.'

'You are the daughter of Sir Thomas Boleyn, I have gathered.'

'Indeed, that was clever of you!' she mocked. 'I am Anne Boleyn.'

'You still do not ask my name. Have you no curiosity to know it?'

'I shall doubtless learn in good time.'

'My name is Henry.'

'It is a good English name.'

'And have you noticed nothing yet?'

She turned innocent eyes upon him. 'What is there that I should have noticed?'

'It is the same as the King's.' He saw the mockery in her eyes now. He blurted out: 'By God! You knew all the time!'

'Having once seen the King's Grace, how could one of his subjects ever forget him?'

He was uncertain now whether to be amused or angry; in vain did he try to remember all she had said to him and he to her. 'Methinks you are a saucy wench!' he said.

'I hope my sauciness has pleased my mighty King.'

He looked at her sternly, for though her words were respectful, her manner was not.

'Too much sauce,' he said, 'is apt to spoil a dish.'

'And too little, to destroy it!' she said, casting down her eyes. 'I had thought that Your Majesty, being a famous epicure, would have preferred a well-flavoured one.'

He gave a snort of laughter and put out a hand which he would have laid on her shoulders, but without giving him a glance she moved daintily away, so that he could not know whether by accident or design.

He said: 'We shall look to see you at court with your sister.'

He was unprepared for the effect of those words; her cheeks were scarlet as her dress, and her eyes lost all their merriment. Her father was coming across the lawn towards them; she bowed low and turning from him ran across the grass and into the castle.

'You have a beautiful daughter there, Thomas!' exclaimed the King. And Thomas, obsequious, smiling, humbly conducted Henry into Hever Castle.

The sight of the table in the great dining-hall brought a glister of pride into Sir Thomas's eyes. On it were laid out in most lavish array great joints of beef, mutton and venison, hare and seasoned peacocks; there were vegetables and fruit, and great pies and pastries. Sir Thomas's harrying of his cooks and scullions had been well worth while, and he felt that the great kitchens of Hever had done him justice. The King eyed this display with an approval which might have been more marked, had not his thoughts been inclined to dwell more upon Sir Thomas's daughter than on his table.

They took their seats, the King in the place of honour at the right hand of his host, the small company he had brought with him ranged about the table. There was one face for which the King looked in vain; Sir Thomas, ever eager to anticipate the smallest wish of his sovereign, saw the King's searching look and understood it; he called a serving-maid to him and whispered sharply to her to go at once to his daughter and bid her to the table without a second's delay. The maid returned with the disconcerting message that Sir Thomas's daughter suffered from a headache and would not come to the table that day. The King, watching this little by-play with the greatest interest, heard every word.

'Go back at once,' said Sir Thomas, 'and tell the lady I command her presence here at once!'

'Stay!' interceded Henry, his voice startling Sir Thomas by its unusual softness. 'Allow me to deal with the matter, good Thomas. Come hither, girl.'

The poor little serving-maid dropped a frightened curtsey and feared she would not be able to understand the King's commands, so overawed was she by his notice.

'Tell the lady from us,' said Henry, 'that we are indeed sorry for the headache. Tell her it doubtless comes from lingering too daringly in the rays of the sun. Tell her we excuse her and wish her good speed in her recovery.'

He did not see Anne again, for she kept to her room. Next morning he left Hever. He looked up at its windows, wondering which might be hers, telling himself that no girl, however haughty, however self-possessed, would be able to prevent herself from taking one glimpse at her King. But there was no sign of a face at any window. Disconsolate, bemused, the King rode away from Hever.

* * *

The great Cardinal, he who was Lord Chancellor of the realm, rode through the crowds. Before him and behind went his gentlemen attendants, for the great man never rode abroad but that he must impress the people with his greatness. He sat his mule with a dignity which would have become a king. What though his body were weak, his digestion poor, that he was very far from robust and suffered many ailments! His mind was the keenest, the most able, the most profound in the kingdom; and thus, first through the King's father, and more effectively through his gracious son, had Thomas Wolsey come to his high office. His success, he knew well, lay with his understanding of the King – that fine robustious animal – and when he

61

was but almoner to his gracious lord he had used that knowledge and so distinguished himself. There had been those counsellors who might urge the King to leave his pleasure and devote more time to affairs of state. Not so Thomas Wolsey! Let the King leave tiresome matters to his most dutiful servant. Let the King pursue his pleasures. Leave the wearisome matters to his most obedient – and what was all-important – to his most able Wolsey! How well the King loved those who did his will! This King, this immense man – in whom all emotions matched his huge body – hated fiercely and could love well. And he had loved Wolsey, in whose hands he could so safely place those matters that were important to his kingdom but so monotonously dull to his royal mind. And never was a man more content than Wolsey that this should be so. He, arrogant, imperious as his master, had had the indignity to be born the son of a poor man of Ipswich, and by his own fine brain had replaced indignity with honour. The Ipswich merchant's son was the best loved friend of the English King, and how doubly dear were those luxuries and those extravagances with which he, who had once suffered from obscurity, now surrounded himself! If he were over-lavish, he forgave himself; he had to wash the taste of Ipswich from his mouth.

As he rode on his ceremonious way, the people watched him. To his nose he held what might appear to be an orange, and what was really a guard against disease; for all the natural matter had been taken from the orange and in its place was stuffed part of a sponge containing vinegar and such concoctions as would preserve a great man from the pestilence which floated in the London air. Perhaps the people murmured against him; there were those who gave him sullen looks. Is this a man of God? they asked each other. This Wolsey – no higher born than you or I – who surrounds himself with elegance and luxury at the expense of the hard-pressed people! This gourmet, who must get special dispensation from the Pope that he need not follow the Lenten observances! They say he never forgives a slight. They say his hands are as red as his robes.

What of brave Buckingham! A marvel it is that the headless ghost of the Duke does not haunt his murderer!

If Wolsey could have spoken to them of Buckingham, he could have told them that a man, who will at any cost hold the King's favour, must often steep his hands in blood. Buckingham had been a fool. Buckingham had insulted Wolsey, and Wolsey had brought a charge against him of treasonable sorcery. Buckingham went to the block, not for his treasonable sorcery; he died because he had committed the unforgivable sin of being too nearly related to the King. He stood too close to the throne, and the Tudors had not been in possession of it long enough to be able to regard such an offence lightly. Thus it was one kept the favour of kings; by learning their unuttered desires and anticipating their wishes; thus one remained the power behind the throne, one's eyes alert, one's ears trained to catch the faintest inflection of the royal voice, fearful lest the mighty puppet might become the master.

In the presence-chamber Wolsey awaited audience of the King. He came, fresh from his Kentish journey, flushed with health, his eyes beaming with pleasure as they rested on his best-loved statesman.

'I would speak with Your Majesty on one or two matters,' said the Chancellor-Cardinal when he had congratulated the King on his healthy appearance.

'Matters of state! Matters of state, eh? Let us look into these matters, good Thomas.'

Wolsey spread papers on the table, and the royal signature was appended to them. The King listened, though his manner was a little absent.

'You are a good man, Thomas,' he said, 'and we love you well.'

'Your Majesty's regard is my most treasured possession.'

The King laughed heartily, but his voice was a trifle acid when he spoke. 'Then the King is pleased, for to be the most treasured of all your possessions, my rich friend, is indeed to be of great price!'

Wolsey felt the faintest twinge of uneasiness, until he saw in his sovereign's face a look he knew well. There was

63

a glaze over the bright little eyes, the cruel mouth had softened, and when the King spoke, his voice was gentle.

'Wolsey, I have been discoursing with a young lady who has the wit of an angel, and is worthy to wear a crown.'

Wolsey, alert, suppressed his smile with the desire to rub his hands together in his glee.

'It is sufficient if Your Majesty finds her worthy of your love,' he whispered.

The King pulled at his beard.

'Nay, Thomas, I fear she would never condescend that way.'

'Sire, great princes, if they choose to play the lover, have that in their power to mollify a heart of steel.'

The King shook his great head in melancholy fashion, seeing her bending over the pond, seeing her proud young head on the small neck, hearing her sweet voice: 'I would never be a king's mistress!'

'Your Majesty has been saddened by this lady,' said Wolsey solicitously.

'I fear so, Wolsey.'

'This must not be!' Wolsey's heart was merry. There was nothing he desired so much at this time as to see his master immersed in a passionate love affair. It was necessary at this moment to keep the fat, jewelled finger out of the French pie.

'Nay, my master, my dear lord, your chancellor forbids such sadness.' He put his head closer to the flushed face. 'Could we not bring the lady to court, and find a place for her among the Queen's ladies?'

The King placed an affectionate arm about Wolsey's shoulders.

'If Your Majesty will but whisper the name of the lady . . .'

'It is Boleyn's daughter . . . Anne.'

Now Wolsey had great difficulty in restraining his mirth. Boleyn's daughter! Anne! Off with the elder daughter! On with the younger!

'My lord King, she shall come to the court. I shall give a banquet at Hampton Court – a masque it shall be! I shall ask my Gracious Liege to honour me with his mighty presence. The lady shall be there!'

The King smiled, well pleased. A prince, had said this wise man, has that power to mollify a heart of steel. Good Wolsey! Dear Thomas! Dear friend and most able statesman!

'Methinks, Thomas,' said the King with tears in his eyes, 'that I love thee well.'

Wolsey fell on his knees and kissed the ruby on the forefinger of the fat hand. And I do love this man, thought the King; for he was one to whom it was not necessary to state crude facts. The lady would be brought to court, and it would appear that she came not through the King's wish. That was what he wanted, and not a word had he said of it; yet Wolsey had known. And well knew the King that Wolsey would arrange this matter with expedience and tact.

* * *

Life at the English court offered amusement in plenty, and the coming of one as vivacious and striking as Anne Boleyn could not pass unnoticed. The ladies received her with some interest and much envy, the gentlemen with marked appreciation. There were two ways of life at court; on the one hand there was the gay merry-making of the King's faction, on the other the piety of the Queen. As Queen's attendant, Anne's actions were restricted; but at the jousts and balls, where the Queen's side must mingle with the King's, she attracted a good deal of attention for none excelled her at the dance, and whether it was harpsichord, virginals or flute she played there were always those to crowd about her; when she sang, men grew sentimental, for there was that in her rich young voice to move men to tears.

The King was acutely aware of her while feigning not to notice her. He would have her believe that he had been not entirely pleased by her disrespectful manners at Hever, and that he still remembered the levity of her conversation with pained displeasure.

65

Anne laughed to herself, thinking – Well he likes a masquerade, when he arranges it; well he likes a joke against others! Is he angry at my appointment to attend the Queen? How I hope he does not banish me to Hever!

Life had become so interesting. As lady-in-waiting to the Queen, she was allowed a woman attendant and a spaniel of her own; she was pleased with the woman and delighted with the spaniel. The three of them shared a breakfast of beef and bread, which they washed down with a gallon of ale between them. Other meals were taken with the rest of the ladies in the great chamber, and at all these meals ale and wine were served in plenty; meat was usually the fare – beef, mutton, poultry, rabbits, peacocks, hares, pigeons – except on fast days when, in place of the meats, there would be a goodly supply of salmon or flounders, salted eels, whiting, or plaice and gurnet. But it was not the abundance of food that delighted Anne; it was the gaiety of the company. And if she had feared to be dismissed from the court in those first days, no sooner had she set eyes on Henry, Lord Percy, eldest son of the Earl of Northumberland, than she was terrified of that happening.

These two young people met about the court, though not as often as they could have wished, for whilst Anne, as maid of honour to Queen Katharine, was attached to the court, Percy was a protégé of the Cardinal. It pleased Wolsey to have in his retinue of attendants various high-born young men, and so great was his place in the kingdom that this honour was sought by the noblest families in the realm. Young Percy must therefore attend the Cardinal daily, accompany him to court, and consider himself greatly honoured by the patronage of this low-born man.

Lord Percy was a handsome young man of delicate features and of courteous manners; and as soon as he saw the Queen's newest lady-in-waiting he was captivated by her personal charms. And Anne, seeing this handsome boy, was filled with such a tenderness towards him, which she had experienced for none hitherto, that whenever she knew the Cardinal to be in audience with the King she would look for the young nobleman. Whenever he came to the palace he was alert for a glimpse of her. They were both young; he was very shy; and so, oddly enough, was she, where he was concerned.

One day she was sitting at a window overlooking a court-yard when into this courtyard there came my lord Cardinal and his attendants; and among these latter was Henry, Lord Percy. His eyes flew to the window, saw Anne, and emboldened by the distance which separated them, flashed her a message which she construed as 'Wait there, and while the Cardinal is closeted with the King I will return. I have so long yearned to hold speech with you!'

She waited, her heart beating fast as she pretended to stitch a piece of tapestry; waiting, waiting, feeling a sick fear within her lest the King might not wish to see the Cardinal, and the young man might thus be unable to escape.

He came running across the courtyard, and she knew by his haste and his enraptured expression that his fear had been as hers.

'I feared to find you gone!' he said breathlessly.

'I feared you would not come,' she answered.

'I look for you always.'

'I for you.'

They smiled, beautiful both of them in the joyful discovery of loving and being loved.

Anne was thinking that were he to ask her, she, who had laughed at Mary for marrying Will Carey, would gladly marry him though he might be nothing more than the Cardinal's Fool.

'I know not your name,' said Percy, 'but your face is the fairest I ever saw.'

'It is Anne Boleyn.'

'You are daughter to Sir Thomas?'

She nodded, blushing, thinking Mary would be in his mind, and a fear came to her that her sister's disgrace might discredit herself in his eyes. But he was too far gone in love to find her anything but perfect.

'I am recently come to court,' she said.

'That I know! You could not have been here a day but that I should have found you.'

She said: 'What would your master say an he found you lingering beneath this window?'

'I know not, nor care I!'

'Were you caught, might there not be those who would prevent you from coming again? Already you may have been missed.'

He was alarmed. To be prevented from enjoying the further bliss of such meetings was intolerable.

'I go now,' he said. 'Tomorrow . . . you will be here at this hour?'

'You will find me here.'

'Tomorrow,' he said, and they smiled at each other.

Next day she saw him, and the next. There were many meetings, and for each of those two young lovers the day was good when they met, and bad when they did not. She learned of his exalted rank, and she could say with honesty that this mattered to her not at all, except of course that her ambitious father could raise no objection to a match with the house of Northumberland.

One day her lover came to her and pleasure was written large on his face.

'The Cardinal is to give a ball at his house at Hampton. All the ladies of the court will be invited!'

'You will be there?'

'You too!' he replied.

'We shall be masked.'

'I shall find you.'

'And then . . . ?' she said.

His eyes held the answer to that question.

Anne had dreamed of such happiness, though of late her observation of those about her had led her to conclude that it was rarely known. But to her it had come; she would treasure it, preserve it, keep it for ever. She could scarcely wait for that day when Thomas Wolsey would entertain the court at his great house at Hampton on the Thames.

*　　*　　*

The King was uneasy. The Cardinal had thought to help him when he had had Anne appointed a maid of honour to the Queen; but had he? Never, for the sake of a woman, had the King been so perplexed. He must see her every day, for how could he deny his eyes a sight of the most charming creature they had ever rested on! Yet he dared not speak with her. And why? For this reason; no sooner had the girl set foot in the Queen's apartments than that old enemy, his conscience, must rear its ugly head to leer at him.

'Henry,' said the conscience, 'this girl's sister, Mary Boleyn, has shared your bed full many a night, and well you know the edict of the Pope. Well you know that association with one sister gives you an affinity with the other. Therein lies sin!'

'That I know well,' answered Henry the King. 'But as there was no marriage . . .'

Such reasoning could not satisfy the conscience; it was the same – marriage ceremony or no marriage ceremony – and well he knew it.

'But there was never one like this girl; never was I so drawn to a woman; never before have I felt myself weak as I would be with her. Were she my mistress, I verily believe I should be willing to dispense with all others, and would not that be a good thing, for in the eyes of Holy Church, is it not better for a man to have one mistress than many? Then, would not the Queen be happier? One mistress is forgivable; her distress comes from there being so many.'

He was a man of many superstitions, of deep religious convictions. The God of his belief was a king like himself, though a more powerful being since, in place of the axe, he was able to wield a more terrifying weapon whose blade was supernatural phenomena. Vindictive was the King's god, susceptible to flattery, violent in love, more violent in hate – a jealous god, a god who spied, who recorded slights and insults, and whose mind worked in the same simple way as that of Henry of England. Before this god Henry trembled as men trembled before Henry. Hence the conscience, the uneasiness, his jealous watchfulness of Anne

Boleyn, and his reluctance to make his preference known.

In vain he tried to soothe his senses. All women are much alike in darkness. Mary is very like her sister. Mary is sweet and willing; and there are others as willing.

He tried to placate his conscience. 'I shall not look at the girl; I will remember there is an affinity between us.'

So those days, which were a blissful heaven to Anne and another Henry, were purgatory to Henry the King, racked alternately by conscience and desire.

* * *

She was clad in scarlet, and her vest was cloth of gold. She wore what had become known at court as the Boleyn sleeves, but they did not divulge her identity, for many wore the Boleyn sleeves since she had shown the charm of this particular fashion. Her hair was hidden by her gold cap, and only the beautiful eyes showing through her mask might proclaim her as Anne Boleyn.

He found her effortlessly, because she had described to him in detail the costume she would wear.

'I should have known you though you had not told me. I should always know you.'

'Then, sir,' she answered pertly, 'I would I had put you to the test!'

'I heard the music on the barges as they came along the river,' he said, 'and I do not think I have ever been so happy in my life.'

He was a slender figure in a coat of purple velvet embroidered in gold thread and pearls. Anne thought there was no one more handsome in this great ballroom, though the King, in his scarlet coat on which emeralds flashed, and in his bonnet dazzling rich with rubies and diamonds, was a truly magnificent sight.

The lovers clasped hands, and from a recess watched the gay company.

'There goes the King!'

'Who thinks,' said Anne, laughing, 'to disguise himself with a mask!'

'None dare disillusion him, or 'twould spoil the fun. It seems as though he searches for someone.'

'His latest sweetheart, doubtless!' said Anne scornfully.

Percy laid his hand on her lips.

'You speak too freely, Anne.'

'That was ever a fault of mine. But do you doubt that is the case?'

'I doubt it not – and you have no faults! Let us steal away from these crowds. I know a room where we can be alone. There is much I would say to you.'

'Take me there then. Though I should be most severely reprimanded if the Queen should hear that one of her ladies hides herself in lonely apartments in the house.'

'You can trust me. I would die rather than allow any hurt to come to you.'

'That I know well. I like not these crowds, and would hear what it is that you have to say to me.'

They went up a staircase and along a corridor. There were three small steps leading into a little antechamber; its one window showed the river glistening in moonlight.

Anne went to that window and looked across the gardens to the water.

'There was surely never such a perfect night!' she exclaimed.

He put his arms about her, and they looked at each other, marvelling at what they saw.

'Anne! Make it the most perfect night there ever was, by promising to marry me.'

'If it takes that to make this night perfect,' she answered softly, 'then now it is so.'

He took her hands and kissed them, too young and mild of nature to trust entirely the violence of his emotion.

'You are the most beautiful of all the court ladies, Anne.'

'You think that because you love me.'

'I think it because it is so.'

'Then I am happy to be so for you.'

'Did you ever dream of such happiness, Anne?'

'Yes, often . . . but scarce dared hope it would be mine.'

'Think of those people below us, Anne. How one pities them! For what can they know of happiness like this!'

She laughed suddenly, thinking of the King, pacing the floor, trying to disguise the fact that he was the King, looking about him for his newest sweetheart. Her thoughts went swiftly to Mary.

'My sister . . .' she began.

'What of your sister! Of what moment could she be to us!'

'None!' she cried, and taking his hand, kissed it. 'None, do we but refuse to let her.'

'Then we refuse, Anne.'

'How I love you!' she told him. 'And to think I might have let them marry me to my cousin of Ormond!'

'They would marry me to Shrewsbury's daughter!'

A faint fear stirred her then. She remembered that he was the heir of the Earl of Northumberland; it was meet that he should marry into the Shrewsbury family, not humble Anne Boleyn.

'Oh, Henry,' she said, 'what if they should try to marry you to the Lady Mary?'

'They shall marry me to none but Anne Boleyn!'

It was not difficult, up here in the little moonlight chamber, to defy the world; but they dare not tarry too long. All the company must be present when the masks were removed, or absent themselves on pain of the King's displeasure.

In the ballroom the festive air was tinged with melancholy. The Cardinal was perturbed, for the King clearly showed his annoyance. A masked ball was not such a good idea as it had at first seemed, for the King had been unable to find her whom he sought.

The masks were removed, the ball over, and the royal party lodged in the two hundred and forty gorgeous bedrooms which it was the Cardinal's delight to keep ready for his guests.

The news might seem a rumour just at first, but before many days had passed the fact was established that Henry, Lord Percy, eldest son and heir to the noble Earl of Northumberland, was so far gone in love with sparkling Anne Boleyn that he had determined to marry her.

And so the news came to the ear of the King.

* * *

The King was purple with fury. He sent for him to whom he always turned in time of trouble. The Cardinal came hastily, knowing that to rely on the favour of a king is to build one's hopes on a quiet but not extinct volcano. Over the Cardinal flowed the molten lava of Henry's anger.

'By Christ!' cried the King. 'Here is a merry state of affairs! I would take the fool and burn him at the stake, were he not such a young fool. How dare he think to contract himself without our consent!'

'Your Majesty, I fear I am in ignorance ...'

'Young Percy!' roared His Majesty. 'Fool! Dolt that he is! He has, an it please you, decided he will marry Anne Boleyn!'

Inwardly the Cardinal could smile. This was a mere outbreak of royal jealousy. I will deal with this, thought the Cardinal, and deplored that his wit, his diplomacy must be squandered to mend a lover's troubles.

'Impertinent young fool!' soothed the Cardinal. 'As he is one of my young men, Your Majesty must allow me to deal with him. I will castigate him. I will make him aware of his youthful ... nay, criminal folly, since he has offended Your Majesty. He is indeed a dolt to think Northumberland can mate with the daughter of a knight!'

Through the King's anger beamed his gratitude to Wolsey. Dear Thomas, who made the way easy! That was the reason, he told his conscience – Northumberland cannot mate with a mere knight's daughter!

' 'Twere an affront to us!' growled mollified Henry. 'We gave our consent to the match with Shrewsbury's girl.'

'And a fitting match indeed!' murmured the Cardinal.

'A deal more fitting than that he should marry Boleyn's girl. My dear Wolsey, I should hold myself responsible to Shrewsbury and his poor child if anything went amiss. . . .'

'Your Grace was ever full of conscience. You must not blame your royal self for the follies of your subjects.'

'I do, Thomas . . . I do! After all, 'twas I who brought the wench to court.'

Wolsey murmured: 'Your Majesty . . . ? Why, I thought 'twas I who talked to Boleyn of his younger daughter. . . .'

'No matter!' said the King, his eyes beaming with affection. 'I thought I mentioned the girl to you. No matter!'

'I spoke to Boleyn, Your Grace, I remember well.'

The King's hand patted the red-clad shoulder.

'I know this matter can be trusted to you.'

'Your Majesty knows well that I shall settle it most expeditiously.'

'They shall both be banished the court. I will not be flouted by these young people!'

Wolsey bowed.

'The Shrewsbury marriage can be hastened,' said the King.

Greatly daring, Wolsey asked: 'And the girl, Your Majesty? There was talk of a marriage . . . the Ormond estates were the issue . . . Perhaps Your Majesty does not remember.'

The brows contracted; the little eyes seemed swallowed up in puffy flesh. The King's voice cracked out impatiently: 'That matter is not settled. I like not these Irish. Suffice it that we banish the girl.'

'Your Majesty may trust me to deal with the matter in accordance with your royal wishes.'

'And, Thomas . . . let the rebuke come from you. I would not have these young people know that I have their welfare so much at heart; methinks they already have too high a conceit of themselves.'

After Wolsey retired, the King continued to pace up and down. Let her return to Hever. She should be punished for daring to fall in love with that paltry boy. How was she in love? Tender? It was difficult to imagine that. Eager? Ah! Eager with a wretched boy! Haughty enough she had been with her lord the King! To test that eagerness he would have given the brightest jewel in his crown, but she would refuse her favours like a queen. And in a brief acquaintance, she had twice offended him; let her see that even she could not do that with impunity!

So she should be exiled to Hever, whither he would ride one day. She should be humble; he would be stern . . . just at first.

He threw himself into a chair, legs apart, hands on knees, thinking of a reconciliation in the rose garden at Hever.

His anger had passed away.

* * *

Immediately on his return to his house at Westminster, Wolsey sent for Lord Percy.

The young man came promptly, and there in the presence of several of his higher servants Wolsey began to upbraid him, marvelling, he said, at his folly in thinking he might enter into an engagement with a foolish girl at the court. Did the young fool not realize that on his father's death he would inherit and enjoy one of the noblest earldoms in the kingdom? How then could he marry without the consent of his father? Did Percy think, he thundered, that either his father or the King would consent to his matching himself with such a one? Moreover, continued the Cardinal, working himself up to a fine frenzy of indignation such as struck terror into the heart of the boy, he would have Percy know that the King had at great trouble prepared a suitable match for Anne Boleyn. Would he flout the King's pleasure!

Lord Percy was no more timid than most, but he knew the ways of the court well enough to quail before the meaning he read into Wolsey's words. Men had been committed to the Tower for refusing to obey the King's command, and Wolsey clearly had the King behind him in this matter. Committed to the Tower! Though the dread Cardinal did not speak the words, Percy knew they were there ready to be pronounced at any moment. Men went to the Tower and were heard of no more. Dread happenings there were in the underground chambers of the Tower of

London. Men were incarcerated, and never heard of again. And Percy had offended the King!

'Sir,' he said, trembling, 'I knew not the King's pleasure, and am sorry for it. I consider I am of good years, and thought myself able to provide me a convenient wife as my fancy should please me, not doubting that my lord and father would have been well content. Though she be but a simple maid and her father a knight, yet she is descended of noble parentage, for her mother is of high Norfolk blood and her father descended from the Earl of Ormond. I most humbly beseech Your Grace's favour therein, and also to entreat the King's Majesty on my behalf for his princely favour in this matter which I cannot forsake.'

The Cardinal turned to his servants, appealing to them to observe the wilful folly of this boy. Sadly he reproached Percy for knowing the King's pleasure and not readily submitting to it.

'I have gone too far in this matter,' said Percy.

'Dost think,' cried Wolsey, 'that the King and I know not what we have to do in weighty matters such as this!'

He left the boy, remarking as he went that he should not seek out the girl, or he would have to face the wrath of the King.

The Earl arrived, coming in haste from the north since the command was the King's, and hastened to Wolsey's house. A cold man with an eye to his own advantage, the Earl listened gravely, touched his neck uneasily as though he felt the sharp blade of an axe there – for heads had been severed for less than this – hardened his face, and said that he would set the matter to rights.

He went to his son and railed at him, cursing his pride, his licentiousness, but chiefly the fact that he had incurred the King's displeasure. So he would bring his father to the block and forfeit the family estate, would he! He was a waster, useless, idle. . . . He would return to his home immediately and proceed with the marriage to the Lady Mary Talbot, to which he was committed.

Percy, threatened by his father, dreading the wrath of

the King, greatly fearing the mighty Cardinal, and not being possessed of the same reckless courage as his partner in romance, was overpowered by this storm he and Anne had aroused. He could not stand out against them. Wretchedly, broken-heartedly he gave in, and left the court with his father.

He was, however, able to leave a message for Anne with a kinsman of hers, in which he begged that she would remember her promise from which none but God could loose her.

And the Cardinal, passing through the palace courtyard with his retinue, saw a dark-eyed girl with a pale, tragic face at one of the windows.

Ah! thought the Cardinal, turning his mind from matters of state. The cause of all the trouble!

The black eyes blazed into sudden hatred as they rested on him, for there had been those who had overheard Wolsey's slighting remarks about herself and hastened to inform her. Wolsey she blamed, and Wolsey only, for the ruin of her life.

Insolently she stared at him, her lips moving as though she cursed him.

The Cardinal smiled. Does she think to frighten me? A foolish girl! And I the first man in the kingdom! I would reprove her, but for the indignity of noting one so lacking in significance!

The next time he passed through the courtyard, he did not see Anne Boleyn. She had been banished to Hever.

* * *

At home in Hever Castle, a fierce anger took possession of her. She had waited for a further message from her lover. There was no message. He will come, she had told herself. They would ride away together, mayhap disguised as country folk, and they would care nothing for the anger of the Cardinal.

She would awake in the night, thinking she heard a tap on her window; walking in the grounds, she would feel her heart hammering at the sound of crackling bracken. She

77

longed for him, thinking constantly of that night in the little chamber at Hampton Court, which they had said should be a perfect night and which by promising each other marriage they had made so; she thought of how sorry they had been for those who were dancing below, knowing nothing of the enchantment they were experiencing.

She would be ready when he came for her. Where would they go? Anywhere! For what did place matter! Life should be a glorious adventure. Taking her own courage for granted, why should she doubt his?

He did not come, and she brooded. She grew bitter, wondering why he did not come. She thought angrily of the wicked Cardinal whose spite had ruined her chances of happiness. Fiercely she hated him. 'This foolish girl . . .' he had said. 'This Anne Boleyn, who is but the daughter of a knight, to wed with one of the noblest families in the kingdom!'

She would show my lord Cardinal whether she was a foolish girl or not! Oh, the hypocrite! The man of God! He who kept house as a king and was vindictive as a devil and hated by the people!

When she and Percy went off together, the Cardinal should see whether she was a foolish girl!

And still her lover did not come.

'I cannot bear this long separation!' cried the passionate girl. 'Perhaps he thinks to wait awhile until his father is dead, for they say he is a sick man. But I do not wish to wait!'

She was melancholy, for the summer was passing and it was sad to see the leaves fluttering down.

The King rode out to Hever. In her room she heard the bustle his presence in the castle must inevitably cause. She locked her door and refused to go down. If Wolsey had ruined her happiness, the King – doubtless at the wicked man's instigation – had humiliated her by banishing her from the court. Unhappy as she was, she cared for nothing – neither her father's anger nor the King's.

Her mother came and stood outside the door to plead with her.

'The King has asked for you, Anne. You must come . . . quickly.'

'I will not! I will not!' cried Anne. 'I was banished, was I not? Had he wished to see me, he should not have sent me from the court.'

'I dare not go back and say you refuse to come.'

'I care not!' sobbed Anne, throwing herself on her bed and laughing and weeping simultaneously, for she was beside herself with a grief that she found herself unable to control.

Her father came to her door, but his threats were as vain as her mother's pleas.

'Would you bring disgrace on us!' stormed Sir Thomas. 'Have you not done enough!'

'Disgrace!' she cried furiously. 'Yes, if it is a disgrace to love and wish to marry, I have disgraced you. It is an honour to be mistress of the King. Mary has brought you honour! An I would not come for my mother, assuredly I will not come for you!'

'The King commands your presence!'

'You may do what you will,' she said stubbornly. 'He may do what he will. I care for nothing . . . now.' And she burst into fresh weeping.

Sir Thomas – diplomatic over a family crisis as on a foreign mission – explained that his daughter was sadly indisposed; and the King, marvelling at his feelings for this wilful girl, replied: 'Disturb her not then.'

The King left Hever, and Anne returned to that life which had no meaning – waiting, longing, hoping, fearing.

One cold day, when the first touch of winter was in the air and a fresh wind was bringing down the last of the leaves from the trees in the park, Sir Thomas brought home the news.

He looked at Anne expressionlessly and said: 'Lord Percy has married the Lady Mary Talbot. This is an end of your affair.'

She went to her room and stayed there all that day. She

did not eat; she did not sleep; she spoke to none; and on the second day she fell into a fit of weeping, upbraiding the Cardinal, and with him her lover. 'They could have done what they would with me,' she told herself bitterly. 'I would never have given in!'

Drearily the days passed. She grew pale and listless, so that her mother feared for her life and communicated her fears to her husband.

Sir Thomas hinted that if she would return to court, such action would not be frowned on.

'That assuredly I will not do!' she said, and so ill was she that none dared reason with her.

She called to mind then the happiness of her life in France, and it seemed to her that her only hope of tearing her misery from her heart lay in getting away from England. She thought of one whom she would ever admire – the witty, sparkling, Duchess of Alençon; was there some hope, with that spritely lady, of renewing her interest in life?

Love she had experienced, and found it bitter; she wanted no more such experience.

'With Marguerite I could forget,' she said; and, fearing for her health, Sir Thomas decided to humour her wishes; so once more Anne left Hever for the court of France.

THE KING'S SECRET MATTER

THE HOUSE at Lambeth was wrapped in deepest gloom. In the great bed which Jocosa had shared with Lord Edmund Howard since the night of her marriage, she now lay dying. She was very tired, poor lady, for her married life had been a wearying business. It seemed that no sooner had one small Howard left her womb than another was growing there; and poverty, in such circumstances, had been humiliating.

Death softened bitter feelings. What did it matter now, that her distinguished husband had been so neglected! Why, she wondered vaguely, were people afraid of death? It was so easy to die, so difficult to live.

'Hush! Hush!' said a voice. 'You must not disturb your mother now. Do you not see she is sleeping peacefully?'

Then came to Jocosa's ears the sound of a little girl's sobbing. Jocosa tried to move the coverlet to attract attention. That was little Catherine crying, because, young as she was, she was old enough to understand the meaning of hushed voices, the air of gloom, old enough to smell the odour of death.

Jocosa knew suddenly why people were afraid of death. The fear was for those they left behind.

'My children . . .' she murmured, and tried to start up from her bed.

'Hush, my lady,' said a voice. 'You must rest, my dear.'

'My children,' she breathed, but her lips were parched, too stiff for the words to come through.

She thought of Catherine, the prettiest of her daughters, yet somehow the most helpless. Gentle, loving little Catherine, so eager to please that she let others override her. Some extra sense told the mother that her daughter Catherine would sorely miss a mother's care.

With a mighty effort she spoke. 'Catherine. . . . Daughter. . . .'

'She said my name!' cried Catherine. 'She is asking for me.'

'C ... Catherine ...'

'I am here,' said Catherine.

Jocosa lifted the baby fingers to her parched lips. Perhaps, she thought, she will acquire a stepmother. Stepmothers are not always kind; they have their own children whom they would advance beyond those of the woman they have replaced, and a living wife has power a dead one lacks. Perhaps her Aunt Norfolk would take this little Catherine; perhaps her Grandmother Norfolk. No, not the Norfolks, a hard race! Catherine, who was soft and young and tender, should not go to them. Jocosa thought of her own childhood at Hollingbourne, in the lovely old house of her father, Sir Richard Culpepper. Now her brother John was installed there; he had a son of his own who would be playing in her nursery. She remembered happy days spent there, and in her death-drugged thoughts it was Catherine who seemed to be there, not herself. It was soothing to the dying mother to see her daughter Catherine in her own nursery, but the pleasure passed and she was again conscious of the big, bare room at Lambeth.

'Edmund ...' she said.

Catherine turned her tearful eyes to the nurse.

'She speaks my father's name.'

'Yes, my lady?' asked the nurse, bending over the bed.

'Edmund ...'

'Go to your father and tell him your mother would speak to him.'

He stood by the bedside – poor, kind, bitter Edmund, whose life with her had been blighted by that pest, poverty. Now he was sorry for the sharp words he had spoken to her, for poverty had ever haunted him, waylaid him, leered at him, goaded him, warping his natural kindness, wrecking that peace he longed to share with his family.

'Jocosa ...' There was such tenderness in his voice when he said her name that she thought momentarily that this was their wedding night, and he her lover; but she heard then the rattle in her throat and was conscious of her body's burning heat, and thus remembered that this was not the prologue but the epilogue to her life with Edmund, and that Catherine – gentlest of her children – was in some danger, which she sensed but did not comprehend.

'Edmund . . . Catherine . . .'

He lifted the child in his arms and held her nearer the bed.

'Jocosa, here is Catherine.'

'My lord . . . let her go . . . let Catherine go . . .'

His head bent closer, and with a great effort the words came out.

'My brother John . . . at Hollingbourne . . . in Kent. Let Catherine . . . go to my brother John.'

Lord Edmund said: 'Rest peacefully, Jocosa. It shall be as you wish.'

She sank back, smiling, for it was to be, since none dared disregard a promise made to a dying woman.

The effort had tired her; she knew not where she lay, but she believed it must be at Hollingbourne in Kent, so peaceful was she. The weary beating of her heart was slowing down. 'Catherine is safe,' it said. 'Catherine is . . . safe.'

* * *

At Hollingbourne, whither Catherine had been brought at her father's command, life was different from that lived in the house at Lambeth. The first thing that struck Catherine was the plenteous supply of good plain country fare. There was a simplicity at Hollingbourne which had been entirely lacking at Lambeth; and Sir John, in his country retreat, was lord of the neighbourhood, whereas Lord Edmund, living his impecunious life among those of equally noble birth, had seemed of little importance. Catherine looked upon her big Uncle John as something like a god.

The nurseries were composed of several airy rooms at the top of the house, and from these it was possible to look over the pleasant Kentish country undisturbed by the sombre grandeur of the great city on whose outskirts the Lambeth house had sat. Catherine had often looked at the forts of the great Tower of London, and there was that in them to frighten the little girl. Servants were not over-careful; and though there were some who had nothing but adulation to give to Lord Edmund and his wife, poverty proved to be a leveller, and there were others who had but little respect for one who feared to be arrested at any moment for debt, even though he be a noble lord; and these servants were careless of what was said before the little Howards. There was a certain Doll Tappit who had for lover one who was a warder at the Tower, and fine stories he could tell her of the bloodcurdling shrieks which came from the torture chambers, of the noble gentlemen who had displeased the King and who were left to starve in the rat-infested dungeons. Therefore Catherine was glad to see green and pleasant hills against the skyline, and leafy woods in place of the great stone towers.

There was comfort at Hollingbourne, such as there had never been at Lambeth.

She was taken to the nurseries, and there put into the charge of an old nurse who had known her mother; and there she was introduced to her cousin Thomas and his tutor.

Shyly she studied Thomas. He, with his charming face in which his bold and lively eyes flashed and danced with merriment, was her senior by a year or so, and she was much in awe of him; but, finding the cousin who was to share his nursery to be but a girl – and such a little girl – he was inclined to be contemptuous.

She was lonely that first day. It was true she was given food; and the nurse went through her scanty wardrobe, clicking her tongue over this worn garment and that one, which should have been handed to a servant long ago.

'Tut-tut!' exclaimed the nurse. 'And how have you been brought up, I should wonder!' Blaming little Catherine Howard for her father's poverty; wondering what the world was coming to, when such beggars must be received in the noble house of Culpepper.

Catherine was by nature easy-going, gay and optimistic;

never saying – This is bad; always – This might be worse. She had lost her mother whom she had loved beyond all else in the world, and she was heartbroken; but she could not but enjoy the milk that was given her to drink; she could not but be glad that she was removed from Lambeth. Her sisters and brothers she missed, but being one of the younger ones, in games always the unimportant and unpleasant rôles were given to her; and if there were not enough parts to go round, it was Catherine who was left out. The afternoon of her first day at Hollingbourne was spent with the nurse who, tutting and clicking her tongue, cut up garments discarded by my lady, to make clothes for Catherine Howard. She stood still and was fitted; was pushed and made to turn about; and she thought the clothes that would soon be hers were splendid indeed.

Through the window she saw Thomas ride by on his chestnut mare, and she ran to the window and knelt on the window seat to watch him; and he, looking up, for he suspected she might be there, waved to her graciously, which filled Catherine with delight, for she had decided, as soon as he had looked down his haughty nose at her, that he was the most handsome person she had ever seen.

She had a bedroom to herself – a little panelled room with latticed windows – which adjoined the main nursery. At Lambeth she had shared her room with several members of her family.

Even on that first day she loved Hollingbourne, but at that time it was chiefly because her mother had talked to her of it so affectionately.

But on the first night, when she lay in the little room all by herself, with the moon shining through the window and throwing ghostly shadows, she began to sense the solitude all about her and her quick love for Hollingbourne was replaced by fear. There was no sound from barges going down the river to Greenwich or up it to Richmond and Hampton Court; there was only silence broken now and then by the weird hooting of an owl. The strange room seemed menacing in this half-light, and suddenly she longed for the room at Lambeth with the noisy brothers and sisters; she thought of her mother, for Catherine Howard had had that sweet companionship which so many in her station might never know, since there was no court life to take Jocosa from her family, and her preoccupations were not with the cut of a pair of sleeves but with her children; that, poverty had given Catherine, but cruel life had let it be appreciated only to snatch it away. So in her quiet room at Hollingbourne, Catherine shed bitter tears into her pillow, longing for her mother's soft caress and the sound of her gentle voice.

'You have no mother now,' they had said, 'so you must be a brave girl.'

But I'm not brave, thought Catherine, and immediately remembered how her eldest brother had jeered at her because she, who was so afraid of ghosts, would listen to and even encourage Doll Tappit to tell tales of them.

Doll Tappit's lover, Walter the warder, had once seen a ghost. Doll Tappit told the story to Nurse as she sat feeding the baby; Catherine had sat, round-eyed, listening.

'Now you know well how 'tis Walter's task to walk the Tower twice a night. Now Walter, as you know, is nigh on six foot tall, near as tall as His Majesty the King, and not a man to be easily affrighted. It was a moonlit night. Walter said the clouds kept hurrying across the moon as though there was terrible sights they wanted to hide from her. There is terrible sights, Nurse, in the Tower of London! Walter, he's heard some terrible groaning there, he's heard chains clanking, he's heard screams and shrieking. But afore this night he never *see* anything . . . And there he was on the green, right there by the scaffold, when . . . clear as I see you now, Nurse . . . the Duke stood before him; his head was lying in a pool of blood on the ground beside him, and the blood ran down all over his Grace's fine clothes!'

'What then?' asked Nurse, inclined to be sceptical. 'What would my lord Duke of Buckingham have to say to Walter the warder?'

'He said nothing. He was just there . . . just for a minute he was there. Then he was gone.'

'They say,' said Nurse, 'that the pantler there is very hospitable with a glass of metheglin . . .'

'Walter never takes it!'

'I'll warrant he did that night.'

'And when the ghost had gone, Walter stooped down where it was . . .'

'Where what was?'

'The head . . . all dripping blood. And though the head was gone, the blood was still there. Walter touched it; he showed me the stain on his coat.'

Nurse might snort her contempt, but Catherine shivered; and there were occasions when she would dream of the headless duke, coming towards her, and his head making stains on the nursery floor.

And here at Hollingbourne there were no brothers and sisters to help her disbelief in ghosts. Ghosts came when people were alone, for all the stories Catherine had ever heard of ghosts were of people who were alone when they saw them. Ghosts had an aversion to crowds of human beings, so that, all through her life, being surrounded by brothers and sisters, Catherine had felt safe; but not since she had come to Hollingbourne.

As these thoughts set Catherine shivering, outside her window she heard a faint noise, a gentle rustling of the creeper; it was as though hands pulled at it. She listened fearfully, and then it came again.

She was sitting up in bed, staring at the window. Again there came that rustle; and with it she could hear the deep gasps of one who struggles for breath.

She shut her eyes; she covered her head with the clothes; then, peeping out and seeing a face at her window, she screamed. A voice said: 'Hush!' very sternly, and Catherine thought she would die from relief, for the voice was the voice of her handsome young cousin, Thomas Culpepper.

He scrambled through the window.

'Why, 'tis Catherine Howard! I trust I did not startle you, Cousin?'

'I . . . thought you . . . to be a . . . ghost!'

That made him rock with merriment.

'I had forgotten this was your room, Cousin,' he lied, for well he had known it and had climbed in this way in order to impress her with his daring. 'I have been out on wild adventures.' He grimaced at a jagged tear in his breeches.

'Wild adventures . . .!'

'I do bold things by night, Cousin.'

Her big eyes were round with wonder, admiring him, and Thomas Culpepper, basking in such admiration that he could find nowhere but in this simple girl cousin, felt mightily pleased that Catherine Howard had come to Hollingbourne.

'Tell me of them,' she said.

He put his fingers to his lips.

'It is better not to speak so loudly, Cousin. In this house they believe me to be but a boy. When I am out, I am a man.'

'Is it witchcraft?' asked Catherine eagerly, for often had she heard Doll Tappit speak of witchcraft.

He was silent on that point, silent and mysterious; but before he would talk to her, he would have her get off her bed to see the height of the wall which he had climbed with naught to help him but the creeper.

She got out, and naked tiptoed to the window. She was greatly impressed.

'It was a wonderful thing to do, Cousin Thomas,' she said.

He smiled, well pleased, thinking her prettier in her very white skin than in the ugly clothes she had worn on her arrival.

'I do many wonderful things,' he told her. 'You will be cold, naked thus,' he said. 'Get back into your bed.'

'Yes,' she said, shivering, half with cold and half with excitement. 'I am cold.'

She leapt gracefully into bed, and pulled the clothes up to her chin. He sat on the bed, admiring the mud on his shoes and the unkempt appearance of his clothes.

'Do tell me,' she said, her knees at her chin, her eyes sparkling.

'I fear it is not for little girls' ears.'

'I am not such a little girl. It is only because you are big that it seems so.'

'Ah!' he mused, well pleased to consider it in that way. 'That may well be so; perhaps you are not so small. I have been having adventures, Cousin; I have been out trapping hares and shooting game!'

Her mouth was a round O of wonder.

'Did you catch many?'

'Hundreds, Cousin! More than a little girl like you could count.'

'I could count hundreds!' she protested.

'It would have taken you days to count these. Do you know that, had I been caught, I could have been hanged at Tyburn?'

'Yes,' said Catherine, who could have told him more gruesome stories of Tyburn than he could tell her, for he had never known Doll Tappit.

'But,' said Thomas, 'I expect Sir John, my father, would not have allowed that to happen. And then again 'twas scarcely poaching, as it happened on my father's land which will be one day mine, so now, Cousin Catherine, you see what adventures I have!'

'You are very brave,' said Catherine.

'Perhaps a little. I have been helping a man whose acquaintance I made. He is a very interesting man, Cousin; a poacher. So I for fun, and he for profit, poach on my father's land.'

'Were he caught, he would hang by the neck.'

'I should intercede for him with my father.'

'I would that I were brave as you are!'

'Bah! You are just a girl . . . and frightened that you might see a ghost.'

'I am not now. It is only when I am alone.'

'Will you be afraid when I have gone?'

'Very much afraid,' she said.

He surveyed her in kingly fashion. She was such a little girl, and she paid such pleasant tribute to his masculine superiority. Yes, assuredly he was glad his cousin had come to Hollingbourne.

'I shall be here to protect you,' he said.

'Oh, will you? Cousin Thomas, I know not how to thank you.'

'You surely do not think I could be afraid of a ghost!'

'I know it to be impossible.'

'Then you are safe, Catherine.'

'But if, when I am alone ...'

'Listen!' He put his head close to hers conspiratorially. 'There' – he pointed over his shoulder – 'is my room. Only one wall dividing me from you, little Cousin. I am ever alert for danger, and very lightly do I sleep. Now listen very attentively, Catherine. Should a ghost come, all you must do is tap on this wall, and depend upon it you will have me here before you can bat an eyelid. I shall sleep with my sword close at hand.'

'Oh, Thomas! You have a sword too?'

'It is my father's, but as good as mine because one day it will be so.'

'Oh, Thomas!' Sweet was her adulation to the little braggart.

'None dare harm you when I am by,' he assured her. 'Dead or living will have to deal with me.'

'You would make yourself my knight then, Thomas,' she said softly.

'You could not have a braver ...'

'Oh, I know it. I do not think I shall cry very much now.'

'Why should you cry?'

'For my mother, who is dead.'

'No, Catherine, you need not cry; for in place of your mother you have your brave cousin, Thomas Culpepper.'

'Shall I then tap on the wall if ...?'

He wrinkled his brows. 'For tonight, yes. Tomorrow we shall find a stick for you ... a good, stout stick I think; that will make a good banging on the wall, and you could, in an emergency, hit the ghost should it be necessary before I arrive.'

'Oh, no, I could not! I should die of fear. Besides, might a ghost not do terrible things to one who made so bold as to hit it?'

'That may be so. The safest plan, my cousin, is to wait for me.'

'I do not know how to thank you.'

'Thank me by putting your trust in me.'

He stood back from the bed, bowing deeply.

'Good night, Cousin.'

'Good night, dear, *brave* Thomas.'

He went, and she hugged her pillow in an ecstasy of delight. Never had one of her own age been so kind to her; never had she felt of such consequence.

As for ghosts, what of them! What harm could they do to Catherine Howard, with Thomas Culpepper only the other side of her bedroom wall, ready to fly to her rescue!

* * *

There was delight in the hours spent at Hollingbourne. Far away in a hazy and unhappy past were the Lambeth days; and the sweetest thing she had known was the ripening of her friendship with her cousin Thomas. Catherine, whose nature was an excessively affectionate one, asked nothing more than that she should be allowed to love him. Her affection he most graciously accepted, and returned it in some smaller measure. It was a happy friendship, and he grew more fond of her than his dignity would allow him to make known; she, so sweet already, though so young, so clingingly feminine, touched something in his manhood. He found great pleasure in protecting her, and thus love grew between them. He taught her to ride, to climb trees, to share his adventures, though he never took her out at night; nor did he himself adventure much this way after her coming, wishing to be at hand lest in the lonely hours of evening she might need his help.

Her education was neglected. Sir John did not believe overmuch in the education of girls; and who was she but a dependant, though the child of his sister! She was a girl, and doubtless a match would be made for her; and bearing such a name as Howard, that match could be made without the unnecessary adornment of a good education. Consider the case of his kinsman, Thomas Boleyn. He had been, so Sir John had heard, at great pains to educate his two younger children who, in the family, had acquired the reputation of possessing some brilliance. Even the girl had been educated, and what had education done for her? There was some talk of a disaster at court; the girl had aspired to marry herself to a very highly born nobleman – doubtless due to her education. And had her education helped her? Not at all! Banishment and disgrace had been her lot. Let girls remain docile; let them cultivate charming manners; let them learn how to dress themselves prettily and submit to their husbands. That was all a girl needed from life. And did she want to construe Latin verse to do these things; did she want to give voice to her frivolous thoughts in six different languages! No, the education of young Catherine Howard was well taken care of.

Thomas tried to teach his cousin a little, but he quickly gave up the idea. She had no aptitude for it; rather she preferred to listen to the tales of his imaginary adventures, to sing and dance and play musical instruments. She was a frivolous little creature, and having been born into poverty, well pleased to have stepped out of it, happy to have for her friend surely the most handsome and the dearest cousin in the world. What more could she want?

And so the days passed pleasantly – riding with Thomas, listening to Thomas's stories, admiring him, playing games in which he took the glorious part of knight and rescuer, she the rôle of helpless lady and rescued; now and then taking a lesson at the virginals, which was not like a lesson at all because she had been born with a love of music; she had singing lessons too which she loved, for her voice was pretty and promised to be good. But life could not go on in this even tenor for ever. A young man such as Thomas Culpepper could not be left to the care of a private tutor indefinitely.

He came to the music room one day while Catherine sat over the virginals with her teacher, and threw himself into a window seat and watched her as she played. Her auburn hair fell about her flushed face; she was very young, but there was always in Catherine Howard, even when a baby, a certain womanliness. Now she was aware of Thomas there, she was playing with especial pains to please him. That, thought Thomas, was so typical of her; she would always care deeply about pleasing those she loved. He was going to miss her very much; he found that watching her brought a foolish lump into his throat, and he contemplated running from the room for fear his sentimental tears should betray him. It was really but a short time ago that she had come to Hollingbourne, and yet she had made a marked difference to his life. Strange it was that that should be so; she was meek and self-effacing, and yet her very wish to please made her important to him; and he, who had longed for this childish stage of his education to be completed, was now sorry that it was over.

The teacher had stood up; the lesson was ended.

Catherine turned a flushed face to her cousin.

'Thomas, do you think I have improved?'

'Indeed yes,' he said, realizing that he had hardly heard what she had played. 'Catherine,' he said quickly, 'let us ride together. There is something I would say to you.'

They galloped round the paddock, he leading, she trying to catch up but never succeeding – which made her so enchanting. She was the perfect female, for ever stressing her subservience to the male, soft and helpless, meek, her eyes ever ready to fill with tears at a rebuke.

He pulled up his horse, but did not dismount; he dared not, because he felt so ridiculously near tears himself. He must therefore be ready to whip up his horse if this inclination became a real danger.

'Catherine,' he said, his voice hardly steady, 'I have bad news. . . .'

He glanced at her face, at the hazel eyes wide now with fear, at the little round mouth which quivered.

'Oh, sweet little Cousin,' he said, 'it is not so bad. I shall come back; I shall come back very soon.'

'You are going away then, Thomas?'

The world was suddenly dark; tears came to her eyes and brimmed over. He looked away, and sought refuge in hardening his voice.

'Come, Catherine, do not be so foolish. You surely did not imagine that my father's son could spend all his days tucked away here in the country!'

'No . . . no.'

'Well then! Dry your eyes. No handkerchief? How like you, Catherine!' He threw her his. 'You may keep that,' he said, 'and think of me when I am gone.'

She took the handkerchief as though already it were a sacred thing.

He went on, his voice shaking: 'And you must give me one of yours, Catherine, that I may keep it.'

She wiped her eyes.

He said tenderly: "It is only for a little while, Catherine.'

Now she was smiling.

'I should have known,' she said. 'Of course you will go away.'

'When I return we shall have very many pleasant days together, Catherine.'

'Yes, Thomas.' Being Catherine, she could think of the reunion rather than the parting, even now.

He slipped off his horse, and she immediately did likewise; he held out his hands, and she put hers into them.

'Catherine, do you ever think of when we are grown up . . . really grown up, not just pretending to be?'

'I do not know, Thomas. I think perhaps I may have.'

'When we are grown up, Catherine, we shall marry . . . both of us. Catherine, I may marry *you* when I am of age.'

'Thomas! Would you?'

'I might,' he said.

She was pretty, with the smile breaking through her tears.

'Yes,' he said, 'I think mayhap I will. And now, Catherine, you will not mind so much that I must go away, for you must know, we are both young in actual fact. Were we not, I would marry you now and take you with me.'

They were still holding hands, smiling at each other; he, flushed with pleasure at his beneficence in offering her such a glorious prospect as marriage with him; she, overwhelmed by the honour he did her.

He said: 'When people are affianced, Catherine, they kiss. I am going to kiss you now.'

He kissed her on either cheek and then her soft baby mouth. Catherine wished he would go on kissing her, but he did not, not over-much liking the operation and considering it a necessary but rather humiliating formality; besides, he feared that there might be those to witness this and do what he dreaded most that people would do, laugh at him.

'That,' he said, 'is settled. Let us ride.'

* * *

Catherine had been so long at Hollingbourne that she came to regard it as her home. Thomas came home occasionally, and there was nothing he liked better than to talk of the wild adventures he had had; and never had he known a better audience than his young cousin. She was so credulous, so ready to admire. They both looked forward to these reunions, and although they spoke not of their marriage which they had long ago in the paddock decided should one day take place, they neither of them forgot nor wished to repudiate the promises. Thomas was not the type of boy to think over-much of girls except when they could be fitted into an adventure where, by their very helplessness and physical inferiority, they could help to glorify the resourcefulness and strength of the male. Thomas was a normal, healthy boy whose thoughts had turned but fleetingly to sex; Catherine, though younger, was conscious of sex, and had been since she was a baby; she enjoyed Thomas's company most when he held her hand or lifted her over a brook or rescued her from some imaginary evil fate. When the game was a pretence of stealing jewels, and she must pretend to be a man, the adventure lost its complete joy for her. She remembered still the quick, shame-faced kisses he had given her in the paddock, and she would have loved to have made plans for their marriage, to kiss now and then. She dared not tell Thomas this, and little did he guess that she was all but a woman while he was yet a child.

So passed the pleasant days until that sad afternoon when a serving-maid came to her, as she sat in the wide window

95

seat of the main nursery, to tell her that her uncle and aunt would have speech with her, and she was to go at once to her uncle's chamber.

As soon as Catherine reached that room she knew that something was amiss, for both her uncle and her aunt looked very grave.

'My dear niece,' said Sir John, who frequently spoke for both, 'come hither to me. I have news for you.'

Catherine went to him and stood before him, her knees trembling, while she prayed: 'Please, God, let Thomas be safe and well.'

'Now that your grandfather, Lord Thomas the Duke, is no more,' said Sir John in the solemn voice he used when speaking of the dead, 'your grandmother feels that she would like much to have you with her. You know your father has married again. . . .' His face stiffened. He was a righteous man; there was nothing soft in his nature; it seemed to him perfectly reasonable that, his sister's husband having married a new wife, his own responsibility for his sister's child should automatically cease.

'Go . . . from here . . . ?' stammered Catherine.

'To your grandmother in Norfolk.'

'Oh . . . but I . . . do not wish . . . Here, I have been . . . so happy. . . .'

Her aunt put an arm about her shoulders and kissed her cheek.

'You must understand, Catherine, your staying here is not in our hands. Your father has married again . . . he wishes that you should go to your grandmother.'

Catherine looked from one to the other, her eyes bright with tears which overflowed, for she could never control her emotion.

Her aunt and uncle waited for her to dry her eyes and listen to them.

Then Sir John said: 'You must prepare yourself for a long journey, so that you will be ready when your grandmother sends for you. Now you may go.'

Catherine stumbled from the room, thinking, When he

comes next time, I shall not be here! And how shall I ever see him . . . he in Kent and I in Norfolk?

In the nursery the news was received with great interest.

'Well may *you* cry!' she was told. 'Why, when you are at your grandmother's house you will feel very haughty towards us poor folk. I have heard from one who served the Duchess that she keeps great state both at Horsham and Lambeth. The next we shall hear of you is that you are going to court!'

'I do not care to go to court!' cried Catherine.

'Ah!' she was told. 'All you care for is your cousin Thomas!'

Then Catherine thought, is it so far from here to Norfolk? Not so far but that *he* could come to me. He will come; and then in a few years we shall be married. The time will pass quickly. . . .

She remembered her grandmother – plumpish, inclined to poke her with a stick, lazy Grandmother who sat about and laughed to herself and made remarks which set her wheezing and chuckling, such as 'You have pretty eyes, Catherine Howard. Keep them; they will serve you well!' Grandmother, with sly eyes and chins that wobbled, and an inside that gurgled since she took such delight in the table.

Catherine waited for the arrival of those who would take her to her grandmother, and with the passage of the days her fears diminished; she lived in a pleasant dream in which Thomas came to Horsham and spent his holidays there instead of at Hollingbourne; and Catherine, being the granddaughter of such a fine lady as the Dowager Duchess of Norfolk, wore beautiful clothes and jewels in her hair. Thomas said: 'You are more beautiful in Norfolk than you were in Kent!' And he kissed her, and Catherine kissed him; there was much kissing and embracing at Horsham. 'Let us elope,' said Thomas. Thus pleasantly passed the last days at Hollingbourne, and when the time came for her departure to Norfolk, she did not greatly mind, for she had planned such a happy future for herself and Thomas.

* * *

The house at Horsham was indeed grand. It was built round the great hall; it had its ballroom, its many bedrooms, numerous small chambers and unpredictable corridors; from its mullioned windows there were views of gracious parklands; there was comfort in its padded window seats; there was luxury in its elegant furniture. One could lose oneself with ease in this house, and so many servants and attendants waited on her grandmother that in the first weeks she spent there, Catherine was constantly meeting strangers.

On her arrival she was taken to her grandmother whom she found in her bed, not yet having risen though the afternoon was advancing.

'Ah!' said the Dowager Duchess. 'So here you are, little Catherine Howard! Let me look at you. Have you fulfilled the promise of your babyhood that you would be a very pretty girl?'

Catherine must climb onto the bed and kiss one of the plump hands, and be inspected.

'Marry!' said the Duchess. 'You are a big girl for your years! Well, well, there is time yet before we must find a husband for you.' Catherine would have told her of her contract with Thomas Culpepper, but the Duchess was not listening. 'How neat you look! That is my Lady Culpepper, I'll swear. Catherine Howard and such neatness appear to me as though they do not belong one to the other. Give me a kiss, child, and you must go away. Jenny!' she called, and a maid appeared suddenly from a closet. 'Call Mistress Isabel to me. I would talk with her of my granddaughter.' She turned to Catherine. 'Now, Granddaughter, tell me, what did you learn at Hollingbourne?'

'I learned to play the virginals and to sing.'

'Ah! That is well. We must look to your education. I will not have you forget that, though your father is a poor man, you are a Howard. Ah! Here is Mistress Isabel.'

A tall, pale young woman came into the room. She had small eyes and a thin mouth; her eyes darted at once to Catherine Howard, sitting on the bed.

'This is my little granddaughter, Isabel. You knew of her coming.'

'Your Grace mentioned it to me.'

'Well, the child has arrived. Take her, Isabel . . . and see that she lacks nothing.'

Isabel curtseyed, and the Duchess gave Catherine a little push to indicate that she was to get off the bed and follow Isabel. Together they left the Duchess's apartment.

Isabel led the way upstairs and along corridors, occasionally turning, as though to make sure that Catherine followed. Catherine began to feel afraid, for this old house was full of shadows, and in unexpected places were doors and sudden passages; all her old fear of ghosts came back to her, and her longing for Thomas brought tears to her eyes. What if they should put her in a bedroom by herself, remote from other rooms! If Hollingbourne might have contained a ghost, this house assuredly would! Isabel, looking over her shoulder at her, alone stopped her from bursting into tears, for there was something about Isabel which frightened Catherine more than she cared to admit to herself.

Isabel had thrown open a door, and they were in a large room which contained many beds; this dormitory was richly furnished, as was every room in this house, but it was an untidy room; across its chairs and beds were flung various garments; shoes and hose littered the floor. There was perfume in the air.

'This room,' said Isabel, 'is where Her Grace's ladies sleep; she has told me that temporarily you are to share it with us.'

Relief flooded Catherine's heart; there was now nothing to fear; her pale face became animated, flushed with pleasure.

'That pleases you?' asked Isabel.

Catherine said it did, adding: 'I like not solitude.'

Another girl had come into the room, big bosomed, wide hipped and saucy of eye.

'Isabel . . .'

Isabel held up a warning hand.

'Her Grace's granddaughter has arrived.'

'Oh . . . the little girl?'

The girl came forward, saw Catherine, and bowed.

'Her Grace has said,' began Isabel, 'that she is to share our room.'

The girl sat down upon a bed, drew her skirts up to her knees, and lifted her eyes to the ornate ceiling.

'It delights her, does it not ... Catherine?'

'Yes,' said Catherine.

The girl, whose name it seemed was Nan, threw a troubled glance at Isabel, which Catherine intercepted but did not understand.

Nan said: 'You are very pretty, Catherine.'

Catherine smiled.

'But very young,' said Isabel.

'Marry!' said Nan, crossing shapely legs and looking down at them in an excess of admiration. 'We must all be young at some time, must we not?'

Catherine smiled again, liking Nan's friendly ways better than the quiet ones of Isabel.

'And you will soon grow up,' said Nan.

'I hope to,' said Catherine.

'Indeed you do!' Nan giggled, and rose from the bed. From a cabinet she took a box of sweetmeats, ate one herself and gave one to Isabel and one to Catherine.

Isabel examined Catherine's clothes, lifting her skirts and feeling the material between thumb and finger.

'She has lately come from her uncle, Sir John Culpepper of Hollingbourne in Kent.'

'Did they keep grand style in Kent?' asked Nan, munching.

'Not such as in this house.'

'Then you are right glad to be here where you will find life amusing?'

'Life was very good at Hollingbourne.'

'Isabel,' laughed Nan, 'the child looks full of knowledge. ... I believe you had a lover there, Catherine Howard!'

Catherine blushed scarlet.

'She did! She did! I swear she did!'

Isabel dropped Catherine's skirt, and exchanged a glance with Nan. Questions trembled on their lips, but these questions went unasked, for at that moment the door opened and a young man put his head round the door.

'Nan!' he said.

Nan waved her hand to dismiss him, but he ignored the signal, and came into the room.

Catherine considered this a peculiar state of affairs, for at Hollingbourne gentlemen did not enter the private apartments of ladies thus unceremoniously.

'A new arrival!' said the young man.

'Get you gone!' said Isabel. 'She is not for you. She is Catherine Howard, Her Grace's own granddaughter.'

The young man was handsomely dressed. He bowed low to Catherine, and would have taken her hand to kiss it, had not Isabel snatched her up and put her from him. Nan pouted on the bed, and the young man said: 'How is my fair Nan this day?' But Nan turned her face to the wall and would not speak to him; then the young man sat on the bed and put his arms round Nan, so that his left hand was on her right breast, and his right hand on her left breast; and he kissed her neck hard, so that there was a red mark there. Then she arose and slapped him lightly on the face, laughing the while, and she leaped across the bed, he after her and so gave chase, till Isabel shooed him from the room.

Catherine witnessed this scene with much astonishment, thinking Isabel to be very angry indeed, expecting her to castigate the laughing Nan; but she did nothing but smile, when, after the young man had left, Nan threw herself onto the bed laughing.

Nan sat up suddenly and, now that the youth was no longer there to claim her interest, once more bestowed it on Catherine Howard.

'You had a lover at Hollingbourne, Catherine Howard! Did you not see how her cheeks were on fire, Isabel, and still are, I'll warrant! I believe you to be a sly wench, Catherine Howard.

Isabel put her hands on Catherine's shoulders.

'Tell us about him, Catherine.'

Catherine said: 'It was my cousin, Thomas Culpepper.'

'He who is son of Sir John?'

Catherine nodded. 'We shall marry when that is possible.'

'Tell us of Thomas Culpepper, Catherine. Is he tall? Is he handsome?'

'He is both tall and handsome.'

'Tell me, did he kiss you well and heartily?'

'But once,' said Catherine. 'And that in the paddock when he talked of marriage.'

'And he kissed you,' said Nan. 'What else?'

'Hush!' said Isabel. 'What if she should tell Her Grace of the way you have talked!'

'Her Grace is too lazy to care what her ladies may say or do.'

'You will be dismissed the house one day,' said Isabel. 'Caution!'

'So your cousin kissed you, Catherine, and promised he would marry you. Dost not know that when a man talks of marriage it is the time to be wary?'

Catherine did not understand; she was aware of a certain fear, and yet a vivid interest in this unusual conversation.

'Enough of this,' said Isabel, and Nan went to her bed and lay down, reaching for the sweetmeats.

'Your bed,' said Isabel, 'shall be this one. Are you a good sleeper?'

'Yes,' said Catherine; for indeed the only occasions when she could not sleep were those when she was afraid of ghosts, and if she were to sleep in a room so full of beds, each of which would contain a young lady, she need have no fear of gruesome company, and she could say with truth that she would sleep well.

Isabel looked at her clothes, asked many questions about Lambeth and Hollingbourne; and while Catherine was answering her, several ladies came in, and some gave her sweetmeats, some kissed her. Catherine thought them all pretty young ladies; their clothes were bright, and they wore gay ribands in their hair; and many times during that afternoon and evening a young man would put his head round the door and be waved away with the words 'The Duchess's granddaughter, Catherine Howard, is come to share our apartment.' The young men bowed and were as kind to Catherine as the ladies were; and often one of the ladies would go outside and speak with them, and Catherine would hear muffled laughter. It was very gay and pleasant, and even Isabel, who at first had appeared to be a little stern, seemed to change and laugh with the rest.

Catherine had food and drink with the ladies and their kindness persisted through the evening. At length she went to bed, Isabel escorting her and drawing the curtains around her bed. She was very soon asleep for the excitement of the day had tired her.

She awoke startled and wondered where she was. She remembered and was immediately aware of whispering voices. She lay listening for some time, thinking the ladies must just be retiring, but the voices went on and Catherine, in astonishment, recognized some of them as belonging to men. She stood up and peeped through the curtains. There was no light in the room but sufficient moonlight to show her the most unexpected sight.

The room seemed to be full of young men and women; some sitting on the beds, some reclining on them, but all of them in affectionate poses. They were eating and drinking, and stroking and kissing each other. They smacked their lips over the dainties, and now and then one of the girls would make an exclamation of surprise and feigned indignation, or another would laugh softly; they spoke in whispers. The clouds, hurrying across the face of the moon which looked in at the windows, made the scene alternately light and darker; and the wind which was driving the clouds whined now and then, mingling its voice with those of the girls and young men.

Catherine watched, wide-eyed and sleepless for some time. She saw the youth who had aroused Nan's displeasure now kissing her bare shoulders, taking down the straps of her dress and burying his face in her bosom. Catherine watched and wondered until her eyes grew weary and her lids pressed down on them. She lay down and slept.

She awakened to find it was daylight and Isabel was drawing her bed curtains. The room was now occupied by girls only, who ran about naked and chattering, looking for their clothes which seemed to be scattered about the floor.

Isabel was looking down at Catherine slyly.

'I trust you slept well?' she asked.

Catherine said she had.

'But not through the entire night?'

Catherine could not meet Isabel's piercing eyes, for she was afraid that the girl should know she had looked on that scene, since something told her it was not meant that she should.

Isabel sat down heavily on the bed, and caught Catherine's shoulder.

'You were awake part of last night,' she said. 'Dost think I did not see thee, spying through the curtains, listening, taking all in?'

'I did not mean to spy,' said Catherine. 'I was awakened, and the moon showed me things.'

'What things, Catherine Howard?'

'Young gentlemen, sitting about the room with the ladies.'

'What else?'

Isabel looked wicked now. Catherine began to shiver, thinking perhaps it would have been better had she spent the night in a lonely chamber. For it was daylight now, and it was only at night that Catherine had great fear of ghosts.

'What else?' repeated Isabel. 'What else, Catherine Howard?'

'I saw that they did eat . . .'

The grip on Catherine's shoulder increased.

'What else?'

'Well . . . I know not what else, but that they did kiss and seem affectionate.'

'What shall you *do*, Catherine Howard?'

'What shall I do? But I know not what you mean, Mistress Isabel. What would you desire me to do?'

'Shall you then tell aught of what you have seen . . . to Her Grace, your grandmother?'

Catherine's teeth chattered, for what they did must surely be wrong since it was done at her grandmother's displeasure.

Isabel released Catherine's shoulder and called to the others. There was silence while she spoke.

'Catherine Howard,' she said spitefully, 'while feigning

sleep last night, was wide awake, watching what was done in this chamber. She will go to Her Grace the Duchess and tell her of our little entertainment.'

There was a crowd of girls round the bed, who looked down on Catherine, while fear and anger were displayed in every face.

'There was naught I did that was wrong,' said one girl, almost in tears.

'Be silent!' commanded Isabel. 'Should what happens here of nights get to Her Grace's ears, you will all be sent home in dire disgrace.'

Nan knelt down by the bed, her pretty face pleading. 'Thou dost not look like a teller of tales.'

'Indeed I am not!' cried Catherine. 'I but awakened, and being awake what could I do but see . . .'

'She will, I am sure, hold her counsel. Wilt thou not, little Catherine?' whispered Nan.

'If she does not,' said Isabel, 'it will be the worse for her. What if we should tell Her Grace of what you did, Catherine Howard, in the paddock with your cousin, Thomas Culpepper!'

'What . . . I . . . did!' gasped Catherine. 'But I did nothing wrong. Thomas would not. He is noble . . . he would do no wrong.'

'He kissed her and he promised her marriage,' said Isabel.

All the ladies put their mouths into round O's, and looked terribly shocked.

'She calls that naught! The little wanton!'

Catherine thought: Did we sin then? Was that why Thomas was ashamed and never kissed me again?

Isabel jerked off the clothes, so that she lay naked before them; she stooped and slapped Catherine's thigh.

'Thou darest not talk!' said Nan, laughing. 'Why 'twould go harder with thee than with us. A Howard! Her Grace's own granddaughter! Doubtless he would be hanged, drawn and quartered for what he did to you!'

'Oh, no!' cried Catherine, sitting up. 'We did no wrong.'

The girls were all laughing and chattering like magpies.

Isabel put her face close to Catherine's: 'You have heard!

Say nothing of what you have seen or may see in this chamber, and your lover will be safe.'

Nan said: ' 'Tis simple, darling. Say naught of our sins, and we say naught of thine!'

Catherine was weeping with relief.

'I swear I shall say nothing.'

'Then that is well,' said Isabel.

Nan brought a sweetmeat to her, and popped it into her mouth.

'There! Is not that good? They were given to me last night by a very charming gentleman. Mayhap one day some fine gentleman will bring sweetmeats to you, Catherine Howard!'

Nan put her arms about the little girl, and gave her two hearty kisses, and Catherine, munching, wondered why she had been so frightened. There was nothing to fear; all that was necessary was to say nothing.

*   *   *

The days passed as speedily as they had at Hollingbourne, and a good deal more excitingly. There were no lessons at Horsham. There was nothing to do during the long, lazy days but enjoy them. Catherine would carry notes from ladies to gentlemen; she was popular with them all, but especially with the young gentlemen. Once one said to her: 'I have awaited this, and 'tis double sweet to me when brought by pretty Catherine!' They gave her sweetmeats too and other dainties. She played a little, played the flute and the virginals; she sang; they liked well to hear her sing, for her voice was indeed pretty. Occasionally the old Duchess would send for her to have a talk with her, and would murmur: 'What a little tomboy you are, Catherine Howard! I declare you are an untidy chit; I would you had the grace of your cousin, Anne Boleyn. . . . Though much good her grace did her!'

Catherine loved to hear of her cousin, for she remembered seeing her now and then at Lambeth before she went to Hollingbourne. When she heard her name she thought of beauty and colour, and sparkling jewels and sweet smiles; she hoped that one day she would meet her cousin again. The Duchess often talked of her, and Catherine knew by the softening of her voice that she liked her well, even though, when she spoke of her disgrace and banishment from court, her eyes would glint slyly as though she enjoyed contemplating her granddaughter's downfall.

'A Boleyn not good enough for a Percy, eh! Marry, and there's something in that! But Anne is part Howard, and a Howard is a match for a Percy at any hour of the day or night! And I would be the first to tell Northumberland so, were I to come face to face with him. As for the young man, a plague on him! They tell me his Lady Mary hates him and he hates her; so much good that marriage did to either of them! Aye! I'll warrant he does not find it so easy to forget my granddaughter. Ah, Catherine Howard, there was a girl. I vow I never saw such beauty . . . such grace. And what did it do for her? There she goes . . . To France! And what has become of the Ormond marriage? She will be growing on into her teens now . . . I hope she will come back soon. Catherine Howard, Catherine Howard, your hair is in need of attention. And your dress, my child! I tell you, you will never have the grace of Anne Boleyn.'

It was not possible to tell the Duchess that one could not hope to have the grace of one's cousin who had been educated most carefully and had learned the ways of life at the French court; who had been plenteously supplied with the clothes she might need in order that Sir Thomas Boleyn's daughter might do her father credit in whatever circles she moved. One could not explain that the brilliant Anne had a natural gift for choosing the most becoming clothes, and knew how to wear them. The Duchess should have known these things.

But she rocked in her chair and dozed, and was hardly aware of Catherine's standing there before her. 'Marry! And the dangers that girl was exposed to! The French court! There were adventures for her, I'll warrant, but she keeps her secrets well. Ah! How fortunate it is, Catherine, that I have taken you under *my* wing!'

And while the Duchess snored in her bedroom, her ladies

held many midnight feasts in their apartments. Catherine was one of them now, they assured themselves. Catherine could be trusted. It was no matter whether she slept or not; she was little but a baby and there were those times when she would fall asleep suddenly. She was popular; they would throw sweetmeats onto her bed. Sometimes she was kissed and fondled.

'Is she not a pretty little girl!'

'She is indeed, and you will keep your eyes off her, young sir, or I shall be most dismayed.'

Laughter, slapping, teasing. . . . It was fun, they said; and with them Catherine said: 'It is fun!'

Sometimes they lay on the tops of the beds with their arms about each other; sometimes they lay under the clothes, with the curtains drawn.

Catherine was accustomed to this strange behaviour by now, and hardly noticed it. They were all very kind to her, even Isabel. She was happier with them than she was when attending her grandmother, sitting at her feet or rubbing her back where it itched. Sometimes she must massage the old lady's legs, for she had strange pains in them and massage helped to soothe the pain. The old lady would wheeze and rattle, and say something must be done about Catherine's education, since her granddaughter, a Howard, could not be allowed to run wild all the day through. The Duchess would talk of members of her family; her stepsons and her numerous stepdaughters who had married wealthy knights because the Howard fortunes needed bolstering up. 'So Howards married with Wyatts and Bryans and Boleyns,' mused the Duchess. 'And mark you, Catherine Howard, the children of these marriages are goodly and wise. Tom Wyatt is a lovely boy . . .' The Duchess smiled kindly, having a special liking for lovely boys. 'And so is George Boleyn . . . and Mary and Anne are pleasant creatures. . . .'

'Ah!' said the Duchess one day. 'I hear your cousin, Anne, is back in England and at court.'

'I should like well to see her,' said Catherine.

'Rub harder, child! There! Clumsy chit! You scratched me. Ah! Back at court, and a beauty more lovely than when she went away . . .' The Duchess wheezed, and was so overcome with laughter that Catherine feared she would choke. 'They say the King is deeply affected by her,' said the Duchess happily. 'They say too that she is leading him a merry dance!'

* * *

When the Duchess had said that the King was deeply affected by Anne Boleyn, she had spoken the truth. Anne had left the court of France and returned to that of England, and no sooner had she made her spectacular appearance than once more she caught the King's eye. The few years that had elapsed had made a great change in Anne; she was not one whit less beautiful than she had been when Henry had seen her in the garden at Hever; indeed she was more so; she had developed a poise which before would have sat oddly on one so young. If she had been bright then, now she was brilliant; her beauty had matured and gained in maturity; the black eyes still sparkled and flashed; her tongue was more ready with its wit, she herself more accomplished. She had been engaged in helping Marguerite to fête François, so recently released from captivity, a François who had left his youth behind in a Madrid prison in which he had nearly died and would have done so but for his sister's loving haste across France and into Spain to nurse him. But François had made his peace treaty with his old enemy, Charles V, although he did repudiate it immediately, and it was the loving delight of his sister and his mother to compensate him for the months of hardship. Anne Boleyn had been a useful addition to the court; she could sing and dance, write lyrics, poetry, music; could always be relied upon to entertain and amuse. But her father, on the Continent with an embassy, had occasion to return to England, and doubtless feeling that a girl of nineteen must not fritter away her years indefinitely, had brought her back to the court of her native land. So Anne had returned to find the entire family settled at the palace. George, now Viscount Rochford, was married, and his wife, who had been Jane Parker and granddaughter to Lord Morley and Monteagle, was still one of the Queen's ladies. Meeting George's wife had been one of the less pleasant surprises on Anne's return, since she saw that George was not very happy in this marriage with a wife who was frivolous and stupid and was not accepted into the brilliant set of poets and intellectuals – most of them cousins of the Boleyns – in which George naturally took a prominent place. This was depressing. Anne, still smarting from the Percy affair – though none might guess it – would have wished for her brother that married happiness which she herself had missed. Mary, strangely enough, seemed happy with William Carey; they had one boy – who, it was whispered, was the King's – and none would guess that their union was not everything that might be desired. Anne wondered then if she and George asked too much of life.

There was no sign of melancholy about Anne. She could not but feel a certain glee – though she reproached herself for this – when she heard that Percy and his Mary were the most wretched couple in the country. She blamed Percy for his weakness; it was whispered that the Lady Mary was a shrew, who never forgave him, being contracted to her, for daring to fall in love with Anne Boleyn and make a scandal of the affair. Very well, thought Anne, let Percy suffer as she had! How many times during the last years had she in her thoughts reproached him for his infidelity! Perhaps he realized now that the easy way is not always the best way. She held her head higher, calling her lost lover weak, wishing fervently that he had been more like Thomas Wyatt who had pursued her ever since her return to court, wondering if she were not a little in love – or ready to fall in love – with her cousin Thomas, surely the most handsome, the most reckless, the most passionate man about the court. There was no doubt as to his feelings for her; it was both in his eyes and in his verses; and he was reckless enough not to care who knew it.

There was one other who watched her as she went about the court; Anne knew this, though others might not, for though he was by no means a subtle man, he had managed so far to keep this passion, which he felt for one of his wife's ladies-in-waiting, very secret.

Anne did not care to think too much of this man. She did not care to feel those little eyes upon her. His manner was correct enough, yet now there were those who were beginning to notice something. She had seen people whispering together, smiling slyly. Now the King is done with the elder sister, is it to be the younger? What is it about these Boleyns? Thomas is advanced as rapidly as my lord Cardinal ever was; George has posts that should have gone to a grey-haired man; Mary . . . of course we understand how it was with Mary; and now, is it to be the same story with Anne?

No! Anne told herself fiercely. Never!

If Thomas Wyatt had not a wife already, she thought, how pleasant it would be to listen to his excellent verses, which were chiefly about herself. She could picture the great hall at Allington Castle decked out for the Christmas festivities, herself and Thomas taking chief parts in some entertainment they had written for the amusement of their friends. But that could not be.

Her position at court had become complicated. She was thinking of a conversation she had had with the King, when he, who doubtless had seen her walking in the palace grounds, had come down to her unattended and had said, his eyes burning in his heated face, that he would have speech with her.

He had asked her to walk with him to a little summer-house he knew of where they could be secret. She had felt limp with terror, had steeled herself, had realized full well that in the coming interview she would have need of all her wits; she must flatter him and refuse him; she must soothe him, pacify him, and pray that he might turn his desirous eyes upon someone more willing.

She had entered the summer-house, feeling the colour in her cheeks, but her fear made her hold her head the higher; her very determination helped to calm her. He had stood looking at her as he leaned against the doors, a mighty man, his padded clothes, glittering and colourful, adding to his great stature. He would have her accept a costly gift of jewels; he told her that he had favoured her from the moment he had seen her in her father's garden, that never had he set eyes on one who pleased him more; in truth he loved her. He spoke with confidence, for at that time he had believed it was but necessary to explain his feelings towards her to effect her most willing surrender. Thus it had been on other occasions; why should this be different?

She had knelt before him, and he would have raised her, saying lightly and gallantly: No, she must not kneel; it was he who should kneel to her, for by God, he was never more sure of his feelings towards any in his life before.

She had replied: 'I think, most noble and worthy King, that Your Majesty speaks these words in mirth to prove me, without intent of degrading your noble self. Therefore, to ease you of the labour of asking me any such question hereafter, I beseech Your Highness most earnestly to desist and take this my answer, which I speak from the depth of my soul, in good part. Most noble King! I will rather lose my life than my virtue, which will be the greatest and best part of the dowry I shall bring my husband.'

It was bold; it was clever; it was characteristic of Anne. She had known full well that something of this nature would happen, and she had therefore prepared herself with what she would say when it did. She was no Percy to be browbeaten, she was a subject and Henry was King, well she knew that; but this matter of love was not a matter for a king and subject – it was for a man and woman; and Anne was not one to forget her rights as a woman, tactful and cautious as the subject in her might feel it necessary to be.

The King was taken aback, but not seriously; she was so beautiful, kneeling before him, that he was ready to forgive her for putting off her surrender. She wanted to hold him off; very well, he was ever a hunter who liked a run before the kill. He bade her cease to kneel, and said, his eyes devouring her since already in his mind he was possessing her, that he would continue to hope.

But her head shot up at that, the colour flaming in her cheeks.

'I understand not, most mighty King, how you should retain such hope,' she said. 'Your wife I cannot be, both in respect of mine own unworthiness and also because you have a Queen already.' And then there came the most disturbing sentence of all: 'Your mistress I will not be!'

Henry left her; he paced his room. He had desired her deeply when she had been a girl of sixteen, but his conscience had got between him and desire; he had made no protest when she had wrenched open the cage door and flown away. Now here she was back again, more desirable, a lovely woman where there had been a delightful girl. This time, he had thought, she shall not escape. He believed he had but to say so and it would be so. He had stifled the warnings of his conscience and now he had to face the refusal of the woman. It could not be; in a long and amorous life it had never been so. He was the King; she the humblest of his Queen's ladies. No, no! This was coquetry; she wished to keep him waiting, that he might burn the fiercer. If he could believe that was all, how happy he would be!

For his desire for Anne Boleyn astonished him. Desire he knew well; how speedily it came, how quickly it could be gratified. One's passion flamed for one particular person; there was a sweet interlude when passion was slaked and still asked to be slaked; then . . . the end. It was the inevitable pattern. And here was one who said with a ring of determination in her voice: 'Your mistress I will not be!' He was angry with her; had she forgotten he was the King? She had spoken to him as though he were a gentleman of the court . . . any gentleman. Thus had she spoken to him in her father's garden at Hever. The King grew purple with fury against her; then he softened, for it was useless to rail against that which enslaved him; it was her pride, it was her dignity which would make the surrender more sweet.

The King saw himself in his mirror. A fine figure of a man . . . if the size of him was considered. The suit he was wearing had cost three thousand pounds, and that not counting all the jewels that adorned it. But she was not the one to say yes to a suit of clothes; it would be the man inside it. He would smile at himself; he could slap his thigh; he was sure enough of eventual success with her.

He too had changed since those days when he allowed his

conscience to come between him and this Anne Boleyn. The change was subtle, but definite enough. The conscience was still the dominating feature in his life. There it was, more than life size. The change was this: The conscience no longer ruled him; he ruled the conscience. He soothed it and placated it, and put his own construction on events before he let the conscience get at them. There was Mary Boleyn; he had done with Mary; he had decided that when Anne returned. He would cease to think of Mary. Oh, yes, yes, he knew there were those who might say there was an affinity between him and Anne, but in the course of many years of amorous adventures had this never happened before? Was there no man at court who had loved two sisters, perhaps unwittingly? Mayhap he himself had! For – and on this point Henry could be very stern – court morals being as they were, who could be sure who was closely related to whom? Suppose these sisters had had a different father! There! Was not the affinity reduced by one half? One could never know the secret of families. What if even the one mother did not give birth to the two daughters! One could never be sure; there had been strange stories of changeling children. This matter was not really worth wasting another moment's thought on. What if he were to eschew Anne on account of this edict, and make a match for her, only to discover then that she was not Mary's sister after all! Would it not be more sinful to take another man's wife? And this desire of his for this unusual girl could but be slaked one way, well he knew. Better to take her on chance that she might be Mary Boleyn's sister. He would forget such folly!

There was another matter too, about which his conscience perturbed him deeply and had done so for some time, in effect ever since he had heard that Katharine could bear no more children. Very deeply was he perturbed on this matter; so deeply that he had spoken of it to his most trusted friends. For all the years he had been married to Katharine there was but one daughter of the union. What could this mean? Why was it that Katharine's sons died one after the other? Why was it that only one of their offspring – and this a girl – had been allowed to live? There was some deep meaning in this, and Henry thought he had found it. There was assuredly some blight upon his union with Katharine, and what had he done, in the eyes of a righteous God, to deserve this? He knew not . . . except it be by marrying his brother's wife. Was it not written in the book of Leviticus that should a man marry his brother's wife their union should be childless? He had broken off all marital relations with Katharine when the doctors had told him she would never have any more children. Ah! Well he remembered that day; pacing up and down his room in a cold fury. No son for Henry Tudor! A daughter! And why? Why? Then his mind had worked fast and furiously on this matter of a divorce. Exciting possibility it had seemed. Divorces – forbidden by Holy Church on principle – could be obtained for political reasons from the Pope, who was ever ready to please those in high places. I must have an heir! Henry told his conscience. What would happen, should I die and not leave an heir? There is mine and Katharine's daughter, Mary; but a woman on the throne of England! No! I must have a male heir! Women are not made to rule great countries; posterity will reproach me, an I leave not an heir.

There in his mirror looked back the great man. He saw the huge head, the powerful, glittering shoulders; and *this* man could not produce a son for England! A short while ago he had had his son by Elizabeth Blount brought to him, and had created him Duke of Richmond, a title which he himself had carried in his youth; that he had done in order to discomfort Katharine. I could have a son, he implied. See! Here *is* my son. It is you who have failed! And all the tears she shed in secret, and all her prayers, availed her little. She had nothing to give him but a daughter, for – and when he thought of this, the purple veins stood out on Henry's forehead – she had lied. She had sworn that her marriage with Arthur had never been consummated; she had tricked him, deceived him; this pale, passionless Spanish woman had tricked him into marriage, had placed in jeopardy the Tudor dynasty. Henry was filled with self-righteous anger, for he wanted a divorce and he wanted it for the noblest of reasons . . . not for himself, but for the house of Tudor; not to establish his manhood and virility in the eyes of his people, not to banish an ageing, unattractive wife . . . not for these things, but because he, who had previously not hesitated to plunge his people into useless war, feared civil war for them; because he feared he lived in sin with one who had never been his wife, having already lived with his brother. This, his conscience – now so beautifully controlled – told Henry. And all these noble thoughts were tinged rose-colour by a beautiful girl who was obstinately haughty, whose cruel lips said: 'I will never be your mistress!' But it was not necessary for his conscience to dwell upon that matter as yet, for a king does not raise a humble lady-in-waiting to be his queen, however desirable she may be. No, no! No thought of that had entered his head . . . not seriously, of course. The girl was there, and it pleased him to think of her in his arms, for such reflections were but natural and manly; and how she was to be got into that position was of small consequence, being a purely personal matter, whereas this great question of divorce was surely an affair of state.

So was his mind active in these matters, and so did he view the reluctance of her whom he desired above all others with a kindly tolerance, like a good hunter contented to stalk awhile, and though the stalking might be arduous, that would be of little account when the great achievement would be his.

Thus was there some truth in the remarks of the Duchess of Norfolk when she had said to her granddaughter, Catherine Howard, that Anne Boleyn was leading the King a merry dance.

*   *   *

In their apartments at the palace Jane Boleyn was quarrelling with her husband. He sat there in the window seat, handsome enough to plague her, indifferent enough to infuriate her. He was writing on a scrap of paper, and he was smiling as he composed the lyrics that doubtless his clever sister would set to music, that they might be sung before the King.

'Be silent, Jane,' he said lightly, and it was his very lightness that maddened her, for well she knew that he did not care sufficiently for her even to lose his temper. He was tapping with his foot, smiling, well pleased with his work.

'What matters it,' she demanded bitterly, 'whether I speak or am silent? You do not heed which I do.'

'As ever,' said George, 'you speak without thought. Were that so, why should I beg you for silence?'

She shrugged her shoulders impatiently.

'Words! Words! You would always have them at your disposal. I hate you. I wish I had never married you!'

'Sentiments, my dear Jane, which it may interest you to know are reciprocated by your most unwilling husband.'

She went over to him, and sat on the window seat.

'George . . .' she began tearfully.

He sighed. 'Since your feelings towards me are so violent, my dear, would it not be wiser if you removed yourself from this seat, or better still from this room? Should you prefer it, of course, I will be the one to go. But you know full well that you followed me hither.'

As he spoke his voice became weary; the pen in his hand moved as though it were bidding him stop this stupid bickering and get on with what was of real moment to him. His foot began to tap.

Angrily she took the quill from him and threw it to the floor.

He sat very still, looking at it, not at her. If she could have roused him to anger, she would have been less angry with him; it was his indifference – it always had been – that galled her.

'I hate you!' she said again.

'Repetition detracts from, rather than adds to vehemence,' he said in his most lightsome tone. 'Venom is best expressed briefly; over-statement was ever suspect, dear Jane.'

'*Dear* Jane!' she panted. 'When have I ever been dear to you?'

'There you ask a question which gallantry might bid me answer one way, truth another.'

He was cruel, and he meant to be cruel; he knew how to hurt her most; he had discovered her to be jealous, possessive and vindictive, and having no love for her he cared nothing for the jealousy, while the possessiveness irked him, and her vindictiveness left him cold; he was careless of himself and reckless as to what harm might come to him.

Her parents had thought it advantageous to link their daughter's fortunes with those of the Boleyns, which were rising rapidly under the warming rays of royal favour; so she had married, and once married had fallen victim to the Boleyn charm, to that ease of manner, to that dignity, to that cleverness. But what hope had Jane of gaining George's love? What did she know of the things for which he cared so deeply? He thought her stupid, colourless, illiterate. Why, she wondered, could he not be content to make merry, to laugh at the frivolous matters which pleased her; why could he not enjoy a happy married life with her, have children? But he did not want her, and foolishly she thought that by quarrelling, by forcing him to notice her, she might attract him; instead of which she alienated him, wearied him, bored him. They were strange people, thought Jane, these two younger Boleyns; amazingly alike, both possessing in a large degree the power of attracting not only those who were of the same genre as themselves, but those who were completely opposite. Jane believed them both to be cold people; she hated Anne; indeed she had never been so wretched in her life until the return of her sister-in-law; she hated her, not because Anne had been unpleasant to her, for indeed Jane must admit that Anne had in the first instance made efforts to be most sisterly; but she hated Anne because of the influence she had over her brother, because he could give her who was merely his young sister much affection and admiration, while for Jane, his wife who adored him, he had nothing but contempt.

So now she tried to goad him, longed for him to take her by the shoulders and shake her, that he might lay hands on her if only in anger. Perhaps he knew this, for he was diabolically clever and understood most uncomfortably the workings of minds less clever than his own. Therefore he sat, arms folded, looking at the pen stuck in the polished floor, bored by Jane, weary of the many scenes she created, and heartlessly careless of her feelings.

'George....'

He raised weary eyebrows in acknowledgment.

'I ... I am so unhappy!'

He said, with the faintest hint of softness in his voice: 'I am sorry for that.'

She moved closer; he remained impassive.

'George, what are you writing?'

'Just an airy trifle,' he said.

'Are you very annoyed that I interrupted?'

'I am not annoyed,' he replied.

'That pleases me, George. I do not mean to interrupt. Shall I get your pen?'

He laughed and, getting up, fetched it himself with a smile at her. Any sign of quiet reason on her part always pleased him; she struggled with her tears, trying to keep the momentary approval she had won.

'I *am* sorry, George.'

'It is of no matter,' he said. 'I'll warrant also that I should be the one to be sorry.'

'No, George, it is I who am unreasonable. Tell me, is that for the King's masque?'

'It is,' he said, and turned to her, wanting to explain what he, with Wyatt, Surrey and Anne, was doing. But he knew that to be useless; she would pretend to be interested; she would try very hard to concentrate, then she would say something that was maddeningly stupid, and he would realize that she had not been considering what he was saying, and was merely trying to lure him to an amorous interlude. He had little amorous inclination towards her; he found her singularly unattractive and never more so than when she tried to attract him.

She came closer still, leaning her head forward to look at the paper. She began to read.

'It is very clever, George.'

'Nonsense!' said George. 'It is very bad and needs a deal of polishing.'

'Will it be sung?'

'Yes, Anne will write the music.'

Anne! The very mention of that name destroyed her good resolutions.

'Anne, of course!' she said with a sneer.

She saw his eyes flash; she wanted to control herself, but she had heard the tender inflection of his voice when he said his sister's name.

'Why not Anne?' he asked.

'Why not Anne?' she mimicked. 'I'll warrant the greatest musician in the kingdom would never write music such as Anne's . . . in your eyes!'

He did not answer that.

'The King's own music,' she said, 'you would doubtless consider inferior to Anne's!'

That made him laugh.

'Jane, you little fool, one would indeed be a poor musician if one was not more talented in that direction than His Majesty!'

'Such things as you say, George Boleyn, were enough to take a man's head off his shoulders.'

'Reported in the right quarter, doubtless. What do you propose, sweet wife? To report in the appropriate quarter?'

'I swear I will one day!'

He laughed again. 'That would not surprise me, Jane. You are a little fool, and I think out of your vindictive jealousy might conceivably send your husband to the scaffold.'

'And he would richly deserve it!'

'Doubtless! Doubtless! Do not all men who go to the scaffold deserve their fate? They have spoken their minds, expressed an opinion, or have been too nearly related to the King . . . all treasonable matters, my dear Jane.'

For this recklessness she loved him. How she would have liked to be as he was, to have snapped her fingers at life and enjoyed it as he did!

'You are a fool, George. It is well for you that you have a wife such as I!'

'Well indeed, Jane!'

'Mayhap,' she cried, 'you would rather I *looked* like your

sister Anne, *dressed* like your sister Anne, wrote as she wrote.... Then I might find approval in your sight!'

'You never could look like Anne.'

She flashed back : 'It is not given to all of us to be perfect!'

'Anne is far from that.'

'What! Sacrilege! In your eyes she is perfect, if ever any woman was in man's eyes.'

'My dear Jane, Anne is charming, rather because of her imperfections than because of her good qualities.'

'I'll warrant you rage against Fate that you could not marry your sister!'

'I never was engaged in such a foolish discussion in all my life.'

She began to cry.

'Jane,' he said, and put a hand on her shoulder. She threw herself against him, forcing the tears into her eyes, for they alone seemed to have the power to move him. And as they sat thus, there was the sound of footsteps in the corridor, and these footsteps were followed by a knock on the door.

George sat up, putting Jane from him.

'Enter!' he called.

They trooped in, laughing and noisy.

Handsome Thomas Wyatt was a little ahead of the others, singing a ballad. Jane disliked Thomas Wyatt; indeed she loathed them all. They were all of the same calibre, the most important set at court these days, favourites of the King every one of them, and all connected by the skein of kinship. Brilliant of course they were; the songsters of the court. One-eyed Francis Bryan, Thomas Wyatt, George Boleyn, all of them recently returned from France and Italy, and eager now to transform the somewhat heavy atmosphere of the English court into a more brilliant copy of other courts they had known. These gay young men were anxious to oust the duller element, the old set. No soldiers nor grim counsellors to the King these; they were the poets of their generation; they wished to entertain the King, to make him laugh, to give him pleasure. There was nothing the King asked more; and as this gay crowd circulated round none other than the lady who interested him so deeply, they were greatly favoured by His Majesty.

Jane's scowl deepened, for with these young men was Anne herself.

Anne threw a careless smile at Jane, and went to her brother.

'Let us see what thou hast done,' she said, and snatched the paper from him and began reading aloud; and then suddenly she stopped reading and set a tune to the words, singing them, while the others stood round her. Her feet tapped, as her brother's had done, and Wyatt, who was bold as well as handsome, sat down between her and George on the window seat, and his eyes stayed on Anne's face as though they could not tear themselves away.

Jane moved away from them, but that was of no account for they had all forgotten Jane's presence. She was outside the magic circle; she was not one of them. Angrily she watched them, but chiefly she watched Anne. Anne, with the hanging sleeves to hide the sixth nail; Anne, with a special ornament at her throat to hide what she considered to be an unbecoming mole on her neck. And now all the ladies at the court were wearing such ornaments. Jane put her hand to her throat and touched her own. Why, why was life made easy for Anne? Why did everyone applaud what she did? Why did George love her better than he loved his wife? Why was clever, brilliant and handsome Thomas Wyatt in love with her?

Jane went on asking herself these questions as she had done over and over again; bitter jealousy ate deeper and deeper into her heart.

*　　*　　*

Wyatt saw her sitting by the pond in the enclosed garden, a piece of embroidery in her hands. He went to her swiftly. He was deeply and passionately in love.

She lifted her face to smile at him, liking well his handsome face, his quick wit.

'Why, Thomas . . .'

'Why, Anne . . .'

He threw himself down beside her.

'Anne, do you not find it good to escape from the weary ceremony of the court now and then?'

'Indeed I do.'

Her eyes were wistful, catching his mood. They were both thinking of Hever and Allington in quiet Kent.

'I would I were there,' he said, for such was the accord between them that they sometimes read the other's thoughts.

'The gardens at Hever will be beautiful now.'

'And at Allington, Anne.'

'Yes,' she said, 'at Allington also.'

He moved closer.

'Anne, what if we were to leave the court . . . together? What if we were to go to Allington and stay there . . . ?'

'You to talk thus,' she said, 'and you married to a wife!'

'Ah!' His voice was melancholy. 'Anne, dost remember childhood days at Hever?'

'Well,' she answered. 'You locked me in the dungeons once, and I declare I all but died of fright. A cruel boy you were, Thomas.'

'I! Cruel . . . and to you! Never! I swear I was ever tender. Anne, why did we not know then that happiness for you and me lay in the one place?'

'I suppose, Thomas, that when we are young we are so unwise. It is experience that teaches us the great lessons of life. How sad that, in gaining experience, we so often lose what we would most cherish!'

He would have taken her hand, but she held him off.

'Methinks we should return,' she said.

'Now . . . when we are beginning to understand each other!'

'You, having married a wife . . .' she began.

'And therein being most unhappy,' he interrupted; but she would have none of his interruptions.

'You are in no position to speak in this wise, Thomas.'

'Anne, must we then say a long farewell to happiness?'

'If happiness would lie in marriage between us two, then we must.'

'You would condemn me to a life of melancholy.'

'You condemned yourself to that, not I!'

'I was very young.'

'You were, I mind well, a most precocious boy.'

He smiled back sadly over his youth. A boy of great precocity, they had sent him to Cambridge when he was twelve, and at seventeen had married him to Elizabeth Brooke, who was considered a good match for him, being daughter of Lord Cobham.

'Why,' he said, 'do our parents, thinking to do well for us, marry us to their choice which may well not be our own? Why is the right sort of marriage so often the unhappy one?'

Anne said: 'You are spineless, all of you!' And her eyes flashed as her thoughts went to Percy. Percy she had loved and lost, for Percy was but a leaf wafted by the winds. The wicked Cardinal whom she hated now as she had ever done, had said, 'It shall not be!' And meekly Percy had acquiesced. Now he would complain that life had denied him happiness, forgetting he had not made any great effort to attain it. And Wyatt, whom she could so easily love, complained in much the same manner. They obeyed their parents; they married, not where they listed, but entered into any match that was found for them; then they bitterly complained!

'I would never be forced!' she said. 'I would choose my way, and, God help me, whatever I might encounter I would not complain.'

'Ah! Why did I not know then that my happiness was with Anne Boleyn!'

She softened. 'But how should you know it . . . and you but seventeen, and I even less?'

'And,' he said, 'most willing to engage yourself to Percy!'

'That!' She flushed, remembering afresh the insults of the Cardinal. 'That . . . Ah! That failed just as your marriage has failed, Thomas, though differently. Perchance I am glad it failed, for I never could abide a chicken-livered man!'

Now he was suddenly gay, throwing aside his melancholy; he would read to her some verses he had written, for they were of her and for her, and it was meet that she should hear them first.

So she closed her eyes and listened and thrilled to his

poetry, and was sad thinking of how she might have loved him. And there in the pond garden it occurred to her that life had shown her little kindness in her love for men. Percy she had lost after a brief glimpse into a happy future they were to have shared; Wyatt she had lost before ever she could hope to have him.

What did the future hold for her? she wondered. Was she going on in this melancholy way, loving but living alone? It was unsatisfactory.

Thomas finished reading and put the poem into his pocket, his face flushed with appreciation for his work. He has his poetry, she mused, and what have I? Yes, the rest of us write a little; it is to us a pleasant recreation, it means not to us what it does to Wyatt. He has that, and it is much. But what have I?

Wyatt leaned forward; he said earnestly: 'I shall remember this day for ever, for in it you all but said you loved me!'

'There are times,' she said, 'when I fear that love is not for me.'

'Ah, Anne! You are gloomy today. Whom should love be for, if not for those who are most worthy to receive it! Be of good cheer, Anne! Life is not all sadness. Who knows but that one day you and I may be together!'

She shook her head. 'I have a melancholy feeling, Thomas.'

'Bah! You and melancholy mate not well together.' He leaped to his feet and held out his hands to her; she put hers in his, and he helped her to rise. He refused to release her hands; his lips were close to hers. She felt herself drawn towards him, but it seemed to her that her sister was between them . . . Mary, lightsome, wanton, laughing, leering. She drew away coldly. He released her hands at once, and they fell to her side; but his had touched a jewelled tablet she wore and which hung from her pocket on a golden chain. He took it and held it up, laughing. 'A memento, Anne, of this afternoon when you all but said you loved me!'

'Give it back!' she demanded.

'Not I! I shall keep it for ever, and when I feel most melancholy I shall take it out and look at it, and remember that on the afternoon I stole it you all but said you loved me.'

'This is foolishness,' she said. 'I do not wish to lose that tablet.'

'Alas then, Anne! For lost it you have. It is a pleasing trinket – it fills me with hope. When I feel most sad I shall look at it, for then I shall tell myself I have something to live for.'

'Thomas, I beg of you . . .'

She would have snatched it, but he had stepped backwards and now was laughing.

'Never will I give it up, Anne. You would have to steal it back.'

She moved towards him. He ran, she after him; and running across the enclosed pond garden, trying to retrieve that which he had stolen was poignantly reminiscent of happy childhood days at Allington and Hever.

*   *   *

The Cardinal rode through the crowds, passing ceremoniously over London Bridge and out of the capital on his way to France, whither he had been bidden to go by the King. Great numbers of his attendants went before him and followed after him; there were gentlemen in black velvet with gold chains about their necks, and with them their servants in their tawny livery. The Cardinal himself rode on a mule whose trappings were of crimson velvet, and his stirrups were of copper and gold. Before him were borne his two crosses of silver, two pillars of silver, the Great Seal of England, his Cardinal's hat.

The people regarded him sullenly, for it was now whispered, even beyond the court, of that which had come to be known as the King's Secret Matter; and the people blamed the Cardinal, whispering that he had put these ideas into the King's head. Whither went he now, but to France? Mayhap he would find a new wife to replace the King's lawful one, their own beloved Queen Katharine. They found new loyalty towards their quiet Queen, for they pictured her as a poor, wronged woman, and the London crowd was a sentimental crowd ever ready to support the wronged.

In the crowd was whispered the little ditty which malicious Skelton had written, and which the public had taken up, liking its simple implication, liking its cutting allusions to a Cardinal who kept state like a king.

> *'Why come ye not to court*
> *To which court?*
> *To the King's court*
> *Or to Hampton Court!'*

He was well hated, as only the successful man can be hated by the unsuccessful. That he had risen from humble circumstances made the hatred stronger. *'We* are as good as this man!' 'With his luck, there might *I* have gone!' So whispered the people, and the Cardinal knew of their whisperings and was grieved; for indeed many things grieved this man as he passed through London on his way to Sir Richard Wiltshire's house in Dartford wherein he would spend the first night of his journey to the coast.

The Cardinal was brooding on the secret matter of the King's. It was for him to smooth the way for his master, to get him what he desired at the earliest possible moment; and he who had piloted his state ship past many dangerous rocks was now dismayed. Well he could agree with His Majesty that the marriages of kings and queens depend for their success on the male issue, and what had his King and Queen to show for years of marriage but one daughter! The Cardinal's true religion was statecraft; thus most frequently he chose to forget that as Cardinal he owed allegiance to the Church. When he had first been aware of the King's passion for Mistress Anne Boleyn, many fêtes had he given at his great houses, that the King and this lady might meet. Adultery was a sin in the eyes of Holy Church; not so in the liberal mind of Thomas Wolsey. The adultery of the King was as necessary as the jousts and tourneys he himself arranged for His Majesty's diversion. And though he was ever ready to give the King opportunities for meeting this lady, he gave but slight thought to the amorous adventures of His Majesty. This affair seemed to him but one of many; to absorb, to offer satiety; that was inevitable. And then . . . the next. So when this idea of divorce had been passed to him by the King, glorious possibilities of advancing England's interests through an advantageous marriage began to take hold of the Cardinal's mind.

Should England decide to ally herself with France against the Emperor Charles, what better foundation for such an alliance could there be than marriage! Already he had put out feelers for Francis's widowed sister, Marguerite of Alençon, but her brother, uncertain of Henry who still had an undivorced wife – and she none other than the aunt of the Emperor Charles himself – had dallied over negotiations, and married his sister to the King of Navarre. There was, however, Renee of France, sister to the late Queen Claude, and Wolsey's heart glowed at the prospect of such a marriage. Had not Claude borne Francis many children? Why, therefore, should Renee not bear Henry many sons? And to make the bargain complete, why not contract the King's daughter Mary to Francis's son, the Duke of Orleans? Of these matters had Wolsey spoken to the King, and craftily the King appeared to consider them, and whilst considering them he was thinking of none but Anne Boleyn, so did he yearn towards her; and so had her reluctance inflamed his passion that already he was toying with the idea of throwing away Wolsey's plans for a marriage which would be good for England; he was planning to defy his subjects' disapproval, to throw tradition to the wind, to satisfy his desires only and marry Anne Boleyn. He knew his Chancellor; wily, crafty, diplomatic; let Wolsey consider this divorce to be a state affair, and all his genius for statecraft would go into bringing it about; let him think it was but to satisfy his master's overwhelming desire for a humble gentlewoman of his court – who persistently and obstinately refused to become his mistress – and could Wolsey's genius then be counted on to work as well? The King thought not; so he listened to Wolsey's plans with feigned interest and approval, but unknown to the Cardinal, he despatched his own secretary as messenger to the Pope, for he wished to appease his conscience regarding a certain matter which worried him a little. This was his love affair with Mary Boleyn, which he feared must create an affinity between himself and Anne, though he had determined it should be of small consequence should his secretary fail to obtain the Pope's consent to remove the impediment.

Riding on to Dartford, the Cardinal was busily thinking. There was within him a deep apprehension, for he was aware that this matter of the divorce was to be a delicate one and one less suited to his genius, which loved best to involve itself in the intricacies of diplomacy and was perhaps less qualified to deal with petty domesticities. Of Anne Boleyn he thought little. To him the King's affair with this foolish girl was a matter quite separate from the divorce, and unworthy of much thought. It appeared to him that Anne was a light o' love, a younger version of her sister Mary, a comely creature much prone to giving herself airs. He smiled on her, for, while not attaching over-much importance to the King's favourites whose influence had ever been transient, it was well not to anger them. Vaguely he remembered some affair with Percy; the Cardinal smiled faintly at that. Could it be then that the King had remained faithful so long?

He fixed his eyes on his Cardinal's hat being borne before him, and that symbol of his power, the Great Seal of England; and his mind was busy and much disturbed, recent events having complicated the matter of divorce. He thought of the three men of consequence in Europe – Henry, Charles and Francis. Francis – even enfeebled as he was just now – had the enviable rôle of looker-on, sly and secret, waiting to see advantage and leap on it; Henry and Charles must take more active parts in the drama, for Henry's wife was Charles's aunt, and it was unlikely that Charles would stand calmly by to see Henry humiliate Spain through such a near relation. Between these two the Pope, a vacillating man, was most sorely perplexed; he dared not offend Henry; he dared not offend Charles. He had granted a divorce to Henry's sister Margaret on the flimsiest of grounds, but that had proved simple; there was no mighty potentate to be offended by such a divorce. Henry, ranting, fuming, urgently wanting what, it seemed to him, others conspired to keep from him, was a dangerous man; and to whom should he look to gratify his whims but Wolsey? And on whom would he vent his wrath, were his desires frustrated?

This sorry situation had been vastly aggravated by a recent event in Europe; the most unexpected, horrible and sacriligious event the Cardinal could conceive, and the most disastrous to the divorce. This was the sack of Rome by the Duke of Bourbon's forces in the name of the Empire.

Over the last few years Wolsey had juggled dexterously in Europe; and now, riding on to Dartford, he must wonder whether out of his cunning had not grown this most difficult situation. For long Wolsey had known of the discord which existed between Francis and one of the most powerful nobles of France, the mighty Duke of Bourbon. This nobleman, to safeguard his life, had fled his country, and being a very proud and high-spirited gentleman was little inclined to rest in exile all his life; indeed for years before his flight he had been in treasonable communication with the Emperor Charles, France's hereditary enemy, and when he left his country he went to Charles with plans for making war on the French King.

Now it had occurred to Wolsey that if the Duke could be supplied secretly with money he could raise an army from his numerous supporters and thus be, as it were, a general under the King of England while none need know that the King of England had a hand in this war. Therefore would England be in secret alliance with Spain against France. Henry had felt the conception of such an idea to be sheer genius, for the weakening of France and the reconquering of that country had ever been a dream of his. A secret ambassador had been sent to Emperor Charles, and the King and Wolsey with their council laughed complacently at their own astuteness. Francis, however, discovered this and sent a secret messenger to make terms with England, with the result that Bourbon's small army – desperate and exhausted – awaited in vain the promised help from England. Wolsey had calculated without the daring of the Duke and the laxity of the French forces, without Francis's poor generalship which alternately hesitated and then was over-bold. At Pavia the French King's forces were beaten, and the King taken prisoner; and among his documents was found the secret treaty under the Great Seal of England. Thus was Francis a prisoner in the hands of the Emperor, and thus was English double-dealing exposed. Francis was to languish and come near to death in a Madrid prison; and Charles would not be over-eager to link himself with England again. So that the master-stroke which was to have put England in the enviable position of being on the winning side – whichever it was to be – had failed.

That had happened two years ago; yet it was still unpleasant to contemplate, as was Wolsey's failure, in spite of bribery, to be elected Pope. And now had come the greatest blow; Bourbon had turned his attentions to the city of Rome itself. True, this had cost the hasty Duke his life, but his men went on with his devilish scheme, and the city was ransacked, laid waste by fire and pillage, its priests desecrated, its virgins raped; and the sacred city was the scene of one of the most terrible massacres in history. But most shocking of all was the fact that the Pope, who was to grant Henry's divorce, was a prisoner at Castle Angell – prisoner of the Emperor Charles, the nephew of that lady who was to be most deeply wronged by the divorce.

Small wonder that the Cardinal's head ached, but even as it ached it buzzed with plans, for it had ever been this man's genius to turn every position in which he found himself to his own advantage; and now an idea had come to him that should make him more famous, make his master love him more. A short while ago it had seemed to him that a vast cloud was beginning to veil the sun of his glory, as yet so vapourish that the sun was but slightly obscured and blazed hotly through. He trusted in the sun's fierce rays to disperse that cloud; and so it should be. The Pope was a prisoner; why not set up a Deputy-Pope while he was thus imprisoned? And who more fitted for the office than Cardinal Wolsey? And would not such a deputy feel kindly disposed towards his master's plea for a divorce?

On rode the Cardinal, renewed and refreshed, until he came to Canterbury; and there he was the leader of a mighty procession that went into the Abbey; and, gorgeously attired, wearing his Cardinal's hat, he prayed for the captive Pope and wept for him, while his mind was busy with the plans for reigning in Clement's stead, granting the divorce, and marrying his master to a French princess.

And so passed the Cardinal on to France where he was received royally by the Regent, Louise of Savoy – who reigned during the absence of her son François – and by the King's gifted sister, Marguerite of Navarre. He assured them of his master's friendship with their country; he arranged the marriage of the King's daughter to the Duke of Orleans; and he hinted at the King's divorce and his marriage with Renee. He was entertained lavishly, well assured of French friendship.

But among the people of France the Cardinal was no more popular than he was in England; and although he came with offers of friendship, and though he brought English gold with him, the humble people of France did not trust him and made his journey through their land an uncomfortable one. He was robbed in many places where he rested, and one morning when he arose from his bed, he went to his window and there saw that on the leaning stone some mischievous person had engraved a cardinal's hat, and over it a gallows.

*   *   *

The whole court whispered of nothing else but the King's Secret Matter. Anne heard it; Katharine heard it. The Queen was afraid. Great pains she took with her toilet, hoping thereby to please the King, that there might yet be a hope of defying the doctors and producing an heir. Katharine was melancholy; she prayed more fervently; she fretted.

Anne heard it and was sorry for the Queen, for though she was as different from Anne as one woman could be from another, a gloomy woman, rarely heard to laugh, yet had Anne a deep respect for such piety as her mistress's while feeling herself unable to emulate it.

But Anne was busy with thoughts of her own affairs. Wyatt was plaguing her, making wild and impossible suggestions; and she feared she thought too much and too often of Wyatt. There came to her little scraps of paper with his handwriting, and in the poems inscribed on these he expressed his passion for her, the unhappiness of his marriage, the hope he might have, would she but give it, of the future. There had been those who had said that Anne was half French; in character this was so. She was frivolous, sentimental, excessively fond of admiration; but mingling with these attributes was something essentially practical. Had Wyatt been unmarried, ready would she have been to listen to him; and now, admitting this to herself – at the same time giving him no hope that his plans would ever reach fruition – she found it impossible to refuse his attentions entirely. She looked for him; she was ever ready to dally with him. With her cousin, Surrey, and her brother to ensure the proprieties, she was often to be found with Wyatt. They were the gayest and most brilliant quartet at the court; their cousinship was a bond between them. Life was pleasant for Anne with such friends as these, and she was enjoying it as a butterfly flutters in the sunshine even when the first cool of evening is setting in.

Preparing herself for the banquet which was to be given at the palace of Greenwich in honour of the departing French ambassadors, Anne thought of Wyatt. This banquet was to be the most gorgeous of its kind as a gesture of friendship towards the new allies. At Hampton these gentlemen had been entertained most lavishly by my lord Cardinal, who had recently returned from France, and so magnificent a feast had the Cardinal prepared for them that the King, jealous that one of his subjects could provide such a feast fit only for a king's palace, would have Wolsey's hospitality paled to insignificance by his own.

George, Anne, Surrey, Bryan and Wyatt had organized a most lavish carnival for the entertainment of these French gentlemen. They were delighted with their work, sure of the King's pleasure. Such events were ever a delight to Anne; she revelled in them, for she knew that, with her own special gifts she excelled every other woman present, and this was intoxicating to Anne, dispersing that melancholy which she had experienced periodically since she had lost Percy and which was returning more frequently, perhaps on account of Wyatt.

Anne's dress was of scarlet and cloth of gold; there were diamonds at her throat and on her vest. She discarded her head-dress, deciding it made her look too much like the others; she would wear her beautiful hair flowing and informal.

She was, as she had grown accustomed to be, the shining light of the court. Men's eyes turned to watch her; there was Henry Norris, the groom of the stole, Thomas Wyatt, smouldering and passionate, the King, his eyes glittering. To Norris she was indifferent; of Thomas Wyatt she was deeply aware; the King she feared a little; but admiration, no matter whence it came, was sweet. George smiled at her with approval; Jane watched her with envy, but there was little to disturb in that, as all the women were envious; though perhaps with Jane the envy was tinged with hatred. But what did Anne care for her brother's foolish wife! Poor George! she thought. Better to be alone than linked with such a one. It could be good to be alone, to feel so many eyes upon her, watching, admiring, desiring; to feel that power over these watching men which their need of her must give her.

About her, at the banquet, the laughter was louder, the fun more riotous. The King would join the group which surrounded her, because he liked to be with gay young people; and all the time his eyes burned to contemplate her who was the centre of this laughing group.

The Queen sat, pale and almost ugly. She was a sad and frightened woman who could not help thinking continually of the suggested divorce; and this feast in itself was a humiliation to her, since she, a Spaniard, could find little joy in friendship with the French!

The King's distaste for his Queen was apparent; and those courtiers who were young and loved gaiety, scarcely paid her the homage due to her; they preferred to gather round Anne Boleyn, because to be there was to be near the King, joining in his fun and laughter.

Now, from his place at the head of the table, the King was

watching Wyatt. Wine had made the poet over-bold and he would not move from Anne's side though he was fully aware of Henry's watching eyes. There was hardly anyone at the table who was ignorant of the King's passion, and there was an atmosphere of tension in the hall, while everyone waited for the King to act.

Then the King spoke. There was a song he wished the company to hear. It was of his own composing. All assumed great eagerness to hear the song.

The musicians were called. With them came one of the finest singers in the court. There was a moment's complete silence, for no one dared move while the King's song was about to be sung. The King sat forward and his eyes never left Anne's face until the song was finished and the applause broke out.

> *'The eagle's force subdues each bird that flies:*
> *What metal can resist the flaming fire?*
> *Doth not the sun dazzle the clearest eyes*
> *And melt the ice, and make the frost retire?*
> *The hardest stones are pierced through with tools,*
> *The wisest are with princes made but fools.'*

There could be no doubt of the meaning of these arrogant words; there could be no doubt for whom they were written. Anne was freshly aware of the splendour of this palace of Greenwich, of the power it represented. The words kept ringing in her ears. He was telling her that he was weary of waiting; princes, such as he was, did not wait over-long.

This evening had lost its joy for her now; she was afraid. Wyatt had heard those words and realized their implication; George had heard them, and his eyes smiled into hers reassuringly. She wanted to run to her brother, she wanted to say: 'Let us go home; let us go back to being children. I am afraid of the glitter of this court. His eyes watch me now. Brother, help me! Take me home!' George knew her thoughts. She saw the reckless tilt of his head, and imitated it, feeling better, returning his smile. George was reassuring. 'Never fear, Anne!' he seemed to convey. 'We are the Boleyns!'

The company was applauding. Great poetry, was the verdict. Anne looked to him who, some said, was the literary genius of the court, Sir Thomas More; his *Utopia* she had just read with much pleasure. Sir Thomas was gazing at his large and rather ugly hands; he did not, she noticed, join in the effusive praise of the others. Was it the poetry or the sentiments, of which Sir Thomas did not approve?

The King's song was the prelude of the evening's entertainment, and Anne with her friends would have a big part in this. She thrust aside her fears; she played that night with a fervour she had rarely expressed before in any of these masquerades and plays which the quartet contrived. Into her fear of the King there crept an element which she could not have defined. What was it? The desire to make him admire her more? The company were over-courteous to her; even her old enemy, Wolsey, whom she had never ceased to hate, had a very friendly smile! The King's favourites were to be favoured by all, and when you had known yourself to be slighted on account of your humble birth . . . when such a man as Wolsey had humiliated you . . . yes, there was pleasure mingling with the fear of this night.

She was like a brilliant flame in her scarlet and gold. All eyes were upon her. For months to come they would talk of this night, on which Anne had been the moon to all these pale stars.

The evening was to end with a dance, and in this each gentleman would choose his partner. The King should take the Queen's hand and lead the dance, whilst the others fell in behind them. The Queen sat heavy in her chair, brooding and disconsolate. The King did not give her a look. There was a moment of breathless silence while he strode over to Anne Boleyn, and thus, choosing her, made public his preference.

His hand held hers firmly; his was warm and strong; she felt he would crush her fingers.

They danced, His eyes burned bright as the jewels on his clothes. Different this from the passion of Wyatt; fiercer, prouder, not sad but angry passion.

He would have speech with her away from these people, he

said. She replied that she feared the Queen's disapproval should she leave the ballroom.

He said: 'Do you not fear mine if you stay!'

'Sir,' she said, 'the Queen is my mistress.'

'And a hard one, eh?'

'A very kind one, Sir, and one whose displeasure I should not care to incur.'

He said angrily: 'Mistress, you try our patience sorely. Did you like our song?'

'It rhymed well,' she said, for now she sat with him she could see that his anger was not to be feared; he would not hurt her, since mingling with his passion there was a tenderness, and this tenderness which she observed, while it subdued her fear, filled her with a strange and exalted feeling.

'What mean you?' he cried, and he leaned closer, and though he would know himself to be observed he could not keep away.

'Your Majesty's rhyme I liked well; the sentiments expressed, not so well.'

'Enough of this folly!' he said. 'You know I love you well.'

'I beg your Majesty . . .'

'You may beg anything you wish an you say you love me.'

She repeated the old argument. 'Your Majesty, there can be no question of love between us . . . I would never be your mistress.'

'Anne,' he said earnestly, pleadingly, 'should you but give yourself to me body and soul there should be no other in my heart I swear. I would cast off all others that are in competition with you, for there is none that ever have delighted me as you do.'

She stood up, trembling; she could see he would refuse to go on taking no for an answer, and she was afraid.

She said: 'The Queen watches us, Your Majesty. I fear her anger.'

He arose, and they joined the dancers.

'Think not,' he said, 'that this matter can rest here.'

'I crave Your Majesty's indulgences. I see no way that it can end that will satisfy us both.'

'Tell me, he said, 'do you like me?'

'I hope I am a loving subject to Your Majesty...'

'I doubt not that you could be a very loving one, Anne, if you gave your mind to it; and I pray you will give your mind to it. For long have I loved you, and for long have I had little satisfaction in others for my thoughts of you.'

'I am unworthy of Your Majesty's regard.'

She thought: Words! These tiresome words! I am frightened. Oh, Percy, why did you leave me! Thomas, if you loved me when you were a child, why did you let them marry you to a wife!

The King towered over her, massive and glittering in his power. He breathed heavily; his face was scarlet; desire in his eyes, desire in his mouth.

She thought: Tomorrow I shall return secretly to Hever.

* * *

The Queen was sulky. She dismissed her maids and went into that chamber wherein was the huge royal bed which she still shared with Henry, but the sharing of which was a mere formality. She lay at one extreme edge; he at the other.

She said: 'It is useless to pretend you sleep.'

He said: 'I had no intention of pretending, Madam.'

'It would seem to be your greatest pleasure to humiliate me.'

'How so?' he said.

'It is invariably someone; tonight it was the girl Boleyn. It was your kingly duty to have chosen me.'

'Chosen you, Madam!' he snorted. 'That would I never have done; not now, nor years ago, an the choice were mine!'

She began to weep and to murmur prayers; she prayed for self-control for herself and for him. She prayed that he might soften towards her, and that she might defy the doctors who had prophesied that he would never get a male heir from her.

He lay listening to her but paying little attention, being much accustomed to her prayers, thinking of a girl's slender body in scarlet and gold, a girl with flowing hair and a clever, pointed face, and the loveliest dark eyes in the court. Anne, he thought, you witch! I vow you hold off to provoke me. . . . Pleasant thoughts. She was holding off to plague him. But enough, girl. How many years since I saw you in your father's garden, and wanted you then! What do you want, girl? Ask for it; you shall have it, but love me, love me, for indeed I love you truly.

The Queen had stopped praying.

'They give themselves such airs, these women you elevate with your desires.'

'Come,' he said, gratified, for did not she give herself airs, and was it then because of his preference for her? 'It is natural, is it not, that those noticed by the King should give themselves airs?'

'There are so many,' she said faintly.

Ah! he thought, there would be but one, Anne, and you that one!

The Queen repeated: 'I would fain Your Majesty controlled himself.'

Oh, her incessant chatter wearied him. He wished to be left alone with his dreams of her whose presence enchanted him.

He said cruelly: 'Madam, you yourself are little inducement to a man to forsake his mistresses.'

She quivered; he felt that, though the width of the vast bed separated them.

'I am no longer young,' she said. 'Am I to blame because our children died?' He was silent; she was trembling violently now. 'I have heard the whispering that goes on in the court. I have heard of this they call The King's Secret Matter.'

Now she had dragged his mind from the sensuous dream which soothed his body. So the whispering had reached her ears, had it! Well, assuredly it must reach them some time; but he would rather the matter had been put before her in a more dignified manner.

She said appealingly: 'Henry, you do not deny it?'

He heaved his great body up in the bed. 'Katharine,' he

said, 'you know well that for myself I would not replace you; but a king's life does not belong to him but to his kingdom. And Katharine, serious doubts have arisen in my mind, not lately but for some time past; and well would I have suppressed them had my conscience let me. I would have you know, Katharine, that when our daughter's marriage with the Duke of Orleans was proposed, the French ambassador raised the question of her legitimacy.'

'Legitimacy!' cried Katharine, raising herself. 'What meant he? My lord, I hope you reproved him most sternly!'

'Ah! That I did! And sorely grieved was I.' The King felt happier now; he was no longer the erring husband being reproved by his too faithful wife; he was the King, who put his country first, before all personal claims; and in this matter, he could tell himself, the man must take second place to the King. He could, lying in this bed with a woman whose pious ways, whose shapeless body had long since ceased to move him except with repugnance, assure himself that the need to remain married to her was removed.

He had married Katharine because there had been England's need to form a deep friendship with Spain, because England had then been weak, and across a narrow strip of channel lay mighty France, a perennial enemy. In those days of early marriage it had been a hope of Henry's to conquer France once more; with Calais still in English hands, this had not seemed an impossibility; he had hoped that with the Emperor's help this might be effected, but since the undignified affair at Pavia, Charles was hardly likely to link himself with English allies; thus was the need for friendship with Spain removed; Wolsey's schemes had been called to a halt; the new allies were the French. Therefore, what could be better for England than to dissolve the Spanish marriage! And in its place . . . But no matter, dissolve the Spanish marriage since it could no longer help England.

These were minor matters compared with the great issue which disturbed his conscience. God bless the Bishop of Tarbes, that ambassador who had the tact at this moment to question the legitimacy of the Princess Mary.

' 'Twere a matter to make a war with France,' said Katharine hotly. 'My daughter ... a bastard! *Your* daughter ...'

'These matters are not for women's wits,' said the King. 'Wars are not made on such flimsy pretexts.'

'Flimsy!' she cried, her voice sharp with fear. Katharine was no fool; to the suppers given in her apartments there came the most learned of men, the more serious courtiers, men such as Sir Thomas More; she was more fastidious than the English ladies, and she had never tried to learn the English ways. She did not enjoy the blood sports so beloved by her husband. At first he had protested when she had told him that Spanish ladies did not follow the hawk and hound. But that was years ago; he thought it well now that she did not attend sporting displays, since he had no wish for her company. But there was that in her which must make him respect her, her calm dignity, her religious faith; and even now, when this great catastrophe threatened her, she had not shown publicly – apart from her melancholy which was natural to her – that she knew what was afoot. But she was tenacious; she would fight, he knew, if not for herself for her daughter. Her piety would tell her that she fought for Henry as well as for herself, that divorce was wrong in the eyes of the Church, and she would fight with all her quiet persistence against it.

'Katharine,' said the King, 'dost thou remember thy Bible?' He began to quote a passage from Leviticus wherein it was said that for a man to take his brother's wife was an unclean thing, for thus had he uncovered his brother's nakedness; they should therefore be childless. He repeated the last sentence.

'Thou knowest I was never truly thy brother's wife.'

'It is a matter which perplexes me greatly.'

'You would say you believe me not?'

'I know not what to say. Your hopes of an heir have been blighted; it looks like Providence. Is it natural that our sons should die one after the other? Is it natural that our efforts should be frustrated?'

'Not all,' she said plaintively.

'A daughter!' he retorted contemptuously.

'She is a worthy girl. . . .'

'Bah! A girl! What good are women on the throne of England! She is no answer to our prayers, Katharine. Sons have been denied to us. . . . The fault does not lie in me. . . .'

Tears were in the Queen's eyes. She would hate this man if most of her natural instincts had not been suppressed by piety; she knew not now whether she hated or loved; she only knew she must do what was right according to her religion. She must not hate the King; she must not hate her husband; for therein was mortal sin. So all through the years when he had slighted her, humiliated her, shown utter carelessness of the hurt his lack of faith might cause her, she had assured herself that she loved him. Small wonder that he found her colourless; small wonder that now he compared this woman of forty-one with a laughing, wilful girl of nineteen years! He was thirty-five; surely a good age for a man – his prime. But he must be watchful of the years, being a king who had so far failed to give his kingdom an heir.

A short while ago he had brought his illegitimate son to court, and heaped honours upon him to the deep humiliation of the Queen, whose fears were then chiefly for her daughter. This huge man cared nothing for her, little for her daughter; he only cared that he should get what he wanted, and that the world should think that in procuring his own needs he did it not for his own, but for duty's sake.

When he said that the fault was not with him, he meant she had lied when she declared herself a virgin; he meant that she had lived with his brother as his wife. She began to weep as she prayed for strength to fight this powerful man and his evil intentions to displace her daughter from the throne with a bastard he might beget through one whom he would call his wife.

'Search your soul!' he said now, his voice trembling with righteousness. 'Search your soul, Katharine, for the truth. Does the blame for this disaster to our kingdom lie with you or with me? *I* have a clear conscience. Ah, Katharine, can you say you have the same?'

'That I can,' she said, 'and will!'

He could have struck her, but he calmed himself and said

in melancholy fashion: 'Nothing would have made me take this step, but that my conscience troubled me.'

She lay down and was silent; he lay down too; and in a very short while he had forgotten Katharine and was thinking of her who, he had determined, should be his.

* * *

Anne arrived at Hever with the words of the King's song still in her thoughts. She found it difficult to analyse her feelings, for to be the object of so much attention from one as powerful as the King was to reflect that power; and to Anne, bold and eager for life, power, though perhaps not the most cherished gift life could bestow, was not to be despised.

She wondered what he would say when the news of her departure reached him. Would he be angry? Would he decide that it was beneath his dignity to pursue such an unappreciative female? Would he banish her from court? She fervently hoped not that, for she needed gaiety as she never had before. She could suppress her melancholy in feverish plans for the joust, and moreover her friends were at court – George and Thomas, Surrey and Francis Bryan; with them she could laugh and frivol; and indeed talk most seriously too, for they were all – perhaps with the exception of Surrey – interested in the new religion of which she had learned a good deal from Marguerite, now the Queen of Navarre. They leaned towards that religion, all of them, perhaps because they were young and eager to try anything that was different from the old way, liking it by virtue of its very novelty.

She had not been at Hever more than a day, when the King arrived. If she had any doubt of his intense feeling for her, she need have no doubt any longer. He was inclined to be angry, but at the sight of her his anger melted; he was humble, which was somehow touching in one in whom humility was such a rare virtue; he was eager and passionate, anxious that she should have no doubt of the nature of his feelings for her.

They walked in that garden which had been the scene of

their first encounter; and that was at his wish, for he was a sentimental man when it pleased him to be so.

'I have seriously thought of this matter of love between us,' he told her. 'I would have you know that I understand your feelings. I must know – so stricken am I in my love for you – what your feelings to me are, and what they would be if I no longer had a wife.'

She was startled. Dazzling possibilities had presented themselves. Herself a Queen! The intoxicating glory of power! The joy of snapping her fingers at the Cardinal! Queen of England. . . !

'My lord . . .' she stammered. 'I fear I am stupid. I understand not . . .'

He put a hand on her arm, and she felt his fingers burning there; they crept up to her forearm, and she faced him, saw the intensity of his desire for her, and thrilled to it because, though he might not be a man she loved, he was King of England, and she felt his power, and she felt his need of her, and while he was in such urgent need it was she who held the power, for the King of England would be soft in her hands.

She cast down her eyes, fearful lest he should read her thoughts. He said she was fairer than any lady he had ever seen, and that he yearned to possess her, body and soul.

'Body and soul!' he repeated, his voice soft and humble, his eyes on her small neck, her slender body; and his voice slurred suddenly with desire as, in his mind, he took her, just as he had when he had lain beside the Queen and conjured up pictures of her so vividly that it had seemed she was there with him.

She was thinking of Percy and of Wyatt, and it seemed to her that these two mingled together and were one, representing love; and before her beckoned this strong, powerful, bejewelled man who represented ambition.

He was kissing her hand with swift, devouring kisses; there was a ring on her forefinger which she wore always; he kissed this ring, and asked that he might have it as a token, but she clenched her hands and shook her head. There was a large diamond on his finger that he would give to her, he said; and these two rings would be symbols of the love between them.

'For now I shall soon be free,' he said, 'to take a wife.'

She lifted her eyes incredulously to his face. 'Your Majesty cannot mean he would take me!'

He said passionately: 'I will take none other!'

Then it was true; he was offering her marriage. He would lift her up to that lofty eminence on which now sat Queen Katharine, the daughter of a King and Queen. She, humble Anne Boleyn, was to be placed there . . . and higher, for Katharine might be Queen, but she had never had the King's regard. It was too brilliant to be contemplated. It dazzled. It gave her a headache. She could not think clearly, and it seemed as though she saw Wyatt smiling at her, now mocking, now melancholy. It was too big a problem for a girl who was but nineteen and who, longing to be loved, had been grievously disappointed in her lovers.

'Come, Anne!' he said. 'I swear you like me.'

'It is too much for me to contemplate. . . . I need . . .'

'You need me to make up your mind for you!' he said, and there and then he had her in his arms, his lips hard and hot against her own. She felt his impatience, and sought to keep her wits. Already she knew something of this man; a man of deep needs, ever impatient of their immediate gratification; now he was saying to her: 'I've promised marriage. Why wait longer? Here! Now! Show your gratitude to your King and your trust in him, and believe that he will keep his promise!'

The Secret Matter . . . would it be granted? And if so . . . what would her old enemy, Wolsey, have to say of such a marriage? There would be powerful people at court who would exert all their might to prevent it. No, she might be falling in love with the thought of herself as Queen, but she was not in love with the King.

She said, with that haughty dignity which while it exasperated him never failed to subdue him: 'Sire, the honour you do me is so great that I would fain . . .'

With a rough edge to his voice he interrupted: 'Enough of such talk, sweetheart! Let us not talk as King and subject, but as man and woman.' One hand was at her throat. She felt his body hot against her own. With both hands she held him off.

'As yet,' she said coldly, 'I am unsure.'

The veins stood out on his forehead.

'Unsure!' he roared. 'Your King has said he loves you . . . aye, and will marry you, and you are unsure!'

'Your Majesty suggested we should talk as man and woman, not as King and subject.'

She had freed herself and was running towards the hedge of fir-trees which enclosed this garden; he ran after her, and she allowed herself to be caught at the hedge. He held both her hands tightly in his.

'Anne!' he said. 'Anne! Dost seek to plague me?'

She answered earnestly: 'I never felt less like plaguing anyone, and why should I plague Your Majesty who has done me this great honour! You have offered me your love, which is to me the greatest honour, you being my King and I but a humble girl; but it was Your Majesty's command that I should cease to think of you as King . .'

He interrupted: 'You twist my words, Anne. You clever little minx, you do!' And, forcing her against the hedge, he put his hands on her shoulders and kissed her lips; then those hands sought to pull apart her dress.

She wriggled free.

He said sternly: 'I would have you regard me now as your King. I would have you be my obedient, loving little subject.'

She was breathless with fear. She said, greatly daring: 'You could never win my love that way! I beg of you, release me.'

He did so, and she stood apart from him, her eyes flashing, her heart beating madly; for she greatly feared that he would force on her that which till now she had so cleverly avoided. But suddenly she saw her advantage, for there he stood before her, not an angry King but a humble man who, besides desiring her, loved her; and thus she knew that it was not for him to say what should be, but for herself to decide. Such knowledge was sweet; it calmed her

146

sorely troubled mind, and calm she was indeed mistress of the situation. Here he was, this great bull of a man, for the first time in his life in love, and therefore inexperienced in this great emotion which swept over him, governing his actions, forcing him to take orders instead of giving them; forcing him to supplicate instead of demanding.

'Sweetheart . . .' he began hoarsely; but she lifted a hand.

'Your rough treatment has grieved me.'

'But my love for you . . .'

She looked at the red marks his hands had made on her shoulder, where he had torn the neck of her gown.

'It frightens me,' she said, looking not the least frightened, but mistress of herself and of him. 'It makes me uncertain . . .'

'Have no uncertainty of me, darling! When I first met you I went back and said to Wolsey: "I have been discoursing with one who is worthy to wear a crown!"'

'And what said my lord Cardinal? He laughed in your face I dare swear!'

'Dost think he would dare!'

'There are many things my lord Cardinal might dare that others would not. He is an arrogant, ill-bred creature!'

'You wrong him, sweetheart . . . nor do we wish to speak of him. I beg of you, consider this matter in all seriousness, for I swear there is none that can make me happy but yourself.'

'But Your Majesty could not make me your Queen! I have said your mistress I would never be.'

Now he was eager, for his mind, which had weighed this point since she began to torment him, was now firmly made up.

'I swear,' he said, 'I would never take another queen but that she was Anne Boleyn. Give me the ring, sweetheart, and take you this so that I may have peace in my mind.'

These were sweet words to her, but still she wavered. Love first; power second. Ah, she thought, could I but love this man!

'Your Grace must understand my need to think this matter over well.'

'Think it over, Anne? I ask you to be my Queen!'

'We do not discuss kings and queens,' she reproved him, and the reproof enchanted him. 'This is a matter between a man and a woman. Would you then wish me to be your Queen and not to be wholly sure that I loved you more than a subject loves a king?'

This was disarming. Where was there a woman who could hesitate over such a matter! Where was one like her! In wit, in beauty, he had known she had no equal; but in virtue too she stood alone. She was priceless, for nothing he could give would buy her. He must win her love.

He was enchanted. This was delightful – for how could he doubt that she would love him! There was none who excelled as he did at the jousts; always he won – or almost always. His songs were admired more than Wyatt's or Surrey's even; and had he not earned the title of Defender of The Faith by his book against Luther! Could More have written such a book? No! He was a king among men in all senses of the words. Take away the throne tomorrow and he would still be king. In love . . . ah! He had but to look at a woman, and she was ripe for him. So it had always been . . . except with Anne Boleyn. But she stood apart from others; she was different; that was why she should be his Queen.

'I would have time to think on this matter,' she said, and her words rang with sincerity, for this man's kisses had aroused in her a desire for those of another man, and she was torn between love and ambition. If Wyatt had not had a wife, if it was a dignified love he could have given her, she would not have hesitated; but it was the King who offered dignity, and he offered power and state; nor was Wyatt such a humble lover as this man, for all his power, could be; and, lacking humility herself, she liked it in others.

'I stay here till I have your answer,' said the King. 'I swear I will not leave Hever till I wear your ring on my finger and you mine on yours.'

'Give me till tomorrow morning,' she said.

'Thus shall it be, sweetheart. Deal kindly with me in your thoughts.'

'How could I do aught else, when from you I and mine have had naught but kindness!'

He was pleased at that. What had he not done for these Boleyns! Aye, and would do more still. He would make old Thomas's daughter a queen. Then he wondered, did she mean to refer to Mary? Quick of speech was his love; sharp of wits; was she perhaps a little jealous of her sister Mary?

He said soberly: 'There shall be none in competition with you, sweetheart.'

And she answered disconcertingly: 'There would need to be none, for I could not believe in the love of a man who amused himself with mistresses.' Then she was all smiles and sweetness. 'Sire, forgive my forwardness. Since you tell me you are a man who loves me, I forget you are the King.'

He was enraptured; she would come to him not for what the coming would mean to her in honour; she would come to him as the man.

That evening was a pleasant one. After the meal in the great dining-hall she played to him and sang a little.

He kissed her hands fervently on retiring.

'Tomorrow,' he said, 'I must have that ring.'

'Tomorrow,' she answered, 'you shall know whether or not you shall have it.'

He said, his eyes on her lips: 'Dost think of me under this roof knowing you so near and refusing me?'

'Perhaps it will not always be so,' she said.

'I will dream you are already Queen of England. I will dream that you are in my arms.'

She was afraid of such talk; she bade him a hasty good night, repeating her promise that he should hear her decision in the morning. She went to her chamber and locked her door.

Anne passed a night that was tortured with doubts. To be Queen of England! The thought haunted her, dominated her. Love, she had lost – the love she had dreamed of. Ambition beckoned. Surely she was meant to be a queen, she on whom the Fates had bestowed great gifts. She saw her ladies about her, robing her in the garments of state; she saw herself stately and gracious, imperious. Ah! she thought, there are so many people I can help. And her thoughts went to a house in Lambeth and a little girl tugging at her skirts.

That would be indeed gratifying, to lift her poor friends and members of her family out of poverty; to know that they spoke of her lovingly and with respect. . . . We owe this to the Queen – the Queen, but a humble girl whose most unusual gifts, whose wit and beauty so enslaved the King that he would make her his Queen. And then . . . there were some who had laughed at her, her enemies who had said: 'Ah! There goes Anne Boleyn; there she goes, the way of her sister!' How pleasant to snap the fingers at them, to make them bow to her!

Her eyes glittered with excitement. The soft girl who had loved Percy, who was inclined to love Wyatt, had disappeared, and in her place was a calculating woman. Ambition was wrestling desperately with love; and ambition was winning.

I do not dislike the King, she thought – for how could one dislike a man who had the good taste to admire one so wholeheartedly.

And the Queen? Ah! Something else to join the fight against ambition. The poor Queen, who was gentle enough, though melancholy, she a queen to be wronged. Oh, but the glitter of queenship! And Anne Boleyn was more fit to occupy a throne than Katharine of Aragon, for queenship is innate; it is not to be bestowed on those who have nothing but their relationship to other kings and queens.

Thomas, Thomas! Why are you not a king, to arrange a divorce, to take a new queen!

Would you be faithful, Thomas? Are any men? And if not, is love the great possession to be prized above all else? Thomas and his wife! George and Jane! The King and the Queen! Look around the court; where has love lasted? Is it not overrated? And ambition . . . Wolsey! How high he had come! From a butcher's shop, some said, to Westminster Hall. From tutor's cold attic to Hampton Court! Ambition beckoned. Cardinals may be knocked down from their proud perches, but it would need a queen to knock them down; and who could displace a queen of the King's choice!

A queen! A queen! Queen Anne!

While Henry, restless, dreamed of her taking off those

elegant clothes, of caressing the shapely limbs, she, wakeful, pictured herself riding in a litter of cloth of gold, while on either side crowds of people bared their heads to the Queen of England.

The next day Henry, after extracting a promise from her that she would return to court at once, rode away from Hever wearing her ring on his finger.

* * *

The Cardinal wept; the Cardinal implored; all his rare gifts were used in order to dissuade the King. But Henry was more determined on this than he had ever been on any matter. As wax in the hands of the crafty Wolsey he had been malleable indeed; but Wolsey had to learn that he had been so because, being clever enough to recognize the powers of Wolsey, he had been pleased to let him have his way. Now he desired the divorce, he desired marriage with Anne Boleyn as he had never desired anything except the throne, and he would fight for these with all the tenacity of the obstinate man he was; and being able to assure himself that he was in the right he could do so with unbounded energy. The divorce was right, for dynastic reasons; Anne was right for him, for she was young and healthy and would bear him many sons. An English Queen for the English throne! That was all he asked.

In vain did Wolsey point out what the reaction in France must surely be. Had he not almost affianced Henry to Renée? And the people of England? Had His Grace, the King, considered their feelings in the matter? There was murmuring against the divorce throughout the capital. Henry did what he ever did when crossed; he lost his temper, and in his mind were sown the first seeds of suspicion towards his old friend and counsellor. Wolsey had no illusions; well he knew his royal master. He must now work with all his zest and genius for the divorce; he must use all his energies to put on the throne one whom he knew to be his enemy, whom he had discovered to be more than a feckless woman seeking admiration and gaiety, whom he knew to be interested in the new religion, to be involved in a powerful party comprising her uncle of Norfolk, her father, her brother, Wyatt and the rest; this he must do, or displease the King. He could see no reward for himself in this. To please the King he must put Anne Boleyn on the throne, and to put Anne Boleyn on the throne was to advance one who would assuredly have the King under her influence, and who was undoubtedly – if not eager to destroy him – eager to remove him from that high place to which years of work had brought him.

But he was Wolsey the diplomat, so he wrote to the Pope extolling the virtues of Anne Boleyn.

Anne herself had returned to court a changed person. Now she must accept the adulation of all; there were those who, disliking her hitherto, now eagerly sought her favour; she was made to feel that she was the most important person at court, for even the King treated her with deference.

She was nineteen – a girl, in spite of an aura of sophistication. Power was sweet, and if she was a little imperious it was because of remembered slights when she had been considered not good enough for Percy – she who was to be Queen of England. If she was a little hard, it was because life had been unkind to her, first with Percy, then with Wyatt. If she were inclined to be overfond of admiration and seek it where it was unwise to do so, was not her great beauty responsible? She was accomplished and talented, and it was but human that she should wish to use these gifts. Very noble it might seem for Queen Katharine to dress herself in sober attire; she was ageing and shapeless, and never, even in her youth, had she been beautiful. Anne's body was perfectly proportioned, her face animated and charming; it was as natural for her to adorn herself as it was for Wyatt to write verses, or for the King in his youth to tire out many horses in one day at the hunt. People care about doing things which they do well, and had Katharine possessed the face and figure of Anne, doubtless she would have spent more time at her mirror and a little less with her chaplain. And if Anne offended some a little at this point, she was but nineteen, which is not very old; and she was gay by nature and eager to live an exciting, exhilarating and stimulating life.

Her pity for the Queen was diminished when that lady, professing friendship for her, would have her play cards every evening to keep her from the King, and that playing she might show that slight deformity on her left hand. Ah! These pious ones! thought Anne. Are they as good as they would seem? How often do they use their piety to hurt a sinner like myself!

She was over-generous perhaps, eager to share her good fortune with others, and one of the keenest joys she derived from her newly won power was the delight of being able to help the needy. Nor did she forget her uncle, Edmund Howard, but besought the King that something might be done for him. The King, becoming more devoted with each day and caring not who should know it, promised to give the Comptrollership of Calais to her uncle. This was pleasant news to her; and she enjoyed many similar pleasures.

But she, seeming over-gay, not for one moment relaxed in the cautious game she must continue to play with the King; for the divorce was long in coming, and the King's desire was hard to check; for ever must she be on her guard with him, since it was a difficult game with a dangerous opponent.

Nor did she forget it, for with her quickness of mind very speedily did she come to know her royal lover; and there were times in this gay and outwardly butterfly existence when fears beset her.

Wyatt, reckless and bold, hovered about her, and though she knew it was unwise to allow his constant attendance, she was very loth to dismiss him from her companionship. Well she had kept her secret, and Wyatt did not yet know of the talk of marriage which had taken place between her and the King. Wyatt himself was similar to Anne in character, so that the relationship between them often seemed closer than that of first cousin. He was reckoned the handsomest man at court; he was certainly the most charming. Impulsive as Anne herself, he would slip unthinking into a dangerous situation.

There was such an occasion when he was playing bowls with the King. The Duke of Suffolk and Sir Francis Bryan completed the quartet. There was a dispute over the game, which any but Wyatt would have let pass; not so Wyatt; he played to win, as did the King, and he would not allow even Henry to take what was not his. Henry was sure he had beaten Wyatt in casting the bowl. Wyatt immediately replied: 'Sire, by your leave, it is not so.'

The King turned his gaze upon this young man whom he could not help but like for his charm, his gaiety and his wit; his little eyes travelled over Wyatt's slim body, and he remembered that he had seen him but that morning hovering about Anne. Wyatt was handsome, there was no denying that. Wyatt wrote excellent verses. The King also wrote verses. He was a little piqued by Wyatt's fluency. And Anne? He had heard it whispered, before it was known that such whispers would madden him, that Wyatt was in love with Anne.

He was suddenly angry with Wyatt. He had dared to raise a dispute over a game. He had dared write better verses than Henry. He had dared to cast his eyes on Anne Boleyn, and was young enough, handsome enough, plausible enough to turn any girl's head.

Significantly, and speaking in the parables he so loved to use, Henry made a great show of pointing with his little finger on which was the ring Anne had given him. Wyatt saw the ring, recognized it and was nonplussed; and that again added fuel to Henry's anger. How dared Wyatt know so well a ring which had been Anne's! How often, wondered Henry, had he lifted her hand to his lips!

'Wyatt!' said the King; and smiling complacently and significantly: 'I tell thee it is mine!'

Wyatt, debonair, careless of consequences, looked for a moment at the ring and with a nonchalant air brought from his pocket the chain on which hung the tablet he had taken from Anne. He said with equal significance to that used by the King: 'And if it may please Your Majesty to give me leave to measure the cast with this, I have good hopes yet it will be mine!'

Gracefully he stooped to measure, while Henry, bursting with jealous fury, stood by.

'Ah!' cried Wyatt boldly. 'Your Majesty will see that I am right. The game is mine!'

Henry, his face purple with fury, shouted at Wyatt: 'It may be so, but then I am deceived!' He left the players staring after him.

'Wyatt,' said Bryan, 'you were ever a reckless fool! Why did you make such a pother about a paltry game?'

But Wyatt's eyes had lost their look of triumph; he shrugged his shoulders. He knew that he had lost, and guessed the ring Anne had given the King to be a symbol.

Henry stormed into the room where Anne was sitting with some of the ladies. The ladies rose at his entrance, curtseyed timidly, and were quick to obey the signal he gave for their departure.

'Your Majesty is angry,' said Anne, alarmed.

'Mistress Anne Boleyn,' said the King, 'I would know what there is betwixt thee and Wyatt.'

'I understand not,' she said haughtily. 'What should there be?'

'That to make him boast of his success with you.'

'Then he boasts emptily.'

He said: 'I would have proof of that.'

She shrugged her shoulders. 'You mean that you doubt my words.'

She was as quick to anger as he was, and she had great power over him because, though he was deeply in love with her, she was but in love with the power he could give her, and she was as yet uncertain that this honour was what she asked of life. That was the secret of her power over him. She wavered, swaying away from him, and he, bewitched and enflamed with the strong sexual passion which coloured his whole existence, was completely at her mercy.

He said: 'Anne, I know well that you would speak the truth. But tell me now with good speed, sweetheart, that there is naught between you and Wyatt.'

'You would blame me,' she said haughtily, 'since he writes his verse to me?'

'Nay, sweetheart. I would blame you for nothing. Tell me

now that I have naught to fear from this man, and restore my happiness.'

'You have naught to fear from him.'

'He had a jewelled tablet of yours.'

'I remember it. He took it one day; he would not return it, and I, valuing it but little, did not press the matter.'

He sat heavily beside her on the window seat, and put an arm about her.

'You have greatly pleased me, sweetheart. You must excuse my jealousy.'

'I do excuse it,' she said.

'Then all is well.' He kissed her hand hungrily, his eyes asking for much that his lips dared not. He had angered her; he could not risk doing so again, for he sensed the uncertainty in her. Thus he marvelled at his infatuation for this girl; as did the court. He had never loved like this; nay, he had never loved before. He was thirty-six, an old thirty-six in some ways, for he lived heartily; this was the last flare-up of youth, and the glow lighted everything about him in fantastic colours. He was the middle-aged man in love with youth; he felt inexpressibly tender towards her; he was obsessed by her; he chafed against the delay of the divorce.

After this affair of the bowls, Anne knew she was committed. Wyatt's glance was sardonic now; Wyatt was resigned. She had chosen the power and the glory; his rival had tempted her with the bait of marriage.

> '*And wilt thou leave me thus*, he wrote,
> *That hath loved thee so long*
> *In wealth and woe among:*
> *And is thy heart so strong*
> *As for to leave me thus?*'

Her heart must be strong; she must cultivate ambition; she must tread warily, since in that court of glittering men and women she now began to find her enemies, and if their malice was cloaked in soft words, they were none-the-less against her. The Cardinal, watchful and wary; the Duke of Suffolk and his wife – that Mary with whom she had gone to France – who now saw her throwing a shadow over the prospects of their descendants' claim to the throne; Chapuys, the Spaniard who was more of a spy for his master, the Emperor Charles, than his ambassador; Katharine, the Queen whom she would displace; Mary, the princess who would be branded as illegitimate. All these there were in high places to fight against her. There was a more dangerous enemy still – the people of London. Discontent was rampant in the city; the harvest had been a poor one, and the sober merchants felt that an alliance with France was folly, since it merely changed old friends for new ones who had previously shown they were not to be trusted. There was famine throughout the country, and though the King might lend to the city corn from his own granaries, still the people murmured. The cloth merchants fretted, for the trouble with Spain meant losing the great Flanders market. The County of Kent petitioned the King, in view of their poverty, to repay a loan made to him two years before. The Archbishop of Canterbury did what he could to soothe these people, but they remained restive.

For these troubles did the people of England blame Wolsey. During the prosperous years the King received the homage of his subjects; he had been taken to their hearts during the period of his coronation when he, a magnificent figure of an Englishman, fair and tall and skilled in sport, had ridden among them – such a contrast to his ugly, mean old father. During the dark years, however, they blamed Wolsey; for Wolsey had committed the sin of being of the people and rising above them. The whispers went round: 'Which court? Hampton Court or the King's court?' This was the twilight hour of Wolsey's brilliant day. And the starving and wretched gazed at a bright and beautiful girl, reclining in her barge or riding out with friends from court; more gaily dressed than the other ladies, she sparkled with rich jewels, presents from the King – a sight to raise the wrath of a starving people. 'We'll have none of Nan Bullen!' they murmured together. 'The King's whore shall not be our Queen. Queen Katharine for ever!'

From the choked gutters there arose evil smells; decaying matter lay about for weeks; rats, tame as cats, walked the cobbles; overhanging gables, almost touching across narrow streets, shut out the sun and air, held in the vileness. And in those filthy streets men and women were taken suddenly sick; many died in the streets, the sweat pouring from their bodies; and all men knew that the dreaded sweating sickness had returned to England. Thus did the most sorely afflicted people of London wonder at this evil which had fallen upon them; thus did they murmur against her who by her witch's fascination had turned the King from his pious ways. The sick and suffering of London whispered her name; the rebellious people of Kent talked of her; in the weaving counties her name was spoken with distaste. Everywhere there was murmuring against the devil's instrument, Wolsey, and her who had led the King into evil ways and brought down the justice of heaven upon their country. Even at Horsham, where the news of the sweating sickness had not yet reached, they talked of Anne Boleyn. The old Duchess chuckled in great enjoyment of the matter.

'Come here, Catherine Howard. Rub my back. I declare I must be full of lice or suffering from the itch! Rub harder, child. Ah! Fine doings at the court, I hear. The King is bewitched, it seems, by your cousin, Anne Boleyn, and I am not greatly surprised to hear it. I said, when she came visiting me at Lambeth: "Ah! There is a girl the King would like!" though I will say I added that he might feel inclined to spank the haughtiness out of her before carrying her off to bed. Don't scratch, child! Gently . . . gently. Now I wonder if . . .' The Duchess giggled. 'You must not look so interested, child, and I should not talk to you of such matters. Why, of course . . . As if he would not . . . From what I know of His Majesty . . . Though there are those that say . . . It is never wise to give in . . . and yet what can a poor girl do . . . and look how Mary kept him dancing attendance all those years! There is something about the Boleyns, and of course it comes from the Howards . . . though I swear I see little of it in you, child. Why, look at your gown! Is that a rent? You should make Isabel look after you better. And what do you do of nights when you should be sleeping?

I declare I heard such a noise from your apartment that I was of good mind to come and lay about the lot of you . . .'

It was merely the Duchess's talk; she would never stir from her bed. But Catherine decided she must tell the others.

'And your cousin, I hear, is to do something for your father, Catherine Howard. Oh, what it is to have friends at court! Why, you are dreaming there . . . Rub harder! Or leave that . . . you may do my legs now.'

Catherine was dreaming of the beautiful cousin who had come to the house at Lambeth. She knew what it meant to be a king's favourite, for Catherine had a mixed knowledge; she knew of the attraction between men and women, and the methods in which such attraction was shown; of books she knew little, as the Duchess, always meaning to have her taught, was somehow ever forgetful of this necessity. The cousin had given her a jewelled tablet, and she had it still; she treasured it.

'One day,' said the Duchess, 'I shall go to Lambeth that I may be near my granddaughter who is almost a queen.'

'She is not really your granddaughter,' said Catherine. 'You were her grandfather's second wife.'

The Duchess cuffed the girl's ears for that. 'What! And you would deny my relationship to the queen-to-be! She who is all but Queen has never shown me such disrespect. Now do my legs, child, and no more impertinence!'

Catherine thought – Nor are you my real grandmother either! And she was glad, for it seemed sacrilege that this somewhat frowsy old woman – Duchess of Norfolk though she might be – should be too closely connected with glorious Anne.

When Catherine was in the room which she still shared with the ladies-in-waiting, she took out the jewelled tablet and looked at it. It was impossible in the dormitory to have secrets, and several of them wanted to know what she had.

'It is nothing,' said Catherine.

'Ah!' said Nan. 'I know! It is a gift from your lover.'

'It is not!' declared Catherine. 'And I have no lover.'

'You should say so with shame! A fine big girl like you!' said a tall, lewd-looking girl, even bolder than the rest.

'I'll swear it is from her lover,' said Nan. 'Why, look! It has an initial on it – A. Now who is A? Think hard, all of you.'

Catherine could not bear their guessings, and she blurted out: 'I will tell you then. I have had it since I was a very little baby. It was given to me by my cousin, Anne Boleyn.'

'Anne Boleyn!' screamed Nan. 'Why, of course, our Catherine is first cousin to the King's mistress!' Nan leaped off the bed and made a mock bow to Catherine. The others followed her example, and Catherine thrust away the tablet, wishing she had not shown it.

Now they were all talking of the King and her cousin Anne, and what they said made Catherine's cheeks flush scarlet. She could not bear that they should talk of her cousin in this way, as though she were one of *them*.

The incorrigible Nan and the lewd-faced girl were shouting at each other.

'We will stage a little play . . . for tonight . . . You may take the part of the King. I shall be Anne Boleyn!'

They were rocking with laughter. 'I shall do this. You shall do that . . . I'll warrant we'll bring Her Grace up with our laughter . . .'

'We must be careful . . .'

'If she discovered . . .'

'Bah! What would she do?'

'She would send us home in disgrace.'

'She is too lazy . . .'

'What else? What else?'

'Little Catherine Howard shall be lady of the bed-chamber!'

'Ha! That is good. She being first cousin to the lady . . . Well, Catherine Howard, we have brought you up in the right way, have we not? We have trained you to wait on your lady cousin, even in the most delicate circumstances, with understanding and . . .'

'Tact!' screamed Nan. 'And discretion!'

'She'll probably get a place at court!'

'And Catherine Howard, unless you take us with you, we shall tell all we know about you and . . .'

'I have done nothing!' said Catherine hastily. 'There is nothing you could say against me.'

'Ah! Have you forgotten Thomas Culpepper so soon then?'

'I tell you there was nothing . . .'

'Catherine Howard! Have you forgotten the paddock and what he did there . . .'

'It was nothing . . . nothing!'

Nan said firmly: 'Those who excuse themselves, accuse themselves. Did you know that, Catherine?'

'I swear . . .' cried Catherine. And then, in an excess of boldness: 'If you do not stop saying these things about Thomas, I will go and tell my grandmother what happens in this room at night.'

Isabel, who had been silent amidst the noise of the others, caught her by her wrist.

'You would not dare . . .'

'Don't forget,' cried Nan, 'we should have something to say of *you*!'

'There is nothing you could say. I have done nothing but look on . . .'

'And enjoyed looking on! Now, Catherine Howard, I saw a young gentleman kiss you last evening.'

'It was not my wish, and that I told him.'

'Oh, well,' said Nan, 'it was not my wish that such and such happened to me, and I told him; but it happened all the same.'

Catherine moved to the door. Isabel was beside her.

'Catherine, take no heed of these foolish girls.'

There were tears in Catherine's eyes.

'I will not hear them say such things of my cousin.'

'Heed them not, the foolish ones! They mean it not.'

'I will not endure it.'

'And you think to stop it by telling your grandmother?'

'Yes,' said Catherine, 'for if she knew what happened here, she would dismiss them all.'

'I should not tell, Catherine. You have been here many nights yourself; she might not hold you guiltless. Catherine, listen to me. They shall say nothing of your cousin again; I will stop them. But first you must promise me that you will not let a word of what happens here get to your grandmother's ears through you.'

'It is wrong of them to taunt me.'

'Indeed it is wrong,' said Isabel, 'and it must not be. Trust me to deal with them. They are but foolish girls. Now promise you will not tell your grandmother.'

'I will not tell unless they taunt me to it.'

'Then rest assured they shall not.'

Catherine ran from the room, and Isabel turned to the girls who had listened open-eyed to this dialogue.

'You fools!' said Isabel. 'You ask for trouble. It is well enough to be reckless when there is amusement to be had, but just to taunt a baby . . . What do you achieve but the fear of discovery?'

'She would not dare to tell,' said Nan.

'Would she not! She has been turning over in her baby mind whether she ought not to tell ever since she came here. Doubtless the saintly Thomas warned her it was wrong to tell tales.'

'She dared not tell,' insisted another girl.

'Why not, you fool? She is innocent. What has she done but be a looker-on? We should be ruined, all of us, were this known to Her Grace.'

'Her Grace cares nothing but for eating, sleeping, drinking, scratching and gossip!'

'There are others who would care. And while she is innocent, there is danger of her telling. Now if she were involved . . .'

'We shall have to find a lover for her,' said Nan.

'A fine big girl such as she is!' said the lewd-faced girl who had promised to take the part of Henry.

The girls screamed together light-heartedly. Only Isabel, aloof from their foolish chatter, considered this.

*   *   *

The King sat alone and disconsolate in his private apartments. He was filled with apprehension. Through the South-eastern corner of England raged that dread disease, the sweating sickness. In the streets of London men took it whilst walking; many died within a few hours. People looked suspiciously one at the other. Why does this come upon us to add to our miseries! Poverty we have; famine; and now the sweat! Eyes were turned to the palaces, threatening eyes; voices murmured: 'Our King has turned his lawful wife from his bed, that he might put there a witch. Our King has quarrelled with the holy Pope. . . .'

Wolsey had warned him, as had others of his council: 'It would be well to send Mistress Anne Boleyn back to her father's castle until the sickness passes, for the people are murmuring against her. It might be well if Your Majesty appeared in public with the Queen.'

Angry as the King had been, he realized there was wisdom in their words.

'Sweetheart,' he said, 'the people are murmuring against us. This matter of divorce, which they cannot understand, is at the heart of it. You must go to Hever for awhile.'

She, with the recklessness of youth, would have snapped her fingers at the people. 'Ridiculous,' she said, 'to associate this sickness with the divorce! I do not want to leave the court. It is humiliating to be sent away in this discourteous manner.'

Was ever a man so plagued, and he a king! To his face she had laughed at his fears, despising his weakness in bowing to his ministers and his conscience. She would have defied the devil, he knew. He had forced himself to be firm, begging her to see that it was because he longed for her so desperately that he wished this matter of the divorce concluded with the minimum of trouble. Ever since she had gone he had been writing letters to her, passionate letters in which he bared his soul, in which he clearly told her more than it was wise to tell her. 'Oh,' he wrote, 'Oh, that you were in my arms!' He was not subtle with the pen; he wrote from the heart. He loved her; he wanted her with him. He told her these things, and so did he, the King of England, place himself at the mercy of a girl of nineteen.

He believed, with his people, that the sweat was a visitation from Heaven. It had come on other occasions; there had been one epidemic just before his accession to the throne. Ominous this! Was God saying he was not pleased that the Tudors should be the heirs of England? Again it had come in 1517, at about the time when Martin Luther was denouncing Rome. Was it God's intention to support the German, and did He thus show disapproval of those who followed Rome? He had heard his father's speaking of its breaking out after Bosworth . . . and now, here it was again when Henry was thinking of divorce. Assuredly it was alarming to contemplate these things!

So he prayed a good deal; he heard mass many times a day. He prayed aloud and in his thoughts. 'Thou knowest it was not for my carnal desires that I would make Anne my wife. There is none I would have for wife but Katharine, were I sure that she *was* my wife, that I was not sinning in continuing to let her share my bed. Thou knowest that!' he pleaded. 'Thou hast taken William Carey, O Lord. Ah! He was a complaisant husband to Mary, and mayhap this is his punishment. For myself, I have sinned in this matter and in others, as Thou knowest, but always I have confessed. I have repented . . . And if I took William's wife, I gave him a place at court beyond his deserts, for, as Thou knowest, he was a man of small ability.'

All his prayers and all his thoughts were tinged with his desire for Anne. 'There is a woman who will give sons to me and to England! That is why I would elevate her to the throne.' It was reassuring to be able to say 'England needs my sons!' rather than 'I want Anne.'

Henry was working on his treatise, in which he was pointing out the illegality of his marriage, and which he would despatch to the Pope. He was proud of it; for its profound and wise arguments; its clarity; its plausibility; its literary worth. He had shown what he had done to Sir Thomas More; had eagerly awaited the man's compliments; but More had merely said that he could not judge it since he knew so little of such matters. Ah! thought Henry. Professional jealousy, eh! And he had scowled at More, feeling suddenly a ridiculous envy of the man, for there was in More an agreeable humour, deep learning, wit, charm and a serenity of mind which showed in his countenance. Henry had been entertained at More's riverside house; had walked in the pleasant garden and watched More's children feed his peacocks; had seen this man in the heart of his family, deeply loved and reverenced by them; he had watched his friendship with men like the learned Erasmus, the impecunious Hans Holbein who, poor as he might be, knew well how to wield a brush. And being there, he the King – though he could not complain that they gave him not his rightful homage – had been outside that magic family circle, though Erasmus and Holbein had obviously been welcomed into it.

A wild jealousy had filled his heart for this man More who was known for his boldness in stating his opinions, for his readiness to crack a joke, for his love of literature and art, and for his practical virtue. Henry could have hated this man, had the man allowed him to, but ever susceptible to charm in men as well as women, he had fallen a victim to the charm of Sir Thomas More; and so he found, struggling in his breast, a love for this man, and even when More refused to praise his treatise, and even though he knew More was amongst those who did not approve of the divorce, he must continue to respect the man and seek his friendship. How many of his people, like More, did not approve of the divorce! Henry grew hot with righteous indignation and the desire to make them see this matter in the true light.

He had written a moralizing letter to his sister Margaret of Scotland, accusing her of immorality in divorcing her husband on the plea that her marriage had not been legal, thus making her daughter illegitimate. He burned with indignation at his niece's plight while he – at that very time – was planning to place his daughter Mary in a similar position. He did this in all seriousness, for his thoughts were governed by his muddled moral principles. He saw himself as noble, the perfect king; when the people murmured against Anne, it was because they did not understand! He was ready to sacrifice himself to his country. He did not see himself as he was, but as he wished himself to be; and, surrounded by those who continually sought his favour, he could not know that others did not see him as he wished to be seen.

One night during this most unsatisfactory state of affairs occasioned by Anne's absence, an express messenger brought disquieting news.

'From Hever!' roared the King. 'What from Hever?'

And he hoped for a letter, for she had not answered his in spite of his entreaties, a letter in which she was more humble, in which she expressed a more submissive mood of sweet reasonableness. It was not however a letter, but the alarming news that Anne and her father had taken the sickness, though mildly. The King was filled with panic. The most precious body in his kingdom was in danger. Carey had died. Not Anne! he prayed. Not Anne!

He grew practical; grieving that his first physician was not at hand, he immediately despatched his second, Doctor Butts, to Hever. Desperately anxious, he awaited news.

He paced his room, forgetting his superstitious fears, forgetting to remind God that it was just because she was healthy and could give England sons that he proposed marrying her; he thought only of the empty life without her.

He sat down and poured out his heart to her in his direct and simple manner.

'The most displeasing news that could occur came to me suddenly at night. On three accounts I must lament it. One, to hear of the illness of my mistress whom I esteem more than all the world, and whose health I desire as I do mine own : I would willingly bear half of what you suffer to cure you. The second, from the fear that I shall have to endure thy wearisome absence much longer, which has hitherto given me all the vexation that was possible. The third, because my physician (in whom I have most confidence) is absent at the very time when he could have given me the greatest pleasure. But I hope, by him and his means, to obtain one of my chief joys on earth; that is the cure of my mistress. Yet from the want of him I send you my second (Doctor Butts) and hope he will soon make you well. I shall then love him more than ever. I beseech you to be guided by his advice in your illness. By your doing this, I hope soon to see you again. Which will be to me a greater comfort than all the precious jewels in the world.

'Written by the hand of that secretary who is, and for ever will be, your loyal and most assured servant. H.R.'

And having written and despatched this, he must pace his apartment in such anxiety as he had never known, and marvel that there could be such a thing as love, all joy and sorrow, to assail even the hearts of princes.

*   *   *

The Queen was jubilant. Was this God's way of answering her prayers? She rejoiced with her daughter, because Anne Boleyn lay ill of the sweating sickness at Hever.

'Oh,' cried the Queen to her young daughter, 'this is the vengeance of the Lord. This is a judgment on the girl's wickedness.'

Twelve-year-old Mary listened wide-eyed, thinking her mother a saint.

'My father . . .' said the girl, 'loves he this woman?'

Her mother stroked her hair. Loving her dearly, she had until now superintended her education, kept her with her, imbued her with her own ideas of life.

'He thinks to do so, daughter. He is a lusty man, and thus it is with men. It is no true fault of his; she is to blame.'

'I have seen her about the court,' said Mary, her eyes narrowed, picturing Anne as she had seen her. That was how witches looked, thought Mary; they had flowing hair and huge dark eyes, and willowy bodies which they loved to swathe in scarlet; witches looked like Anne Boleyn!

'She should be burned at the stake, Mother!' said Mary.

'Hush!' said her mother. 'It is not meet to talk thus. Pray for her, Mary. Pity her, for mayhap at this moment she burns in hell.'

Mary's eyes were glistening; she hoped so. She had a vivid picture of flames the colour of the witch's gown licking her white limbs; in her imagination she could hear the most melodious voice at court, imploring in vain to be freed from hideous torment.

Mary understood much. This woman would marry her father; through her it would be said that Mary's mother was

167

no wife, and that she, Mary, was a bastard. Mary knew the meaning of that; she would no longer be the Princess Mary; she would no longer receive the homage of her father's subjects; she would never be Queen of England.

Mary prayed each night that her father would tire of Anne, that he would banish her from the court, that he would grow to hate her, commit her to the Tower where she would be put in a dark dungeon to be starved and eaten by rats, that she might be put in chains, that her body might be grievously racked for every tear she had caused to fall from the eyes of Mary's saintly mother.

Mary had something of her father in her as well as of her mother; her mother's fanaticism perhaps, but her father's cruelty and determination.

Once her mother had said: 'Mary, what if your father should make her his Queen?'

Mary had answered proudly: 'There could be but one Queen of England, Mother.'

Katharine's heart had rejoiced, for deeply, tenderly, she loved her daughter. While they were together there could not be complete despair. But all their wishes, all their prayers, were without effect.

When the news came to Henry that Anne had recovered, he embraced the messenger, called for wine to refresh him, fell on his knees and thanked God.

'Ha!' said he to Wolsey. 'This is a sign! I am right to marry the lady; she will give me many lusty sons.'

Poor Katharine! She could but weep silently; and then her bitterness was lost in fear, for her daughter had taken the sickness.

Anne convalesced at Hever. At court she was spoken of continually. Du Bellay, the witty French ambassador, joked in his light way. He wagered the sickness of the lady had spoiled her beauty in some measure; he was certain that during her absence some other one would find a way to the King's susceptible heart. Chapuys, the Spanish ambassador, laughed with him, and gleefully wrote to his master of the 'concubine's' sickness. Blithely he prophesied an end of this – in Spain's eyes – monstrous matter of the divorce.

But Henry did not wait for her convalescence to end. How could he wait much longer! He had waited enough already. Privately he would ride from Greenwich or from Eltham to Hever Castle, and Anne, from the castle grounds, hearing his bugle call on a nearby hill, would go out to meet him. They would walk the gallery together, or sit in the oak-panelled chamber while he told her how the matter of the divorce progressed; he would talk of his love, would demand in fierce anger – or meek supplication – why now she could not make him the happiest of men.

And when the pestilence had passed over and she returned to court, Du Bellay reported to his government: 'I believe the King to be so infatuated with her that God alone can abate his madness.'

* * *

Thomas Wolsey, knowing sickness of heart, feigned sickness of body. He knew his master; sentimental as a girl, and soft as wax in the fiery hands of Anne Boleyn.

Wolsey saw his decline now, as clearly as he had so often seen the sun set; for him though, there would be no rising again after the coming of night.

He did not complain; he was too wise for that. Well he knew that he had made his mistake, and where. He had humiliated her who had now the King's ear. And she was no soft, weak woman; she was strong and fierce, a good friend and a bad enemy. Oh! he thought, There is a night crow that possesses the royal ear and misrepresents all my actions.

He must not complain. He remembered the days of his own youth. He could look back to the humble life when he was tutor to the sons of Lord Marquess Dorset. Then there had been a certain knight, one Sir Amyas Pawlet, who had dared to humiliate young Wolsey; and had young Wolsey forgotten? He had not! Sir Amyas Pawlet grew to wish he had considered awhile before heaping indignities upon a humble tutor. So it was with Mistress Anne Boleyn and Thomas Wolsey. He could go to her; he could say: 'I would explain to you. It was not I who wished to hurt you. It was not I who would have prevented your marriage with Percy.

It was my lord King. I was but his servant in this matter.' It might well be that she, who was noted for her generous impulses, would forgive him; it might be that she would not continue to plan against him. It might be . . . but she was not his only enemy. Her uncle, Norfolk, was with her in this matter; the Duke of Suffolk, also; and that Percy of Northumberland who had loved her and still brooded on his loss. These powerful men had had enough of Wolsey's rule.

He was very weary; defeated by this divorce, feigning sickness that he might appeal to the sentiment of the King, that he might make him sorry for his old friend; hiding himself away until Campeggio whom the Pope was sending from Rome was due to arrive. This was Wolsey in decline.

Foolishly he had acted over this matter of Eleanor Carey. He was in disgrace with the King over that matter, and he had received such a rebuke as he had never had before, and one which told him clearly that the King was no longer his to command. The night crow and her band of vultures watched him, waiting for his death. Yet stupidly and proudly he had acted over the Eleanor Carey affair; she was the sister-in-law of Anne, and with characteristic generosity, when the woman had asked Anne to make her Abbess of Wilton – which place had fallen vacant – Anne had promised she should have her wish. And he, Wolsey, had arrogantly refused Eleanor Carey and given the place to another. Thus was Mistress Anne's anger once more raised against him; how bitterly had she complained of his action to the King! Wolsey had explained that Eleanor was unfit for the post, having had two illegitimate children by a priest. Knowing that, Henry, whose attitude towards others was rigorously moral, must see the point of this refusal. Gently and with many apologies for the humiliation she had suffered in the matter, the King explained this to Anne. 'I would not,' wrote Henry to his sweetheart, 'for all the gold in the world clog your conscience and mine to make her a ruler of a house . . .'

Anne, who was by nature honest, had no great respect for her lover's conscience; she was impatient, and showed it; she insisted that Wolsey's arrogance should not be allowed to pass. And Henry, fearing to lose her, ready to give her anything she wished, wrote sternly to Wolsey; and that letter showed Wolsey more clearly than anything that had gone before that he was slipping dangerously, and he knew no way of gaining a more steady foothold on the road of royal favour.

Now at last he understood that she who had the King's ear was indeed a rival to be feared. And he was caught between Rome and Henry; he had no plans; he could see only disaster coming out of this affair. So he feigned sickness to give himself time to prepare a plan, and sick at heart, he felt defeat closing in on him.

*　　*　　*

The legate had arrived from Rome, and old gouty Campeggio was ready to try the case of the King and Queen. Crowds collected in the streets; when Queen Katharine rode out, she was loudly cheered, and so likewise was her daughter Mary. Katharine, pale and wan from worry, Mary, pale from her illness, were martyrs in the eyes of the people of London; and the King begged Anne not to go abroad for fear the mob might do her some injury.

Anne was wretched, longing now to turn from this thorny road of ambition; not a moment's real peace had she known since she had started to tread it. The King was continually trying to force her surrender, and she was weary with the fight she must put up against him. And when Henry told her she must once more go back to Hever, as the trial was about to begin, she was filled with anger.

Henry said humbly: 'Sweetheart, your absence will be hard to bear, but my one thought is to win our case. With you here . . .'

Her lips curled scornfully, for did she not know that he would plead his lack of interest in a woman other than his wife? Did she not know that he would tell the Cardinals of his most scrupulous conscience?

She was wilful and cared not; she was foolish, she knew, for did she not want the divorce? She was hysterical with fear sometimes, wishing fervently that she was to marry someone who was more agreeable to her, seeing pitfalls yawning at the feet of a queen.

'An I go back,' she said unreasonably, 'I shall not return. I will not be sent back and forth like a shuttlecock!'

He pleaded with her. 'Darling, be reasonable! Dost not wish this business done with? Only when the divorce is complete can I make you my Queen.'

She went back to Hever, having grown suddenly sick of the palace, since from her window she saw the angry knots of people and heard their sullen murmurs. 'Nan Bullen! The King's whore . . . We want no Nan Bullen!'

Oh, it was shameful, shameful! 'Oh, Percy!' she cried. 'Why did you let them do this to us?' And she hated the Cardinal afresh, having convinced herself that it was he who, in his subtle, clever way, had turned the people against her. At Hever her father treated her with great respect — more respect than he had shown to Mary; Anne was not to be the King's mistress, but his wife, his Queen. Lord Rochford could not believe in all that good fortune; he would advise her, but scornfully she rejected his advice.

Two months passed, during which letters came from the King reproaching her for not writing to him, assuring her that she was his entirely beloved; and at length telling her it would now be safe for her to return to court.

The King entreated her; she repeated her refusals to all the King's entreaties.

Her father came to her. 'Your folly is beyond my understanding!' said Lord Rochford. 'The King asks that you will return to court! And you will not!'

'I have said I will not be rushed back and forth in this uncourtly way.'

'You talk like a fool, girl! Dost not realize what issues are at stake?'

'I am tired of it all. When I consented to marry the King, I thought 'twould be but a simple matter.'

'When you consented. . . !' Lord Rochford could scarcely believe his ears. She spoke as though she were conferring a favour on His Majesty. Lord Rochford was perturbed. What if the King should grow weary at this arrogance of his foolish daughter!

'I command you to go!' he roared; which made her laugh at him. Oh, how much simpler to manage had been his daughter Mary! He would have sent Anne to her room, would have said she was to be locked in there, but how could one behave so to the future Queen of England!

Lord Rochford knew a little of this daughter. Wilful and unpredictable, stubborn, reckless of punishment, she had been from babyhood; he knew she wavered even yet. Ere long she would be telling the King she no longer wished to marry him.

'I command you go!' he cried.

'You may command all you care to!' And at random she added: 'I shall not go until a very fine lodging is found for me.'

Lord Rochford told the King, and Henry, with that pertinacity of purpose which he ever displayed when he wanted something urgently, called in Wolsey; and Wolsey, seeking to reinstate himself, suggested Suffolk House in place of Durham House which the King had previously placed at her disposal.

'For, my lord King, my own York House is next to Suffolk House, and would it not be a matter of great convenience to you, if, while the lady is at Suffolk House, Your Highness lived at York House?'

'Thomas, it is a plan worthy of you!' The fat hand rested on the red-clad shoulder. The small eyes smiled into those of his Cardinal; the King was remembering that he had ever loved this man.

* * *

Anne came to Suffolk House. Its grandeur overawed even her, for it was the setting for a queen. There would be her ladies-in-waiting, her trainbearer, her chaplain; she would hold levees, and dispense patronage to church and state.

'It is as if I were a queen!' she told Henry who was there to greet her.

'You are a queen,' he answered passionately.

Now she understood. The fight was over. He who had waited so long had decided to wait no longer.

They would eat together informally at Suffolk House, he told her. Dear old Wolsey had lent him York House, next door, that he might be close and could visit her unceremoniously. Did she not think she had judged the poor old fellow too harshly?

There was about the King an air of excitement this day. She understood it, and he knew she understood it.

'Mayhap we judge him too hardly,' she agreed.

'Darling, I would have you know that you must lack nothing. Everything that you would have as my Queen – which I trust soon to make you – shall be yours.' He put burning hands on her shoulders. 'You have but to ask for what you desire, sweetheart.'

'That I know,' she said.

Alone in her room, she looked at herself in her mirror. Her heart was beating fast. 'And what have you to fear, Anne Boleyn?' she whispered to her reflection. 'Is it because after tonight there can be no turning back, that you tremble? Why should you fear? You are beautiful. There may be ladies at court with more perfect features, but there is none so intoxicatingly lovely, so ravishingly attractive as Anne Boleyn! What have you to fear from this? Nothing! What have you to gain? You have made up your mind that you will be Queen of England. There is nothing to fear.'

Her eyes burned in her pale face; her beautiful lips were firm. She put on a gown of black velvet, and her flesh glowed as lustrous as the pearls that decorated it.

She went out to him, and he received her with breathless wonder. She was animated now, warmed by his admiration, his passionate devotion.

He led her to a table where they were waited upon discreetly; and this *tête à tête* meal, which he had planned with much thought, was to him complete happiness. Gone was her wilfulness now; she was softer; he was sure of her surrender; he had waited so long, he had lived through this so often in his dreams; but nothing he had imagined, he was sure, could be as wonderful as the reality.

He tried to explain his feelings for her, tried to tell her of how she had changed him, how he longed for her, how she was different from any other woman, how thoughts of her coloured his life; how, until she came, he had never known love. Nor had he, and Henry in love was an attractive person; humility was an ill-fitting garment that sat oddly on those great shoulders, but not less charming because it did not fit. He was tender instead of coarse, modest instead of arrogant; and she warmed towards him. She drank more freely than was her custom: she had confidence in herself and the future.

Henry said, when they rose from the table: 'Tonight I think I am to be the happiest man on Earth!' Apprehensively he waited for her answer, but she gave no answer, and when he would have spoken again he found his voice was lost to him; he had no voice, he had no pride; he had nothing but his great need of her.

She lay naked in her bed, and seeing her thus he was speechless, nerveless, fearful of his own emotion; until his passion rushed forth and he kissed her white body in something approaching a frenzy.

She thought: I have nothing to fear. If he was eager before, he will be doubly eager now. And, as she lay crushed by his great weight, feeling his joy, his ecstasy, she laughed inwardly and gladly, because now she knew there was to be no more wavering and she, being herself, would pursue this thing to the end.

His words were incoherent, but they were of love, of great love and desire and passion and pleasure.

'There was never one such as thee, my Anne! Never, never I swear . . . Anne . . . Queen Anne . . . My Queen. . . .'

He lay beside her, this great man, his face serene and completely happy, so she knew how he must have looked when a very small boy; his face was purged of all that coarseness against which her fastidiousness had turned in disgust; and she felt she must begin to love him, that she almost did love him, so that on impulse she leaned over to him and kissed him. He seized her then, laughing, and told her again that she was beautiful, that she excelled his thoughts of her.

'And many times have I taken you, my Queen, in my thoughts. Dost remember the garden at Hever? Dost remember thy haughtiness? Why, Anne! Why I did not take thee there and then I do not know. Never have I wanted any as I wanted thee, Anne, my Queen, my little white Queen!'

She could laugh, thinking – Soon he will be free, and I shall be truly Queen . . . and after this he will never be able to do without me.

'Aye, and I wonder I was so soft with you, my entirely beloved, save that I loved you, save that I could not hurt you. Now you love me truly . . . not as your King, you said, but as a man. . . . You love me as I love you, and you find pleasure in this, as I do. . . .'

And so he would work himself to a fresh frenzy of passion; so he would stroke and caress her, lips on her body, his hands at her hair and her throat and her breasts.

'There was never love like this!' said Henry of England to Anne Boleyn.

HAPPIEST OF WOMEN

AT HORSHAM there was preparation for the Christmas festivities; excitement was high in the ladies' dormitory. There should be a special Yuletide feast, they said, a good deal more exciting than that one which would be held in the great hall to be enjoyed by all; the ladies were busy getting together gifts for their lovers, speculating as to what they would receive.

'Poor little Catherine Howard!' they said, laughing. 'She has no lover!'

'What of the gallant Thomas? Alas, Catherine! He soon forgot thee.'

Catherine thought guiltily that, though she would never forget him, she had thought of him less during the last months; she wondered if he ever thought of her; if he did, he evidently did not think it necessary to let her know.

'It is unwise,' said Isabel, 'to think of those who think not of us.'

In the Duchess's rooms, where Catherine often sat with her grandmother, the old lady fretted about the monotony of life in the country.

'I would we were at Lambeth. Fine doings I hear there are at court.'

'Yes,' answered Catherine, rubbing her grandmother's back. 'My cousin is a most important lady now.'

'That I swear she is! Ah! I wonder what Lord Henry Algernon Percy . . . I beg his pardon, the Earl of Northumberland . . . has to say now! He was too high and mighty to marry her, was he? "Very well," says Anne, "I'll take the King instead." Ha! Ha! And I declare nothing delights me more than to hear the haughty young man is being made wretched by his wife; for so does anyone deserve who thinks himself too fine for my granddaughter.'

'The granddaughter of your husband,' Catherine reminded her once more; and was cuffed for her words.

'How I should like to see her at Suffolk House! I hear that she holds daily levees, as though she is already Queen. She dispenses charity, which is the Queen's task. There are those who storm against her, for, Catherine, my child, there will always be the jealous ones. Ah! How I should love to see my granddaughter reigning at Greenwich! I hear the Queen was most discomfited, and that last Christmas Anne held her revels apart from those of Katharine – which either shocked or delighted all. Imagine *her* revels! Imagine poor Katharine's! Herself, my granddaughter, the centre of attraction, with George and Wyatt and Surrey and Bryan with her; and who could stand up against them, eh? And the King so far gone in love, dear man, that everything she asks must be hers. Ah! How I should love to be there to see it! And Wolsey, that old schemer, trembling in his shoes, I dare swear. And so he should . . . trying to keep our sovereign lord from marrying her who should be his Queen – for if ever woman was born to be a queen, that woman was my granddaughter Anne! '

'I should love to see her too,' said Catherine wistfully. 'Grandmother, when will you go to court?'

'Very soon. I make my plans now. Why, I have only to let her know my desires, and she would send for me. She was ever my favourite granddaughter, and it has always seemed to me that I was a favourite of hers. Bless her! God bless Queen Anne Boleyn!'

'God bless her!' said Catherine.

Her grandmother regarded the girl through narrowed eyes.

'I declare I never saw one so lacking in dignity. I would hear you play to me awhile, Catherine. Music is the only thing for which you seem to have the least aptitude. Go over and play me a tune.'

Catherine eagerly went to the virginals; she hated the ministrations to her grandmother, and regretted that they must be an accompaniment to her racy conversation which she always enjoyed.

The Duchess, her foot tapping, was only half listening, for her thoughts were far away, at Greenwich, at Eltham, at Windsor, at Suffolk House, at York House. She saw her beautiful granddaughter, queening it in all these places; she saw the King, humble in his love; the colour, the music, the gorgeous clothes, the masques; the terror of that man Wolsey whom she had ever hated; and Anne, the loveliest woman in the kingdom, queen of the court.

To be there! To be favoured of her who was most favoured of the King! 'My granddaughter, the Queen.' To see her now and then, lovely, vital; to think of her, loved passionately by the King; mayhap to be on the best of terms oneself with His Majesty, for he would be kind to those beloved of his beloved; and Anne had always had a regard for her scandal-loving, lazy old grandmother – even if she were only the wife of her grandfather!

'I shall go to Lambeth!' said the Duchess. And little Catherine there should have a place at court, she thought. . . . Attendant to her cousin, the Queen? Why not? As soon as this wearisome divorce was done with, she would go to Lambeth. And surely it would not be long now; it had been dragging on for more than two years; and now that the King's eyes were being opened to that Wolsey's wickedness, surely it could not be long.

Yes, little Catherine should have a place at court. But how very unfitted she was for that high honour! Anne, my child, you were at the French court at her age, a little lady delighting all who beheld you, I swear, with your grace and your charm and your delicious clothes and the way you wore them. Ah, Catherine Howard! You will never be an Anne Boleyn; one could not hope for that. Look at the child! Sitting humped over the virginals.

And yet she was not unattractive; she already had the air of a woman; her little body had that budding look which meant that Catherine might well flower early. But she had about her a neglected look, and it was that which made the Duchess angry. What right had Catherine Howard to look neglected! She lived in the great establishment of the Duchess; she was in the charge of the Duchess's ladies. Something should be done about the child, thought the Duchess, and knowing herself to blame – had she not often taken herself to task about the girl's education, promised herself that it should be attended to and then forgotten all about it? – she felt suddenly angry with Catherine, and rising from her chair, went over and slapped the girl at the side of her head.

Catherine stopped playing and looked up in surprise; she was not greatly disturbed by the blow, as the Duchess often cuffed her and there was no great strength in her flabby muscles.

'Disgraceful!' stormed the old lady.

Catherine did not understand. Playing musical instruments was one of the few things she did really well; she did not know that the Duchess, her thoughts far away at Suffolk House where another granddaughter was a queen in all but name, had not heard what she played; she thought that her playing was at fault, for how should she realize that the Duchess was comparing her with Anne and wondering how this child could possibly go to court uneducated as she was.

'Catherine Howard,' said the Duchess, trying to convince herself that she was in no way to blame for the years of neglect, 'you are a disgrace to this house! What do you think Queen Anne would say if I asked for a place at court for you – which she of course would find, since I asked it – and then I presented you to her . . . her cousin? Look at your hair! You are bursting forth from your clothes, and your manners are a disgrace! I declare I will give you such a beating as you never had, you untidy, ignorant little chit! And worse, it seems to me that were you less lazy, you might be quite a pretty girl. Now we shall begin your education in earnest; we are done with this dreaming away of the days. You will work, Catherine Howard, and if you do not, you shall answer to me. Did you hear that?'

'I did hear, Grandmother.'

The Duchess rang a bell, and a serving maid appeared.

'Go bring to me at once young Henry Manox.'

The maid complied, and in a very short time a young man with hair growing low upon his brow but a certain handsome swagger in his walk and an elegance about his person, combined with a pair of very bold black eyes to make him an attractive creature, appeared and bowed low before the Duchess.

'Manox, here is my granddaughter. I fear she needs much tuition. Now I would you sat down at the virginals and played awhile.'

He flashed a smile at Catherine which seemed to suggest that they were going to be friends. Catherine, ever ready to respond to friendship, returned the smile, and he sat down and played most excellently, so that Catherine, loving music as she did, was delighted and clapped her hands when he ended.

'There. child!' said the Duchess. 'That is how I would have you play. Manox, you shall teach my granddaughter. You may give her a lesson now.'

Manox stood up and bowed. He came to Catherine, bowed again, took her hand and led her to the virginals.

The Duchess watched them; she liked to watch young people; there was something, she decided, so delightful about them; their movements were graceful. Particularly she liked young men, having always had a fondness for them from the cradle. She remembered her own youth; there had been a delightful music master. Nothing wrong about that of course; she had been aware of her dignity at a very early age. Still it had been pleasant to be taught by one who had charm; and he had grown quite fond of her, although always she had kept him at a distance.

There they sat, those two children – for after all he was little more than a child compared with her old age – and they seemed more attractive than they had separately. If Catherine were not so young, thought the Duchess, I should have to watch Manox; I believe he has quite a naughty reputation and is fond of adventuring with the young ladies.

Watching her granddaughter take a lesson, the Duchess thought – From now on I shall superintend the child's education myself. After all, to be cousin to the Queen means a good deal. When her opportunity comes, she must be ready to take it.

Then, feeling virtuous, grandmotherly devotion rising within her, she told herself that even though Catherine was such a child, she would not allow her to be alone with one of Manox's reputation; the lessons should always take place in this room and she herself would be there.

For the thousandth time the Duchess assured herself that it was fortunate indeed that little Catherine Howard should have come under her care; after all, the cousin of a Queen needs to be very tenderly nurtured, for who can say what honours may await her?

* * *

Anne was being dressed for the banquet. Her ladies fluttered about her, flattering her. Was she happy? she asked herself, as her thoughts went back over the past year which had seen her rise to the height of glory, and which yet had been full of misgivings and apprehensions, even fears.

She had changed; none knew this better than herself; she had grown hard, calculating; she was not the same girl who had loved Percy so deeply and defiantly; she was less ready with sympathy, finding hatreds springing up in her, and with them a new, surprising quality which had not been there before – vindictiveness.

She laughed when she saw Percy. He was changed from that rather delicate, beautiful young man whom she had loved; he was still delicate, suffering from some undefined disease; and such unhappiness was apparent in his face that should have made her weep for him. But she did not weep; instead she was filled with bitter laughter, thinking: You fool! You brought this on yourself. You spoiled your life – and mine with it – and now you must suffer for your folly, and I shall benefit from it!

But did she benefit? She was beginning to understand her royal lover well; she could command him; her beauty and her wit, being unsurpassed in his court, must make him their slave. But how long does a man, who is more polygamous than most, remain faithful? That was a question that would perplex her now and then. Already there was a change in his attitude towards her. Oh, he was deeply in love, eager to please, anxious that every little wish she expressed should be granted. But who was it now who must curse the delay,

Anne or Henry? Henry desired the divorce; he wanted very much to remove Katharine from the throne and put Anne on it, but he was less eager than Anne. Anne was his mistress; he could wait to make her his wife. It was Anne who must rail against delay, who must fret, who must deplore her lost virtue, who must ask herself, Will the Pope ever agree to the divorce?

Sometimes her thoughts would make her frantic. She had yielded in spite of her protestations that she would never yield. She had yielded on the King's promise to make her Queen; her sister Mary had exacted no promise. Where was the difference between Anne and Mary, since Mary had yielded for lust, and Anne for a crown! Anne had a picture of herself returning home to Hever defeated, or perhaps married to one as ineffectual as the late William Carey.

Henry had given Thomas Wyatt the post of High Marshal of Calais, which would take him out of England a good deal. Anne liked to dwell on that facet of Henry's character; he loved some of his friends, and Wyatt was one of them. He did not commit Wyatt to the Tower – which would have been easy enough – but sent him away . . . Oh, yes, Henry could feel sentimental where one he had really loved was concerned, and Henry did love Thomas. Who could help loving Thomas? asked Anne, and wept a little.

Anne tried now to think clearly and honestly of that last year. Had it been a good year? It had . . . of course it had! How could she say that she had not enjoyed it . . . she had enjoyed it vastly! Proud, haughty, as she was, how pleasant it must be to have such deference shown to her. Aware of her beauty, how could she help but wish to adorn it! Such as Queen Katharine might call that vanity; is pride in a most unusual possession, then, vanity? Must she not enjoy the revels when she herself was acclaimed the shining light, the star, the most beautiful, the most accomplished of women, greatly loved by the King?

She had her enemies, the Cardinal the chief among them. Her Uncle Norfolk was outwardly her friend, but she could never like and trust him, and she believed him now to be annoyed because the King had not chosen to favour his daughter, the Lady Mary Howard, who was of so much nobler birth than Anne Boleyn. Suffolk! There was another enemy, and Suffolk was a dangerous, cruel man. Her thoughts went back to windy days and nights in Dover Castle, when Mary Tudor talked of the magnificence of a certain Charles Brandon. And this was he, this florid, cruel-eyed, relentless and ambitious man! An astute man, he had married the King's sister and placed himself very near the throne, and because a strange fate had placed Anne even nearer, he had become her enemy. These thoughts were frightening.

How happy she had been, dancing with the King at Greenwich last Christmas, laughing in the faces of those who would criticize her for holding her revels at Greenwich in defiance of the Queen; hating the Queen, who so obstinately refused to go into a nunnery and to admit she had consummated her marriage with Arthur! She had danced wildly, had made brilliantly witty remarks about the Queen and the Princess, had flaunted her supremacy over them – and afterwards hated herself for this, though admitting the hatred to none but the bright-eyed reflection which looked back at her so reproachfully from the mirror.

The Princess hated her and took no pains to hide the fact; and had not hesitated to whisper to those who had been ready to carry such talk to the ears of Anne, of what she would do to Anne Boleyn, were she Queen.

'I would commit her to the Tower, where I would torture her; we should see if she would be so beautiful after the tormentors had done with her! I should turn the rack myself. We should see if she could make such witty remarks to the rats who came to The Pit to gnaw her bones and bite her to death. But I would not leave her to die that way; I would burn her alive. She is all but a witch, and I hear that she has those about her who are of the new faith. Aye! I would pile the faggots at her feet and watch her burn, and before she had burnt, I would remove her that she might burn and burn again, tasting on Earth that which she will assuredly meet in hell.'

The eyes of the Princess, already burning with fanatical

fervour, rested on Anne with loathing, and Anne laughed in the face of the foolish girl and feigned indifference to her, but those eyes haunted her when she was awake and when she slept. But even as she professed scorn and hatred for the girl, Anne well understood what her coming must have meant to Mary, who had enjoyed the privileges of being her father's daughter, Princess Mary and heiress of England. Now the King sought to make her but a bastard, of less importance than the Duke of Richmond who was at least a boy.

As she lay in the King's arms, Anne would talk of the Princess.

'I will not be treated thus by her! I swear it. There is not room for both of us at court.'

Henry soothed her while he put up a fight for Mary. His sentimental streak was evident when he thought of his daughter; he was not without affection for her and, while longing for a son, he had become – before the prospect of displacing Katharine had come to him, and Anne declared she would never be his mistress – reconciled to her.

Anne said: 'I shall go back to Hever. I will not stay to be insulted thus.'

'I shall not allow you to go to Hever, sweetheart. Your place is here with me.'

'Nevertheless,' said Anne coldly, 'to Hever I shall go!'

The fear that she would leave him was a constant threat to Henry, and he could not bear that she should be out of his sight; she could command him by threatening to leave him.

When Mary fell into disgrace with her father, there were those who, sorry for the young girl, accused Anne of acute vindictiveness. It was the same with Wolsey. It was true that she did not forget the slights she had received from him, and that she pursued him relentlessly, determined that he should fall from that high place on which he had lodged himself. Perhaps it was forgotten by those who accused her that Anne was fighting a desperate battle. Behind all the riches and power, all the admiration and kingly affection which was showered upon her, Anne was aware of that low murmur of the people, of the malicious schemes of her enemies who even now were seeking to ruin her. Prominent among these enemies were Wolsey and Princess Mary. What therefore could Anne do but fight these people, and if she at this time held the most effective weapons, she merely used them as both Wolsey and Mary would have done, had they the luck to hold them.

But her triumphs were bitter to her. She loved admiration; she loved approval, and she wanted no enemies. Wolsey and she, though they flattered each other and feigned friendship, knew that both could not hold the high positions they aspired to; one must go. Anne fought as tenaciously as Wolsey had ever fought, and because Wolsey's star was setting and Anne's was rising, she was winning. There were many little pointers to indicate this strife between them, and perhaps one of the most significant – Anne was thinking – was the confiscation of a book of hers which had found its way into the possession of her equerry, young George Zouch. Anne, it was beginning to be known – and this knowledge could not please the Cardinal – was interested in the new religion which was becoming a matter of some importance on the Continent, and one of the reformers had presented her with Tindal's translation of the holy scriptures.

Anne had read it, discussed it with her brother and some of her friends, found it of great interest and passed it on to one of the favourite ladies of her retinue, for Mistress Gaynsford was an intelligent girl, and Anne thought the book might be of interest to her. However, Mistress Gaynsford was loved by George Zouch who, one day when he had come upon her quietly reading, to tease her snatched the book and refused to return it; instead he took it with him to the King's chapel, where, during the service, he opened the book and becoming absorbed in its contents attracted the attention of the dean who, demanding to see it and finding it to be a prohibited one, lost no time in conveying it to Cardinal Wolsey. Mistress Gaynsford was terrified at the course of events, and went trembling to Anne, who, ever ready to complain against the Cardinal, told the King that he had confiscated her book and demanded its immediate return. The book was brought back to Anne at once.

'What book is this that causes so much pother?' Henry wanted to know.

'You must read it,' Anne answered and added: 'I insist!'

Henry promised and did; the Cardinal was disconcerted to learn that His Majesty was as interested as young George Zouch had been. This was a deeply significant defeat for Wolsey.

This year, reflected Anne as the coif was fixed upon her hair and her reflection looked back at her, had been a sorry one for the Cardinal. The trial had gone wrong. Shall we ever get this divorce, wondered Anne. The Pope was adamant; the people murmured: 'Nan Bullen shall not be our Queen!'

Henry would say little of what had happened at Blackfriars Hall, but Anne knew something of that fiasco; of Katharine's coming into the court and kneeling at the feet of the King, asking for justice. Anne could picture it – the solemn state, the May sunshine filtering through the windows, the King impatient with the whole proceedings, grey-faced Wolsey praying that the King might turn from the folly of his desire to marry Anne Boleyn, gouty old Campeggio procrastinating, having no intention of giving a verdict. The King had made a long speech about his scrupulous conscience and how – Anne's lips curled with scorn – he did not ask for the divorce out of his carnal desires, how the Queen pleased him as much as any woman, but his conscience . . . his conscience . . . his most scrupulous conscience . . .

And the trial had dragged on through the summer months, until Henry, urged on by herself, demanded a decision. Then had Campeggio been forced to make a statement, then had he been forced to show his intention – which was, of course, not to grant the divorce at all. He must, he had said – to Henry's extreme wrath – consult with his master, the Pope. Then had Suffolk decided to declare open war on the Cardinal, for he had stood up and shouted: 'It was never merry in England whilst we had cardinals among us!' And the King strode forth from the court in an access of rage, cursing the Pope, cursing the delay, cursing Campeggio and with him Wolsey, whom he was almost ready to regard as Campeggio's confederate. Anne's thoughts went to two men who, though obscure before, had this year leaped into prominence – the two Thomases, Cromwell and Cranmer. Anne thought warmly of them both, for from these two did she and Henry hope for much. Cranmer had distinguished himself because of his novel views, particularly on this subject of the divorce. He was tactful and discreet, clever and intellectual. As don, tutor, priest and Cambridge man, he was interested in Lutherism. He had suggested that Henry should appeal to the English ecclesiastical courts instead of to Rome on this matter of the divorce; he voiced this opinion constantly, until it had been brought to Henry's notice.

Henry, eager to escape from the meshes of Rome, was ready to welcome anyone who could wield a knife to cut him free. He liked what he heard of Cranmer. 'By God!' he cried. 'That man hath the right sow by the ear!'

Cranmer was sent for. Henry was crafty, clever enough when he gave his mind to a matter; and never had he given as much thought to anything as he had to this matter of the divorce. Wolsey, he knew, was attached to Rome, for Rome had its sticky threads about the Cardinal as a spider has about the fly in its web. The King was crying out for new men to take the place of Wolsey. There could never be another Wolsey; of that he was sure; but might there not be many who together could carry the great burdens which Wolsey had carried alone? When Cranmer had talked with Henry a few times, Henry saw great possibilities in the man. He was obedient, he was docile, he was loyal; he was going to be of inestimable value to a Henry who had lost his Wolsey to the Roman web.

Anne's thoughts went to that other Thomas – Cromwell. Cromwell was of the people, just as Wolsey had been, but with a difference. Cromwell bore the marks of his origins and could not escape from them; Wolsey, the intellectual, had escaped, though there were those who said that he showed the marks of his upbringing in his great love of splendour, in his vulgar displays of wealth. (But, thought Anne, laughing to herself, had not the King even greater delight in flamboyant display!) Cromwell, however – thickset, impervious to insult, with his fish-like eyes and his ugly hands – could not hide his origins and made but little attempt to do so. He was serving Wolsey well, deploring the lack of fight he was showing. Cromwell was not over-nice; Henry knew this and, while seeing in him enormous possibilities, had never taken to him. 'I love not that man!' said Henry to Anne. 'By God! He has a touch of the sewer about him. He sickens me! He is a knave!'

There was a peculiar side to Henry's nature which grew out of an almost childish love and admiration for certain people, which made him seek to defend them even while he planned their destruction. He had had that affection for Wolsey, Wolsey the wit, in his gorgeous homes, in his fine clothes; he had liked Wolsey as a man. This man Cromwell he could never like, useful as he was; more useful as he promised to be. Cromwell was blind to humiliation; he worked hard and took insults; he was clever; he helped Wolsey, advised him to favour Anne's friends, placated Norfolk, and so secured a seat in parliament. Would there always be those to spring up and replace others when the King needed them? What if she herself lost the King's favour! It was simpler to replace a mistress than a Wolsey ...

Pretty Anne Saville, Anne's favourite attendant, whispered that she was preoccupied tonight. Anne answered that indeed she was, and had been thinking back over the past year.

Anne Saville patted Anne's beautiful hair lovingly.

'It has been a great and glorious year for your ladyship.'

'Has it?' said Anne, her face so serious that the other Anne looked at her in sudden alarm.

'Assuredly,' said the girl. 'Many honours have come your ladyship's way, and the King grows more in love with you with the passing of each day.'

Anne took her namesake's hand and pressed it for awhile, for she was very fond of this girl.

'And you grow more beautiful with each day,' said Anne Saville earnestly. 'There is no lady in the court who would not give ten years of her life to change places with you.'

In the mirror the coif glittered like a golden crown. Anne trembled a little; in the great hall she would be gayer than any, but up here away from the throng she often trembled, contemplating the night before her, and afraid to think further than that.

Anne was ready; she would go down. She would take one last look at herself – The Lady Anne Rochford now, for recently her father had been made Earl of Wiltshire, George became Lord Rochford, and she herself was no longer plain Anne Boleyn. The Boleyns had come far, she thought, and was reminded of George, laughing-eyed and only sad when one caught him in repose.

When she thought of George she would feel recklessness stealing over her, and the determination to live dangerously rather than live without adventure.

Thoughts of George were pleasant. She realized with a pang that of all her friends who now, with the King at their head, swore they would die for her, there was only one she could really trust. There was her father, her Uncle Norfolk, the man who would be her husband . . . but on those occasions when Fear came and stood menacingly before her, it was of her brother she must think. 'There is really none but George!'

'Thank God for George!' she said to herself, and dismissed gloomy thoughts.

In the great hall the King was waiting to greet her. He was magnificent in his favourite russet, padded and sparkling, larger than any man there, ruddy from the day's hunting, flushed already and flushing more as his eyes rested on Anne.

He said: 'It seems long since I kissed you!'

' 'Tis several hours, I'll swear!' she answered.

'There is none like you, Anne.'

He would show his great love for her tonight, for of late she had complained bitterly of the lack of courtesy shown her by the Queen and Princess.

He had said: 'By God! I'll put an end to their obstinacy. They shall bow the knee to you, sweetheart, or learn our displeasure!' The Princess should be separated from her mother, and they should both be banished from court; he had said last night that he was weary of them both; weary of the pious obstinacy of the Queen, who stuck to her lies and refused to make matters easy by going into a nunnery; weary of the rebellious daughter who refused to behave herself and think herself fortunate – she, who was no more than a bastard, though a royal one – in receiving her father's affection. 'I tell thee, Anne,' he had said, his lips on her hair, 'I am weary of these women.'

She had answered: 'Need I say I am too?' And she had thought, They would see me burn in hell; nor do I blame them for that, for what good have I done them! But what I cannot endure is their attitude of righteousness. They burn with desire for revenge, and they pray that justice shall be dealt me; they pray to God to put me in torment. Hearty sinful vengeance I can forgive; but when it is hidden under a cloak of piety and called justice . . . never! Never! And so will I fight against these two, and will not do a thing to make their lot easier. I am a sinner; and so are they; nor do sins become whiter when cloaked in piety.

But this she did not tell her lover, for was he not inclined to use that very cloak of piety to cover his sins? When he confessed what he had done this night, last night, would he not say: 'It is for England; I must have a son!' Little eyes, greedy with lust; hot straying hands; the urgent desire to possess her again and again. And this, not that she might give the King pleasure, but that she should give England a son!

Was it surprising that sometimes in the early hours of the morning, when he lay beside her breathing heavily in sleep, his hand laid lightly on her body, smiling as he slept the smile of remembrance, murmuring her name in his sleep – was it surprising that then she would think of her brother's handsome face, and murmur to herself: 'Oh, George, take me home! Take me to Blickling, not to Hever, for at Hever I should see the rose garden and think of him. But take me to Blickling where we were together when we were very young . . . and where I never dreamed of being Queen of England.'

But she could not go back now. She must go on and on. I want to go on! I want to go on! What is love? It is ethereal, so that you cannot hold it; it is transient, so that you cannot keep it. But a queen is always a queen. Her sons are kings. I want to be a queen; of course I want to be a queen! It is only in moments of deepest depression that I am afraid.

Nor was she afraid this night as he, regardless of all these watching ladies and gentlemen, pressed his great body close to hers and showed that he was impatient for the night.

Tonight he wished to show her how greatly he loved her; that he wished all these people to pay homage to this beautiful girl who had pleased him, who continued to please him, and whom, because of an evil Fate in the shape of a weak Pope, an obstinate Queen, and a pair of scheming Cardinals, he could not yet make his Queen.

He would have her take precedence over the two most noble ladies present, the Duchess of Norfolk and his own sister of Suffolk.

These ladies resented this, Anne knew, and suddenly a mood of recklessness came over her. What did she care! What mattered it, indeed. She had the King's love and none of her enemies dared oppose her openly.

The King's sister? She was ageing now; different indeed from the giddy girl who had led poor Louis such a dance, who had alternated between her desire to bear a king of France and marry Brandon; there was nothing left to her but ambition; and ambition for what? Her daughter Frances Brandon? Mary of Suffolk wanted her daughter on the throne. And now here was Anne Boleyn, young and full of life, only waiting for the divorce to bear the King many sons and so set a greater distance between Frances Brandon and the throne of England.

And the Duchess of Norfolk? She was jealous, as was her husband, on account of the King's having chosen Anne instead of their daughter the Lady Mary Howard. She was angry because of Anne's friendship with the old Dowager Duchess of Norfolk.

What do I care? What have I to fear!

Nothing! For the King was looking at her with deep longing; nor could he bear that she should not be with him. She only had to threaten to leave him, and she could have both of these arrogant ladies banished from court.

So she was bold and defiant, and flaunted her supremacy in the faces of all those who resented her. Lady Anne Rochford, beloved of the King, leader of the revels, now taking precedence over the highest in the land as though she were already Queen.

She had seen the Countess Chateau-briant and the Duchess D'Estampes treated as princesses by poor little Claude at the court of Francis. So should she be treated by these haughty Duchesses of Norfolk and Suffolk; yes, and by Katharine of Aragon and her daughter Mary!

But of course there was a great difference between the French ladies and the Lady Anne Rochford. They were merely the mistresses of the King of France; the Lady Anne Rochford was to be Queen of England!

*　　*　　*

In her chair the Dowager Duchess of Norfolk dozed; her foot tapped automatically, but she was not watching the pair at the virginals. She was thinking of the court and the King's passion for that gorgeous lady, her dear granddaughter. Ah! And scheming Thomas now has his Earldom and all that goes with it; and well pleased he is, I'll swear, for money means more to Thomas than aught else. And she is the Lady Anne Rochford, if you please, and George on very pleasant terms with the King . . . though not with his own sly little wife! Poor George! A pity there can't be a divorce. Why not a princess wife for your brother, eh, Queen Anne? Eh? Of course you are Queen! But she'll look after George . . . those two would stick together no matter what befell. Ah, how I wish she would send for me! I trow she would if she knew how eager I am to be gone . . . What if I sent a messenger . . . Ah! The court, the masques . . .

though indeed I am a little old for such pleasures. Charming, if she came to visit me at Lambeth ... We would sit in the gardens, and I would make her talk to me of the King ... My granddaughter, the Queen of England! My granddaughter ... Queen Anne ...

She was asleep, and Henry Manox, sensing this, threw a sly glance over his shoulder at her.

'There!' said Catherine. 'Was that better?'

He said, moving nearer to Catherine: 'That was perfect!'

She flushed with pleasure, and he noticed the delicate skin and the long, fair lashes, and the charming strand of auburn hair that fell across her brow. Her youth was very appealing; he had never made love to one so young before; and yet, in spite of her youth, already she showed signs of an early ripening.

'Never,' he whispered, 'have I enjoyed teaching anyone as I have enjoyed our lessons!'

The Duchess snored softly.

Catherine laughed, and he joined in the laugh; he leaned forward suddenly and kissed the tip of her nose. Catherine felt a pleasurable thrill; it was exciting because it had to be done while the Duchess slept; and he was handsome, she thought, with his dark, bold eyes; and it was flattering to be admired by one so much older than herself; it was gratifying to be treated as though one were charming, after the reproaches her grandmother had showered upon her.

'I am glad I am a good pupil.'

'You are a very good pupil!' he said. 'Right glad I am that it is my happy lot to teach you.'

'Her Grace, my grandmother, thinks me very stupid.'

'Then it is Her Grace, your grandmother, who is stupid!'

Catherine hunched her shoulders, laughing.

'I take it, sir, that you do not then think me stupid.'

'Indeed not; but young, very young, and there is much you have to learn yet.'

The Duchess awoke with a start, and Catherine began to play.

'That was better,' said the Duchess, 'was it not, Manox?'

'Indeed, Your Grace, it was!'

'And you think your pupil is improving?'

'Vastly, Madam!'

'So thought I. Now you may go, Catherine. Manox, you may stay awhile and talk with me.'

Catherine went, and he stayed and talked awhile; they talked of music, for they had nothing in common but music. But the Duchess did not mind of what her young men talked as long as they talked and entertained her. It was their youth she liked; it was their flattery. And as Manox talked to her, she drifted back to the days of her own youth, and then forward again to the court as it was today, ruled by her loveliest of granddaughters.

'Methinks I shall go to Lambeth,' she announced, and dismissed Manox.

Catherine went to the apartment, where she found Isabel.

'How went the lesson?' asked Isabel.

'Very well.'

'How you love your music!' said Isabel. 'You look as if you had just left a lover, not a lesson.'

Their talk was continually of lovers; Catherine did not notice this, as it seemed natural enough to her. To have lovers was not only natural but the most exciting possibility; it was all part of the glorious business of growing up, and now Catherine longed to be grown-up.

She still thought of Thomas Culpepper, but she could only with difficulty remember what he looked like. She still dreamed that he rode out to Horsham and told her they were to elope together, but his face, which for so long had been blurred in her mind, now began to take on the shape of Henry Manox. She looked forward to her lessons; the most exciting moment of her days was when she went down to the Duchess's room and found him there; she was always terrified that he would not be there, that her grandmother had decided to find her a new teacher; she looked forward with gleeful anticipation to those spasmodic snores of the Duchess which set both her and Manox giggling, and made his eyes become more bold.

As he sat very close to her, his long musician's fingers would come to rest on her knee, tapping lightly that she might keep in time. The Duchess nodded; her head shook; then she would awake startled and look round her defiantly, as though to deny the obvious fact that she had dozed.

There was one day, some weeks after the first lesson, which was a perfect day, with spring in the sunshine filtering through the window, in the songs of the birds in the trees outside it, in Catherine's heart and in Manox's eyes.

He whispered: 'Catherine! I think of you constantly.'

'Have I improved so much then?'

'Not of your music, but of you, Catherine . . . of you.'

'I wonder why you should think constantly of me.'

'Because you are very sweet.'

'Am I?' said Catherine.

'And not such a child as you would seem!'

'No,' said Catherine. 'Sometimes I think I am very grown-up.'

He laid his delicate hands on the faint outline of her breasts.

'Yes, Catherine, I think so too. It is very sweet to be grown-up, Catherine. When you are a woman you will wonder how you could ever have borne your childhood.'

'Yes,' said Catherine, 'I believe that. I have had some unhappy times in my childhood; my mother died, and then I went to Hollingbourne, and just when I was beginning to love my life there, that was over.'

'Do not look so sad, sweet Catherine! Tell me, you are not sad, are you?'

'Not now,' she said.

He kissed her cheek.

He said: 'I would like to kiss your lips.'

He did this, and she was astonished by the kiss, which was different from those Thomas had given her. Catherine was stirred; she kissed him.

'I have never been so happy!' he said.

They were both too absorbed in each other to listen for the Duchess's snores and heavy breathing; she awoke suddenly, and hearing no music, looked towards them.

'Chatter, chatter, chatter!' she said. 'I declare! Is this a music lesson!'

Catherine began to play, stumbling badly.

The Duchess yawned; her foot began to tap; in five minutes she was asleep again.

'Do you think she saw us kiss?' whispered Catherine.

'Indeed I do not!' said Manox, and he meant that, for he well knew that if she had he would have been immediately turned out, possibly dismissed from the house; and Mistress Catherine would have received a sound beating.

Catherine shivered ecstatically.

'I am terrified that she might, and will stop the lessons.'

'You would care greatly about that?'

Catherine turned candid eyes upon him. 'I should care very much!' she said. She was vulnerable because her mind was that of a child, though her body was becoming that of a woman; and the one being so advanced, the other somewhat backward, it was her body which was in command of Catherine. She liked the proximity of this man; she liked his kisses. She told him so in many ways; and he, being without scruples, found the situation too novel and too exciting not to be exploited.

He was rash in his excitement, taking her in his arms before the sleeping Duchess and kissing her lips. Catherine lifted her face eagerly, as a flower will turn towards the sun.

The Duchess was sleeping, when there was a faint tap on the door and Isabel entered. The lesson had extended beyond its appointed time, and she, eager to see the teacher and pupil together, had an excuse ready for intruding. Isabel stood on the threshold, taking in the scene – the sleeping Duchess, the young man, his face very pale, his eyes very bright; Catherine, hair in some disorder, her eyes wide, her lips parted, and with a red mark on her chin. Where he has kissed her, the knave! thought Isabel.

The Duchess awoke with a start.

'Come in! Come in!' she called, seeing Isabel at the door.

Isabel approached and spoke to the Duchess. Catherine rose, and so did Manox.

'You may go, Catherine,' said the Duchess. 'Manox! Stay awhile. I would speak to you.'

Catherine went, eager to be alone, to remember everything he had said, how he had looked; to wonder how she was going to live through the hours until the next lesson on the morrow.

When Isabel was dismissed, she waited for Manox to come out.

He bowed low, smiling when he saw her, thinking that he had made an impression on her, for his surface charm and his reputation had made him irresistible to quite a number of ladies. He smiled at Isabel's pale face and compared it with Catherine's round childish one. He was more excited by Catherine than he had been since his first affair; for this adventuring with the little girl was a new experience, and though it was bound to be slow, and needed tact and patience, he found it more intriguing than any normal affair could be.

Isabel said: 'I have never seen you at our entertainments.'

He smiled and said that he had heard of the young ladies' revels, and it was a matter of great regret that he had never attended one.

She said: 'You must come . . . I will tell you when. You know it is a secret!'

'Never fear that I should drop a hint to Her Grace.'

'It is innocent entertainment,' said Isabel anxiously.

'I could not doubt it!'

'We frolic a little; we feast; there is nothing wrong. It is just amusing.'

'That I have heard.'

'I will let you know then.'

'You are the kindest of ladies.'

He bowed courteously, and went on his way, thinking of Catherine.

* * *

Through the gardens at Hampton Court Anne walked with Henry. He was excited, his head teeming with plans, for the Cardinal's palace was now his. He had demanded of a humiliated Wolsey wherefore a subject should have such a palace; and with a return of that wit which had been the very planks on which he had built his mighty career, the

Cardinal, knowing himself lost and hoping by gifts to re-instate himself a little in the heart of the King, replied that a subject might build such a palace only to show what a noble gift a subject might make to his King.

Henry had been delighted by that reply; he had all but embraced his old friend, and his eyes had glistened to think of Hampton Court. Henry had inherited his father's acquisitive nature, and the thought of riches must ever make him lick his lips with pleasure.

'Darling,' he said to Anne, 'we must to Hampton Court, for there are many alterations I would make. I will make a palace of Hampton Court, and you shall help in this.'

The royal barge had carried them up the river; there was no ceremony on this occasion. Perhaps the King was not eager for it; perhaps he felt a little shame in accepting this magnificent gift from his old friend. All the way up the river he laughed with Anne at the incongruity of a subject's daring to possess such a place.

'He was another king . . . or would be!' said Anne. 'You were most lenient with him.'

' 'Twas ever a fault of mine, sweetheart, to be over-lenient with those I love.'

She raised her beautifully arched eyebrows, and surveyed him mockingly.

'I fancy it is so with myself.'

He slapped his thigh – a habit of his – and laughed at her; she delighted him now as ever. He grew sentimental, contemplating her. He had loved her long, nor did his passion for her abate. To be in love was a pleasant thing; he glowed with self-sacrifice, thinking: She shall have the grandest apartments that can be built! I myself will plan them.

He told her of his ideas for the alterations.

'Work shall be started for my Queen's apartments before aught else. The hangings shall be of tissue of gold, sweetheart. I myself will design the walls.' He thought of great lovers' knots with the initials H and A intwined. He told her of this; sentimental and soft, his voice was slurred with affection. 'Intwined, darling! As our lives shall be and have been ever since we met. For I would have the world know that naught shall come between us two.'

Unceremoniously they left the barge. The gardens were beautiful – but a cardinal's gardens, said Henry, not a king's!

'Dost know I have a special fondness for gardens?' he asked. 'And dost know why?'

She thought it strange and oddly perturbing that he could remind her of his faithfulness to her here in this domain which he had taken – for the gift was enforced – from one to whom he owed greater loyalty. But how like Henry! Here in the shadow of Wolsey's cherished Hampton Court, he must tell himself that he was a loyal friend, because he had been disloyal to its owner.

'Red and white roses,' said the King, and he touched her cheek. 'We will have this like your father's garden at Hever, eh? We will have a pond, and you shall sit on its edge and talk to me, and watch your own reflection. I'll warrant you will be somewhat kinder to me than you were at Hever, eh?'

'It would not surprise me,' she laughed.

He talked with enthusiasm of his plans. He visualized beds of roses – red and white to symbolize the union of the houses of York and Lancaster, to remind all who beheld them that the Tudors represented peace; he would enclose those beds with wooden railings painted in his livery colours of white and green; he would set up posts and pillars which should be decorated with heraldic designs. There would be about the place a constant reminder to all, including himself, that he was a faithful man; that when he loved, he loved deeply and long. H and A! Those initials should be displayed in every possible spot.

'Come along in, sweetheart,' he said. 'I would choose your apartments. They shall be the most lavish that were ever seen.'

They went up the staircase, across a large room. It was Anne who turned to the right and descended a few steps into the panelled rooms which had been Wolsey's own. Henry had not wished to go into those rooms, but when he saw their splendid furnishings, their rich hangings, the magnificent plate, the window seats padded with red window carpets, the twisted gold work on the ceilings, he was loth to leave them. He had seen this splendour many times before; but then it had been Wolsey's, now it was his.

Anne pointed to the damask carpets which lay about the floors, and reminded the King of how, it was whispered, Wolsey had come by these.

Henry was less ready to defend his old favourite than usual. He recounted the story of the Venetian bribe, and his mouth was a thin line, though previously he had laughed at it, condoned it.

They went through the lavishly furnished bedrooms, admired the counterpanes of satin and damask, the cushions of velvet and satin and cloth of gold.

'Good sweetheart,' said Henry, 'I think your apartment shall be here, for I declare it to be the finest part of Hampton Court. The rooms shall be enlarged; I will have new ceilings; everything here shall be of the best. It shall be accomplished as soon as possible.'

'It will take many years,' said Anne, and added: 'So therefore it is just possible that the divorce may be done with by then, if it ever is!'

He put an arm about her shoulders.

'How now, darling! We have waited long, and are impatient, but methinks we shall not wait much longer. Cranmer is a man of ideas . . . and that knave, Cromwell, too! My plans for your apartments may take a year or two completely to carry out, but never fear, long ere their accomplishment you shall be Queen of England!'

They sat awhile on the window seat, for the day was warm. He talked enthusiastically of the changes he would make. She listened but listlessly; Hampton Court held memories of a certain moonlit night, when she and Percy had looked from one of those windows and talked of the happiness they would make for each other.

She wondered if she would ever occupy these rooms which he planned for her. Wolsey had once made plans in this house.

'Our initials intwined, sweetheart,' said the King. 'Come! You shiver. Let us on.'

*   *   *

In his house at Westminster, Wolsey awaited the arrival of Norfolk and Suffolk. His day was over, and Wolsey knew it; this was the end of his brightness; he would live the rest of his life in the darkness of obscurity, if he were lucky; but was it not a proven fact that when great men fell from favour their heads were not long in coming to the block? Those who lived gloriously must often die violently. Wolsey was sick, of mind and body; there was a pain in his solar plexus, a pain in his throat; and this was what men called heartbreak. And the most heartbreaking moment of his career was when he had arrived at Grafton with Campeggio, to find that there was no place for him at the court. For his fellow cardinal there were lodgings prepared in accordance with his state, but for Thomas Wolsey, once beloved of the King, there was no bed on which to rest his weary body. Then did he know to what depths of disfavour he had sunk. But for young Henry Norris, he knew not what he would have done; already had he suffered enough humiliation to break the heart of a proud man.

Norris, groom of the stole, a young handsome person with compassion in his pleasant eyes, had offered his own apartment to the travel-stained old man; such moments were pleasant in a wretched day. And yet, next day when he and Campeggio had had audience with the King, had not His Majesty softened to him, his little eyes troubled, his little mouth pursed with remembrance? Henry would never hate his old friend when he stood face to face with him; there were too many memories they shared; between them they had given birth to too many successful schemes for all to be forgotten. It is the careless, watching, speculating eyes which hurt a fallen man. He knew those callous courtiers laid wagers on the King's conduct towards his old favourite. Wolsey had seen the disappointment in their faces when Henry let his old affection triumph; and Lady Anne's dark eyes had glittered angrily, for she believed that the resuscitation of Wolsey's dying influence meant the strangulation of her own. Her beautiful face had hardened, though she had smiled graciously enough on the Cardinal; and Wolsey, returning her smile, had felt fear grip his heart once more, for what hope had he with such an enemy!

It had come to his ears, by way of those who had waited on her and the King when they dined, that she had been deeply offended by Henry's show of affection for the Cardinal; and she, bold and confident in her power over the King, did not hesitate to reprove him. 'Is it not a marvellous thing,' so he had heard she said, 'to consider what debt and danger the Cardinal hath brought you in with your subjects?' The King was puzzled. 'How so, sweetheart?' Then she referred to that loan which the Cardinal had raised from his subjects for the King's use. And she laughed and added: 'If my lord Norfolk, my lord Suffolk, my lord my father, or any other noble person within your realm had done much less than he, they should have lost their heads ere this.' To which the King answered: 'I perceive ye are not the Cardinal's friend.' 'I have no cause!' she retorted. 'Nor more any other that love Your Grace, if ye consider well his doings!'

No more had been heard at the table, but Wolsey knew full well how gratifying it would be for the King to imagine her hatred for the Cardinal had grown out of her love for the King. She was an adversary to beware of. He had no chance of seeing the King again, for the Lady Anne had gone off riding with him next morning, and had so contrived it that His Majesty did not return until the cardinals had left. What poison did this woman pour into his master's ears by day and night? But being Wolsey he must know it was himself whom he must blame; he it was who had taken that false step. He was too astute not to realize that had he been in Lady Anne's place he would have acted as she did now. Imagination had helped to lift him, therefore it was easy to see himself in her position. He could even pity her, for her road was a more dangerous one than his, and those who depend for prosperity upon a prince's favour – and such a prince – must consider each step before they take it, if they wish to survive. He had failed with the divorce, and looking back, that seemed inevitable, for as Cardinal he owed allegiance to Rome, and the King was straining to break those chains which bound him to the Holy See. He, who was shrewd, diplomatic, had failed. She was haughty, imperious, impulsive; what fate awaited her? Where she was concerned he had been foolish; he had lacked imagination. A man does not blame himself when enemies are made by his greatness; it is only when they are made by his folly that he does this. Perhaps humiliation was easier to bear, knowing he had brought it on himself.

His usher, Cavendish, came in to tell him that the Dukes of Norfolk and Suffolk had arrived. The Cardinal received them ceremoniously – the cold-eyed Norfolk, the cruel-eyed Suffolk, both rejoicing in his downfall.

'It is the King's pleasure,' said Suffolk, 'that you should hand over the Great Seal into our hands, and that you depart simply unto Esher.'

Esher! To a house near splendid Hampton Court which was his through the Bishopric of Winchester. He summoned all his dignity.

'And what commission have you, my lords, to give me such commandment?'

They said they came from the King, that they had received the commission from his royal mouth.

'Then that is not sufficient,' said Wolsey, 'for the Great Seal of England was delivered me by the King's own person, to enjoy during my life. I have the King's letters to show it.'

The Dukes were angered by this reply, but seeing the King's letters, all they could do was return to Henry.

Wolsey knew he but put off the evil day. The Great Seal, the symbol of his greatness, remained in his hands for but one more day; on the morrow the Dukes returned from Windsor with letters from the King, and there was nothing more that Wolsey could do but deliver up the seal.

The ex-chancellor was filled with deep foreboding and set his servants to make inventories of all the rich possessions in his house; these goods he would give to the King, for if his master could not be touched by affection it might well be that he could by rich gifts; many times had Wolsey noted that the little eyes glinted with envy when they rested on these things. When a man is in danger of drowning, thought Wolsey, he throws off all his fine apparel that he may swim more easily. What are possessions, compared with life itself!

He took his barge at his privy stairs, having ordered horses to be awaiting him at Putney; and the river, he saw, was crowded with craft, for news had travelled quickly and there were those who find the spectacle of a fallen man pleasurable indeed. He saw their grins; he heard their jeers; he sensed the speculation, the disappointment that he was not going straightway to the Tower.

Riding through Putney town, he saw Norris coming towards him, and his heart was lightened, since he had come to look upon Norris as a friend. And so it proved, for the King's peace of mind had been profoundly disturbed by the story which Norfolk and Suffolk had told him of the giving up of the seal. The King could not forget that he had once loved Wolsey; he was haunted by a pale, sick face under a cardinal's hat; and he remembered how this man had been his friend and counsellor; and though he knew that he had done with Wolsey, he wanted to reassure his conscience that it was not he who had destroyed his old friend, but others. Therefore, to appease that conscience, he sent Norris to Putney with a gold ring which Wolsey would recognize by the rich stone it contained, as they had previously used this ring for a token. He was to be of good cheer, Norris told him, for he stood as high as ever in the King's favour.

Wolsey's spirits soared; his body gained strength; the old fighting spirit came back to him. He was not defeated. He embraced Norris, feeling great affection for this young man, and took a little chain of gold from his neck to give to him; on this chain there hung a tiny cross. 'I desire you to take this small reward from my hand,' he said, and Norris was deeply moved.

Then did the Cardinal look about his retinue; and saw one who had been close to him, and in whom he delighted, for the man's wit and humour were of the subtlest, and many times had he brought mirth into the Cardinal's heaviest hours.

'Take my Fool, Norris,' he said. 'Take him to my lord the King, for well I know His Majesty will like well the gift. Fool!' he called. 'Here, Fool!'

The man came, his eyes wide with fear and with love for his master; and seeing this, the Cardinal leaned forward and said almost tenderly: 'Thou shalt have a place at court, Fool.'

But the Fool knelt down in the mire and wept bitterly. Wolsey was much moved that his servant should show such love, since to be Fool to the King, instead of to a man who is sinking in disgrace, was surely a great step forward.

'Thou art indeed a fool!' said Wolsey. 'Dost not know what I am offering thee?'

All foolery was gone from those droll features; only tears were in the humorous eyes now.

'I will not leave you, master.'

'Didst not hear I have given thee to His Majesty?'

'I will not serve His Majesty. My lord, I have but one master.'

With tears in his eyes the Cardinal called six yeomen to remove the man; and struggling, full of rage and sorrow, went the Fool.

Then on rode Wolsey, and when he reached his destination to find himself in that barren house in which there were not even beds nor dishes, plates nor cups, his heart was warmed that in this world there were those to love a man who is fallen from his greatness.

*　　*　　*

Lady Anne Rochford sat in her apartment, turning the leaves of a book. She had found this book in her chamber, and even as she picked it up she knew that someone had put it there that she might find it. As she looked at this book, the colour rose from her neck to her forehead, and she was filled with anger. She sat for a long time, staring at the open page, wondering who had put it there, how many of her attendants had seen it.

The book was a book of prophecies; there were many in the country, she knew, who would regard such prophecies as miraculous; it was alarming therefore to find herself appearing very prominently in them.

She called Anne Saville to her, adopting a haughty mien, which was never difficult with her.

'Nan!' she called. 'Come here! Come here at once!'

Anne Saville came and, seeing the book in her mistress's hand, grew immediately pale.

'You have seen this book?' asked Anne.

'I should have removed it ere your ladyship set eyes on it.'

Anne laughed.

'You should have done no such thing, for this book makes me laugh so much that it cannot fail to give me pleasure.'

She turned the pages, smiling, her fingers steady.

'Look, Nan! This figure represents me . . . and here is the King. And here is Katharine. This must be so, since our initials are on them. Nan, tell me, I do not look like that! Look, Nan, do not turn away. Here I am with my head cut off!'

Anne Saville was seized with violent trembling.

'If I thought that true, I would not have him were he an emperor!' she said.

Anne snapped her fingers scornfully, 'I am resolved to have him, Nan.'

Anne Saville could not take her eyes from the headless figure on the page.

'The book is a foolish book, a bauble. I am resolved that my issue shall be royal, Nan . . .' She added: '. . . whatever may become of me!'

'Then your ladyship is very brave.'

'Nan! Nan! What a little fool you are! To believe a foolish book!'

If Anne Saville was very quiet all that day as though her thoughts troubled her, Lady Anne Rochford was especially gay, though she did not regard the book as lightly as she would have those about her suppose. She did not wish to give her enemies the satisfaction of knowing that she was disturbed. For one thing was certain in her mind – she was surrounded by her enemies who would undermine · her security in every possible way; and this little matter of the book was but one of those ways. An enemy had put the book where she might see it, hoping thereby to sow fear in her mind. What a hideous idea! To cut off her head!

She was nervous; her dreams were disturbed by that picture in the book. She watched those about her suspiciously, seeking her enemies. The Queen, the Princess, the Duke and Duchess of Suffolk, the Cardinal . . . all of the most important in the land. Who else? Who had brought the book into her chamber?

Those about her would be watching everything she did; listening to everything she said. She felt very frightened. Once she awoke trembling in a cold sweat; she had dreamed that Wolsey was standing before her, holding an axe, and the blade was turned towards her. The King lay beside her, and terrified, she awoke him.

'I had an evil dream . . .'

'Dreams are nothing, sweetheart.'

She would not let him dismiss her dream so. She would insist that he put his arms about her, assure her of his undying love for her.

'For without your love, I should die,' she told him. He kissed her tenderly and soothed her.

'As I should, without yours.'

'Nothing could hurt you,' she said.

'Nothing could hurt you, sweetheart, since I am here to take care of you.'

'There are many who are jealous of your love for me, who seek to destroy me.' She blurted out the story of her finding the book.

'The knave who printed it shall hang, darling. We'll have his head on London Bridge. Thus shall people see what happens to those who would frighten my sweetheart.'

'This you say, but will you do it, when you suffer those who hate me, to enjoy your favour?'

'Never should any who hated you receive my favour!'

'I know of one.'

'Oh, darling, he is an old, sick man. He wishes you no ill. . . .'

'No!' she cried fiercely. 'Has he not fought against us con-

208

sistently! Has he not spoken against us to the Pope! I know of those who will confirm this.'

She was trembling in his arms, for she felt his reluctance to discuss the Cardinal.

'I fear for us both,' she said. 'How can I help but fear for you too, when I love you! I have heard much of his wickedness. There is his Venetian physician, who has been to me....'

'What!' cried the King.

'But no more! You think so highly of him that you will see him my enemy, and leave him to go unpunished. He is in York, you say. Let him rest there! He is banished from Westminster; that is enough. So in York he may pursue his wickedness and set the people against me, since he is of more importance to you than I am.'

'Anne, Anne, thou talkest wildly. Who could be of more importance to me than thou?'

'Your late chancellor, my lord Cardinal Wolsey!' she retorted. She was seized with a wild frenzy, and drew his face close to hers and kissed him, and spoke to him incoherently of her love and devotion, which touched him deeply; and out of his tenderness for her grew passion such as he had rarely experienced before, and he longed to give her all that she asked, to prove his love for her and to keep her loving him thus.

He said: 'Sweetheart, you talk with wildness!'

'Yes,' she said, 'I talk with wildness; it is only your beloved Cardinal who talks with good sense. I can see that I must not stay here. I will go away. I have lost those assets which were dearer to me than aught else – my virtue, my honour. I shall leave you. This is the last night I shall lie in your arms, for I see that I am ruined, that you cannot love me.'

Henry could always be moved to terror when she talked of leaving him; before he had given her Suffolk House, she had so often gone back and forth to Hever. The thought of losing her was more than he could endure; he was ready to offer her Wolsey if that was the price she asked.

He said: 'Dost think I should allow thee to leave me, Anne?'

She laughed softly. 'You might force me to stay; you could force me to share your bed!' Again she laughed. 'You are big and strong, and I am but weak. You are a king and I am a poor woman who from love of you has given you her honour and her virtue. . . . Yes, doubtless you could force me to stay, but though you should do this, you would but keep my body; my love, though it has destroyed me, would be lost to you.'

'You shall not talk thus! I have never known happiness such as I have enjoyed with you. Your virtue . . . your honour! My God, you talk foolishly, darling! Shall you not be my Queen?'

'You have said so these many years. I grow weary of waiting. You surround yourself with those who hinder you rather than help. I have proof that the Cardinal is one of these.'

'What proof?' he demanded.

'Did I not tell you of the physician? He knows that Wolsey wrote to the Pope, asking him to excommunicate you, an you did not dismiss me and take back Katharine.'

'By God! And I will not believe it.'

She put her arms about his neck, and with one hand stroked his hair.

'Darling, see the physician, discover for yourself. . . .'

'That will I do!' he assured her.

Then she slept more peacefully, but in the morning her fears were as strong as ever. When the physician confirmed Wolsey's perfidy, when her cousin, Francis Bryan, brought her papers which proved that Wolsey had been in communication with the Pope, had asked for the divorce to be delayed; when she took these in triumph to the King and saw the veins stand out on his forehead with anger against the Cardinal, still she found peace of mind elusive. She remembered the softness of the King towards this man; she remembered how, when he had lain ill at Esher, he had sent Butts, his physician – the man he had sent to her at Hever – to attend his old friend. She remembered how he had summoned Butts, recently returned from Esher, and had asked after Wolsey's health; and when Butts had said he feared the old man would die unless he received some token of the King's regard, then had the King sent him a ruby ring, and – greater humiliation – he had turned to her and bidden her send a token too. Such was the King's regard for this man; such was his reluctance to destroy him.

But she would not let her enemy live; and in this she had behind her many noblemen, at whose head were the powerful Dukes of Norfolk and Suffolk, men such as would not let the grass grow under their feet in the matter. George had talked with her of Wolsey. 'There will be no peace for us, Anne, while that man lives. For, if ever you had an enemy, that man is he!' She trusted George completely. He had said: 'You can do this, Anne. You have but to command the King. Hesitate not, for well you know that had Wolsey the power to destroy you, he would not hesitate.'

'That I do know,' she answered, and was suddenly sad. 'George,' she went on, 'would it not be wonderful if we could go home and live quietly, hated by none!'

'I would not wish to live quietly, sister,' said George. 'Nor would you. Come! Could you turn back now, would you?' She searched her mind and knew that he was right. 'You were meant to be Queen of England, Anne. You have all the attributes.'

'I feel that, but I could wish there were not so much hating to be done!'

But she went on hating furiously; this was a battle between herself and Wolsey, and it was one she was determined to win. Norfolk watched; Suffolk watched; they were waiting for their opportunity.

There was a new charge against the Cardinal. He had been guilty of asserting and maintaining papal jurisdiction in England. Henry must accept the evidence; he must appease Anne; he must satisfy his ministers. Wolsey was to be arrested at Cawood Castle in York, whither he had retired these last months.

'The Earl of Northumberland should be sent to arrest him,' said Anne, her eyes gleaming.

This was to be. She went to her apartment, dismissed her ladies, and flung herself upon her bed overcome by paroxysms of laughter and tears. She felt herself to be, not the woman who aspired to the throne of England, but a girl in love who through this man had lost her lover.

Now he would see! Now he should know! 'That foolish girl!' he had said. 'Her father but a knight, and yours one of the noblest houses in the land. . . .'

Her father was an earl now; and she all but Queen of England.

Oh, you wise Cardinal! How I should love to see your face when Percy comes for you! You will know then that you were not so wise in seeking to destroy Anne Boleyn.

*　　*　　*

As the Cardinal sat at dinner in the dining-hall at Cawood Castle, his gentleman usher came to him and said: 'My lord, His Grace, the Earl of Northumberland is in the castle!'

Wolsey was astounded.

'This cannot be. Were I to have the honour of a visit from such a nobleman, he would surely have warned me. Show him in to me that I may greet him.'

The Earl was brought into the dining-hall. He had changed a good deal since Wolsey had last seen him, and Wolsey scarcely recognized him as the delicate, handsome boy whom he had had occasion to reprimand at the King's command because he had dared to fall in love with the King's favourite.

Wolsey reproached Northumberland: 'My lord Earl, you should have let me know, that I might have done you the honour due to you!'

Northumberland was quiet; he had come to receive no honour, he said. His eyes burned oddly in his pallid face. Wolsey remembered stories he had heard of his unhappy marriage with Shrewsbury's daughter. A man should not allow a marriage to affect him so strongly; there were other things in life. A man in Northumberland's position had much; was he not reigning lord of one of the noblest houses in the land! Bah! thought Wolsey enviously, an I were earl . . .

He had an affection for this young man, remembering him well when he had served under him. A docile boy, a charming boy. He had been grieved when he had to send him away.

'It is well to meet again,' said Wolsey. 'For old times' sake.'

'For old times' sake!' said Northumberland, and he spoke as a man speaks in his sleep.

'I mind thee well,' said Wolsey. 'Thou wert a bright, impetuous boy.'

'I mind thee well,' said Northumberland.

With malice in his heart, he surveyed the broken old man. So were the mighty fallen from their high places! This man had done that for which he would never forgive him, for he had taken from him Anne Boleyn whom in six long years of wretched marriage he had never forgotten; nor had he any intention of forgiving Wolsey. Anne should have been his, and he Anne's. They had loved; they had made vows; and this man, who dared now to remind him of the old times, had been the cause of all his misery. And now that he was old and broken, now that his ambition had destroyed him, Wolsey would be kind and full of tender reminiscence. But Percy also remembered!

'I have often thought of you,' he said, and that was true. When he had quarrelled with Mary, his wife, whom he hated and who hated him, he thought of the Cardinal's face and the stern words that he had used. 'Thou foolish boy ...' Would he never forget the bitter humiliation? No, he never would; and because he would never cease to reproach himself for his own misery, knowing full well that had he shown sufficient courage he might have made a fight for his happiness, he hated this man with a violent hatred. He stood before him, trembling with rage, for well he knew that *she* had contrived this, and that she would expect him to show now that courage he had failed to show seven years ago.

Northumberland laid his hand on Wolsey's arm. 'My lord, I arrest you of High Treason!'

The Earl was smiling courteously, but with malice; the Cardinal began to tremble.

Revenge was a satisfying emotion, thought the Earl. He who had made others to suffer, must now himself suffer.

'We shall travel towards London at the earliest possible moment,' he said.

This they did; and, trembling with his desire for vengeance, the Earl caused the Cardinal's legs to be bound to the stirrups of his mule; thus did he proclaim to the world: 'This man, who was once great, is now naught but a common malefactor!'

About Cawood the people saw the Cardinal go; they wept; they called curses on his enemies. He left Cawood with their cries ringing in his ears. 'God save Your Grace! The foul evil take them that have taken you from us! We pray God that a very vengeance may light upon them!'

The Cardinal smiled sadly. Of late weeks, here in York, he had led that life which it would have become him as a churchman to have led before. Alms had he given to the people at his gates; his table had been over-flowing with food and wine, and at Cawood Castle had he entertained the beggars and the needy to whom he had given scarcely a thought at Hampton Court and York House; for Wolsey, who had once sought to placate his sense of inferiority, to establish his social standing, now sought a place in Heaven by his good deeds. He smiled at himself as he rode down to Leicester; his body was sick, and he doubted whether it would – indeed he prayed that it would not – last the journey to London. But he smiled, for he saw himself a man who has climbed high and has fallen low. Pride was my enemy, he said, as bitter an enemy as ever was the Lady Anne.

* * *

The rejoicing of the Boleyn faction at the death of Wolsey was shameless. None would have believed a year before that the greatest man in England could be brought so low. Wolsey, it was said, had died of a flux, but all knew he had died of a broken heart, for melancholy was as sure a disease as any other; and having lost all that he cared to live for, why should the Cardinal live? He to be taken to the Tower! He, who had loved his master, to be tried for High Treason!

Here was triumph for Anne. People sought her more than ever, flattered her, fêted her. To be favoured by Anne was to be favoured by the King. She enjoyed her triumph and gave special revels to commemorate the defeat of her enemy. She was led into the bad taste of having a play enacted which treated the great Cardinal as a figure of fun.

George was as recklessly glad about Wolsey's fall as she was. 'While that man lived, I trembled for you,' he said. He laughed shortly. 'I hear that near his end he told Kingston that had he served God as diligently as he had served the King, he would not have been given over in his grey hairs. I would say that had he served his God as diligently as he served himself, he would have gone to the scaffold long ere this!' People hearing this remark, took it up and laughed over it.

The King did not attend these revels of the Boleyns. Having given the order for the arrest of Wolsey, he wished to shut the matter from his mind. He was torn between remorse and gladness. Wolsey had left much wealth, and into whose hands should this fall but the King's!

Henry prayed: 'O Lord, thou knowest I loved that man. I would I had seen him. I would I had not let his enemies keep him from me. Did I not send him tokens of my regard? Did I not say I would not lose the fellow for twenty thousand pounds?'

But he could not stop his thoughts straying to the Cardinal's possessions. There was more yet that he must get his hands upon. Hampton Court was his; York House was his, for he had never given it back after Anne went to Suffolk House, liking it too well.

But he wept for the old days of friendship; he wept for Wolsey; and he was able to deplore his death whilst considering how much more there was in gold to come to him.

Soon after this there were two matters which caused Anne some misgiving. The first came in the form of a letter which the Countess of Northumberland had written to her father, the Earl of Shrewsbury. Shrewsbury had thought it wise to show this letter to the Duke of Norfolk, who had brought it to his niece with all speed.

Anne read the letter. There was no doubt of its meaning. Mary of Northumberland was leaving her husband; she told her father that in one of their more violent quarrels her husband had told her that he was not really married to her, being previously contracted to Anne Boleyn.

Anne's heart beat fast. Here was yet another plot to discredit her in the eyes of the King. She had been his mistress for nearly two years, and it seemed to her that she was no nearer becoming Queen than she had been on that first night in Suffolk House. She was becoming anxious, wondering how long she could expect to keep the King her obedient slave. For a long time she had watched for some lessening of his affection; she had found none; she studied herself carefully for some deterioration of her beauty; if she were older, a little drawn, there were many more gorgeous clothes and priceless jewels to set against that. But she was worried, and though she told herself that she longed for a peaceful life and would have been happy had she married Percy or Wyatt she knew that the spark of ambition inside her had been fanned into a great consuming fire; and when she had said to Anne Saville that she would marry the King, no matter what happened to herself, she meant that. She was quite sure that, once she was Queen, she would give the King sons, that not only could she delight him as his mistress, but as mother of the future Tudor King of England. Having tasted power, how could she ever relinquish it! And this was at the root of her fear. The delay of the divorce, the awareness of powerful enemies all about her – this was what had made her nervous, imperious, hysterical, haughty, frightened.

Therefore she trembled when she read this letter.

'Give it to me,' she commanded.

'What will you do with it?' asked her uncle. She was unsure. He said: 'You should show it to the King.'

She studied him curiously. Cold, hard, completely without sentiment, he despised these families which had sprung up, allied to his own house simply because the Norfolk fortunes were in decline at Henry the Seventh's accession on account of the mistake his family had made in backing Richard the Third. She weighed his words. He was no friend of hers; yet was he an enemy? It would be more advantageous to see his niece on the throne of England than another's niece.

She went to the King.

He was sitting in a window seat, playing a harp and singing a song he had written.

'Ah! Sweetheart, I was thinking of you. Sit with me, and I will sing to you my song . . . Why, what ails you? You are pale and trembling.'

She said: 'I am afraid. There are those who would poison your mind against me.'

'Bah!' he said, feeling in a merry mood, for Wolsey had left riches such as even Henry had not dreamed of, and he had convinced himself that the Cardinal's death was none of his doing. He had died of a flux, and a flux will attack a man, be he chancellor or beggar. 'What now, Anne? Have I not told you that naught could ever poison my mind against you!'

'You would not remember, but when I was very young and first came to court, Percy of Northumberland wished to marry me.'

The King's eyes narrowed. Well he remembered. He had got Wolsey to banish the boy from court, and he had banished Anne too. For years he had let her escape him. She was a bud of a girl then, scarce awake at all, but very lovely. They had missed years together.

Anne went on: 'It was no contract. He was sent from the court, being pre-contracted to my Lord Shrewsbury's daughter. Now they have quarrelled, and he says he will leave her, and she says he tells her he was never really married to her, being pre-contracted to me.'

The King let out an exclamation, and put aside his harp.

'This were not true?' he said.

'Indeed not!'

'Then we must put a stop to such idle talk. Leave this to me, sweetheart. I'll have him brought up before the Archbishop of Canterbury. I'll have him recant this, or 'twill be the worse for him!'

The King paced the floor, his face anxious.

'Dost know, sweetheart,' he said, 'I fear I have dolts about me. Were Wolsey here . . .'

She did not speak, for she knew it was unnecessary to rail against the Cardinal now; he was done with. She had new enemies with whom to cope. She knew that Henry was casting a slur on the new ministry of Norfolk and More; that he was reminding her that though Wolsey had died, he had had nothing to do with his death. She wished then that she did not know this man so well; she wished that she could have been as light-heartedly gay as people thought her, living for the day, thinking not of the morrow. She had set her skirts daintily about her, aware of her grace and charm, knowing that they drew men irresistibly to her, wondering what would happen to her when she was old, as her grandmother Norfolk. Then I suppose, she thought, I will doze in a chair and recall my adventurous youth, and poke my granddaughters with an ebony stick. I would like my grandmother to come and see me; she is a foolish old woman assuredly, but at least she would be a friend.

'Sweetheart,' said the King, 'I shall go now and settle this matter, for there will be no peace of mind until Northumberland admits this to be a lie.'

He kissed her lips; she returned his kiss, knowing well how to enchant him, being often sparing with her caresses so that when he received them he must be more grateful than if they had been lavished on him. He was the hunter; although he talked continually of longing for peace of mind, she knew that that would never satisfy him. He must never be satisfied, but always be looking for satisfaction. For two years she had kept him thus in difficult circumstances. She must go on keeping him thus, for her future depended on her ability to do so.

Fain would he have stayed, but she bid him go. 'For,' she said, 'although I know this matter to be a lie, until my lord of Northumberland admits it I am under a cloud. I could not marry you unless we had his full confession that there is no grain of truth in this claim.'

She surveyed him through narrowed eyes; she saw return to him that dread fear of losing her. He was easy to read, simple in his desires, ready enough to accept her own valuation of herself. What folly it would have been to have wept, to have told him that Northumberland lied, to have caused him to believe that her being Queen of England was to her advantage, not to his. While he believed she was ready to return to Hever, while he believed that she wished to be his wife chiefly because she had given way to his desires and sacrificed her honour and virtue, he would fight for her. She had to make him believe that the joy she could give him was worth more than any honours he could heap on her.

And he did believe this. He went storming out of the room; he had Northumberland brought before the Archbishops; he had him swear there had never been a contract with Anne Boleyn. It was made perfectly clear that Northumberland was married to Shrewsbury's daughter, and Anne Boleyn free to marry the King.

Anne knew that her handling of that little matter had been successful.

It was different with the trouble over Suffolk.

Suffolk, jealous, ambitious, seeking to prevent her marriage to the King, was ready to go to any lengths to discredit Anne, provided he could keep his head on his shoulders.

He started a rumour that Anne had had an affair with Thomas Wyatt even while the King was showing his preference for her. There was real danger in this sort of rumour, as there was no one at court who had not witnessed Thomas's loving attitude towards Anne; they had been seen by all, spending much time together, and it was possible that she had shown how she preferred the poet.

Anne, recklessly deciding that one rumour was as good as another, repeated something completely damaging to Suffolk. He had, she had heard, and she did not hesitate to say it in quarters where it would be quickly carried to Suffolk's ears, more than a fatherly affection for his daughter, Frances Brandon, and his love for her was nothing less than incestuous. Suffolk was furious at the accusation; he confronted Anne; they quarrelled; and the result of this quarrel was that Anne insisted he should absent himself from the court for a while.

This was open warfare with one who – with perhaps the exception of Norfolk – was the most powerful noble in the land, and the King's brother-in-law to boot. Suffolk retired in smouldering anger; he would not, Anne knew, let such an accusation go unpaid for, and she had always been afraid of Suffolk.

She shut herself in her room, feeling depressed; she wept a little and told Anne Saville that whoever asked for her was not to be admitted, even should it be the King himself.

She lay on her bed, staring at the ornate ceiling, seeing Suffolk's angry eyes wherever she looked; she pictured his talking over with his friends the arrogance of her who, momentarily, had the King's ear. Momentarily! It was a hideous word. The influence of all failed sooner or later. Oh, my God, were I but Queen! she thought. Were I but Queen, how happy I should feel! It is this perpetual waiting, this delay. The Pope will never give in; he is afraid of the Emperor Charles! And how can I be Queen of England while Katharine lives!

There was a tap on the door, and Anne Saville's head appeared.

'I told you I would see no one!' cried Anne impatiently. 'I told you – no one! No one at all! Not the King himself . . .'

'It is not the King,' said Anne Saville, 'but my Lord Rochford. I told him you might see him . . .'

'Bring him to me,' said Anne.

George came in, his handsome face set in a smile, but she knew him well enough to be able to see the worried look behind the smile.

'I had the devil's own job to get them to tell you I was here, Anne.'

'I had said I would see no one.'

He sat on the bed and looked at her.

'I have been hearing about Suffolk, Anne,' he said, and she shivered. 'It is a sorry business.'

'I fear so.'

'He is the King's brother-in-law.'

'Well, what if that is so? I am to be the King's wife!'

'You make too many enemies, Anne.'

'I do not make them! I fear they make themselves.'

'The higher you rise, sister, the more there will be, ready to pull you down.'

'You cannot tell me more than I know about that, George.'

He leaned towards her.

'When I saw Suffolk, when I heard the talk . . . I was afraid. I would you had been more reasonable, Anne.'

'Did you hear what he said of me? He said Wyatt and I were, or had been, lovers!'

'I understand your need to punish him, but not your method.'

'I have said he shall be banished the court, and so he is. I have but to say one shall be banished, and it is done.'

'The King loves you deeply, Anne, but it is best to be wise. A queen will have more need of friends than Anne Rochford, and Anne Rochford could never have too many.'

'Ah, my wise brother! I have been foolish . . . that I well know.'

'He will not let the matter rest here, Anne; he will seek to work you some wrong.'

'There will always be those who seek to do me wrong, George, no matter what I do!'

'It is so senseless to make enemies.'

'Sometimes I am very weary of the court, George.'

'So you tell yourself, Anne. Were you banished to Hever, you would die of boredom.'

'That I declare I would, George!'

'If you were asked what was your dearest wish, and spoke truthfully, you would say "I would I were settled firmly on the throne of England." Would you not?'

'You know me better than I know myself, George. It is a glorious adventure. I am flying high, and it is a wonderful, exhilarating, joyous flight; but when I look down I am sometimes giddy; then I am afraid.' She held out a hand and he took it. 'Sometimes I say to myself "There is no one I trust but George."'

He kissed her hand. 'George you can always trust,' he said. 'Others too, I'll warrant; but always George.' Suddenly his reserve broke down, and he was talking as freely as she did.

'Anne, Anne, sometimes I too am afraid. Whither are we going, you and I? From simple folk we have become great folk; and yet ... and yet ... Dost remember how we scorned poor Mary? And yet ... Anne, whither are we going, you and I? Are you happy? Am I? I am married to the most vindictive of women; you contemplate marrying the most dangerous of men. Anne, Anne, we have to tread warily, both of us.'

'You frighten me, George.'

'I did not come to frighten you, Anne,'

'You came to reprove me for my conduct toward Suffolk. And I have always hated the man.'

'When you hate, Anne, it is better to hide your hatred. It is only love that should be shown.'

'There is nothing to be done about Suffolk now, George. In future I shall remember your words. I shall remember you coming to my room with a worried frown looking out from behind your smiles.'

The door opened and Lady Rochford came in. Her eyes darted to the bed.

'I thought to find you here.'

'Where is Anne Saville?' said Anne coldly, for she hated to have this *tête-à-tête* disturbed; there was much yet that she wished to say to her brother.

'Do you want to reprove her for letting me in?' asked Jane maliciously. 'Marry! I thought when my husband came into a lady's chamber, there should I follow him!'

'How are you, Jane?' said Anne.

'Very well, I thank you. You do not look so, sister. This affair of Suffolk must have upset you. I hear he is raging. You accused him of incest, so I heard.'

Anne flushed hotly. There was that in her sister-in-law to anger her even when she felt most kindly towards the world; now, the woman was maddening.

Jane went on: 'The King's sister will be most put about. She retains her fiery temper. . . . And what Frances will say I cannot think!'

'One would not expect you to think about any matter!'

said Anne cuttingly. 'And I do not wish you to enter my apartment without announcement.'

'Indeed, Anne, I am sorry. I thought there would be no need to stand on ceremony with your brother's wife.'

'Let us go, Jane,' said George wearily; and she was aware that he had not looked at her since that one first glance of distaste when she entered the room.

'Oh, very well. I am sure I know when I am not wanted; but do not let me disturb your pleasant conversation – I am sure it was most pleasant . . . and loving.'

'Farewell, Anne,' said George. He stood by the bed, smiling at her, his eyes flashing a message: 'Be of good cheer. All will be well. The King adores you. Hast forgotten he would make you Queen? What of Suffolk! What of any, while the King loves you!'

She said: 'You have done me so much good, George. You always do.'

He stooped and kissed her forehead. Jane watched jealously. When had he last kissed her – kissed her voluntarily, that was – a year ago, or more? I hate Anne, she thought, reclining there as though she were a queen already; her gowns beautifully furred – paid for by the King doubtless! Herself bejewelled as though for a state function, here in her private apartments. I hope she is never Queen! Katharine is Queen. Why should a man put away his wife because he is tired of her? Why should Anne Boleyn take the place of the true Queen, just because she is young and sparkling and vivacious and witty and beautifully dressed, and makes people believe she is more handsome than anyone at court? Everyone speaks of her; everywhere one goes one hears her name!

And he loves her . . . as he never loved me! And am I not his wife?

'Come, Jane!' he said, and his voice was different now that he spoke to her and not to his sister.

He led her out, and they walked silently through the corridors to their apartments in the palace.

She faced him and would not let him walk past her.

'You are as foolish about her as is the King!'

He sighed that weary sigh which always made her all but want to kill him, but not quite, because she loved him, and to kill him would be to kill her hopes of happiness.

'You will talk such nonsense, Jane!'

'Nonsense!' she cried shrilly, and then burst into weeping, covering her face with her hands, and waited for him to take her hands, plead with her to control herself. She wept noisily, but nothing happened; and taking down her hands, she saw that he had left her.

Then did she tremble with cold rage against him and against his sister.

'I would they were dead, both of them! They deserve to die; she for what she has done to the Queen; he for what he has done to me! One day . . .' She stopped, and ran to her mirror, saw her face blotched with tears and grief, thought of the cool, lovely face of the girl on the bed, and the long black hair which looked more beautiful in its disorder than it did when neatly tied. 'One day,' she went on muttering to herself, 'I believe I shall kill one of them . . . both of them, mayhap.'

They were foolish thoughts, which George might say were worthy of her, but nevertheless she found in them an outlet for her violent feelings, and they brought her an odd comfort.

*　　*　　*

A barge passed along the river. People on the banks turned to stare after it. In it sat the most beautiful lady of the King's court. People saw how the fading sunlight caught her bejewelled person. Her hair was caught up in a gold coif that sat elegantly on her shapely head.

'Nan Bullen!' The words were like a rumble of thunder among the crowd.

'They say the poor Queen, the true Queen, is dying of a broken heart . . .'

'As is her daughter Mary.'

'They say Nan Bullen has bribed the Queen's cook to administer poison unto Her Most Gracious Majesty . . .'

'They say she has threatened to poison the Princess Mary.'

'What of the King?'

'The King is the King. It is no fault of his. He is bewitched by this whore.'

'She is very lovely!'

'Bah! That is her witchery.'

''Tis right. A witch may come in any guise . . .'

Women in tattered rags drew their garments about them and thought angrily of the satins and velvets and cloth of gold worn by the Lady Anne Rochford . . . who was really plain Nan Bullen.

'Her grandfather was but a merchant in London town. Why should we have a merchant's daughter for our Queen?'

'There cannot be a second Queen while the first Queen lives.'

'I lost two sons, of the sweat . . .'

They trampled through the muck of the gutter, rats scuttled from under their feet, made bold by their numbers and the lack of surprise and animosity their presence caused. In the fever-ridden stench of the cobbled streets, the people blamed Anne Boleyn.

Over London Bridge the heads of traitors stared out with glassy eyes; offal floated up the river; beggars with sore-encrusted limbs asked for alms; one-legged beggars, one-eyed beggars and beggars all but eaten away with some pox.

''Tis a poor country we live in, since the King would send the rightful Queen from his bed!'

'I mind the poor lady at her coronation; beautiful she was then, with her lovely long hair flowing, and her in a litter of cloth of gold. Nothing too good for her then, poor lady.'

'Should a man, even if he be a king, cast off his wife because she is no longer young?'

It was the cry of fearful women, for all knew that it was the King who set examples. It was the cry of ageing women against the younger members of their sex who would bewitch their husbands and steal them from them.

The murmurs grew to a roar. 'We'll have no Nan Bullen!'

There was one woman with deep cadaverous eyes and her

front teeth missing. She raised her hands and jeered at the women who gathered about her.

'Ye'll have no Nan Bullen, eh? And what'll ye do about it, eh? You'll be the first to shout "God save Your Majesty" when the King makes his whore our Queen!'

'Not I!' cried one bold spirit, and the others took it up.

The fire of leadership was in the woman. She brandished a stick.

'We'll take Nan Bullen! We'll go to her and we'll take her, and when we've done with her we'll see if she is such a beauty, eh? Who'll come? Who'll come?'

Excitement was in the air. There were many who were ever ready to follow a procession, ever ready to espouse a cause; and what more worthy than this, for weary house-wives who had little to eat and but rags to cover them, little to hope for and much to fear?

They had seen the Lady Anne Rochford in her barge, proud and imperious, so beautiful that she was more like a picture to them than a woman; her clothes looked too fine to be real . . . And she was not far off . . . her barge had stopped along the river.

Dusk was in the sky; it touched them with adventure, dangerous adventure. They were needy; they were hungry; and she was rich, and doubtless on her way to some noble friends' house to supper. This was a noble cause; it was Queen Katharine's cause; it was the cause of Princess Mary.

'Down with Nan Bullen!' they shouted.

She would have jewels about her, they remembered. Cupidity and righteousness filled their minds. 'Shall we let the whore sit on the throne of England? They say she carries a fortune in jewels about her body!'

Once, it was said, in the days of the King's youth when he feasted with his friends, the mob watched him; and so dazzled were they by his person, that they were unable to keep away from him; they seized their mighty King; they seized Bluff King Hal, and stripped him of his jewels. What did he do? He was a noble King, a lover of sport. What did he do? He did naught but smile and treat the matter as a joke. He was a bluff King! A great King! But momentarily he was in the hands of a witch. There were men who had picked up a fortune that night. Why should not a fortune be picked up from Nan Bullen? And she was no bluff, good king, but a scheming woman, a witch, a poisoner, a usurper of the throne of England! It was a righteous cause; it was a noble cause; it might also prove a profitable cause!

Someone had lighted a torch; another sprang up, and another. In the flickering glow from the flares the faces of the women looked like those of animals. Cupidity was in each face . . . cruelty, jealousy, envy. . . .

'Ah! What will we do to Nan Bullen when we find her? I will tear her limbs apart . . . I will tear the jewels off her. Nan Bullen shall not be our Queen. Queen Katharine for ever!'

They fell into some order, and marched. There were more flares; they made a bright glow in the sky.

They muttered, and each dreamed of the bright jewel she would snatch from the fair body. A fortune . . . a fortune to be made in a night, and in the righteous cause of Katharine the Queen.

'What means this?' asked newcomers.

'Nan Bullen!' chanted the crowd. 'We'll have no Nan Bullen! Queen Katharine for ever!'

The crowd was swollen now; it bulged and sprawled, but it went forward, a grimly earnest, glowing procession.

Anne, at the riverside house where she had gone to take supper, saw the glow in the sky, heard the low chanting of voices.

'What is it they say?' she asked of those about her. 'What is it? I think they come this way.'

Anne and her friends went out into the riverside garden, and listened. The voices seemed thousands strong.

'Nan Bullen . . . Nan Bullen. . . . We'll not have the King's whore . . .'

She felt sick with fear. She had heard that cry before, never at such close quarters, never so ominous.

'They have seen you come here,' whispered her hostess, and trembled, wondering what an ugly mob would do to the friends of Anne Boleyn.

'What do they want?'

'They say your name. Listen. . . .'

They stood, straining their ears.

'We'll have none of Nan Bullen. Queen Katharine for ever!'

The guests were pale; they looked at each other, shuddering. Outwardly calm, inwardly full of misery, Anne said: 'Methinks I had better leave you, good people. Mayhap when they find me not here they will go away.'

And with the dignity of a queen, unhurried, and taking Anne Saville with her, she walked down the riverside steps to her barge. Scarcely daring to breathe until it slipped away from the bank, she looked back and saw the torches clearly, saw the dark mass of people, and thought for a moment of what would have happened to her if she had fallen into their hands.

Silently moved the barge; down the river it went towards Greenwich. Anne Saville was white and trembling, sobbing, but Lady Anne Rochford appeared calm.

She could not forget the howls of rage, and she felt heavy with sadness. She had dreamed of herself a queen, riding through the streets of London, acclaimed on all sides. 'Queen Anne. Good Queen Anne!' She wanted to be respected and admired.

'Nan Bullen, the whore! We'll not have a whore on the throne. . . . Queen Katharine for ever!'

'I will win their respect,' she told herself. 'I must . . . I must! One day . . . one day they shall love me.'

Swiftly went the barge. She was exhausted when she reached the palace; her face was white and set, more haughty, more imperious, more queenly than when she had left to join the river-side party.

*   *   *

There was a special feast in the dormitory at Horsham. The girls had been giggling together all day.

'I hear,' said one to Catherine Howard, 'that this is a special occasion for you. There is a treat in store for you!'

Catherine, wide-eyed, listened. What? she wondered.

Isabel was smiling secretly; they were all in the secret but Catherine.

She had her lesson that day, and found Manox less adventurous than usual. The Duchess dozed, tapped her foot, admonished Catherine – for it was true she stumbled over her playing. Manox sat upright beside her – the teacher rather than the admiring and passionate friend. Catherine knew then how much she looked forward to the lessons.

She whispered to him: 'I have offended you?'

'Offended me! Indeed not; you could never do aught but please me.'

'Methought you seemed aloof.'

'I am but your instructor in the virginals,' he whispered. 'It has come to me that were the Duchess to discover we are friends, she would be offended; she might even stop the lessons. Would that make you very unhappy, Catherine?'

'Indeed it would!' she said guilelessly. 'More than most things I love music.'

'And you do not dislike your teacher?'

'You know well that I do not.'

'Let us play. The Duchess is restive; she will hear our talking at any moment now.'

She played. The Duchess's foot tapped in a spritely way; then it slowed down and stopped.

'I think of you continually,' said Manox. 'But with fear.'

'Fear?'

'Fear that something might happen to stop these lessons.'

'Oh, nothing must happen!'

'And yet how easily it could! Her Grace has but to decide that she would prefer you to have another teacher.'

'I would beg her to let you stay.'

His eyes showed his alarm.

'You should not do that, Catherine!'

'But I should! I could not bear to have another teacher.'

'I have been turning over in my mind what I would say to you today. We must go cautiously, Catherine. Why, if Her Grace knew of our . . . our friendship . . .'

'Oh, we will be careful,' said Catherine.

'It is sad,' he said, 'for only here do we meet, under the Duchess's eyes.'

He would talk no more. When she would have spoken, he said: 'Hush! Her Grace will awaken. In future, Catherine, I shall appear to be distant to you, but mistake me not, though I may seem merely your cold, hard master, my regard for you will be as deep as ever.'

Catherine felt unhappy; she thrived on caresses and demonstrations of affection, and so few came her way. When the Duchess dismissed her, she returned to the young ladies' apartments feeling deflated and sad at heart. She lay on her bed and drew the curtains round it; she thought of Manox's dark eyes and how on several occasions he had leaned close to her and kissed her swiftly.

In the dormitory she could hear the girls laughing together, preparing for tonight. She heard her own name mentioned amidst laughter.

'A surprise . . .'

'Why not . . .'

'Safer too . . .'

She did not care for their surprises; she cared only that Manox would kiss her no more. Then it occurred to her that he had merely liked her as a young and attractive man might like a little girl. It was not the same emotion as the older people felt for each other; that emotion of which Catherine thought a good deal, and longed to experience. She must live through the weary years of childhood before that could happen; the thought made her melancholy.

Through her curtains she listened to running footsteps. She heard a young man's voice; he had brought sweetmeats and dainties for the party tonight, he said. There were exclamations of surprise and delight.

'But how lovely!'

'I declare I can scarce keep my hands off them.'

'Tonight is a special occasion, didst know? Catherine's coming of age. . . .'

What did they mean? They could laugh all they liked; she was not interested in their surprises.

Evening came. Isabel insisted on drawing back the curtains of Catherine's bed.

'I am weary tonight,' said Catherine. 'I wish to sleep.'

'Bah!' laughed Isabel. 'I thought you would wish to join in the fun! Great pains have I taken to see that you should enjoy this night.'

'You are very kind, but really I would rather retire.'

'You know not what you say. Come, take a little wine.'

The guests began to arrive; they crept in, suppressing their laughter. The great room was filled with the erotic excitement which was always part of these entertainments. There were slapping and kisses and tickling and laughter; bed curtains pulled back and forth, entreaties for caution, entreaties for less noise.

'You'll be the death of me, I declare!'

'Hush! Her Grace . . .'

'Her Grace is snoring most elegantly. I heard her.'

'People are often awakened by their snores!'

'The Duchess is. I've seen it happen.'

'So has Catherine, has she not, when she is having her lesson on the virginals with Henry Manox!'

That remark seemed to be the signal for great laughter, as though it were the most amusing thing possible.

Catherine said seriously: 'That is so. Her snores do awaken her.'

The door opened. There was a moment's silence. Catherine's heart began to hammer with an odd mixture of fear and delight. Henry Manox came into the room.

'Welcome!' said Isabel. Then: 'Catherine, here is your surprise!'

Catherine raised herself, and turned first red, then white. Manox went swiftly to her and sat on her bed.

'I had no notion . . .' began Catherine breathlessly.

'We decided it should be a secret. . . . You are not displeased to see me?'

'I . . . of course not!'

'Dare I hope that you are pleased?'

'Yes, I am pleased.'

His black eyes flashed. He said: ''Twas dangerous, little

Catherine, to kiss you there before the Duchess. I did it because of my need to kiss you.'

She answered: 'It is dangerous here.'

'Bah!' he said. 'I would not fear the danger here . . . among so many. And I would have you know, Catherine, that no amount of danger would deter me.'

Isabel came over.

'Well, my children? You see how I think of your happiness!'

'This was your surprise, Isabel?' said Catherine.

'Indeed so. Are you not grateful, and is it not a pleasant one?'

'It is,' said Catherine.

One of the young gentlemen came over with a dish of sweetmeats, another with wine.

Catherine and Manox sat on the edge of Catherine's bed, holding hands, and Catherine thought she had never been so excited nor so happy, for she knew that she had stepped right out of an irksome childhood into womanhood, where life was perpetually exciting and amusing.

Manox said: 'We can be prim now before Her Grace, and what care I! I shall be cold and aloof, and all the time you will know that I long to kiss you.' Thereupon he kissed her and she kissed him. The wine was potent; the sweetmeats pleasant. Manox put an arm about Catherine's waist.

Darkness came to the room, as on these occasions lights were never used for fear they should be detected in their revels.

Manox said: 'Catherine, I would be alone with you completely. . . . Let us draw these curtains.' And so saying he drew the curtains, and they were shut in, away from the others.

* * *

October mists hung over Calais. Anne was reminded of long ago feasting at Ardres and Guisnes, for then, as now, Francis and Henry had met and expressed their friendship; then Queen Katharine had been his Queen; now the chief lady from England was the Marchioness of Pembroke, Anne herself. Anne felt more at ease than she had for four years. Never had she felt this same certainty that her ambition would be realized. The King was ardent as ever, impatient with the long delay; Thomas Cromwell had wily schemes to present to His Majesty; there was something ruthless about the man; he was the sort one would employ to do any deed, however dangerous, however murky – and, provided the reward was great enough, one felt the deed would be done.

So, at the highest peak of glory she had so far reached, she could enjoy the pomp and ceremony of this visit to France, which was being conducted as a visit of a king and his queen. The King was ready to commit to the Tower any who did not pay her full honour. When, a month ago, she had been created Marchioness of Pembroke she had acquired with this high honour the establishment of a queen. She must have her train-bearer, her ladies of the bedchamber, her maids of honour, her gentlemen-in-waiting, her officers, and at least thirty domestics for her own use. What Henry wished the world to know was that the only thing that kept the Marchioness from being Queen in name was the marriage ceremony. 'By God!' said Henry to Anne. 'That shall take place before you are much older, sweetheart!'

They had stayed four days at Boulogne, and there Anne had met with some slight rebuff, being unable to attend the festivities which the French arranged for Henry, as the French ladies had not come with Francis. It was understandable that Francis's wife should not come, for, on the death of Claude he had married Charles's sister Eleanor, and Henry was known to have said, when the visit was being discussed, that he would rather see a devil than a lady in Spanish dress. The Queen of France therefore could not come. There remained Francis's sister, the Queen of Navarre, but she had pleaded illness. Consequently there were no ladies of the French court to greet Henry and his Marchioness. Doubtless it was a slight, but such slights would be quickly remedied once Anne wore a crown.

Now they were back at Calais and very soon, with her

ladies, Anne would go down to the great hall for the masked ball; she must however wait until supper was concluded, since the banquet was attended only by men. Contentedly she browsed, thinking of the past months, thinking of that state ceremony at Windsor, when the King had made her Marchioness of Pembroke – the first woman ever to be created a peer of the realm. What a triumph that had been! And how she, with her love of admiration and pomp, of which she was the centre, had enjoyed every minute of it! Ladies of noble birth, who previously had thought themselves so far above her, had been forced to attend her in all humility; Lady Mary Howard to carry her state robes; the Countesses of Rutland and Sussex to conduct her to the King; my lords of Norfolk and Suffolk with the French ambassador to attend the King in the state apartments. And all this ceremony that they might do honour to Anne Boleyn. She pictured herself afresh, in her surcoat of crimson velvet that was lined with ermine, her lovely hair flowing; herself kneeling before the King while he very lovingly and tenderly placed the coronet on the brow of his much loved Marchioness.

And then to France, with Wyatt in their train, and her uncle Norfolk and, best of all, George. With George and Wyatt there, she had felt secure and happy. Wyatt loved her as he ever did, though now he dared not show his love. He poured it out in his poetry.

> 'Forget not! O, forget not this!—
> How long ago hath been, and is,
> The mind that never meant amiss—
> Forget not yet!
>
> Forget not then thine own approved,
> The which so long hath thee so loved,
> Whose steadfast faith yet never moved:
> Forget not this!'

She quoted those words as her ladies helped to dress her. Wyatt would never forget; he asked her not to. She smiled happily. No, she would not forget Wyatt; but she was happy tonight for she was assured of the King's steadfastness in his intention to marry her. He had declared this, but actions speak so much louder than words; would he have created her Marchioness of Pembroke, would he have brought her to France if he were not even more determined to make her his Queen than he had been two years ago? She felt strong and full of power, able to bind him to her, able to keep him. How could she help but be happy, knowing herself so loved! George was her friend; Wyatt had said he would never forget. Poor Wyatt! And the King had met the disapproval of his people, even faced the possibility of a tottering throne, rather than relinquish her.

Courage made her eyes shine the brighter, made her cheeks to glow. Tonight she was dressed in masquing costume; her gown was of cloth of gold with crimson tinsel satin slashed across it in unusual fashion, puffed with cloth of silver and ornamented with gold laces. All the ladies were dressed in this fashion, and they would enter the hall masked, so that none should know who was who. And then, after the dancing, Henry himself would remove the masks, and the ladies would be exhibited with national pride, for they had been chosen for their beauty.

The Countess of Derby came in to tell her it was time they went down, and four ladies in crimson satin, who were to lead them into the hall, were summoned, and they descended the stairs.

There was an expectant hush as they entered the hall which at great cost Henry had furnished specially for this occasion. The hangings were of tissue of silver and gold; and the seams of these hangings had been decorated with silver, pearls and stones.

Each masked lady was to select her partner, and Anne chose the King of France.

Francis had changed a good deal since Anne had last seen him; his face was lined and debauched; she had heard alarming stories of him when she had been in France, and she remembered one of these was of the daughter of a mayor at whose house Francis had stayed during one of his campaigns. He had fancied the girl, and she, dreading his advances and knowing too well his reputation, had ruined her looks with acid.

Francis said he could think of no more delight to follow supper than the English King's idea of a ball in which the ladies were masked.

'One is breathless with suspense, awaiting that moment when the masks are removed.' He tried to peer lasciviously beneath hers, but laughingly she replied that she was surprised he should be breathless. 'It is the inexperienced, not the connoisseur, is it not, who is more likely to be reduced to such a state?'

'Even connoisseurs are deeply moved by masterpieces, Madam!'

'This is what our lord King would doubtless call French flattery.'

' 'Tis French truth nevertheless.'

Henry watched her, jealous and alert, knowing well the French King's reputation, distrusting him, disliking to see him in conversation with Anne.

Francis said: 'It is indeed exciting to contemplate that we have the Lady Anne here with us tonight. I declare I long to see the face that so enchants my brother of England.'

'Your curiosity will be satisfied ere long,' she said.

'I knew the lady once,' he said, feigning not to know it was with none other that he now danced.

'That must have been very long ago.'

'A few years. But such a lady, Madam, one would never forget, you understand.'

She said: 'Speak French, if you wish it. I know the language.'

He spoke French; he was happier in it. He told her she spoke it enchantingly. He told her that he would wager she was more fair than the Lady Anne herself, for he had never set eyes on such a lithesome figure, nor heard such a melodious voice; and he trusted she had the fairest face in England and France, for he would be disappointed if she had not!

Anne, feeling Henry's eyes upon her, rejoiced in Henry.

236

He was a king and a great king; she could not have endured Francis for all the kingdoms in the world.

Henry, impatient of watching, would now remove the masks; and did so, going first to Anne.

'Your Majesty has been dancing with the Marchioness of Pembroke,' he told Francis, who declared himself astonished and delighted.

Henry moved on, leaving Anne with Francis.

'And what did I say of my old friend, little Anne Boleyn?' he said.

Anne laughed. 'Your Majesty was fully aware with whom he danced.'

'I should have known that one so full of grace, so pleasant to the eye and the ear, could be none other than she who will soon, I trust, be my sister of England. I congratulate myself that she chose to dance with me.'

'Ceremony, as Your Majesty will well understand, demanded it.'

'You were ever unkind, fair lady! That I well remember.'

'Tell me of your sister.'

They talked long together; Anne's laughter rang out now and then, for they had many reminiscences to share of the French court, and each could bring back memories to the other.

Henry watched, half proud, half angry. He had ever been jealous of Francis; he wondered whether to join them or leave them together. He did not care to see Anne in such close conversation with the lecher Francis, and yet it must be so for he was the King of France, and honour shown to Anne was honour shown to Henry. Francis's approval at Rome could mean a good deal, for though Charles was the most important man in Europe, might not Henry and Francis together carry more weight than Katharine's nephew?

The dance broke up; the ladies retired. Henry talked with his royal guest. Francis suggested he should marry Anne without the Pope's consent. Henry did not see how this could be, but enjoyed such talk; it was pleasant to think he had French support behind him.

He went to Anne's chamber, and dismissed her ladies.

'You were indeed a queen tonight!' he said.

'I trust I did not disgrace my King.'

She was gay tonight, savouring the success of the evening; adorable in her costume of cloth of gold and crimson.

He went to her and put his arms about her.

'The dresses were the same, but you stood out among them all. Had one not known who you were, it would have been easily seen that you were she who should be Queen.'

'You are very gracious to me.'

'And you are glad I love you, eh?'

She was so very happy this night that she wanted to shower happiness all about her; and on whom should it fall but on her royal benefactor!

'I was never happier in my life!' she said.

Later, when she lay in his arms, he confessed to jealousy of the French King.

'You seemed to like him too well, sweetheart.'

'Would you have had me ungracious to him? If I seemed to like him, it was because he was your guest.'

'Methought you appeared to coquette with him a little.'

'I did only what I thought would please you.'

' 'Twould never please me, Anne, to see your smiles given to another!'

'My smiles! Bah! If I smiled too warmly then 'twas because I compared him with you and was happy in the comparing.'

Henry was overjoyed.

'I declare he puts on years as one would put on state robes; he is weighed down with them. I never thought him handsome. . . .'

'Debauchery is apparent in his face,' said Anne.

Henry's prudish little mouth lifted into a smile.

'I would not care to own his reputation!'

Then she amused him with an imitation of the French King, recounting what he had said and what she had answered; and the King laughed and was very happy with her.

In the morning Francis sent Anne a jewel as a gift. Henry examined it, was delighted with its worth, and jealous that it had not come from himself.

He gave her more jewellery; he gave of his own and Katharine's and even his sister's, Mary of Suffolk. The King was more deeply in love than ever.

When it was time for them to leave Calais there was a high wind and it was unsafe to cross the Channel. Anne was reminded of that stay at Dover; but then she had been a seven-year-old girl of no importance whatever, trying to listen to those about her and learn something of life. Pleasant it was to think back, when one had come so far.

They beguiled the days with dice and cards, at which the King lost heavily and Anne almost always won; nor did it matter if she lost, for the King would pay her debts. One of the players was a handsome young man named Francis Weston, for whom Anne conceived a genuine liking, and he for her. They played by day and danced at night; they were hilarious over the cards; there was much fun to be had at 'Pope Julius', the favourite game of the court, with its allusions to matrimony, intrigue and the Pope – they all found it so apt in view of the pending divorce. Thus passed the days, with Anne happier than she had been since deciding to occupy the throne, more secure, more content.

* * *

The old year was dying, and Christmas came. Still the Pope was adamant; still action hung fire. Four years ago Anne had become the King's mistress, and now, at Christmas of the year 1532, still she waited to be his Queen.

She was pale and listless.

'Does aught ail thee, sweetheart?' the King asked her.

'Much ails me,' she told him.

The King was alarmed.

'Darling, tell me instantly. I would know what is wrong, and right it.'

She said very clearly: 'I fear he who should follow Your Majesty as King of England will after all be but a bastard.'

Henry was beside himself with the importance of this news. Anne was pregnant! A son was what he wanted more than anything – next to Anne herself – on Earth. Anne, who should have been the Queen long ere this – and had they married she would have given him a son by now, for it had ever been her wish that no children should be born to them until she was Queen – Anne was with child. His child! His *son*! He who should be King of England!

'And by God,' said the King, 'he shall be!' Now he was all tenderness, all loving care; that body which sheltered his son had become doubly precious. 'Fret not, sweetheart. Be done with fretting for evermore. I declare I'll endure this delay no longer. I'll be cut free from that canting Pope, or, by God, much blood will flow!'

Anne could smile; this was the happiest thing that could have happened; this would decide him. She was determined that her son should be born in wedlock; and so was Henry.

Well he remembered how he had looked with something like fury on his son, the Duke of Richmond – that fine boy so like himself, who, had he been born of Katharine instead of Elizabeth Blount would have spared him much heart-burning. No! There should be no repetition of that!

He called Cromwell to him; he would see Cranmer; he would leave nothing undone, no way out unexplored. Divorce he must have, and quickly, for Anne was pregnant with a son.

Henry's determination was vital; it swept all opposition before it; none who valued his future, or his head, dared go against him, whilst those who worked with him and were blessed with success were sure of favour.

Warham had died in August, and who should replace him but Cranmer, the man who, when the idea of divorce was first being considered, had the right sow by the ear! The Archbishopric of Canterbury could therefore be placed in good hands. Then Cromwell: Cromwell's daring scheme of separating England from Rome, which had on first hearing seemed too wild to be put into action, now presented itself as the only sure solution. Cromwell, unlike so many, suffered not at all from a superstitious dread of consequences; he was not by any means scrupulous; he could bring in evidence against Rome as fast as his master cared to receive it. What had Henry to lose by the separation? he demanded of his King. And see what he had to gain!

Henry's eyes glistened, contemplating the dissolution of those storehouses of treasure, the monasteries . . . treasures which would naturally be thrown into the King's chests. The state would be free of Rome; it would be strong, beholden to no one. Moreover, free from the Pope, why should Henry care for his verdict on the divorce? Henry, all-powerful, might make his own divorce! The Continent, in the grip of the reformation, had weakened the Church. Everywhere in Europe men were challenging the Pope's authority; a new religion was springing up. It was simple; it merely meant that the headship was transferred from the Pope to Henry. Henry had hesitated, turning this truly delightful plan over and over in his mind. He had to consider his conscience, which troubled him incessantly. He was afraid of isolation. How would it affect him politically? Wolsey – the wisest man he had ever known – would have opposed Cromwell's scheme; he did not like Cromwell, he considered him a knave. Was Cromwell right? Could Cromwell be trusted? Cromwell might be a knave, but was he a wise man?

Henry shilly-shallied. He had always considered his accession to be influenced by the Holy See, and through the Holy See, by God; but he was ever ready to support an idea he liked. He was superstitious to a great degree; he had looked upon the Pope as holy; it was not easy for a superstitious man with a conscience to overthrow a lifetime's tradition. He was afraid of God's wrath, although he did not fear the vacillating Clement. He had been proud of his title 'Defender of the Faith'. Who was it who had written the most brilliant denouncement of Luther? Henry of England. How could he then overthrow that which he had so ardently defended!

Cromwell had talked slyly and persuasively, for if he would keep in favour, this matter of the divorce must be settled, and he saw no way of settling it but this. He explained this was nothing to do with Lutherism; the religion of the country remained the same; it was merely the headship of the church that was involved. Was it not more seemly that a nation's great good King should lead its Church?

Henry tried to justify this procedure morally. Once he had

made a case for the break-away, it would be done. Warham had died at the most convenient moment; that was a sign perhaps. Who better to head a country's Church than its King! Anne was pregnant. This was a sign. He must have the divorce if he was to legitimize Anne's child. The time was short. There was no longer occasion for conferences, for shilly-shallying. Sir Thomas More, a few months previously, had retired from the office of Chancellor. More had ever been one to discountenance Henry. He liked the man, he could not help it, but he had been rather shaken when More had said, on taking office, that he would 'first look unto God and after God to his Prince,' for that was a most uncomfortable thing for a minister to say; but More was an uncomfortable man; he was beloved by the people, he was honest, religious in that true sense to which so few do, or even try to attain. He had calmly walked out and gone home to his family and friends; he begged to be allowed to do this on the plea of ill health, and Henry had to accept that plea; but he had always liked the man, and he knew his lack of ease was more mental than bodily. More could not reconcile himself to the divorce; that was why he had resigned and gone to the peace of his Chelsea home. The King had outwardly taken his resignation in good part; he had visited Chelsea; but at the same time he was disturbed on More's account, since More was known as a good man, and the King would have preferred him to be less arbitrary.

Cromwell was whispering in the King's ear. Cromwell was smart; Cromwell was cunning; any delicate job could be left to Cromwell.

Divorce! Why divorce? When a marriage has not been valid, what need of divorce? He had never been married to Katharine! She was his brother's wife, and therefore the ceremony was illegal.

Henry dared delay no longer. Anne's child must be legitimate. So, on a January day, he summoned one of his chaplains to a quiet attic of White Hall, and when the chaplain arrived, he found there – much to his astonishment, for he had been told he was merely to celebrate mass – the King attended by two grooms of the chamber, one of them being

242

that Norris whose sympathy for Wolsey had lightened the Cardinal's last hours. The chaplain had not been there more than a few minutes when who should arrive but the Marchioness of Pembroke accompanied by Anne Saville!

The King then took the chaplain aside, and told him he would be required to marry him to the Marchioness.

The chaplain began to tremble at this, looking fearfully about him, at which the King stamped impatiently. Greatly did the chaplain fear the King, but more so did he fear Rome. Henry, seeing himself in a quandary, hastily told the man that the Pope had granted the divorce, and he need fear nothing. The ceremony was over before the light of morning, and all the party went secretly away.

Henry was disturbed and not a little alarmed; he had done a bold thing, and not even Cranmer knew he had intended to do it in this way. For, by marrying Anne as he had, he had irrevocably broken with Rome and placed himself at the head of the English Church. The Council could do nothing but accept this state of affairs; Henry was their King. But what of the people, that growling mass of the populace who had come through pestilence and poverty, and were less inclined to bend the knee than his courtiers? In the streets they murmured against Anne. Some murmured against the King.

If the King trembled, Anne was triumphant. She was Queen after four years of waiting; Queen of England. Already she carried the King's child within her. She was mentally exhausted by the long struggle, and only now did she realize what a struggle it had been, what nervous energy she had put into maintaining it, how she had feared she would never reach this pinnacle of power. She could now relax and remember that she was to be a mother. Love was not to be denied her then. She carried a child, and the child would inherit the throne of England. She slept peacefully, dreaming the child – a son – was already born, that her attendants laid it in her arms; and her heart was full of love for this unborn child. 'September!' she said on waking. 'But September is such a long way off!'

George Boleyn was preparing for a journey; he would leave

the palace before dawn. Jane came gliding to him as he buttoned his coat.

'George . . . where are you going?'

'A secret mission,' he said.

'So early?'

'So early.'

'Could I not accompany you?'

He did not answer such folly.

'George, is it very secret? Tell me where you go.'

He contemplated her; he always felt more kindly towards her when he was going to leave her.

'It is a secret, so if I tell you, you must keep it entirely to yourself.'

She clasped her hands, feeling suddenly happy because he smiled in such a friendly way.

'I will, George! I swear I will! I can see it is good news.'

'The best!'

'Tell me quickly, George.'

'The King and Anne were married this morning. I go to carry the news to the King of France.'

'The King . . . married to Anne! But the Pope has not given the divorce, so how can that be possible?'

'With God – and the King – all things are possible.'

She was silent, not wishing to spoil this slight friendliness he was showing towards her.

'So you are the Queen's brother now, George, and I am her sister-in-law!'

'That is so. I must away. I must leave the palace before the day begins.'

She watched him go, smiling pleasantly; then all her bitter jealousy burst forth. It was so unfair. So she was Queen of England, and she would be more arrogant than ever now. Why should a man displace his wife because he tired of her!

* * *

A marriage had been arranged for Isabel; she was leaving the Duchess's retinue. Catherine was not really sorry, never having liked Isabel; and then she was too absorbed in Henry Manox to care much what happened to anyone else.

Manox had been to the dormitory on several occasions; he was recognized now as Catherine's lover. There was much petting and caressing and whispering, and Catherine found this a delightful state of affairs. She was grown up at last, revelling in intrigue, receiving little gifts from Manox; she never wrote to him, since she had never been taught how to write properly; but oral messages were exchanged between her and Manox by way of their friends.

During the lessons they were very conventional in their behaviour – which seemed to Catherine a great joke. The old Duchess might fall into a deep sleep, and all Manox and Catherine would do was exchange mischievous glances.

'I declare, Manox,' said the Duchess on one occasion, 'you are too stern with the child. You do nothing but scold!'

They would laugh at that when she lay in his arms in her bed with the curtains drawn. Catherine, though a child in years, was highly sexed, precocious, a budding woman; over-excitable, generous, reckless, this affair with Manox seemed the high spot of her life. He said he had loved her ever since he had first set eyes on her; Catherine was sure she had loved him ever since her very first lesson. Love was the excuse for everything they did. He brought her sweetmeats and ribands for her hair; they laughed and joked and giggled with the rest.

It was the Duchess who told Catherine that she was engaging another woman in place of Isabel.

'She is from the village, and her name is Dorothy Barwicke. She will take Isabel's place among the ladies. She is a serious young lady, as Isabel was, and I feel I can trust her to keep you young people in some sort of order. I'll whisper something else to you, Catherine . . . We really are going to Lambeth ere the month is out! I declare I grow weary of the country, and now that my granddaughter is in truth the Queen . . .'

She never tired of talking of Anne, but Catherine who had loved to hear such talk was hardly interested now.

'Imagine poor old Katharine's face when he took Anne to

245

France! If ever a king proclaimed his queen, he did then! And I hear she was a great success. How I should have loved to see her dancing with the French King! Marchioness of Pembroke, if you please! I'll warrant Thomas – I beg his pardon, the Earl of Wiltshire – is counting what this means in gold. Oh, Thomas, Earl of Wiltshire, who would not have beautiful daughters!'

'Grandmother, will you really go to Lambeth?'

'Don't look so startled, child. Assuredly I shall go. Someone must assist at the dear Queen's coronation. I feel sure I shall be invited, in view of my rank and my relationship to Her Majesty the Queen.'

'And . . . will you take the whole household?' asked Catherine, her voice trembling. But the Duchess was too absorbed by her thoughts and plans for the coronation to notice that.

'What foolish questions you ask, child! What matter . . .'

'You would take your musicians, would you not, Grandmother? You would take me?'

'Ah! So that is what you are thinking, is it? You fear to be left out of the excitement. Never fear, Catherine Howard, I doubt not the Queen your cousin will find a place at court for you when you are ready.'

There was no satisfaction to be gained from the Duchess; in any case she changed her plans every day.

'Isabel! Isabel!' said Catherine. 'Do you think the whole household will remove to Lambeth?'

'Ah!' cried Isabel, who in view of her coming marriage was not interested in the Duchess's household. 'You are thinking of your lover!' She turned to Dorothy Barwicke, a dark woman with quick, curious eyes and a thin mouth. 'You would think Catherine Howard but a child, would you not? But that is not so; she has a lover; he visits her in our bedroom of nights. He is a very bold young man, and they enjoy life; do you not, Catherine?'

Catherine flushed and, looking straight at Dorothy Barwicke, said: 'I love Henry and he loves me.'

'Of course you do!' said Isabel. 'And a very loving little girl she is, are you not, Catherine? She is very virtuous, and

246

would not allow Manox in her bed an she did not love him!'

'And, loving him,' said Dorothy Barwicke, 'I'll warrant she finds it difficult to refuse his admittance.'

The two young women exchanged glances, and laughed.

'You will look after Catherine when I leave, will you not?' said Isabel.

'I do not need looking after.'

'Indeed you do not!' said Dorothy. 'Any young lady not yet in her teens, who entertains gentlemen in her bed at night, is quite able to look after herself, I'd swear!'

'Not gentle*men*,' said Isabel ambiguously. 'It is only Manox.'

Catherine felt they were mocking her, but she always felt too unsure of all the ladies to accuse them of so doing.

'I shall expect you to look after Catherine when I have gone,' said Isabel.

'You may safely leave that to me.'

Catherine lived in agony of fear while the Duchess set the household bustling with preparations for her journey to Lambeth. She talked perpetually of 'my granddaughter, the Queen', and having already heard that she was to attend the coronation – fixed for May – was anxious to get to Lambeth in good time, for there would be her state robes to be put in order, and many other things to be seen to; and she hoped to have a few informal meetings with the Queen before the great event.

Catherine was wont to lie in bed on those nights when there were no visitors to the dormitory and ask herself what she would do were the Duchess to decide not to take Manox. Catherine loved Manox because she needed to love someone; there were two passions in Catherine's life; one was music, and the other was loving. She had loved her mother and lost her; she had loved Thomas Culpepper, and lost him; now she loved Manox. And on all these people had she lavished unstintingly her capacity for loving, and that was great. Catherine must love; life for her was completely devoid of interest without love. She enjoyed the sensational excitement of physical love in spite of her youth; but her love for Manox was not entirely a physical emotion.

247

She loved to give pleasure as well as to take it, and there was nothing she would not do for those she loved. All that she asked of life was to let her love; and she was afraid of life, for it seemed to her that her love was ill-fated; first her mother, then Thomas Culpepper, now Manox. She was terrified that she would have to go to Lambeth without Manox.

There came a day when she could no longer bear the suspense. She asked her grandmother outright.

'Grandmother, what of my lessons at Lambeth?'

'What of them, child?'

'Shall Henry Manox accompany us, that he may continue to instruct me?'

The Duchess's reply sent a shiver down her spine.

'Dost think I would not find thee a teacher at Lambeth?'

'I doubt not that you would, but when one feels that one can do well with one teacher . . .'

'Bah! I know best who will make a good teacher. And why do you bother me with lessons and teachers? Dost not realize that this is to be the coronation of your own cousin Anne!'

Catherine could have wept with mortification, and her agony of mind continued.

Manox came often to the dormitory.

'Do you think I could ever leave you?' he asked. 'Why, should you go to Lambeth without me I would follow.'

'And what would happen to you if you so disobeyed?'

'Whatever the punishment it would be worth it to be near you, if but for an hour!'

But no! Catherine would not hear of that. She remembered the tales Doll Tappit had gleaned of Walter the warder. She remembered then that, though she ran wild through the house and her clothes were so shabby as to be almost those of a beggar, she was Catherine Howard, daughter of a great and noble house, while he was plain Henry Manox, instructor at the virginals. Though he seemed so handsome and clever to her, there would be some – and her grandmother and her dreaded uncle the Duke among them – who would consider they had done great wrong in loving. What if they, both, should be committed to the Tower! It was for Manox she trembled, for Catherine's love was complete. She could endure separation, but not to think of Manox's body cramped in the Little Ease, or rotting, and the food of rats in the Pit. She cried and begged that he would do nothing rash; and he laughed and said did she not think he did something rash every night that he came to her thus, for what did she think would happen to him if her grandmother were to hear of their love?

Then was Catherine seized with fresh fears. Why must the world, which was full of so many delights, hold so much that was cruel! Why did there have to be stern grandmothers and terrifying uncles! Why could not everybody understand what a good thing it was to love and be loved in this most exciting and sensational way which she had recently discovered!

Then Catherine found the world was indeed a happy place, for when she left for Lambeth in her grandmother's retinue, Manox was in it too.

* * *

Lambeth was beautiful in the spring, and Catherine felt she had never been so completely happy in her life. The fruit trees in the orchards which ran down to the river's brink were in blossom; she spent whole days wandering through the beautiful gardens, watching the barges go down the river.

With Manox at Lambeth, they were often able to meet out of doors; the Duchess was even more lax than she had been at Horsham, so busy was she with preparations for the coronation. Anne visited her grandmother, and they sat together in the garden, the Duchess's eyes sparkling to contemplate her lovely granddaughter. She could not resist telling Anne how gratified she was, how lucky was the King, and how, deep in her heart, she had ever known this must happen.

Catherine was brought to greet her cousin.

'Your Majesty remembers this one?' asked the Duchess. 'She was doubtless but a baby when you last saw her.'

'I remember her well,' said Anne. 'Come hither, Catherine, that I may see you more closely.'

Catherine came, and received a light kiss on her cheek. Catherine still thought her cousin the most beautiful person she had ever seen, but she was less likely to idealize, because all her devotion was for Manox.

'Curtsey, girl!' thundered the Duchess. 'Do you not know that you stand before your Queen?'

Anne laughed. 'Oh, come! No ceremony in the family ... No, Catherine, please ...'

Anne thought, Poor little thing! She is pretty enough, but how unkempt she looks!

'Perhaps Your Majesty will find a place for her at court ...'

'Assuredly I will,' said Anne, 'but she is young yet.'

'On your knees, girl, and show some gratitude!'

'Grandmother,' laughed the Queen, 'I would have you remember this is but our family circle. I am weary of ceremony; let me drop it awhile. What do you like doing, Catherine? Are you fond of music?'

Catherine could glow when she talked of music. They remembered how they had once felt affection, which was spontaneous, for one another, and as they talked it came back to them.

After Catherine had been dismissed, Anne said: 'She is a sweet child, but a little gauche. I will send her some clothes; they could be altered to fit her.'

'Ah! You would dress up Catherine Howard! She is a romp, that child. And what a sheltered life she has led! I have kept her away in the country, perhaps too long.'

A new woman joined the Duchess's household while they were at Lambeth. Her name was Mary Lassells, and she was of lower birth than most of the Duchess's attendants; she had been nurse to Lord William Howard's first child, and on the death of his wife, the Duchess had agreed to take her in. During her first week in the Duchess's establishment, Mary Lassells met a young man who was dark and handsome with bold roving eyes, and to whom she felt immediately drawn. She was sitting on an overturned tree-trunk in the Lambeth orchard, when he strolled by.

'Welcome, stranger!' he said. 'Or am I wrong in calling you stranger? I declare I should recognize you, had I ever seen you before!'

And so saying he sat down beside her.

'You are right in supposing me to be a stranger. I have been in the Duchess's establishment but a few days. You have been here long?'

'I made the journey up from Norfolk.'

His bold eyes surveyed her. She was well enough, but not worth risking trouble with little Catherine, who, with her naïvety, her delight, her willingness, was giving him the most amusing and absorbing affair he had enjoyed for a long time.

'I rejoice to see you here,' he continued.

'Indeed, sir, you are very kind.'

'It is you who are kind, to sit thus beside me. Tell me, how do you like it here?'

She did not greatly like it, she told him; she found the behaviour of some of the ladies shocking. She was rather bitter, acutely feeling herself to be low-born, inexperienced in the ways of etiquette, having been merely a nurse before she entered the Duchess's household. She had been delighted when she was offered the position, and owing to the unconventional ways of the household Mary had been accepted into it without ceremony. But among these ladies she felt awkward – awkward in speech, awkward in manners; she fancied that they watched her, sneered at her behind her back. This was pure imagination on Mary's part, for in actual fact the ladies were much too absorbed in their own affairs to give much attention to her; but she nursed her grievances, aired them to herself with great bitterness, until they grew out of all proportion to the truth. She occupied a bed in the dormitory with the rest, but there had been no feasting nor love-making in her presence yet, as at the Lambeth house the dormitory was not so conveniently situated. Still, she could not help but notice the levity of the ladies; young gentlemen had looked in on some of them during the day; she had seen many a kiss and indications of greater familiarity. Mary had thought bitterly: And these are those who would look down on a good woman such as I am!

She told him that she did not like what she had so far seen of the conduct of those who were called ladies.

He raised his eyebrows.

'There is much familiarity between them and the young men.'

Manox laughed inwardly, thinking it would be amusing to lead her on. He feigned shocked surprise.

Warming to the subject, she went on: 'Gentlemen – or those who would call themselves gentlemen – look in at the dormitory at all hours of the day. I was never more startled in my life. There was one, who would doubtless call herself a lady, changing her dress, and a gentleman looked round the door and she pretended to hide herself by running behind a screen and was much delighted when he peeped over the top. I declare I wondered whether I should not go at once to Her Grace!'

Manox looked sharply at her. The severely practical head-dress, the thin disapproving lips, the pale eyes – all these belonged to a bearer of tales. She was a virgin, he doubted not – a virgin of necessity! he thought cynically; and of such material were made the tale-bearers, the really dangerous women.

He laid a hand over hers. She started, and a flush spread over her face, beginning at her modest collar and running swiftly to her flat and simply-arranged hair. She was nearer to being pretty at that moment than she would ever be.

He said gently: 'I understand . . . of course I understand. But would you take a word of advice?'

She turned her eyes upon him, smiling, thinking him the handsomest and most charming person she had met since entering the house.

'I am ever ready to take good advice,' she said.

'It would be most unwise to carry tales of this matter to Her Grace.'

'Why so?'

'You have told me that you were a nurse before you came

here. I am but a musician. I instruct ladies at whichever musical instrument it is decreed they shall learn to play.' His voice became caressing. 'You and I are but humble folk; do you think we should be believed? Nay! It is you who would be turned from the house, were you to tell Her Grace what you have seen!'

This was fuel to the bitterness in her; she had lived in noble houses, and had longed to be one of the nobility; she saw every situation from this angle. I am as good as they are . . . Why should I have to serve them, just because I was born in a humble house, and they in castles!

'Well I can believe that the blame would be put on me, rather than on those delinquents.'

He leaned closer to her. 'Depend upon it, it most assuredly would! That is the way of life. Be silent about what you see, fair lady.'

'I cannot tell you what it means to me to have met you,' she said. 'Your sympathy warms me, gives me courage.'

'Then I am indeed glad that I walked this way.'

Mary Lassells was trembling with excitement. No young man had ever taken notice of her before. The eyes of this one were warm and friendly, one might say bold. Mary began to feel very happy, very glad that she had joined the Duchess's retinue after all.

'Do you often walk this way?' she asked.

He kissed her hand. 'We shall meet again ere long.'

She was anxious to make it definite. 'I shall doubtless walk here tomorrow.'

'That is well to know,' he said.

They walked through the orchards down to the river's edge. It was a lovely spring day, and she thought there had never been any scene more beautiful than that of the river gliding by the blossoming trees. The sun, she was sure, was warmer today, and the birds seemed to sing more joyously. Manox sang too; he sang pleasantly; music was his passion, the only one to which he could remain faithful through his life. Mary thought: He means he is happy too, to sing thus.

They went into the house. That encounter had changed Mary; everything to her looked different, and people looked at her and thought her less plain than they had imagined. She hummed the song which Manox had sung; she was pleasant and smiling, forgetting the social barriers between her and most of the others. She smiled in a kindly way on the Duchess's little granddaughter. It is well, thought Mary, that I am not of noble birth; a musician would be a tolerable match for me.

In less than a week she was rudely awakened. She had seen Manox on several occasions, and on each he had continued to charm her. On this day she went to the dormitory in the middle of the morning, having been down to the orchards, having sat for a full hour on the overturned tree-trunk, waiting in vain. She opened the door of the dormitory; the curtains were drawn back from most of the beds, and on one in a corner – young Catherine Howard's – sat the little girl, and with her Henry Manox. They sat side by side, their arms about each other; he was caressing the child, and Catherine was flushed and laughing. It was a great shock to Mary; she stood still, staring at them. Then Manox rose and said: 'Ah! Here is Mistress Lassells!'

Mary stood, struggling with her emotions, thinking: How foolish of me! He likes children; he doubtless came here on some errand, saw the child, and made much of her. But what business could Henry Manox have in the ladies' dormitory? And had he not known that this was the hour when she would be waiting to see him in the orchards!

Manox was plausible. In his numerous love affairs he had found himself in many a delicate situation; with grace he had ever managed to set matters right, if only temporarily.

He went swiftly to Mary and said to her: 'I had a message to bring here; I am really but a servant; and when I came here, the little girl needed comforting.'

She accepted his explanation; because she felt Catherine to be but a child, it did not occur to her that they could possibly be lovers. She smiled again, quite happy. Manox thought, My God! She would be a vindictive woman! And he cursed himself for having light-heartedly indulged in this mild flirtation with her. She had been so prim, so seemingly virtuous, that he could not resist the temptation; he had wanted to show her that what she lacked was, not the desire to sin, but the opportunity.

He escaped, and the situation was saved; but this could not always be so, and he would not give up Catherine for Mary Lassells.

There came a night when Manox, unable to stay away longer, recklessly went to Catherine though he knew Mary would discover this. Mary pulled the curtains about her bed, and wept tears of bitter humiliation. If she had hated the world before she had met Manox, now she hated it a thousand times more; and her hatred was directed, not against Manox, but against Catherine Howard. The wanton! The slut! she thought. And she a great lady to be! A Howard! So much for the nobility – a cousin to the Queen! And who is the Queen? Another such as Catherine Howard. Why, in this wicked world does sin go unpunished and virtue unrewarded?

Her eyes were narrow with weeping. She would go to the Duchess at once, were it not that Manox would suffer. Catherine Howard would be beaten, possibly sent away, but they would hush the matter up so that scandal should not be brought to the house of Howard. It would be Manox who would suffer most, for he was low-born like herself, of no importance; it was such as they who suffered for the sins of the nobility.

Who knew that Manox might not come to his senses, that he might not learn to cherish virtue, that he might discard that vile slut, Catherine Howard, who was not yet in her teens and yet had sunk to the very depths of wickedness! Sexual immorality was surely the most violent form of sin; for such did one burn in hell. To steal and to murder were to commit evil crimes, it was true; but what crime could compare with the wickedness of Catherine Howard!

She would not tell though, for Manox's sake; she would hope that one day he would see his folly, that he would repent . . . that before the blossom gave way to leaves on the trees in the orchard, he would come to her and tell her he had been a fool.

He did not, and there was mockery in his eyes. One day

she met him by the river, and telling herself that she must save him from his folly, she went to him, and with burning eyes and lips that trembled demanded: 'Man, what meanest thou to play the fool of this fashion! Knowest thou not that an my lady of Norfolk knew of the love between thee and Mistress Howard she will undo thee? She is of a noble house; and if thou should'st marry her, some of her blood will kill thee.'

Manox threw back his head and laughed, knowing full well what had caused her to utter such warning, mocking her, laughing at her. He said that she need have no fear for him, since his intentions were strictly of a dishonourable nature.

Angry and humiliated, Mary went into the house. If Manox would not accept her warning against the folly of pursuing this affair, perhaps Catherine would. She found Catherine stitching at a piece of tapestry in the sewing-room.

'I would have speech with you, Mistress Howard.'

Catherine looked up; she knew little of Mary Lassells, and had not greatly liked what she did know, agreeing with most of the others that the woman was prudish and dull.

'Yes?' said Catherine.

'I have come to warn you. You are very young, and I do not think you realize what you do. What you do with Manox is . . . criminal!'

'I understand you not,' said Catherine haughtily, and would have moved away, but Mary caught her arm.

'You must listen. Manox is amusing himself with you. He jokes about your willingness.'

'You lie!' said Catherine.

'I have just come from him,' said Mary with a virtuous air, 'having wished – for indeed I feel it would be but Her Grace's pleasure – to beg him to cease his attentions to yourself. I pointed out to him what reckless folly this was, and how, if he married you, one of your house would surely work his ruin. He boasted that his intentions were only dishonourable.'

Catherine flushed hotly, hating the pale prim face of

Mary Lassells, suddenly afraid, suddenly seeing this beautiful love of hers in a different light. It was sordid now, not beautiful at all. She had been wrong to indulge in it. Manox despised her; many people would despise her; Heaven help her if what she had done should ever get to her grandmother's ears! But chiefly she suffered from Manox's words: His intentions were dishonourable! What a wicked thing for him to have said! Could it be that he was not the adoring, the faithful and gallant, the courteous lover she had believed him to be?

Catherine was hot with rage.

'Fie upon him!' she cried. 'Where is he now? I will go to him, and you shall come with me. I will demand of him whether you have spoken the truth.'

There was nothing Mary could do but conduct Catherine to him there in the orchards, where the thick trees helped to shield those who wished to meet clandestinely. Mary had one thought – and that to break up this foolish affair of Manox's with Catherine Howard. She visualized Manox's repentance, her own great understanding; a marriage between them would be so suitable.

Manox looked startled to see them both; Catherine flushed and angry, Mary smiling secretly.

'I would have you know,' said Catherine in such a fine temper that she could not control it, 'that I despise you, that I hate you, that I never wish to see you again!'

'Catherine!' gasped Manox. 'What does this mean?'

'I know what you have said to this ... woman, of me.'

He was shaken. There was something tremendously attractive about Catherine Howard; her complete enjoyment of physical contact made for his enjoyment; never had he known one so innocently abandoned and responsive; she was a lovely child; her youth was enchanting, and must add piquancy to the affair; he had never had such an experience. And he was not going to lose her if he could help it. He threw a venomous glance at Mary Lassells, which she saw, and which wounded her deeply.

'Catherine,' he said, and would have embraced her there in front of Mary Lassells, but she held off haughtily.

'Do not touch me! I would have you know that I shall never again allow you to do so.'

'I must make you understand,' said Manox, covering his face with his hands and forcing tears into his eyes. 'I love you entirely, Catherine. I have said nothing that could offend. How could I, when my only thought is for your happiness!'

She repeated what Mary had told her. Mary burst out spitefully: 'Thou canst not deny it, Manox, to my face!'

'I know not what I say,' said Manox, his voice shaking with anguish. 'All I know is that my passion for you so transports me beyond the bounds of reason that I wist not what I say!'

Catherine could never bear to see anyone in distress; her heart softened at once.

'I am very displeased,' she said, and it was obvious that she was weakening.

Ignoring Mary Lassells, Manox slipped an arm about Catherine; Mary, in bitter defeat, turned and ran into the house.

Catherine walked in friendly fashion through the orchards, listening to his protestations of love, but although she said she forgave him, it not being in her nature to harbour ill-feeling for long, as she was always ready to believe the best of people and could not happily see anyone suffer, she was shaken, and badly shaken.

Mary Lassells had made her see this love affair in a different light. She never felt the same towards Manox again; and, being Catherine, in need of love, she must look about her for a more worthy object on which to lavish her affection.

* * *

Every citizen who could find a boat to hold him was on the Thames that May morning; along the banks of the river the crowd thronged. Beggars had come into the city to view the procession, and pickpockets hoped to ensure a profitable day's work among the press of people. The taverns were full and over-flowing; at all points of vantage people stood, sat or knelt, mounted posts or one another's shoulders to get a good view of the celebrations in honour of Queen Anne's coronation.

From the river bank, Catherine watched with some of the ladies, among them Dorothy Barwicke and Mary Lassells. There was festivity and recklessness in the air today. All the ladies giggled and looked for someone with whom to flirt; they had decked themselves out in their gayest clothes in order to do honour to the new Queen. Most of the young people were ready to admire her; it was chiefly the old ones who continued to murmur against her, and even they were lethargic in their disapproval on this day. When she had been the King's mistress it was one thing; now she was Queen it was another. The King had married her; the Pope had not sanctioned the divorce; Rome considered the marriage illegal; but what matter! England was no longer under the Pope; it owed allegiance to none but its own great King. Weighty matters these, which the people did not fully understand; they worshipped in the same way as before, and the same religious rites were observed, so what matter! And even those who pitied sad Katharine and reviled flaunting, wicked Anne, enjoyed a day's pleasure. And this honour which the King would do to his newly made Queen was to be such a spectacle, so lavish in its display, as to outdo even Tudor splendour.

The Queen was to come from Greenwich to the Tower, and the coronation would take place at Westminster; there would be days of rejoicing, days of processions, and the citizens of London ever loved such occasions.

Mary Lassells would have liked to voice her opinions of the new Queen, but thought it wise to keep quiet. Here was another example of sin's being lauded and fêted; but she knew well enough the folly of talking too freely. The King was determined to have no opposition; already she had heard that the dungeons at the Tower of London were full of those who spoke rashly; well she knew that the instruments of torture were being over-worked. It was not for a humble person to run into danger.

Silly Catherine Howard was filled with childish glee, talking incessantly of her dear, beautiful cousin whom she loved devotedly. 'I declare I shall die of pride . . .' babbled Catherine Howard. 'I declare I can scarce wait for her royal barge . . .'

Mary Lassells talked with Dorothy Barwicke about the wickedness of Manox and Catherine. Dorothy listened and feigned disgust, not mentioning that she had carried many a message from Manox to Catherine, had helped to make their meetings easy, that she had taken over Isabel's task of advancing Catherine's love affair so that she, Catherine, might be involved in the practices which occurred in the ladies' apartments and thereby be prevented from carrying stories to her grandmother. Not, thought Dorothy, that Isabel need have feared. Catherine was no tale-bearer, but the last person in the world to wish to make trouble for others. With Mary Lassells it was quite another matter; Dorothy knew she must go cautiously with Mary.

Catherine's bright eyes had seen a little group of gentlemen along the river bank. The gentlemen looked interested in the party of young ladies, recognizing them as of the Duchess's retinue.

'I can tell you who they are,' whispered one laughing-eyed girl to Catherine, 'They are your uncle the Duke's young gentlemen.'

This was so, for the Duke of Norfolk kept in his household certain gentlemen of good birth and low fortune, most of whom could claim some connection – however distant – with himself. He called them his household troop; they were really pensioners; their only duty was to guard his interests wherever they might be, in time of war to follow him in the field, to back him in his quarrels, to be ever ready to defend him should the need arise. For this he paid them well, fed and clothed them, and gave them little to do – except when he should need them – but amuse themselves. The Earl of Northumberland had a similar retinue in his house; they had always had such, and found it difficult to discard this relic of the feudal system. The gentlemen, having nothing to do but amuse themselves, did this with gusto; they were a high-spirited group, reckless and daring, seeking adventure in any form.

It was a little band of these gentlemen who now found an opportunity of speaking to the ladies of the Duchess's household whom they had seen often, for the Duke's residence was close by his stepmother's, and its gardens and orchards also ran down to the river.

'Look!' cried Dorothy Barwicke, and Catherine's attention was taken from the young men to the river. Numerous barges, containing the chief citizens of London with their Lord Mayor, were passing by on their way to greet the Queen. The merchants presented a brilliant sight in their scarlet clothes and the great heavy chains about their necks. A band of musicians was playing in the city state barge.

Catherine began to sing, keeping time with the band; one of the young men on the river bank joined in. Catherine noticed that he was quite the handsomest of the group, and as she sang, she could not take her eyes from him. He pointed to a barge, calling her attention to what appeared to be a dragon which capered about the deck, shaking its great tail and spitting fire into the river, to the intense delight of all who beheld it. Catherine laughed gleefully, and the young man laughed; she believed he was urging his companions to get nearer to her and her friends. Catherine shrieked with excitement, watching the monsters who were helping the dragon to entertain the citizens. Catherine's eyes filled with ready tears as a barge came into view containing a choir of young girls, singing softly. Catherine could hear the words they sang, which were of the beauty and virtue of Queen Anne.

There was a long wait before the return of the procession bringing with it the Queen. There was however plenty with which to beguile themselves on such a day.

Sweetmeats were handed round; there was wine to drink and little cakes to nibble. It was all very pleasant, especially when Catherine found the handsome young man standing beside her, offering sweets.

'I watched you from the crowd,' he said.

'Indeed, sir, you need not tell me that, for I saw that you watched!'

She looked older than her years; she was flushed with

pleasure; her experience with Manox had matured her. Francis Derham judged her to be about fifteen – a delightful age, he thought.

'I thought you might care to sample these sweetmeats.'

'Indeed I do care.' She munched them happily, childishly. 'I long for the moment when the Queen comes by!'

'Have you ever seen Her Majesty? I hear she is wondrously beautiful.'

'Have I ever seen her! I would have you know, sir, that the Queen is first cousin to me.'

'Cousin to you! I know you are of my lady of Norfolk's house. Tell me, are you then her granddaughter?'

'I am.'

He was surprised that Her Grace of Norfolk should allow her granddaughter – so young and so attractive – to run wild in this way, but he suppressed his surprise. He said in tones of excitement: 'Then verily I believe you to be a kinswoman of mine!'

Catherine was delighted. They talked of their relations; he was right, there was a connection, though distant.

'Ah!' said Catherine. 'I feel safe then with you!'

That was a pleasant reflection, for she was realizing that she could feel safe no longer with Manox, that she was beginning to fear his embraces, that she sought excuses not to be with him. His sordid words to Mary Lassells had shocked and frightened her, and though she did not wish to hurt him, she had no desire to see him. Moreover, now that she had met Francis Derham, she felt more estranged from Manox than before, for Francis was an entirely different type – a gentleman, a man of good manners, good breeding – and being with him, even in those first hours, and seeing that he was attracted by her as Manox had been, she could not help but compare the two; and every vestige of admiration she had had for the musician vanished.

Francis thought: Her grandmother is waiting on the Queen, and that accounts for her freedom; but she is young to be abroad alone. He made up his mind to protect her .

He stayed at her side; they wandered along the bank of the river, they saw the Queen in her royal barge from which issued sweet music; and there followed the Queen, the barges of her father, the Duke of Suffolk, and all the nobility.

'She goes to the Tower!' said Derham.

'The Tower!' Catherine shivered, and he laughed at her. 'Why do you laugh?' she asked.

'Because you look afraid.'

Then she was telling him of her childhood, of Doll Tappit and Walter the warder, of the Little Ease and the Pit; and the screams the warder had heard coming from the torture chambers.

'I would,' said Catherine simply, 'that my sweet cousin were not going to the Tower.'

He laughed at this simplicity. 'Do you not know that all our sovereigns go to the Tower on their coronation? The state apartments there are very different from the dungeons and torture chambers, I'll warrant you!'

'Still, I like it not.'

'You are a dear little girl.' He thought again: She should not be allowed to run free like this! And he was angry towards those who were in charge of her. He liked her company; she was so youthful, so innocent, and yet . . . womanly. She would attract men, he knew, perhaps too strongly for her safety. He said: 'You and I should see the celebrations together, should we not? We could meet and go together.'

Catherine was ever eager for adventure, and she liked this young man because he inspired her with trust. She wanted someone to think of affectionately, so that she might no longer brood on Manox.

'You are very kind.'

'You would need to wear your plainest garments, for we should mingle with the crowds.'

'My plainest! They are all plain!'

'I mean you would cease to be Catherine Howard of Norfolk in a crowd of citizens; you would be plain Catherine Smith or some such. How like you this plan?'

'I like it vastly!' laughed Catherine.

And so they made their plans, and it was with him that Catherine saw the Queen's procession after her sojourn at the Tower; it was with Derham that she watched the royal progress through the city. In Gracechurch Street, hung with crimson and scarlet, they mingled with the crowd; they marvelled at the sight of the Chepe decorated with cloth and velvet. They saw the Lord Mayor receive the Queen at the Tower Gate; they saw the French ambassador, the judges, the knights who had been newly honoured in celebration of the coronation; they saw the abbots and the bishops; they espied the florid Duke of Suffolk, who must bury his animosity this day, bearing the verge of silver which showed him to hold the office of High Constable of England.

Catherine looked at this man, and held Derham's hand more firmly. Her companion looked down at her questioningly.

'What ails Catherine Smith?'

'I but thought of his wife, the King's sister, who I have heard is dying. He shows no sorrow.'

'He shows nothing,' whispered Derham. 'Not his antagonism to the Queen. . . . But let us not speak of such matters.'

Catherine shivered, then burst into sudden laughter.

'I think it more pleasant to wear a plain hood and be of the crowd, than to be a queen. I trow I'm as happy as my cousin!'

He pressed her hand; he had begun by feeling friendship, but friendship was deepening into warmer feelings. Catherine Howard was so sweet, such a loving and entrancing little creature!

Catherine gasped, for now came none but the Queen herself, breath-takingly lovely, borne by two white palfreys in white damask in an open litter covered with cloth of gold. Her beautiful hair was flowing in her favourite style, and on her head was a coif whose circlet was set with precious stones. Her surcoat was of silver tissue, and her mantle of the same material lined with ermine. Even those who had murmured against her must stop their murmurings, for never had they beheld such beauty, and while she was among them they must come under her spell.

Catherine was entirely fascinated by her; she had no eyes for those following; she did not see the crimson-clad ladies nor the chariots that followed, all covered in red cloth of gold, until Derham pointed out her grandmother in the first of these with the Marchioness of Dorset. Catherine smiled, wondering what the old lady would say, could she see her in this crowd. But the old Duchess would be thinking of nothing but the lovely woman in the litter, her granddaughter Queen of England, and that this was the proudest day of her long life.

Through the city the pageant continued. In Gracechurch Street they fought their way through the crowd clustered round a fountain from which spurted most lavishly good Rhenish wine. The pageant of the white falcon was enchanting, thought Catherine, for the white falcon represented Anne, and it sat uncrowned among the red and white roses; and then, as the Queen came close, there was a burst of sweet music and an angel flew down and placed a golden crown on the falcon's head. In Cornhill the Queen must pause before a throne on which sat the Three Graces, and in front of which was a spring which ran continually with wine; and she rested there while a poet read a poem which declared that the Queen possessed the qualities represented by the three ladies on the throne. The conduits of Chepe Side ran at one end white wine, and at the other claret, during the whole of that afternoon.

All through this pageantry rode Anne, her eyes bright with triumph – this was the moment for which she had waited four long years – on to Westminster Hall to thank the Lord Mayor and those who had organized the pageantry. Weary and very happy, she ate, and changed from the state garments, staying there at Westminster with the King that night.

Next morning – the coronation day itself, the first of June and a glorious Sunday – Catherine and Derham were again together. They caught a glimpse of the Queen in her surcoat and mantle of purple velvet lined with ermine, with rubies glistening in her hair.

'There is my grandmother!' whispered Catherine. And so it was, for on this day it was the old Duchess's delight and joy to hold the train of her granddaughter. Following the Dowager Duchess were the highest ladies in the land, clad splendidly in scarlet velvet, and the bars of ermine which decorated their stomachers denoted by their number the degree of nobility possessed by each; after these ladies came the knights' wives and the Queen's gentlewomen all clad in gay scarlet. Neither Catherine nor Derham went into the Abbey to see Cranmer set the crown on Anne's head. Mingling with the crowd outside, they both thought they had never been so happy in their lives.

'This is a great adventure indeed for me!' said Derham. 'And glad I am I saw thee!'

'Glad I am too!'

They looked at each other and laughed. Then he, drawing her into an alley, laid his lips against hers. He was surprised by the warmth with which she returned his kiss. He kissed her again and again.

Passers-by saw them and smiled.

'The city is as full of lovers as pickpockets this day!' said one.

'Aye! All eager to follow the royal example doubtless!'

There was laughter, for who could but laugh at such a time, when these streets, in which but a few years before people had died of that plague called the sweating sickness, were now running with good wine!

* * *

There was one member of Anne's family who did not attend the coronation. Jane Rochford's jealousy had become uncontrollable, and in her mad rage against her sister-in-law she was even more indiscreet than was habitual with her.

She had said: 'This marriage ... it is no marriage. A man may not take a wife while he has another. Anne is still the King's mistress, no matter what ceremonies there may be. There is only one Queen, and she is Queen Katharine.'

There were many in support of Queen Katharine, many who shook their heads sadly over the melancholy fate which had befallen the woman whom they had respected as Queen for over twenty years; indeed even those who supported Anne through love or fear could have little to say against Queen Katharine. She must be admired for that calm and queenly dignity which had never deserted her throughout her reign; she had suffered deeply; she had been submitted to mental torture by her unfaithful husband, even before he had brutally told her he would divorce her since she was of no more use to him; she had, by her tactful behaviour, managed to endow the King with some of her own dignity, covering his blatant amours, saying and believing 'This is but the way of kings!' She who suffered bitter humiliations at the hands of Henry the Seventh during those years which had elapsed between Arthur's death and her marriage with Henry, bore few grudges; she was meek and submissive when she considered it her duty to be so; when she considered it her duty to be strong she could be as firm and tenacious as Henry himself. Duty was the keynote of her life. She would suffer the severest torture rather than deviate from what she considered right. She had been taught her religion by her mother, Isabella, who in her turn had been taught by that grim zealot, Torquemada.

In these great people – Katharine, Isabella, Torquemada – there burned fierce fires of fanaticism which purged them of fear. Their religion was the rock to which they clung; life on Earth was to them but a dream, compared with the reality to come. Katharine, bound irrevocably to Rome, believing there could be no divorce, was ready to go to the stake rather than give Henry what he demanded; for to her mind earthly torment was a small price to pay for that eternal bliss which was reserved only for those true servants of the Roman Catholic Faith. With all the strength she had possessed she had stood out against her blustering, furious husband, so nobly, so fearlessly, so assured of the right, that even in defeat she appeared to triumph, and there was none who could go into her presence and not treat her as a queen. There was her passionate devotion to her daughter to touch the hearts of all; to this daughter she had given all the affection her husband did not want; she lived for this daughter, and delighted in the belief that one day she would sit on the throne of England; she had superintended her education with the greatest care, had glowed with pleasure at Mary's aptitude for learning, at her youthful charm, at her father's affection for her.

The only earthly joy which had lighted Katharine's sombre life was in her daughter, the Princess Mary. Henry, raging against her, cursing her obstinacy, unable to believe she could not see what was so clear to his scrupulous conscience, cursing her because she would not admit having consummated her marriage with his brother, hating her because she could have solved the whole difficulty by going into a nunnery, had struck at her in the most effective way possible, when he had separated her from her daughter.

In doing this he had acted foolishly, for the sympathy of the great mass of people was ever ready to be given to the victim of injustice, and they were all for Katharine and Mary. Mothers wept for them and, with their own children beside them, though they might be humble fishwives, could well understand the sufferings of a queen.

Henry, whose nature demanded homage and admiration, was hurt and alarmed by the sympathy shown to Katharine. Previous to the time when the divorce was mooted, it was he who had strutted across the stage, he on whom all attention was focussed – he, large and magnificent, the goodliest of princes, the most handsome of princes, the most sporting of princes, the most loved and admired prince in the world. Katharine had been beside him, but only as a satellite shining with the reflected brilliance from his blazing personality. And now in the hearts of the susceptible and sentimental people she was enshrined as a saint, while he was looked upon as a bully, a promiscuous husband, a brutal man. He could not bear it; it was so unfair. Had he not told them he had merely obeyed the promptings of his conscience? They judged him as a man, not as a king. Then he grew angry. He had explained patiently; he had bared his soul; he had suffered the humiliation of a trial at Westminster Hall; and they did not understand! He had done with patience. He would have all these sullen people know who was their absolute master! A word, a look, would be enough to send any one of them, however high, however low, to the Tower.

Jane's motives were not of the highest, since it was her

jealousy which overcame her prudence. She was a little hysterical. George was so often with the Queen; she had seen emotion in his face at a fancied slight to his sister; he was alert, anxious for her, admonishing her for her impulsiveness, and ridiculously, as people do when they love, loving her the more for it. My faults, thought Jane tearfully, are treated as such; hers are considered virtues.

People were looking furtively at her. When she railed against the Queen, they moved away from her, not wishing to be involved in such recklessness. Jane was too unhappy to care what she said, and gave herself up to the bitter satisfaction of reviling Anne.

Now in her apartment at the palace, she felt about her an ominous calm; those of her associates who had been wont to chat with her or sit with her, were not to be found. Her jealousy burned out, she had time to be frightened, and as she sat and brooded, longing for the return of George that she might tell him of her fears – feeling that he, seeing her in danger, might find her at least worthy of his pity – she heard on the staircase close to her door the sound of footsteps. She leaped up, for there was something in those footsteps of precision and authority; they stopped outside her door; there was a peremptory knocking.

Suppressing a desire to hide, Jane called in a trembling voice: 'Come in!'

She knew him. His face was hard; he would have seen much suffering and grown accustomed to it; for he was Sir William Kingston, the Constable of the Tower of London.

Jane's fingers clutched the scarlet hangings. Her face was drained of colour, her lips trembled.

'Lady Jane Rochford, I am to conduct you to the Tower of London on a charge of High Treason.'

Treason! That dreaded word. And she was guilty of it, for it was treason to speak against the King, and in speaking against Anne, this was what she had done.

She felt the room swing round her; one of Sir William's attendants caught her. They held her head down until the blood rushed back, and they did this naturally, as though they expected it. The room righted itself, but there was a rushing sound in her ears, and the faces of the men were blurred.

She faltered: 'There is some mistake.'

'There is no mistake,' Sir William told her. 'Your ladyship is requested to leave immediately.'

'My husband . . .' she began. 'My sister the Queen . . .'

'I have a warrant for your ladyship's arrest,' she was told. 'I must obey orders. And I must ask your ladyship to accompany us at once.'

Quietly she went out, across the courtyard to the waiting barge. Silently they went up the river. She looked back at the sprawling palace on the river bank with its squat towers and its mullioned windows – the favourite palace of the King, for he was born there and he liked its situation which gave him a perfect view of the rising and falling of the river. When, wondered Jane, would she see Greenwich again?

Past the riverside houses of the rich went the barge until it came to that great fortress which now looked sullen in the grey light, forbidding and ominous. How many had passed through the Traitor's Gate and been swallowed up by that grey stone monster, and so lost to the world outside! It could not happen to me, thought Jane. Not to me! What have I done? Nothing . . . nothing. I did but voice an opinion.

Then she remembered some cynical remark of George's about those who voiced their opinions and those who were too nearly related to the King, deserving to die.

The barge was made fast; up the stone stairs Jane was led. She felt stifled by the oppressive atmosphere of the place. She was taken through a postern, across a narrow stone bridge, and was brought to the entrance of a grey tower. Trembling, Jane entered the Tower of London and was led up narrow spiral staircases, along cold corridors, to the room she would have to occupy. The door was locked on her. She ran to the window and looked out; below her was the dark water of the Thames.

Jane threw herself onto the narrow bed and burst into hysterical tears. This was her own folly! What did she care for Queen Katharine! What did she care for the Princess Mary! She wished to be no martyr. Well did she know that, had she tried to be Anne's friend, she could have been, for Anne did not look for enemies – she only fought those who stood against her. And how could poor little Jane Rochford stand against Queen Anne!

She was a fool. Looking back over her married life, she could see how foolish she had been. Oh, for another chance! She was humble, she was repentant, blaming herself. If she went to Anne, confessed her folly, asked for forgiveness, it would be granted, she knew well. She resolved that if she came out of the Tower she would overcome her jealousy of her brilliant sister-in-law; who knew, by so doing might she not gain a little of George's affection?

She was soothed and calmed, and so remained for some time, until that day which marked the beginning of the celebrations. And then, gazing from her window, she saw the arrival at the Tower, of Anne, dressed in cloth of gold and attended by many ladies; and at the sight of her, all Jane's enmity returned, for the contrast between herself and her sister-in-law was too great to be endured stoically. *She* had arrived by way of the Traitor's Gate, while Anne had come in triumph as the Queen. No! Jane could not endure it. Here in this very place was her sister-in-law, fêted and honoured, adored openly by that mighty and most feared man, Henry the Eighth. It was too much. Jane was overcome by fresh weeping.

'She has many enemies,' said Jane aloud. 'There is the true Queen and her daughter; there is Suffolk, Chapuys . . . to name but a few, and all of them powerful people. But Anne Boleyn, though there are many who hate you,' she sobbed bitterly, 'none does so as whole-heartedly as your despised Jane Rochford!'

*　　*　　*

The King was not happy. All through the hot month of June he had been aware of his dissatisfaction with life. He had thought that when Anne became his Queen he would know complete happiness; she had been that for five months, and instead of his happiness growing it had gradually diminished.

The King still desired Anne, but he was no longer in love with her; which meant that he had lost that tenderness for her which had dominated him for six years, which had softened him and mellowed his nature. Never had the King loved any but himself, for even his love for Anne was based on his need of her. She had appeared on his horizon, a gay, laughing girl; to him she represented delightful youth; she was unique in her refusal to surrender; she appeared to be unimpressed by his kingship, and had talked of the need to love the man before the king. In his emotions Henry was as simple as a jungle lion; he stalked his quarry, and at these times stalking was his main preoccupation. The stalking of Anne was finished; she had managed to make it arduous; she had made him believe that the end of the hunt was not her surrender, but her place beside him on the throne; together they had stalked a crown for Anne; now it was hers, and they were both exhausted with the effort.

The relationship of mistress and lover was more exciting to a man of Henry's temperament than that of wife and husband; though his conscience would never allow him to admit this. The one was full of excitement, with clandestine meetings, with doubts and fears, and all the ingredients of romance; the other was prosaic, arranged, and – most objectionable of all – inescapable, or almost. Gradually the relationship had been changing ever since January. She could still arouse in him moments of wild passion; she would always do that, she would always be to him the most attractive woman in his life; but he was essentially polygamous, and he possessed a wonderful and elastic conscience to explain all his actions.

Anne was clever; she could have held him; she could have kept him believing he had achieved happiness. But she had always been reckless, and the fight had tired her far more than it had Henry; she had more to gain and more to lose; now she felt she had reached her goal and needed to rest. Moreover she was able now to see this man she had married, from a different angle. She was no longer the humble subject climbing up to the dizzy heights on which he stood secure as King; she was level with him now, not a humble knight's daughter, but a Queen looking at a King – and the closer view was less flattering to him. His youthful looks had gone. He was in his forties, and he had lived too well; he had done most things to excess, and this was apparent; stripped of his glittering clothes he was by no means wholesome; he had suffered the inevitable consequences of a promiscuous life. His oblique gaze at facts irritated Anne beyond endurance. She rebelled against his conscience; she looked at him too closely, and he knew she did. He had seen her lips curl at certain remarks of his; he had seen her face harden at some display of coarseness. This would enrage him, for he would remind himself that he was the son of a king, and that it was entirely due to him that she had gained her high eminence.

They quarrelled; they were both too easily roused to anger to avoid it; but so far the quarrels were little more than tiffs, for she could still enchant him, and moreover he did not forget that she carried the Tudor heir. Anne did not forget it either; in fact it absorbed her; she was experiencing the abandonment of the mother – all else was of small importance, set beside the life that moved within her. She was obsessed by it; she wished to be left alone that she might dream of this child, this son, for whom she must wait for three long dreary months.

This was all very right, thought Henry; the child *was* all-important, but there was no need for her to change so completely. He rejoiced to see her larger; it was a goodly sight. The boy was well and happy inside her, and God speed his coming! But . . . she should not forget the baby's father, as she appeared to do. She was languid, expressing no delight in the attentions he paid to her, preferring to talk of babies with her ladies than to have him with her. Henry was disappointed. He missed too their passionate love-making. He was in the forties; he could not expect to enjoy his manly vigour for many more years. Sometimes he felt quite old; then he would say to himself: 'What I have endured these last years for her has done this to me; brought me a few years nearer the grave, I trow!' Then he would be indignant with her, indignant that she, while carrying his child, must deny him those blissful moments which he could enjoy with none as he could with her. He would think back over his faithfulness to her. This was astonishing; it amazed him. Ah, well, a man must be faithful to a mistress if he wishes to keep her, but a wife is a different matter altogether!

The thought took hold of Henry, haunting his mind. He thought of the days before Anne had come to Suffolk House; they had a piquancy, a charm, since the excitement of adventure is in its unexpectedness. 'It is more pleasing to pluck an apple from the branch which you have seized, than to take one up from a graven dish.' There was truth enough in that, he assured himself, thinking of sudden amorous adventures.

There came a day in July when the rain was teeming down and there was little to do. One played the harp, one sang ... but the day flagged, for he was uneasy in his mind. Affairs of state weighed heavily upon him. In spite of his separation from Rome, he was eager that the Pope should sanction his marriage; he was disappointed of this, for instead of the sanction there came an announcement that Cranmer's sentence on Henry's former marriage was to be annulled; unless, he was threatened, he left Anne before September and returned to Katharine, both he and she he called his new Queen would be excommunicated.

This was disquieting news which set Henry trembling; Anne's defiance of Rome, her lack of superstitious dread, angered him against her, for he did not care that she should show more courage than he; although his conscience explained that his feeling was not fear but eagerness to assure himself that he had acted within the will of God. Some priests, particularly in the North, were preaching against the new marriage. At Greenwich, Friar Peyto had even had the temerity to preach before Henry and Anne, hinting at the awful judgment that awaited them. Cardinal Pole, who had decided it would be well to live on the Continent owing to his close relationship to the King, wrote reproachful letters abusing Anne. Henry did not trust the Spanish ambassador; the man was sly and insolent and over-bold; he had dared to ask Henry if he could be sure of having children, making a reference to the state of the kingly body which was outwardly manifested by a malignant sore on the leg, which refused to heal.

Henry had reason to believe that Chapuys had reported to his master on the state of English defences; and if this were so, might he not advise the Emperor to make an attack?

Would a conquest of England be difficult for such a skilled general as Charles? Henry knew that most of his nobles – with perhaps the exception of Norfolk – would be ready to support Katharine's side; the Scots were ever eager to be troublesome. Why should not Charles, on the pretext of avenging an ill-treated aunt, do that which would be of inestimable advantage to himself – subdue England? There was one gleam of hope in this prospect; Charles was fully occupied in his scattered possessions, and he was too cautious to stretch his already overstrained resources in another cause. Henry raged and fumed and said he would send Chapuys home, but that was senseless, he knew well; better to have the spy whose evil ways were known to him than another sent in his place who might be possessed of even greater cunning. Henry bottled up his indignation temporarily, holding in his anger, but storing it, nourishing it. The only brightness on the political horizon was that Francis had sent congratulations to both himself and Anne; Henry had invited the French King to sponsor his son, which Francis had cordially agreed to do. Henry felt that, once his son was born, the mass of the people – the element he feared most – would be so overjoyed that it would be forgotten that various unorthodox methods had been followed in order to bring about such a joyous event. Astrologers and physicians had assured him that there could be no doubt of the sex of the child, so all Henry needed to do was to wait for September; but never had a month seemed so long in coming, and it was but July, and wet. The King therefore felt himself in need of diversion.

It came in the voluptuous form of one of the ladies attending Anne. This girl was in complete contrast to her mistress, round-faced, possessed of large baby blue eyes, plump and inviting. No haughtiness there; no dignity; Henry was ever attracted by change.

She glanced at him as she flitted about the chamber, and Anne, absorbed in maternity, did not at first notice what was going on. The girl curtseyed to him, glanced sideways at him; he smiled at her, forgetting Chapuys and astute Charles, and all those who preached against him.

He came upon her suddenly in the quiet of a corridor. She curtseyed, throwing at him that bold glance of admiration which he remembered so well from the days before his thoughts had been given entirely to Anne. He kissed the girl; she caught her breath; he remembered that too; as though they were overwhelmed by him! He felt a king again; pleasant indeed to bestow favours like a king, instead of having to beg for them like a dog.

He left her though, for Anne still largely occupied his thoughts. There was none to be compared with Anne, and he was afraid of her still, afraid of her reactions should she discover any infidelity. He could not forget how she had gone back to Hever; moreover she was to bear him a son. He felt sentimental towards her still; but a kiss was nothing.

The weather cleared, and he felt better. August came. Invitations to the christening of the prince were made ready. Anne, languid on her couch, watched the King obliquely, wondering what gave him that secret look, noting the sly glances of her attendant, noting a certain covert boldness in the girl's manner towards herself. Anne could not believe that he who had been faithful for so many years in the most difficult circumstances had so quickly lapsed, and at such a time, when she was to give him a son. But the secretiveness of him, that irritability towards herself which a man of his type would feel towards someone he had wronged or was about to wrong made her feel sure of what was afoot.

Anne was no patient Griselda, no Katharine of Aragon. She was furious, and the more so because her fury must be tinged with fear. What if history were to repeat itself! What if that which had happened to Queen Katharine was about to happen to Queen Anne! Would she be asked to admit that her marriage was illegal? Would she be invited to go into a nunnery? She must remember that she had no powerful Emperor Charles behind her.

She watched the King; she watched the girl. Henry was over-wrought; he drank freely; the days seemed endless to him; he was nervous and irritable sometimes, at others over-exuberant. But this was understandable, for the birth of a son was of the utmost importance since not only would it ensure the Tudor dynasty, but to Henry it would come like a sign from heaven that he had been right to displace Katharine.

Anne lived uncomfortably through the hot days, longing for the birth of her child. She felt upon her the eyes of all; she felt them to be waiting for that all-deciding factor, the birth of a male child. Her friends prayed for a son; her enemies hoped for a daughter or a still-born child.

One day at the end of August it seemed to her that the girl whom she watched with such suspicion was looking more sly and a trifle arrogant. She saw Henry give her a look of smouldering desire.

'Shall I endure this before my very eyes?' Anne asked herself. 'Am I not Queen?'

She waited until Henry was alone in the chamber with her; then she said, her eyes blazing: 'If you must amuse yourself, I would prefer you did not do it under my eyes and with one of my own women!'

Henry's eyes bulged with fury. He hated being caught; he had had this matter out with his conscience; it was nothing, this light little affair with a wench who had doubtless lost her virginity long ago; it was hardly worth confessing. It was a light and airy nothing, entered into after the drinking of too much wine, little more than a dream.

'Am I to be defied by one wife,' he asked himself, 'dictated to by another?'

He had had enough of this; he was the King, he would have her know. It was not for her to keep up her arrogance to him now.

As he struggled for words to express his indignation, one of Anne's attendants entered; that did not deter him. It should be known throughout the court that he was absolute

King, and that the Queen enjoyed her power through him.

He shouted: 'You close your eyes, as your betters did before you!'

Her cheeks flushed scarlet; she lifted herself in the bed; angry retorts rose to her lips, but something in the face of the King subdued her suddenly, so that her anger left her; she had no room for any other emotion than deadly fear. His face had lost its flushed appearance too; his eyes peered out from his quivering flesh, suddenly cold and very cruel.

Then he continued to speak, slowly and deliberately: 'You ought to know that it is in my power in a single instant to lower you further than I raised you up.'

He went from the room; she sank back, almost fainting. The attendant came to her hastily, ministering to her anxiously, knowing the deep humiliation that must have wounded one so proud. Had Anne been alone she would have retorted hotly; she would have flayed him with her tongue; but they were not alone – yet he had not cared for that! In the court her enemies would hear of this; they would talk of the beginning of the end of Anne Boleyn.

Her hands were cold and wet; she overcame a desire to burst into passionate tears. Then the child began to move inside her, reassuring her. Her son. Once he was born, she was safe, for Henry would never displace the mother of his son whatever the provocation.

Henry did not go near her again for several days. He found a fresh and feverish excitement in the knowledge that to be in lust was satisfying and more congenial to his nature than to be in love. The girl was a saucy wench, God knew, but ready enough, over-ready, to obey her King. To love was to beg and plead; to lust was but to demand satisfaction.

He thought of Anne often, sometimes when he was with the girl. His thoughts were so mixed he could not define them. Sometimes he thought, When the confinement's over, she'll be herself again. Then he thought of a lithesome girl leaning over a pond at Hever, a lovely woman entertaining him at Suffolk House. Anne, Anne . . . there is none on Earth as delightful as Anne! This is naught, Anne; this is forgotten once you are with me again.

Then at mass or confession his thoughts would be tinged with fear. Suppose the Almighty should show his displeasure by a daughter or a still-born child! Marriage with Katharine had been a succession of still-born children, because his marriage with Katharine had been no marriage. He himself had said that. What if his marriage with Anne should be no marriage either?

But God would show him, for God would always be ready to guide one who followed His laws and praised Him, as did Henry the Eighth of England.

* * *

Throughout the city the news was awaited. People in the barges that floated down the Thames called one to the other.

'Is the prince come yet then?'

There was scarcely a whisper against the new Queen; those who had been her most violent enemies thought of her now, not as the Queen, but as a mother.

'I heard her pains had started, poor lady . . .'

'They say his name will be Henry or Edward . . .'

Mothers remembered occasions when they had suffered as the Queen suffered now, and even those who cared nothing for motherhood were fond of pageantry. They remembered the coronation, when wine had flowed free from fountains. Pageants, feasting, rejoicing would mark the birth of a son to a king who had waited twenty-four years for it; it would be a greater event than a coronation.

'God save the little prince!' cried the people.

The Dowager Duchess of Norfolk scarcely slept at all, so eager was she for the event. She was full of pride and misgivings, assuring herself that Anne was a healthy girl, that the delivery must be effected efficiently, pushing to the back of her mind those fears which came from her knowledge of the King. Poor Katharine had had miscarriage after miscarriage; they said she was diseased, and whence did she come by such diseases? Might it not have been through close contact with His Majesty? One did not speak such thoughts, for it were treason to do so, but how could the most loyal subjects help their coming to mind! But Anne was a healthy girl; this was her first child. She had come safely through the nine months of pregnancy, and everything must be well.

*　　*　　*

In the orchard, sheltered by the trees whose fruit was beginning to ripen, Catherine Howard and Francis Derham lay in each other's arms with scarcely a thought for the momentous events which would shape the course of history.

Francis said: 'Why should they not consent to our marriage? It is true I am poor, but my birth is good.'

'They will assuredly consent,' murmured Catherine. 'They must consent!'

'And why should it not be soon? When the Duchess is recovered from this excitement, she will surely listen to me, Catherine. Do you think that I might approach her?'

'Yes,' said Catherine happily.

'Then we are betrothed!'

'Yes.'

'Then call me husband.'

'Husband,' said Catherine, and he kissed her.

'I would we were away from here, wife, that we were in our own house. I get so little opportunity for seeing you.'

'So little,' she sighed.

'And I hear that the Duchess's ladies are unprincipled in some ways, that they are over-bold with men. I like it not that you should be among them.'

'I am safe,' she said, 'loving thee.'

They kissed again, Catherine drew him closer, feeling that excessive excitement which physical contact with one who attracted her must always give her.

Derham kissed her fervently, enchanted by her as Manox had been; but he was genuinely in love with her, and his feelings were governed by affection as well as the need to gratify his senses. She was very young, but she was ready for passion. He was a reckless young man, courageous and virile; and Catherine's obvious longing to complete their intimacy was so alluring that he – while tenderly thinking of her age – must seek to arrange it.

He insisted they would marry. He could think of nothing more delightful. They were really married, he told her, because according to the law of the Church it was only necessary for two free people to agree to a contract and it was made. It soothed his fears that she was too young, when he called her wife; when she called him husband, he was transported with joy.

He meant to be tactful and kind. He knew nothing of her experience with Manox. Catherine did not tell him, not because she wished to hide it, but because Manox no longer interested her. She had asked her grandmother if she might have a new music teacher, and the old lady, too full of court matters to care what her granddaughter did, had nodded, and when Catherine had named an ascetic, middle-aged man, her grandmother had nodded again. In any case the Duchess no longer sat as chaperon during the music lessons. Manox had almost passed from Catherine's thoughts, except on those unpleasant occasions when he would try to see her – for he was furious that she had ended the affair so abruptly, blaming Mary Lassells for this and making no secret of his hatred and contempt for the girl. Catherine wished of course that she had never known Manox, but she was too blissful to think of much else but the completion of her love with Francis Derham.

'I have a plan,' said Derham.

'Tell me of it.'

'What if I were to ask Her Grace to take me into her house?'

'Dost think she would?' Catherine was trembling at the thought.

'I think she might.' He smiled complacently, remembering how on one occasion Her Grace had singled him out – as a most personable young man – for her special attention. 'I can but try. Then we shall be under the same roof; then I may speak for you. Oh, Catherine, Catherine, how I long for that day!'

Catherine longed for it with equal intensity.

He almost whispered to her that they need not wait; why should they, when they were husband and wife? Catherine was waiting for him to say that; but he did not . . . yet. They lay on the grass, looking up at the ripening fruit.

'I shall never forget the day you first called me husband,' he said. 'I shall remember it when I die!'

Catherine laughed, for death seemed far away and a most absurd topic for two young people in love.

'I shall never forget it either,' she told him, and turned her face to his. They kissed; they trembled; they yearned for each other.

'Soon,' he said, 'I shall be in the Duchess's house. Then I shall see you often . . . often.'

Catherine nodded.

* * *

On the gorgeous bed, which had been part of a French Prince's ransom, Anne lay racked with the agony of child-birth. The King paced up and down in an adjoining room. He could hear her groans. How he loved her! For her groaning set his heart beating with fear that she would die. He was that same lover to whom news of her illness had been brought during the pestilence. 'I would willingly endure half of what you suffer to cure you.' Memories of her came and went in his mind; her laughter, her gaiety; Anne, the centre of attraction at the jousts and masques; sitting beside him watching the jousts in the tiltyard, so beautiful, so apart from all others that he found it difficult to turn his attention from her to the jousting; he thought of her in his arms, his love and his Queen.

He was filled with remorse for that lapse, for the quarrel which had upset her, and – this made him break out into a clammy sweat – might have had some effect on the birth of his son.

He paced up and down, suffering with her. How long? How long? The veins stood out on his forehead. 'By God! If anything happens to her, blood will flow – that I swear!'

The girl with whom he had dallied recently, looked in at the door, smiling; she had been sent to soothe him. He looked at her without recognizing her.

Up and down he went, straining his ears and then putting

his hands over them to shut out the sound of Anne's pain. His fear was suddenly swept away, for distinctly he heard the cry of a child, and in a second he was at the bedside, trembling with eagerness. In the chamber there was a hushed silence. The attendants were afraid to look at him. Anne lay white and exhausted, aware neither of him, nor her room, nor perhaps herself.

'What is it?' he shouted.

They hesitated, one looking at another, hoping that some other would take on the delicate task of breaking unpleasant news.

His face was purple; his eyes blazing. He roared in his anguish.

'A daughter!' His voice was almost a sob; he was defeated; he was humiliated.

He stood, his hands clenched, words pouring from his mouth, abuse and rage; and his eyes were on Anne, lying still on the bed. This to happen to him! What had he done to deserve it? What had he ever done to deserve it? Had he not always sought to do right? Had he not spent hours of labour, studying theology; had he not written *A Glasse of the Truth*? Had he not delved deep into this matter before he had taken action? Had he not waited for the promptings of his conscience? And for whom had he worked and suffered? Not for himself, but for his people, to save them from the rigours of civil war which during the last century had distressed and ravaged the land. For this he had worked, sparing himself not at all, defying the wrath of his simple people who could not be expected to understand his high motives. And this was his reward . . . a daughter!

He saw tears roll from Anne's closed eyes; her face was white as marble; she looked as though all life had gone from her; those tears alone showed him that she had heard. And then suddenly his disappointment was pushed aside. She too had suffered deeply; she was disappointed as he was. He knelt down and put his arms about her.

He said earnestly: 'I would rather beg from door to door than forsake you!'

When he had gone, she lay very still, exhausted by the

effort of giving birth to her daughter, her mind unable to give her body the rest it needed. She had failed. She had borne a daughter, not a son! This then was how Katharine of Aragon had felt when Mary was born. The hope was over; the prophecies of the physicians and the soothsayers had proved to be meaningless. 'It will be a boy,' they had assured her; and then . . . it was a girl!

Her heartbeats, which had been sluggish, quickened. What had he said? 'I would rather beg from door to door than forsake you!' Forsake you! Why should he have said that? He would surely only have said it if the thought of forsaking her had been in his mind! He had forsaken Katharine.

Her cheeks were wet; then she must have shed tears. I could never live in a nunnery, she thought, and she remembered how she had once believed that Katharine ought to have gone to such a place. How different the suggestion seemed when applied to oneself! She had never understood Katharine's case until now.

Someone bent over her and whispered: 'Your Majesty must try to sleep.'

She slept awhile and dreamed she was plain Anne Boleyn at Blickling; she was experiencing great happiness, and when she awoke she thought, Happiness then is a matter of comparison; I never knew such complete happiness, for my body was in agony and now I scarce know I have a body, and that in itself is enough.

Fully conscious, she remembered that she was no longer a girl at Blickling, but a queen who had failed in her duty of bearing a male heir. She remembered that throughout the palace – throughout the kingdom – they would now be talking of her failure, speculating as to what effect it would have upon her relationship with the King. Her enemies would be rejoicing, her friends mourning. Chapuys would be writing gleefully to his master. Suffolk would be smiling, well content. Katharine would pray for her; Mary would gloat: She has failed! She has failed! What will the King do now?

The sleep had strengthened her; her weakness of spirit

was passing. She had fought to gain her place, she would fight to keep it.

'My baby . . .' she said, and they brought the child and laid it in her arms.

The red, crumpled face looked beautiful to her, because the child was hers; she held it close, examining it, touching its face lightly with her fingers, murmuring: 'Little baby . . . my little baby!'

It mattered little to her now that the child was a girl, for, having seen her, she was convinced that there never had been such a beautiful child – so how could she wish to change it! She held her close, loving her and yet feeling fearful for her, for was not the child a possible Queen of England? No, there would be sons to follow. The first child had been a girl; therefore she would never sit on the throne of England, because Anne would have sons, many sons. Still, the mother must tremble for her child, must wish now that she were not the daughter of a king and queen. Suppose this baby had been born in some other home than royal Greenwich, where her sex would not have been a matter of such great importance. How happy she would have been then! There would have been nothing to think of but tending the child.

They would have taken the baby from her, but she would not let her go. She wanted her with her, to hold her close, to protect her.

She thought of Mary Tudor's fanatical eyes. How the birth of this child would add fuel to the fierce fires of Mary's resentment! Another girl to take her place, when she had lost it merely by being a girl! Before, there had been many a skirmish with Mary Tudor; now there must be deciding warfare between her and Queen Anne. For what if there were no more children! What if the fate of Queen Anne was that of Queen Katharine? Then . . . when the King was no more, there would be a throne for this child, a throne which would be coveted most ardently by Mary Tudor; and might not the people of England think Mary had the greater claim? Some considered that Katharine was still Queen, and that this newly born child was the bastard, not Mary Tudor.

'Oh, baby,' murmured Anne, 'what a troublesome world it is that you have been born into!' Fiercely she kissed the child. 'But it shall be as happy for you as I can make it. I would kill Mary Tudor rather than that she should keep from you that which is your right!'

One of the women bent over the bed.

'Your Majesty needs to rest. . . .'

Hands took the baby; reluctantly Anne let her go.

She said: 'She shall be called Elizabeth, after my mother and the King's.'

* * *

The court was tense with excitement. In lowered tones the birth of Elizabeth was discussed, in state apartments, in the kitchens; women weeding in the gardens whispered together. In the streets, the people said: 'What now? This is God's answer!' Chapuys was watchful, waiting; he sounded Cromwell. Cromwell was noncommittal, cool. He felt that the King was as yet too fond of the lady to desire any change in their relationship. He was unlike Wolsey; Wolsey shaped the King's policy while he allowed the King to believe it was his own; Cromwell left the shaping to the King, placing himself completely at the royal disposal. Whatever the King needed, Thomas Cromwell would provide. If he wished to disinherit Mary, Cromwell would find the most expeditious way of doing it; if the King wished to discard Anne, Cromwell would work out a way in which this could be done. Cromwell's motto was: 'The King is always right.'

The King still desired Anne ardently, but though he could be the passionate lover, he wished her to realize that it was not hers to command but to obey. A mistress may command, a wife must be submissive. Yet he missed his mistress; he even felt a need to replace her. He could not look upon Anne – young, beautiful and desirable – as he had looked on Katharine. And yet it seemed to him that wives are always wives; one is shackled to them by the laws of holy church, and to be shackled is a most unpleasant condition. There was an element of spice in sin, which virtue lacked; and even though a man had a perfectly good answer to offer his conscience, the spice was there. Anne could no longer threaten to return home; this was her home, the home of which she was indubitably master. She had given him a daughter – a further proof that she was not all he had believed her to be when he had pursued her so fanatically.

And so, in spite of his still passionate desire for her, when this was satisfied he would quickly change from lover into that mighty figure, King and master.

This was apparent very soon after Elizabeth's birth. Anne wanted to keep the child with her, to feed her herself, to have her constantly in her care. Apart from her maternal feelings which were strong, she feared ill might befall her daughter through those enemies whom the child would inherit from the mother.

Seeing his daughter's cradle in the chamber which he shared with Anne, the King was startled.

'How now!' he growled. 'What means this?'

'I would have her with me,' said Anne, used to command, continuing to do so.

'You would have her with you!' he repeated ominously.

'Yes. And I shall feed her myself, for I declare I shall trust no one else with this task.'

The King's face was purple with rage.

He stamped to the door and called to a startled maid of honour. She came in, trembling.

'Take the child away!' he roared.

The girl looked from the King to the Queen; the Queen's face was very pale, but she did not speak. She was trembling, remembering what he had said before the child's birth; at that time he had not waited until they were alone. 'You ought to know that it is in my power in a single instant to lower you further than I raised you up!' And later, 'I would rather beg from door to door than forsake you.' He cared not what he said before whom; he was so careless of her feelings that it mattered not to him if, in the court, people speculated as to whether her influence was waning. Therefore she watched the girl remove her baby, and said nothing.

'She would disturb our rest!' said the King.

When they were alone, Anne turned on him fiercely.

'I wished to keep her with me. I wished to feed her my-self. What could it matter . . .'

He looked at her squarely. 'Remember,' he said slowly, 'that I lifted you up to be Queen of England. I ask that you do not behave as a commoner.'

His voice matched his eyes for coldness; she had never noticed how very cold they could be, how relentless and cruel was the small mouth.

Still trembling, she turned away from him, holding her head high, realizing that she, who a short while ago would have blazed at him demanding that her wishes be gratified, now dared do nothing but obey.

The King watched; her hair loose about her shoulders, she reminded him suddenly of the girl in the Hever rose garden. He went to her and laid a heavy hand on her shoulder.

'Come, Anne!' he said, and turning her face to his kissed her. Hope soared in her heart then; she still had power to move him; she had accepted defeat too easily. She smiled.

'You were very determined about that!' she said, trying to infuse a careless note into her voice, for she was afraid to insist on keeping Elizabeth with her, and realized the folly of showing fear to one who was naturally a bully.

'Come, sweetheart!' His voice was thick with the be-ginnings of passion; she knew him so well; she recognized his moods. 'A queen does not suckle her babes. Enough of this!' He laughed. 'We have a daughter; we must get our-selves a boy!'

She laughed with him. As he caressed her, her thoughts moved fast. She had believed that, with the birth of her child her great fight would be over; she would sink back, re-freshed by new homage, into a security which could not be shaken. But Fate had been unkind; she had given the King, not that son who would have placed her so securely on the throne, but a daughter. The fight was not over; it was just beginning; for what had gone before must be a skirmish compared with what must follow. She would need all her skill now, since the very weapons which had won for her her first victories were grown blunt; and it was now not only for herself that she must fight.

How she pitied Katharine of Aragon, who had gone through it all before her! Who was still going through it; a veteran whose weapons were endurance and tenacity. Anne would have need of equal endurance, equal tenacity, for she fought in the opposite camp. She was a mother now; she was a tigress who sees her cub in mortal danger. Katharine of Aragon she had thought of as a pitiable woman, Mary as a wilful, outspoken girl; now they were her bitterest enemies, and they stood on their guard, waiting to dishonour her daughter.

She returned Henry's kisses.

He said: 'Anne, Anne, there's no one like you, Anne!'

And hot anger rose within her, for she sensed that he was comparing her with the woman whom he had dallied with before her delivery. Once she would have repulsed him, stormed at him, told him what she thought; now she must consider; she must lure him afresh, she must enchant him. It would be more difficult now, but she would do it, because it was imperative that she should.

As he lay beside her, she entwined her fingers in his.

'Henry,' she said.

He grunted.

Words trembled on her lips. What if she asked to have the baby in! No, that would be unwise; she could not make conditions now. She must tread very carefully; she was only the King's wife now. The Queen of England lacked the power of Anne Rochford and the Marchioness of Pembroke; but the Queen had all the cunning of those ladies, and she would laugh yet in the faces of her enemies who prophesied her destruction.

'Henry, now that we have a child, would it not be well to declare Mary illegitimate? We know well that she is, but it has never been so stated.'

He considered this. He was feeling a little hurt with Mary, who had applauded and supported her mother ever since the divorce had been thought of. Mary was an obstinate girl, an unloving daughter who had dared to flout her father, the King.

'By God!' he said. 'I've been too lenient with that girl!'

'Indeed you have! And did I not always tell you so; you must announce her illegitimacy at once, and every man of note in the country must agree to it.'

'If they do not,' growled Henry, ''twill be the worse for them!'

She kissed his cheek; she had been foolish to worry. She still had the power to manage him.

He said: 'We must go cautiously. I fear the people will not like it. They have made a martyr of Katharine, and of Mary too.'

She did not attach over-much importance to the will of the people. They had shouted: 'We'll have no Nan Bullen!' And here she was, on the throne in spite of them. The people gathered together and grumbled; sometimes they made disturbances; sometimes they marched together with flaming torches in their hands. . . . Still, they should not pay too much attention to the people.

'Mary is a stupid, wayward girl,' said Anne. And as the King nodded in agreement, she added: 'She should be compelled to act as maid to Elizabeth. She should be made to understand who is the true Princess!'

Then she threw herself into his arms, laughing immoderately. He was pleased with her; he was sure that ere long they would have a healthy boy.

* * *

Sir Thomas More's daughter, Margaret Roper, was full of fear, for peace had been slowly filched from her home. April was such a pleasant month at Chelsea; in the garden of her father's house, where she had spent her happy childhood and continued to live with her husband Will Roper, the trees were blossoming; the water of the Thames lapped gently about the privy stairs; and how often had Margaret sat on the wooden seat with her father, listening to his reading to her and her brother and sisters, or watching him as he discoursed most wittily with his good friend Erasmus!

Change had crept into the house like a winter fog, and Margaret's heart was filled with a hatred alien to it; the hatred was for one whom she thought of as a brown girl, a girl with a sixth nail on her left hand and a disfiguring mark on her throat, a girl who had bewitched the King, who had cut off England from the Pope, and who had placed Margaret's father in mortal danger.

When Anne Boleyn had gone to court from Hever Castle, the first shadow had been cast over the Chelsea house. Her father would reprove her for her hatred, but Margaret could not subdue it. She was no saint, she reasoned. She had talked of Anne Boleyn most bitterly to her sisters, Elizabeth and Cecily; and now, sitting in the garden watching the river, calm today, bringing with it the mingled smells of tar and seaweed and rotting wood and fish, with the willow trees abudding and drooping sadly over it, she felt fear in the very air. When her adopted sister, Mercy, came running out to sit with her awhile, she had started violently and begun to tremble, fearing Mercy had brought news of some disaster. When her step-sister, Alice, appeared beside her, she felt her knees shake, though Alice had merely come to ask if Margaret would care to help her feed the peacocks.

Margaret recalled this house a few years back; she remembered seeing her father in the heart of his family, reading to them in long summer evenings out of doors, saying prayers in the house; and so often with a joke on his lips. Her father was the centre of his household; they all moved round him; were he removed, what then of the More family? 'Twould be like Earth without the sun, thought Margaret. She remembered writing letters to him when he was away from home on an embassy. He had been proud of her, showing her letters to the great scholar, Reginald Pole, who had complimented him on possessing such a daughter. He had told her this, for he knew well when a compliment might be passed to do the object good, and not to foster pride. He was a saint. And what so often was the end of saints? They became martyrs. Margaret wept softly, controlledly, for she dared not show the others she had wept; it would displease her father. Why must she now recall the memories of her childhood and all those sunny days in which her father moved, the centre of her life, the best loved one? Fear made her do it; fear of what was coming swiftly towards him. What was waiting for this adored father, tomorrow or the next day, or the next? Gloom had settled in the house; it was in the eyes of her step-mother, usually not eager to entertain it, usually eager to push it away; but it had come too close to be pushed away. Her sisters . . . were they over-gay? Their husbands laughed a little louder than was their wont; and in the garden, or from the windows of the house, their eyes would go to the river as though they were watching, watching for a barge that might come from Westminster or the Tower, and stop at the privy steps of Sir Thomas More's garden.

Her father was the calmest of the household; though often he would look at them all sadly and eagerly, as though he would remember the details of each face, that he might recall them after he would be unable to see them. A great calm had settled upon him of late, as though he had grappled with a problem and found the solution. He was a great, good man; and yet he was full of fun. One would have expected a saint to be a little melancholy, not fond of partaking of pleasure nor seeing those about him doing so. He was not like that; he loved to laugh, to see his children laugh; he was full of kindly wit. Oh, there was never such a one as Father! sighed Margaret.

He was fifty-six years of age now, and since he had given up the chancellorship he had looked every year of it. As a boy he had been taken into the household of Cardinal Morton who was then Archbishop of Canterbury; from thence he had gone to Oxford, become a lawyer, gone into Parliament, had lectured on the subject of theology, and was soon recognized as a brilliant young man. There was in him the stuff of the martyr; at one time he had come very near to becoming a monk, but he decided to marry. 'Did you ever regret that decision, Father?' Margaret once asked, and he laughed and pretended to consider; and she had been filled with happiness to know he did not. That was well, for if ever a man was meant to be a father, that man was Sir Thomas More. There was never such a family as ours, thought Margaret. We were happy . . . happy . . . before Anne Boleyn went to court. Wolsey had admired Sir Thomas, had made use of him; the King had met him, taken a liking to him, sought his help in denouncing the doctrines of Luther. Thus, when Wolsey was discarded, it was on this man that the King's choice fell. 'More shall be Chancellor. More shall have the Great Seal of England,' said the King. 'For rarely liked I a man better!' And so he achieved that high office; but he was never meant to go to court. Had he not remarked that he would serve God first, the Prince second? He would ever say that which would lead to trouble, because honesty was second nature to him. He was a saint; please God he need never show the world that he could be a martyr too! Margaret had been frightened when he became Chancellor, knowing his views on the divorce.

'Anne Boleyn will never be Queen,' she had said often enough to her husband, Will. 'How can she be, when the Pope will not sanction the divorce?'

'Indeed,' had answered Will, 'you speak truth, Meg. How can that be! A man who has one wife may not marry another.'

She had been afraid for Will then, for he was interested in the new Faith and would read of it secretly, being unsure in his mind; she trembled, for she could not have borne that her beloved father and her dear husband should not be in agreement on these matters. She had discussed Martin Luther and his doctrines with her father, for he was ever ready to talk with her on any serious subject, holding that though she was a woman she had the power to think and reason.

'Father,' she had said, 'there have been times when I have heard you discourse against the ways of Rome.'

'That I have done, Meg. But this is how I see it, daughter. Rome's ways are not always good, but I hold the things we value most in life may best be held to under Rome.'

She had not dared to tell him of Will's flirting with the new faith. She did not understand it fully. She supposed that

Will, being young, would prefer to try the new, and her father, being not so young, must like the old ways best. She had thought it a great tragedy when she discovered this tendency in Will; but what was that, compared with this which threatened!

The giving up of the Great Seal had been like the first clap of thunder that heralds an unexpected storm on a fine summer's day. After that there was quiet, until that April day a year ago, when three bishops came to the house one morning to bring twenty pounds for his dress, that he might attend the coronation of her who was set up as Queen, and who could never be accepted as Queen in this household. He had refused that invitation. She shivered at the memory. A few days later that refusal brought forth its results; he was charged with bribery and corruption. A ridiculous charge against the most honest man in England; but nothing was too ridiculous to bring against one so prominent who failed to do honour to Anne Boleyn. And recently there had come a further and more alarming charge; a mad nun of Kent, named Elizabeth Barton, had been shocking Anne's supporters and heartening those of Katharine with her lurid prophecies of the evil fates which would await the King and Anne, should they continue in their ungodly ways. The rightful Queen, declared the nun, was Katharine. She had seen visions; she went into trances and then gave voice to prophecies which she declared were put into her mouth by the Holy Ghost. As she had been in touch with Queen Katharine and the Emperor Charles, she was considered dangerous, but on her arrest and examination in the Star Chamber she had confessed she was an imposter. And Sir Thomas More was accused of having instigated this woman to pretend the future had been revealed to her, that she might frighten the King into taking back Katharine and abandoning Anne.

Margaret remembered how they had sat about the table, pretending to eat, pretending it would be well, telling each other that the innocence of the guiltless was their best defence. He had been taken before the Council; he had been questioned by the new Archbishop, by His Grace of Norfolk

– whom she feared for his cold eyes and his hard, cruel mouth – before Thomas Cromwell, whose thick hands looked as though they would not hesitate to turn on one slow to answer his questions; his fish-like eyes held no warmth, only cunning. But he was clever as well as good, this most loved father; he had outwitted them, for his wit was sharper than theirs; and she had heard that there was none equal to him apart from Cranmer, and on this occasion Cranmer was on the wrong side, so right must prevail. They had dismissed him in exasperation, for they could not trip him; and it was *his* arguments, she was sure, that had dumb-founded *them,* not theirs him.

Will had travelled down with him, and told her about this afterwards. Will had said that he knew all must be well, and rejoiced to see him so merry.

Her father had replied that truly he was merry, and would Will know why? He had taken the first step and the first step was the hardest. He had gone so far with those lords that without great shame he could never turn back.

This then had been the cause of his merriment. The step was taken down that path which he believed to be the right one; but what a path, where danger lurked at every turn! And what was at the end of it? That had happened a year ago, and now he had come far along that path; and this gloom which hung over them now – did it mean that he was nearing its end?

Mercy was running out to the garden now.

'Meg!' she called. 'Meg!' And Margaret dared not turn to look at her, so strong was her fear, so numbing the suspense.

Mercy's pleasant face was hot with running.

'Dinner, Meg! Of what are you thinking . . . dreaming here? We are all waiting for you. Father sent to call you. . . .'

She thought she had never heard more beautiful words than those, and their beauty was in their sweet normality. 'Father sent to call you.' She went with Mercy into the house.

They sat round the large table, her stepmother Alice, Cecily and her husband Giles, Elizabeth and her husband,

John and his wife, Mercy and Clement, Margaret and Will. And there at the head of the table he sat, his face more serene than any, as though he were unaware of the dark patches of sorrow that hung about his house. He was laughing, pretending to chide her for day-dreaming, giving her a lecture on the evils of unpunctuality which was spattered with fun; and she laughed with the rest, but not daring to meet his eyes for fear he should see the tears there. He knew why she would not look at him, for they were closer than any in the household, and though he loved well his family, it was his daughter Meg who was closest to his heart. So the others laughed, for he was a sorcerer where laughter was concerned, conjuring it up out of nowhere, but not for her; she was too close to the magician, she knew his tricks, she saw the sleight of hand; she knew the merry eyes watched the window, listened for a sign.

It came with a loud knocking on the outer door.

Gillian, their little maid, came running in, her mouth open. There was one outside who must see Sir Thomas.

Sir Thomas arose, but the man was already in the room. He carried the scroll in his hands. He bowed most courteously. His face was sad, as though he did not greatly love his mission, which was a command that Sir Thomas must appear next day before the Commissioners in order to take the Oath of Supremacy.

There was silence round the table; Margaret stared at the dish before her, at the worn wood of the table which she remembered so well, since she had sat at this particular place for as long as she could recall. She wished the birds would not sing so loudly, showing they did not know this was a day of doom; she wished the sun would not shine so hotly on her neck, for it made her feel she would be sick. She wanted perfect clarity of mind to remember for ever each detail of that well loved face.

Her stepmother had turned deathly pale; she looked as if she would faint. The whole family might have been petrified; they did not move; they sat and waited.

Margaret looked at her father; his eyes had begun to twinkle. No, no! she thought. Not now! I cannot bear that you should turn this into a joke. Not even for them. Not now!

But he was smiling at her, imploring her. Margaret! You and I, we understand. We have to help one another.

Then she arose from the table and went to the messenger, and looking closely at his face, she said: 'Why . . . Dick Halliwell! Mother . . . Everybody . . . 'Tis only Dick!'

And they fell upon her father, chiding him, telling him he went too far with his jokes. And there he was, laughing among them, believing that it is well not to look at unhappiness until it is close upon you, having often said that once you have passed it, every day lends distance between it and yourself.

Margaret went to her nursery where she stayed with her small daughter, finding solace in the charm of the child and thinking of the child's future when she would have children of her own, so that she might not think of this day and the days that would immediately follow it.

Later, hearing voices beneath her window, she looked out and saw her father walking below with the Duke of Norfolk who, she guessed, had come to have a word with him about the morrow. Margaret, her hand on her heart, as though she feared those below would hear its wild beating, listened to their voices which were wafted up to her.

' 'Tis perilous striving with princes,' said His Grace. 'I could wish you as a friend to incline to the King's pleasure.'

Then she heard her father's voice, and it seemed to her that it held little of sorrow. 'There will be only this difference between Your Grace and me, that I shall die today and you tomorrow.'

That night, she could not sleep. Death seemed already to be hovering over the house. She recalled what she had heard of those committed to the Tower; she thought of that gloomy prison and compared it with this happy home. He would say: 'All these years of happiness have I had; I should be grateful to have known them, not sorrowful that because I have loved them well I now must grieve the more to lose them.'

She wept bitter tears, and took her child in her arms, seeking comfort from that small body. But there was no comfort for Margaret Roper. Death hung over the house, waiting to snatch its best loved member.

He left next day. She watched him go down the privy steps with Will, his head held high; already he looked a saint. He did not cast a look behind him; he would have them all believe that soon he would be returning to them.

* * *

Catherine Howard was in the orchard, looking through the trees at the river. She was plumper than she had been almost a year ago when she had first met Francis Derham at the coronation. Now she deplored the state of her clothes, longed for rich materials, for ribands and flowers to adorn her hair.

She was not yet thirteen years old and looked seventeen – a plump, ripe, seventeen; she was very pretty, very gay, fond of laughter; in love with Francis.

Life was beautiful, she thought, and promised to be more so. Francis was husband to her, she wife to him. One day – and that not far distant – they would be so in earnest.

As she stood gazing at the river, a pair of hands were placed over her eyes; she gave a little cry of pleasure, assured this was Francis. Often he came to her, and they met here in the orchards, for he was still of her uncle's house.

'Guess who!' said the loved and familiar voice.

'Guess!' she cried shrilly. 'I do not have to guess – I know!'

She pulled away his hands and swung round to face him; they kissed passionately.

He said: 'Such good news I have today, Catherine! I can scarce wait to tell you.'

'Good news!'

'The best of news. I hope that you will agree that it is.'

'Tell me, tell me! You must tell me.'

He stood, surveying her, laughing, harbouring his secret, longing so deeply for the moment of revelation that he must keep it back, savouring afresh the pleasure it would give him to tell her.

'Very well, I will tell you, Catherine. Her Grace is to have a new gentleman usher. What do you think his name is?'

'Francis . . . you!'

He nodded.

'Then you will be here . . . under this very roof! This is wonderful news, Francis.'

They embraced.

'It will be so much simpler to meet, Catherine.'

She was smiling. Yes, indeed, it would be much easier to meet. There would be many opportunities of which he did not as yet dream.

She was flushed with pleasure, bright-eyed, dreaming of them.

Some young ladies and gentlemen came upon them kissing there. Among them was Francis's great friend Damport.

Francis and Catherine broke free on seeing them, and were greeted with laughter. One of the young men said in mock dismay: 'You often kiss Mrs Catherine Howard, Derham. Is it not very bold of you?'

Derham answered: 'Who should hinder me from kissing my wife?'

'I trow this matter will come to pass!' said one of the ladies.

'What is that?' asked Derham.

'Marry! That Mr Derham shall have Mrs Catherine Howard.'

Derham laughed with pleasure. 'By St John!' he cried. 'You may guess twice and guess worse!'

They were all laughing merrily, when Catherine broke up their mirth by pointing to a barge that went down the river.

'Look ye all!' she cried. 'Is that not Sir Thomas More!'

They all fell silent, thinking of the man. They knew he had come near to the block when the nun of Kent had burned for her heresies. What now? they wondered, and a gloom was cast over their merriment. They watched the barge pass along the river on its way to Westminster; and when it was out of sight, they sought to laugh again, but they found they had no mirth in them.

*   *   *

Jane Rochford's brief sojourn in the Tower had frightened her considerably. There, in her prison, as she looked down on the river at the pomp of the coronation, she had realized that only her own folly had brought her to this pass, and that in future she must be wiser. She would always hate Anne, but that was no reason why she should shout the dangerous fact abroad. Her short incarceration had been in the nature of a warning to herself and others, but she came out chastened, determined to curb her hysterical jealousy. She apologized to Anne, who accepted her apology, her dislike for Jane being but mild, and she thinking her too colourless to feel much interest in her. So Jane came back to court as attendant to Anne, and though they were never even outwardly friends, there was a truce between them.

It was about a year after the coronation when Jane, who had a habit of discovering the secrets of those around her, made a great discovery.

There was among Anne's attendants a young girl of some beauty, of modest, rather retiring demeanour, somewhat self-effacing; a member of what had come to be known as the anti-Boleyn faction – that set which had held out for Katharine, and were quiet now, though seeming to be watching and waiting for a turn in events.

Jane had intercepted a glance the King had given this girl, and she had felt a deep exultation. Could it be, wondered Jane, that the King was contemplating taking a mistress . . . that he had already been unfaithful to Anne? The thought made Jane laugh aloud when she was alone. How foolish she had been to murmur against Anne! What a poor sort of revenge, that merely put oneself into the Tower! Revenge should be taken subtly; she had learned that now.

How amusing to carry the news to Anne, to falter, to shed a tear, to murmur: 'I am afraid I have some terrible news for you. I am not certain that I should tell . . . I am grieved that it should fall to my lot to bring you such news . . .'

She must watch; she must peep; she must go cautiously. She listened at doors; she hid behind curtains. She was really very bold, for well she knew what the wrath of the King could be like. But it was worth it; she discovered what she had hoped to discover.

She then must turn over in her mind how she would use this. She could go to Anne; she could have the story dragged from her seemingly reluctant lips; it would do her good to see the proud eyes flash, the anger burn in those cheeks, to see haughty Anne humiliated. On the other hand, what if she went to George with the news? She would have his complete attention; she would have his approval, as he would say she had done right in coming to him. She could not make up her mind what she wanted most, and she must do so quickly, for there were others in the court who pried and peeped, and would be only too glad to have the pleasure of doing that which she had worked for.

In the end she went to George.

'George, I have something to tell you. I am afraid. I hardly know what to do. Perhaps you can advise me.'

He was not very interested, she noticed with a sudden jealous rage; he thought it was her own affair. But wait until he learned it concerned his sister Anne!

'The King is indulging in a love affair with one of Anne's ladies.'

George, who had been writing when she came in, hardly looked up from his work. He was perturbed by this news, but not greatly. Knowing the King, he considered such affairs inevitable; they were bound to come sooner or later. The main point was that Anne should realize this and not irritate the King further than he was already irritated by the birth of a daughter. If she remained calm, understanding, she could keep her hold on him; if she were jealous, demanding, she might find herself in a similar position to that of Katharine. He would warn her to treat this matter with the lightness it deserved.

'Well,' said Jane, 'do you not think it was clever of me to have discovered this before most?'

He looked at her with distaste. She could not hide the triumph in her eyes. He pictured her, spying; he discovered early in their married life that she had a gift for spying. And now she was all excitement, happy – and showing it – because she had knowledge which was certain to hurt Anne.

'I am sure,' he said, 'that you enjoyed making the discovery and were clever in doing so.'

'What mean you?' she demanded.

'Just what I say, Jane.'

He stood up, and would have walked past her; she stopped him, putting her hands on his coat.

'I thought to please you, George. I wish I had gone straight to Anne now.'

He was glad she had not done that. Anne was nervous; she was irritable; she was inclined to do the first rash thing that came into her head these days.

He forced himself to smile at Jane. He patted her hand.

'I am glad you told me first.'

She pouted.

'You seemed angry with me a moment ago. Why, George? Why? Why does everything I do anger you?'

He could feel blowing up, one of those scenes which he dreaded. He said: 'Of course I was not angry. You imagine these things.'

'You were angry because you think she will be hurt. It does not matter that *I* risk my life . . .'

'To spy on the King!' he finished. He burst into sudden laughter. 'By God, Jane, I should like to have seen His Majesty, had he come upon you peeping through a crack in the door!'

She stamped her foot; her face was white with rage.

'You find this comic!' she said.

'Well, in a measure. The King, taking his guilty pleasure, and you doing that for which you have a perfect genius . . . spying, congratulating yourself . . .'

'Congratulating myself!'

'Oh, come! I swear I never saw you so pleased with anything.'

Her lips trembled; tears came into her eyes.

'I know I'm not clever, but why should you laugh at everything I do!'

'Everything?' he said, laughing. 'I assure you, Jane, that it is only on rare occasions that I can laugh at what you do.'

She turned on him angrily.

'Perhaps you will not find this such a laughing matter when I tell you who the lady is!'

He was startled now, and she had the joy of seeing that she had all his attention.

'I forget her name. She is so quiet, one scarcely notices her. She is a friend of Chapuys; she is of those who would very gladly see the Queen displaced from the throne . . .'

She saw now that he was deeply perturbed; this was not merely a king's light love affair; this was high politics. It was very likely that the girl had been primed to do this by the enemies of Anne.

George began to pace up and down; Jane sat in a window seat, watching him. Quite suddenly he went towards the door, and without a glance at Jane strode from the room. Jane wanted to laugh; but there was no laughter in her; she covered her face with her hands and began to cry.

George went to Anne. She was in her room, reading quietly, making marks with her thumbnail at those passages which she meant Henry to read. She was interesting herself in theology, because the subject interested him. She was trying now to bind him to her in every way she knew; she was uneasy; she thought often of Katharine and what had happened to her; she now wondered why she had not previously been more sympathetic towards Henry's first Queen. Bitterly she would laugh at herself; did she not understand the old Queen's case because her own was becoming distressingly similar?

'You look alarmed, George,' she said, laying aside her book.

'I have alarming news.'

'Tell me quickly.' She gave a somewhat hysterical laugh. 'I think I am prepared for anything.'

'The King is philandering.'

She threw back her head and laughed.

'I cannot say I am greatly surprised, George.'

'This is no ordinary philandering. It is important, when we consider who the girl is.'

'Who?'

'Jane does not remember her name.'

'Jane!'

They exchanged glances of understanding.

'Jane made it her affair to discover this matter,' said George. 'This time I think Jane has done us a service. She described the girl as meek and mild as milk.'

'Ah!' cried Anne. 'I can guess who she is!'

'She is of our enemies,' said George. 'It may well be that she has been made to do this to work your ruin, Anne.'

Anne stood up, her cheeks flaming.

'She shall be banished from the court! I myself will see her. She shall come to me at once ... I ...'

He lifted a restraining hand.

'Anne, you terrify me. These sudden rages ...'

'Sudden! Rages! Have I not good cause ...'

'You have every cause in the world, Anne, to go carefully. You must do nothing rash; everything you do is watched; everything you say is listened to. The throne shakes under you! You must say nothing of this to the King; you must feign ignorance for awhile. We must go secretly and in great quiet, for this is no ordinary light flirtation.'

'There are times,' she said, 'when I feel I should like nothing better than to walk out of the palace and never set eyes on the King again.'

'Be of good cheer. We'll think of something. There is one point you must not forget: Give no sign to the King that you know anything. We will, between us, think of a plan.'

'It is so ... humiliating!' she cried. 'By my faith! I have suffered more indignities since I have been the Queen than I ever did before.'

'One of the penalties of being Queen, Anne! Promise ... promise you will go cautiously!'

'Of course, of course! Naturally I shall ...'

'No,' he said, with a little grimace, 'not naturally, Anne; most unnaturally! Remember Mary ...'

'What of Mary?'

'You know well to what I refer. How could you have been so wild, so foolish, as to say that if the King went to France and you were Regent, you would find a reason for putting Mary out of the way!'

'This girl maddens me. She is foolish, obstinate . . . and . . .'

'That we well know, but the greater foolishness was yours, Anne, in making such unwise statements.'

'I know . . . I know. And you do well to warn me.'

'I warn you now. Remember previous follies, and keep in good temper with the King.'

'I had thought he seemed more tender of late,' she said, and began to laugh suddenly. 'To think it was naught but his guilty conscience!'

'Ah!' said George. 'He was ever a man of much conscience. But, Anne, he is simple; you and I know that, and together we can be frank. He has great pride in himself. His verses . . . If he thought we did not consider them the best ever written in his court, he would be ready to have our heads off our shoulders!'

'That he would! He has indeed great pride in himself and all his works. George . . .' She looked over her shoulder. 'There is none other to whom I could say this.' She paused, biting her lips, her eyes searching his face. 'Katharine had a daughter, and then . . . all those miscarriages! George, I wonder, might it not be that the King cannot breed sons?'

He stared at her.

'I understand not,' he said.

'Not one son,' she said, 'but Richmond. And Richmond . . . have you noticed? There is a delicate air about him; I do not think he will live to a great age. He is the King's only son. Then there is Mary who is normal, but Mary is a girl and they say that girls survive at birth more easily than boys. There is my own Elizabeth; she is also a girl . . .' She covered her face with her hands. 'And all those stillborn boys, and all those boys who lived to breathe for an hour or so before they died . . . George, was it due to any weakness in Katharine, think you, or was it . . . ?'

He silenced her with a look. He read the terror behind her words.

She said in a whisper: 'He is not wholly well . . . The place on his leg . . .' She closed her eyes and shivered. 'One feels unclean . . .' She shivered again. 'George, what if . . . he . . . cannot have sons?'

He clenched his hands, begging her with his eyes to cease such talk. He got up and strode to the door. Jane was in the corridor, coming towards the room. He wondered, Had she heard that? Had she heard him rise from his seat and stride to the door? Had she retreated a few paces from the door, and then, just as it opened, commenced to walk leisurely towards it? He could not tell from her face; her eyes glistened; she had been weeping. It seemed to him that she was always weeping. He would have to be careful with her; he was sure she could be dangerous.

'Oh . . . Jane . . . I was just telling Anne . . .'

Anne threw a haughty glance at her sister-in-law, but Jane did not care, as George was smiling at her.

'Come inside,' said George.

Jane went in, and the three of them sat together; but Anne would not speak of this matter before Jane. She wondered at her brother's show of friendship for his wife. Could it be that he was reconciling himself to his unhappy marriage, trying to make something out of it at last?

* * *

The King hummed a snatch of a song. Anne watched him. He sparkled with jewels; he looked enormous; he was getting corpulent, he was no longer the handsomest prince in Christendom; he was no longer the golden prince. He was a coarse man whose face was too red, whose eyes were bloodshot, and whose leg was a hideously unwholesome ulcer. His eyes were gleaming; he was the lover now, and she remembered the lover well. How often had she seen that look in his eyes! Always before, the look had been for her. Strange indeed to know his desires were fixed on someone else – strange and terrifying.

She said: 'The song is charming. Your own?'

He smiled. She was reclining on the bed he had given her before her confinement. It was a beautiful bed, he thought. By God, she should think herself lucky to have such a fine bed! He doubted whether there was such another bed in the world. Its splendour suited her, he thought indulgently. Anne! There was no one like her, of course; not even little . . . Well, he had never thought she was, but she was sweet, and Anne was fractious and could be maddening – and a man needed a change, if but to prove his manhood. He felt tender towards Anne at moments like this, when she said: 'The song is charming. Your own?' It was when those great black eyes of hers seemed to look right through him and see more of his mind than he cared for anyone to see, that he was angry with her. She was more clever than a woman ought to be! Learned foreigners delighted to talk to her of the new Lutheran theories, and did great homage to her because she could converse naturally and easily with them. He liked that not. Any glory that came to a queen should come through her king. Her beauty might be admired; the splendid clothes she wore, also; but her cleverness, her sharp retorts that might be construed as gibes . . . No, no; they angered him.

He would have her keep in mind that he had raised her up, that she owed all she now enjoyed to him. By God, there were moments when she would appear to forget this! She could please him still, could make him see that there never had been any like her, nor ever would be. That in itself irritated him; it bound him, and he did not like to be bound. He could think with increasing longing of the days before he had known Anne, before this accursed leg began to trouble him, when he was a golden-haired, golden-bearded giant of a man, excelling all others in any sport that could be named; riding hard, eating, drinking, loving, all in a grander manner than that of other men; with Wolsey – dear old Wolsey – to take over matters of state. She had killed Wolsey as surely as if she had slain him with her own hands, since but for her Wolsey would have been alive to this day.

More was in the Tower. And she had done this. And yet . . . there was none could satisfy him as she could; haughty, aloof, as she well knew how to be, always he must feel the longing to subdue her. Sometimes his feeling for her was difficult to explain; sudden anger and fury she aroused in him, and then as suddenly desire, blinding desire that demanded satisfaction at any price. Nay, there was no one like her, but she had cut him off from the days of his glowing manhood. He had met her and changed from that bright youth; during the years of his faithfulness he had been steadily undergoing a change; now he would never be the same man again.

But enough of introspection! He was trying hard to regain his youth. There was one – and she soon to be in his arms, looking up at him with sweet humility – who would assure him that he was the greatest of men as well as the mightiest of kings; who asked for nothing but the honour of being his mistress. Sweet balm to the scorching wounds the black-eyed witch on the bed had given him. But at the moment the witch was sweetly complimenting him, and he had ever found her irresistible in that mood. The other could wait awhile.

'My own, yes,' he said. 'You shall hear me sing it, but not now.'

'I shall await the hearing with pleasure.'

He looked at her sharply. Did she mock? Did she like his songs? Did she compare them with her brother's, with Wyatt's, with Surrey's? Did she think they suffered by comparison?

She was smiling very sweetly. Absently she twirled a lock of her hair. Her eyes were brilliant tonight, and there was a flush in her cheeks. He was taken aback at the contemplation of her beauty, even though he had come to know it too familiarly.

The little one would be awaiting him. Her homage was very sweet. He would sing his song to her, and have no doubts of her approval – but for that reason it was not as sweet as Anne's. She thought him wonderful. She was not clever; a woman should not be clever; her mission in life was to please her lord. And yet . . . he was proud of his Queen. But what matter? It was but manly to love; there was little harm in a dash of light loving here and there; the ladies expected it, and a king should please his subjects.

'Henry . . .' she said. He paused, patting the diamond

which was the centre button of his coat. 'There is something I would say to you.'

'Can it not wait?'

'I think you would rather hear it now.'

'Then tell me quickly.'

She sat up on the bed and held out her hands to him, laughing.

'But it is news I would not care to hurry over.' She was watching his face eagerly.

'What!' said the King. 'Anne . . . what meanest thou?'

He took her hands, and she raised herself to a kneeling position.

'Tell me,' she said, putting her face close to his, 'what news would you rather I gave, what news would please you more than any?'

His heart was beating wildly. Could it be what he had longed to hear? Could it really be true? And why not? It was the most natural . . . it was what all expected, what all were waiting for.

'Anne!' he said.

She nodded.

He put his arms about her; she slid hers about his neck.

'I thought to please you,' she said.

'Please me!' He was hilarious as a schoolboy. 'There could be naught to give me greater pleasure.'

'Then I am happy.'

'Anne, Anne, when . . . ?'

'Not for eight long months. Still . . .'

'You are sure?'

She nodded, and he kissed her again.

'This pleases me more than all the jewels in the world,' he told her.

'It pleases me as much as it pleases you. There have been times of late . . . when I have felt . . .'

He stopped her words by kissing her.

'Bah! Then thou wert indeed a foolish girl, Anne!'

'Indeed I was. Tell me, were you about to go on an important mission? For I would fain talk of this . . .'

He laughed. 'Important mission! By God! I would desert the most important of missions to hear this news!'

He had forgotten her already, thought Anne exultantly. Here was the tender lover returned. It had only needed this.

He did not leave her, not that night, nor the next. He had forgotten the demure little girl; he had merely been passing the time with her. Anne was with child. This time a son; certainly a son. Why not! All was well. He had done right to marry Anne. This was God's answer!

* * *

Henry felt sure of his people's joy, once his son was born. It would but need that to have done with the murmuring and grumbling. He forgot the girl with whom he had been pleasing himself; he was the loyal husband now; the father of a daughter, about to be the father of a son. He gave up the idea of going to France, and instead went on a tour through the midlands with Anne – belligerent and mighty. This is the Queen I have chosen. Be good subjects, and love her – or face my wrath!

Subjects *en masse* were disconcerting. A king might punish a few with severity, but what of that? The Dacres affair was proof that the people were not with Anne. Dacres was devoted wholeheartedly to the Catholic cause, and thus to Katharine; and for this reason, Northumberland – still a great admirer of Anne – had quarrelled with the man and accused him of treason. To Cromwell and Cranmer it seemed a good moment to conduct Lord Dacres to the block, so they brought him to London, where he was tried by his peers. The Lords, with unexpected courage and with a defiance unheard of under Henry's despotic rule, had acquitted Dacres. This would seem to Henry like treason on the part of the peers, but it was much more; it meant that these gentlemen knew they had public support behind them, and that was backed up by hatred of Anne – whether she was with child or not made no difference. It shook Henry; it shattered Anne and her supporters. It seemed that everyone was waiting now for the son she promised to produce; that of course would make all the difference; Henry could never displace the mother of his son. Once Anne gave birth to a boy, who showed some promise of becoming a man, she was safe; until then she was tottering.

Anne was very uneasy; more so than anyone, with perhaps the exception of George, could possibly guess. She would wander in the grounds around Greenwich, and brood on the future. She wished to be alone; sometimes when she was in the midst of a laughing crowd she would steal away. Anne was very frightened.

Each day she hoped and prayed for some sign that she might be pregnant; there was none. She had planned boldly, and it seemed as if her plan had failed. What will become of me? she wondered. She could not keep her secret much longer.

She had believed, when she told the King that she was with child, that soon she must be. Why was it that she was not? Something told her the fault lay with him, and this idea was supported by Katharine's disastrous experiences and her own inability to produce another child. There was Elizabeth, but Elizabeth would not do. She murmured: 'Oh, Elizabeth, my daughter, why wast thou not born a boy!'

She watched the clouds drifting across the summer sky; she looked at the green leaves on the trees and murmured: 'Before they fall I shall have to tell him. A woman cannot go on for ever pretending she is pregnant!'

Perhaps by then . . . Yes, that had been the burden of her thoughts. . . . Perhaps by then that which had been a fabrication of her tortured mind would be a reality. Perhaps by then there would be a real child in her womb, not an imaginary one.

The days passed. Already people were glancing at her oddly. Is the Queen well? How small she is! Can she really be with child? What think you? Is something wrong? Is this her punishment for the way she treated poor Queen Katharine?

She sat under the trees, praying for a child. How many women had sat under these trees, frightened because they were to bear a child! And now here was one who was terrified because she was not to bear one, because she, feeling herself in a desperate situation, had seen in such a lie a possible way out of her difficulties.

Her sister Mary came and sat beside her. Mary was plumper, more matronly, but still the same Mary although perhaps over ripe now. Still unable to say No, I'll warrant, thought Anne, and was suddenly filled with sharp envy.

'Anne,' said Mary, 'I am in great trouble.'

Anne's lips curled; she wondered what Mary's trouble was, and how it would compare with her own.

'What trouble?' asked Anne, finding sudden relief as her thoughts necessarily shifted from herself to her sister.

'Anne, dost know Stafford?'

'What!' cried Anne. 'Stafford the gentleman usher?'

'The very one,' said Mary. 'Well ... he and I ...'

'A gentleman usher!' said Anne.

'All the world seemed to set so little by me, and he so much,' said Mary. 'I thought I could take no better way out but to take him and forsake all other ways.'

'The King will never consent,' said Anne.

'Perhaps when he knows I am to have a child ...'

Anne turned on her sister in horror. Mary had been a widow for five years. Naturally one would not expect her to live a nun's life, but one did expect her to show a little care. Oh, thought Anne, how like Mary! How like her!

Mary hastened to explain. 'He was young, and love overcame us. And I loved him as he did me....'

Anne was silent.

'Ah!' went on Mary, 'I might have had a man of higher birth, but I could never have had one who could have loved me so well ... nor a more honest man.'

Anne looked cold, and Mary could not bear coldness now; she did not know of her sister's trials; she pictured her happy and secure, rejoicing in her queenly state. It seemed unkind to have from her no word of reassurance.

Mary stood up. 'I had rather be with him than I were the greatest queen!' she cried, and began to run across the grass into the palace.

Anne watched her. Mary – a widow – was with child, and afraid because of it. Anne – a queen and a wife – was not, and far, far more afraid than Mary could understand, because of it! Anne threw back her head and laughed immoderately; and when she had done, she touched her cheeks and there were tears upon them.

*   *   *

When Anne told Henry there was not to be a child, he was furious.

'How could such a mistake occur!' he demanded suspiciously, his little eyes cold and cruel.

'Simply!' she flared back. 'And it did, so why argue about it!'

'I have been tricked!' he cried. 'It seems that God has decreed I shall never have a son.'

And he turned away, for there was a certain speculation in his eyes which he did not wish her to see. He went to the demure little lady-in-waiting.

'Ha!' he said. 'It seems a long time since I kissed you, sweetheart!'

She was meek, without reproaches. How different from Anne! he thought, and remembered resentfully how she had commanded him during the days of his courtship, and how when she had become his mistress she continued to berate him.

By God, he thought, I'll have none of that. Who brought her up, eh? Who could send her back whence she came? Women should be meek and submissive, as this one was.

Anne watched angrily, trying to follow her brother's advice and finding herself unable to do so.

'Madge,' she said to her cousin, a lovely girl of whom she was very fond, 'go to that girl and tell her I would see her this minute.'

Madge went, and awaiting the arrival of the girl, Anne paced up and down, trying to compose herself, trying to rehearse what she would say to her.

The girl came, eyes downcast, very frightened, for Anne's eyes were blazing in spite of her efforts to remain calm.

'I would have you know,' said Anne, 'that I have been hearing evil reports of my ladies. I am sending you back to your home. Be ready to start as soon as you hear from me that you are to do so.'

The girl scarcely looked at Anne; she blushed scarlet, and her lips quivered.

Sly creature! thought Anne angrily. And she the King's mistress! What he can see in the girl I do not understand, except that she is a trifle pretty and very meek. Doubtless she tells him he is wonderful! Her lips twisted scornfully, and then suddenly she felt a need to burst into tears. Here was she, the Queen, and must resort to such methods to rid herself of her rivals! Was everyone in this court against her? Her father was anxious now, she knew, wondering how long she would retain her hold on the King; Norfolk no longer troubled to be courteous; they had quarrelled; he had stamped out of the room on the last occasion she had seen him, muttering that of her which she would prefer not to remember; Suffolk watched, sly, secretly smiling; the Princess Mary was openly defiant. And now this girl!

'Get you gone from my presence!' said Anne. 'You are banished from court.'

The girl's reply was to go straight to the King, who immediately countermanded the Queen's order.

He left the girl and went to Anne.

'What means this?' he demanded.

'I will not have you parade your infidelities right under my nose!'

'Madam!' roared the King. 'I would have you know I am master here!'

'Nevertheless,' she said, 'you cannot expect me to smile on your mistresses and to treat them as though they were the most faithful of my attendants.'

He said coarsely: 'If that is what I wish, you shall do it ... as others did before you!'

'You mistake me,' she answered.

'I mistake you not. From where do you derive your authority if not from me! Consider from what I lifted you. I have but to lift my finger to send you back whence you came!'

'Why not lift it then?' she blazed. 'Your pretty little mistress doubtless would grace the throne better than I. She is so brilliant! Her conversation is so witty! The people would acclaim her. But, Henry, do you not think she might put you a little in the shade. . . . Such wit . . . such brilliance!'

He looked at her with smouldering eyes; there were occasions when he could forget he was a king and put his hands about that little neck, and press and press until there was no breath left in her. But a king does not do murder; others do it for him. It was a quick thought that passed through his mind and was gone before he had time to realize it had been there.

He turned and strode out of the room.

Jane Rochford had overheard that quarrel. She was excited; it gave her a pleasurable thrill to know that Anne was having difficulties with her husband, just as she herself had with George, though with a difference.

Jane crept away and came back later, begging a word with the Queen. Could the ladies be dismissed? Jane whispered. What she had to say was for Anne's ear alone.

She expresssed her sympathy.

'Such a sly wench! I declare she deliberately sets out to trap the King. All that modesty and reluctance . . .' Jane glanced sideways at Anne; had her barb struck a vulnerable spot? Oh, how did it feel, when you have shown reluctance to a king and complete indifference to the feelings of his wife, to find your position suddenly reversed; yourself the neglected wife, and another careless of your feelings? Jane was so excited she could scarcely talk; she wanted to laugh at this, because it seemed so very amusing.

'But I have not come to commiserate with you, dear sister. I want to help. I have a plan. Were I to let her people know that she is in danger of disgracing herself – oh, I need not mention His Majesty – it might be a friendly warning. . . . I would try. I trow that, were she removed from court, the King would be the most loyal of husbands; and how can a woman get children when her husband has no time for her, but only for other women!'

Jane spoke vehemently, but Anne was too sick at heart to notice it. Everywhere she looked, disaster was threatening.

She was young and healthy, but her husband was neither so young nor so healthy; she could not get a child, when the most urgent matter she had ever known was that she should first get with child, and that the child should be a son. The King's health was doubtless to blame, but the King never blamed himself; when he was in fault he blamed someone else. There was evidence of that all about him, and had been for years. Francis had made an alarming move; he had begun to talk once more of a match between his son and Mary. What could that mean, but one thing! Mary was a bastard; how could a bastard marry the son of the King of France?

There was only one answer: The King of France no longer regarded Mary as a bastard. Her hopes had soared when Clement died and Paul III took his place; Paul had seemed more inclined to listen to reason, but what did she know of these matters? Only what it was deemed wise to tell her! Francis, whom she had regarded as a friend to herself, who had shown decided friendship when they had met at Calais, had decided it was unsafe to quarrel with Charles and with Rome. France was entirely Catholic – that was the answer. Francis could not stand out against his people; his sympathy might be with Anne, but a king's sympathy must be governed by diplomacy; Francis was showing a less friendly face to Anne. She saw now that the whole of Europe would be against the marriage; that would have meant nothing, had Henry been with her, had Henry been the devoted lover he had remained during the waiting years. But Henry was turning from her; this sly, meek, pretty girl from the opposite camp was proof of that. She was filled with terror, for she remembered the negotiations which had gone on before news of a possible divorce had reached Katharine. Everyone at court had known before Katharine; they had whispered of The King's Secret Matter. Was the King now indulging once more in a secret matter? Terrified, she listened to Jane; she was ready to clutch at any straw. That was foolish – she might have known Jane was no diplomatist. Jane's art was in listening at doors, slyly setting one person against another.

Henry discovered what Jane was about.

'What!' he shouted. 'This is the work of Rochford's wife. She shall be committed to the Tower by the Traitor's Gate.' She wept and stormed, cursing herself for her folly. To think she had come to this by merely trying to help Anne! What would become of her now? she wondered. If ever she got out of the Tower alive, she would be clever, subtle. . . . Once before she had been careless; this time she had been equally foolish, but she had learned her lesson at last. George would bear her no gratitude for what she had done; he would say: 'What a clumsy fool you are, Jane!' Or if he did not say it, he would think it.

All this she had done for George really . . . and he cared not, had no feeling for her at all. 'Methinks I begin to hate him!' she murmured, and looked through her narrow windows onto the cobbles beneath.

George came to see his sister; he was secretly alarmed.

'Jane has been sent to the Tower!' he said. Anne told him what had happened. 'This grows mightily dangerous, Anne.'

'You to tell *me* that! I assure you I know it but too well.'

'Anne, you must go very carefully.'

'You tell me that persistently,' she answered pettishly. 'What must I do now? I have gone carefully, and I have been brought to this pass. What is happening to us? Mary in disgrace, our father quite often absenting himself from court, shamefaced, hardly looking at me! And Uncle Norfolk becoming more and more outspoken! You, alarmed that I will not be cautious, and I . . .'

'We have to go carefully, that is all. We have to stop this affair of the King's with this girl; it must not be allowed to go on.'

'I care not! And it were not she, it would be another.'

'Anne, for God's sake listen to reason! It matters not if it were another one; it only matters that it should be *she*!'

'You mean . . . there is more in this than a simple love affair?'

'Indeed I do.'

Madge Shelton looked in at the door.

'I beg your pardon. I had thought Your Majesty to be

alone.' She and George exchanged cousinly greetings, and Madge retired.

'Our cousin is a beautiful girl,' said George.

Anne looked at him sharply.

He said: 'You'll hate what I am about to say, Anne. It is a desperate remedy, but I feel it would be effective. Madge is delightful, so young and charming. The other affair may well be beginning to pall.'

'George! I do not understand. . . .'

'We cannot afford to be over-nice, Anne.'

'Oh, speak frankly. You mean – throw Madge to the King, that he may forget that other . . .'

'It is not a woman we have to fight, Anne. It is a party!'

'I would not do it,' she said. 'Why, Madge . . . she is but a young girl, and he . . . You cannot know, George. The life he has lived. . . .'

'I do know. Hast ever thought we are fighting for thy life?'

She tried to throw off her fears with flippancy. She laughed rather too loudly; he noticed uneasily that of late she had been given to immoderate laughter.

'Ever since I had thought to be Queen, there have been those ready to thrust prophecies under my eyes. I mind well one where I was depicted with my head cut off!' She put her hands about her throat. 'Fret not, George. My husband, after the manner of most, amuses himself. He was all eagerness for me before our marriage; now?' She shrugged her shoulders and began to laugh again.

'Be silent,' said George. 'What of Elizabeth?'

She stopped laughing.

'What of Elizabeth?'

'It has been decreed that Mary Tudor is a bastard, because the King tired of her mother and decided – as she could no longer hope to give him a son – that he was no longer married to her. Oh, we know of his conscience, we know of his treatise . . . we know too well the story. But, Anne, we are alone and we need not fear each other. . . . Ah! What a good thing it is to have in this world one person of whom you need not cherish the smallest fear! Anne, I begin to think we are not so unlucky, you and I.'

'Please stop,' she said. 'You make me weep.'

'This is no time for tears. I said Mary has been decreed a bastard, though her mother is of Spain and related to the most powerful man in Europe. Anne, you are but the daughter of the Earl of Wiltshire – Sir Thomas Boleyn not long since – and he was only raised to his earldom to do honour to you; he could be stripped of that honour easily enough. He is no Emperor, Anne! Dost see what I mean? Mary was made a bastard; what of Elizabeth? Who need fear *her* most humble relations?'

'Yes,' said Anne breathlessly. 'Yes!'

'If the King has no sons, Elizabeth will be Queen of England . . . or Mary will! Oh, Anne, you have to fight this, you have to hold your place for your daughter's sake.'

'You are right,' she said. 'I have my daughter.'

'Therefore . . .'

She nodded. 'You are right, George. I think you are often right. I shall remember what you said about our being lucky. Yes, I think we are; for who else is there, but each other!'

The next day she sent Madge Shelton with a message to the King. From a window she watched the girl approach him, for he was in the palace grounds. Yes, he was appreciative; who could help being so, of Madge! Madge had beauty; Madge had wit. She had made the king laugh; he was suggesting they should take a turn round the rose garden.

Anne soothed her doubts with the reflection that Madge was a saucy wench, able to take care of herself, and had probably had love affairs before. Besides . . . there was Elizabeth!

* * *

The Dowager Duchess of Norfolk was uneasy. Rumours came from the court, and one could not ignore them. All was not well with the Queen. She herself had quarrelled with her stepson, the Duke, because he had spoken as she did not care to hear him speak, and it had been of the Queen. I never did like the man, she mused. Cruel, hard, opportunist! One could tell which way the wind was blowing, by what he would have to say. Which way was the wind blowing? She liked not these rumours.

She was to be state governess to the Princess Elizabeth, a further sign of Anne's friendship for her. 'I do hope the dear child is well and happy. It is a terrible trial to be a queen, and to such a king!' she murmured to herself.

The Duchess was fractious in her own household. Those girls were noisy in their room at night, and she had heard it whispered that they were over-free with the young men.

She sent for Mary Lassells, whom she did not like over-much. The girl was of humble birth, apt to look sullen; she was really a serving-maid, and should not be with the ladies. I must see to that one day, thought the duchess, and filed the matter away in that mental pigeon-hole which was crammed full of forgotten notes.

'Mary Lassells,' she said, when the girl came to her, 'there is much noise in the ladies' sleeping apartments at night. These ladies are under my care, and as since my grand-daughter's coronation I find myself with less and less leisure, I am going to take a few precautions to make sure of correct behaviour on the part of these young people.'

The girl was smiling primly, as though to indicate that there was every reason for the Duchess to take precautions. This angered the Duchess; she did not wish to be reminded that she had been lax; she would have preferred the girl to look as though this were a quite unnecessary precaution being taken by an over-careful duenna.

'It will be your duty, Mary Lassells, every night when the ladies have retired, to see that the key of their apartment is placed in the lock outside the door. Then at a fixed hour I shall send someone to lock the door, and the key will be brought to me.'

The Duchess sat back in her chair, well pleased.

'I think that will be a very excellent plan, Your Grace,' said Mary Lassells unctuously.

'Your opinion was not asked, Mary Lassells,' said the Duchess haughtily. 'That will do. Now remember please, and I will send someone for the key this very night.'

Mary said nothing. It was shocking to consider what

went on in that room at night. Catherine Howard behaved quite shamelessly now with Francis Derham; he would bring fruit and wine for her, and they would sit on her bed and laugh and chatter, telling everyone that as they were really married there was no harm in what they were doing. Derham was very much in love with the child – that was obvious – and she with him; he salved his conscience by pretending they were married. It was very silly, thought Mary Lassells, and certainly time such wickedness was stopped.

They were planning for tonight. Let them plan! What a shock for them, when they were waiting to receive their lovers, to find the door locked, keeping them out! And so would it be every night. No more games, no more of such wicked folly.

Though Manox never came to the room now, she often thought of him. Some said he was sorely troubled because he had lost little Catherine Howard. And she not fourteen! Thirteen at the most. Was ever such crass wickedness allowed to go unpunished! She will go to hell and suffer eternal torment when she dies, I'll swear! And Mary Lassells felt happier at the thought.

They were all laughing, chattering in their silly way, when Mary Lassells went to the door to obey the Duchess's instructions. 'Where go you?' asked one girl.

'Merely to act on Her Grace's orders.' Mary put the key in the outer lock. Inside the room they heard her exchanging a few words with someone outside the door. Mary came back into the room, and the door was immediately locked on the outside.

There was a chorus of excitement. 'What means this?' 'Is it a joke?' 'What said you, Mary Lassells?' 'Why did you take the key?'

Mary Lassells faced them, her prim mouth working. 'Her Grace the Duchess is much displeased. She has heard the laughing and chatter that goes on here of nights. She has taken me on one side and told me what she will do. Every night the door of this apartment is to be locked and the key taken to her.'

There were cries of rage.

'Mary Lassells! You have been bearing tales!'

'Indeed I have not!'

'What can one expect of a cook's daughter!'

'I am not a cook's daughter.'

'Oh, well . . . something such!'

'This is shameful. Her Grace merely asked me to put the key outside. . . . I suppose because she sees I am more virtuous than the rest of you.'

Dorothy Barwicke said: 'Do you swear, Mary Lassells, that you have said nothing to Her Grace of what happens in this room?'

'I swear!'

'Then why . . . ?'

'She has heard the noise in here. She says too that she has heard whispers of what goes on. . . . Doubtless the servants. . . .'

'They may have heard the gentlemen creeping up the stairs!' said one girl with a giggle. 'I declare Thomas made one devil of a row last time.'

'The truth remains,' said Mary Lassells, 'that you are under suspicion. I only hope Her Grace does not think I have been a party to your follies!'

'Impossible!'

'You would find it difficult, Mary, to discover one who would be a partner.'

The girls were rocking on their beds, laughing immoderately.

'Poor Mary!' said Catherine. 'I am sure Manox likes you very well.'

Everyone shrieked with laughter at that. Catherine was hurt; she had not meant to be unkind. She had seen Manox and Mary together before she had broken with him, and she had thought they seemed friendly. She would have liked Manox to find someone he could care for. Mary too. It seemed a satisfactory settlement, to Catherine.

Mary threw her a glance of hatred.

'Well,' said Dorothy Barwicke, 'this is an end of our little frolics . . . unless . . .'

'Unless what?' cried several voices.

'There are some very rash and gallant gentlemen among our friends; who knows, one might find a way of stealing the keys!'

'Stealing the keys!' The adventures would have an additional spice if keys had first to be stolen.

The young ladies settled into their beds and talked for a long time. Mary Lassells lay in hers, trembling with rage against them all, and particularly against Catherine Howard.

* * *

In his prison room in the Tower of London, Margaret Roper stood before her father. He was hollow-eyed, but he was smiling bravely, and she saw that he was more serene in his mind than he had been for a long time. Margaret flung herself at him, reproaches on her lips for those who had brought him to this, for her hatred of them she could not express in his presence, knowing it would disturb him.

They could only look at each other, drinking in each detail of the well-loved faces, knowing that only with the greatest good luck could they hope for another interview. He was braver than she was. Perhaps, she thought, it is easier to die than to be left. He could laugh; she could not. When she would have spoken, tears ran from her eyes.

He understood her feelings. Had he not always understood her?

'Let me look at thee, Meg! Thou hast been too long in the sun. There are freckles across thy nose. Look after the children, Meg. Let them be happy. Meg, thou and I may speak frankly together.'

She nodded. She knew that all pretence between them was at an end. He would not say to her, as he might have said to any of the others: 'This will pass!' They were too close; they could hide nothing. He knew that it was but a matter of time before he must lay his head on the block.

'Take care of the children, Meg. Frighten them not with gloomy tales of death. Tell them of bright chariots and of beauty. Make them see death as a lovely thing. Do this for me, Meg. Grieve not that I must leave this gloomy prison.

My spirit is enclosed in a shell. It longs for the hatching. It longs to be born. Oh, let that shell be cracked. What matter by whom, by the King or his mistress!'

'Speak not of her, Father . . . But for her . . .'

He must lay his hands on her lips, and say a word for the creature.

'Judge her not, Meg. For how do we know what she may be suffering at this moment?'

She burst out: 'At the court there is sport and dances. What do they care that you – the noblest of men – shall die! They must amuse themselves; they must destroy those who would stand in the way of their pleasure. Father, do not ask me not to curse them . . . for I do, I do!'

'Poor Anne Boleyn!' he said sadly. 'Alas, Meg, it pitieth me to consider what misery, poor şoul, she will shortly come to. These dances of hers will prove such dances that she will spurn our heads off like footballs, but 'twill not be long ere her head will dance the like dance.'

He was saint indeed, thought Margaret, for he could defend her who was to cause his death; he could be sorry for her, could weep a little for her. He talked of the King more frankly than she had ever heard him spoken of. He said there was always cruelty in a man who cannot restrain his passions.

'Be not troubled, sweet daughter, even when you see my head on London Bridge. Remember it is *I* who will look down on *thee* and feel pity.'

He asked of family affairs, of the garden, of the house, of the peacocks. He could laugh; he could even jest. And sick at heart, yet comforted, she left him.

After his trial she saw him brought back to the Tower. He walked with his head erect; though she noticed his clothes were creased and looked shabby; well she remembered the gold chain ornamented with double roses, the dark green coat with its fur collar and big sleeves which he favoured as his hands were of awkward shape; she looked at his hands, loving him afresh for his one vanity. Anger surged through her that they should have made him walk between the guards, their bills and halberts ready lest he should attempt an escape. Fools, to think he would try to escape! Did they not know he welcomed this, that he had said to Will: 'I am joyful because the first step which is the worst and most difficult, is taken!' Had he not said that to stand out against the King was to lose one's body, but to submit to him was to lose one's soul!

She ran to him, breaking through the guards; she flung her arms about his neck. And the guards turned away that they might not see this which brought tears to their eyes.

'Meg!' he whispered. 'For Christ's sake don't unman me!'

She remembered nothing more until she was lying on the ground while those about her chafed her hands and whispered words of comfort; she was conscious of nothing but the hateful sultry July heat, and the fact that she would never see him alive again.

From the Tower he wrote to her, using a piece of coal, to tell her which day he would be executed. He could not forbear to jest even then. 'It will be St. Thomas's Eve, a day very meet and convenient for me. And I never liked your manners better than when you kissed me last. For I like when daughterly love and dear charity hath no leisure to look to worldly courtesy.'

She was to go to his burial. The King had given written consent – and this was a privilege – providing that at his execution Sir Thomas would promise not to use many words.

So he died; and his head was impaled on London Bridge to show the people he was a traitor. But the people looked at it with anger; they murmured sullenly; for these people knew they looked at the head of one who was more saint than traitor.

*　　*　　*

Henry was uneasy; he was tired of women. Women should be a pleasant diversion; matters of state should be those affairs to claim the attention of a king.

The French King was trying to renew negotiations for a marriage with Mary. More was in prison awaiting execution; so was Fisher. He had postponed execution of these men, knowing of the popular feeling towards them. He had ever been afraid of popular feeling.

Anne coloured all his thoughts; he was angry with her who had placed him in this position; angry with his desire for her, brief though it might be, without which his life would be incomplete. Anne had brought him to this pass; he could wish she had never entered his life, yet he could not imagine it without her. He hated her; he loved her. She was a disturbance, an irritation; he could never escape from her; he fancied he never would; worse still, he was not entirely sure that he wanted to. Obviously a most unfortunate state of affairs for a mighty king to find himself in. He had broken with Rome for Anne's sake; the Pope's name had been struck from the prayer books, and it was not mentioned at Divine Service; yet in the streets the people never ceased to talk of the Pope, and with reverence. Wolsey was gone, and with his going, the policy of England was changed. Wolsey it was who had believed that England must preserve the balance of power in Europe; Henry had pursued a new policy, he had cut off England from Europe. England stood alone.

Those matters, which had once been the concern of the Cardinal's, were now the King's. Cromwell was sly and cunning, but a servant, no leader; Cromwell did what he was told. Why should a man with so much on his shoulders be pestered by women! Madge Shelton was a bright wench, but he had had enough of her. Anne was Anne . . . none like her, but a witch – a nagging witch at that. Too clever, trying to dictate to England through him; advising rashness here, there and everywhere. This state of affairs was such as to make a man's blood – which was ever ready to simmer – bubble and boil over.

He was going to be firm. Anne could not get children; he would be better without Anne; she disturbed him, distracted him from state matters. Women were for bedtime, not to sidle between a king and his country.

The people were dissatisfied. There were too many noble lords ready to support the Catholic cause, possibly conspiring with Chapuys. These were not dangerous at the moment, but there were inevitable perils in such a situation. He had his daughter Mary watched; he believed there was a plot afoot to smuggle her out of the country to the Emperor. What if that warrior thought to raise an army against the King, with the replacement of Katharine and Mary as its cause! How many nobles of England, who now did honour to its King, would slip over to the Emperor's banner? Henry asked himself uneasily. His conscience told him that he had embarked on this matter of divorce that he might produce a son and save England from civil war, but he had produced no son, and his actions had put England nearer to civil war than she had been since the conflicts between the houses of York and Lancaster.

He sounded a few of his most trusted counsellors on a new line of action. What if he divorced Anne? It looked as if she could not have a son. Might not this be a sign from Almighty God that the union with Anne had not found favour in the sight of heaven? It was astonishing; a healthy girl to be so barren. One daughter! One pretended pregnancy! His lips curled. How she had fooled him! How she continued to fool him! How, when he was thinking he would be better without her, she would lure him and tempt him, so that instead of occupying his mind with plans to rid himself of her, he found himself making love to her.

His counsellors shook their heads at the suggestion of a second divorce. There were points beyond which even the most docile men could not go, and the most despotic of kings could not carry them with him. Perhaps these men were thinking of Sir Thomas More and John Fisher, awaiting death stoically in the Tower; perhaps they were thinking that the people were murmuring against the doings of the King.

Divorce Anne he might, his counsellors thought, but only on condition that he took Katharine back.

Katharine! That made the King roar like a wounded animal. Katharine back! Anne angered him, Anne plagued him, but at least she excited him. Let matters rest. Not for anything would he have Katharine back.

These matters all tended to arouse the wrath of the King.

The new Pope aggravated him still further, by raising John Fisher – a man who was in prison for treason – to cardinal's rank. When Henry heard the news, he foamed with rage.

'I'll send the head to Rome for the cap!' he cried fiercely. He had had enough. Fisher was executed. Sir Thomas More was to follow. Nor were these the only traitors; those monks of the Charterhouse who had refused to acknowledge him Supreme Head of the Church, were to be punished with the utmost severity. This should be a sign to the people that all those who would not do the will of Henry the Eighth of England should suffer thus. He would have the people heartily aware of this. There should be public executions; there should be hangings; there should be burnt flesh offerings to the supremacy of the King. Murder was in the King's heart; he murdered now with a greater ferocity than when he had murdered men like Empson, Dudley, and Buckingham; the murders of these men were calculated, cold blooded; now he murdered in revenge and anger. The instruments of torture in those gloomy dungeons of pain beneath the grey buildings of the Tower should be worked night and day. The King was intent on the complete subjugation of all who raised a voice against him.

A pall of smoke hung over London. The people huddled together, watching the mutilation, listening to the shrieks and groans of martyrs.

The Continent was aghast at the news of the death of Fisher and More; the Church infuriated by the murder of Fisher, the political world shocked beyond expression by that of More. The Vatican found its voice, and sent forth vituperation against the monster of England. The Emperor, astonished at the stupidity of a king who could rid himself of the ablest man in the country, said: 'Had we been master of such a servant, we would rather have lost the fairest city in our dominion than such a counsellor.'

Europe mourned wise men, but London mourned its martyrs, and the King was shaken, afraid. But his blood was up; he was shrewd enough to know that any sign of weakness would not help him now; he had gone too far to retrace his steps. When More had said that a man who cannot restrain his passions is essentially cruel, he spoke the truth. The real Henry emerged from behind the fair, flushed, good-tempered hail-fellow-well-met personality which his people – as good Englishmen – had admired so long. The cold, cruel, implacable, relentless egoist was exposed.

But there was still the conscience, which could make him tremble. 'What I have done,' he told it, 'has been done for Anne.' He did not say 'I am a great hater!' but 'I am a great lover.'

They brought the news of Thomas More's execution to him while he played at the tables with Anne; as he sat opposite her, he pictured beside her brilliant beauty the calm ascetic face of the man whose death he had just brought about.

He stood up. He had no stomach for the game now. He knew that he had murdered a great man, a good man; and he was afraid.

Then he saw Anne sitting there opposite him. The answer to his conscience was clear; he knew how to stifle that persistent voice inside him.

He said: 'Thou art the cause of this man's death!'

Then he left the table and shut himself in his private chamber in sudden fright which nothing would allay.

* * *

Crossing London Bridge, people could not look up without seeing the ghastly sights exhibited there. The heads of brave men dripped blood; to this pass had their bravery brought them, since it was unwise to be brave in the reign of bluff King Hal.

On the lips of all were the names of More and Fisher. These men were saints enshrined in the hearts of the people; there could be no open worship of such saints. Many of the monks of the Charterhouse preferred death to admitting that Henry was Supreme Head of the Church. A large number of them went to the Tower; some were tortured on the rack, that they might betray their friends; many found their way into the embrace of the Scavenger's Daughter, that vile instrument recently invented by Thomas Skevington, which contracted the body in a manner exactly opposite to that of the rack, so that blood was forced from the nose and ears; some were hung from the ceilings of dungeons by their wrists, which were encased in gauntlets, until their hands were bleeding and paralysed; some had their teeth forced out by the brakes; some were tortured with the thumb-screws or the bilboes. People whispered together of the dreadful things that befell these saintly men in the Tower of London. Some were chained in airless dungeons, and left to starve; some were paralysed by continued confinement in one of those chambers called the Little Ease, the walls of which were so contrived that its inmate could neither walk, nor sit, not lie full length; some were put into the Pit, a noisome deep cavern in which rats were as ferocious as wild beasts and lived on those human wrecks who, chained and helpless, standing knee deep in filthy water, must face them while being unable to defend themselves. Some of the more obstinate monks were given an execution which was public and shameful; taken to Tyburn, they were half-hanged, cut down, and while they were conscious their abdomens were ripped open and their bowels dragged forth from their mutilated bodies and burned. Even after death their bodies were further desecrated.

This, the King would have the people know, might be the fate of any who questioned his supremacy. The people of London heard the screams of the Anabaptists as the flames leaped from the faggots at their feet, scorching and frizzling their bodies. In Europe the people talked of the terror which had befallen England; they talked in hushed, shocked whispers. When Henry heard this he laughed savagely, calling to mind the Spaniards' way of dealing with heretics, and how, but a few months before, Francis and his family had marched through Paris chanting piously while Lutherans were burned before the doors of Notre-Dame.

Henry knew how to suppress rebellion; he knew how to make the people knuckle under. 'I will have this thing an it cost me my crown!' he had been known to say, and he meant it. He was strong and ruthless; all men trembled before him. He was no longer the young and lusty boy seeking pleasure while a cardinal ruled; he was master. He would force all to recognize that, however much blood should flow.

He had a plan now which intrigued him; it was to make Thomas Cromwell his Vicar-general, and as such let him visit all the churches and monasteries of England. The Supreme Head of the church would know the state of these monasteries; it worried his conscience that stories he had heard from time to time of the profligacy of the monks and nuns might have some truth in them! What if these monasteries were the bawdy houses he had often heard it whispered that they were! What if there were men living licentious lives, sheltered by their monks' robes! Those nuns, wrapped up in the garments of piety – what of them? He remembered the case of Eleanor Carey, that relative of Anne's who had had two illegitimate children by a priest. These things had come to light, and if there was one thing the Supreme Head of the Church of England would not tolerate in his land, it was immorality! He would suppress it, he would stamp it out! Once it had been no concern of his, but now by God's will he was the head of the Church, and by God, he would put an end to all evil practices.

Thomas Cromwell should go to these places; he should bring back evidence of what he found – and Thomas Cromwell could always be relied upon to bring back the evidence that was expected of him – and if that evidence warranted the dissolution of these places, then dissolved they should be! A list of their valuables, should Thomas bring back; it was said they had some fine treasures in their chests – jewels, works of art only suited to a king's palace. This was a good plan; later he would talk with Cromwell.

From his palace he saw the smoke over London. This was done in the name of righteousness. The Anabaptists denied the divinity of Christ; they deserved to die.

In the courtyards of the palace men talked together in whispers. Something was afoot. The King was nervous to-day; there had been a time in the days of his youth when he had gone among his people unafraid, but now it was not so. If he stayed in a house, even for a night, he took a locksmith with him that new bolts might be put on the door of his sleeping apartment; he had the straw of his bed searched every night for hidden daggers.

'Now what?' he said, and leaning from his windows roared down to be told what fresh news was exciting them.

A little group of courtiers looked up at him in some alarm.

'There is some news. Hide it not!' he shouted.

''Tis naught, Your Majesty, but that the head of Sir Thomas More is no longer on the bridge.'

'What!' cried the King, roaring, that none might guess his voice shook. 'Who moved it then?'

There was no answer.

'Who moved it then?' he roared again.

''Tis not known, Your Majesty . . . 'Tis but known that it is gone.'

He shut the window. His knees trembled; the whole of his great body shook. The head of More the martyr had been removed from the bridge, where it should have remained with the heads of other traitors. What meant this? What meant it? A miracle, was it? There had been One who had risen from the dead; what if this man, More, were such another!

He could see the shrewd, kind face, did he but close his eyes; he could recall the humour, the mocking kindliness. He remembered the man so well; often had he walked in the Chelsea garden, his arms about the fellow's neck. He remembered when he had written his book denouncing Luther, who had worked with him, whose lucid style, whose perfect Latin knowledge had largely made the book. And because he had had need to show this man he could not disobey his master, he had murdered him. True he had not wielded the axe; true he had not been the one to place the head among the heads of traitors; but he was the murderer nevertheless. His old friend More – the brightest light in his realm! He remembered how the man had walked with him and Katharine on the terraces of the palace, and talked of the stars, pointing them out to the royal pair, for he and Katharine had been interested in astronomy then. Now he was dead, he who had never wanted to sun himself in the brilliance of court life; who would have preferred to live quietly in the heart of his family with his books. He was dead; and his head had disappeared. This might be a miracle, a sign!

Anne came in, saw that he was distressed, and was unusually soft and ready to comfort him.

'You have had some shock.'

He looked at her eagerly; she thought he had the air of a frightened boy who is afraid to be left in the dark.

'More's head has gone from London Bridge!'

She was taken aback; she looked at him, wide-eyed; and they were drawn together in their fear.

'Anne,' he said, groping for her hand, 'what means this, thinkest thou?'

She took his hand and pressed it firmly; she forgot the miracle of the missing head, since the fear which had been with her night and day was evaporating. Henry needed her; at moments such as this, it was to her he turned; she had been too easily humiliated, too ready to show her humiliation. She had nothing to fear. She was the wife of a man who, having absolute power, would have his way, but a clever woman might manage him still. She could see her folly stretching right back to her coronation; she thought she saw why she had appeared to lose her power over him. Now here he was, trembling and afraid, superstitious in an age of superstition, lacking that courage which had made her the reckless creature she was.

She smiled at him.

'My lord, someone has removed the head.'

'But who would dare?'

'He was a man who had many friends, and one of these might be ready to take his head from where it belonged.'

'I see that, Anne.' He was feeling better already; he looked at her through softly sentimental eyes. She was very beautiful, and now she was gentle and very reassuring; she was clever too; the others palled quickly. When Anne reassured, there was a good deal that was truth in the reassurance; the others flattered; it was good to be with Anne. 'That was where the head belonged,' he said fiercely. 'He was a traitor, Anne.'

'As all who seek to disobey Your Majesty's commands,' she said.

'Thou speakest truth. 'Twas a friend of his that took the head. By God, that in itself was a traitorous act, was it not!'

She stroked his hand.

'Indeed it was. There will be those simple people who ever look on traitors as saints. Mayhap it would be well to leave this matter. Why should it worry us? We know the man deserved to die.'

'By God, you're right!' he cried. ''Tis a matter of small importance.'

He did not wish to leave her; she distracted his thoughts from the memory of that severed head with its kindly mocking eyes.

It was reconciliation. In the court it was said: 'She has a power over him, which none other could exercise.'

Her enemies cursed her. If she but give him a son, they said, she is Queen of England till her death.

Chapuys wrote home to the Emperor, Charles, telling him that the King of England was over and over again unfaithful, but that the concubine was cunning and knew how to manage the King. It would be unwise to attach too much importance to his brief infatuations for court ladies.

*　　*　　*

Anne was preparing the most splendid banquet the court had yet seen. She was feverish with delight. She felt as though she had come through a nightmare of terror, and now here was the morning to prove that the shadows had been conjured up out of her imagination, that they had no existence in truth. How could she have been so foolish; how could she have believed that she who had held the King so well in check, could have lost control now! She was supreme; his need of her was passionate and lasting; now that – as her husband – he was conscious of the shackles that held him to her, all she need do was lengthen the tether. Her fault had been in trying to keep it as tight as a mistress might. All a wife needed was a little more subtlety, and it had taken her two years of doubts and nightmares to realize this. Let him wander away from her, let him dally with others – it would but be to compare them with his incomparable Queen.

She was gayer than she had ever been. She designed new costumes; she called to her the most brilliant courtiers to arrange an entertainment that should enchant the King; Witty Wyatt, subtle George, gentle Harry Norris, amusing Francis Bryan, Henry Howard, those gay courtiers Francis Weston and William Brereton; others too, all the brightest stars of the court clustered about her, and she the dazzling centre as it used to be. The King was with her constantly; she planned and thrilled to her plans.

One day she found one of the youngest of the musicians sitting alone playing, and she paused to listen, delighting in his delicate touch, thinking, He is more than ordinarily good. She had Madge Shelton bring him to her. He was young and slender, a rather beautiful boy with long tapering fingers and dreamy, dark eyes.

'Her Majesty heard your music,' said Madge. 'She thought it good.'

The boy was overcome with the honour of being noticed by the Queen, who smiled on him most graciously.

'I would have you play awhile,' she said. 'I feel you could be of use to us in the revels, for it would seem to me that we have not so many musicians of your talent in the court that we can afford to leave out one who plays as you do.'

She was charming, because she at once saw that his admiration was not merely that which he would give to his Queen. Her long sleeves hung over the hand with its slight malformation; the other, with long, white, jewel-decked fingers, rested lightly on her chair. He could not take his wondering eyes from her, for he had never been so close to her before.

'What is his name?' she asked, when he had been dismissed.

'It is Smeaton, Your Majesty. Mark Smeaton.'

'He was poorly clad,' she said.

'He is one of the humbler musicians, Your Majesty.'

'See that he has money with which to procure himself clothes. He plays too well to be so shabbily attired. Tell him

335

he may play before me; I will have a part for him to take at the entertainment.'

She dismissed him from her mind, and gave herself over to fresh plans. There was an air of lightheartedness among her friends; George seemed younger, excessively gay. The Queen herself was as sparkling as she had ever been when she was the King's mistress. She was the centre of the brilliant pageant, the pivot round which the wit and laughter revolved; she was the most lovely performer. The King watched the entertainment, his eyes for her alone. Anne! he thought, inwardly chuckling. By God, she was meant to be a Queen. She could amuse him, she could enchant him, she could divert him, she could cast unpleasant thoughts from his mind.

He had forgotten Fisher; More too almost, for the removal of his head from London Bridge had been no miracle but the bold action of his daughter, Margaret Roper, who had gone stealthily and by night. Anne had learned this, and brought him the news.

'By God!' he had cried. ' 'Tis a treasonable offence to go against the King's command!' She had soothed him. 'Let be! Let be! 'Twas a brave action. Doubtless the girl loved her father well. People are full of sentiment; they would not care that a girl should be punished because she loved her father well. Let us have done with this gruesome affair of a traitor's head. To please me, I would ask Your Majesty not to pursue the matter.'

He had frowned and feigned to be considering it, knowing full well that his people would not care for interference with Margaret Roper; then she had wheedled, and kissed him, and he had patted her thighs and said: 'Well then, sweetheart, since you ask it, it shall be done. But I like not treason . . . I like it not at all!' She had smiled, well pleased, and so had he. An unpleasant business was done with.

He watched her now – the loveliest woman in the court – and too many of these young profligates had their eyes upon her, ready to be over-bold an they dared. He liked to know that they fancied her, even while it filled him with this smouldering rage. He could laugh. None dared to give her

more than covert looks, for it would be treason to cast over-
desirous eyes on what belonged to the King; and well they
knew this King's method of dealing with traitors! He called
to her, would have her sit by him, would let his hands
caress her.

It was borne home to the Queen's enemies that their hopes
had been premature, and to her friends that they had feared
too soon.

*   *   *

Catherine Howard was joyous as a lark; like the lively
young grasshopper, she danced all through the summer
months without a thought of winter. She was discovering
that she was more than ordinarily pretty; she was the prettiest of all the ladies; she had, said some, a faint resemblance
to her cousin the Queen. She developed a love of finery, and
being kept short of decorative clothes or the money with
which to provide herself with even the smallest addition to
her wardrobe, she looked to her lover to provide these. Derham was only too delighted. He was enchanted by the lovely
child, who was so very youthful at times, at others completely mature. He would provide her with many little luxuries
besides – wines and sweetmeats, fruit and flowers. So when
Catherine yearned to possess an ornament called the French
Fennel, which was being worn by all the court ladies who
would follow the latest fashion, Derham told her that he
knew a little woman in London with a crooked back who
was most skilled in the making of flowers of silk. Catherine
begged him to get this done for her. 'I will pay you when I
have the means,' she told him, which set him smiling and
begging her that it should be a present. And so it was, but
when she had the precious ornament, she was afraid to wear
it until she had let it be known that one of the ladies had
given it to her, for the Duchess was more watchful than she
had been at Horsham.

It was tiresome of the old lady to have taken that precaution of locking the chamber door each night. Derham
was an adventurous young man; he was passionately in
love. He was not going to let a key separate him from

Catherine. A little planning, a little scheming, a little nodding and looking the other way by those who liked to see good sport, and it was not such a difficult matter to steal the key after it had been brought to the Duchess.

There was the additional spice of planning what should be done, should there be a sudden intrusion.

'You would have to hurry into the gallery and hide there!' said Catherine.

'That I could do with the greatest of ease!' said Derham.

He would come to the chamber at any hour of the night; it was a highly exciting adventure they were both enjoying.

The others watched, rather wistfully. Derham was such a handsome young man and so much in love with the child; there were some, such as Dorothy Barwicke and a newcomer, Jane Acworth, who whispered to each other that Catherine Howard was the sort who would always find men to love her. What use to warn her? She was too addicted to physical love to heed any warning. If she realized that the path she was treading might be dangerous, she might try to reform, but she would surely slip back. She was a lusty little animal, irresistible to men because she found them irresistible. Mary Lassells thought the Duchess should be told, in secret so that she could come up and catch them in the act, but the others were against this. They wanted no probings, no inquiries. They pointed out that they would all be implicated – even Mary Lassells, since she had been months in the house and had not seen fit to warn Her Grace before.

The Duchess was less comfortable in her mind than she had been. Apart from the rumours she heard at court, she sensed the presence of intrigue in her own household. She watched Catherine, flaunting her new French Fennel. Heaven knew there were plenty of men all too eager to take advantage of a young girl. She saw something in Catherine's face, something secret and knowledgeable, and the memory of it would recur in her uneasy thoughts. Her other granddaughter, she believed, was not happy; the Duchess preferred not to think of what might be happening at court; better to turn her attention to her own house. Were the young men too free with the girls? She would have to be arranging a marriage for young Catherine soon; when she next saw the Queen, she would have a word with her about this. In the meantime the greatest care must be exercised.

Sometimes the Duchess did not sleep very well; sometimes she would wake in the night and fancy she heard foot-steps on the stairs, or a muffled burst of laughter overhead. She knew now that for some time she had been suspicious of what went on in the girls' apartments; there were some over-bold wenches there, she believed. I must bestir myself; I must look into this. There is my little granddaughter, Catherine to be considered. That French Fennel . . . She had said she got it from Lady Brereton. Now did she? Would her ladyship give such a handsome gift? What if one of the young gentlemen was seeking Catherine's favours by offer-ing gifts! It was not a very pleasant reflection.

Forced by a sense of impending danger both at court and at Lambeth, she roused herself one night soon after twelve, and went to the place where the key of the ladies' apart-ment should be. It was not there. Puffing and panting with the fear of what she would find if she went to the room, she nevertheless could make no excuse for not going. It had ever been her habit to avoid the unpleasant, but here was something for the avoidance of which it would be most difficult to find an adequate excuse.

She put on a robe and went out of her sleeping apartment to the corridor. Slowly she mounted the staircase. She was distressed, for she was sure she could hear muffled voices coming from that room; she paused outside the door. There was no sound inside the room now. She opened the door and stood on the threshold. All the ladies were in their beds, but there was in that room an atmosphere of such tenseness that she could not but be aware of it, and she was sure that, though they had their eyes shut, they but feigned sleep.

She went first to Catherine's bed. She drew off the clothes and looked at the naked body of her granddaughter. Catherine feigned sleep too long for innocence.

The Duchess thought she heard the faintest creak of boards in the gallery which ran along one side of the room.

She had an alarmed feeling that if she had that gallery searched, the search would not be fruitless. It would set tongues wagging though, and she dared not let that happen.

Her panic made her angry; she wished to blame someone for the negligence of which she knew herself to be guilty. Catherine was lying on her back; the Duchess rolled her over roughly and brought her hand across the girl's buttocks. Catherine yelled; the girls sat up in bed, the curtains were drawn back.

'What has happened? What is this?'

Did their exclamations ring true? wondered the old lady.

Catherine was holding her bruised flesh, for the Duchess's rings had cut into her.

'I would know,' said the Duchess sharply, 'who it was who stole my keys and opened this door.'

'Stole Your Grace's keys. . . .'

'Opened the door. . . .'

Oh, yes! The sly wenches . . . they knew well enough who it was. Thank God, she thought, I came in time!

Mary Lassells was trying to catch her eye, but she would not look at the sly creature. Didn't the fool realize that what she just did not want to hear was the truth . . . providing of course that the truth was disturbing!

'Tomorrow,' said the Duchess, 'I shall look into this matter. If any of you had aught to do with this matter of my keys, you shall be soundly whipped and sent home in disgrace. I shall make no secret of your sins, I warn you! I thought I heard noises here. Let me warn you that if I hear more noises it will be the worse for you.'

She went out and left them.

'There!' she said, as she settled down to sleep. 'I have done my duty. I have warned them. After such a threat, none of them would dare to misbehave herself, and if any of them have already done so, they will take good care to keep quiet about it.'

In the morning she found her keys; they were not in their rightful place, which led her to hope and believe that they must have been there all the time, and that there had been an oversight, the doors having been left unlocked all that night.

Still, she was resolved to keep an eye on the young women, and particularly on Catherine.

There came a day when, entering what was known as the maids' room, she saw Catherine and Derham together. The maids' room was a long, pleasant, extremely light room in which the ladies sat to embroider, or to work tapestry, or to spin. Such a room was certainly forbidden to gentlemen.

The Duchess had come to the room, taking her usual laboured steps, and had Derham and Catherine not been noisily engaged in a romp, they would assuredly have heard her approach.

Derham had come in to talk to Catherine, and she feigning greater interest in her piece of needlework than in him, had goaded him to snatch it from her; after which, Catherine immediately sought to retrieve it. They were not interested in the piece of needlework, except as an excuse for titillating their senses by apparent haphazard physical contacts. Derham ran round the room, flourishing the piece of needlework, and Catherine gave chase. Cornering him behind the spinning wheel, she snatched it from him, but he caught her round the waist and she slid to the floor, at which he did likewise. They rolled on the floor together, he with his arms about her, Catherine shrieking her delighted protests. And thus the Duchess found them.

She stood in the doorway, shouting at them for some seconds before they heard her angry voice.

Then she stalked over to them. They saw her and were immediately quiet, standing abashed before her.

She was trembling with rage and fury. Her granddaughter to be guilty of such impropriety! The girl's gown was torn at the neck, noted Her Grace, and that doubtless on purpose! She narrowed her eyes.

'Leave us at once, Derham!' she said ominously. 'You shall hear further of this.'

He threw Catherine a glance and went out.

The Duchess seized her frightened granddaughter by her sleeve and ripped the clothes off her shoulders.

'You slut!' she cried. 'What means this behaviour ... after all my care!'

She lifted her ebony stick, and would have brought it down on Catherine's head had she not dodged out of the way. The Duchess was growing a little calmer now, realizing it would not do to make too violent a scene.

She cornered Catherine, pushed her onto a couch and, bending over her, said: 'How far has this gone?'

'It was nothing,' said Catherine, fearful for Derham as well as for herself. 'It was just that he ... stole my piece of needlework, and I ... sought to retrieve it ... and then ... you came in.'

'His hands were on your neck!'

'It was to retrieve the needlework which I had snatched from him.'

The Duchess preferred to believe it was but a childish romp. She wanted no scandal. What if it came to the hard-faced Duke's ears, of what went on in her house, what tricks and pranks those under her care got up to! He would not hesitate to whisper it abroad, the wicked man, and then would she be considered the rightful state governess for the Princess Elizabeth!

It must go no further than this room; but at the same time she must make Catherine understand that she must have no dangerous friendships with young men under her roof.

She said: 'An I thought there was aught wrong in this romping between thee and Derham, I would have thee sent to the Tower; him too! As it is, I will content myself with giving you the biggest beating you have ever had in your life, Catherine Howard!'

She paused, horror-stricken; sitting in a corner, quietly trembling with fear, was one of her attendants, and she must have witnessed the whole scene.

The Duchess turned from Catherine and went over to her

'Jane Acworth! You think to sit there and allow such behaviour! What do you think your task is? To watch young men make free with Catherine Howard?'

The girl, trembling, said: 'Your Grace, it was naught ...'

But a stinging blow at the side of her head silenced the girl. The Duchess continued to slap her for some seconds.

'Let me hear no more of this, girl, or you shall feel a whip across your shoulders. Catherine, go to my private chamber; you shall receive your punishment there!'

She went puffing from the room, very ill at ease. But having beaten Catherine, while Catherine writhed and shrieked, she felt she had done her duty.

She summoned one Margaret Morton, when she had done with Catherine.

'I would have speech with Francis Derham. Send him to me without delay!'

He came. She did not know how to punish him. She should banish him of course. But she had always liked him; he was quite the most charming young man of her household. If anything, he was over-bold, but there is something very attractive about over-boldness. He was a distant kinsman too . . . so perhaps it would be enough to warn him.

'I would have you know that you are without prospects. You could not marry my granddaughter. I would have you remember your position in this house, Francis Derham!'

'Your Grace, I must humbly apologize. It was but animal spirits. . . .'

The animal spirits of youth, she thought. There was something delightful about them. Memories came back, softening her. Suppose she allowed him to stay this time! She had warned him; he would not dare to presume again. He was such a handsome, courtly, charming boy!

* * *

With the coming of the autumn, Anne's spirits soared, for she discovered that at last she was pregnant. The King was overjoyed. He was sure that if he would but show the people a male heir, everything that had gone to the producing of it might be forgotten.

Anne, eager to be brought to bed of a healthy child, gave up her life of gaiety and spent a good deal of time reading and thinking of the past. She could not look back with much pride on the two years which had seen her Queen. It seemed to her that much of her time had been spent in worthless machinations and sordid subterfuge. The affair of Madge Shelton stood out from those years, filling her with shame. She herself was now with child again; should she be delivered of a son, her dearest wish would be granted; she would then ask nothing more of life.

She was thoughtfully sitting over her tapestry with her ladies, asking questions about the poor of London. She said: 'Would it not be better if, instead of stitching this fine tapestry, we made shirts and suchlike garments for the poor?'

It was strange to see her who had been known to occupy herself at great length with the planning of her own gowns, to see her who had given orders how should be cut and made yards of black satin and gold arras, now stitching contentedly at garments for the poor. She had changed, and the change had a good deal to do with the terrible fear which had beset her and which had been removed, first by the King's returning affection for her, and then by her pregnancy.

Hugh Latimer had been largely instrumental in her change of heart. She had been interested in the great reformer ever since she had heard of him, and when Stokesley, Bishop of London, had had him committed to the Tower, she used all her influence to get him released. The King, reluctant and yet unable in a fresh return of his passion to refuse what she asked, agreed on the release, and thus postponed Latimer's martyrdom for twenty-five years. On his release, Anne had desired to hear him preach and forthwith did so, when, much to her astonishment, instead of receiving the gratitude she might have expected from the man, he delivered for her benefit a stormy lecture advising those who placed too much reliance on treasures upon Earth to turn from their folly and repent. Anne saw the man afterwards and characteristically asked him where he thought she had erred. He answered unflinchingly that she should by her morality and piety set an example to those under her command. Greatly impressed by his honesty – a virtue by which she set great store – she appointed him one of her chaplains and began to veer towards a more spiritual way of life. Always generous in the extreme, she delighted in looking into deserving cases about her, and helping those whom she considered would benefit by such help. She had always done this when cases were brought to her notice, but now she looked for them systematically.

Although less superstitious than the King, she was not entirely free from this weakness. As she stitched at garments for the poor, she asked herself if she were not doing this in return for a healthy boy. Was she placating the Powers above, as Henry did? Was she, she wondered, getting a little like him? She had her moments of fear. Was Henry capable of begetting a healthy boy? His body was diseased. What if this were the reason Katharine had failed, and she too, so far! Perhaps she was, in a way, placating Providence, making conditions.

She was worried about the Princess Mary. She was still afraid of the Princess and of Katharine. It had seemed to her that if these two were together they might plot something against her, and through her against Elizabeth. Chapuys she feared. She knew well there were many powerful nobles who deeply resented the break with Rome. They were all only waiting to rise up and destroy her. She must not allow her new favour with the King to blind her to this.

And as she stitched, she prayed for a son.

The King prayed too. He was pleased with the change in Anne. It was well to see her calmer, quieter; it was well to feel this peace stealing over him because at last their union was flavoured with hope. He needed such hope; the people were being difficult once more. They were saying that it had not rained since More had died; they would always find a reason for a bad harvest, and the crops had failed once more. The Flanders trade was not good. In fact it looked as if the country was getting together a collection of grievances and irritations in order to make trouble.

The King needed distraction. It suddenly dawned on him that one of his wife's attendants was – well, not so much an attractive girl as a different kind of girl. Perhaps he meant that she was quite different from Anne; she was so quiet, she moved about like a little mouse; she was very fair; she had a prim little mouth and quick, glancing eyes. She would never be leader of the revels, she would never shine, she would never outwit a man with her sharp tongue! She was as different from Anne as any woman could be. That was why he first noticed her.

If she caught his eyes upon her, she would drop hers quickly; a soft rose-pink blush would steal into her cheeks. She was very demure.

On one occasion he was sitting alone, thinking that it was a long time before his son could be born, and wondering if there was some holy relic the soothsayers could give him as protection against another girl child. He had some holy water, a tear which Christ had shed over Lazarus, and a phial of the sweat of St Michael; all of which he had purchased at great cost during the sweating sickness. But in spite of these, Anne's first child had been a girl, and he wondered whether he should buy something especially which might ensure the birth of a boy. As he considered this, the demure maid of honour came into the room and, seeing him, curtseyed in a frightened way and would have hurried off had he not detained her with a 'Hi, there! What want you?'

'Her Grace, the Queen . . .' said the girl, so low that he could scarcely hear her.

'What of Her Grace, the Queen?' He studied her from head to toe. Small where Anne was tall; slow of movement where Anne was quick; meek where Anne sparkled; slow of speech instead of bright; modest instead of coquettish; willing to listen humbly rather than disconcert a man with her wit.

'I had thought to find her . . .'

'Come hither!' said the King. 'And are you very disturbed to come upon the King when you looked for the Queen?'

'Yes, Your Majesty . . . I mean no, Your Majesty. . . .'

'Well,' said Henry pleasantly, 'make up your mind.'

She would not come too close. He did not force her, liking suddenly her demureness, since there were so many of them who were too ready.

She could think of nothing to say, which pleased him and made him remember that Anne was over-ready with her retorts.

'Sit there awhile and I will play. You may listen. Bring my lute to me.'

She brought it, cautiously. He tried to touch her fingers over the lute, but she was quick; she had leaped back as though he had tried to sting her. He was not angry. His thoughts were chiefly of his son, and therefore with Anne. But he liked the girl; he was, he told himself, always touched by modesty; he liked and respected it in the young people about his court.

He commanded her to sit; she did so, modestly letting her hands fall into her lap; her mild eyes watched him, and then seemed full of admiration.

When he had finished he saw that her eyes were filled with tears, so moved was she by his music, and he realized that he had not felt so gratified for a long time.

He asked her name. She told him it was Jane Seymour.

He dismissed her then. 'You may go. We shall meet again. I like you, Jane!'

It was not a quarrel with Anne, just a slight irritation. A petty argument, and she, in her overpowering way, had proved herself right. Jane Seymour would never be one to prove herself right. She's all woman, thought Henry. And that's how a woman should be. Women are women, and men are men. When the one will dabble with that which is solely within the province of the other, it is a sad thing.

He sent for Jane Seymour. She should have the honour of hearing his new song before he allowed anyone else to hear it. She sat listening, her feet scarce reaching the floor; which made her seem helpless. She was very meek.

He made inquiries about her. She was the daughter of Sir John Seymour of Wolf Hall in Wiltshire; he was by no means a powerful nobleman, but it was interesting to discover that there was a tiny root of royalty in his family tree, provided one dug deep enough to find it. Henry stored such knowledge. And as he played his lute, he thought about Jane; a quiet, mild bed-fellow, he thought, pleasant enough, and white-skinned; unawakened and virginal. He grew sentimental; virtue had that effect on him. All women, he told himself, should be virtuous.

The court noticed his preoccupation with the maid of honour. Chapuys and the French ambassador laughed together. They were cynical. The King had been noted of late to extol virginity. 'He refers to Jane Seymour!' said the French ambassador, to whom the Spanish ambassador replied that he greatly doubted Jane possessed that quality, having been some time at court. He added that the King might be pleased though that she did not, for then he could marry her on condition that she was a virgin, and when he needed a divorce he could then find many witnesses to the contrary.

But the King continued to view Jane through sentimental eyes. She had been primed by her father and her brothers, when dazzling possibilities had occurred to the minds of these very ambitious men who had the example of the Earl of Wiltshire and the young Lord Rochford before their eyes. They advised Jane: 'Do this . . .' 'On no account do that . . .' Jane herself was not without ambition. She had watched many a quarrel between the King and Queen, and she understood the King more than he would have thought from the demure eyes that met his with such seeming sincerity.

When he tried to kiss her, she was overcome with blushes; she ran away and hid herself, and the King, having become the champion of virtue, could not satisfy his conscience if he forced the girl to anything. His mind began to scheme with his conscience once again. What if this marriage with Anne had been wrong? What if God should show his disapproval over the child? The plans were not very well shaped as yet – they were misty shadows of thought, which allowed him to dally with Jane, while respecting her virtue.

He gave her a locket bearing his picture; she wore it on a chain round her throat, intending this to be a sign that were she not of such unbending virtue she would readily consider his advances, having the greatest admiration for his person. He wanted Jane; he could not have her; and this made her seem very desirable to him.

The story of Anne was to Jane a long object lesson: what to do before, what not to do after. But though Jane knew what she must do, she was not very intelligent, and she could not prevent a new haughtiness creeping into her manner, which Anne was quick to notice. She saw the locket which Jane was wearing, and asked mildly enough if she might see it.

Jane flushed guiltily, and put her hand over the locket; whereat Anne's suspicions flared up. She took the locket, breaking its chain as she did so, and on snapping it open beheld the smiling face of the King crowned in a jewelled cap.

A year ago she would have raged against him; now she was silent and undecided. She saw in sly Jane Seymour, with her much-paraded virtue, a more deadly enemy than any other woman who had taken the King's fancy.

She prayed urgently. A son! I must have a son!

*   *   *

At Kimbolton Castle, Katharine lay dying. She had lived wretchedly during her lingering illness, for money due to her was not paid. She was full of sorrow; not only had she been separated from her beloved daughter, but when she had asked that she might see the Princess before she died, even this request was denied her. She was deeply disturbed by the fate of her former confessor, Father Forrest, who though an old man had, through his allegiance to her, been cruelly treated at the hands of the King; he had been imprisoned and tortured in such a manner that she could not bear to contemplate; she longed to write and comfort him, but she feared that if a letter from her was intercepted, it might cause the old man's execution, and though, in his case, death might be the happiest release from his misery, she could not bring it about. Abell, her other confessor, was treated with equal cruelty; it was unbearable that her friends should suffer thus.

Chapuys had got the King's reluctant permission to visit

her, and arrived on New Year's Day. She was delighted to see one whom she knew to be her friend. She was very ill, and looked ten years older than her fifty years. He sat by her bed and she, while expressing genuine sorrow for all those who had suffered in her cause, said that she had never thought for one instant that she had been wrong in her struggle against the King.

To the man who had caused the chief miseries of her life she had no reproaches to offer. She was the daughter of a king and queen, and she believed in the divine right of royalty. The King would bastardize a princess, because he was bewitched; he would, she believed, emerge from that witchery and see the folly of his ways. It was her duty in the interests of royalty to uphold herself and her daughter – not for any personal reasons, but because they were Queen and Princess. Katharine was adamant now as ever, and would have suffered any torture rather than admit that her daughter was not the legitimate heir to the throne of England.

She talked with tears of Fisher, with regret of More; she talked of Abell and Forrest, mercifully knowing nothing of the more horrible deaths that awaited these two of her faithful adherents.

Chapuys, the cynic, thought, She is dying by his hand as surely as More and Fisher did. He thought of the years of misery this woman had endured, the mental torture that had been inflicted on her by her husband. Here was yet another victim of the murderer's hand. What though the method was different!

Chapuys had no real comfort to give her. His master would not wish to be embroiled in a war with England for the sake of Katharine of Aragon and her daughter, since he had his hands full elsewhere.

To comfort her though, he hinted at some action from outside on her behalf. She brightened. His visit did much to revive her; it was so rarely that the King allowed her to be visited by her friends.

After he left, another incident occurred which helped to lighten her grief in being denied the comfort of her daughter's presence.

It was evening of a bitterly cold day, when through the castle there echoed the sound of loud knocking. Her maid came to tell her that it was a poor woman who, making a journey across country, had lost her way and begged to be allowed to spend the night at the castle for fear she and her attendant should freeze to death.

Katharine bade them bring in the poor souls and give them food.

She was dozing, when her bedroom door was opened and a woman came in. Katharine looked at the newcomer in astonishment for one moment, and then the tears began to flow from her eyes. She held out her arms, feeling that she was a girl again, riding the rough seas of the Bay of Biscay, thinking fearfully of the fate which awaited her in an unknown country where she was to marry a boy husband; she was young again, watching the land grow less blurred, as she sailed into Plymouth. With her there had been a band of beautiful Spanish girls, and there was one among them who, during the unhappy years which England had given her, had ever been her faithful friend. This girl had married Lord Willoughby; and they had been together until, by the King's command, Katharine had been banished from the court and cut off from all those she loved. And here was Lady Willoughby coming by stealth, as a stranger lost in the snow, that she might be with Katharine during her last hours in England as she had been during her first.

This was wonderful; she was almost happy.

'If I could but have seen my little daughter . . .' she murmured.

But the coming of her friend had put her in high spirits, and she revived so much that she was well enough to sit up in her bed, though she was too far gone in sickness of body, which had grown out of sickness of mind, to make any real recovery. During the first week of January her condition grew worse. She had mass said in her room on the afternoon of the sixth, and then, ill as she was, asked for materials that she might write a last letter to the King. She did not blame him; she accepted her fate meekly; she

351

only asked that he should be a good father to their daughter Mary, and that he should do right by her servants.

Henry was hilarious when he heard the news of Katharine's death; there followed one moment of apprehension when in a blurred fashion he remembered her sad, pale face, heard her strong voice pleading for justice. He did then what he ever did when remorse touched him; he made the persecution of Katharine someone else's burden, not his own; he assured himself that he had acted from the highest and most disinterested of motives.

'Praise be to God!' he cried. 'We are delivered from all fear of war. The time has come for me to manage the French better than before, because in wondering whether I may now ally myself to the Emperor, they will do all I want.'

He would now show that he had never been married to Katharine. He dressed himself in yellow, having a white feather set in his cap, for why should a man go into mourning for one not his wife!

'Bring me my daughter!' he cried, and the nurses brought Elizabeth to him. Although little more than two years old, she was already a very bright and intelligent child who enjoyed being exhibited, and surveyed her great dazzling father with the utmost interest.

He called for all the musical instruments to play; the courtiers must dance. He went from one to the other, demanding they do homage to their little Princess. 'For,' he exclaimed again and again, 'we are now delivered from the evil threat of war!'

Anne rejoiced when she heard the news. It was a great relief. For the first time, she thought, I can feel myself to be really Queen; there is no shadowy Queen in the background to whom some could still look. I am Queen. There is no other Queen but me!

She was inordinately gay; she imitated the King's action, and dressed in yellow.

She did not know that he had once discussed the question of divorcing her, with his most trusted counsellors; she did not know that he had refrained from doing so because they had said he might divorce her, but if he did, he would surely have to take back Katharine.

* * *

Now that Katharine was dead, and Anne felt more secure, she decided she could be less harsh to the Princess Mary, so she sent one of her ladies to the girl with a message. Would Mary come to court? Could they not be friends?

'Tell her,' said Anne, 'that if she will be a good daughter to her father, she may come to court and count me her friend. Tell her she may walk beside me, and I shall not need her to hold my train.'

Mary, grief-stricken by the death of her mother, broken-hearted so that she cared not what became of her, sent back word that if being a good daughter to her father meant denying that for which martyrs' blood had been shed, she could not accept Anne's offer.

'The foolish girl!' said Anne. 'What more can I do?'

Then she was angry, and at the root of her anger was the knowledge that she herself had helped to make this motherless girl's unhappy lot harder than it need have been. She could not forget what she had heard of Katharine's miserable death, and in her new and chastened mood she felt remorse as well as anger.

She tried again with Mary, but Mary was hard and stubborn, neither ready to forgive nor forget. Mary was fanatical; she would have all or nothing. She wanted recognition: Her mother to be recognized as the true Queen, Anne to be displaced, Elizabeth to be acknowledged a bastard. And on these terms only, would Mary come to court.

Anne shrugged impatient shoulders, really angry with the girl because she would not let her make amends. When my son is born, thought Anne, I shall be in such a strong position that she will do as I say. If I say she shall come to court, she shall come to court, and it will not be so easy for her to find favour with the King when she is forced to do that which she might have done more graciously.

The beginning of that year was disastrously eventful for

Anne. The first disturbance was when Norfolk came hurrying into her chamber to tell her that the King had taken such a toss from his horse that he feared he was killed. This upset Anne – not that the King, during their married life, had given her any reasons to love him – but in her condition she felt herself unable to cope adequately with the situation which must inevitably arise if he died. She had the interests of her daughter and the child as yet unborn, to look to, and she was greatly disturbed. This however proved to be a minor accident; the King's fall had done scarcely any harm, and he was too practised a horseman to suffer much shock from such a fall.

After this escape, the King was in excellent spirits. He found Jane Seymour alone in one of the Queen's apartments. People had a way of disappearing from Jane Seymour's side when the King approached. Demure as she was, she had permitted certain liberties. He was somewhat enamoured of the pretty, pale creature, and she was a pleasant diversion for a man who can scarcely wait to hear that his son is born.

'Come hither, Jane!' he said in the soft, slurred voice of a lover, made husky with good ale and wine. And she came to him most cautiously, until he, seizing her, pulled her on to his knee.

'Well, what did you think, Jane, when that fool Norfolk ran around telling the world I was done for, eh?'

Jane's eyes filled with tears.

'There, there!' he said. ' 'Tis no matter for weeping. Here I am, hale and hearty as ever, except for a sore leg . . .'

He liked to talk of his leg; he spent a good deal of time thinking about it.

'Every physician in London has had a go at it, Jane! And to no avail. I've tried charms and potions . . . no avail . . . no avail.'

Jane was timidly sympathetic; he stroked her thighs caressingly.

He liked Jane; he could sit thus happily with her, feeling a mild pleasure in her, without that raging desire which must put a man in torment till it was slaked; it was just pleasant, stroking and patting and going so far and then drawing back.

The door opened, and Anne was watching them. All the fears which she had successfully pushed away came rushing back. She knew Jane Seymour . . . sly, waiting, watchful of her opportunities. Anne suddenly realized why they waited, why Henry could be content to wait. They were waiting to see whether she bore a son. If she did, then Jane Seymour would be the King's mistress. If not. . . .

Anne's self-control broke. She began to storm and rage. She now said to the King all those things which had been in her mind and which, even in her most frank moments, she had never mentioned before. It was as though she dragged him away from that bright and pleasant picture he had made of himself, and held up her picture of him. She was laughing at his conscience, at his childish method of putting himself right. Did he not think she saw through that! Did he not think that the great men about him did not either!

She was maddened with rage and grief and terror, so that she knew not what she said.

Henry's one idea was to calm her, for he must think of the son, whom she was so soon to bear.

'Be at peace, sweetheart,' he pleaded, 'and all shall go well for thee.'

But Anne was not at peace. Jane Seymour ran and hid herself behind the hangings, covering her face with her hands and audibly murmuring: 'Oh, what have I done!' while she rejoiced at what she had done.

For what could she have done to suit herself and her supporters more, since, after that sudden shock, prematurely Anne's son was born dead!

*   *   *

Trembling, they brought the news to the King. He clenched his hands; his eyes seemed to sink into the flesh about them, while the veins stood out knotted on his forehead. In uncontrollable rage he strode into Anne's room. He stood over her as she lay limp, exhausted and defeated.

355

Words flowed from that cruel little mouth. She had done this! She had humiliated him! She had deceived him into thinking she would give him sons! She was a witch, a sorceress . . .

Enfeebled as she was by hours of agony, yet she answered with spirit: 'There was none to blame but yourself. This is due to the distress of mind you caused me through your philanderings with that sly Seymour wench!'

Henry roared back wrathfully: 'You shall have no more boys by me!' And then, cunning and pious: 'I see well that God does not wish to give me male children.'

But he did not really believe this, not seeing how he himself could possibly be at fault in this matter.

'When you are on your feet, I will speak to you,' he said coldly.

Then he went from the room, his thoughts with Jane Seymour. It might well be that this marriage was a mistake, he was thinking. By God, I was forced into it by sorcery! She was irresistible, with her long hair and her wicked little pointed face. It was beyond the power of man to say nay to her. Sorcery! This is why God does not permit me to have male children. Might it not be that I should make a new match?

*　　*　　*

Jane Seymour sat in her apartments at the palace, awaiting the King. These apartments which were splendid and hung with rich arras and cloth of gold, had a short while before belonged to Thomas Cromwell, but he had vacated them that Jane might use them, because adjoining those of the King they could most easily and secretly be reached by His Majesty.

Jane was rather frightened by the great happenings which had come about ever since that day when the King had glanced in her direction. Her brothers, Thomas and Edward, had planned ambitiously, and their plans, they told their sister, were all for her. Edward was clever, subtle and ambitious; Thomas was fascinating, dashing and also ambitious. Look what came to Anne Boleyn! said these two.

Why not to Jane Seymour? True, Jane had not the obvious attractions of Anne Boleyn, but men were strange in their fancies, and was it Anne's beauty and wit that had charmed the King as much as her reluctance? If Jane had not beauty and wit, she could be as reluctant as Anne, and in all probability with more effect, for shyness would seem more natural in Jane than it ever could be in Anne.

So Jane must bow to the wishes of her family. Chapuys and the imperialists were with Jane too, eager to support any who would bring disfavour on the partisans of Martin Luther.

So here was Jane, meek and mild, yet not being entirely without ambition, feeling that it would be somewhat pleasant to wear a crown, and that to discountenance the haughty Anne Boleyn would be most gratifying. She was therefore ready enough to step into her mistress's shoes, yet a little frightened, for she could not but be aware that this role which was being forced upon her – even though she was not altogether reluctant to take it – was a very dangerous one. Anne was losing her place; Anne who had wit and beauty; Anne who had kept the King for five long years after she had become his mistress; and when she remembered this, Jane dared not think more than a month or two ahead. Her brothers had assured her that all she need do was obey their orders. She admired her brothers; they were clever, which Jane had never been; they were men, whereas Jane was just a weak woman. She was afraid of the King; when he put his face near hers and she smelt the wine on his breath, when she looked at the great face with its purple veins, when the little bloodshot eyes twinkled at her, she did not have to feign a desire to run. Jane, without pity, thought of the Queen who would have to be displaced if she were to sit on the throne; it was not that Jane was cruel or hard-hearted, but merely that she was without imagination. Children could move her a little; they were small and helpless like Jane herself, and she understood their doubts, their fear of their elders, their gropings for enlightenment. She had wept a little for the Princess Mary, for surely that child had suffered a very hard fate; if Jane were ever Queen, she would do her best to see that even little Elizabeth was treated fairly, for bastard though she was, she was at least a child, and a little child at that.

Jane's thoughts went back to that important day when the King's messenger had come to her with a letter and purse of gold from the King. Her brothers had been expecting some such approach from the King, and had primed her as to what she must do. Jane was ever obedient; her nature demanded that she should be; so she obeyed her brothers. She kissed the letter to show how greatly she esteemed the King's person, how if he were but free to pay honourable courtship to her, she would so willingly have linked her fortune with his. The purse she refused.

'Kneel to His Grace the King,' said Jane, 'beseeching him to consider that I am a gentlewoman of good and honourable family. I have no greater wealth than mine honour, and for a thousand deaths I would not sully it. If my lord the King desires to make me a present of money, I pray it shall be when God sends me a good offer of marriage.'

The King had evidently not been displeased with this response. Jane had made it tremblingly, doubting whether her brothers had not gone too far and might have displeased His Majesty. But no! Her brothers had been right; the King was enchanted by such modesty and virtue. He would have the world know that the virtue of the ladies of his court was their most admired possession in the eyes of their King. The Seymours were honoured; they should have apartments in the palace near the King, for with Jane's family and friends he was more at ease than with Anne and hers. He was never sure of Anne's friends; they were too clever, too subtle. In future, give him good practical jokes; give him hearty humour that all could understand; he had done with mockery and smartness, and people who wrote and talked in a manner that he was not at all sure did not put him in the shade. No, he liked the company of the Seymours; they soothed him, and it was pleasant to contemplate a good and virtuous woman who appealed to him without arousing too insistent a passion.

He knew what the Seymours were after. Well, well, Anne could not have boys. A daughter from Katharine, a daughter from Anne! He wondered what he would get from Jane. With Anne he had scarcely thought of children at first, so greatly had he desired her, but he would not marry Jane on the chance that she might have a child; he would have to make sure that she was capable of doing so, before he committed himself again. This was a delicate situation for the Seymours, which while it was full of the most dazzling possibilities, was rampant with danger. Jane's strength had been in her aloofness, and how could she remain aloof and at the same time prove to the King that she was capable of bearing his child? The Seymours had to act with extreme tact; the had to take a risk, and they took it boldly. Hence the apartments close to those of His Majesty; hence the secret visits of the King, when he found Edward Seymour and his wife discreetly absent, and Jane alone and not so demure, waiting to receive him.

His courtship of her was a sober matter when he compared it with his courtship of Anne Boleyn. There was something restful about Jane; he never forgot for a moment when he was with her that he was the King, and never did he lose sight of the real meaning of this love-making. If Jane was unlike Anne, she was also unlike the King; he looked at their reflections, side by side in the mirror; himself large and red, she small and white; he completely master of the situation, she shrinking, a little afraid. She did not shrink from his coarseness as Anne had often done; cleverly she feigned such innocence as not to understand it; if she made a false move, if she said anything to arouse his anger, she would be meekly apologetic. With Jane Seymour he was enjoying a period of domestic peace which he had not enjoyed since he had banished Katharine and taken Anne to live beside him. In the turbulent years he had longed for that peace which would be brought about by what he thought of as Anne's sweet reasonableness; it had been a goal to which he, in his sentimental hours, had reached out with yearning hands, and never did he succeed in attaining it. Now here was Jane, offering it to him; he could lie back, close his eyes, enjoy it, say what he liked, and be sure of approbation.

The girl was a bit insipid though; he realized that, after the first few nights with her. She was too passive; neither eager nor repulsing him; just meek and submissive. All that a Queen should be to a King of course, but . . . Ah! he thought, I think of Anne. I gave too much of myself to that witch, for witch she is, with the devil's own power over me, so that even when I lie with another I cannot forget her. There will be no peace for me, while Anne lives, for the power of a witch is far-reaching, and she can cast spells even when her victim is in a good woman's arms.

Jane was not a little troubled by this most secret love affair between herself and the King; she was terrified of the Queen, whose rages could be awful; she had been maid of honour long enough to witness many a scene between their Majesties, and at these scenes the Queen had been known to outwit the King. The Queen was more physically attractive than any woman at court; it was impossible to be near her and not see the effect she could have on those about her. There were men who, conceiving passions for her ladies, would visit them, and on the coming of the Queen would be unable to take their eyes from her; she had but to throw a stray word in their direction, or a quick smile, and they were ready to do anything for her. She had that power. There might be those who said the King was tired of her; and so he was . . . at times. There might be those who would say that her only hope of holding the King was to give him a son; that was true in part, but not wholly. Jane had seen the many and conflicting moods that had come to the King as he watched this woman; anger and hatred had been there, strong enough to let in murder; but something else too, passionate hunger which Jane could not understand but vaguely feared. 'What if through Your Majesty's visits I should be with child?' she had asked. He had patted her thigh indulgently. 'Then, my Jane, you would please me mightily; you would show yourself worthy to be my Queen.' 'But how may I be your Queen when you have already a Queen?' His eyes glinted like tiny diamonds. 'Let not thy head bother with matters too big for it, Jane!' A warning, that had been; Do not meddle in state affairs, child. It is a dangerous thing for a woman to do.

All the same, Jane was uneasy. She would tell herself that the King was bewitched, the Queen had sorcery in her eyes; it was not necessary to be clever to see that. Those huge, black, flashing eyes had more witchery than was natural for a woman to have; and the Queen was careless of what she said, as though she had some hidden power to protect her; she could draw men to her with a speed and an ease that had magic in their roots. She would weave spells round the King who, having realized her wickedness and his folly in submitting to it, would now escape. She had brought evil into the court when she entered it. She had brought misery and great humiliation to the true Queen and her daughter Mary. Jane could weep to think of the child. And now her spells were less potent, for though she could weave them about men, she could bring no son to the King, since children were of heaven and Anne's powers came from hell. This was how Jane saw it. When the King caressed her, she would close her eyes tightly and say to herself: 'I must endure this, for in this way can I save our lord the King from a witch.' She prayed that her body might be fruitful, for she saw that thus could she fulfil her mission.

She thought continually of the Princess Mary. She had known her when she had been a maid to Katharine, before the coming of Anne Boleyn; she had ever deplored the King's mad infatuation for Anne; she had secretly adhered to Katharine all through the dangerous years, and so had she won the approval of Chapuys and many of the nobles who condemned the break with Rome. Thus they had been pleased when the King's fancy had lighted on her, and had sought to help and advise her.

She said to the King when he came to her: 'I have been thinking of the Princess Mary.'

'What of her?' he asked indifferently.

'I but thought of the hardship of her life, and how sad it is that she should be banished from the court. I wondered if Your Majesty would most graciously allow her to be brought back; I fear she suffers deeply from the humiliation which has been heaped upon her.'

The King looked at Jane with narrowed eyes. He said with exasperation: 'You are a fool! You ought to solicit the advancement of the children we shall have between us, and not others.'

When he left her Jane assured herself that her duty was to rescue the Supreme Head of the English Church from a wanton witch who would never release him in this life. And as Jane did not know how she could rescue him, except by bearing him a child, she knelt down by her bed and prayed that her union with the King might bring forth fruit.

*　　*　　*

The Queen was gay, recklessly so. Her eyes were enormous in her pale face; she was almost coquettish; she was lavish with the smiles she bestowed on those about her. The King was spending more and more time with the Seymours, and there was no doubt in Anne's mind that Jane was his mistress; moreover she knew this to be no light affair; there was deep meaning behind it. Those two brothers of Jane's were eager and apprehensive; they watched, they waited; indeed all the court was watching and waiting for something to happen. The loss of her boy, they whispered, had finished Anne. Cynical courtiers murmured together: 'Is he trying out Jane? If the King is waiting to produce a child before divorcing Anne, he may wait a very long time!'

It would have been a humiliating position for anyone; for Anne it was agonizing. She thought, This happened to Katharine while we tried for the divorce; it happened to Wolsey when he awaited his downfall; this is how More and Fisher must have waited in their homes . . . waited for a doom they felt coming to them, but knew not from which direction it would come. She was not the sort to show her fear; if during the lonely nights she would awake startled, the sweat on her forehead, having dreamed some nightmare in which the doom was upon her; if she lay awake for hours staring into darkness, thinking of the King with Jane Seymour, wondering if he ever thought of her, she never showed this. After such nightmares, such nocturnal wondering, she would be gayer than ever. Her clothes were still the talk of the court; she would throw herself feverishly into the planning of a new gown; she could no longer sit silently stitching for the poor, though she did not forget them. She would gather round her the most brilliant of the young men and women. Just as there had been Katharine's sober friends in the old days who had held aloof from that set over which she and the King ruled together, so now there was yet another set, and this time it was the Seymour party, but the King was of the Seymour party. Round Anne fluttered the poets and the wits, not seeming to care that they scorched their wings. Her revels were still the wittiest; the Seymours' were heavy and clumsy in comparison, but the King could not be lured from them. Handsome Henry Norris, who was supposed to be in love with Madge Shelton, had eyes for none but the Queen; people smiled at this man who was supposed to be engaging himself to Madge but was for ever postponing his marriage. 'What good does that do poor Norris?' they asked. 'Surely he cannot hope to marry the Queen!' Francis Weston and William Brereton, younger and more sophisticated, were equally enamoured of her; Wyatt was faithful as ever. She encouraged their attentions, finding great solace in the love of these men, finding a balm to her pride which had been so deeply wounded when she discovered that the King preferred dull Jane Seymour. She was reckless; she accepted the homage of those who loved her; she would dance and laugh immoderately; she was wittier than ever, and the wildness of her looks gave her beauty a new strangeness that for some augmented it. It would seem that she wished to lure all to her side, that only when she was surrounded by those who admired her did she feel safe. She sought to build up a wall of friendship round her. She had with her, in addition to Madge Shelton, those two friends, Margaret Lee and her sister Mary Wyatt, in whom she placed the greatest trust. Her own sister Mary came to attend her, and it was good to contemplate the serene happiness of Mary who, happy in her love for Stafford whom she had married, was as comfortable to be near as a glowing fire in winter. Anne felt secure with these people. Even Mark Smeaton, whom she had raised to be one of her chief musicians, might show his passionate admiration of her, and go unreproved.

There were always those to watch her slyly. The black eyes of the Spanish ambassador would meet those of the King's vicar-general, and the Spaniard would guess what thoughts went round and round in Cromwell's ugly shaven head. Jane Rochford was now openly unsympathetic towards Anne, not caring if she did invite her husband's disapproval.

As for George, he seemed to have caught his sister's recklessness; he rarely warned Anne now; he was like a man who had been running from danger and, feeling suddenly there is no escape, turns to face it.

It was pleasant to sit with George and Mary, Margaret Lee, Mary and Thomas Wyatt, talking of childhood days before they had been scattered and lost touch with each other.

'Well I remember,' said Anne on one occasion, 'how we all played together in Norfolk, and then again in Kent, how we all talked of our ambitions and what we would do.'

'Ambition,' laughed George, 'is like the moon; it looks so close, so easy to grasp, but the nearer knowledge takes you to it, the more unattainable you realize it to be. Ambition is a pernicious thing!'

'You said you would be a great poet,' said Anne. 'Wyatt too.'

'And he at least achieved his ambition,' said George.

'Much good did it do him!' said Wyatt, looking meaningly at Anne.

'We hoped for too much,' she said; 'all of us except Margaret and my sister Mary and your sister Mary. They are the happiest ones.'

They could look at those three. Margaret who was happily married to Sir Henry Lee, Mary Wyatt who had no husband but a serene countenance, Mary Boleyn who had many lovers, not for gain but for pleasure. The ambition of these three was happiness; they had found it. For the other three it had been power, and in a measure they had realized it too. There they were – Wyatt whose joy was in his verses and yet, being never satisfied with them, they could not give him complete happiness; Anne who would be a queen and had achieved her ambition and now listened for some sign to herald in disaster, as she scanned people's faces and tried to read behind their eyes; George who through the fortunes of his sisters had come to fame. Three of those children who had played together – the ordinary ones who were not clever or brilliant, or made for greatness – had succeeded; it was the clever ones who had asked for much – though in a measure they had found what they desired – to whom failure had come.

Anne said: 'We chose the wrong things; they chose the right. . . .' And none answered her, for this was a matter which it was unwise to discuss.

Mary would talk to her comfortingly.

'The King . . . ah! How well I knew him! Almost as well as you do, Anne.' Mary would smile at the memory. 'He is wayward; none dare stand between him and his desires, but an a woman pleases she need fear naught.'

Ah, but Mary had known him as a mistress; Anne knew him as a wife.

The winter of that year passed into spring. Anne danced and sang as though she had not a care in the world; she would wander through the park at Greenwich, would watch the barges on the river, would sit under the trees; sometimes she would romp with the dogs, laughing gaily at their antics, throwing herself about in a frenzy of enjoyment, but her heart was sad and heavy; she would weep sometimes and mingle her tears with her laughter; this was a dangerous mood, for in it she cared nothing for what she said or what she did, and so laid herself open to attack from all her enemies. She would call Smeaton to her and bid him play, play something gay, something to which she could dance, something to make her gay and joyous; play music that told of love and laughter, not of sorrow. And the musician's great dark eyes watched her passionately, and his long tapering fingers played for her, soothing her.

She gave him a fine ring, for his talent, she said, was great, and those with talent should not go unrewarded. She thought, He may sell it and buy himself clothes, poor man; he has little reward for his labours. But she knew he would never sell the ring, since she had worn it on her finger; and she laughed and was pleased that though the King appeared to be indifferent to her, a poor musician was deep in hopeless love for her.

'Come!' she would cry suddenly. 'Let us have a masque. Let us do a witty play. Thomas, you and George shall put your heads together; I would be amused. Mark, you shall play for the dancing; you shall play for my singing. Let us dance and be merry. . . . I am tired of melancholy.'

*   *   *

Cromwell had retired from court life for several days, on the plea of sickness. Cromwell needed solitude; he had to work out his next moves in this game of politics most carefully. He was no inspired genius; everything that had come to him had been the result of unflagging labour, of cautiously putting one foot forward and waiting until it was securely in its rightful place before lifting the other. He was fully aware that now he faced one of the crises of his career. His master commanded, and he obeyed, though the command of course was not given in so many words. Henry was too conscience-ridden to mention his more vile thoughts, so it was the duty of a good servant to discover his master's wishes though not a word be spoken between them. Murder is a dangerous business, and Cromwell must consider whilst carrying out the King's wishes, not what was good for the King and the country, but what was good for Cromwell. Cromwell had a very good head on a pair of sturdy shoulders, and he did not intend that those should part company. The farther one climbed, the more steep the road, the easier it was to slip; one false step now, and Cromwell would go slipping down to the dark valley where waited the block and the executioner's axe.

It had seemed to Emperor Charles that, on the death of Katharine, new friendship with Henry might be sought, and for this reason Chapuys came to Greenwich for a special audience with the King. But how could Henry become the ally of Charles, when Henry had broken so definitely with Rome, and Charles supported Rome? Rome, it seemed, stood between the Emperor and Henry. Cranmer trembled; he got as near blazing forth his anger as Cranmer could get; he preached a reckless sermon. Cromwell did not feel so deeply. Cranmer made up his mind which course he would take, and was loyal to that course; Cromwell was ready to examine any course; he would use any members of any sect if necessary; he would support them one day, burn them at the stake the next. Cromwell could see that there was some advantage to accrue from a new bond of friendship with the Emperor; therefore he was ready to explore this course of action. Cromwell was at this time very busily engaged in ransacking the monasteries, but he could see that if the Emperor and Henry should cease to be enemies, this could easily be held up for a time. He was prepared for anything. Anne was furious; naturally she would be. A possible reconciliation with the Emperor was a direct insult to her; she had not been over-cautious in her treatment of Cromwell, never liking nor trusting him. Until now Cromwell had been meek enough, but he did not believe that he need now treat the Queen with over-much humility. The King had hinted that Jane Seymour was with child, and Cromwell must think of this matter very seriously. What if this were so? What if there was need for Henry to marry the girl quickly in order to legitimize a possible heir to the throne? Cromwell would be expected to bring this about, and if Cromwell failed to do it in the time at his disposal, what then? It was not so long ago when the King had desired a divorce most urgently, and Cromwell's late master had blundered. Cromwell was ready to profit by the Cardinal's mistakes, for he was resolved that he should not be caught as Wolsey had been. Cromwell would be ready. It was easy to see – and this applied particularly if Jane

Seymour was really pregnant – that he need fear nothing from the wrath of Queen Anne. This secret matter of the King's was conducted rather differently from that other secret matter. This was a series of hints and innuendoes: the lady was so demure, so shy, that the King must respect her reserve. She must not suffer – nor the King through her – the pain and scandal of divorce. How did one rid oneself of a wife one no longer wants, if not by divorce?

Cromwell knew a great deal about that peculiar burden of the King's – his conscience. Cromwell knew that it was capable of unexpected twists and turns; Cromwell knew that it must always be placated, and how comparatively easy it was to placate it; how one turned a subject to show the side which the conscience might like and approve; how one carefully covered that which was unpleasant. The conscience was obliging; it could be both blind and deaf when the need arose; therefore, he did not propose to lose much sleep over that accommodating creature.

Cromwell decided to favour alliance with Spain. The Emperor was a better ally than Francis; alliance with the French had never brought gain to England. Henry had been very difficult at the meeting – which had seemed to Cromwell and to most of the counsellors deplorable. It showed cunning Cromwell one thing – the King was still under the influence of Anne. In spite of Jane Seymour, he would listen to Anne; in spite of her failure to give him an heir, he still hankered after her. It was an alarming state of affairs; Cromwell knew his master well enough to realize that if something was not soon done, he would have Henry throwing aside Jane Seymour, buying fresh holy relics, reconciling himself to his black-browed witch, in one more effort to get himself a son. Were the Queen secure again, what would happen to Thomas Cromwell? What had happened to Thomas Wolsey! It was not so long ago that one could forget.

There must be alliance with Spain, for it meant the downfall of Anne; how disconcerting therefore, when the King must abuse the Emperor before Chapuys himself, must recall all he had done to delay the divorce, must announce here and now that not for a hundred alliances would he give way to Rome! He had made himself head of the Church, and head of the Church he would stay. If there was any humility to be shown, then Emperor Charles must show it. He even went so far as to tell Chapuys that he believed Francis had first claim on Burgundy and Milan.

This seemed to Cromwell sheer folly. The King was not acting with that shrewdness a statesman must always display. Henry was smarting under insults which he had received from Clement and Paul and Charles. He was not thinking of the good of England; he could only think: 'They want my friendship – these people who have been against me, who have worked against me, who have humiliated me for years!'

Anne had said: 'Ah! So you would be friends with your enemies as soon as they whistle for you, would you! Have you forgotten the insults of Clement? And why did he insult us? Would Clement have dared, had he not been supported? And by whom was he supported? By whom but this Charles who now comes and asks for your friendship, and in a manner that is most haughty! Oh, make friends, accept your humble rôle, remember not the insults to your kingship, to your Queen!'

He had ever been afraid of her tongue; it could find his weakness. Well he knew that she feared alliance with Spain more than anything, for it would mean her personal defeat; and yet he knew there was something in what she said; they had humiliated him and her, and as he had made her Queen, insults to her were insults to him. They had doubly insulted him!

This he remembered as he paced the floor with Chapuys, as he talked to Cromwell and Audley – that chancellor who had followed More – both of whom were urging him to sink his grievances and snatch a good thing while he could. But no! It was the Emperor who must come humbly to him. The egoist was wounded; he needed the sweet balm of deference from one he feared to be more mighty than himself, to lay upon his wounds.

Cromwell, for the first time in a long obsequious association, lost his temper; his voice cracked as he would explain; Cromwell and the King shouted at each other.

'Danger, Cromwell! Danger!' said a small voice inside the man, and he had to excuse himself and move away that he might regain control of his temper. He was trembling from head to foot at his folly; he was sick with fear and anger. How simple to abandon his quarrel with Rome! What need to continue it now Katharine was dead. Only the gratification of Henry's personal feelings came into this. Anne and her supporters were at the bottom of it; they would keep alive the King's anger. Could it be that Anne's falling into disfavour really was but a temporary thing? Such thoughts were fraught with great terror for Thomas Cromwell. For the first time in his career with the King, he must act alone; thus he feigned sickness that he might shut himself away from the King, that he might make a plan, study its effect, its reverberations, from all sides before daring to put it into practice.

He emerged from his isolation one mild April day, and asked for permission to see the King.

The King scowled at him, never liking him, liking him less remembering the man's behaviour when he had last seen him. He, who had ever been meek and accommodating, daring to shout at him, to tell him he was wrong! Was this secretary – whom he had made his vicar-general – was humble Thomas Cromwell a spy of Chapuys!

'Sir,' said Thomas Cromwell, 'I am perplexed.'

His Majesty grunted, still retaining his expression of distaste.

'I would have Your Majesty's permission to exceed the powers I now enjoy.'

Henry regarded his servant with some shrewdness. Why not? he wondered. He knew his Cromwell – cunning as a fox, stealthy as a cat; since he had attained to great power, he had his spies everywhere; if one wanted to know anything, the simplest way was to ask Cromwell; with speed and efficiency he would bring the answer. He was the most feared man at court. A good servant, thought Henry, though a maddening one; and there'll come a day, was the royal mental comment, when he'll anger me so much by his uncouth manners and his sly, cunning ways, that I'll have his head off his shoulders . . . and doubtless be sorry afterwards, for though he creeps and crawls and is most wondrous sly, I declare he knows what he is about.

Cromwell should have his special powers. Cromwell bowed low and retired well pleased.

A few nights later, he asked Mark Smeaton to come up to dinner at his house at Stepney.

* * *

When Mark Smeaton received an invitation to dine at the house of the King's secretary, he was delighted. Here was great honour indeed. The Queen had shown him favour, and now here was Master Secretary Thomas Cromwell himself seeking his company!

It must be, thought Mark, my exceptional skill at music – though he had not known that Master Cromwell was fond of music. He knew very little of Cromwell; he had seen him now and then at the court, his cold eyes darting everywhere, and he had shivered a little, for he had heard it said that none was too insignificant to be of interest to that man. He would know a good deal of most people, and usually of matters they would prefer to keep secret; and every little piece of information he gathered, he would store, cherishing it until he might lay it beside another bit of information, and so make up a true picture of what was happening at court.

Mark had never been so happy as he had this last year or so. He had begun life most humbly in his father's cottage; he had watched his father at work on his bench, mending chairs and such things as people brought to him to be mended. He had heard music in his father's saw and plane; he had heard music in his mother's spinning wheel. Mark had been born with two great gifts – beauty and a love of music. He had a small pointed face with great luminous dark eyes, and hair that hung in curls about his face; his hands were delicate, his fingers tapering; his skin was white. He had danced gracefully from the time he was a small boy, though he had never been taught to dance. He was noticed, and taken to the house of a neighbouring knight where he had taught the knight's daughter to play various musical instruments; and when she had married, his benefactor had found him a place at court – a very humble place, it was true – so that Mark thought himself singularly blessed, which indeed he was, to have gained it. He had seen poor beggars wander past his father's door with never a bite to eat, and their feet sore and bleeding; no such fate for clever Mark! An opening at court; what next?

What next, indeed! He had never known how beautiful a thing life could be until one day when the Queen had passed so close to him that he had seen her long silken lashes lying against her smooth skin, and had heard her sing in the most exquisite voice he had ever heard, very softly to herself. Then she had caught sight of him, noticed his beauty of face, would have him play to her. He had wondered how he had been able to play, so deep had been his emotion.

Not only was she his idol, she was his benefactress. He was in his teens, at that age when it is possible to worship from afar some bright object, and to be completely happy in such worship, to be amply rewarded by a smile; and the Queen was generous with her smiles, especially to those who pleased her – and who could please her more readily than those who played excellently the music she loved!

Sometimes she would send for him and have him play to her when she was sad; he had seen her eyes fill with tears, had seen her hastily wipe them. Then he had yearned to throw himself at her feet, to say: 'Let Your Majesty command me to die for you, and gladly will I do it!'

But that was foolish, for what good could his death do her? There were rumours in the court, and thinking he knew the cause of her unhappiness, he longed to comfort her. He could do so by his music, and he played to the Queen as he had never played before in his life. So pleased was she that she gave him a ring with a ruby in it, a most valuable ring which never, never would he remove from his finger.

That was some weeks ago, and it seemed to him as he

considered this invitation to dine at Stepney, that events were moving so fast that he could not guess to what they pointed.

There were many about the Queen who loved her and made no great effort to hide their love; playing the virginals close by, he had heard their conversation with her. There was Sir Henry Norris whose eyes never left her, and whom she baited continually, pretending to scold him because he was a careless lover – since he was supposed to be in love with her cousin, Madge Shelton, yet was ever at the Queen's side. There were Brereton and Weston too, whom she scolded happily enough as though the scolding was not meant to be taken seriously. There was Wyatt with whom she exchanged quips; they laughed together, those two, and yet there was such sadness in their eyes when they looked on each other, that Mark could not but be aware of it. As for Mark himself, he was but humbly born, unfit to be the companion of such noble lords and their Queen, but he could not help his emotions nor could he hide them completely, and those lovely black eyes must see his feelings and regard him with more indulgence because of them.

Two days before Mark had received the invitation, Brereton did not come to the presence chamber. He heard the nobles' speculating on what had happened to him. He had been seen in his barge – going whither? None could be sure.

'On some gay adventure, I'll warrant,' said the Queen. 'We shall have to exact a confession from gay William, when he again presents himself!' And she was piqued, or feigned to be so; Mark was not sure; he could never be sure of the Queen; when she laughed most gaily, he sensed she was most near tears.

She found him sitting in the window seat, his lute idle in his hands.

She said softly: 'Mark, you look sad! Tell me why.'

He could not tell her that he had been thinking he was but a foolish boy, a boy whose father was a carpenter, a boy who had come far because of his skill in music, and he at the height of his triumph must be melancholy because he loved a queen.

He said that it was of no importance that he was sad, for how could the sadness of her humblest musician affect so great a lady!

She said then that she thought he might be sad because she may have spoken to him as an inferior person, and he would wish her to speak to him as though he were a nobleman.

He bowed low and, overcome with embarrassment, murmured: 'No, no, Madam. A look sufficeth me.'

That was disturbing, because she was perhaps telling him that she knew of his ridiculous passion. She was clever; she was endowed with wit and subtlety; how was it possible to keep such a mighty secret from her!

The next day he took barge to Stepney. Cromwell's house stood back from the river, which lapped its garden. Smeaton scrambled out and ascended the privy steps to the garden. A few years ago he would have been overawed by the splendour of the house he saw before him, but now he was accustomed to Greenwich and Windsor and Hampton Court; he noted it was just a comfortable riverside house.

He went through the gates and across the courtyard. He knocked, and a servant opened the door. Would he enter? He was expected. He was led through the great hall to a small chamber and asked to sit. He did so, taking a chair near the window, through which he gazed at the sunshine sparkling on the river, thinking what a pleasant spot this was.

The door must have been opened some time before he realized it, so silently was it done. In the doorway stood Thomas Cromwell. His face was very pale; his eyes were brilliant, as though they burned with some excitement. Surely he could not be excited by the visit of a humble court musician! But he was. This was decidedly flattering. In the court there were many who feared this man; when he entered a room, Mark had noticed, words died on people's lips; they would lightly change a dangerous subject. Why had the great Thomas Cromwell sent for Mark Smeaton?

Mark was aware of a hushed silence throughout the house. For the first time since he had received the invitation, he began to wonder if it was not as a friend that Cromwell had asked him. He felt the palms of his hands were wet with sweat; he was trembling so much that he was sure that if he were asked to play some musical instrument he would be unable to do so.

Cromwell advanced into the room. He said: 'It was good of you to come so promptly and so punctually.'

'I would have you know, my lord,' said Mark humbly, 'that I am by no means insensible of the honour . . .'

Cromwell waved his thick and heavy hands, as though to say 'Enough of that!' He was a crude man; he had never cultivated court graces, nor did he care that some might criticize his manners. The Queen might dislike him, turning her face from him fastidiously; he cared not a jot. The King might shout at him, call him rogue and knave to his face; still Thomas Cromwell cared not. Words would never hurt him. All he cared was that he might keep his position in this realm, that he might keep his head safely in the place where it was most natural for it to be.

He walked silently and he gave the impression of creeping, for he was a heavy man. Once again Mark was aware of the silence all about him, and he felt a mad desire to leap through the window, run across the gardens to the privy stairs and take barge down the river . . . no, not back to court where he could never be safe from this man's cold gaze, but back to his father's cottage, where he might listen to the gentle sawing of wood and his mother's spinning-wheel.

He would have risen, but Cromwell motioned him to be seated, and came and stood beside him.

'You have pleasant looking hands, Master Smeaton. Would they not be called musician's hands?' Cromwell's own hands were clammy as fish skin; he lifted one of Mark's and affected to study it closely. 'And what a pleasant ring! A most valuable ring; a ruby, is it not? You are a very fortunate young man to come by such a ring.'

Smeaton looked at the ring on his finger, and felt that his

face had flushed almost to the stone's colour; there was something so piercing in the cold eyes; he liked not to see them so close. The big, clumsy fingers touched the stone.

'A gift, was it, Master Smeaton?'

Mark nodded.

'I should be pleased to hear from whom.'

Mark tried to conceal the truth. He could not bear those cold hands to touch the ring; he could not bear to say to this crude man, 'It was a gift from the Queen.' He was silent therefore, and Cromwell's fingers pressed into his wrist.

'You do not answer. Tell me, who gave you that most valuable ring?'

'It was . . . from one of my patrons . . . one who liked my playing.'

'Might I ask if it was a man . . . or a lady?'

Mark slipped his hands beneath the table.

'A man,' he lied.

His arms were gripped so tightly that he let out a shriek for Cromwell's hands were strong, and Mark was fragile as a girl.

'You lie!' said Cromwell, and his voice was quiet and soft as silk.

'I . . . no, I swear . . . I . . .'

'Will you tell me who gave you the ring?'

Mark stood up. 'Sir, I came here on an invitation to dine with you. I had no idea that it was to answer your questions.'

'You came here to dine,' said Cromwell expressionlessly. 'Well, when you dine, boy, will depend on how readily you answer my questions.'

'I know not by what authority . . .' stammered the poor boy, almost in tears.

'On the authority of the King, you fool! Now will you answer my questions?'

Sweat trickled down Smeaton's nose. He had never before come face to face with violence. When the beggars had passed his father's door, when he had seen men in the pillory or hanging from a gibbet, he had looked the other way. He could not bear to look on any distressing sight. He was an artist; when he saw misery, he turned from it and tried

376

to conjure up music in his head that he might disperse his unhappy thoughts. And now, looking at Cromwell, he realized that he was face to face with something from which it was not possible to turn.

'Who gave you the ring?' asked Cromwell.

'I . . . I told you. . . .' Smeaton covered his face with his hands, for tears were starting to his eyes, and he could not bear to look longer into the cold and brutal face confronting him.

'Have done!' said Cromwell. 'Now . . . ready?'

Mark uncovered his eyes and saw that he was no longer alone with Cromwell. On either side of him stood two big men dressed as servants; in the hands of one was a stick and a rope.

Cromwell nodded to these men. One seized Smeaton in a grip that paralysed him. The other placed the rope about his head, making a loop in the rope through which was placed the stick.

'Tighten the rope as I say,' commanded Cromwell.

The boy's eyes were starting in terror; they pleaded with Cromwell: Do not hurt me; I cannot bear it! I could not bear physical pain . . . I never could. . . .

The eyes of Cromwell surveyed his victim, amused, cynical. One of the thick fingers pulled at his doublet.

'Indeed it is a fine doublet . . . a very fine doublet for a humble musician to wear. Tell me, whence came this fine doublet?'

'I . . . I . . .'

'Tighten the rope,' said Cromwell. It cut into the pale skin of Mark's forehead. He felt as though his head was about to burst.

'The doublet . . . whence did it come?'

'I . . . I do not understand. . . .'

'Tighter . . . tighter! I have not all the day to spend on such as he.'

Something was trickling down his face, something warm and thick. He could see it on his nose, just below his eyes.

'Who gave you the doublet? Tighten the rope, you fools!'

Mark screamed. His head was throbbing; black spots, like notes of music, danced before his eyes.

'Please . . . stop! I . . . will tell you . . . about the doublet . . . Her Majesty . . .'

'Her Majesty!' said Cromwell, smiling suddenly. 'Loosen the rope. Bring him a little water. Her Majesty?' he prompted.

'Her Majesty thought I was ill-clad, and since I was to be her musician, she gave money for the doublet. . . .'

'The Queen gave you money. . . .' One large cold finger pointed to the ruby. 'And the ring. . . ?'

'I . . .'

'The rope, you fools! Tighten it! You were too soft before. . . .'

'No!' screamed Mark. 'You said . . . water . . .'

'Then who gave you the ring?'

'The Queen . . .'

'Give him water. The Queen then gave you the ruby ring.'

Mark drank; the room was swimming round and round; the ceiling dipped. He could see the river through the window – it looked faint and far away; he heard the sound of singing on a passing barge. Oh, were I but there! thought Mark.

'I would know why the Queen gave you the ruby.'

That was easy. 'She was pleased with my playing . . . She is a most generous lady . . .'

'Over-generous with her favours, I'll warrant!'

He felt sick. This was no way to speak of the Queen. He wanted to stand up, push aside that bland, smiling face, run out into the fresh air, run to the Queen.

'You were most friendly with the Queen?'

'She was most gracious . . .'

'Come, no evasions! You know full well my meaning. The Queen gave you money, clothes, and a ruby ring. Well, why not? She is young, and so are you. You are a handsome boy.'

'I understand not . . .'

'Subterfuge will not help you. You are here, on the King's command, to answer questions. You are the Queen's lover!'

The shock of those words set his head throbbing anew; he

could still feel the tight pressure of the rope about his head, although in actual fact it was quite loose now; the torture had stopped for awhile. He felt very ill; the blood was still trickling down his face from the cut which the rope had made. Oh, why had he accepted an invitation to dine with Thomas Cromwell! Now he knew what people meant when they talked with fear of Cromwell. Now he knew why they would suddenly stop talking when Cromwell appeared.

Cromwell rapped on the table with his knuckles.

'Tighten the rope.'

'No!' screamed Mark.

'Now. Speak the truth, or it will be worse for you. You are the Queen's lover. You have committed adultery with the Queen. Answer! Answer yes!'

'No!' sobbed Mark.

He could not bear this. He was screaming with the pain; it seemed to him that his blood was pounding against the top of his head, threatening to burst it. It gushed from his nose. He alternately moaned and screamed.

Cromwell said: 'You must tell the truth. You must admit this crime you and she have committed.'

'I have committed no crime! She . . . she . . . is a queen . . . No, no! Please . . . please . . . I cannot bear it . . . I cannot . . .'

One of the men was putting vinegar beneath his nose, and he realized that he had enjoyed a second or two of blessed unconsciousness.

Cromwell gripped his chin and jerked his head up violently, so that it seemed as if a hundred knives had been plunged into his head.

'This is nothing to what will follow, if you do not answer my questions. Admit that you have committed adultery with the Queen.'

' 'Twould be but an untruth . . .'

Cromwell banged on the table; the noise was like hammer blows on his aching head.

'You committed adultery with the Queen . . . Tighten up . . . Tighter, you fools! Tighter . . .'

'No!' screamed Mark. And then the smell of vinegar,

mingling with that of blood, told him he had lost consciousness again.

He sobbed: 'I cannot ... I cannot ...'

'Listen,' snarled Cromwell, 'you committed adultery with the Queen ...' The great hand shot up and seized the stick from the hands of his servant 'There! There! You committed adultery with the Queen. You committed adultery with the Queen ... Admit it! Admit it!'

Mark screamed. 'Anything ... anything ... Please ... I cannot ... I cannot ... endure ... my head ...'

'You admit it then?'

'I admit ...'

'You committed adultery with the Queen ...'

He was crying, and his tears mingled with the blood and sweat ... and that hateful smell of vinegar would not let him sink into peace. He had longed to die for her, and he could not bear a little pain for her. A little pain! Oh, but it was such exquisite torture; his head was bursting, bleeding; he had never known there could be agony like this.

Cromwell said: 'He admits adultery with the Queen. Take him away.'

They had to carry him, for when he stood up he could see nothing but a blur of panelled walls, and light from the window, and a medley of cruel faces. He could not stand; so they carried him to a dark chamber in which they left him, locked in. And as he sank to the floor, he lost consciousness once more.

He lay there, half fainting, not aware of the room nor even what had gone before. He knew nothing except that there was a pain that maddened him, and that it was in his head. In his mouth he tasted blood; the smell of vinegar clung to his clothes, devilishly not allowing him to rest in that dark world for which he longed.

He was semi-conscious, thinking he was in his father's cottage, thinking he sat at the feet of the Queen, and that darkness for which he longed was her eyes, as black as night, as beautiful as forgetfulness.

But now someone was beating with a hammer on his head, and it was hurting him abominably. He awakened screaming, and knew suddenly that he was not in his father's cottage, nor at the feet of the Queen; he was in a dark room in Thomas Cromwell's house at Stepney, and he had been tortured . . . and what had he said? What *had* he said?

He had lied; he had lied about her for whom he would have died! Sobs shook his slender body. He would tell them . . . he would tell them he lied; he would explain. It hurt me so that I knew not what I said. She is a great, good lady. How could I have said that of her! How could I so demean her . . . and myself! But I could not bear the pain in my head; it was maddening. I could not endure it, Your Most Gracious Majesty! For that reason I lied.

He must pray for strength. He must do anything, but he must explain that he had lied. He could not let them believe . . .

He lay groaning in the dark, misery of body forgotten because he mourned so sincerely what he had done. Even though I assure them it is not so, I said it . . . I failed her.

He was almost glad when they came to him. That cruel man was with them.

Mark stammered: 'I lied . . . It was not so. The pain was too much for me.'

'Can you stand?' asked Cromwell in a voice that was almost solicitous.

He could stand. He felt better. There was a terrible throbbing in his head, but the frightening giddiness had passed. He felt strengthened. No matter what they did to him, he would tell no more lies. He was ready to go to the scaffold for the Queen.

'This way,' said Cromwell.

The cool air fanned his burning face, setting his wounds to smart. He reeled, but there were those to support him. He was too dazed to wonder where he was going. They led him down the privy stairs to a barge.

He could feel the river breeze; he could smell the river, tar and sea salt mingling with blood and vinegar. He felt steady with purpose; he pictured himself going to the scaffold for her sake; but first though, he must make it clear that he had lied, that only such frightening, maddening torture could have made him lie about her.

The river was shot with darkness, for evening was advancing. The barge was being moored; he was prodded and told to get out. Above him loomed a dark, grey tower; he mounted the steps and went over the stone bridge. They were going to put him in the Tower! He was suddenly sick; the sight of the Tower had done that to him. What now? Why should they take him to the Tower? What had he done? He had accepted money, he had accepted a ring; they were gifts from a queen to one whose music had pleased her. He had committed no crime.

'This way,' said Cromwell. A door was unlocked; they passed through it. They were in a dark passage whose walls were slimy; and there was a noisome smell coming up from below the dismal spiral staircase which they were descending.

A man with a lanthorn appeared. Their shadows were grotesque on the walls.

'Come along,' said Cromwell, almost gently.

They were in one of the many passages which ran under the great fortress. The place was damp and slimy; little streams trickled across the earthen floor, and rats scuttled away at their approach.

'You are in the Tower of London, Smeaton.'

'That I have realised. For what reason have I been brought here?'

'You will know soon enough. Methought I would like to show you the place.'

'I would rather go back. I would have you know that when I said ... when I said what I did ... that I lied ...'

Cromwell held up a thick finger.

'An interesting place, this Tower of London. I thought you would enjoy a tour of inspection before we continue with our cross-examination.'

'I ... I understand not ...'

'Listen! Ah! We are nearer the torture chambers. How that poor wretch groans! Doubtless 'tis the rack that stretches his body. These rogues! They should answer questions, and all would be well with them.'

Mark vomited suddenly. The smell of the place revolted him, his head was throbbing, he was in great pain, and he felt he could not breathe in this confined space.

'You will be better later,' said Cromwell. 'This place has a decided effect on those who visit it for the first time . . . Here! Someone comes . . .'

He drew Mark to one side of the loathsome passage. Uncanny screams, like those of a madman, grew louder, and peering in the dim light, Mark saw that they issued from the bloody head of what appeared to be a man who was coming towards them; he walked between two strong men in the uniform of warders of the Tower, who both supported and restrained him. Mark gasped with horror; he could not take his eyes from that gory thing which should have been a head; blood dripped from it, splashing Mark's clothes as the man reeled past, struggling in his agony to dash his head against the wall and so put an end to his misery.

Cromwell's voice was silky in his ear.

'They have cut off his ears. Poor fool! I trow he thought it smart to repeat what he'd heard against the King's Grace.'

Mark could not move; it seemed to him that his legs were rooted to this noisome spot; he put out a hand and touched the slimy wall.

'Come on!' said Cromwell, and pushed him.

They went on; Mark was dazed with what he had seen. I am dreaming this, he thought. This cannot be; there could never be such things as this!

The passages led past cells, and Cromwell would have the man shine his lanthorn into these, that Mark might see for himself what befell those who saw fit to displease the King. Mark looked; he saw men more dead than alive, their filthy rags heaving with the movement of vermin, their bones protruding through their skin. These men groaned and blinked, shutting their eyes from that feeble light, and their clanking chains seemed to groan with them. He saw what had been men, and were now mere bones in chains. He saw death, and smelt it. He saw the men cramped in the Little Ease, so paralysed by this form of confinement that when Cromwell called to one of them to come out, the man, though his face lit up with a sudden hope of freedom, could not move.

The lanthorn was shone into the gloomy pits where rats swam and squeaked in a ferocious chorus as they fought one another over dying men. He saw men, bleeding and torn from the torture chambers; he heard their groans, saw their bleeding hands and feet, their mutilated fingers from which the nails had been pulled, their poor, shapeless, bleeding mouths from which their teeth had been brutally torn.

'These dungeons have grown lively during the reign of our most Christian King,' said Cromwell. 'There will always be fools who know not when they are fortunate . . . Come, Master Smeaton, we are at our destination.'

They were in a dimly lighted chamber which seemed to Mark's dazed eyes to be hung with grotesque shapes. He noticed first the table, for at this table sat a man, and set before him were writing materials. He smelt in this foul air the sudden odour of vinegar, and the immediate effect of this – so reminiscent of his pain – was to make him retch. In the centre of this chamber was a heavy stone pillar from which was projected a long iron bar, and slung around this was a rope at the end of which was a hook. Mark stared at this with wonder, until Cromwell directed his gaze to that ponderous instrument of torture nick-named The Scavenger's Daughter; it was a simple construction, like a wide iron hoop, which by means of screws could be tightened about its victim's body.

'Our Scavenger's Daughter!' said Cromwell. 'One would not care for that wench's embrace. Very different, Smeaton, from the arms of her who is thought by many to be the fairest lady of the court!'

Mark stared at his tormentor, as a rabbit stares at a stoat. He was as if petrified, and while he longed to scream, to run to dash himself against the walls in an effort to kill himself – as that other poor wretch had done – he could do nothing but stand and stare at those instruments of torture which Cromwell pointed out to him.

'The gauntlets, Smeaton! A man will hang from these ... Try them on? Very well. I was saying ... they would be fixed on yonder hook which you see there, and a man would hang for days in such torture as you cannot ... yet imagine. And all because he will not answer a few civil questions. The folly of men, Smeaton, is past all believing!'

Mark shuddered, and the sweat ran down his body.

'The thumbscrews, Smeaton. See, there is blood on them. The Spanish Collar ... see these spikes! Not pleasant when pressed into the flesh. How would you like to be locked into such a collar and to stay there for days on end? But no, you would not be unwise, Smeaton. Methinks you are a cultured man; you are a musician; you have musician's hands. Would it not be a pity were those beautiful hands fixed in yon gauntlets! They say men have been known to lose the use of their hands after hanging from that beam.'

Mark was trembling so that he could no longer stand.

'Sit here,' said Cromwell, and sat with him. Regaining his composure to some small extent, Mark looked about him. They were sitting on a wooden frame shaped like a trough, large enough to contain a human body. At each end of this frame were fixed windlasses on which rope was coiled.

Smeaton screamed aloud. 'The rack!' he cried.

'Clever of you, Smeaton, to have guessed aright. But fear not. You are a wise young man; you will answer the questions I ask, and you will have no need of the rack nor her grim sister, the Scavenger's Daughter.'

Mark's mouth was dry, and his tongue was too big for it.

'I ... I cannot ... I lied ...'

Cromwell lifted a hand. Two strong men appeared and, laying hands on the shivering boy, began stripping off his clothes.

Mark tried to picture the face of the Queen; he could see her clearly. He must keep that picture before him, no matter what they did to him. If he could but remember her face ... if ...

He was half fainting as they laid him in the frame and fastened the loops of the ropes to his wrists and ankles.

Cromwell's face was close to his.

'Smeaton, I would not have them do this to you. Dost know what happens to men who are racked? Some lose their reason. There are some who never walk again. This is pain such as you cannot dream of, Smeaton. Just answer my questions.' He nodded to his attendants to be ready. 'Smeaton, you have committed adultery with the Queen.'

'No!'

'You have admitted it. You admitted it at Stepney; you cannot go back on that.'

'I was tortured ... The pain ... it was too much ...'

'So you admitted the truth. Did I not tell you that what you have known so far was naught? You are on the rack, Smeaton. One sign from me, and those men will begin to work it. Will you answer my questions?'

'I lied ... I did not ...'

He could see her face clearly, smiling at him; her eyes were great wells of blessed darkness; to lose oneself in that darkness would be to die, and death was the end of pain.

'Begin,' said Cromwell. The windlasses turned outwards ... Smeaton felt his body was being torn apart; he screamed, and immediately lost consciousness.

Vinegar. That hateful smell that would not let a man rest.

'Come, Smeaton! You committed adultery with the Queen.'

He could still see her face, but it was blurred now.

'You committed adultery with the Queen ...'

There was nothing but pain, pain that was a thousand red hot needles pressing into the sockets of his arms and legs; he could feel his joints cracking; he felt they must be breaking. He began to groan.

'Yes, yes ... yes ... anything ... But ...'

'Enough!' said Cromwell, and the man at the table wrote.

Mark was sobbing. It seemed to him that they poured the accursed vinegar over his face. They sprinkled it on with the brush he had seen hanging on the wall, adding fresh smarts to his bleeding head; causing him to shrink, which in its turn made him scream afresh, for every movement was acute torture.

Cromwell's voice came from a long way off.

'There were others, beside yourself, Smeaton.'

Others? He knew not what the man meant. He knew nothing but pain, pain, excruciating pain that shot all over his flesh; this was all the pain he had ever thought there could be; this was all the pain in the world. And more than pain of the body – pain of the mind. For he would have died for her, and he had betrayed her; he had lied; he had lied about her; he had said shameful things of her because . . . he . . . could not bear the pain.

'Their names?' said Cromwell.

'I know . . . no names.'

Not vinegar again! I cannot bear it . . . I cannot bear pain and vinegar . . . not both! He broke into deep sobs.

'You shall rest if you but tell us their names.'

How could he know of what the man was speaking? Names? What names? He thought he was a little boy at his mother's spinning-wheel. 'Little Mark! He is a pretty boy. Here is a sweetmeat, Mark . . . And he sings prettily too. And he plays the virginals . . . Mark, how would you like a place at court? The King loves music mightily . . .'

'Begin again!' ordered Cromwell.

'No!' shrieked Mark.

'The names,' murmured Cromwell.

'I . . . I . . . know . . . not . . .'

It was coming again, the agony. There was never agony such as this. Burning pincers . . . the wrenching apart of his muscles . . . the wicked rack was tearing off his limbs. Vinegar. Accursed vinegar.

'Mark Smeaton, you have committed adultery with the Queen. Not you alone! You were not to blame, Mark; the Queen tempted you, and who were you, a humble musician, to say nay to the Queen! But you were not alone in this, Mark; there were others. There were noble gentlemen, Mark . . . Come now, you have had enough of this rack; men cannot be racked forever – you know that, Mark. It drives men mad. Just say their names, Mark. Come! Was it Wyatt?'

'There was none . . . I know not. I lied. Not I . . . I . . .'

No, not again. He was going mad. He could not endure more. Her face was becoming blurred. He must stop, stop. He was going mad. He would not say what they told him to. He must not say Wyatt's name . . .

They were putting vinegar under his nose. They were going to turn the rack again.

He saw the court, as clearly as though he were there. She was smiling, and someone was standing beside her.

'Norris!' he screamed. 'Norris!'

Cromwell's voice was gentle, soothing.

'Norris, Mark. That is good. That is right. Who else, Mark? Just whisper . . .'

'Norris! Brereton! Weston!' screamed Mark.

He was unconscious as they unbound him and carried his tortured body away.

Cromwell watched them, smiling faintly. It had been a good day's work.

* * *

The next day was the first of May. May Day was a favourite court festival which the King never failed to keep. At one time he had been the hero of the tiltyard, but now that his leg was troublesome, he must sit back and watch others take the glory of the day. The chief challenger on this day would be Lord Rochford, and the chief of the defenders, Henry Norris. It was not pleasant, when one had been more skilful than they, to realize age was creeping on, turning one into a spectator instead of a brilliant performer who had held the admiration of the entire court.

Cromwell came to see the King before he went to the tilt-yard. Henry frowned on the man, not wishing to see him now, but for once Cromwell would not be waved aside; he had news, disturbing news, news which should not be with-held from His Majesty one second longer than necessary. Cromwell talked; the King listened. He listened in silence, while his eyes seemed to sink into his head and his face grew as purple as his coat.

Down in the tiltyard they were awaiting the arrival of the

King. The Queen was already in her place, but obviously the jousts could not start without the King. He went to the yard, and took his place beside her. The tilt began.

He was aware of her beside him; he was trembling with jealous rage. He was thinking. This is the woman to whom I have given everything; the best years of my life, my love, my throne. For her I broke with Rome; for her I risked the displeasure of my people. And how does she reward me? She betrays me with any man that takes her fancy!

He did not know who tilted below; he did not care. Red mist swam before his eyes. He glanced sideways at her; she was more beautiful than she had ever seemed, and more remote than she had been in her father's garden at Hever. She had tricked him; she had laughed at him; and he had loved her passionately and exclusively. He was a king, and he had loved her; she was a nobody, the daughter of a man who owed his advancement to the favour of his king . . . and she had flouted him. Never had she loved him; she had loved a throne and a crown, and she had reluctantly taken him because she could not have them without him. His throat was dry with the pain she had caused him; his heart beat wildly with anger. His eyes were murderous; he wanted her to suffer all the pain she had inflicted on him – not as he had suffered, but a thousand times more so. It galled him that even now she was not one half as jealous of Jane Seymour as he was of Norris down there in the yard.

He looked at Norris – one of his greatest and most intimate friends – handsome, not as young as those others, Weston, Brereton and Smeaton, but with a distinguished air, a charm of manner, a gracious, gentle, knightly air. He loathed Norris, of whom a short while ago he had been very fond. There was her brother, Rochford; he had liked that young man; he had been glad to raise him for his own sake as well as his sister's; gay, amusing, devilishly witty and attractive . . . and now Cromwell had discovered that Rochford had said unforgivable, disloyal, treasonable things of his royal master; he had laughed at the King's verses, laughed at the King's clothes; he had most shamefully – and for this he deserved to die – disparaged the King's manhood, had laughed at him and whispered that the reason why the King's wives could not have children successfully was that the King himself was at fault.

Smeaton . . . that low-born creature who had nothing to recommend him but his pretty face and his music had pleased her more than he himself had. He, King of England, had begged her, had implored her, had bribed her with offers of greatness, and reluctantly she had accepted – not for love of him, but because she could not refuse a glittering crown.

He was mad with rage, mad with jealousy; furious with her that she could still hurt him thus, and that he was so vulnerable even now when he planned to cast her off. He could leap on her now . . . and if he had a knife in his hand he would plunge it into her heart; nothing would satisfy him, nothing . . . nothing but that her blood should flow; he would stab her himself, rejoicing to see her die, rejoicing that no one else should enjoy her.

The May sunshine was hot on his face; the sweat glistening across his nose. He did not see the jousts; he could see nothing but her making such voluptuous love with others as she had never given him. He had been jealous of her before; he had been ready to torture those who had glanced at her, but that had been complacent jealousy; now he could be jealous by reason of his knowledge, he could even fill in the forms of her lovers – Norris! Weston! Brereton! Wyatt? And that Smeaton! How dare she, she whom he had made a Queen! Even a humble boy could please her more than he could!

His attention was suddenly caught, for her handkerchief had fluttered from her hand; she was smiling, smiling at Norris; and Norris picked up the handkerchief, bowed, handed it to her on the point of his lance while they exchanged smiles that seemed like lovers' smiles to Henry's jealous eyes.

The joust continued. His tongue was thick, his throat was dry; he was filled with mad rage which he knew he could not continue to control. If he stayed here he would shout at her, he would take her by the beautiful hair which he had loved to twine about his fingers, and he would twist it about that small white neck, and tighten it and tighten it until there was no life left in the body he had loved too well.

She spoke to him. He did not hear what she said. He stood up; he was the King, and everything he did was of importance. How many of those people, who now turned startled eyes on him, had laughed at him for the complaisant husband he had appeared to be, had laughed at his blind devotion to this woman who had tricked him and deceived him with any man she fancied in his court!

It was the signal for the jousting to end. How could it go on, when the King no longer wished to see it? Anne was not so surprised, that she would attach too much importance to the strange behaviour of the King; he had been curt with her often enough of late; she guessed he had left Greenwich for White Hall, as he often went to London to see Jane Seymour.

The King was on his way to White Hall. He had given orders that Rochford and Weston should be arrested as they were leaving the tiltyard. Norris he had commanded to ride back with him.

He could not take his eyes from that handsome profile; there was a certain nobility about Norris that angered the King; he was tall and straight, and his gentle character was apparent in the finely cut profile and the mobile mouth. He was a man to be jealous of. The King had heard that Norris was about to engage himself to Madge Shelton who at one time – and that not so long ago – had pleased the King himself. Henry had wished him well of Madge; she was a very attractive woman, lively and clever and good-looking. The King had tired of her quickly; the only woman he did not tire of quickly was Anne Boleyn. And she . . . The anger came surging up again. The wanton! The slut! To think that he, who had always admired virtue in women, should have been cursed with a wife who was known throughout his court for her wanton ways! It was too much. She had known that he admired virtue in those about him; and she had laughed at him, jeered at him . . . with her brother and Weston and Brereton and Norris . . .

He leaned forward in his saddle and said, his voice quivering with rage: 'Norris, I know thee for what thou art, thou traitor!'

Norris almost fell from the saddle, so great was his surprise.

'Your Majesty . . . I know not . . .'

'You know not! I'll warrant you know well enough. Ha! You start, do you! Think you not that I am a fool, a man to stand aside and let his inferiors amuse themselves with his wife. I accuse you of adultery with the Queen!'

'Sir . . . this is a joke . . .'

'This is no joke, Norris, and well you know it!'

'Then it is the biggest mistake that has ever been made.'

'You would dare to deny it?' foamed the King.

'I deny it utterly, Your Majesty.'

'Your lies and evasions will carry little weight with me, Norris.'

'I can only repeat, Sir, that I am guiltless of that of which you accuse me,' said Norris with dignity.

All the rich blood had left the King's usually florid face, showing a network of veins against a skin grown pallid.

' 'Twill be better if you do not lie to me, Norris. I am in no mood to brook such ways. You will confess to me here and now.'

'There is naught I can confess, my lord. I am guiltless of this charge you bring against me.'

'Come, come! You know, as all in the court know, how the Queen conducts herself.'

'I assure Your Most Gracious Majesty that I know naught against the Queen.'

'You have not heard rumours! Come, Norris, I warn you I am not in the mood for dalliance.'

'I have heard no rumours, Sir.'

'Norris, I offer you pardon, for you know that I have loved you well, if you will confess to your adultery.'

'I would rather die a thousand deaths, my lord, than accuse the Queen of that which I believe her, in my conscience, innocent.'

The King's fury almost choked him. He said no more until

they reached Westminster. Then, calling to him the burly bully Fitzwilliam, whom Cromwell had chosen to be his lieutenant, he bade the man arrest Norris and despatch him to the Tower.

* * *

Anne, sitting down to supper in Greenwich Palace, felt the first breath of uneasiness.

She said to Madge Shelton: 'Where is Mark? He does not seem to be in his accustomed place.'

'I do not know what has happened to Mark, Your Majesty,' answered Madge.

'If I remember aright, I did not notice him last night. I hope he is not sick.'

'I do not know, Madam,' said Madge, and Anne noticed that her cousin's eyes did not meet hers; it was as though the girl was afraid.

Later she said: 'I do not see Norris. Madge, is it not strange that they should both absent themselves? Where is Norris, Madge? You should know.'

'He has said nothing to me, Madam.'

'What! He is indeed a neglectful lover; I should not allow it, Madge.'

Her voice had an edge to it. She well knew, and Madge well knew that though Norris was supposed to be in love with Madge, it was the Queen who received his attention. Madge was charming; she could attract easily, but she could not hold men to her as her cousin did. Weston had been attracted by Madge once, until he had felt the deeper and irresistible attraction of the Queen.

'I know not what is holding him,' said Madge.

Anne said: 'You know not *who* is holding him, you mean!' And when she laughed, her laughter was more than usually high-pitched.

It was a strange evening; people whispered together in the corridors of the palace.

'What means this?'

'Did you see the way His Majesty left the tiltyard?'

'They say Norris, Weston and Brereton are missing.'

'Where is Mark Smeaton? Surely they would not arrest little Mark!'

The Queen was aware of this strange stillness about her; she called for the musicians, and while they played to her, sat staring at Mark's empty place. Where was Norris? Where was Weston? Why did Brereton continue to absent himself?

She spent a sleepless night, and in the early morning fell into a heavy doze from which she awakened late. All during the morning the palace abounded in rumour. Anne heard the whispering voices, noted the compassionate glances directed at her, and was increasingly uneasy.

She sat down to dinner, determined to hide the terrible apprehension that was stealing over her. When she did not dine with the King, His Majesty would send his waiter to her with the courteous message: 'Much good may it do you!' On this day she waited in vain for the King's messenger; and as soon as the meal was over and the surnap was removed, there came one to announce the arrival at Greenwich of certain members of the council, and with them, to her disgust, was her uncle the Duke of Norfolk.

Her uncle looked truculent and self-righteous, pleased with himself, as though that which he had prophesied had come to pass. He behaved, not as a courtier to a queen, but as a judge to a prisoner.

'What means this?' demanded Anne.

'Pray be seated,' said Norfolk.

She hesitated, wanting to demand of him why he thought he might give her orders when to sit and when to stand; but something in his eyes restrained her. She sat down, her head held high, her eyes imperious.

'I would know why you think fit to come to me at this hour and disturb me with your presence. I would know . . .'

'You shall know,' said Norfolk grimly. 'Smeaton is in the Tower. He has confessed to having committed adultery with you.'

She grew very pale, and stood up, her eyes flashing.

'How dare you come to me with such vile accusations!'

'Tut, tut, tut!' said Norfolk, and shook his head at her.

'Norris is also in the Tower.' He lied: 'He also admits to adultery with you.'

'I will not believe that he could be guilty of such falsehood! I will not believe it of either. Please leave me at once. I declare you shall suffer for your insolence.'

'Forget not,' said Norfolk, 'that we come by the King's command to conduct you to the Tower, there to abide His Highness's pleasure.'

'I must see the King,' said Anne. 'My enemies have done this. These stories you would tell me would be tragic, were they not ridiculous. . . .'

'It is not possible for you to see the King.'

'It is not possible for *me* to see the King. You forget who I am, do you not? I declare you will wish . . .'

'You must await the King's pleasure, and he has said he does not wish to see you.'

She was really frightened now. The King had sent these men to arrest her and take her to the Tower; he had said he did not wish to see her. Lies were being told about her. Norris? Smeaton? Oh, no! Not those two! They had been her friends, and she would have sworn to their loyalty. What did this mean. . . . George, where was George? She needed his advice now as never before.

'If it be His Majesty's pleasure,' she said calmly, 'I am ready to obey.'

In the barge she felt very frightened. She was reminded of another journey to the Tower, of a white falcon which had been crowned by an angel, of the King, waiting to receive her there . . . eager that all the honour he could give her should be hers.

She turned to her uncle. 'I am innocent of these foul charges. I swear it! I swear it! If you will but take me to the King, I know I can convince him of my innocence.'

She knew she could, if she could but see him . . . if she could but take his hands. . . . She had ever been able to do with him what she would . . . but she had been careless of late. She had never loved him; she had not much cared that he had strayed; she had thought that she had but to flatter him and amuse him, and he would be hers. She had never thought that this could happen to her, that she would be removed from him, not allowed to see him, a prisoner in the Tower.

Norfolk folded his arms and looked at her coldly. One would have thought he was her bitterest enemy rather than her kinsman.

'Your paramours have confessed,' he said, shrugging his shoulders. ' 'Twould be better if you did likewise.'

'I have naught to confess. Have I not told you! What should I confess? I do not believe that these men have made confessions; you say so to trap me. You are my enemy; you always have been.'

'Calm yourself!' said Norfolk. 'Such outbursts can avail you nothing.'

They made fast the barge; they led her up the steps; the great gate opened to admit her.

'Oh, Lord, help me,' she murmured, 'as I am guiltless of that whereof I am accused.' Sir William Kingston came out to receive her, as he had on that other occasion. 'Mr Kingston,' she asked, 'do I go into a dungeon?'

'No, Madam,' answered the constable, 'to your own lodgings where you lay at your coronation.'

She burst into passionate weeping, and then she began to laugh hysterically; and her sobs, mingling with her laughter, were pitiful to hear. She was thinking of then and now – and that in but three short years. A queen coming to her coronation; a queen coming to her doom.

'It is too good for me!' she cried, laughing as the sobs shook her. 'Jesus have mercy on me!'

Kingston watched her until her hysteria passed. He was a hard man but he could not but be moved to pity. He had seen some terrible sights in these grey, grim buildings, but he thought that this girl, laughing and crying before him, presented one of the most pathetic he had ever witnessed. He had received her on her first coming to the Tower, thought her very beautiful in her coronation robes with her hair flowing about her; he could not but compare her then with this poor weeping girl, and so was moved in spite of himself.

She wiped her eyes, controlled her laughter, and her dignity returned to her. She listened to a clock strike five, and such a familiar, homely sound reminded her of ordinary matters. Her family – what of them?

She turned to the members of the council, who were about to leave her in Kingston's care.

'I entreat you to beseech the King in my behalf that he will be a good lord unto me,' she said; and when they had taken their leave, Kingston conducted her to her apartments.

She said: 'I am the King's true wedded wife.' And added: 'Mr Kingston, do you know wherefore I am here?'

'Nay!' he answered.

'When saw you the King?'

'I saw him not since I saw him in the tiltyard,' he said.

'Then Mr Kingston, I pray you tell me where my lord father is.'

'I saw him in the court before dinner,' said Kingston.

She was silent awhile, but the question she had longed to ask, now refused to be kept back longer. Oh, where is my sweet brother?'

He could not look at her; hard as he was he could not face the passionate entreaty in her eyes which pleaded with him to tell her that her brother was safe.

Kingston said evasively that he had last seen him at York Place.

She began to pace up and down, and as though talking to herself, she murmured: 'I hear say that I shall be accused with three men, and I can say no more than "Nay!"' She began to weep softly, as if all the wildness had been drained out of her, and there was only sadness left. 'Oh, Norris, hast thou accused me? Thou art in the Tower, and thou and I shall die together; and Mark, thou art here too? Oh, my mother, thou wilt die for sorrow.'

She sat brooding awhile, and then turning to him asked: 'Mr Kingston, shall I die without justice?'

He tried to comfort her. 'The poorest subject the King hath, has that,' he assured her.

She looked at him a moment before she fell into prolonged and bitter laughter.

*　　*　　*

Silence hung over the palace; in the courtyards men and women stood about whispering together, glancing furtively over their shoulders, fearful of what would happen next. Wyatt was in the Tower; who next? No man in the Queen's set felt safe. In the streets the people talked together; they knew that the Queen was a prisoner in the Tower; they knew she was to be tried on a charge of adultery. They remembered how the King had sought to rid himself of Katharine; did he seek to rid himself of Anne? Those who had shouted 'Down with Nan Bullen!' now murmured 'Poor lady! What will become of her?'

Jane Rochford, looking from her window, watched the courtiers and the ladies crossing the courtyard. She had expected trouble, but not such trouble. Anne in the Tower, where she herself had spent many an uneasy hour! George in the Tower! It was Jane's turn to laugh now, for might it not be that her whispered slander had put Cromwell on the scent? Had she not seen grave Norris and gay Weston cast their longing glances at the Queen? Yes, and she had not hesitated to laugh at these matters, to point them out to others. 'Ah! The Queen was born gay, and my husband tells me that the King . . . no matter, but what is a woman to do when she cannot get children. . . .' Proud George was in the Tower now, though it was whispered that no harm could come to him. It was those others, who had been her lovers, who would die.

Jane threw back her head, and for some moments she was weak with hysterical laughter. Poor little Jane! they had said. Silly little Jane! They had not bothered to explain their clever remarks to her; they had cut her out, considering her too stupid to understand. And yet she had had quite a big part to play in bringing about this event. Ah, Anne! she thought, when I was in the Tower you came thither in your cloth of silver and ermine, did you not! Anne the Queen, and Jane the fool whose folly had got her accused of treason. Now, who is the fool, eh, Anne? You, you and your lovers . . . dear sister! Not Jane, for Jane is free, free of you all . . . yes, even free of George, for now she does not cry and fret for him; she can laugh at him and say 'I hate you, George!'

And he will be freed, for what has he done to deserve death! And he was ever a favourite with the King. It is only her lovers who will die the deaths of traitors. . . . But he loved her as well as any.

Her eyes narrowed; her heart began to pound against her side, but her mind was very calm. She could see his face clearer in her mind's eye – calm and cynical, ever courageous. If he could stand before her, his eyes would despise her, would say 'Very well, Jane, do your worst! You were always a vindictive, cruel woman.' Vindictive! He had used that word to describe her. 'I think you are the most vindictive woman in the world!' He had laughed at her fondness for listening at doors.

Her cheeks flamed; she ran down the staircase and out into the warm May sunshine.

People looked at her in a shamefaced way, as they looked at those whose loved ones were in danger. They should know that George Boleyn meant nothing to her; she could almost scream at the thought of him. 'Nothing! Nothing! He means nothing to me, for if I loved him once, he taught me to hate him!' She was a partisan of the true Queen Katharine. Princess Mary was the rightful heir to the throne, not the bastard Elizabeth!

She joined a little group by a fountain.

'Has aught else happened?'

'You have heard about Wyatt. . . .' said one.

'Poor Wyatt!' added another.

'Poor Wyatt!' Jane's eyes flashed in anger. 'He was guilty if ever one was!'

The man who had spoken moved away; he had been a fool to say 'Poor Wyatt!' Such talk was folly.

'Ah! I fear they will all die,' said Jane. 'Oh, do not look to be sorry for me. She was my sister-in-law, but I always knew. My husband is in the Tower, and he will be released 'because ... because ...' And she burst into wild laughter.

'It is the strain,' said one. 'It is because George is in the Tower.'

'It is funny,' said Jane. 'He will be released ... and he ... he is as guilty as any. ...'

They stared at her. She saw a man on the edge of that group, whom she knew to be Thomas Cromwell's spy.

'What mean you?' he asked lightly, as though what she meant were of but little importance to him.

'He was her lover as well as any!' cried Jane. 'He adored her. He could not keep his hands from her ... he would kiss and fondle her ...'

'George. ... ?' said one, looking oddly at her. 'But he is her brother. ...'

Jane's eyes flashed. 'What mattered that ... to such ... monsters! He was her lover. Dost think I, his wife, did not know these things? Dost think I never saw? Dost think I could shut my eyes to such obvious evidence? He was for ever with her, for ever shut away with her. Often I have surprised them ... together. I have seen their lovers' embrace. I have seen ...'

Her voice was shrill as the jealousy of years conjured up pictures for her.

She closed her eyes, and went on shouting. 'They were lovers, I tell you, lovers! I, his wife, meant nothing to him; he loved his sister. They laughed together at the folly of those around them. I tell you I know. I have seen ... I have seen ...'

Someone said in a tone of disgust: 'You had better go to your apartment, Lady Rochford. I fear recent happenings have been too much for you; you are overwrought.'

She was trembling from head to foot. She opened her eyes and saw that Cromwell's spy had left the group.

* * *

The King could not stop thinking of Anne Boleyn. Cromwell had talked to him of her; Cromwell applied enthusiasm to this matter as to all others; he had closed his eyes, pressed his ugly lips together, had begged to be excused from telling the King of all the abominations and unmentionable things that his diligent probing had brought to light. The King dwelt on these matters which Cromwell had laid before him, because they were balm to his conscience. He hated Anne, for she had deceived him; if she had given him the happiest moments of his life, she had given him the most wretched also. He had, before Cromwell had forced the confession from Smeaton, thought of displacing Anne by Jane Seymour; and Jane was with child, so action must take place promptly. He knew what this meant; it could mean but one thing; he was embarking on no more divorces. There were two counts which he could bring forward to make his marriage with Anne null and void; the first was that pre-contract of hers with Northumberland; the second was his own affinity with Anne through his association with her sister Mary. Both of these were very delicate matters, since Northumberland had already sworn before the Archbishop of Canterbury that there had been no pre-contract, and this before he himself had married Anne; moreover he was in full knowledge of the matter. Could he now say that he believed her to have been pre-contracted to Northumberland when he had accepted her freedom and married her? Not very easily. And this affair with Mary; it would mean he must make public his association with Anne's sister; and there was of course the ugly fact that he had chosen to forget about this when he had married Anne. It seemed to him that two opportunities of divorcing Anne were rendered useless by these very awkward circumstances; how could a man, who was setting himself up as a champion of chastity, use either? On the other hand how – unless he could prove his marriage to Anne illegal – could he marry Jane in time to make her issue legitimate?

There was one other way, and that was the way he wanted. He wanted it fiercely. While she lived he would continue to think of her enjoyed by and enjoying others; he could never bear that; she had meant too much to him, and still did. But their marriage had been a mistake; he had been completely happy with her before it, and he had never known a moment's true peace since; and it was all her fault.

She could not get a male child, which meant that heaven disapproved of the marriage. He could see no other way out of this but that that charming head should be cut from those elegant shoulders. His eyes glistened at the thought. Love and hatred, he knew, were closely allied. None other shall have her! was his main thought. She shall enjoy no more lovers; she shall laugh at me no more with her paramours! She shall die ... die ... die, for she is a black-browed witch, born to destroy men; therefore shall she be destroyed. She was guilty of adultery, and, worse still, incest; he must not forget that.

Ah, it grieved him that one he had once loved dearly should be too unworthy to live; but so it was ... so it was. It was his painful duty to see justice done.

He said to Cranmer: 'This is painful to me, Cranmer. I would such work as this had not fallen to my bitter lot!'

Cranmer was grieved too; he was terrified that this might turn back the King towards Rome. And then what of those who had urged the break? Cranmer imagined he could smell the pungent smell of burning faggots and feel the hot flames creeping up his legs.

He said that he was hurt and grieved as was His Majesty, for next to the King's Grace he was most bound unto her of all creatures living. He would ask the King's permission to pray for her; he had loved her for the love he had supposed her to bear to God and the gospel. He hastened to add that all who loved God must now hate her above all others, for there could never have been one who so slandered the gospel.

Poor chicken-hearted Cranmer went in fear and trembling for the next few weeks. He could wish his courage was as strong as his beliefs. What if he who had been helped by the Queen, whose duty really lay towards her now, were clapped into the Tower! Those who were high one day, were brought low the next. He thought of a girl he had loved and married in Nuremberg, whither he had gone to study Lutheran doctrines, and whom he had left in Nuremberg because he had been called home to become Archbishop of Canterbury. It had been heartbreaking to leave her behind;

she was sweet and clinging; but Henry believed in the celibacy of priests, and what would he have said to a priest who had married a wife? He had left her for Henry; had left a bride for an archbishopric, had sacrificed love for a high place at court. What if he should fall from that high place to a dungeon in the Tower! From the Tower to the stake or the block was a short step indeed.

Henry found it comforting to talk with Cranmer; Cranmer was eager as he himself to do what was right.

'If she has done wrong,' said Cranmer, 'then Your Grace will punish her through God.'

'Through God,' said Henry. 'Though I trust she may yet prove her innocence. I would say to you, my lord, that I have no desire in the world to marry again unless constrained to do so by my subjects.'

'Amen!' said Cranmer, and tried not to show by his expression that he must think of Jane Seymour and those reports he had heard that she was already with child.

Henry patted the Archbishop's shoulder, called him his good friend; and Cranmer begged that this sad matter should not cause the King to think less of the gospel.

'I but turn to it more, good Cranmer.'

Cranmer left happier, and the King was relieved by his visit.

He called to his son, the young Duke of Richmond, and would have him stand before him that he might embrace him.

'For I feel tender towards you this night, my son.'

He was thinking of Anne even as he spoke. How often had she discountenanced him! How often had she disturbed him! And she, laughing at him . . . in the arms of his courtiers. . . . Norris . . . Weston. . . . Their faces leaped up in his mind, and were beside Anne's, laughing at him.

Fiercely he embraced his son; tears of self-pity came into his eyes and brimmed over onto the boy's head.

'Your Majesty is deeply disturbed,' said the young Duke.

Henry's voice broke on a sob. He remembered a rumour that when he had thought of going to France and leaving

403

Anne as Regent, she had talked wildly of getting rid of Mary; some had said she meant to poison her.

He held the boy against his chest.

'You and your sister Mary ought to thank God for escaping that cursed and venomous whore who tried to poison you both!' he declared.

* * *

Anne was desolate. The weary days were passing. There were with her two women, day and night, whom she hated and knew to be her enemies. These had been sent as her attendants by command of the King. They were a certain Mrs Cosyns, a spy and a talebearer, and her aunt, Lady Boleyn, who was the wife of her uncle, Sir Edward. This aunt had always been jealous of her niece, right from the time when she was a precocious child considered in the family to be clever. These two, at Cromwell's instigation, wore her down with their questions as they tried to trap her into admissions; they were sly-faced, ugly women, envious, jealous women who enjoyed their position and were made most gleeful by the distress of the Queen. Every chance remark that fell from her lips was repeated with some distortion to make it incriminating. This was just what Cromwell wanted, and he was therefore pleased with these two women. Those ladies whom she would have liked to have beside her, were not allowed to come to her. She longed to talk with Margaret Lee and Mary Wyatt, with her own sister Mary, with Madge; but no, she must be followed, no matter where she went, by these two odious females or by Lady Kingston who was as cold as her husband and had little sympathy, having seen too much suffering in her capacity of wife of the Constable of the Tower to have much to spare for one who, before this evil fate had befallen her, had enjoyed in plenty the good things of life.

But news filtered through to Anne. Her brother had been arrested. On what charge? Incest! Oh, but this was grotesque! How could they say such things! It was a joke; George would laugh; they could not hurt George. What had George done to deserve this? 'For myself,' she cried, 'I have been foolish and careless and over-fond of flattery. I have been vain and stupid. . . . But oh, my sweet brother, what have you ever done but help me! I would die a thousand deaths rather than you should suffer so through me.'

The sly women nodded, carefully going over what she had said. By eliminating a word here, a sentence there, they could give a very good account of themselves to Thomas Cromwell.

'Wyatt here!' she exclaimed. 'Here in the Tower?' And she wept for Wyatt, calling him Dear Thomas, and was over-wrought, recalling the happy days of childhood.

'Norris is here. Norris accused me. . . . Oh, I cannot believe it of Norris. . . . Oh, I cannot! He would never betray me.'

She could not believe that Norris would betray her! Then, argued Cromwell, if she cannot believe he would betray her, is not that an admission that there is something to betray?

When she was tired, they would pretend to soothe her, laying wily traps.

'What of the unhappy gentlemen in the Tower?' she wanted to know. 'Will any make their beds?'

'No, I'll warrant you; they'll have none to make their beds!'

She showed great solicitude for the comfort of her paramours, they reported.

'Ballads will be made about me,' she said, smiling suddenly. 'None can do that better than Wyatt.'

She spoke with great admiration and feeling of Thomas Wyatt, they then told Cromwell.

She wept bitterly for her baby. 'What will become of her? Who will care for her now? I feel death close to me, because I know of her whom the King would set up in my place, but how can he set up a new queen when he has a queen already living? And what of my baby? She is not yet three. It is so very young, is it not? Could I not see her? Oh, plead for me please! Have you never thought how a mother might long for a last glimpse of her daughter! No, no. Bring her not to me. What would she think to see me thus! I should weep over her and frighten her, since the thought of her frightens me, for she is so very young to be left alone in a cruel world. . . . Say not that I wish to see my baby.'

Her eyes were round with fear. They would be so clever at thinking up fresh mental torture for her to bear. Not that though! Not Elizabeth!

'She will be playing in her nursery now. What will become of her? After all, is she not the King's daughter?'

Then she began to laugh shrilly, and her laughter ended in violent weeping. For she thought, They will call her bastard now perhaps . . . and this is a judgment on me for my unkindness to Katharine's daughter Mary. Oh, Katharine, forgive me. I knew not then what it meant to have a daughter. And what if the King . . .

But she could not think; she dared not. Oh, but she knew him, cold and relentless and calculating, and having need to rid himself of her. Already she was accused with five men, and one of them her own, and so innocently loved, brother. What if he said Elizabeth were not his child? What will he care for her, hating her mother? And if he marries Jane Seymour . . . if she is Queen, will she be kind to my baby daughter . . . as I was to Mary? Jesus, forgive me. I was wicked. I was wrong . . . and now this is my punishment. It will happen to me as it happened to Katharine, and there will be none to care for my daughter, as there was none to care for Mary.

Such thoughts must set her weeping; then remembering that when she had become Henry's Queen she had chosen as her device 'Happiest of Women', she laughed bitterly and long.

'How she weeps! How she laughs!' whispered the women. 'How unstable she is . . . hysterical and afraid! Does not her behaviour tend to show her guilt?'

She talked a good deal; she did not sleep; she lay staring into the darkness, thinking back over the past, trying to peer into the future. Despair enveloped her. The King is cruel and cold; he can always find a righteous answer when he wishes to do some particularly cruel deed. I am lost.

There is naught can save me now! Hope came to her. But he loved me once; once there was nothing he would not do for me. Even to the last I could amuse him, and I tried hard enough. . . . I could delight him more than any an I gave myself up to it. He does this but to try me. He will come to me soon; all will be well.

But no! I am here in the Tower and they say evil things of me. My friends are here. George, my darling, my sweet brother, the only one I could truly trust in the whole world. And they know that! That is why they have sent you here, George; that is why they imprison you; so that I shall have none to help me now.

She asked for writing materials. She would write; she would try to forget his cruel eyes; she would try to forget him as he was now and remember him as he used to be when he had said the name of Anne Boleyn was the sweetest music in his ears.

The words flowed impulsively from her pen.

'Your Grace's displeasure and my imprisonment are things so strange unto me, that what to write or what to excuse, I am altogether ignorant. . . .'

She wrote hastily, hope coming back to her as her pen moved swiftly along.

'Never a prince had wife more loyal in all duty, and in all true affection, than you have ever found in Anne Boleyn – with which name and place I could willingly have contented myself if God and your Grace's pleasure had so been pleased. Neither did I at any time so far forget myself in my exaltation, or received queenship, but that I always looked for such alteration as I now found; for the ground of my preferment being on no surer foundation than your Grace's fancy, the least alteration was fit and sufficient (I knew) to draw that fancy to some other subject.'

She paused. Was she over-bold? She felt death close to her and cared not.

'You have chosen me from low estate to be your Queen and companion, far beyond my desert or desire; if then you found

407

me worthy of such honour, good your Grace, let not any light fancy or bad counsel of my enemies, withdraw your princely favour from me, neither let that stain – that unworthy stain – of a disloyal heart towards your good Grace, ever cast so foul a blot on me and on the infant Princess your daughter Elizabeth.

'Try me, good King, but let me have a lawful trial and let not my sworn enemies sit as my accusers and as my judges; yea, let me receive an open trial, for my truth shall fear no open shames; then shall you see either my innocency cleared, your suspicions and conscience satisfied, the ignominy and slander of the world stopped, or my guilt openly declared. So that whatever God and you may determine of, your Grace may be freed from an open censure, and mine offence being so lawfully proved, your Grace may be at liberty, both before God and man, not only to execute worthy punishment on me, as an unfaithful wife, but to follow your affection already settled on that party, for whose sake I am now as I am; whose name I could, some good while since, have pointed unto; your Grace being not ignorant of my suspicion therein.'

Her cheeks burned with anger as her pen flew on.

'But if you have already determined of me, and that not only my death, but an infamous slander, must bring you the joying of your desired happiness, then, I desire of God that he will pardon your great sin herein, and, likewise, my enemies, the instruments thereof, and that He will not call you to a strait account of your unprincely and cruel usage of me, at his general judgment seat, where both you and myself must shortly appear; and in whose just judgment I doubt not (whatsoever the world may think of me) mine innocency shall be openly known, and sufficiently cleared.'

She laid down her pen, a bitter smile about her lips. That would touch him as she knew so well how to touch him, and as she, among all those around him, alone had the courage to touch him. She was reckless of herself, and though she may have been foolish and vain she clung to her magnificent courage. If he ever read those words with their reference to the judgment of God he would tremble in his shoes, and no matter how he might present them to his conscience, they would disturb him to the end of his days. He would think of them when he lay with Jane Seymour; and she exulted in that power over him which she would wield from the grave. She was sure that he intended to murder her; in cold blood he planned this, as any commoner might plan to put away a wife of whom he had tired, by beating her to death or stabbing her with a knife or throwing her body into the dark river. She was terrified, experiencing all the alarm of a woman who knows herself to be followed in the dark by a footpad with murder in his heart. Such women, who were warned of an impending fate, might call for help; but there was none who could come to her aid, for her murderer would be the mightiest man in England whose anger none could curb, for whose crimes the archbishops themselves would find a righteous excuse.

She began to cry in very fear, and her thoughts went from her own troubles to those of the men who would be required to shed their blood with her, and she blamed herself, for was it not her love of flattery that had led them to express their feelings too openly? Was it not her desire to show the King that though he might prefer others, there were always men to prefer her, which had brought about this tragedy?

She took up her pen once more.

'My last and only request shall be, that myself may only bear the burden of your Grace's displeasure, and that it may not touch the innocent souls of those poor gentlemen, who, as I understand, are likewise in strait imprisonment for my sake.

'If ever I have found favour in your sight – if ever the name of Anne Boleyn have been pleasing in your ears – then let me obtain this request; and so I will leave to trouble your Grace any further: with mine earnest prayer to the Trinity to have your Grace in his good keeping, and to direct you in all your actions.

'From my doleful prison in the Tower, the 6th of May.
                                        ANNE BOLEYN.'

She felt better after having written that letter; she would keep the writing materials with her that she might write now and then. She was wretched though, wondering how her letter would reach the King. She pictured its falling into Cromwell's hands, which was likely, for he had his spies all about her, and it could hardly be hoped that the letter would find its way through them to the King. If by good luck it did, he could not be unmoved by her words, she felt sure. He who had once upbraided her for not writing frequently enough, surely would read this last letter.

But she was afraid, sensing her doom, knowing her husband too well, knowing how he was placed, how he must find a way to marry Jane Seymour and appease his conscience; and thinking on these matters, hope, which had come to her through the writing of the letter, was swallowed up once more in deepest despondency.

*　　*　　*

Smeaton lay in his cell. He was no longer a beautiful boy; his dark curls were tangled and matted with blood and sweat; his delicate features were swollen with pain and grief. It seemed to him that there were but two emotions in the world – that of suffering pain and that of having no pain. One was agony; the other bliss.

He had scarcely been aware of the solemn atmosphere of the courtroom of the men who stood on trial with him; he had answered when he had been questioned, answered mechanically as they wanted him to answer, for he knew that not to do so would be to invite pain to come to him once more.

'Guilty!' he cried. 'Guilty! Guilty!' And before his eyes he saw, not the judge and the jurymen, but the dark room with the smell of blood and death about it, mingling with the odour of vinegar; he saw the dim light, heard the sickening creak of rollers, felt again the excruciating pain of bones being torn from their sockets.

He could but walk slowly to the place assigned to him; every movement was agony; he would never stand up straight again; he would never walk with springy step; he would never let his fingers caress a musical instrument and draw magic from it.

A big bearded man came to him as he lay in his cell and

would have speech with him. He held a paper in his hand. He said Mark must sign the paper.

'Dost know the just reward of low born traitors, Mark?' a voice whispered in his ear.

No! He did not know; he could not think; pain had robbed him of his power to use both his limbs and his mind.

Hung by the neck, but not to die. Disembowelled. Did Mark wish him to go on? Had not Mark seen how the monks of the Charterhouse had died? They had died traitors' deaths, and Mark was a traitor even as they had been.

Pain! He screamed at the thought of it; it was as though every nerve in his body cried out in protest. A prolongation of that torture he had suffered in that gloomy dungeon? No, no! Not that!

He was sobbing, and the great Fitzwilliam, leaning over him, whispered: ' 'Tis not necessary, Mark. 'Tis not necessary at all. Just pen your name to this paper, and it shall not happen to you. You shall have naught to fear.'

Paper? 'Where is it?' asked Mark, not What is it? He dared not ask that, though he seemed to see the Queen's beautiful black eyes reproaching him. He was not quite sure whether he was in the cell or in her presence chamber; he was trying to explain to her. Ah, Madam, you know not the pains of the torture chamber; it is more than human flesh can stand.

'Sign here, Mark. Come! Let me guide your hand.'

'What then? What then?' he cried. 'No more . . . no more. . . .'

'No more, Mark. All you need do is sign your name. Subscribe here, Mark, and you shall see what will come of it.'

His hand guided by Fitzwillian, he put his name to the statement prepared for him.

Sir Francis Weston, the beautiful and very rich young man, whose wife and mother offered the King a very large ransom for his freedom, could face death more stoically. So it was with Sir William Brereton. Handsome, debonair, full of the spirit of adventure they had come to court; they had seen others go to the block on the flimsiest of excuses. They lived in an age of terror and had been prepared for the death sentence from the moment they entered the Tower. Guiltless they were, but what of that? Their jury was picked; so were the judges; the result was a foregone conclusion and the trial a farce; and they were knowledgeable enough to know this. They remembered Buckingham who had gone to the block ostensibly on a charge of treason, but actually because of his relationship to the King; now they, in their turn, would go to the block on a charge of treason, when the real reason for their going was the King's desire to rid himself of his present Queen and take another before her child was born. It was brutal, but it was simple. Court law was jungle law, and the king of beasts was a roaring man-eating lion who spared none – man nor woman – from his lustful egoistical demands.

They remembered that they were gentlemen; they prayed that no matter what befell them, they might go on remembering it. Mark Smeaton had perjured his soul and sullied his honour; they trusted that whatever torment they were called upon to face, they would not sink so low. They took their cue from their older companion, Norris, who, grave and stoical, faced his judges.

'Not guilty!' said Norris.

'Not guilty!' echoed Weston and Brereton.

It mattered not; they were found guilty, and sentenced to death, all four of them – the block for three of them and the hangman's noose for Mark on account of his low birth.

The King was angry with these three men. How dared they stand up in the courtroom, looking such haughty heroes, and pronounce in ringing tones that they were not guilty! The people were sentimental, and he thanked God that Anne had ever been disliked and resented by them. They would not have a word to say in favour of her now; they would be glad to see the end of her, the witch, the would-be-poisoner, the black-browed sorceress, the harlot. He thanked God there would be none ready to defend her. Her father? Oh, Thomas, Earl of Wiltshire, was not very much in evidence these days. He was sick and sorry, and ready to obey his King, fearful lest he should be brought in to face trial with his wicked daughter and son. Norfolk?

There was none more pleased than Norfolk to see Anne brought low. They had been quarrelling for years. Suffolk, her old enemy, was rubbing his hands in glee. Northumberland? A pox on Northumberland! Sick and ailing! A fine champion, he! He should be appointed one of her judges and he should see what would happen to him were he to oppose his King. He had been in trouble over Anne Boleyn before; doubtless he would be so again. There was none to fear. My Lord Rochford, that foul, unnatural monster, was safe under lock and key, and what had he with which to defend himself and his sister but a tongue of venom! Anne should see what price she would pay for laughing at the King, first bewitching him and then deceiving him. No one else, girl, he said viciously, shall kiss your pretty lips, unless they like to kiss them cold; nor would they find the head of you so lovely without the body that goes with it!

But a pox on these men, and all would-be-martyrs! There they stood, side by side, on trial for their lives, and though Cromwell could be trusted to find evidence against them, though they were traitors, lechers, all of them, people would murmur: 'So young to die! So handsome! So noble! Could such bravery belong to guilty men? And even if they are guilty, who has not loved recklessly in his life? Why, the King himself . . .'

Enough! He called Cromwell to him.

'Go to Norris!' he commanded. 'I liked that man. Why, he was an intimate friend of mine. Tell him I know the provocation of the Queen. Tell him I know how she could, an she wished it, be wellnigh irresistible. Go to him and tell him I will be merciful. Offer him his life in exchange for a full confession of his guilt.'

Cromwell went, and returned.

'Ah, Your Most Clement Majesty, that there should be such ungrateful subjects in your realm!'

'What said he then?' asked Henry, and he was trembling for the answer. He wanted to show Norris's confession to his court; he would have it read to his people.

'His reply is the same as that he made Your Majesty before. He would rather die a thousand deaths than accuse the Queen who is innocent.'

Henry lost control.

'Hang him up then!' he screamed. 'Hang him up!'

He stamped out of the room and he seemed to see the bodyless head of More and there was a mocking smile about the mouth.

'A thousand curses on all martyrs!' muttered Henry.

* * *

The room in which Anne and her brother would be tried had been hastily erected within the great hall of the Tower. Courageously she entered it, and faced that row of peers who had been selected by the King to try her, and she saw at once that he had succeeded in confronting her with her most bitter enemies. Chief among them was the Duke of Suffolk, his hateful red face aglow with pleasure; there was also the young Duke of Richmond who was firmly against her, because he had had hopes of the throne, illegitimate though he might be; he was influenced by his father the King, and the Duke of Norfolk who had become his father-in-law when he had married the Lady Mary Howard, the Duke's daughter.

Anne had schooled herself for the ordeal; she was determined that she would not break down before her enemies; but she almost lost control to see Percy among those whom the King had named Lord-Triers. He looked at her across the room, and it seemed to them both that the years were swept away and that they were young and in love and from the happiness of a little room in Hampton Court were taking a terrified peep into a grim future. Percy, weak with his physical defects, turned deathly pale at the sight of her; but she lifted her head higher and smiled jauntily, shaming him with her readiness to face whatever life brought her. Percy was not of her calibre. He crumpled and fell to the floor in a faint. How could he condemn her whom he had never been able to forget? And yet, how could he not condemn her, when it was the King's wish that she should be condemned? Percy could not face this, as years before he had not been able to face the wrath of Wolsey, his father and the King. He was genuinely ill at the prospect and had to be carried out of the courtroom.

Thank God, thought Anne, that her father was not among those who were to try her! She had feared he would be, for it would have been characteristic of Henry to have forced him to this and characteristic of her father that he would have obeyed his King and sent his daughter to her death. She had escaped the shame of seeing her father's shame.

She listened to the list of crimes for which she was being tried. She had, they were saying, wronged the King with four persons and also with her brother. She was said to have conspired with them against the King's life. Cromwell's ingenuity had even supplied the dates on which the acts had taken place; she could smile bitterly at these, for the first offence – supposed to have been committed with Norris – was fixed for an occasion when she, having just given birth to Elizabeth, had not left the lying-in chamber.

As she faced her accusers she seemed to see the doubts that beset them. There could not be any of these men who did not know that she was here because the King wished to replace her with Jane Seymour. Oh, justice! she thought. If I could but be sure of justice!

The decision of the peers was not required to be unanimous; a majority was all that was necessary to destroy her. But Suffolk's hot eyes were surveying those about him as though to tell them he watched for any who would disobey the King's desires.

Outside in the streets, where men and women stood about in groups, the atmosphere was stormy. If Anne could have seen these people her spirits would have been lightened. Many eyes wept for her, though once their owners had abused her. At the height of her power they had called her whore; now they could not believe that one who carried herself with such nobility and courage could be anything but innocent. Mothers remembered that she had a child scarcely three years old. A terrible, tragic fate overhung her, and she had the pity of the people as Katharine and Mary had had it before her.

Suffolk knew what people were thinking; he knew what some of the Lord-Triers were thinking. This was a reign of terror. Bluff Hal had removed his mask and shown a monster who thought nothing of murder and of inhuman torture to herald it in. A man would be a fool to run his body into torment for the sake of Anne Boleyn. Suffolk won the day and they pronounced her guilty.

'Condemned to be burnt or beheaded, at the King's pleasure!' said the Duke of Norfolk, savouring each word as though it held a flavour very sweet to his palate.

She did not change colour; she did not flinch. She could look into the cruel eyes of her enemies and she could say, her voice firm, her head high, her eyes imperious: 'God hath taught me how to die, and he will strengthen my faith.'

She smiled haughtily at the group of men. 'I am willing to believe that you have sufficient reasons for what you have done, but then they must be other than those which have been produced in court.'

Even Suffolk must squirm at those words; even Norfolk must turn his head away in shame.

But her voice broke suddenly when she mentioned her brother.

'As for my brother and those others who are unjustly accused, I would willingly suffer many deaths to deliver them.'

The Lord Mayor was very shaken, knowing now for certain what he had before suspected, that they had found nothing against her, only that they had resolved to make an occasion to get rid of her.

* * *

Back in her room, Anne relived it over and over again; she thanked God for the strength which had been hers; she prayed that she might have sustained courage.

Lady Kingston unbent a little now that she had been condemned to die and Mary Wyatt was allowed to come to her.

'You cannot know what comfort it is to me to see you here, Mary,' she said.

416

'You cannot know what comfort it gives me to come,' answered Mary.

'Weep not, Mary. This was inevitable. Do you not see it now? From the first moments in the garden of Hever. . . . But my thoughts run on. You know not of that occasion; nor do I wish to recall it. Ah, Mary, had I been good and sweet and humble as you ever were, this would never have befallen me. I was ambitious, Mary. I wanted a crown upon my head. Yet, looking back, I know not where I could have turned to tread another road. You must not weep, dear Mary, for soon I shall be past all pain. I should not talk of myself. What of George, Mary? Oh, what news of my sweet brother?'

Mary did not answer, but the tears which she could not restrain, were answer enough.

'He defended himself most nobly, that I do not need to be told,' said Anne. Her eyes sparkled suddenly. 'I wonder he did not confound them. Mary, dost remember old days at Blickling and Hever! When he had done aught that merited punishment, could he not always most convincingly defend himself? But this time . . . what had he done? He had loved his sister. May not a brother love his sister, but there must be those to say evil of him? Ah, George, this time when you were truly innocent, you could not save yourself. This was not Blickling, George! This was not Hever! This was the wicked court of Henry, my husband, who now seeks to murder me as he will murder you!'

'Be calm,' said Mary. 'Anne, Anne, you were so brave before those men. You must be brave now.'

'I would rather be the victim of a murderer, Mary, than be a murderer. Tell me of George.'

'He was right noble in his defence. Even Suffolk could scarce accuse him. There was much speculation in court. It was said: "None could name this man guilty!"'

'And what said they of . . . me and George?'

'They said what you would have expected them to say! Jane was there . . . a witness against him.'

'Jane!' Anne threw back her head and laughed. 'I would not be in Jane's shoes for years of life. Liar and perjurer that she is. She . . . out of jealousy, to bear false witness against her husband! But what could she say of him and me? What *could* she say?'

'She said that on one occasion he did come to your chamber while you were abed. He came to make some request and he kissed you. There seemed little else. It was shameful. They had naught against him. They could not call him guilty, but he . . .'

'Tell me all, Mary. Hold nothing back from me. Know you not what this means to me to have you here with me at last, after my dreary captivity with them that hate me? Be frank with me, Mary. Hold nothing back, for frankness is for friends.'

'They handed him a paper, Anne, for on it was a question they dared not ask and he . . .'

'Yes? What did he?'

'He, knowing how it would sorely discountenance them, should he read aloud what was written, read it aloud, in his reckless and impulsive way.'

'Ah! I know him well. For so would I have done in an unguarded moment. He had nothing but contempt for that group of selected peers – selected by the King whose one object is to destroy us – and he showed it by reading aloud that which was meant to be kept secret. It was of the King?'

Mary nodded. 'That the King was not able to have children; that there was no virtue or potency in him. He was asked if he had ever said such things. And he read that aloud. No man could be allowed to live after that. But he meant to show his contempt for them all; he meant to show that he knew he had been condemned to die before the trial began. He asked then to plead Guilty, solely that he might prevent his property passing into the hands of the King. The King could have his life but he should not have his goods.'

'Oh, George!' cried Anne. 'And you to scold me for reckless folly! Mary, I cannot but weep, not for myself but for my brother. I led the way; he followed. I should go to the block for my careless ambition, for my foolish vanity. But that I should take him with me! Oh, Mary, I cannot bear that, so I weep and am most miserable. Oh, Mary, sit by me.

Talk to me of our childhood. Thomas! What of Thomas? I cannot bear to think on those I have loved and brought to disaster.'

'Grieve not for Thomas. He would not have it so. He would not have you shed one tear for him, for well you know he ever loved you dearly. We hope for Thomas. He was not tried with the rest. Perhaps he will just be a prisoner awhile, for it is strange that he should not be tried with the others.'

'Pray for him, Mary. Pray that this awful fate may not befall him. Mayhap they have forgotten Thomas. Oh, pray that they have forgotten Thomas.'

When Mary left her she lay on her bed. She felt happier. Rather my lot, she thought, than the King's. Rather my lot, than Jane Rochford's. I would rather mine were the hapless head that rolled in the straw, than mine the murderous hand that signs the death warrant.

*   *   *

She was preparing herself for a journey. A summons had been brought to her that she was to make ready to go to the Archbishop at Lambeth. She was to go quietly; this was the King's order. He wanted no hysterical crowds on the river's bank to cheer her barge. He himself had received a copy of the summons, but he would not go; he would send his old proctor, Doctor Sampson, to represent him. Come face to face with Anne Boleyn! Never! There were too many memories between them. What if she tried her witcheries on him once more!

He felt shaken and ill at ease. He was sleeping badly; he would wake startled from bad dreams, calling her name and, with the daze of sleep still on him, think she was there beside him. He had despatched Jane Seymour to her father's house, since that was the most seemly place for her to be in. He did not wish to have her with him during the critical days, as he had announced that he was deeply grieved at the falseness of his wife and would not take another unless his people wished it. Jane should therefore not attract much attention. Her condition – early in pregnancy though she was – must be considered. So Henry sat alone, awaiting news from Lambeth; whilst Anne, who would have liked to refuse to answer the summons, left the Tower and went quietly up the river.

She was conducted to the crypt of the Archbishop's residence and awaiting her there were Cranmer, looking troubled but determined to do his duty, Cromwell, looking more sly and ugly than ever, Doctor Sampson, to represent the King, and two doctors Wotton and Barbour, who, most farcically, were supposed to represent her.

She had not been there for more than a few moments when she realized their cunning purpose.

Cranmer's voice was silky. There was no man who could present a case as he could. His voice almost caressed her, expressing sympathy for her most unhappy state.

She was under the sentence of death, he said, by beheading . . . or burning.

Did he mean to stress that last word, or did she imagine this? The way in which he said it made her hot with fear; she felt as though the flames were already scorching her flesh.

The King's conscience, went on Cranmer, troubled him sorely. She had been pre-contracted to Northumberland! That, she would understand, would make her marriage with the King illegal.

She cried: 'Northumberland was brought before you. You yourself accepted . . .'

Cranmer was quiet and calm, so capable of adjusting his opinion, so clever, so intellectual, so impossible to confound.

The King himself had been indiscreet. Yes, His Majesty was ready to admit it. An association with Anne's sister. An affinity created.

Cranmer spread his hands as though to say, Now, you see how it is. You were never really married to the King!

She could hold her head high in the crypt at Lambeth as she had in that other court where they had condemned her. They would need her acknowledgment of this, would they not? Well, they should never get it.

420

Cranmer was pained and sad. He had loved her well, he said.

She thought, How I hate all hypocrites! Fool I may be but I am no hypocrite. How I hate you, Cranmer! I helped you to your present position. You too, Cromwell. But neither of you would think of helping me! But Cranmer I hate more than Cromwell for Cranmer is a hypocrite, and perhaps I hate this in men because I am married to the most shameless one that ever lived.

Cranmer was talking in his deep sonorous voice. He had a gift for making suggestions without expressing actual statements. She was thinking, I have my little daughter to consider. She shall never be called bastard.

Cranmer's voice went droning on. He was hinting at her release. There was a pleasant convent at Antwerp. What of the young men whose fate she deplored and whose innocence she proclaimed? All the country knew how she esteemed her brother, and he her. Was he to go to the block? What of her daughter? The King would be more inclined to favour a child whose mother had impressed him with her good sense.

Anne's mind was working quickly. It was painfully clear. She must make a choice. If her marriage to the King were proved null and void then that was all he need ask of her. He could marry Jane Seymour immediately if his marriage with Anne Boleyn had been no marriage at all. The child Jane carried would be born in wedlock. And for this, Anne was offered a convent in Antwerp, the lives of her brother and those innocent men who were to die with him. And if not ... Once more she was hot with the imaginary fire that licked her limbs. And what would her refusal mean in any case? If the King had decided to disinherit Elizabeth, he would surely do so. He had ever found excuses for what he wished to do.

She had something to gain and nothing to lose, for if she had not been married to the King, how could she have committed adultery? The affairs of Lady Anne Rochford and the Marchioness of Pembroke could not be called treason to the King.

Her hopes were soaring. She thought, Oh, George, my darling, I have saved you! You shall not die. Gladly I will throw away my crown to save you!

Cromwell went back to his master rubbing his ugly hands with pleasure. Once more he had succeeded. The King was free to take a new wife whenever he wished, for he had never been married to Anne Boleyn. She herself had agreed upon it.

* * *

It was over. They had tricked her. At the King's command she had stood and watched them as they passed by her window on their way to Tower Hill. She had sacrificed her own and her daughter's rights in vain. Although she was no queen, these men had died. It was not reasonable; it was not logical; it was simply murder.

She herself had yet another day to live through. Mary Wyatt came to tell her how nobly these men had died, following the example of George, how they had made their speeches, which etiquette demanded, on the scaffold, how they had met their deaths bravely.

'What of Smeaton?' she asked. She thought of him still as a soft-eyed boy, and she could not believe that he would not tell the truth on the scaffold. Mary was silent and Anne cried out: 'Has he not cleared me of the public shame he hath done me!' She surveyed Mary's silent face in horror. 'Alas,' she said at length and in great sorrow, ' I fear his soul will suffer from the false witness he hath borne.'

Her face lightened suddenly.

'Oh, Mary,' she cried, 'it will not be long now. My brother and the rest are now, I doubt not, before the face of the greater King, and I shall follow tomorrow.'

When Mary left her her sadness returned. She wished they had not given her fresh hope in the Lambeth Crypt. She had resigned herself to death, and then they had promised her she should live, and life was so sweet. She was twenty-nine and beautiful; and though she had thought herself weary of living, when they had given her that peep into a possible future, how eagerly she had grasped at it!

She thought of her daughter, and trembled. Three is so very young. She would not understand what had happened to her mother. Oh, let them be kind to Elizabeth.

She asked that Lady Kingston might come to her, and when the woman came she locked the door and with tears running down her cheeks, asked that Lady Kingston would sit in her chair of state.

Lady Kingston herself was moved in face of such distress.

'It is my duty to stand in the presence of the Queen, Madam,' she said.

'That title is gone,' was the answer. 'I am a condemned person, and I have no estate left me in this life, but for the clearing of my conscience, I pray you sit down.'

She began to weep, and her talk was incoherent, and humbly she fell upon her knees and begged that Lady Kingston would go to Mary, the daughter of Katharine, and kneel before her and beg that she would forgive Anne Boleyn for the wrong she had done her.

'For, my Lady Kingston,' she said, 'till this be accomplished, my conscience cannot be quiet.'

After that she was more at peace and did not need to thrust the thought of her daughter from her mind.

The news was brought to her that her death should not take place at the appointed hour; there had been a postponement. She had been almost gay, and to learn that she was to have a few more hours on Earth was a disappointment to her.

'Mr Kingston,' she said, 'I hear I shall not die afore noon, and I am very sorry therefore, for I thought to be dead by this time and past my pain.'

'The pain will be little,' he told her gently, 'it is so subtle.'

She answered: 'I have heard say the executioner is very good, and I have a little neck.'

She embraced it with her hands and laughed; and when her laughter had subsided, a great peace came to her. She had another day to live and she had heard that the King wished the hour of her execution to be kept secret, and that it was not to take place on Tower Hill where any idle spectator might see her die, but on the enclosed green; for the King feared the reactions of the people.

The evening passed; she was gay and melancholy in turns; she joked about her end. 'I shall be easily nick-named – "Queen Anne . . . *sans tête*".'

She occupied herself in writing her own dirge.

> '*Oh death, rock me asleep,*
> *Bring on my quiet rest,*
> *Let pass my very guiltless ghost*
> *Out of my careful breast.*
> *Ring out the doleful knell*
> *Let its sound my death tell;*
> *For I must die,*
> *There is no remedy,*
> *For now I die . . .*'

*   *   *

She dressed herself with such care that it might have been a state banquet to which she was going instead of to the scaffold. Her robe of grey damask was trimmed with fur and low cut; beneath this showed a kirtle of crimson. Her head-dress was trimmed with pearls. She had never looked more beautiful; her cheeks were flushed, her eyes brilliant, and all the misery and fear of the last weeks seemed to have been lifted from her face.

Attended by four ladies, among them her beloved Mary Wyatt, with much dignity and grace she walked to the green before the church of St Peter ad Vincula. Slowly and calmly she ascended the steps to that platform which was strewn with straw; and she could smile because there were so few people to witness her last moments, smile because the hour and place of her execution had had to be kept secret from the people.

Among those who had gathered about the scaffold she saw the Dukes of Suffolk and Richmond, but she could feel no enmity towards these two now. She saw Thomas Cromwell whose eldest son was now married to Jane Seymour's sister. Ah, thought Anne, when my head has rolled into the sawdust, he will feel an impediment lifted and his relationship to the King almost an accomplished fact.

She called to her one whom she knew to be of the King's privy chamber, and said she would send a message by him to the King.

'Commend me to His Majesty,' she said, 'and tell him that he hath ever been constant in his career of advancing me; from a private gentlewoman, he made me a marchioness, from a marchioness a queen, and now he hath left no higher degree of honour, he gives my innocency the crown of martyrdom.'

The messenger trembled for she was a woman about to die, and how could he dare carry such a message to the King!

Then she would, after the etiquette of the scaffold, make her dying speech.

'Good Christian people,' she said, 'I am come hither to die, according to law, for by the law I am judged to die, and therefore I will speak nothing against it . . .'

Her ladies were so overcome with weeping that she, hearing their sobs, was deeply moved.

'I come hither to accuse no man,' she continued, 'nor to speak anything of that whereof I am accused, as I know full well that aught that I say in my defence doth not appertain to you . . .'

When she spoke of the King, her words were choked. Cromwell moved nearer to the scaffold. This was the moment he and the King had most feared. But with death so near she cared nothing for revenge. All the bitterness had gone out of her. Cromwell would arrange the words she spoke, not only as they should best please the King, but also that they should mislead the public into thinking she had died justly. The people must be told that at the end she had only praise for the King, that she spoke of him as a merciful prince and a gentle sovereign lord.

Her voice cleared and she went on: 'If any person will meddle with my cause I require them to judge the best. Thus I take my leave of the world and of you, and I heartily desire you all to pray for me.'

It was time for her now to lay her head upon the block and there was not one of her attendants whose hands were steady enough to remove her headdress; they could only turn from her in blind misery. She smiled and did this herself; then she spoke to each of them gently, bidding them not to grieve and thanking them for their services to her. Mary she took aside and to her gave a little book of devotions as a parting gift and whispered into her ear a message of good cheer that she might give it to her brother in the Tower.

Then she was ready. She laid her head upon the block. Her lips were murmuring her own verses.

> 'Farewell my pleasures past,,
> Welcome my present pain,
> I feel my torments so increase
> That life cannot remain.
> Sound now the passing bell,
> Rung is my doleful knell,
> For its sound my death doth tell.
> Death doth draw nigh,
> Sound the knell dolefully,
> For now I die.'

She was waiting now, waiting for that swift stroke, that quick and subtle pain.

'Oh, Lord God have pity on my soul. Oh, Lord God . . .'

Her lips were still moving as her head lay on the straw.

* * *

The Dowager Duchess of Norfolk was weeping bitterly as she went about the Lambeth House. Catherine Howard flung herself onto her bed and wept. Over the city of London hung silence. The Queen was dead.

At Richmond the King waited for the booming of the gun which would announce the end of Anne Boleyn. He waited in anxiety; he was terrified of what she might say to those watching crowds. He knew that the people who had never accepted her as their Queen, were now ready to make of her a martyr.

His horse was restive, longing to be off; but not more so

than he. Would he never hear the signal! What were they at, those fools? What if some had planned a rescue! He was hot at the thought. There had been men who loved her dearly and none knew better than he did, how easy it was to do that. She had changed his life when she came into it; what would she do when she went out of it?

He pictured her last moments; he knew she would show great courage; he knew she would show dignity; he knew she would be beautiful enough to stir up pity in the hearts of all who beheld her. It was well that but few were sure of hour and place.

Around him were hounds and huntsmen. This night the hunt would end at Wolf Hall whether the stag led them there or not. But the waiting was long, and try as he might he could not forget Anne Boleyn.

He spoke to his conscience, 'Thank God I can now leave Mary without constant fear that she will meet a horrible end. Thank God I discovered the evil ways of this harlot.'

He had done right, he assured himself. Katharine had suffered through her; Mary had suffered. Thank God he had found out in time! Thank God he had turned his affections on a more worthy object!

What would the people say when they heard the gun booming from the Tower? What would they say of a man who went to a new bride before the body of his wife was cold?

Along the river came the dismal booming of the gun. He heard it; his mouth twisted into a line of mingling joy and apprehension.

'The deed is done!' he cried. 'Uncouple the hounds and away!'

So he rode on, on to Wolf Hall, on to marriage with Jane Seymour.

THE DOWAGER DUCHESS of Norfolk was in bed and very sad. A new queen reigned in the place of her granddaughter; a pale-faced creature with scarcely any eyebrows so that she looked for ever surprised, a meek, insipid, vapid woman; and to put her on the throne had the King sent beautiful Anne to the block. The Duchess's dreams were haunted by her granddaughter, and she would awaken out of them sweating and trembling. She had just had such a dream, and thought she had stood among those spectators who had watched Anne submit her lovely head to the Executioner's sword.

She began to weep into her bedclothes, seeing again Anne at court, Anne at Lambeth; she remembered promised favours which would never now be hers. She could rail against the King in the privacy her bedchamber offered her. Fat! Coarse! Adulterer! And forty-five! While Anne at twenty-nine had lost her lovely head that that slut Seymour might sit beside him on the throne!

'Much good will she do him!' murmured the Duchess. 'Give the King a son quickly, Mistress Seymour, or your head will not stay on your shoulders more than a year or two, I warrant you! And I'll be there to see the deed done; I swear it!' She began to chuckle throatily, remembering that she had heard but a week or so after his marriage to Jane had been announced, the King, on meeting two very beautiful young women, had shown himself to be – and even mentioned this fact – sorry that he had not seen them before he married Jane. It had not been so with Anne. She had absorbed his attention, and it was only when she could not produce a son that her enemies had dared to plot against her. 'Bound to Serve and Obey.' That was the device chosen by Jane. 'You'll serve, my dear!' muttered the Duchess. 'But whether you produce a son or not remains to be seen, and if you do not, why then you must very meekly obey, by laying your head on the block. You'll have your enemies just as my sweet Anne did!' The Duchess dried her eyes and set her lips firmly together as she thought of one of the greatest of those enemies, both to Anne and herself, and one with whom she must continually be on her guard – her own stepson and Anne's uncle, the Duke of Norfolk.

Some of the Duchess's ladies came in to help her dress. Stupid girls they were. She scolded them, for she thought their hands over-rough as they forced her bulk into clothes too small for it.

'Katharine Tylney! I declare you scratch me with those nails of yours. I declare you did it apurpose! Take that!'

Katharine Tylney scowled at the blow. The old Duchess's temper had been very bad since the execution of the Queen, and the least thing sent it flaring up. Katharine Tylney shrugged her shoulders at Mistress Wilkes and Mistress Baskerville, the two who were also assisting with the Duchess's toilet. When they were beyond the range of the Duchess's ears they would curse the old woman, laughing at her obscenity and her ill-temper, laughing because she who was so fat and old and ugly was vain as a young girl, and would have just the right amount of embroidered kirtle showing beneath her skirt, and would deck herself in costly jewels even in the morning.

The Duchess wheezed and scolded while her thoughts ran on poor Anne and sly Jane and that absurd fancy of the King's, which had made him change the one for the other; she brooded on the cunning of that low-born brute Cromwell, and the cruelty of Norfolk and Suffolk, until she herself felt as though she were standing almost as near the edge of that active volcano as Anne herself had stood.

She dismissed the women and went slowly into her presence chamber to receive the first of her morning callers. She was fond of ceremony and herself kept an establishment here at Lambeth – as she had at Norfolk – like a queen's. As she entered the chamber, she saw a letter lying on a table, and going to it, read her own name. She frowned at it, picked it up, looked at the writing, did not recognize this, unfolded it and began to read; and as she read a dull anger set her limbs shaking. She re-read it.

'This is not true!' she said aloud, and she spoke to re-assure herself, for had she not for some time suspected the possibility of such a calamity! 'It is not true!' she repeated fiercely. 'I'll have the skin beaten off the writer of this letter. My granddaughter to behave in this way! Like some low creature in a tavern!'

Puffing with that breathlessness which the least exertion aroused in her, she once more read the letter with its sly sug-gestion that she should go quietly and unannounced to the ladies' sleeping apartments and see for herself how Cath-erine Howard and Francis Derham, who called themselves wife and husband, behaved as such.

'Under my roof!' cried the Duchess. 'Under my roof!' She trembled violently, thinking of this most sordid scan-dal's reaching the ears of her stepson.

She paced up and down not knowing what it would be best for her to do. She recalled a certain night when the key of the ladies' apartment had not been in its rightful place, and she had gone up to find the ladies alone, but seeming guilty; she remembered hearing suspicious creaking noises in the gallery. There had been another occasion when going to the maids' room she had found Catherine and Derham romping on the floor.

She sent for Jane Acworth, for Jane had been present and had had her ears boxed in the maids' room for looking on with indifference while Catherine and Derham behaved so improperly.

Jane's eyes glinted with fear when she saw the wrath of the Duchess.

'You know this writing?'

Jane said she did not, and a slap on her cheek told her that she had better think again; but Jane Acworth, seeing Catherine's and Derham's names on that paper, was not go-ing to commit herself. The writing, she said, was doubtless disguised, and she knew it not.

'Get you gone then!' said the Duchess; and left alone once more began her pacing up and down. What would this mean? Her granddaughter, Catherine Howard, had been seduced by a young man, who, though of good family, being a connection of the Howards, was but a member of an obscure branch of theirs. Catherine, for all her illiteracy, for all that she had been allowed to run wild during her childhood, was yet the daughter of Lord Edmund Howard; and she had been so reckless and foolish, that she had doubtless ruined her chances of making a good marriage.

'The little slut!' whispered the Duchess. 'To have that young man in her bed! This will cost him his life! And her ... and her ...' The Duchess's fingers twitched. 'Let her wait till I lay hands on her. I'll make her wish she had never been so free with Mr Derham. I'll make her wish she had never been born. After all my care of her...! I always told myself there was a harlot in Catherine Howard!'

Jane Acworth sought Catherine Howard and found her on the point of going to the orchard to meet Derham.

'A terrible thing has happened,' said Jane. 'I would not care to be in your shoes!'

'What mean you, Jane?'

'Someone has written to Her Grace, telling her what you and Derham are about.'

Catherine turned pale.

'No!'

'Indeed yes! Her Grace is in a fury. She showed me the letter and asked if I knew the handwriting. I swore I did not, nor could I be sure, but to my mind ...'

'Mary Lassells!' whispered Catherine.

'I could not swear, but methought. Let us not waste time. What do you think is going to happen to you and Derham and to us all?'

'I dare not think.'

'We shall all be brought into this. I doubt not but that this is the end of our pleasant days and nights. The Duchess cannot ignore this, much as she may wish to do. I would not be you, Catherine Howard; and most assuredly I would not be Derham.'

'What dost think they will do to him?'

'I could not say. I could only guess. They will say what he

431

has done to you is criminal. Mayhap he will go to the Tower. Oh, no, it will not be the block for him, because then it would be known that he had seduced Catherine Howard. He would be taken to the dungeons and allowed to rot in his chains, or perhaps be tortured to death. The Howards are powerful, and I would not be in the shoes of one who had seduced a member of their house!'

'Please say no more. I must go!'

'Yes. Go and warn Derham. He must not stay here to be arrested and committed to the Tower.'

Fear made Catherine fleet; tears gushed from her eyes and her childish mouth was trembling; she could not shut from her mind terrible pictures of Francis in the Tower, groaning in his chains, dying a lingering death for her sake.

He was waiting in the orchard.

'Catherine!' he cried on seeing her. 'What ails thee, Catherine?'

'You must fly,' she told him incoherently. 'You must wait for nothing. Someone has written to Her Grace, and you will be sent to the Tower.'

He turned pale. 'Catherine! Catherine! Where heard you this?'

'Jane Acworth has seen the letter. Her Grace sent for her that she might tell her who wrote it. It was there . . . all about *us* . . . and my grandmother is furious.'

Bold and reckless, very much in love with Catherine, he wished to thrust such unpleasantness aside. He could not fly, and leave Catherine?'

'Dost think I would ever leave thee?'

'I could not bear that they should take thee to the Tower.'

'Bah!' he said. 'What have we done? Are we not married – husband and wife?'

'They would not allow that to be.'

'And could they help it? We are! That is good enough for me.'

He put his arms about her and kissed her, and Catherine kissed him in such desire that was none the less urgent because danger threatened, but all the more insistent. She took his hand and ran with him into that part of the orchard where the trees grew thickest.

'I would put as far between us and my grandmother as possible,' she told him.

He said: 'Catherine, thou hast let them frighten thee.'

She answered: 'It is not without cause.' She took his face into her hand and kissed his lips. 'I fear I shall not see thee for a long time, Francis.'

'What!' he cried, throwing himself onto the grass and pulling her down beside him. 'Dost think aught could keep me from thee?'

'There is that in me that would send thee from me,' she sighed, 'and that is my love for thee.'

She clung to him, burying her face in his jerkin. She was picturing his young healthy body in chains; he was seeing her taken from him to be given to some nobleman whom they would consider worthy to be her husband. Fear gave a new savour to their passion, and they did not care in those few moments of recklessness whether they were discovered or not. Catherine had ever been the slave of the moment; Derham was single-minded as a drone in his hymeneal flight; death was no deterrent to desire.

The moment passed, and Catherine opened her eyes to stare at the roof of branches, and her hand touched the cold grass which was her bed.

'Francis . . . I am so frightened.'

He stroked her auburn hair that was turning red because the sun was glinting through the leaves of the fruit tree onto it.

'Do not be, Catherine.'

'But they know, Francis. They know!'

Now he seemed to feel cold steel at his throat. What would the Norfolks do to one who had seduced a daughter of their house? Assuredly they would decide he was not worthy to live. One night at dusk, as he came into this very orchard, arms mayhap would seize him. There would be a blow on the head, followed by a second blow to make sure life was extinct, and then the soft sound of displaced water and the ripples would be visible on the surface of the river at the spot where his body had fallen into it. Or would it be a charge of treason? It was simple enough for the Norfolks to find a poor man guilty of treason. The Tower . . . the dreaded Tower! Confinement to one who was ever active! Living a life in one small cell when one's spirit was adventurous; one's limbs which were never happy unless active, in heavy chains.

'You must fly from here,' said Catherine.

'Thou wouldst have me leave thee?'

'I shall die of sorrow, but I would not have them hurt thee. I would not have thee remember this love between us with aught but the utmost delight.'

'I could never think on it but with delight.'

She sat up, listening. 'Methought I heard . . .'

'Catherine! Catherine Howard!' It was the voice of Mistress Baskerville calling her.

'You must go at once!' cried Catherine in panic. 'You must leave Lambeth. You must leave London.'

'And leave you! You know not what you ask!'

'Do I not! An you lose me, do I not lose you? But I would rather not keep you with me if it means that they will take you. Francis, terrible things happen to men in the Tower of London, and I fear for you.'

'Catherine!' called Mistress Baskerville. 'Come here, Catherine!'

Her eyes entreated him to go, but he would not release her.

'I cannot leave you!' he insisted.

'I will come with you.'

'We should then be discovered at once.'

'An you took me,' she said sagely, 'they would indeed find us. They would search for us and bring me back, and oh, Francis, what would they do to you?'

Mistress Baskerville was all but upon them.

'I will go to her,' said Catherine.

'And I will wait here until you come back to me.'

'Nay, nay! Go now, Francis. Do not wait. Something tells me each moment is precious.'

They embraced; they kissed long and broken-heartedly.

'I shall wait here awhile and hope that you will come back to me, Catherine,' he said. 'I cannot go until we are certain this thing has come to pass.'

Catherine left him and ran to Mistress Baskerville.

'What is it?' asked Catherine.

'Her Grace wants you to go to her at once . . . you and Derham. She is wellnigh mad with rage. She has had a whip brought to her. Some of us have been questioned. I heard Jane Acworth crying in her room. I believe she has been whipped . . . and it is all about you and Derham.'

Catherine said: 'What do you think they will do to Derham?'

'I know not. It is a matter of which one can only guess. They are saying he deserves to die.'

Catherine's teeth began to chatter. 'Please help me,' she pleaded. 'Wait here one moment. Will you give me one last moment with him?'

The girl looked over her shoulder. 'What if we are watched?'

'Please!' cried Catherine. 'One moment. . . . Stay here. . . . Call my name. Pretend that you are still looking for me. I swear I will be with you after one short minute.'

She ran through the trees to Derham. 'It is all true!' she cried. 'They will kill thee, Francis. Please go. . . . Go now!'

He was thoroughly alarmed now, knowing that she did not speak idly. He kissed her again, played with the idea of taking her with him, knew the folly of that, guessing what hardships she would have to face. He must leave her; that was common sense; for if he disappeared they might not try very hard to find him, preferring to let the matter drop, since with him gone, it would be easier to hush up the affair. Besides, he might be able to keep in touch with Catherine yet.

'I will go,' said Francis, 'but first promise me this shall not be the end.'

'Dost think I could bear it an it were?' she demanded tearfully.

'I shall write letters, and thou wilt answer them?'

She nodded. She could not wield a pen very happily, but that there would be those to help her in this matter she doubted not.

'Then I leave thee,' he said.

435

'Do not return to the house for aught, Francis. It would not be safe. Where shall you go?'

'That I cannot say. Mayhap I shall go to Ireland and turn pirate and win a fortune so that I may then come back and claim Catherine Howard as my wife. Never forget, Catherine, that thou art that.'

The tears were streaming down Catherine's cheeks. She said with great emotion: 'Thou wilt never live to say to me "Thou hast swerved!"'

One last kiss; one last embrace.

'Not farewell, Catherine. Never that. *Au revoir*, sweet Catherine. Forget not the promise thou hast made to me.'

She watched him disappear through the trees before she ran back to Mistress Baskerville. Fearfully they went into the house and to the Duchess's rooms.

When the old woman saw Catherine, her eyes blazed with rage. She seized her by the hair and flung her against the wall, shouting at her, after first shutting the door: 'You little harlot! At your age to allow such liberties! What dost think you have done! Do not look at me so boldly, wench!'

The whip came down on Catherine's shoulders while she cowered against the wall, covering her face with her hands. Across her back, across her thighs, across her legs, the whip descended. There was not much strength behind the Duchess's blows, but the whip cut into Catherine's flesh, and she was crying, not from the infliction of those strokes, but for Derham, since she could know no pain that would equal the loss of him.

The Duchess flung away the whip and pushed Catherine onto a couch. She jerked the girl's head up, and looked into her grief-swollen face.

'It was true then!' cried the Duchess in a fury. 'Every word of it was true! He was in your bed most nights! And when you were disturbed he hid in the gallery!' She slapped Catherine's face, first one side, then the other. 'What sort of marriage do you expect after this? Tell me that! Who will want Catherine Howard who is known for a slut and a harlot!' She slapped Catherine's face. 'We shall marry you to a potman or a pantler!'

436

Catherine was hysterical with the pain of the blows and the mental anxiety she suffered concerning Derham's fate.

'You would not care!' stormed the Duchess. 'One man as good as another to you, eh? You low creature!'

The slapping began again. Catherine had wept so much that she had no more tears.

'And what do you think we shall do with your fine lover, eh? We will teach him to philander. We shall show him what happens to those who creep stealthily into the beds of their betters ... or those who should be their betters....'

Down came the heavy ringed hands again. Catherine's bodice was in tatters, her flesh red and bruised; and the whip had drawn blood from her shoulders.

The Duchess began to whisper of the terrible things that would be done to Francis Derham, were he caught. Did she think she had been severely punished? Well, that would be naught compared with what would be done to Francis Derham. When they had done with him, he would find himself unable to creep into young ladies' beds of night, for lascivious wenches like Catherine Howard would find little use for him, when they had done with him ... when they had done with him...!

Saliva dripped from Her Grace's lips; her venom eased her fear. What if the Duke heard of this? Oh, yes, his own morals did not bear too close scrutiny and there were scandals enough in the Norfolk family and to spare. What of the washerwoman Bess Holland who was making a Duchess of Norfolk most peevish and very jealous! And the late Queen herself had had Howard blood in her veins and stood accused of incest. But oddly enough it was those who had little cause to judge others who most frequently and most loudly did. The King himself who was over-fond of wine and women was the first to condemn such excesses in others; and did not courtiers ever take their cue from a king! If the Duke heard of this he would laugh his sardonic laugh and doubtless say evil things of his old enemy his step-mother. She was afraid, for this would be traced to her neglect. The girl had been in her charge and she had allowed irreparable harm to be done. What of Catherine's sisters? Such a scandal would impair their chances in the matrimonial field. Then, there must be no scandal, not only for Catherine's sake, but for that of her sisters – and also for the sake of the Dowager Duchess of Norfolk. She quietened her voice and her blows slackened.

'Why,' she said slyly, 'there are those who might think this thing had gone farther than it has. Why, there are those who will be ready to say there was complete intimacy between you and Francis Derham.' She looked earnestly into Catherine's face, but Catherine scarcely heard what she said; much less did she gather the import of her words. 'Derham shall suffer nevertheless!' went on the Duchess fiercely; and she went to the door and called to her Mary Lassells and Katharine Tylney. 'Take my granddaughter to the apartment,' she told them, 'and put her to bed. She will need to rest awhile.'

They took Catherine away. She winced as they removed her clothes. Katharine Tylney brought water to bathe her skin where the Duchess's ring had broken it.

While Catherine cried softly, Mary Lassells surveyed with satisfaction the plump little body which had been so severely beaten. Her just deserts! thought Mary Lassells. It was a right and proper thing to have done, to have written to the Duchess. Now this immorality would be stopped. No more petting and stroking of those soft white limbs. Mary Lassells did not know how she had so long borne to contemplate such wickedness.

In her room the Duchess was still shaking with agitation. She must have advice, she decided, and she asked her son, Lord William Howard, to come to see her. When he arrived she showed him the letter and told him the story. He grumbled about mad wenches who could not be merry among themselves without falling out.

'Derham,' said Her Grace, 'has disappeared.'

Lord William shrugged. Did his mother not attach too much importance to a trifling occurrence, he would know. Young men and women were lusty creatures and they would always frolic. It need not necessarily mean that although

438

Derham had visited the girl's sleeping apartment, there was anything to worry about.

'Forget it! Forget it!' said Lord William. 'Give the girl a beating and a talking to. As for Derham, let him go. And pray keep all this from my lord Duke.'

It was sound advice. There was no harm done, said the Duchess to herself, and dozed almost serenely in her chair. But out of her dozes she would awake startled, worried by dreams of her two most attractive granddaughters, one dead, and the other so vitally alive.

Then the Duchess made a resolution, and this she determined to keep, for she felt that it did not only involve the future of Catherine Howard, but that of her own. Catherine should be kept under surveillance; she should be coached in deportment so that she should cease to be a wild young hoyden and become a lady. And some of those women, whose sly ways the Duchess did not like over-much, should go.

On this occasion the Duchess carried out her resolutions. Most of the young ladies who had shared the main sleeping apartment with Catherine were sent to their homes. Jane Acworth was among those who remained, for a marriage was being arranged for her with a Mr Bulmer of York, and, thought the Duchess, she will soon be going in any case.

The Duchess decided to see more of Catherine, to school her herself, although, she admitted ruefully, it was hardly likely that Jane Seymour would find a place at court for Anne's cousin. Never mind! The main thing was that Catherine's unfortunate past must be speedily forgotten, and Catherine prepared to make the right sort of marriage.

* * *

It seemed to the Princess Mary that the happiest event that had taken place since the King had cast off her mother, was the death of Anne Boleyn. Mary was twenty years old, a very serious girl, with bitterness already in her face, and fanaticism peering out through her eyes. She was disappointed and frustrated, perpetually on the defensive and whole-heartedly devoted to Roman Catholicism. She was

439

proud and the branding of illegitimacy did not make her less so. She had friends and supporters, but whereas, while Anne Boleyn lived, these did not wish to have their friendship known, they now were less secretive. The King had put it on record that not in any carnal concupiscence had he taken a wife, but only at the entreaty of his nobility, and he had chosen one whose age and form was deemed to be meet and apt for the procreation of children. His choice had been supported by the imperialists, for he had chosen Jane Seymour who was one who still clung to the old catholicism; moreover Jane was known to be kindly disposed towards Mary.

It was, as ever, necessary to tread very cautiously, for the King had changed since the death of Anne; he was less jovial; he had aged considerably and looked more than his forty-five years; he did not laugh so frequently, and there was a glitter in his eyes, which could send cold shivers down the spine of a man though he might have no knowledge of having displeased the King. His matrimonial adventures had been conspicuously unsuccessful, and though Jane had been reported to be pregnant before the death of Anne – well, Katharine of Aragon had been pregnant a good many times without much result; and Anne had had no success either. Young Richmond, on whom the King doted, as his only son, had ever since the death of Anne been spitting blood. 'She has cast a spell on him,' said Mary. 'She would murder him as she tried to murder me, for Richmond has death in his face if ever one had.' And what if Richmond died and Jane Seymour was without issue! Elizabeth was a bastard now, no less then Mary.

'It is time,' said her friends to Mary, 'that you began to woo the King.'

'And defame my mother!' cried Mary.

'She who was responsible for your mother's position is now herself cast off and done with. You should try to gain His Majesty's friendship.'

'I do not believe he will listen to me.'

'There is a way of approaching him.'

'Which way is that?'

'Through Cromwell. It is not only the best, but the only possible way for you.'

The result was that Cromwell came to visit Mary at Hunsdon whither she had been banished. Cromwell came eagerly enough, seeing good reasons for having Mary taken back into favour. He knew that the King would never receive his daughter unless she agreed that her mother's marriage had been unlawful and incestuous; and if Mary could be brought to such admission, she would cease to have the sympathy of the people. There were many nobles in the land who deplored the break with Rome; who were silently awaiting an opportunity to repair the link. If they were ever able to do this, what would happen to those who had worked for the break! And was not the greatest of them Thomas Cromwell! Cromwell could therefore see much good in the King's reconciliation with his daughter.

Henry's eyes were speculative regarding the prospect laid out before him by Cromwell. How he loathed that man! But what good work he was doing with the smaller abbeys, and what better work he would do with the larger ones! If there was to be a reconciliation with Mary, Cromwell was right in thinking this was the time to make it. Many people considered Mary had been badly treated; the common people were particularly ready to be incensed on her behalf. He had separated her from her mother, had not allowed her to see Katharine on her death-bed. He could not help feeling a stirring of his conscience over Mary. But if he effected a reconciliation at this moment, he himself would emerge from the dangerous matter, not as a monster but as a misguided man who had been under the influence of a witch and a sorceress. Anne, the harlot and would-be-poisoner, could be shown to have been entirely responsible for the King's treatment of his daughter. 'Why,' people would say, 'as soon as the whore was sent to her well-deserved death, the King becomes reconciled to his daughter!' A well-deserved death! Henry liked that phrase. He had suffered many disturbed nights of late; he would awaken and think she lay beside him; he would find sleep impossible for hours at a time; and once he dreamed of her looking into a pool at Hever: and when he looked too, he saw her head with its black hair, and blood was streaming from it. A well-deserved death! thought Henry complacently, and he sent Norfolk to see his daughter at Hunsdon.

'Tell the girl,' he said, 'that she is wilful and disobedient, but that we are ever ready to take pity on those who repent.'

Mary saw that she was expected to deny all that she had previously upheld, and was frightened by the storm that she had aroused.

'My mother was the King's true wife,' she insisted. 'I can say naught but that!'

She was reminded ominously that many had lost their heads for saying what she had said. She was not easily frightened and she tried to assure herself that she would go to the block as readily as More and Fisher had done.

Mary could see now that she had been wrong in blaming Anne for her treatment. Norfolk was brusque with her, insulting even; she had never been so humiliated when Anne was living. It was Anne who had begged that they might bury their quarrel, that Mary should come to court, and had told her that she should walk beside her and need not carry her train. Lady Kingston had come to her with an account of Anne's plea for forgiveness and Mary had shrugged her shoulders at that. Forgiveness! What good would that do Anne Boleyn! When Mary died she would look down on Anne, burning in hell, for burn in hell she assuredly would. She had carried out the old religious rites until her death, but she had listened to and even applauded the lies of Martin Luther and so earned eternal damnation. Mary was not cruel at heart; she knew only two ways, the right and the wrong, and the right way was through the Roman Catholic Church. No true Catholic burned in hell; but this was a fate which those who were not true Catholics could not possibly escape. But she saw that though Anne would assuredly burn in hell for her responsibility in the severance of England from Rome, she could not in all truth be entirely blamed for the King's treatment of his elder daughter. Mary decided that although she could not forgive Anne, she would at least be as kind as she could to Anne's daughter.

Henry was furious at the reports brought back to him. He swore that he could not trust Mary. He was an angry man. It was but a matter of days since he had married Jane Seymour and yet he was not happy. He could not forget Anne Boleyn; he was dissatisfied with Jane; and he was enraged against Mary. A man's daughter to work against him! He would not have it! He called the council together. A man cannot trust those nearest to him! was his cry. There should be an inquiry. If he found his daughter guilty of conspiracy she should suffer the penalty of traitors.

'I'll have no more disobedience!' foamed Henry. 'There is one road traitors should tread, and by God, I'll see that they tread it!'

There was tension in court circles. It was well known that, while Anne lived, Mary and her mother had had secret communications from Chapuys; and that the ambassador had had plans for – with the Emperor's aid – setting Katharine or Mary on the throne.

The King, as was his custom, chose Cromwell to do the unpleasant work; he was to go secretly into the houses of suspected persons and search for evidence against the Princess.

The Queen came to the King.

'What ails thee?' growled the newly married husband. 'Dost not see I am occupied with matters of state!'

'Most gracious lord,' said Jane, not realizing his dangerous mood, 'I would have speech with you. The Princess Mary has ever been in my thoughts, and now that I know she repents and longs to be restored in your affections . . .'

Jane got no further.

'Be off!' roared the King. 'And meddle not in my affairs!'

Jane wept, but Henry strode angrily from her, and in his mind's eye, he seemed to see a pair of black eyes laughing at him, and although he was furious he was also wistful. He growled: 'There is none I can trust. My nearest and those who should be my dearest are ready to betray me!'

Mary's life was in danger. Chapuys wrote to her advising her to submit to the King's demands, since it was unsafe for her not to do so. She must acknowledge her father Supreme

Head of the Church; she must agree that her mother had never been truly married to the King. It was useless to think that as his daughter she was safe, since there was no safety for those who opposed Henry. Let her think, Chapuys advised her, of the King's last concubine to whom he had been exclusively devoted over several years; he had not hesitated to send her to the block; nor would he hesitate in his present mood to send his own daughter.

But the shrewd man Henry had become knew that the unpopularity he had incurred, first by his marriage with Anne and then by his murder of her, would be further increased if he shed the blood of his daughter. The enmity of the people, ever a dark bogey in his life since he felt his dynasty to be unsafe, seemed as close as it had when he broke from the Church of Rome. He told Cromwell to write to her telling her that if she did not leave all her sinister councils she would lose her chance of gaining the King's favour.

Mary was defeated, since even Chapuys was against her holding out; she gave in, acknowledged the King Supreme Head of the Church, admitted the Pope to be a pretender, and agreed that her mother's marriage was incestuous and unlawful. She signed the papers she was required to sign and she retired to the privacy of her rooms where she wept bitterly, calling on her saintly mother to forgive her for what she had done. She thought of More and Fisher. 'Ah! That I had been brave as they!' she sobbed.

Henry was well pleased; instead of a recalcitrant daughter, he had a dutiful one. Uneasy about the death of Anne, he wished to assure himself and the world that he had done right to rid himself of her. He was a family man; he loved his children. Anne had threatened to poison his daughter, his beloved Mary. Did his people not now see that Anne had met a just fate? Was not Mary once more his beloved daughter? It mattered not that she had been born out of wedlock. She was his daughter and she should come to court. With the death of the harlot who had tried to poison his daughter, everything was well between her and her father.

Jane was jubilant.

'You are the most gracious and clement of fathers,' she told Henry.

'You speak truth, sweetheart!' he said and warmed to Jane, liking afresh her white skin and pale eyelashes. He loved her truly, and if she gave him sons, he would love her all the more. He was a happy family man.

Mary sat at the royal table, next in importance to her step-mother, and she and Jane were the best of friends. Henry smiled at them benignly. There was peace in his home, for his obstinate daughter was obstinate no longer. He tried to look at her with love, but though he had an affection for her, it was scarcely strong enough to be called love.

When Jane asked that Elizabeth should also come to court, he said he thought this thing might be.

'An you wish it, sweetheart,' he said, making it a favour to Jane. But he liked to see the child. She was attractive and spirited, and there was already a touch of her mother in her.

'The King is very affectionate towards the young Elizabeth,' it was said.

*　　*　　*

When his son the Duke of Richmond died, Henry was filled with sorrow. Anne, he declared, had set a spell upon him, for it was but two months since Anne had gone to the block, and from the day she died, Richmond had begun to spit blood.

Such an event must set the King brooding once more on the succession. He was disturbed because young Thomas Howard, half brother to the Duke of Norfolk had dared to betroth himself, without Henry's permission, to Lady Margaret Douglas, daughter of Henry's sister Margaret of Scotland. This was a black crime indeed. Henry knew the Howards – ambitious to a man. He was sure that Thomas Howard aspired to the throne through this proposed marriage with Henry's niece and he was reminded afresh of what a slight hold the Tudors had upon the throne.

'Fling young Howard into the Tower!' cried Henry, and this was done.

He was displeased with the Duke also, and Norfolk was

terrified, expecting that at any moment he might join his half brother.

If the Howards were disturbed so was Henry; he hated trouble at home more than trouble abroad. The Henry of this period was a different person from that younger man whose thoughts had been mainly occupied in games and the hunting of women and forest creatures. He had come into the world endowed with a magnificent physique and a shrewd brain; but as the former was magnificent and the latter merely shrewd, he had developed the one at the expense of the other. Excelling as he did in sport, he had passed over intellectual matters; loving his great body, he had decked it in dazzling jewels and fine velvets and cloth of gold; for the glory of his body he had subdued his mind. But at forty-five he was well past his active youth; the ulcer in his leg was bad enough to make him roar with pain at times; he was inclined to breathlessness being a heavy man who had indulged too freely in all fleshly lusts. His body being not now the dominating feature in his life, he began to exercise his mind. He was chiefly concerned in the preservation and the glorification of himself, and as this must necessarily mean the preservation and the glorification of England, matters of state were of the utmost interest to him. Under him, the Navy had grown to a formidable size; certain monies were set aside each year for the building of new ships and that those already built might be kept in good fighting order; he wished to shut England off from the Continent, making her secure; while he did not wish England to become involved in war, he wished to inflame Charles and Francis to make war on one another, for he feared these two men; but he feared them less when they warred together than when they were at peace. His main idea was to have all potential enemies fighting while England grew out of adolescence into that mighty Power which it was his great hope she would one day be. If this was to happen, he must first of all have peace at home, for he knew well that there was nothing to weaken a growing country like civil war. In severing the Church of England from that of Rome, he had done a bold thing, and England was still shaking

446

from the shock. There were many of his people who deplored the break, who would ask nothing better than to be reunited with Rome. Cleverly and shrewdly, Henry had planned a new religious programme. Not for one moment did he wish to deprive his people of those rites and ceremonies which were as much a part of their lives as they were of the Roman Catholic faith. But their acceptance of the King as Supreme Head of the Church must be a matter of life and death.

Peace at home and peace abroad therefore, was all he asked, so that England might grow in the best possible conditions to maturity. Wolsey had moulded him into a political shape very like his own. Wolsey had believed that it was England's task to keep the balance of power in Europe, but Wolsey had been less qualified to pursue this than was Henry. Wolsey had been guilty of accepting bribes; he could never resist adding to his treasures; Henry was not so shortsighted as to jeopardize England's position for a gift or two from foreign Powers. He was every bit as acquisitive as Wolsey, but the preservation of himself through England was his greatest need. He had England's treasures at his disposal, and at this moment he was finding the dissolution of the abbeys most fruitful. Wolsey never forgot his allegiance to Rome; Henry knew no such loyalty. With Wolsey it was Wolsey first, England second; with Henry, England and Henry meant the same thing. Cromwell believed that England should ally herself with Charles because Charles represented the strongest Power in Europe, but Henry would associate himself with neither Charles nor Francis, clinging to his policy of preserving the balance of power. Neither Wolsey nor Cromwell could be as strong as Henry, for there was ever present with these two the one great fear which must be their first consideration, and this was fear of Henry. Henry therefore was freer to act; he could take advantage of sudden action; he could do what he would, without having to think what excuse he should make if his action failed. It was a great advantage in the subtle game he played.

Looking back, Henry could see whither his laziness had

led him. He had made wars which had given nothing to England, and he had drained her of her strength and riches, so that the wealth so cautiously and cleverly amassed by his thrifty father, had slowly dwindled away. There was the example of the Field of the Cloth of Gold, on which he could now look back through the eyes of a wiser and far more experienced man, and be shocked by his lack of statecraft at that time. Kings who squandered the treasure and the blood of their subjects also squandered their affections. He could see now that it was due to his father's wealth that England had become a Power in Europe, and that with the disappearance of that wealth went England's power. By the middle of the twenties England was of scarcely any importance in Europe, and at home Ireland was being troublesome. When Henry had talked of divorcing his Queen, and was living openly with Anne Boleyn, his subjects had murmured against him, and that most feared of all calamities to a wise king – civil war – had threatened. At that time he had scarcely been a king at all, but when he had broken from Rome he had felt his strength, and that was the beginning of Henry VIII as a real ruler.

He would now continue to rule, and brute strength would be his method; never again should any other person than the King govern the country. He was watchful; men were watchful of him. They dreaded his anger, but Henry was wise enough to realize the wisdom of that remark of his Spanish ambassador's: 'Whom many fear, must fear many.' And Henry feared many, even if many feared him.

His great weakness had its roots in his conscience. He was what men called a religious man, which in his case meant he was a superstitious man. There was never a man less Christian; there was never one who made a greater show of piety. He was cruel; he was brutal; he was pitiless. This was his creed. He was an egoist, a megalomaniac; he saw himself not only as the centre of England but of the world. In his own opinion, everything he did was right; he only needed time to see it in its right perspective, and he would prove it to be right. He took his strength from this belief in himself; and as his belief was strong, so was Henry.

One of the greatest weaknesses of his life was his feeling for Anne Boleyn. Even now, after she had died at his command, when his hands were stained with her innocent blood, when he had gloated over his thoughts of her once loved, now mutilated body, when he knew that could he have her back he would do the same again, he could not forget her. He had hated her so violently, only because he had loved her; he had killed her out of passionate jealousy, and she haunted him. Sometimes he knew that he could never hope to forget her. All his life he would seek a way of forgetting. He was now trying the obvious way, through women.

Jane! He was fond enough of Jane. What egoist is not fond of those who continually show him he is all that he would have people believe he is! Yes, he liked Jane well enough, but she maddened him; she irritated him because he always knew exactly what she would say; she submitted to his embraces mildly, and he felt that she did so because she considered it her duty; she annoyed him because she offered him that domestic peace which had ever been his goal, and now having reached it, he found it damnably insipid; she angered him because she was not Anne.

Moreover, now she had disappointed him. She had had her first miscarriage, and that very reason why he had been forced to get rid of Anne so speedily, to resort to all kinds of subterfuge to pacify his subjects, and to tell his people that it was his nobles who had begged him to marry Jane before Anne's mutilated body was cold, had proved to be no worthwhile reason at all. He could have waited a few months; he could have allowed Cromwell and Norfolk to have persuaded him; he could have been led self-sacrificingly into marriage with Jane instead of scuffling into it in the undignified way he had done. It was irritating.

It was also uncanny. Why did all his wives miscarry? He thought of the old Duke of Norfolk's brood, first with one wife, then with another. Why should the King be so cursed? First with Katharine, then with Anne. Katharine he had discarded; Anne he had beheaded; still, he was truly married to Jane, for neither of these two had been living when he married Jane; therefore he could have done no wrong. If he had displeased God in marrying Anne while Katharine was alive, he could understand that; but he had been a true widower when he had married Jane. No, he was worrying unduly; he would have children yet by Jane, for if he did not ... why, why had he got rid of Anne?

In his chamber at Windsor, he was brooding on these matters when he was aware of a disturbance in the courtyard below his window; even as he looked out a messenger was at his door with the news that certain men had ridden with all speed to the King as they had alarming news for him.

When they were brought in they fell on their knees before him.

'Sir, we tremble to bring such news to Your Majesty. We come hot speed to tell you that trouble has started, so we hear, in Lincoln.'

'Trouble!' cried Henry. 'What mean you by trouble?'

'My Lord, it was when the men went into Lincoln to deal with the abbeys there. There was a rising, and two were killed. Beaten and roughly handled, please Your Majesty, unto death.'

Henry's face was purple; his eyes blazed.

'What means this! Rebellion! Who dares rebel against the King!'

Henry was astounded. Had he steered the country away from civil war, only to find it breaking out at last when he had been congratulating himself on his strength. The people, particularly those in the north, had been bewildered by the break with Rome; but by the pillaging of the abbeys, they had been roused to action. Already bands of beggars were springing up all over the country; they who had been sure of food and shelter from the monks were now desolate, and there was but one sure way for a destitute man to keep himself fed in Tudor England, and that was to rob his fellow men. Over the countryside there roamed hordes of desperate starving men, and to their numbers were added the displaced monks and nuns. There was more boldness in the north than in the south because those far removed from his presence could fear Henry less. So they, smarting from the break with Rome, sympathizing with the monks, resenting the loss of the monasteries, decided that something should be done. They were joined by peasants who, owing to the enclosure acts, and the prevailing policy of turning arable into pasture land, had been rendered homeless. Lords Darcy and Hussey, two of the most powerful noblemen of the north, had always supported the old Catholic faith; the rebels therefore could feel they had these men behind them.

Henry was enraged and apprehensive. He felt this to be a major test. Should he emerge from it triumphant, he would have achieved a great victory; he would prove himself a great King. Two ways lay before him. He could return to Rome and assure peace in his realm; he could fight the rebels and remain not only head of the Church but truly head of the English people. He chose the second course. He would risk his crown to put down the rebels.

It meant reconciliation with Norfolk, for whenever there was a war to be fought, Norfolk must be treated with respect. He would send Suffolk to Lincoln. He stormed against those of his counsellors who advised him against opposing the rebels. Fiercely he reminded them that they were bound to serve him with their lives, lands and goods.

Jane was afraid. She was very superstitious and it seemed to her that this rising was a direct reproach from heaven because of Cromwell's sacrilegious pillaging of the monasteries.

She came to the King and knelt before him, and had her head not been bent she would have seen her danger from his blazing eyes.

'My lord husband,' she said, 'I have heard the most disquieting news. I fear it may be a judgment on us for ridding ourselves of the abbeys. Could not Your Most Gracious Majesty consider the restoring of them?'

For a few seconds he was speechless with rage; he saw Jane through the red haze in his eyes, and when he spoke his voice was a rumble of thunder.

'Get up!'

She lifted terrified eyes to his face and stood. He came

closer to her, breathing heavily, his jowls quivering, his lower lip stuck out menacingly.

'Have I not told you never to meddle in my affairs!' he said very slowly and deliberately.

Tears came into Jane's eyes; she was thinking of all those people who were wandering homeless about the country; she thought of little babies crying for milk. She had pictured herself saving the people from a terrible calamity; moreover, her friends who longed for the return of the old ways, would rejoice in the restoration of the monasteries, and would be very pleased with Queen Jane. Therefore she felt it to be her duty to turn the King back to Rome, or at least away from that wickedness which had sprung up in the world since Martin Luther had made himself heard.

The King gripped her shoulder, and put his face to hers.

'Dost remember what happened to your predecessor?' he asked meaningly.

She stared at him in horror. Anne had gone to the block because she was guilty of high treason. What could he mean?

His eyes were hot and cruel.

'Forget it not!' he said, and threw her from him.

* * *

The men of the north had followed the example of the men from Lincolnshire. This was no mob rising; into the ranks of the Pilgrimage of Grace went sober men of the provinces. The most inspiring of its leaders was a certain Robert Aske, and this man, whose integrity and honesty of purpose were well known, had a talent for organization; he was a born commander, and under him, the northern rebels were made into a formidable force.

Henry realized too well how very formidable. The winter was beginning; he had no standing army. He acted with foresight and cunning. He invited Aske to discuss the trouble with him.

It did not occur to Aske that one as genial as Henry appeared to him could possibly not be as honest as Aske himself. On the leader, Henry unloosed all his bluffness, all his honest down-to-earth friendliness. Did Aske wish to spread bloodshed over England? Aske certainly did not. He wanted only hardship removed from the suffering people. Henry patted the man affectionately. Why then, Aske and the King had the same interests at heart. Should they quarrel! Never! All they must do was to find a way agreeable to them both of doing what was right for England.

Aske went back to Yorkshire to tell of the King's oral promises, and the insurgents were disbanded; there was a truce between the north and the King.

There were in the movement less level-headed men than such leaders as Aske and Constable, and in spite of Aske's belief in the King's promises he could not prevent a second rising. This gave Henry an excuse for what followed. He had decided on his action before he had seen Aske; his promises to the leader had meant that he wished to gain time, to gather his strengh about him, to wait until the end of winter. He had never swerved from the policy he intended to adopt and which he would continue to follow to the end of his reign. It was brute strength and his own absolute and un-questioned rule.

He decided to make a bloody example and show his people what happened to those who opposed the King. Up to the north went Norfolk and the blood-letting began. Darcy was beheaded; Sir Thomas Percy was brought to Tyburn and hanged; honest men who had looked upon the Pilgrimage of Grace as a sacred movement were hanged, cut down alive, disembowelled, and their entrails burned while they still lived; then they were beheaded. Aske learned too late that he had accepted the promises of one to whom a promise was naught but a tool to be picked up and used for a moment when it might be useful and then to be laid aside and forgotten. In spite of his pardon, he was executed and hanged in chains on one of the towers of York that all might see what befell traitors. Constable was taken to Hull and hanged from the highest gate in the town, a grim warn-ing to all who beheld him.

The King licked his lips over the accounts of cruelties done in his name. 'Thus shall all traitors die!' he growled, and warned Cromwell against leniency, knowing well that he could leave bloody work in those ugly hands.

The Continent, hearing of his internal troubles, was on tiptoe waiting and watching. Henry's open enemy Pope Paul could state publicly his satisfaction; Henry's secret enemies, Charles and Francis, though discreetly silent, were none the less delighted.

The Pope, deeply resenting this King who had dared set an example which he feared others might follow, began to plan. What if the revolt against Henry were nourished outside England? Reginald Pole was on the Continent; he had left England for two reasons; he did not approve of the divorce and break with Rome; and he being the grandson of that Duke of Clarence who was brother to Edward IV, was too near the throne to make residence in England safe for him. He had written a book against Henry, and Henry feigning interest suggested Pole return to England that they might discuss their differences of opinion. Pole was no careless fly to walk into the spider's web. He declined his sovereign's offer and went to Rome instead where the Pope made him a Cardinal and discussed with him a plan for fanning the flames which were at this time bursting out in the North of England. If Pole succeeded in displacing Henry, why should he not marry the Princess Mary, restore England to the papacy and rule as her king?

Henry acted with cunning and boldness. He demanded from Francis, Pole's extradition, that he might be sent to England and stand his trial as a traitor. Francis, who did not wish to defy the Pope not to annoy Henry, ordered Pole to leave his domains. Pole went to Flanders, but Charles was as reluctant as Francis to displease the King of England. Pole had to disguise himself.

The attitude of the two great monarchs showed clearly that they were very respectful towards the island lying off the coast of Europe, for never had a papal legate been so humiliated before.

Henry could purr with pleasure. He was treated with respect abroad and he had crushed a revolt which threatened his throne. The crown was safe for the Tudors, and England was saved from civil war. He knew how to rule his country. He had been strong and he had emerged triumphant from the most dangerous situation of his reign.

There was great news yet. The Queen was paler than usual; she had been sick; she had fancies for special foods.

Henry was joyful. He once more had hopes of getting a son.

* * *

While Henry was strutting with pleasure, Jane was beset with fear. There were many things to frighten Jane. Before her lay the ordeal of childbirth. What if it should prove unsuccessful? As she lay in those Hampton Court apartments which the King had lovingly planned for Anne Boleyn, she brooded on these matters. From her window she could see the initials entwined in stone work – J and H, and where the J was there had once been an A, and the A had had to be taken away very suddenly indeed.

The King was in high humour, certain that this time he would get a son. He went noisily about the palace, eating and drinking with great heartiness; and hunting whenever his leg was not too painful to deter him. If Jane gave him a son, he told himself, he would at last have found happiness. He would know that he had been right in everything he had done, right to rid himself of Katharine who had never really been his wife, right to execute Anne who was a sorceress, right to marry Jane.

He jollied the poor pale creature, admonishing her to take good care of herself, threatening her that if she did not, he would want to know the reason why; and his loving care was not for her frail body but for the heir it held.

The hot summer passed. Jane heard of the executions and shuddered, and whenever she looked from her windows she saw those initials. The J seemed to turn into an A as she looked, and then into something else, blurred and indistinguishable.

Plague came to London, rising up from the fetid gutters and from the dirty wash left on the river banks with the fall of the tide. People died like flies in London. Death came close to Jane Seymour during those months.

She was wan and sickly and she felt very ill, though she dared not mention this for fear of angering the King; she was afraid for herself and the child she carried. She had qualms about the execution of Anne, and her dreams became haunted with visions. She could not forget an occasion when Anne had come upon her and the King together. Then Anne must have felt this sickness, this heaviness, this fear, for she herself was carrying the King's child at that time.

Jane could not forget the words the King had used to her more than once. 'Remember what happened to your predecessor!' There was no need to ask Jane to remember what she would never be able to forget.

She became more observant of religious rites, and as her religion was of the old kind, both Cranmer and Cromwell were disturbed. But they dared not approach the King with complaints for they knew well what his answer would be. 'Let the Queen eat fish on Fridays. Let her do what she will an she give me a son!'

All over the country, people waited to hear of the birth of a son. What would happen to Jane, it was asked, if she produced a stillborn child? What if she produced a girl?

Many were cynical over Henry's matrimonial affairs, inclined to snigger behind their hands. Already there were Mary and Elizabeth – both proclaimed illegitimate. What if there was yet another girl? Perhaps it was better to be humble folk when it was considered what had happened to Katharine of Aragon and Anne Boleyn.

The Dowager Duchess of Norfolk waited eagerly for the news. Her mouth was grim. Would Jane Seymour do what her granddaughter had failed to do? That pale sickly creature succeed, where glowing, vital Anne had failed! She thought not!

Catherine Howard fervently hoped the King would get a son. She had wept bitterly at the death of her cousin, but unlike her grandmother she bore no resentment. Let poor Queen Jane be happy even if Queen Anne had not. Where was the good sense in harbouring resentment? She scarcely listened to her grandmother's grim prophecies.

Catherine had changed a good deal since that violent beating her grandmother had given her. Now she really looked like a daughter of the house of Howard. She was quieter; she had been badly frightened by the discovery. She had received lectures from Lord William who insisted on looking on the episode as a foolish girlish prank; she had received a very serious warning from her grandmother who, when they were alone, did not hide from her that she knew the worst. Catherine must put all that behind her, must forget it had happened, must never refer to it again, must deny what she had done if she were ever questioned by anyone. She had been criminally foolish; let her remember that. Catherine did remember; she was restrained.

She was growing very pretty and her gentle manners gave a new charm to her person. The Duchess was ready to forget unsavoury incidents; she hoped Catherine was too. She did not know that Catherine was still receiving letters from Derham, that through the agency of Jane Acworth, whose pen was ever ready, the correspondence was being kept up.

Derham wrote: 'Do not think that I forget thee. Do not forget that we are husband and wife, for I never shall. Do not forget you have said, "You shall never live to say I have swerved." For I do not, and I treasure the memory. One day I shall return for you. . . .'

It appealed strongly to Catherine's adventure-loving nature to receive love letters and to have her replies smuggled out of the house. She found it pleasant to be free from those women who had known about her love affair with Derham and who were for ever making sly allusions to it. There were no amorous adventures these days, for the Duchess's surveillance was strict. Catherine did not want them; she realized her folly and she was very much ashamed of the freedom she had allowed Manox. She still loved Francis, she insisted; she still loved receiving his letters; and one day he would return for her.

October came, and one morning, very early, Catherine

was awakened by the ringing of bells and the sound of guns. Jane Seymour had borne the King a son.

*   *   *

Jane was too ill to feel her triumph. She was hardly aware of what was going on in her chamber. Shapes rose up and faded. There was a huge red-faced man, whose laughter was very loud, drawing her away from the peaceful sleep she sought. She heard whispering voices, loud voices, laughter.

The King would peer at his son anxiously. A poor puny little thing he was, and Henry was terrified that he would, as others of his breed before him, be snatched from his father before he reached maturity. Even Richmond had not survived, though he had been a bonny boy; this little Edward was small and white and weak.

Still, the King had a son and he was delighted. Courtiers moved about the sick room. They must kiss Jane's hand; they must congratulate her. She was too tired? Nonsense! She must rejoice. Had she not done that which her predecessors had failed to do, given the King a son!

Fruit and meat were sent to her, gifts from the King. She must show her pleasure in His Majesty's attentions. She ate without knowing what she ate.

The ceremony of the christening began in her chamber. They lifted her from her bed to the state pallet which was decorated with crowns and the arms of England in gold thread. She lay, propped on cushions of crimson damask, wrapped in a mantle of crimson velvet furred with ermine; but Jane's face looked transparent against the rich redness of her robes. She was exhausted before they lifted her from the bed; her head throbbed and her hands were hot with fever. She longed to sleep, but she reminded herself over and over again that she must do her duty by attending the christening of her son. What would the King say, if he found the mother of his prince sleeping when she should be smiling her pleasure!

It was midnight as the ceremonial procession with Jane in its midst went through the draughty corridors of Hampton Court to the chapel. Jane slipped into unconsciousness, recovered and smiled about her. She saw the Princess Mary present the newly born Prince at the font; she saw her own brother carrying the small Elizabeth, whose eyes were small with sleepiness and in whose fat little hands was Edward's crysom; she saw Cranmer and Norfolk who were the Prince's sponsors; she saw the nurse and the midwife; and so vague was this scene to her that she thought it was but a dream, and that her son was not yet born and her pains about to begin.

Through the mist before her eyes she saw Sir Francis Bryan at the font, and she was reminded that he had been one of those who had not very long ago delighted in the wit of Anne Boleyn. Her eyes came to rest on the figure of a grey old man who carried a taper and bore a towel about his neck; she recognized him as Anne's father. The Earl looked shamefaced, and had the unhappy air of a man who knows himself to be worthy of the contempt of his fellow-men. Was he thinking of his brilliant boy and his lovely girl who had been done to death for the sake of this little Prince to whom he did honour because he dared do nothing else?

Unable to follow the ceremony because of the fits of dizziness which kept overwhelming her, Jane longed for the quiet of her chamber. She wanted the comfort of her bed; she wanted darkness and quiet and rest.

'God, in His Almighty and infinite grace, grant good life and long, to the right high, right excellent, and noble Prince Edward, Duke of Cornwall and Earl of Chester, most dear and entirely beloved son of our most dread and gracious Lord Henry VIII.'

The words were like a rushing tide that swept over Jane and threatened to drown her; she gasped for breath. She was only hazily aware of the ceremonial journey back to her chamber.

A few days after the christening, Jane was dead.

'Ah!' said the people in the streets, 'His Majesty is desolate. Poor dear man! At last he had found a queen he could love; at last he has his heart's desire, a son to follow him; and now this dreadful catastrophe must overtake him.'

Certain rebels raised their heads, feeling the King to be too sunk in grief to notice them. The lion but feigned to sleep. When he lifted his head and roared, rebels learned what happened to those who dared raise a voice against the King. The torture chambers were filled with such. Ears were cut off; tongues were cut out; and the mutilated victims were whipped as they were driven naked through the streets.

Before Jane was buried, Henry was discussing with Cromwell whom he should next take for a wife.

* * *

Henry was looking for a wife. Politically he was at an advantage; he would be able to continue with his policy of keeping his two enemies guessing. He would send ambassadors to the French court; he would throw out hints to the Emperor; for both would greatly fear an alliance of the other with England.

Henry was becoming uneasy concerning continental affairs. The war between Charles and Francis had come to an end; and with these two not at each other's throats, but in fact friends, and Pole persisting in his schemes to bring about civil war in England with the assistance of invasion from the Continent, he had cause for anxiety. To be able to offer himself in the marriage market was a great asset at such a time and Henry decided to exploit it to the full.

Although Henry was anxious to make a politically advantageous marriage, he could not help being excited by the prospect of a new wife. He visualized her. It was good to be a free man once more. He was but forty-seven and very ready to receive a wife. There was still in his mind the image of Anne Boleyn. He knew exactly what sort of wife he wanted; she must be beautiful, clever, vivacious; one who was high-spirited as Anne, meek as Jane. He reassured himself that although it was imperative that he should make the right marriage, he would not involve himself unless the person of his bride was pleasing.

He asked Chatillon, the French ambassador who had taken the place of du Bellay at the English court, that a selection of the most beautiful and accomplished ladies of the French court be sent to Calais; Henry would go there and inspect them.

'Pardie!' mused Henry. 'How can I depend on any but myself! I must see them myself and see them sing!'

To this request, Francis retorted in such a way as to make Henry squirm, and he did not go to Calais to make a personal inspection of prospective wives.

There were among others the beautiful Christina of Milan who was a niece of Emperor Charles. She had married the Duke of Milan who had died leaving her a virgin-widow of sixteen. Henry was interested in reports of her, and after the snub from Francis not averse to looking around the camp of the Emperor. He sent Holbein to make a picture of Christina and when the painter brought it back, Henry was attracted, but not sufficiently so to make him wish to clinch the bargain immediately. He was still keeping up negotiations with the French. It was reported that Christina had said that if she had had two heads one should be at the English King's service, but having only one she was reluctant to come to England. She had heard that her great-aunt Katharine of Aragon had been poisoned; that Anne Boleyn had been put innocently to death; and that Jane Seymour had been lost for lack of keeping in childbirth. She was of course at Charles's command, and these reports might well have sprung out of the reluctance of the Emperor for the match.

Henry's uneasiness did not abate. He was terrified that the growing friendship between Charles and Francis might be a prelude to an attack on England. He knew that Pope Paul was trying to stir up the Scots to invade England from the North; Pole was moving slyly, from the Continent.

Henry's first act was to descend with ferocity on the Pole family in England. He began by committing Pole's young brother Geoffrey to the Tower and there the boy was tortured so violently that he said all Henry wished him to say. The result was that his brother Lord Montague and his cousin the Marquis of Exeter were seized. Even Pole's mother, the ageing Countess of Salisbury, who had been governess to the Princess Mary and one of the greatest friends of Katharine of Aragon, was not spared.

These people were the hope of those Catholics who longed for reunion with Rome, and Henry was watching his people closely to see what effect their arrest was having. He had had enough of troubles within his own domains, and with trouble threatening from outside he must tread very cautiously. At this time, he selected as his victim a scholar named Lambert whom he accused of leaning too far towards Lutheranism. The young man was said to have denied the body of God to be in the sacrament in corporal substance but only to be there spiritually. Lambert was tried and burned alive. This was merely Henry's answer to the Catholics; he was telling them that he favoured neither extreme sect. Montague and Exeter went to the block as traitors, not as Catholics. Catholic or Lutheran, it mattered not. No favouritism. No swaying from one sect to another. He only asked allegiance to the King.

Francis thought this would be a good moment to undermine English commerce which, while he and Charles had been wasting their people's energy in war, Henry had been able to extend. Henry shrewdly saw what was about to happen and again acted quickly. He promised the Flemish merchants that for seven years Flemish goods should pay no more duty than those of the English. The merchants – a thrifty people – were overjoyed, seeing years of prosperous trading stretching before them. If their Emperor would make war on England he could hardly hope for much support from a nation benefiting from good trade with that country on whom Charles wished them to make war.

This was a good move, but Henry's fears flared up afresh when the Emperor, visiting his domains, decided to travel through France to Germany, instead of going by sea or through Italy and Austria as was his custom. This seemed to Henry a gesture of great friendship. What plans would the two old enemies formulate when they met in France? Would England be involved in those plans?

Cromwell, to whose great interest it was to turn England from the Catholics and so make more secure his own position, seized this chance of urging on Henry the selection of a wife from one of the German Protestant houses. Cromwell outlined his plan. For years the old Duke of Cleves had wanted an alliance with England. His son had a claim to the Duchy of Guelders, which Duchy was in relation to the Emperor Charles very much what Scotland was to Henry, ever ready to be a cause of trouble. A marriage between England and the house of Cleves would therefore seriously threaten the Emperor's hold on his Dutch dominions.

Unfortunately, Anne, sister of the young Duke, had already been promised to the Duke of Lorraine, but it was not difficult to waive this. Holbein was despatched; he made a pretty picture of Anne, and Henry was pleasurably excited and the plans for the marriage went forward.

Henry was impatient. Anne! Her very name enchanted him. He pictured her, gentle and submissive and very very loving. She would have full awareness of her duty; she was no daughter of a humble knight; she had been bred that she might make a good marriage; she would know what was expected of her. He could scarcely wait for her arrival. At last he would find matrimonial happiness, and at the same time confound Charles and Francis.

'Anne!' he mused, and eagerly counted the days until her arrival.

* * *

Jane Acworth was preparing to leave.

'How I shall miss you!' sighed Catherine.

Jane smiled at her slyly. 'It is not I whom you will miss but your secretary!'

'Poor Derham!' said Catherine. 'I fear he will be most unhappy. For I declare it is indeed a mighty task for me to put pen to paper.'

Jane shrugged her shoulders; her thoughts were all for the new home she was to go to and Mr Bulmer whom she was to marry.

'You will think of me often, Jane?' asked Catherine.

Jane laughed. 'I shall think of your receiving your letters. He writes a pretty letter and I dare swear seems to love you truly.'

463

'Ah! That he does. Dear Francis! How faithful he has always been to me.'

'You will marry him one day?'

'We are married, Jane. You know it well. How else . . .'

'How else should you have lived the life you did together! Well, I have heard it whispered that you were very lavish with your favours where a certain Manox was concerned.'

'Oh, speak not of him! That is past and done with. My love for Francis goes on for ever. I was foolish over Manox, but I regret nothing I have done with Francis, nor ever shall.'

'How lonely you will be without me!'

'Indeed, you speak truthfully.'

'And how different this life from that other! Why, scarce anything happens now, but sending letters to Derham and receiving his. What excitement we used to have!'

'You had better not speak of that to Mr Bulmer!' warned Catherine; and they laughed.

It was well to laugh, and she was in truth very saddened by Jane's departure; the receiving and despatching of letters had provided a good deal of excitement in a dull existence.

With Jane's going the days seemed long and monotonous. A letter came from Francis; she read it, tucked it into her bodice and was aware of it all day; but she could not read it very easily and it was not the same without Jane, for she, as well as being happy with a pen was also a good reader. She must reply to Derham, but as the task lacked appeal, she put it off.

The Duchess talked to her of court matters.

'If the King would but take him a wife! I declare it is two years since Queen Jane died, and still no wife! I tell you, Catherine, that if this much talked of marriage with the Duchess of Cleves materializes, I shall look to a place at court for you.'

'How I wish I could go to court!' cried Catherine.

'You will have to mind your manners. Though I will say they have improved since . . . since . . .' The Duchess's brows were dark with memory. 'You would not do so badly now at court, I trow. We must see. We must see.'

Catherine pictured herself at court.

'I should need many new clothes.'

'Dost think Lord William would allow you to go to court in rags! Why even His Grace the Duke would not have that! Ha! I hear he is most angry at this proposed marriage. Master Cromwell has indeed put my noble stepson's nose out of joint. Well, all this is not good for the Howards, and it is a mistake for a house to war within its walls. And so . . . it may not be so easy to find you a place at court. And I know that the King does not like the strife between my stepson and his wife. It is not meet that a Duke of noble house should feel so strongly for a washer in his wife's nurseries that he will flaunt the slut in the face of his lady Duchess. The King was ever a moral man, as you must always remember. Ah! Pat my back, child, lest I choke. Where was I? Oh, yes, the Howards are not in favour while Master Cromwell is, and this Cleves marriage is Cromwell-made. Therefore, Catherine, it may not be easy to find you a place at court, for though I dislike my lord Duke with all my heart, he is my stepson, and if he is out of favour at court, depend upon it, we shall be too.'

On another occasion the Duchess sent for Catherine. Her old eyes, bright as a bird's, peered out through her wrinkles.

'Get my cloak, child. I would walk in the gardens and have you accompany me.'

Catherine obeyed, and they stepped out of the house and strolled slowly through the orchards where Catherine had lain so many times with Derham. She had ever felt sad when she was in the orchards being unable to forget Derham, but now she scarcely thought of him, for she knew by the Duchess's demeanour that she had news for her, and she was hoping it was news of a place at court.

'You are an attractive child,' wheezed the Duchess. 'I declare you have a look of your poor tragic cousin. Oh . . . it is not obvious. Her hair was black and so were her eyes, and her face was pointed and unforgettable. You are auburn-haired and hazel-eyed and plump-faced. Oh, no, it is not in

465

your face. In your sudden laughter? In your quick movements? She had an air of loving life, and so have you. There was a little bit of Howard in Anne that looked out from her eyes; there is a good deal of Howard in you; and there is the resemblance.'

Catherine wished her grandmother would not talk so frequently of her cousin, for such talk always made her sad.

'You had news for me?' she reminded her.

'Ah, news!' The Duchess purred. 'Well, mayhap it is not yet news. It is a thought. And I will whisper this in your ear, child. I doubt not that the stony-hearted Duke would give his approval, for it is a good match.'

'A match!' cried Catherine.

'You do not remember your dear mother, Catherine?'

'Vaguely I do!' Catherine's large eyes glistened with tears so that they looked like pieces of topaz.

'Your dear mother had a brother, and it is to his son, your cousin, whom we feel you might be betrothed. He is a dear boy, already at court. He is a most handsome creature. Thomas Culpepper, son of Sir John, your mother's brother . . .'

'Thomas Culpepper!' whispered Catherine, her thoughts whirling back to a room at Hollingbourne, to a rustle of creeper, to a stalwart protector, to a kiss in the paddock. She repeated: 'Thomas Culpepper!' She realized that something very unusual was about to happen. A childhood dream was about to come true. 'And he . . . ?' she asked eagerly.

'My dear Catherine, curb your excitement. This is a suggestion merely. The Duke will have to be consulted. The King's consent will be necessary. It is an idea. I was not to tell you yet . . . but seeing you so attractive and marriageable, I could not resist it.'

'My cousin . . .' murmured Catherine. 'Grandmother . . . when I was at Hollingbourne . . . we played together. We loved each other then.'

The Duchess put her finger to her lips.

'Hush, child! Be discreet. This matter must not be made open knowledge yet. Be calm.'

Catherine found that very difficult. She wanted to be

alone to think this out. She tried to picture what Thomas would be like now. She had only a hazy picture of a little boy, telling her in a somewhat shame-faced way that he would marry her.

Derham's letter scraped her skin. The thought of Thomas excited her so much that she had lost her burning desire to see Francis. She was wishing that all her life had been spent as she had passed the last months.

The Duchess was holding her wrists and the Duchess's hands were hot.

'Catherine, I would speak to you very seriously. You will have need of great caution. The distressing things which have happened to you . . .'

Catherine wanted to weep. Oh, how right her grandmother was! If only she had listened even to Mary Lassells! If only she had not allowed herself to drift into that sensuous stream which at the time had been so sweet and cooling to her warm nature and which now was so repulsive to look back on. How she had regretted her affair with Manox when she had found Francis! Now she was beginning to regret her love for Francis as her grandmother talked of Thomas.

'You have been very wicked,' said her grandmother. 'You deserve to die for what you have done. But I will do my best for you. Your wickedness must never get to the Duke's ears.'

Catherine cried out in misery rather than in anger: 'The Duke! What of him and Bess Holland!'

The Duchess was on her dignity. She might say what she would of her erring kinsman, not so Catherine.

'What if his wife's washerwoman be his mistress! He is a man; you are a woman. There is all the difference in the world.'

Catherine was subdued; she began to cry.

'Dry your eyes, you foolish girl, and forget not for one instant that all your wickedness is done with, and it must be as though it never was.'

'Yes, grandmother,' said Catherine, and Derham's letter pricked her skin.

Derham continued to write though he received no answers. Catherine had inherited some of her grandmother's

467

capacity for shifting her eyes from the unpleasant. She thought continually of her cousin Thomas and wondered if he remembered her, if he had heard of the proposed match and if so what he thought of it.

One day, wandering in the orchard, she heard a rustle of leaves behind her, and turning came face to face with Derham. He was smiling; he would have put his arms about her but she held him off.

'Catherine, I have longed to see thee.'

She was silent and frightened. He came closer and took her by the shoulders. 'I had no answer to my letters,' he said.

She said hastily: 'Jane has married and gone to York. You know I was never able to manage a pen.'

'Ah!' His face cleared. 'That was all then? Thank God! I feared . . .' He kissed her on the mouth; Catherine trembled; she was unresponsive.

His face darkened. 'Catherine! What ails thee?'

'Nothing ails me, Francis. It is . . .' But her heart melted to see him standing so forlorn before her, and she could not tell him that she no longer loved him. Let the break come gradually. 'Your return is very sudden. Francis . . .'

'You have changed, Catherine. You are so solemn, so sedate.'

'I was a hoyden before. My grandmother said so.'

'Catherine, what did they do to thee?'

'They beat me with a whip. There never was such a beating. I was sick with the pain of it, and for weeks I could feel it. I was locked up, and ever since I have scarce been able to go out alone. They will be looking for me ere long, I doubt not.'

'Poor Catherine! And this you suffered for my sake! But never forget, Catherine, you are my wife.'

'Francis!' she said, and swallowed. 'That cannot be. They will never consent, and what dost think they would do an you married me in actual fact?'

'We should go away to Ireland.'

'They would never let me go. We should die horrible deaths.'

'They would never catch us, Catherine.'

He was young and eager, fresh from a life of piracy off the coast of Ireland. He had money; he wished to take her away. She could not bear to tell him that they were talking of betrothing her to her cousin, Thomas Culpepper.

She said: 'What dost think would happen to you if you showed yourself?'

'I know not. To hold you in my arms would suffice for anything they could do to me afterwards.'

Such talk frightened her. She escaped, promising to see him again.

She was disturbed. Now that she had seen Derham after his long absence, she knew for truth that which she had begun to suspect. She no longer loved him. She cried herself to sleep, feeling dishonoured and guilty, feeling miserable because she would have to go to her cousin difiled and unclean. Why had she not stayed at Hollingbourne! Why had her mother died! What cruel fate had sent her to the Duchess where there were so many women eager to lead her into temptation! She was not yet eighteen and she had been wicked ... and all so stupidly and so pointlessly.

She determined to break with Francis; there should be no more clandestine meetings. She would marry Thomas and be such a good wife to him, that when set against years and years of the perfect happiness she would bring him, the sinful years would seem like a tiny mistake on a beautifully written page.

Francis was hurt and angry. He had come back full of hope; he loved her and she was his wife, he reminded her. He had money from his spell of piracy; he was in any case related to the Howards.

She told him she had heard she was to go to court.

'I like that not!' he said.

'But I like it,' she told him.

'Dost know the wickedness of court life?' he demanded.

She shrugged her shoulders. She hated hurting people and being forced to hurt Francis who loved her so truly was a terrible sorrow to her; she found herself disliking him because she had to hurt him.

'You ... to talk of wickedness ... when you and I ...'

He would have no misunderstanding about that.

'What we did, Catherine, is naught. Thou art my wife. Never forget it. Many people are married at an early age. We have done no wrong.'

'You know we are not husband and wife!' she retorted. 'It was a fiction to say we are; it was but to make it easy. We have sinned, and I cannot bear it. I wish we had never met.'

Poor Derham was heartbroken. He had thought of no one else all the time he had been away. He begged her to remember how she had felt towards him before he went away. Then he heard the rumour of her proposed betrothal to Culpepper.

'This then,' he said angrily, 'is the reason for your change of heart. You are going to marry this Culpepper?'

She demanded what right he had to ask such a question, adding: 'For you know I will not have you, and if you have heard such report, you heard more than I do know!'

They quarrelled then. She had deceived him, he said. How could she, in view of their contract, think of marrying another man? She must fly with him at once.

'Nay, nay!' cried Catherine, weeping bitterly. 'Francis, please be reasonable. How could I fly with you? Dost not see it would mean death to you! I have hurt you and you have hurt me. The only hope for a good life for us both is never to see each other again.'

Someone was calling her. She turned to him imploringly. 'Go quickly. I dare not think what would happen to you were you found here.'

'They could not hurt me, an they put me on the rack, as you have hurt me.'

Such words pierced like knives into the soft heart of Catherine Howard. She could not be happy, knowing she had hurt him so deeply. Was there to be no peace for her, no happiness, because she had acted foolishly when she was but a child?

The serving-maid who had called her told her her grandmother would speak to her at once. The Duchess was excited.

'I think, my dear, that you are to go to court. As soon as

the new queen arrives you will be one of her maids of honour. There! What do you think of that? We must see that you are well equipped. Fear not! You shall not disgrace us! And let me whisper a secret. While you are at court, you may get a chance to see Thomas Culpepper. Are you not excited?'

Catherine made a great effort to forget Francis Derham and think of the exciting life which was opening out before her. Court . . . and Thomas Culpepper.

* * *

Henry was on his way to Rochester to greet his new wife. He was greatly excited. Such a wise marriage this was! Ha! Charles! he thought. What do you think of this, eh? And you, Francis, who think yourself so clever? I doubt not, dear Emperor, that Guelders is going to be a thorn in your fleshy side for many a long day!

Anne! He could not help his memories. But this Anne would be different from that other. He thought of that exquisite miniature of Holbein's; the box it had arrived in was in the form of a white rose, so beautifully executed, that in itself it was a fine work of art; the carved ivory top of the box had to be unscrewed to show the miniature at the bottom of it. He had been joyful ever since the receipt of it. Oh, he would enjoy himself with this Anne, thinking, all the time he caressed her, not only of the delights of her body, but of sardonic Francis and that Charles who believed himself to be astute.

He had a splendid gift of sables for his bride. He was going to creep in on her unceremoniously. He would dismiss her attendants, for this would be the call of a lover rather than the visit of a king. He chuckled. It was so agreeable to be making the right sort of marriage. Cromwell was a clever fellow; his agents had reported that the beauty of Anne of Cleves exceeded that of Christina of Milan as the sun doth the moon!

Henry was fast approaching fifty, but he felt twenty, so eager he was, as eager as a bridegroom with his first wife. Anne was about twenty-four; it seemed delightfully young when one was fifty. She could not speak very much English; he could not speak much German. That would add piquancy to his courtship. Such a practised lover as himself did not need words to get what he wanted from a woman. He laughed in anticipation. Not since his marriage to Anne Boleyn, said those about him, had the King been in such high humour.

When he reached Rochester, accompanied by two of his attendants he went into Anne's chamber. At the door he paused in horror. The woman who curtseyed before him was not at all like the bride of his imaginings. It was the same face he had seen in the miniature, and it was not the same. Her forehead was wide and high, her eyes dark, her lashes thick, her eyebrows black and definitely marked; her black hair was parted in the centre and smoothed down at the sides of her face. Her dress was most unbecoming with its stiff high collar resembling a man's coat. It was voluminous after the Flemish fashion, and English fashions had been following the French ever since Anne Boleyn had introduced them at court. Henry started in dismay, for the face in the miniature had been delicately coloured so that the skin had the appearance of rose petals; in reality Anne's skin was brownish and most disfiguringly pock-marked. She seemed quite ugly to Henry, and as it did not occur to him that his person might have produced a similar shock to her, he was speechless with anger.

His one idea was to remove himself from her presence as quickly as possible; his little scheme to 'nourish love' as he had described it to Cromwell, had failed. He was too upset to give her the sables. She should have no such gift from his hands! He was mad with rage. His wise marriage had brought him a woman who delighted him not. Because her name was Anne, he had thought of another Anne, and his vision of his bride had been a blurred Anne Boleyn, as meek as Jane Seymour. And here he was, confronted by a creature whose accents jarred on him, whose face and figure repelled him. He had been misled. Holbein had misled him! Cromwell had misled him. Cromwell! He gnashed his teeth over that name. Yes, Cromwell had brought about this unhappy

472

state of affairs. Cromwell had brought him Anne of Cleves.

'Alas!' he cried. 'Whom shall men trust! I see no such thing as hath been shown me of her pictures and report. I am ashamed that men have praised her as they have done, and I love her not!'

But he was polite enough to Anne in public, so that the crowds of his subjects to whom pageantry was the flavouring in their dull dish of life, did not guess that the King was anything but satisfied. Anne in her cloth of gold and rich jewellery seemed beautiful enough to them; they did not know that in private the King was berating Cromwell, likening his new bride to a great Flanders mare, that his conscience was asking him if the lady's contract with the Duke of Lorraine did not make a marriage between herself and the King illegal.

Poor Anne was deliberately delayed at Dartford whilst Henry tried to find some excuse for not continuing with the marriage. She was melancholy. The King had shown his dislike quite clearly; she had seen the great red face grow redder; she had seen the small eyes almost disappear into the puffy flesh; she had seen the quick distaste. She herself was disappointed, such accounts had she had of the once handsomest prince in Christendom; and in reality he was a puffed-out, unwieldy, fleshy man with great white hands overloaded with jewels, into whose dazzling garments two men could be wrapped with room to spare; on his face was the mark of internal disease; and bandages bulged about his leg; he had the wickedest mouth and cruellest eyes she had ever seen. She could but, waiting at Dartford, remember stories she had heard of this man. How had Katharine met her death? What had she suffered before she died? All the world knew the fate of tragic Anne Boleyn. And poor Jane Seymour? Was it true that after having given the King a son she had been so neglected that she had died?

She thought of the long and tiring journey from Dusseldorf to Calais, and the Channel crossing to her new home; she thought of the journey to Rochester; until then she had been reasonably happy. Then she had seen him, and seeing him it was not difficult to believe there was a good deal of truth in the stories she had heard concerning his treatment of his wives. And now she was to be one of them, or perhaps she would not, for, having seen the distaste in his face, she could guess at the meaning of this delay. She did not know whether she hoped he would marry her or whether she would prefer to suffer the humiliation of being sent home because her person was displeasing to him.

Meanwhile Henry was flying into such rages that all who must come into contact with him went in fear for their lives. Was there a previous contract? He was sure there was! Should he endanger the safety of England by producing another bastard? His conscience, his most scrupulous conscience, would not allow him to put his head into a halter until he was sure.

It was Cromwell who must make him act reasonably, Cromwell who would get a cuff for his pains.

'Your most Gracious Majesty, the Emperor is being fêted in Paris. An you marry not this woman you throw the Duke of Cleves into an alliance with Charles and Francis. We should stand alone.'

Cromwell was eloquent and convincing; after all he was pleading for Cromwell. If this marriage failed, Cromwell failed, and he knew his head to be resting very lightly on his shoulders, and that the King would be delighted to find a reason for striking it off. But Henry knew that in this matter, Cromwell spoke wisely. If Henry feared civil war more than anything, then next he feared friendship between Charles and Francis, and this was what had been accomplished. He dared not refuse to marry Anne of Cleves.

'If I had known so much before, she should not have come hither!' he said, looking menacingly at Cromwell, as though the meetings between Charles and Francis had been arranged by him. Henry's voice broke on a tearful note. 'But what remedy now! What remedy but to put my head in the yoke and marry this . . .' His cheeks puffed with anger and his eyes were murderous. . . . 'What remedy but to marry this great Flanders mare!'

There followed the ceremony of marriage with its gorgeously apparelled men and women, its gilded barges and banners and streamers. Henry in a gown of cloth of gold raised with great silver flowers, with his coat of crimson satin decorated with great flashing diamonds, was a sullen bridegroom. Cromwell was terrified, for he knew not how this would end, and he had in his mind such examples of men who had displeased the King as would make a braver man than he was tremble. The Henry of ten years ago would never have entered into this marriage; but this Henry was more careful of his throne. He spoke truthfully when he had said a few hours before the ceremony that if it were not for the sake of his realm he would never have done this thing.

Cromwell did not give up hope. He knew the King well; it might be that any wife was better than no wife at all; and there were less pleasant looking females than Anne of Cleves. She was docile enough and the King liked docility in women; the last Queen had been married for that very quality.

The morning after the wedding day he sought audience with the King; he looked in vain for that expression of satiety in the King's coarse red face.

'Well?' roared Henry, and Cromwell noticed with fresh terror that his master liked him no better this day than he had done on the previous one.

'Your Most Gracious Majesty,' murmured the trembling Cromwell, 'I would know if you are any more pleased with your Queen.'

'Nay, my lord!' said the King viciously, and glared at Cromwell, laying the blame for this catastrophe entirely upon him. 'Much worse! For by her breasts and belly she should be no maid; which, when I felt them, strake me so to the heart that I had neither will nor courage to prove the rest.'

Cromwell left his master, trembling for his future.

*   *   *

Catherine Howard could not sleep for excitement. At last she had come to court. Her grandmother had provided her with the garments she would need, and Catherine had never

475

felt so affluent in the whole of her eighteen years. How exciting it was to peep through the windows at personages who had been mere names to her! She saw Thomas Cromwell walking through the courtyards, cap in hand, with the King himself. Catherine shuddered at the sight of that man. 'Beware of the blacksmith's son!' her grandmother had said. 'He is no friend of the Howards.' Always before Catherine had seen the King from a great distance; closer he seemed larger, more sparkling than ever, and very terrifying, so that she felt a greater urge to run from him than she did even from Thomas Cromwell. The King was loud in conversation, laughter and wrath, and his red face in anger was an alarming sight. Sometimes he would hobble across the courtyards with a stick, and she had seen his face go dark with the pain he suffered in his leg, and he would shout and cuff anyone who annoyed him. His cheeks were so puffed out and swollen that his eyes seemed lost between them and his forehead, and were more like the flash of bright stones than eyes. This King made Catherine shiver. Cranmer she saw too – quiet and calm in his archbishop's robes. She saw her uncle and would have hidden herself, but his sharp eyes would pick her out and he would nod curtly.

Catherine was enjoying life, for Derham could not pester her at court as he had done at the Duchess's house, and when she did not see him she could almost forget the sorrow that had come to her through him. She loved the Queen, and wept for her because she was so unhappy. The King did not love her; he was with her only in public. The ladies whispered together that when they went to the royal bedchamber at night the King said Good night to the Queen and that nothing passed between them until the morning when he said Good morning. They giggled over the extraordinary relationship of the King and Queen; and Catherine was too inexperienced and too much in awe of them not to giggle with them, but she was really sorry for the sad-eyed Queen. But Catherine did refrain from laughing with them over the overcrowded and tasteless wardrobe of the Queen.

'Ah!' whispered the ladies. 'You should have seen the other Queen Anne. What clothes she had, and how she knew the way to wear them! But this one! No wonder the King has no fancy for her. Ja, ja, ja! That is all she can say!'

Catherine said: 'But she is very kind.'

'She is without spirit to be otherwise!'

But that was not true. Catherine, who had been often beaten by the hard-handed Duchess, was susceptible to kindness; she sat with the Queen and learned the Flemish style of embroidery, and was very happy to serve Anne of Cleves.

There was something else that made Catherine happy. Thomas Culpepper was at court. She had not yet seen him, but each day she hoped for their reunion. He was, she heard, a great favourite with the King himself and it was his duty to sleep in the royal apartment and superintend those who dressed the King's leg. She wondered if he knew she was here, and if he were waiting for the reunion as eagerly as she was.

Gardiner, the Bishop of Winchester, gave a banquet one evening. Catherine was very excited about this, for she was going to sing, and it would be the first time she had ever sung alone before the King.

'You are a little beauty!' said one of the ladies. 'What a charming gown!'

'My grandmother gave it to me,' said Catherine, smoothing the rich cloth with the pleasure of one who has always longed for beautiful clothes and has never before possessed them.

'If you sing as prettily as you look,' she was told, 'you will be a successful young woman.'

Catherine danced all the way down to the barge; she sang as they went along the river; she danced into the Bishop's house. Over her small head smiles were exchanged; she was infectiously gay and very young.

'Mind you do not forget your words.'

'Oh, what if I do! I feel sure I shall!'

'Committed to the Tower!' they teased her, and she laughed with them, her cheeks aglow, her auburn curls flying.

She sat at the great table with the humblest of the ladies.

The King, at the head of the table, was in a noisy mood. He was eating and drinking with great heartiness as was his custom, congratulating the Bishop on his cook's efforts, swilling great quantities of wine, belching happily.

Would His Most Gracious Majesty care for a little music? the Bishop would know.

The King was ever ready to be entertained, and there was nothing he liked better, when he was full of good food and wine, than to hear a little music. He felt pleasantly sleepy; he smiled with benevolent eyes on Gardiner. A good servant, a good servant. He was in a mellow mood; he would have smiled on Cromwell.

He looked along the table. A little girl was singing. She had a pretty voice; her flushed cheeks reminded him of June roses, her hair gleamed gold; she was tiny and plump and very pretty. There was something in her which startled him out of his drowsiness. It was not that she was the least bit like Anne. Anne's hair had been black as had her eyes; Anne had been tall and slender. How could this little girl be like Anne? He did not know what could have suggested such a thought to him, and yet there it was ... but elusive, so that he could not catch it, could not even define it. All he could say was that she reminded him. It was the tilt of her head, the gesture of the hands, that graceful back bent forward, and now the pretty head tossed back. He was excited, as for a long time he had wanted to be excited. He had not been so excited since the early days of marriage with Anne.

'Who is the girl now singing?' he asked Gardiner.

'That, Your Majesty, is Norfolk's niece, Catherine Howard.'

The King tapped his knee reflectively. Now he had it. Anne had been Norfolk's niece too. The elusive quality was explained by a family resemblance.

'Norfolk's niece!' he said, and growled without anger, so that the growl came through his pouched lips like a purr. He watched the girl. He thought, By God, the more I see of her the more I like her!

He was comparing her with his pock-marked Queen. Give him English beauties, sweet-faced and sweet-voiced. He liked sonorous English on the tongue, not harsh German. Like a rose she was, flushed, laughing and happy.

'She seems little more than a child,' he said to Gardiner.

Norfolk was beside the King. Norfolk was cunning as a monkey, artful as a fox. He knew well how to interpret that soft look in the royal eyes; he knew the meaning of the slurring tones. Norfolk had been furious when the King had chosen Anne Boleyn instead of his own daughter, the Lady Mary Howard. Every family wanted boys, but girls, when they were as pleasant to the eye as Anne Boleyn and Catherine Howard, had their uses.

'We liked well your little niece's playing,' said the King.

Norfolk murmured that His Majesty was gracious, and that it gave him the utmost delight that a member of his family should give some small pleasure to her sovereign.

'She gives us much pleasure,' said the King. 'We like her manners and we like her singing. Who is her father?'

'My brother Edmund, sir. Your Majesty doubtless remembers him. He did well at Flodden Field.'

The King nodded. 'I remember well,' he said kindly. 'A good servant!' He was ready to see through a haze of benevolence, every member of a family which could produce such a charming child as Catherine Howard.

'Doubtless Your Most Gracious Majesty would do my little niece the great honour of speaking to her. A royal compliment on her little talents would naturally mean more to the child than the costliest gems.'

'Right gladly I will speak to her. Let her be brought to me.'

'Your Majesty, I would humbly beg that you would be patient with her simplicity. She has led but a sheltered life until recently she came to court. I fear she may seem very shy and displease you with her gaucherie. She is perhaps too modest.'

'Too modest!' The King all but shouted. 'How is it possible, my lord, for maidens to be too modest!' He was all impatience to have her close to him, to study the fresh young skin, to pat her shoulder and let her know she had pleased her King. 'Bring her to me without delay.'

479

Norfolk himself went to Catherine. She stopped playing and looked at him in fear. He always terrified her, but now his eyes glittered speculatively and in the friendliest manner.

Catherine stood up. 'Have I done aught wrong?'

'Nay, nay!' said his Grace. 'Your singing has pleased His Majesty and he would tell you how much. Speak up when he talks to you. Do not mumble, for he finds that most irritating. Be modest but not shy.'

The King was waiting impatiently. Catherine curtseyed low and a fat, white, jewelled hand patted her shoulder.

'Enough!' he said, not at all unkindly, and she rose and stood trembling before him.

He said: 'We liked your singing. You have a pretty voice.'

'Your Majesty is most gracious. . . .' she stammered and blushed sweetly. He watched the blood stain her delicate cheeks. By God, he thought, there never has been such a one since Anne. And his eyes filled with sudden self-pity to think how ill life had used him. He had loved Anne who had deceived him. He had loved Jane who had died. And now he was married to a great Flanders mare, when in his kingdom, standing before him so close that he had but to stretch out his hands and take her, was the fairest rose that ever grew in England.

'We are glad to be gracious to those who please us,' he said. 'You are lately come to court? Come! You may sit here . . . close to us.'

'Yes, please Your Majesty. I . . . I have lately come . . .'

She was a bud just unfolding, he thought; she was the most perfect creature he had ever seen, for while Anne had been irresistible, she had also been haughty, vindictive and demanding, whereas this little Catherine Howard with her doe's eyes and gentle frightened manner, had the beauty of Anne and the docility of Jane. Ah, he thought, how happy I should have been if instead of that Flemish creature I had found this lovely girl at Rochester. How I should have enjoyed presenting her with costly sables; jewels too; there is naught I would not give to such a lovely child.

He leaned towards her; his breath, not too sweet, warmed

her cheek, and she withdrew involuntarily; he thought this but natural modesty and was enchanted with her.

'Your uncle has been talking to me of you.'

Her uncle! She blushed again, feeling that the Duke would have said nothing good of her.

'He told me of your father. A good man, Lord Edmund. And your grandmother, the Dowager Duchess is a friend of ours.'

She was silent; she had not dreamed of such success; she had known her voice was moderately good, nothing more, certainly not good enough to attract the King.

'And how do you like the court?' he asked.

'I like it very much, please Your Majesty.'

'Then I am right glad that our court pleases you!' He laughed and she laughed too. He saw her pretty teeth, her little white throat, and he felt a desire to make her laugh some more.

'Now we have discovered you,' he said, 'we shall make you sing to us often. How will you like that, eh?'

'I shall find it a great honour.'

She looked as if she meant this; he liked her air of candid youth.

He said: 'Your name is Catherine, I know. Tell me, how old are you?'

'I am eighteen, sir.'

Eighteen! He repeated it, and felt sad. Eighteen, and he close fifty. Getting old; short of breath; quick of temper; often dizzy; often after meals suffering from divers disorders of the body; his leg getting worse instead of better; he could not sit his horse as once he had done. Fifty . . . and eighteen!

He watched her closely. 'You shall play and sing to us again,' he said.

He wanted to watch her without talking; his thoughts were busy. She was a precious jewel. She had everything he would look for in a wife; she had beauty, modesty, virtue and charm. It hurt him to look at her and see behind her the shadow of his Queen. He wanted Catherine Howard as urgently as once he had wanted Anne Boleyn. His hunger

481

for Catherine was more pathetic than that he had known for Anne, for when he had loved Anne he had been a comparatively young man. Catherine was precious because she was a beacon to light the dark days of his middle-age with her youthful glow.

Sweetly she sang. He wanted to stretch out his hands and pet her and keep her by him. This was cold age's need of warm youth. He thought, I would be a parent and a lover to her, for she is younger than my daughter Mary, and she is lovely enough to make any but the blind love her, and those she would enchant with her voice.

He watched her and she played again; then he would have her sit with him; nor did she stir from his side the evening through.

* * *

A ripple of excitement went through the court.

'Didst see the King with Mistress Catherine Howard last night?'

'I declare I never saw His Majesty so taken with a girl since Anne Boleyn.'

'Much good will it do her. His mistress? What else since he has a Queen?'

'The King has a way with queens, has he not?'

'Hush! Dost want to go to the Tower on a charge of treason?'

'Poor Queen Anne, she is so dull, so German! And Catherine Howard is the prettiest thing we have had at court for many years!'

'Poor Catherine Howard!'

'*Poor*, forsooth!'

'Would *you* change places with her? Remember ...'

'Hush! They were unfortunate!'

Cromwell very quickly grasped the new complications brought about by the King's infatuation for Catherine Howard, and it seemed to him that his end was in sight. Norfolk could be trusted to exploit this situation to the full. Catherine was a Catholic, a member of the most devout Catholic family in England. Continental events loomed up darkly for Cromwell. When the Emperor had passed through France there were signs that his friendship with Francis was not quite as cordial as it had been. Charles was no longer thinking of attacking England, and it was only when such plans interested him that he would be eager to take Francis as an ally. Trouble was springing up over Charles's domains and he would have his hands tied very satisfactorily from Henry's point of view if not from Cromwell's. When the Duke of Cleves asked for help in securing the Duchy of Guelders, Henry showed that he was in no mood to give it.

Cromwell saw the position clearly. He had made no mistakes. He had merely gambled and lost. When the marriage with Anne of Cleves had been made it was necessary to the safety of England; now England had passed out of that particular danger and the marriage was no longer necessary, and the King would assuredly seize an excuse to rid himself of his most hated minister. Cromwell had known this all the time. He could not play a good game if he had not the cards. With Charles and Francis friendly, he had stood a chance of winning; when relations between these two were strained, Cromwell was unlucky. On Cromwell's advice Henry had put a very irritating yoke about his neck. Now events had shown that it was no longer necessary that the yoke should remain. And there was Norfolk, making the most of Cromwell's ill luck, cultivating his niece, arranging meetings between her and the King, offering up the young girl as a sacrifice from the House of Howard on that already blood-stained altar of the King's lusts.

Henry's mind was working rapidly. He must have Catherine Howard. He was happy; he was in love. Catherine was the sweetest creature in the world, and there was none but Catherine who could keep him happy. She was delightful; she was sweetly modest; and the more he knew her, the more she delighted him. Just to see her skipping about the Hampton Court gardens which he had planned with her cousin Anne, made him feel younger. She would be the perfect wife; he did not want her to be his mistress – she was too sweet and pure for that – he wanted her beside him on the throne, that he might live out his life with none other but her.

She was less shy with him now; she was full of laughter, but ready to weep for other people's sorrows. Sweet Catherine! The sweetest of women! The rose without a thorn! Anne had perhaps been the most gorgeous rose that ever bloomed, but oh, the thorns! In his old age this sweet creature should be beside him. And he was not so old! He could laugh throatily, holding her hand in his, pressing the cool, plump fingers against his thigh. He was not so old. He had years of pleasant living in front of him. He did not want riotous living, he told himself. All he had ever wanted was married happiness with one woman, and he had not found her until now. He must marry Catherine; he must make her his Queen.

His conscience began to worry him. He realized that Anne's contract with the Duke of Lorraine had ever been on his mind, and it was for this reason that he had never consummated the marriage. So cursed had he been in his matrimonial undertakings, that he went cautiously. He had never been Anne's true husband because of his dread of presenting another bastard to the nation. Moreover the lady was distasteful to him and he suspected her virtue. Oh, he had said naught about it at the time, being over-merciful perhaps, being anxious not to accuse before he was sure. He had not been free when he entered into the marriage; only because he had felt England to be defenceless against the union of Charles and Francis had he allowed it to take place. England owed him a divorce, for had he not entered into this most unwelcome engagement for England's sake? And he owed England children. He had one boy and two girls – both of these last illegitimate; and the boy did not enjoy the best of health. He had failed to make the throne secure for Tudors; he must have an opportunity of doing so. Something must be done.

* * *

The Dowager Duchess of Norfolk could scarcely believe her ears when she heard the news. The King and her granddaughter! What a wonderful day this was to bring her such news!

She would bring out her most costly jewels. 'If Catherine could attract him in those simple things,' she babbled, 'how much more so will she when I have dressed her!'

For once she and the Duke were in agreement. He visited her, and the visit was the most amiable they had ever shared. The Dowager Duchess had never thought she and the Duke would one day put their heads together over the hatching of a plot. But when the Duke had gone, the Duchess was overcome with fears, for it seemed to her that another granddaughter looked at her from out of the dark shadows of her room and would remind her of her own tragic fate. How beautiful and proud that Queen Anne had been on the day of her coronation! Never would the Duchess be able to forget the sight of her entering the Tower to be received by her royal lover. And then, only three years later....

The Duchess called for lights. 'I declare the gloom of this house displeases me. Light up! Light up! What are you wenches thinking of to leave me in the dark!'

She felt easier when the room was lighted. It was stupid to imagine for a moment that the dead could return. 'She cannot die for what was done before,' she muttered to herself; and she set about sorting out her most valuable jewels – some for Catherine in which to enchant the King; and some for herself when she should go to another coronation of yet another granddaughter.

*   *   *

The Earl of Essex, who had been such a short time before plain Thomas Cromwell, was awaiting death. He knew it was inevitable. He had been calculating and unscrupulous; he had been devilishly cruel; he had tortured men's bodies and sacrificed their flesh to the flames; he had dissolved the monasteries, inflicting great hardship on their inmates, and he had invented crimes for these people to have committed, to justify his actions; with Sampson, Bishop of Chichester, he had worked out a case against Anne Boleyn, and had brought about her death through the only man who would talk against her, a poor delicate musician who had had to be violently tortured first; all these crimes – and many others – had he committed, but they had all been done at the command of his master. They were not Cromwell's crimes; they were Henry's crimes.

And now he awaited the fate which he had so many times prepared for others. It was ten years since the death of Wolsey, and they had been ten years of mounting power for Cromwell; and now here was the inevitable end. The King had rid himself of Wolsey – for whom he had had some affection – because of Anne Boleyn; now he would rid himself of Cromwell – whom, though he did not love him, he knew to be a faithful servant – for Catherine Howard. For though this young girl, whom the King would make his Queen, bore no malice to any, and would never ask to see even an enemy punished but rather beg that he should be forgiven, yet was it through her that Cromwell was falling; for cruel Norfolk and Gardiner had risen to fresh power since the King had shown his preference for Norfolk's niece, and these two men, who represented Catholicism in all its old forms, would naturally wish to destroy one who, with staunch supporters like Thomas Wyatt, stood more strongly for the new religion than he would dare admit. Whilst he was despoiling the monasteries, he had been safe, and knowing this he had left one very wealthy institution untouched, so that in an emergency he might dangle its treasure before the King's eyes and so earn a little respite. This he had done, and in throwing in this last prize he had earned the title of Earl of Essex.

It was a brief triumph, for Cromwell's position was distressingly similar to that in which Wolsey had found himself. Had not Wolsey flung his own treasure to the King in a futile effort to save himself? Hampton Court and York House; his houses and plate and art treasures. Cromwell, as Wolsey before him, if it would please the King, must rid his master of a wife whom he, Cromwell, supported; but if he succeeded in doing this, he would put on the throne a member of the Howard family who had sworn to effect his destruction.

When the King realized that Cromwell was hesitating to choose between two evils, since he could not be certain as to which was the lesser, he lost patience, and declared that Cromwell had been working against his aims for a settlement of the religious problem, and this was, without a doubt, treason.

Now, awaiting his end, he recalled that gusty day when as he travelled with the members of the privy council to the palace a wind had blown his bonnet from his head. How significant had it been when they, discourteously, did not remove their bonnets, but had kept them on whilst he stood bareheaded! And their glances had been both eager and furtive. And then later he had come upon them sitting round the council chamber, talking together, insolently showing him that they would not wait for his coming; and as he would have sat down with them, Norfolk's voice had rung out, triumphant, the voice of a man who at last knows an old enemy is defeated. 'Cromwell! Traitors do not sit with gentlemen!'

He had been arrested then and taken to the Tower. He smiled bitterly, imagining the King's agents making inventories of his treasures. How often had he been sent to do a similar errand in the King's name! He had gambled and lost; there was a small grain of comfort in the knowledge that it was not due to lack of skill, but ill luck which had brought about his end.

A messenger was announced; he came from the King. Cromwell's hopes soared. He had served the King well; surely His Majesty could not desert him now. Perhaps he could still be useful to the King. Yes! It seemed he could. The King needed Cromwell to effect his release from the marriage into which he had led him. Cromwell must do as he was bid. The reward? The King was ever generous, ever merciful, and Cromwell should be rewarded when he had freed the King. Cromwell was a traitor and there were two deaths accorded to traitors. One was the honourable and easy death by the axe. The other? Cromwell knew better than most. How many poor wretches had he condemned to die that way? The victim was hanged but not killed; he was disembowelled and his entrails were burned while the utmost care was taken to keep him alive; only then was he beheaded. This should be Cromwell's reward for his last service to his master: In his gracious mercy, the most Christian King would let him choose which way he would die.

Cromwell made his choice. He would never fail to serve the King.

* * *

Anne had been sent to Richmond. It was significant that the King did not accompany her. She was terrified. This had happened before, with another poor lady in the rôle she now must play. What next? she wondered. She was alone in a strange land, among people whose language she could not speak, and she felt that death was very close to her. Her brother the Duke of Cleves was far away and he was but insignificant compared with this great personage who was her husband, and who thought little of murder and practised it as lightly as some people eat, drink and sleep.

She had endured such mental anguish since her marriage that she felt limp and unequal to the struggle she would doubtless have to put up for her life. Her nights were sleepless; her days were so full of terror that a tap on a door would set her shivering as though she suffered from some ague.

She had been Queen of England for but a few months and she felt as though she had lived through years of torment. Her husband made no attempt to hide his distaste for her. She was surrounded by attendants who mimicked her because they were encouraged in this unkindness by the King who was ready to do any cruel act to discredit her, and who found great satisfaction in hurting her – and inspiring others to hurt her – as she declared her unpleasant appearance hurt him. The Lady Rochford, one of her ladies, who had been the wife of another queen's late brother, was an unpleasant creature, who listened at doors and spied upon her, and reported all that she said to the other ladies and tittered unkindly about her; they laughed at her clothes which she was ready to admit were not as graceful as those worn in

England. The King was hinting that she had led an immoral life before she came to England; this was so unjust and untrue that it distressed her more than anything else she had been called upon to endure, because she really believed Henry did doubt her virtue. She did not know him well enough to realize that this was characteristic of him, and that he accused others of his own failings because he drew moral strength from this attitude and deceived himself into thinking that he could not be guilty of that which he condemned fiercely in others. So poor Queen Anne was a most unhappy woman.

There was one little girl recently come to court whom she could have loved; and how ironical it was that this child's beauty and charm should have increased the King's animosity towards herself. The King would rid himself of me, she thought, to put poor little Catherine Howard on the throne. This he may well do, and how I pity that poor child, for when I am removed, she will stand in my most unhappy shoes!

As she sat in the window seat a message was brought to her that my lords Suffolk and Southampton with Sir Thomas Wriothesley were without, and would speak with her.

The room began to swing round her; she clutched at the scarlet hangings to steady herself. She felt the blood drain away from her head. It had come. Her doom was upon her!

When Suffolk with Southampton and Wriothesley entered the room they found the Queen lying on the floor in a faint. They roused her and helped her to a chair. She opened her eyes and saw Suffolk's florid face close to her own, and all but fainted again; but that nobleman began to talk to her in soothing tones and his words were reassuring.

What he said seemed to Anne the happiest news she had ever heard in her life. The King, out of his regard for her – which meant his regard for the house of Cleves, but what did that matter! – wished to adopt her as his sister, providing she would resign her title of Queen. The King wished her no ill, but she well knew that she had never been truly married to His Majesty because of that previous contract with the Duke of Lorraine. This was why His Most Cautious

Majesty had never consummated the marriage. All she need do was to behave in a reasonable manner, and she should have precedence at court over every lady, excepting only the King's daughters and her who would become his Queen. The English taxpayers would provide her with an income of three thousand pounds a year.

The King's sister! Three thousand pounds a year! This was miraculous! This was happiness! That corpulent, perspiring, sullen, angry, spiteful, wicked monster of a man was no longer her husband! She need not live close to him! She could have her own establishment! She need not return to her own dull country, but she could live in this beautiful land which she had already begun to love in spite of its King! She was free.

She almost swooned again, for the reaction of complete joy after absolute misery was overwhelming.

Suffolk and Southampton exchanged glances with Wriothesley. The King need not have been so generous with his three thousand pounds. It had not occurred to him that Anne would be so eager to be rid of him. They would keep that from the King; better to let His August Majesty believe that their tact had persuaded the woman it would be well to accept.

Anne bade her visitors a gay farewell. Never had Henry succeeded in making one of his wives so happy.

* * *

Catherine was bewildered. Quite suddenly her position had changed. Instead of being the humblest newcomer, she was the most important person at court. Everyone paid deference to her; even her grim old uncle had a pleasant word for her, so that Catherine felt she had misjudged him. The Dowager Duchess, her grandmother, would deck her out in the most costly jewels, but these were poor indeed compared with those which came from the King. He called her 'The Rose without a Thorn'; and this he had had inscribed on some of the jewels he had given her. He had chosen her device which was 'No other Will but His.'

Catherine was sorry for the poor Queen, and could not

bear to think that she was displacing her; but when she heard that Anne appeared to be happier at Richmond than she had ever been at court, she began to enjoy her new power.

Gifts were sent to her, not only from the King, but from the courtiers. Her grandmother petted, scolded and warned at the same time. 'Be careful! No word of what has happened with Derham must ever reach the King's ears.'

'I would prefer to tell him all,' said Catherine uneasily.

'I never heard such folly!' Her Grace's black eyes glinted. 'Do you know where Derham is?' she asked. And Catherine assured her that she did not know.

'That is well,' said the Duchess. 'I and Lord William have spoken to the King of your virtues and how you will make a most gracious and gentle queen.'

'But shall I?' asked Catherine.

'Indeed you shall. Now, no folly. Come let me try this ruby ring on your finger. I would have you know that the King, while liking well our talk, would have been most displeased with us had we done aught but sing your praises. Oh, what it is to be loved by a king! Catherine Howard, I declare you give yourself graces already!'

Catherine had thought that she would be terrified of the King, but this was not so. There was nothing for her to fear in this great soft man. His voice changed when he addressed her, and his hard mouth could express nothing but kindness for her. He would hold her hand and stroke her cheek and twine her hair about his fingers; and sometimes press his lips against the flesh on her plump shoulders. He told her that she would mean a good deal to him, that he wished above all things to make her his Queen, that he had been a most unhappy man until he had set eyes on her. Catherine looked in wonder at the little tear-filled eyes. Was this the man who had sent her beautiful cousin to her death? How could simple Catherine believe ill of him when she stood before him and saw real tears in his eyes?

He talked of Anne, for he saw that Anne was in Catherine's thoughts; she was, after all, her own cousin, and the two had known and been fond of one another.

491

'Come and sit upon my knee, Catherine,' he said, and she sat there while he pressed her body against his and talked of Anne Boleyn. 'Wert deceived as I was by all that charm and beauty, eh? Ah! but thou wert but a child and I a man. Didst know that she sought to take my life and poison my daughter Mary? Dost know that my son died through a spell she cast upon him?'

'It is hard to believe that. She was so kind to me. I have a jewelled tablet she gave me when I was but a baby.'

'Sweet Catherine, I too had gifts from her. I too could not believe . . .'

It was easier for Catherine to believe the King who was close to her, when Anne was but a memory.

It was at this time that she met Thomas Culpepper. He was one of the gentlemen of the privy chamber, and had great charm of manner and personal beauty which had pleased the King ever since he had set eyes upon him. Thomas's intimate duties of superintending the carrying out of the doctor's orders regarding the King's leg kept him close to Henry, who had favoured him considerably, and had given him several posts which, while they brought little work, brought good remuneration; he had even given him an abbey. He liked Culpepper; he was amused by Culpepper. In his native Kent, the boy had involved himself in a certain amount of scandal, for it seemed he was wild and not over-scrupulous, but the King was as ready to forgive the faults of those he wished to keep around him, as he was to find fault with those he wished removed.

The knowledge that his cousin was at court soon reached Thomas Culpepper, for since her elevation, everyone was discussing Catherine Howard. Seeing her in the pond garden one afternoon, he went out to her. She was standing by a rose tree, the sun shining on her auburn hair. Thomas immediately understood the King's infatuation.

'You would not remember me,' he said. 'I am your cousin, Thomas Culpepper.'

Her eyes opened very wide and she gave a little trill of pleasure; she held out both her hands.

'Thomas! I had hoped to see you.'

They stood holding hands; studying each other's faces.

How handsome he is! thought Catherine. Even more handsome than he was as a boy!

How charming she is! thought Thomas. How lovable – and in view of what has happened to her during the last weeks, how dangerously lovable! But to Thomas nothing was ever very interesting unless it held an element of danger.

He said greatly daring: 'How beautiful you have grown, Catherine!'

She laughed delightedly. 'That is what everyone says to me now! Do you remember the stick you gave me with which to tap on the wall?'

They were laughing over their memories.

'And the adventures you used to have . . . and how we used to ride in the paddock . . . and how you . . .'

'Said I would marry you!'

'You did, you know, Thomas, and then you never did anything about it!'

'I never forgot!' he lied. 'But now . . .' He looked across the garden and over the hedge to the windows of the palace. Even now, he thought, little hot jealous eyes might have caught sight of him. Living close to the King he knew something of his rages. Dangerously sweet was this contact with Catherine.

'It is too late now,' she said soberly, and she looked very sad. She saw Thomas as the lover to whom she had been betrothed for many years; she forgot Manox and Derham and believed that she had loved Thomas always.

'Suppose that we had married when it was suggested a year or so ago,' said Thomas.

'How different our lives would have been then!'

'And now,' he said, 'I risk my life to speak to you.'

Her eyes widened with terror. 'Then we must not stay here.' She laughed suddenly. They did not know the King, these people who were afraid of him. His Majesty was all kindness, all eagerness to make people happy really. As if he would hurt her cousin if she asked him not to!

'Catherine,' said Thomas, 'I shall risk my life again and again. It will be worth it.'

493

He took her hand and kissed it, and left her in the pond garden.

They could not resist meeting secretly. They met in dark corridors; they feared that if it reached the ears of the King that they were meeting thus, there would be no more such meetings. Sometimes he touched her fingers with his, but nothing more; and after the first few meetings they were in love with each other.

There was a similarity in their natures, both were passionate, reckless people; they were first cousins and they knew now that they wished to enjoy a closer relationship; and because, when they had been children, they had plighted their troth in the paddock of Hollingbourne, they felt life had been cruel to them to keep them apart and bring them together only when it was too late for them to be lovers.

Catherine had little fear for herself, but she feared for him. He, a reckless adventurer who had been involved in more than one dangerous escape, was afraid not for himself but for her.

They would touch hands and cry out to each other: 'Oh, why, oh, why did it have to happen thus!'

She would say to him: 'I shall be passing along the corridor that leads to the music room at three of the clock this afternoon.'

He would answer: 'I will be there as if by accident.'

All their meetings were like that. They would long for them all day, and then when they reached the appointed spot, it might be that someone was there, and it was impossible for them to exchange more than a glance. But to them both this danger was very stimulating.

There was one occasion when he, grown more reckless by the passing of several days which did not bring even a glimpse of her, drew her from the corridor into an antechamber and shut the door on them.

'Catherine,' he said, 'I can endure this no longer. Dost not realize that thou and I were meant one for the other from the first night I climbed into thy chamber? We were but children then, and the years have been cruel to us, but I have

494

a plan. Thou and I will leave the palace together. We will hide ourselves and we will marry.'

She was pale with longing, ever ready to abandon herself to the passion of the moment, but it seemed to her that she heard her cousin's voice warning her. Catherine would never know the true story of Anne Boleyn, but she had loved her and she knew her end had been terrible. Anne had been loved by the same huge man; those eyes had burned hotly for Anne; those warm, moist hands had caressed her. Anne had had no sad story of a cousin to warn her.

Culpepper was kissing her hands and her lips, Catherine's healthy young body was suggesting surrender. Perhaps with Manox or Derham she would have surrendered; but not with Culpepper. She was no longer a lighthearted girl. Dark shadows came pursuing her out of the past. Doll Tappit's high voice. 'The cries of the torture chambers are terrible. . . .' Catherine knew how the monks of the Charterhouse had died; she could not bear to think of others suffering pain, but to contemplate one she loved being vilely hurt was sufficient to stem her desire. She remembered how Derham had run for his life; but then she had been plain Catherine Howard. What of him who dared to love her whom the King had chosen for his Queen!

'Nay, nay!' she cried, tears falling from her eyes. 'It cannot be! Oh, that it could! I would give all my life for one year of happiness with you. But I dare not. I fear the King. I must stay here because I love you.'

She tore herself away; there must be no more such meetings.

'Tomorrow . . .' she agreed weakly. 'Tomorrow.'

She ran to her apartment, where, since Anne had left for Richmond, she enjoyed the state of a queen. She was greeted by one of her attendants, Jane Rochford, widow of her late cousin George Boleyn. Lady Rochford looked excited. There was a letter for Catherine, she said.

'A letter?' cried Catherine. 'From whom?'

Catherine did not receive many letters; she took this one and opened it; she frowned for she had never been able to read very easily.

Jane Rochford was at her side.

'Mayhap I could assist?'

Jane had been very eager to ingratiate herself with Catherine; she had not liked the last Queen; Jane had decided to adhere to the Catholic cause and support Catherine Howard against Anne of Cleves.

Catherine handed her the letter.

'It is from a Jane Bulmer,' said Jane, 'and it comes from York.'

'I remember. It is from Jane Acworth who went to York to marry Mr Bulmer. Tell me what she says.'

Jane Bulmer's letter was carefully worded. She wished Catherine all honour, wealth and good fortune. Her motive in writing was to ask a favour of Catherine, and this was that she should be found a place at court. Jane was unhappy in the country; she was desolate. A command from the future Queen to Jane's husband to bring his wife to court would make Jane Bulmer very happy, and she begged for Catherine's help.

The threat was in the last sentence.

'I know the Queen of Britain will not forget her secretary. . . .'

Her secretary! Jane Bulmer it was who had written those revealing, those intimate and passionate letters to Derham; Jane Bulmer knew everything that had happened.

Catherine sat very still as Jane Rochford read to her; her face was rosy with shame.

Jane Rochford was not one to let such signs pass unnoticed. She, as well as Catherine, read into those words a hint of blackmail.

* * *

On a hot July day Cromwell made the journey from the Tower to Tyburn. Tyburn it was because it was not forgotten that he was a man of lowly origins; he could smile at this, though a short while ago it would have angered him; but what does a man care when his head is to be cut off, whether it be done at Tower Hill or Tyburn?

He had obeyed his master to the last; he had been more than the King's servant; he had been the King's slave. But to his cry for mercy, had his most gracious Prince been deaf. He had done with Cromwell. He had not allowed Cromwell to speak in his own defence. Cromwell's fall would help to bring back Henry's popularity, for the people of England hated Cromwell.

His friends? Where were they? Cranmer? He could laugh at the thought of Cranmer's being his friend. Only a fool would expect loyalty in the face of danger from weak-kneed Cranmer. He knew that the Archbishop had declared himself smitten with grief; he had told the King that he had loved Cromwell, and the more for the love he had believed him to bear His Grace the King; he had added that although he was glad Cromwell's treason was discovered, he was very sorrowful, for whom should the King trust in future?

He had said almost the same words when Anne Boleyn had been taken to the Tower. Poor Cranmer! How fearful he was. He must have faced death a thousand times in his imagination. There was never a man quicker to dissociate himself from a fallen friend!

Crowds had gathered to see Cromwell's last moments. He recognized many enemies. He thought of Wolsey who would have faced this, had he lived long enough. He had walked in the shadow of Wolsey, had profited by his example, by his brilliance and his mistakes; he had followed the road to Power and had found it led to Tyburn.

There was one in the crowd who shed a tear for him. It was Thomas Wyatt who had been as eager as Cromwell himself that the Lutheran doctrines should be more widely understood. Their eyes met. Cromwell knew that Wyatt was trying to reassure him, to tell him that cruelties he had inflicted on so many had been done at Henry's command and that Cromwell was not entirely responsible for them. This young man did not know of the part Cromwell had played in the destruction of Anne Boleyn. Cromwell hoped then that he never would. His heart warmed to Wyatt.

'Weep not, Wyatt,' he said, 'for if I were not more guilty

than thou wert when they took thee, I should not be in this pass.'

It was time for him to make his last speech, to lay his head upon the block. He thought of all the blood he had caused to be shed, and tried to pray, but he could think of nothing but blood, and the screams of men in agony and the creaking of the rack.

Onto his thick neck, the axe descended; his head rolled away from his body as four years before, had Anne Boleyn's.

*   *   *

The King was enchanted with his bride. In the great hall at Hampton Court, he proclaimed her Queen. None had known the King in such humour for years; he was rejuvenated.

A few days after the proclamation, he took her from Hampton Court to Windsor, and astonished everyone by cutting himself off from the court that he might enjoy the company of his bride in private. Catherine seemed doubly pleasing in the King's eyes, coming after Anne of Cleves; she was gentle yet ever ready to laugh; she had no disconcerting wit to confound him; her conversation held not a trace of cleverness, only kindness. She was a passionate creature, a little afraid of him, but not too much so; she was responsive and womanly; and never had the King felt such drowsy and delicious peace. If she had a fault it was her generosity, her kindness to others. She would give away her clothes and jewels, explaining, her head a little on one side, her dewy lips parted, 'But it becomes her so, and she had so little. . . .' Or, 'She is poor, if we could but do something for her, how happy I should be!' She was irresistible and he could not bring himself to reprimand her for this over-lavishness; he liked it; for he too came in for his share of her generosity. He would kiss her and stroke her and tickle her; and have her shrieking with laughter. Never had he dreamed of such blessedness.

Anne of Cleves was ordered to come to court to pay homage to the new Queen. There was a good deal of speculation in the court as to how the displaced queen would feel when kneeling to one who had but a short time ago been her maid of honour. It was expected that Catherine would demand great homage from Anne of Cleves to prove to herself and to the court that she was safely seated on the throne and had command of the King's affection. But when Anne came and knelt before the new Queen, Catherine impulsively declared that there should be no ceremony.

'You must not kneel to me!' she cried, and the two Queens embraced each other with tears of affection in their eyes, and it was Anne of Cleves who was moved to pity, not Catherine Howard.

Catherine would do honour to her cousin's daughter, Elizabeth, partly because she was her cousin's daughter, and partly because, of all her step-children, she loved Elizabeth best.

Mary was disposed to be friendly, but only because Catherine came from a family which adhered to the old Catholic faith, and Mary's friendship for people depended entirely on whether or not they were what she called true Catholics. Mary was six years older than her father's wife, and she thought the girl over-frivolous. Catherine accepted Mary's disapproval of her at first because she knew the Princess had suffered so much, but eventually she was goaded into complaining that Mary showed her little respect; she added that if only Mary would remember that although she was young she was the Queen, she would be ready to be friendly. This resulted in a sharp reprimand to Mary from the King; but friendship was not made that way, and how could poor, plain, frustrated Mary help feeling certain twinges of jealousy for sparkling Catherine whose influence over the King appeared to be unlimited. Mary was more Spanish than English; she would often sink into deepest melancholy; she would spend hours on her knees in devotion, brooding on her mother's dreary tragedy and the break with Rome; preferring to do this rather than sing and dance and be gay. On her knees she would pray that the King might come back to the true faith in all its old forms, that he might follow the example of her mother's country and earn the approval of heaven by setting up an Inquisition in this careless island

and torturing and burning all those who deserved such a fate, since they were heretics. How could soft-hearted, frivolous Catherine ever bring the King to take this duty upon himself! No, there could be no real friendship between Catherine and Mary.

Little Edward was not quite two years old; pale of face; solemn-eyed, he was watched over by his devoted nurse, Mrs Sibell Penn, who was terrified that some cold breath of air might touch him and end his frail life.

Of course it was Elizabeth whom Catherine must love most, for the child already had a look of Anne, for all that she had inherited her father's colouring. She would have Elizabeth at the table with them, occupying the place of honour next to Mary. She begged privileges for Elizabeth.

'Ah!' said Henry indulgently. 'It would seem that England has a new ruler, and that Queen Catherine!'

'Nay!' she replied. 'For how could I, who am young and foolish, rule this great country? That is for one who is strong and clever to do.'

He could not show his love sufficiently. 'Do what thou wilt, sweetheart,' he said, 'for well thou knowest, I have heart to refuse thee naught.'

He liked to watch them together – his favourite child and his beloved Queen. Seeing them thus, he would feel a deep contentment creep into his mind. Anne's child is happy with my new Queen, he would tell himself; and because it would seem to him that there might be a plea for forgiveness in that thought, he would hastily assure himself that there was nothing for Anne to forgive.

He and Catherine rode together in the park at Windsor. He had never wandered about so unattended before; and he enjoyed to the full each day he shared with this lovely laughing girl. It was pleasant to throw off the cares of kingship and be a lover. He wished he were not so weighty, though he never could abide lean men; still, to puff and pant when you were the lover of a spritely young girl was in itself a sad state of affairs. But Catherine feigned not to notice the puffing and looked to it that he need not exert himself too much in his pursuit of her. She was perfect; his rose without a single thorn.

He was almost glad that the low state of the treasury would not allow for ceremony just at this time, for this enabled him to enjoy peace with his young bride.

They made a happy little journey from Windsor to Grafton where they stayed until September, and it was while they were at Grafton that an alarming incident took place.

Cranmer noted it and decided to make the utmost use of it, although, knowing the amorous nature of the King, he could hope for little from it yet. Cranmer was uneasy, and had been since the arrest of Cromwell, for they had walked too long side by side for the liquidation of one not to frighten the other seriously. Norfolk was in the ascendant, and he and Cranmer were bitterly engaged in the silent subtle warring of two opposing religious sects. Such as Catherine Howard were but counters to be moved this way and that by either side; and the fight was fierce and deadly. Cranmer, though a man of considerable intellectual power, was at heart a coward. His great aim was to keep his head from the block and his feet from the stake. He could not forget that he had lost his ally Cromwell and had to play this wily Norfolk single-handed. Cranmer was as determined to get Catherine Howard off the throne as the Catholics had been to destroy Anne Boleyn. At this time, he bowed before the new Queen; he flattered her; he talked of her in delight to the King, murmuring that he trusted His Majesty had now the wife his great goodness deserved. And now, with this incident coming to light and the marriage not a month old, Cranmer prayed that he might be able to make the utmost use of it and bring Catherine Howard to ruin and so serve God in the way He most assuredly preferred to be served.

It had begun with a few words spoken by a priest at Windsor. He had talked slightingly of the Queen, saying that he had been told once, when she was quite a child, she had led a most immoral life. This priest was immediately taken prisoner and put into the keep of Windsor Castle, while

Wriothesley, at the bidding of the Council, was sent to lay these matters before the King.

Catherine was in a little antechamber when this man arrived; she heard the King greet him loudly.

'What news?' cried Henry. 'By God! You look glum enough!'

'Bad news, Your Majesty, and news it grieves me greatly to bring to Your Grace.'

'Speak up! Speak up!' said the King testily.

'I would ask Your Majesty to be patient with me, for this concerns Her Majesty the Queen.'

'The Queen!' Henry's voice was a roar of fear. The sly manner and the feigned sorrow in the eyes of the visitor were familiar to him. He could not bear that anything should happen to disturb this love idyll he shared with Catherine.

'The dribblings of a dotard doubtless,' said Wriothesley. 'But the Council felt it their duty to warn Your Majesty. A certain priest at Windsor has said that which was unbefitting concerning the Queen.'

Catherine clutched the hangings, and felt as though she were about to faint. She thought, I ought to have told him. Then he would not have married me. Then I might have married Thomas. What will become of me? What will become of me now?

'What's this? What's this?' growled the King.

'The foolish priest – doubtless a maniac – referred to the laxity of Her Majesty's behaviour when she was in the Dowager Duchess's care at Lambeth.'

The King looked at Wriothesley in such a manner as to make that ambitious young man shudder. The King was thinking that if Catherine had been a saucy wench before he had set eyes on her, he was ready to forget it. He wanted no disturbance of this paradise. She was charming and good-tempered, a constant delight, a lovely companion, a most agreeable bedfellow; she was his fifth wife, and his fourth had robbed him of any desire to make a hasty change. He wanted Catherine as he had made her appear to himself. Woe betide any who tried to destroy that illusion!

'Look ye here!' he said sternly. 'I should have thought you would have known better than to trouble me with any foolish tale of a drunken priest. You say this priest but repeated what he had heard. You did right to imprison him. Release him now, and warn him. Tell him what becomes of men who speak against the King . . . and by God, those who speak against the Queen speak against the King! Tongues have been ripped out for less. Tell him that, Wriothesley, tell him that. As for him who spoke these evil lies to the priest, let him be confined until I order his release.'

Wriothesley was glad to escape.

Catherine, trembling violently, thought: I must speak to my grandmother. I must explain to the King.

She half expected the King to order her immediate arrest, and that she would be taken to the Tower and have to lay her head on the block as her cousin had done. She was hysterical when she ran out to the King; she was flushed with fear; impulsively she threw her arms about his neck and kissed him.

He pressed her close to him. He might still be doubtful, but he was not going to lose this. By God, he thought, if anyone says a word against my Queen, he shall pay for it!

'Why, sweetheart?' he said, and turned her face to his, determined to read there what he wished to read. Such innocence! By God, those who talked against her deserved to have their heads on London Bridge – and should too! She was pure and innocent, just as Lord William and her grandmother had assured him. He was lucky – even though he were a King – to have such a jewel of womanhood.

The happy honeymoon continued.

*　　*　　*

The Dowager Duchess was closeted with the Queen.

'I declare,' said Catherine, 'I was greatly affrighted. I heard every word, and I trembled so that I scarce dared go out to the King when the man had gone!'

'And the King, said he naught to you?'

'He said naught.'

'He has decided to ignore this, depend upon it.'

'I feel so miserable. I would prefer to tell him. You understand, with Derham, it was as though we were married...'

'Hush! Do not say such things. I am an old woman and an experienced one; you are young and unwise. Take my advice.'

'I will,' said Catherine. 'Of course I will. It was yours I took when I did not tell the King before my marriage.'

'Pish!' said the Duchess, and then dropping her voice to a whisper: 'I have heard from Derham.'

'From Derham!'

'I said from Derham. He is back in my house. He is such a charming boy and I could not find it in my heart to keep up my anger against him. He still speaks of you with indiscreet devotion, and he has asked for something which I cannot advise you to refuse him. He says that he must see you now and then, that you have nothing to fear from him. He loves you too well to harm you.'

'What does he ask?'

'A place at court!'

'Oh, no!'

'Indeed yes; and I feel that you would be very unwise to refuse it. Do not look so frightened. Remember you are the Queen.'

Catherine said slowly: 'I have Jane Bulmer here and Katharine Tylney as well as Margaret Morton. I would that I had refused them.'

'Refuse them! You speak without thought. Have you forgotten that these people were at Lambeth and actually witnessed what took place between you and Derham!'

'I had rather they were not here. They are inclined to insolence as though they know I dare not dismiss them.'

She did not tell the Duchess that Manox had approached her too, that he had demanded a place at court. There was no need to disturb the Duchess further, and tell her that Manox, now one of the court musicians, had once been Catherine's lover.

'Now,' said the Duchess, 'you must listen to me. Derham must come to court. You cannot refuse him.'

'I see that you are right,' said Catherine wearily.
So came Derham.

*　　*　　*

The King's delight in his Queen did not diminish with the passing of the months. They left Ampthill for More Park where they could enjoy an even more secluded life; Henry was impatient with any minister who dared disturb him, and gave special instructions that no one was to approach him; any matter which was urgent was to be set out in writing. He was happy, desperately warming himself by the fire of Catherine's youth; he doted on her; he caressed her even in public, declaring that at last he had found conjugal happiness. He felt this to be a reward for a life of piety. There was one further blessing he asked, and that was children. So far, there was little success, but what matter? Catherine in herself was as much as any man could reasonably ask.

She was such a soft-hearted little thing and could bear to hurt no one. She hated to hear of the executions which were taking place every day; she would put her plump little fingers into her ears, and he would pet her and murmur; 'There, there, sweetheart, wouldst have me fête these traitors?'

'I know traitors must be severely dealt with,' she said. 'They must die, but let them die by the axe or the rope, not these lingering, cruel deaths.'

And he, forgetting how he had spurned Jane Seymour and threatened her when she would meddle, could deny his new Queen little.

Those Catholics who still hoped for reunion with Rome thought the moment ripe to strike at the men who had supported Cromwell, and Wyatt, among others, was sent to the Tower. He, bold as ever, had dared defend himself, and Catherine angered her uncle Norfolk by pleading for leniency towards Wyatt. She took warm clothes and food to the old Countess of Salisbury who was still in the Tower.

The King remonstrated with her.

'It will not do, sweetheart, it will not do.'

'Would you have me leave such a poor old lady to starve?'

He took her onto his knee, and touched her cheek in a

505

manner meant to reprove her, but she, with a characteristic gesture, seized his finger and bit it softly, which amused him, so that he found himself laughing instead of scolding.

He could not help it. She was irresistible. If she would take clothes and food to the old Countess, then she must. He would try pleading with her again concerning the greater indiscretion of asking pardon for Wyatt.

'Now listen to me,' he said. 'Wyatt is a traitor.'

'He is no traitor. He is a brave man. He does not cringe nor show fear, and is not afraid to state his opinions.'

'Aye!' said the King slyly. 'And he is the handsomest man in court, you are about to add!'

'He is assuredly, and I am certain he is a true friend to Your Majesty.'

'So you find him handsomer than your King, eh?'

'The handsomest *man*, you said. We did not speak of *kings*!' She took his great face in her hands and surveyed him saucily. 'Nay,' she said, 'I will say that Thomas Wyatt is the handsomest man in the court, but I would not include the King in that!' Which made him laugh and feel so gratified that he must kiss her and say to himself, A plague on Norfolk! Does he think to rule this realm! Wyatt is indeed a bold spirit and I was ever one to look for boldness in a man. If he is too anti-Catholic, he is at least honest. How does a King know when men will plot against him? Wyatt is too pleasant a man to die; his head is too handsome to be struck off his shoulders. Doubtless we can pardon Wyatt on some condition.

Norfolk was furious over the affair of Wyatt. He quarrelled with his step-mother.

'What means the Queen? Wyatt is our enemy. Has she not sense enough to know that!'

'Speak not thus of the Queen in my presence!' said the Dowager Duchess. 'Or 'twill go ill with thee, Thomas Howard.'

'You are an old fool. Who put the wench on the throne, I would ask you?'

'You may ask all you care to. I am willing to answer. The

King put Catherine Howard on the throne because he loves her sweet face.'

'Bah! You will go to the block one day, old woman, and that wench with you.'

'This is treason!' cried Her Grace.

'Tut, tut,' said the Duke and left her.

The Duchess was so furious that she went straight to the Queen.

'He was but feigning friendship for us,' said Catherine. 'I believe I ever knew it . . .'

'I fear him,' said the Duchess. 'There is that in him to terrify a woman, particularly when . . .'

They looked at each other; then glanced over their shoulders. The past was something they must keep shut away.

'Tread warily with the Duke!' warned the Duchess.

But it was not in Catherine's nature to tread warily. She showed her displeasure in her coolness to the Duke. The King noticed it and was amused. He liked to see proud Norfolk slighted by this vivacious Queen of his whose power flowed from himself.

Norfolk was filled with cold fury. This Catherine was every bit as unruly as his niece Anne Boleyn. If there was anything in that rumour which had risen up within a few weeks of her marriage, by God, he would not be the one to hold out a helping hand to Catherine Howard.

Sly Cranmer watched the trouble between Norfolk and his niece, and was pleased by it, for Norfolk was a worthy ally, and that they, enemies to one another, should be joined in common cause against Catherine Howard, was not an unsatisfactory state of affairs. But even if he had a case against Catherine, he would have to wait awhile, since it would be folly to present it to the King in his present amorous state. How much longer was the fat monarch going on cooing like a mating pigeon?

There was no sign of a change in the King's attitude towards Catherine. All through spring and summer as they journeyed from place to place, he was her devoted husband.

He preferred comparative retirement in the country to state balls and functions.

Henry was, however, jolted out of his complacency by news of a papist revolt in the north. This was headed by Sir John Neville and there was no doubt that it had been strongly influenced from the Continent by Cardinal Pole. Up rose Henry, roaring like a lion who has slumbered too long. He would restrain his wrath no longer. He had, in his newly found happiness, allowed himself to be over-lenient. How could he go on enjoying bliss with Catherine if his throne was imperilled and snatched from him by traitors!

The old Countess of Salisbury could no longer be allowed to live. Her execution had been delayed too long. Catherine had pleaded for her, had conjured up pitiful pictures of her freezing and starving in the Tower. Let her freeze! Let her starve! So perish all traitors! She was the mother of a traitor – one of the greatest and most feared Henry had ever known. Cardinal Pole might be safe on the Continent, but his mother should suffer in his stead.

'To the block with her!' shouted Henry, and all Catherine's pleas could not deter him this time. He was gentle with her, soothing her. 'Now now, sweetheart, let such matters rest. She is not the poor old lady you might think her to be. She is a traitor and she has bred traitors. Come, come, wouldst thou have thy King and husband tottering from his throne? Thrones have to be defended now and then with blood, sweetheart.'

So the old Countess was done to death in cruel fashion, for she, the last of the Plantagenets, kept her courage to the violent end. She refused to lay her head on the block, saying the sentence was unjust and she no traitor.

'So should traitors do,' she said, 'but I am none, and if you will have my head, you must win it if you can.'

Of all murders men had committed at the King's command this was the most horrible, for the Countess was dragged by her hair to the block, and since she would not then submit her head peaceably, the executioner hacked at her with his axe until she, bleeding from many wounds, sank in her death agony to the ground, where she was decapitated.

Such deaths aroused Henry's wrath. The people loved to gloat over bloody details; they whispered together, ever fond of martyrs.

It had always been Henry's plan, since the break with Rome, to play the Catholics off against the Lutherans, just as he played Charles against Francis. The last insurrection had put the Catholics out of favour, and his conscience now gave him several twinges about Cromwell. He replied to his conscience by mourning that, acting on false accusations which those about him had made, he had put to death the best servant he had ever had. Thus could he blame the Catholics for Cromwell's death and exonerate himself. Norfolk was out of favour; Cranmer in the ascendant. Henry left the administration of his affairs in the hands of a few chosen anti-papists headed by Cranmer and Chancellor Audley, and proceeded North on a punitive expedition, accompanied by the Queen.

* * *

Henry was whole-hearted in most things he undertook. When he set out to stamp the impression of his power on his subjects, he did so with vigour; and as his method was cruelty, Catherine could not help being revolted by that tour to the north.

Loving most romantically the handsome Culpepper, she must compare him with Henry; and while she had been prepared to do her best and please the indulgent man she had so far known, she was discovering that this was not the real man, and she was filled with horror. There was no kindness in him. She was forced to witness the grovelling of those who had rebelled because they wished to follow what they believed to be true. As they went through county after county and she saw the cruelty inflicted, and worse still was forced to look on his delight in it, it seemed to her, that when he came to her, his hands dripped blood. She wished the King to be a loving monarch; she wished the people to do homage to him; but she wanted them to respect him without fearing him, as she herself was trying so desperately to do.

509

There had been many compensations which had come to her when she forsook Culpepper to marry Henry. Mary, Joyce and Isabel, her young sisters, had been lifted from their poverty; indeed, there was not one impecunious member of her family who had not felt her generosity. This did not only apply to her family but to her friends also. She wanted to feel happiness about her; she wanted to make the King happy; she wanted no one worried by poverty, inconvenienced by hardship, smitten with sorrow. She wanted a pleasant world for herself and everyone in it.

When they came to Hull and saw what was left of Constable, a prey to the flies, hanging on the highest gate where Norfolk had gleefully placed him full four years ago, she turned away sickened, for the King had laughingly pointed out this grim sight to her.

'There hangs a traitor . . . or what is left of him!'

She turned from the King, knowing that however she tried she would never love him.

'Thou art too gentle, sweetheart!' The King leaned towards her and patted her arm, showing that he liked her gentleness, even though it might make her shed a tear for his enemies.

Often she thought of Thomas Culpepper who was in the retinue accompanying them. Often their eyes would meet, exchanging smiles. Jane Rochford noted this, and that peculiar twist of her character which had ever made her court danger though through doing so she could bring no gain to herself, made her say: 'Your cousin Culpepper is a handsome young man. He loves you truly. I see it there in his eyes. And methinks Your Majesty is not indifferent to him, for who could be to such a handsome boy! You never meet him. You are over-cautious. It could be arranged. . . .'

This was reminiscent of the old days of intrigue, and Catherine could not resist it. She felt that only could she endure Henry's caresses if she saw Thomas now and then. She carried in her mind every detail of Thomas's face so that when the King was with her, she could, in her imagination, put Thomas in his place, and so not show the repugnance to his caresses which she could not help but feel.

Derham came to her once or twice to write letters for her. He watched her with smouldering, passionate eyes, but she was not afraid of harm coming from Derham. He was devoted as ever, and though his jealousy was great, he would never do anything, if he could help it, to harm the Queen. Derham knew nothing of her love for Culpepper, and Catherine, not wishing to cause him pain, saw to it that he should not know, and now and then would throw him soft glances to show that she remembered all they had been to each other. In view of this Derham could not forbear to whisper to his friend Damport that he loved the Queen, and he was sure that if the King were dead he might marry her.

During that journey there were many meetings with Culpepper. Lady Rochford was in her element; she carried messages between the lovers; she listened at doors. 'The King will be in council for two hours more. It is safe for Culpepper to come to the apartment. . . .' Catherine did not know that her relations with Culpepper were becoming a sly joke throughout the court and were discussed behind hands with many a suppressed giggle.

When they were at Lincoln she all but surrendered to Culpepper. He would beg; she would hesitate; and then be firm in her refusals.

'I dare not!' wept Catherine.

'Ah! Why did you not fly with me when I asked it!'

'If only I had done so!'

'Shall we go on spoiling our lives, Catherine?'

'I cannot bear this sorrow, but never, never could I bear that harm should come to you through me.'

Thus it went on, but Catherine was firm. When she felt weak she would seem to feel the presence of Anne Boleyn begging her to take care, warning her to reflect on her poor cousin's fate.

Because no one showed that the love between them was known, they did not believe it was known, and they grew more and more reckless. There was a time at Lincoln when they were alone until two in the morning, feeling themselves safe because Lady Rochford was keeping guard. They revelled in their secret meetings with ostrich-like folly. As long as they denied themselves the satisfaction their love demanded, they felt safe. No matter that people all around them were aware of their intrigue. No matter that Cranmer was but waiting an opportunity.

On this occasion at Lincoln, Katharine Tylney and Margaret Morton had been loitering on the stairs outside the Queen's apartment in a fever of excitement lest the King should come unexpectedly, and they be involved.

'Jesus!' whispered Katharine Tylney as Margaret came gliding into the corridor, 'is not the Queen abed yet?'

Margaret, who a moment before had seen Culpepper emerge, answered: 'Yes, even now.' And the two exchanged glances of relief, shrugging their shoulders and smiling over the Queen's recklessness and frivolity, reminding each other of her behaviour at Lambeth.

Many such dangerous meetings took place, with Lady Rochford always at hand, the Queen's trusted attendant, always ready with suggestions and hints. Catherine had been indiscreet enough to write to Culpepper before this journey began. This was an indication of the great anxiety she felt for him, because Catherine never did feel happy with a pen, and to write even a few lines was a great effort to her. She had written this letter before the beginning of the tour when she and the King were moving about close to London and Culpepper was not with them. It was folly to write; and greater folly on Culpepper's part to keep the letter; but being in love and inspired by danger rather than deterred by it, they had done many foolish things and this was but one of them.

'I heartily recommend me unto you, praying you to send me word how that you do,' wrote Catherine. 'I did fear you were sick and I never longed for anything so much as to see you. It makes my heart to die when I think that I cannot always be in your company. Come to me when Lady Rochford be here for then I shall be best at leisure to be at your commandment...'

And such like sentences all written out laboriously in Catherine's untrained hand.

She lived through the days, waiting for a glimpse of Culpepper, recklessly, dangerously, while the foolish Lady Rochford sympathized and arranged meetings.

The King noticed nothing. He felt pleased; once more he was showing rebels what happened to those who went against their King. He could turn from the flattery of those who sought his good graces to the sweet, youthful charm of Catherine Howard.

'Never was man so happy in his wife!' he said; and he thought that when he returned he would have the nation sing a Te Deum, for at last the Almighty had seen fit to reward his servant with a perfect jewel of womanhood.

*　　*　　*

Cranmer was so excited he could scarcely make his plans. At last his chance had come. This was too much even for the King to ignore.

There was a man at court who was of little importance, but towards whom Cranmer had always had a kindly feeling. This man was a Protestant, stern and cold, a man who never laughed because he considered laughter sinful, a man who had the makings of a martyr, one who could find more joy in a hair-shirt than in a flagon of good wine. This man's name was John Lassells, a protégé of Cromwell's who had remained faithful to him; he preached eternal damnation for all those who did not accept the teachings of Martin Luther.

This John Lassells came to Cranmer with a story which set Cranmer's hopes soaring, that made him feel he could embrace the man.

'My lord,' said Lassells most humbly, 'there is on my conscience that which troubles me sorely.'

Cranmer listened half-heartedly, feeling this was doubtless some religious point the man wished explained.

'I tremble for what this may mean,' said Lassells, 'for it concerns Her Grace the Queen.'

Gone was Cranmer's lethargy; there was a flicker of fire in his eyes.

'My lord Archbishop, I have a sister Mary, and Mary being nurse to Lord William Howard's first wife, was after her death taken into the service of the Dowager Duchess of Norfolk.'

'Where the Queen was brought up,' said Cranmer eagerly.

'I asked my sister Mary why she did not sue for service with the Queen, for I saw that many who had been in the Dowager Duchess's household now held places at court. My sister's answer was most disturbing. "I will not," she said. "But I am very sorry for the Queen." I asked why, and she answered, "Marry, for she is both light in living and behaviour." I asked how so, and she did tell me a most alarming story.'

'Yes, yes?'

'There was one Francis Derham who had slept in bed with her for many nights, and another, Manox, had known her.'

'Derham!' cried Cranmer. 'Manox! They are both in the Queen's household.'

He questioned Lassells further, and when he had learned all the man had to tell, he dismissed him after telling him he had indeed done the King a great service.

Cranmer was busy, glad of the absence of the King to give him a free hand. He sent Southampton to question Mary Lassells. Manox was arrested and brought before him and Wriothesley. Derham went to the Tower. Cranmer was going to garner each grain he gleaned, and when they were laid side by side he doubted not he would have a good harvest. He waited impatiently for the return of the royal pair.

Henry was filled with satisfaction when he returned to Hampton Court. He was full of plans which he would lay before his confessor. A public thanksgiving should be prepared that the whole country might know, and thank God, that he had been blessed with a loving, dutiful and virtuous wife.

But Henry's satisfaction was shortlived. He was in the chapel at Hampton Court when Cranmer came to him; Cranmer's eyes were averted and in his hand he carried a paper.

'Most Gracious King,' said Cranmer, 'I fear to place this grave matter set out herein in your hands, and yet the matter being so grave I dare do naught else. I pray that Your Grace will read it when you are alone.'

Henry read the report on Catherine; his anger was terrible, but it was not directed against Catherine but those who had given evidence against her. He sent for Cranmer.

'This is forged!' he cried. 'This is not truthful! I have conceived such a constant opinion of her honesty that I know this!'

He paced up and down so that Cranmer's chicken heart was filled with fear. It was too soon. The King would not give up the Queen; rather he would destroy those who sought to destroy her.

'I do not believe this!' cried the King, but Cranmer had heard the quiver of doubt in his master's voice and rejoiced. 'But,' went on the King, 'I shall not be satisfied until the certainty is known to me.' He glowered at Cranmer. 'There must be an examination. And . . . no breath of scandal against the Queen.'

The King left Hampton Court, and Catherine was told to stay in her rooms. Her musicians were sent away and told that this was no time for music.

Over Hampton Court there fell a hush of horror like a dark curtain that shut away gaiety and laughter; thus it had been at Greenwich less then six years ago when Anne Boleyn had looked in vain for Brereton, Weston, Norris and Smeaton.

Catherine was chilled with horror; and when Cranmer with Norfolk, Audley, Sussex and Gardiner, came to her, she knew that the awful doom she had feared ever since she had become the King's wife was about to fall upon her.

* * *

Wriothesley questioned Francis Derham in his cell.

'You may as well tell the truth,' said Wriothesley, 'for others have already confessed it for you. You have spent a hundred nights naked in the bed of the Queen.'

'Before she was Queen,' said Derham.

'Ah! Before she was Queen. We will come to that later.

You admit that there were immoral relations between you and the Queen?'

'No,' said Derham.

'Come, come, we have ways of extracting the truth. There were immoral relations between you and the Queen.'

'They were not immoral. Catherine Howard and I regarded each other as husband and wife.'

Wriothesley nodded slowly.

'You called her "wife" before others?'

'Yes.'

'And you exchanged love tokens?'

'We did.'

'And some of the household regarded you as husband and wife?'

'That is so.'

'The Dowager Duchess and Lord William Howard regarded you as husband and wife?'

'No; they were ignorant of it.'

'And yet it was no secret.'

'No, but . . .'

'The entire household knew, with the exception of the Dowager Duchess and Lord William?'

'It was known among those with whom it was our custom to mix.'

'You went to Ireland recently, did you not?'

'I did.'

'And there were engaged in piracy?'

'Yes.'

'For which you deserve to hang, but no matter now. Did you not leave rather abruptly for Ireland?'

'I did.'

'Why?'

'Because Her Grace had discovered the relationship between Catherine and me.'

'Was there not another occasion when she discovered you with her granddaughter?'

'Yes.'

'It was in the maids' room and she entered and found you romping together, in arms kissing?'

516

He nodded.

'And what were Her Grace's reactions to that?'

'Catherine was beaten; I was warned.'

'That seems light punishment.'

'Her Grace believed it to be but a romp.'

'And you joined the Queen's household soon after her marriage with the King? Mr Derham, I suggest that you and the Queen continued to live immorally, in fact in adultery, after the Queen's marriage with His Majesty.'

'That is not true.'

'Is it not strange that you should join the Queen's household, and receive special favours, and remain in the rôle of Queen's attendant only?'

'It does not seem strange.'

'You swear that no immoral act ever took place between you and the Queen after her marriage with the King?'

'I swear it.'

'Come, Mr Derham. Be reasonable. Does it seem logical to you in view of what you once were to the Queen?'

'I care not what it may seem. I only know that no act of immorality ever took place between us since her marriage.'

Wriothesley sighed. 'You try my patience sorely,' he said, and left him.

He returned in half an hour accompanied by two burly men.

'Mr Derham,' said the King's secretary softly, 'I would ask you once more to confess to adultery with the Queen.'

'I cannot confess what is not so.'

'Then I must ask you to accompany us.'

Derham was no coward; he knew the meaning of that summons; they were going to torture him. He pressed his lips together, and silently prayed for the courage he would have need of. He had led an adventurous life of late; he had faced death more than once when he had fought on the rough sea for booty. He had taken his chances recklessly as the inevitable milestones on the road of adventure; but the cold-blooded horror of the torture chamber was different.

In the corridors of the Tower was the sickening smell of death; there was dried blood on the floor of the torture rooms. If he admitted adultery, what would they do to Catherine? They could not hurt her for what was done before. They could not call that treason, even though she had deceived the King into thinking her a virgin. They could not hurt Catherine if he refused to say what they wished. He would not swerve. He would face all the torture in the world rather than harm her with the lies they wished him to tell. She had not loved him since his return from Ireland; but he had continued to love her. He would not lie.

They were stripping him of his clothes. They were putting him on the rack. Wriothesley, one of the cruellest men in all England, was standing over him implacably.

'You are a fool, Derham. Why not confess and have done!'

'You would have me lie?' asked Derham.

'I would have you save yourself this torture.'

The ropes were about his wrists; the windlasses were turned. He tried to suppress his cries, for it was more cruel than his wildest imaginings. He had not known there could be such pain. He shrieked and they stopped.

'Come, Derham. You committed adultery with the Queen.'

'No, no.'

Wriothesley's cruel lips were pressed together; he nodded to the tormentors. It began again. Derham fainted and they thrust the vinegar brush under his nose.

'Derham, you fool. Men cannot endure much of this.'

That was true; but there were men who would not lie to save themselves from death, even if it must be death on the rack; and Derham, the pirate, was one of them.

When it would have been death to continue with the torture they carried him away; he was fainting, maimed and broken; but he had told them nothing.

*　　*　　*

When the Dowager Duchess heard what had happened at Hampton Court she shut herself into her chamber and was sick with fear. The Queen under lock and key! Derham in the Tower! She remembered her sorrow when Anne was sent to the Tower; but now side by side with sorrow went fear, and out of these two was born panic.

She must not stay idle. She must act. Had she not assured His Majesty of Catherine's purity and goodness! And yet had she not beaten Catherine for her lewdness! Had she not warned Derham first, and had he not, later, run away to escape her anger when it had been discovered that he and Catherine had been living as husband and wife in her house!

She paced up and down her room. What if they questioned her! Her teeth chattered. She pictured the terrible end of the Countess of Salisbury, and saw herself running from the headsman's axe. She was rich; her house was chock-full of treasure. Was not the King always ready to despatch those who were rich, that their goods might fall into his hands! She pictured the Duke's sly eyes smiling at her. 'That wench will go to the block!' he had said; and she had berated him, telling him he had better take care how he spoke of the Queen. Her stepson was her most deadly enemy and now he would have a chance of working openly against her.

She must waste no time. She must act. She went down to the great hall and called a confidential servant to her. She told him to go to Hampton Court, glean the latest news, and come back to her as fast as he could. She waited in mental anguish for his return, but when he came he could only tell her what she knew already. The Queen and Derham were accused of misconduct, and some of the Queen's attendants were accused of being in the guilty secret.

She thought of Derham's friend Damport, who doubtless knew as much of Derham's secrets as any. She had some hazy plan of bribing him to silence on all he knew.

'I hear Derham is taken,' she said plaintively, 'and also the Queen; what is the matter?'

Damport said he thought Derham had spoken with indiscretion to a gentleman usher.

Her Grace's lips quivered; she said that she greatly feared that in consequence of evil reports some harm should fall the Queen. She looked fearfully at Damport and said she would like to give him a little gift. Thereupon she presented him with ten pounds. It was stupid and clumsy, but she was too frightened to know what she did. She murmured something about his saying nothing of Catherine Howard's friendship with Derham.

Her fear becoming hysterical, the Dowager Duchess paced from room to room. What if Catherine and Derham had exchanged letters when he had gone away to Ireland!

There were here in her house some trunks and coffers of Derham's, for before he had gone to court she had taken him back into her house; several of the trunks were those which he had left behind when he fled. He had not removed them when he went to court, for his lodging there was not large enough to accommodate them. What if in Derham's trunks and coffers there was some incriminating evidence?

Her legs shaking, her voice high with hysteria, she called to some of her most trusted servants. She told them that she feared a visit from the King's ambassadors at any moment; the Queen was in danger; all Derham's belongings must be searched for fear there might be something in them to incriminate the Queen; she implored her attendants to show their loyalty and help her.

There was a great bustling throughout the house; trunks were forced open; coffers were rifled. There were found some of those letters written by Jane Bulmer on Catherine's behalf, and which had been preserved by Derham; of these there was made a bonfire; the Duchess even destroyed articles which she suspected had been gifts from Catherine to Derham.

When this work was done she retired to her chamber, feeling old and very weary. But there was no rest for her. A knocking on her door heralded the advent of fresh trouble, the worst possible trouble.

'His Grace the Duke is below,' said her frightened maid, 'and he demands to see you immediately.'

❈ ❈ ❈

Catherine, facing those five dreaded men, was numb with terror. Her limbs trembled so much, and her countenance was so wild, that they thought she would lose her reason. She had had a wild fit of laughing which had ended in weeping; she was more hysterical than had been her cousin, for Anne had not had a terrible example in her mind all the time.

There was one thing which terrified her beyond all others, and gave her great agony of mind. She could think of no way of warning Culpepper. She was almost mad with anxiety on his behalf.

Norfolk's cold eyes mocked her, seeming to say – So you thought yourself so clever, did you! You are another such as your cousin Anne Boleyn. Oh, did ever a man have such a pair of nieces!

Her uncle was more terrifying than the other four.

'Compose yourself! Compose yourself!' said Norfolk. 'Think not to drown your guilt in tears!'

Cranmer seemed much kinder; he was ever cautious, knowing well the King's great tenderness for her; he was determined to go cautiously for fear he had to retrace his steps. It was to Cranmer whom she would talk if she talked at all.

In his soft voice he told her how grieved he was that this should have befallen her. Francis Derham had confessed to having lived with her as her husband. Manox had also known her. It would be better for her to tell the truth, for the King, heartbroken at her deception, was inclined towards leniency.

Her answers were scarcely audible. She caught her breath every time one of them spoke, terrified that she would hear Culpepper's name. But when they did not speak of him, she came to the conclusion that they knew nothing of her love for him and his for her; and this so lightened her spirits that she seemed suddenly happy. She confessed readily to what she had done before her marriage to the King. Yes, Derham had called her wife; she had called him husband. Yes . . . yes. . . .

Norfolk, with never a thought of his own adultery with Bess Holland, tut-tutted in horror at such wickedness; but in comparison with him, the others seemed almost kind, and her hysteria was passing. They knew nothing against Thomas. They could send her to the block as they had her cousin, but Thomas Culpepper should not suffer through his love for her.

The council of five left her, and Cranmer prepared a report of the examination that he might show it to the King.

Henry was awaiting the report in feverish impatience. He could not hide his agitation. He had changed since he had read that paper containing the news which Cranmer had declared he was too moved to give his master by word of mouth. His usually purple face had gone a shade of grey the colour of parchment, and the veins, usually so full of rich red blood, now looked like brown lines drawn upon it.

Cranmer's voice took on those pained tones he could always assume on certain occasions. He talked of the abominable, base, and carnal life of the Queen; voluptuous and vicious were the words he used to describe her; and this woman had led the King to love her, had arrogantly coupled herself in marriage with him.

Norfolk watched the King and Cranmer uneasily. After all the wanton wench was his niece, and it was he who had helped to recommend her to the King. Norfolk was worried. He was possessed of great worldly riches. When a queen was found guilty of treason, members of her family often found themselves in like trouble. He had spoken with disgust of his niece whenever he could; he had whispered slander about her; his great wish was to dissociate himself from her. He was grieved, he told all; his house was plunged into deepest mourning because it had produced two such wanton and abandoned women as Anne Boleyn and Catherine Howard. He said he thought the only just fate that should be meted out to Catherine Howard was death by burning. He would be there to savour every one of her screams as she had a foretaste of the torment that would be eternally hers. His pity, he had announced, went to the King whom he loved and whom he hoped would not hold him in any way responsible for the vile creatures his house had produced to deceive his most loved monarch. He had quarrelled with his stepmother, whom all knew had had the confidence of the Queen; all were aware that he had never been a friend of that old woman nor of her vile granddaughter.

The King could do nothing but sit leaden-eyed. His dream was over; reality faced him. He had been deceived in her. She was not his jewel of womanhood; she was not entirely his. Others had enjoyed her; he was tortured by thoughts of them. He had loved her; she was to have been his last wife; she was to have made all his miserable matrimonial engagements worth while. He could not bear it. He put his hands to his face and tears gushed from his eyes.

Chapuys summed up the King's feelings when writing to his master. 'This King,' he wrote. 'has wonderfully felt the case of the Queen, his wife, and has certainly shown greater sorrow at her loss than at the faults, loss or divorce of his preceding wives. It is like the case of the woman who cried more bitterly at the loss of her tenth husband than at the deaths of all the others together, though they had all been good men, but it was because she had never buried one of them before, without being sure of the next; and as yet this King has formed no plan or preference.'

That was true. At the height of his jealousy of Anne, Jane had been waiting to comfort him; but in between Jane and Catherine he had had the disappointing experience of Anne of Cleves. He had lost Catherine and he felt cheated, since there was no beautiful and much desired young woman waiting to console him. And indeed he wanted consolation from no one but Catherine herself. He was no longer a rambling bull; he was a staid domesticated animal who wished only to spend his last days in peace with the mate he loved.

So he wept bitterly and unashamedly before his council, and Cranmer quaked to see those tears, for it seemed to him that there was a possibility of the King's trying to hush up this matter and take back the Queen. 'The faults have been committed,' those tears seemed to be telling Cranmer. 'Let be!'

But what of Cranmer if Catherine Howard regained her influence with the King? Cranmer knew of two ways to stop this. He could have the scandal bruited abroad. How would Henry feel if those foreign princes knew that Henry had kept a wife who had deceived him? Spread the news abroad then; make it hard for him to take her back. There was another and even more satisfactory alternative: Discover that she had had a lover even as she had loved with and been loved by the King.

*   *   *

Damport was arrested. He had been the greatest friend of Derham's; he had been in the Dowager Duchess's household; he had recently received a sum of money from Her Grace.

Damport was sweating with fear.

'My lords, I know nothing . . . nothing. . . .'

It is a terrible predicament for a man who knows nothing and yet must tell something. What could he tell them? Nothing! Nothing, but that which they knew already.

'Why did the Dowager Duchess of Norfolk give you money?'

'I know not! I know not!'

There was nothing they could extract from this young man but what they already knew, and Cranmer himself had given orders that they must get confessions.

'Come, Damport, you were the special friend of this man Derham.'

'Yes, yes, yes . . .'

'It will be much better for you if you talk.'

'But I swear I know nothing . . . nothing. . . .'

They led him down to the torture chamber where Derham had gone before him, where Mark Smeaton had moaned in agony.

'Come, Damport. What is it to you? You have naught to lose. We do but ask for truth.'

Damport's hair was wet on his forehead; sweat ran down his nose; he could but stare open-mouthed at those vile instruments; he could but retch from the stench of death.

'Why, Damport, that is a very fine set of teeth you have, and doubtless you are very proud of them!'

Damport looked about him as though seeking escape from such a situation, but the dark and slimy walls had no suggestion to offer; there was nothing to learn from them except that within them men had descended for many many years to the level of the lowest animals. It seemed to Damport that the evil shadows that hung about the dim chamber were the ghosts of those who, having died in agony, had returned to watch the anguish of those doomed to follow them. These cruel tormentors, these examiners, felt not the presence of those sad ghosts; cruelty was commonplace to them; they had learned indifference to the groans of tortured men; one had but to look into their brute faces to know this.

Damport whimpered: 'An I knew aught, I would tell it.'

'We were saying those teeth were fine, Damport. Let us see whether they will look as fine when the brakes have done with them!'

It seemed that his head was being torn from his body; he felt a sickening crunch; his jerkin was wet and he felt its damp warmness on his chest; he smelt his own blood, and swooned. Words were like the beating of the blunt end of an axe on his head.

'Come, Damport, you know Derham committed adultery with the Queen.'

They had torn out most of his teeth and all he could remember was that Derham had said that if the King were dead he would marry Catherine Howard. He told them this, fearing further torture. They were disappointed, but the man was bleeding badly and he could not stand for the pain; and his mouth was so swollen that if he would, he could not speak.

They led him from the torture chamber. They would have to tell Cranmer that they could get nothing from Damport and believed he had nothing to tell. Cranmer would be filled with that cold fury that was more terrifying than the hot rage of some men.

From Manox they could get nothing of interest. There

was not sufficient evidence against him; he had been one of the humblest musicians, and there was really nothing against him; he had not been in the Queen's presence, even while her ladies were with her. As for his relations with her at Horsham and Lambeth he was ready enough to talk of these. He was such an obvious rogue, that torture would be wasted on him.

But Cranmer was not angry. He was in fact delighted. The King of France had sent condolences to Henry, telling him how grieved he was to hear news of the faults of her, so recently his Queen. That was good; but there was better still.

Why, thought Cranmer, should the Queen wish to surround herself with those who had helped her in her wantonness before her marriage, if it was not to help her in the same capacity after marriage? He would examine thoroughly all those women at the court of the Queen who had been in the service of the Dowager Duchess of Norfolk. There were several of them – Katharine Tylney, Margaret Morton, Jane Bulmer, and two named Wilkes and Baskerville being the chief among them. It was from Katharine Tylney and Margaret Morton that Cranmer learned of a certain night at Lincoln; Thomas Culpepper's name was mentioned. Lady Rochford had arranged interviews. There had been several meetings before the tour to the north and during it.

'Bring in Culpepper!' ordered Cranmer, and they brought in Culpepper.

He was a bold youth, fearless and courageous, such as Francis Derham.

A plague on courageous, gallant men! thought Cranmer, the coward. What trouble they give us!

Head held high, Culpepper admitted his love for the Queen, admitted that he would have married her if he could. No wrong, he said, had passed between them.

Cranmer laughed at that. He must admit that wrong had passed between them! How else could Cranmer be sure of enraging this love-sick King.

'Rack him until he confesses!' he ordered.

Derham had been a pirate; he had faced death more than once, and it held less horror for him than for a man like

Cranmer who had never seen it come close to himself; it was with Culpepper as with Derham. Culpepper was a wild boy and had ever been a plague to his father; he was a rebellious, unruly boy with a taste for adventure and getting into trouble. There was one quality he had in common with Derham and that was bravery.

They put him on the rack. He endured that excruciating pain, that most exquisite of tortures, pressing his lips firmly together, and only now and then, and most shamefacedly, let out a groan of pain. He even smiled on the rack and tried to remember her face, anxious for him. 'Oh, take care, Thomas. Take care lest thou shouldst suffer for love of me.'

He thought she was with him, talking to him now. In his thoughts he answered her. 'Sweet Catherine, dost think I would do aught that might hurt thee? Thou shalt never suffer through me, Catherine. Let them do what they will.'

'Culpepper! Culpepper, you young fool! Will you speak?'

He gasped, for the pain was such as to make speech difficult.

'I have spoken.'

'Again! Again! Work faster, you fools! He *has* to confess!'

But he did not confess, and they carried his poor suffering body away most roughly, for they had worked themselves weary over him in vain.

* * *

The King's rage was terrible when he heard that Culpepper was involved. Rage, misery, jealousy, self-pity, humiliation maddened him. He wept; he shut himself up; he would see no one. This . . . to happen to the King of England.

His face was clothed in grief; his sick leg throbbed with pain; his youth was gone, taking with it his hope of happiness. He was an old sick man and Culpepper was a young and beautiful boy. He himself had loved to watch the grace of Culpepper; he had favoured the lad; he had winked at his wickedness and had said that what happened in Kent need not be remembered at court. He had loved that boy –

loved him for his wit and his beauty; and this same boy, fair of face and clean of limb had looked frequently on the unsightly weeping sore on the royal leg, and doubtless had laughed that all the power and riches in England could not buy youth and health such as he enjoyed.

Mayhap, thought the King angrily, he is less beautiful now his graceful limbs have been tortured; The King laughed deep sobbing laughter. Culpepper should die the death of a traitor; he should die ignobly; indignities should be piled upon his traitor's body; and when his head was on London Bridge, would she feel the same desire to kiss his lips? The King tormented himself with such thoughts of them together that could only come to a very sensual man, and the boiling blood in his head seemed as if it would burst it.

'She never had such delight in her lovers,' he said, 'as she shall have torture in death!'

Catherine, in those apartments which had been planned for Anne Boleyn and used so briefly by Jane, and briefer still by Anne of Cleves, was in such a state of terror that those who guarded her feared for her reason. She would fling herself onto her bed, sobbing wildly; then she would arise and walk about her room, asking questions about her death; she would have those who had witnessed the death of her cousin come to her and tell her how Anne had died; she would weep with sorrow, and then her laughter would begin again for it seemed ironical that Anne's fate should be hers. She was crazy with grief when she heard Culpepper was taken. She prayed incoherently. 'Let them not harm him. Let me die, but let him be spared.'

If I could but see the King, she thought, surely I could make him listen to me. Surely he would spare Thomas, if I asked him.

'Could I have speech with His Majesty? Just one moment!' she begged.

'Speech with His Majesty!' They shook their heads. How could that be! His Majesty was incensed by her conduct; he would not see her. And what would Cranmer say, Cranmer who would not know real peace until Catherine Howard's head was severed from her body!

She remembered the King as he had always been to her, indulgent and loving; even when he had reprimanded her for too much generosity, even when he, angered by the acts of traitors, had listened to her pleas for leniency, he had never shown a flicker of anger. Surely now he would listen to her.

She made plans. If she could but get to the King, if she could but elude her jailors, she would know how to make herself irresistible.

She was calm now, watching for an opportunity. One quick movement of the hand to open the door, and then she would dash down the back stairs; she would watch and wait and pray for help.

The opportunity came when she knew him to be at mass in the chapel. She would run to him there, fling herself onto her knees, implore his compassion, promise him life-long devotion if he would but spare her and Culpepper and Derham.

Those who were guarding her, pleased with her calmness, were sitting in a window seat, conversing among themselves of the strange happenings at court. She moved swiftly towards the door; she paused, threw a glance over her shoulder, saw that their suspicions had not been aroused, turned the handle, and was on the dark staircase before she heard the exclamation of dismay behind her.

Fleet with fear she ran. She came to the gallery; she could hear the singing in the chapel. The King was there. She would succeed because she must. Culpepper was innocent. He must not die.

Her attendants were close behind her, full of determination that her plan should not succeed, fully aware that no light punishment would be meted out to them should they let her reach the King. They caught at her gown; they captured her just as she reached the chapel door. They dragged her back to the apartment. Through the gallery her screams rang out like those of a mad creature, mingling uncannily with the singing in the chapel.

529

A few days later she was taken from Hampton Court; she sailed down the river to a less grand prison at Sion House.

*   *   *

The Dowager Duchess lay in bed. She said to her attendants: 'I cannot get up. I am too ill. I feel death approaching fast.'

She was sick and her disease was fear. She had heard that Culpepper and Derham had been found guilty of treason. She knew that they had had no true trial, for how could men be sentenced to death for what could not be proved, and for that which they would not admit under the vilest torture! But these two brave men had not convinced their torturers that they would not eventually respond to the persuasions of the rack, and even after their sentence, daily they were taken to the torture chambers to suffer fresh agonies. But not once did either of them swerve from their protestations of the Queen's innocence since her marriage.

Never in the Dowager Duchess's memory, had men been tried like this before. For those accused with Anne Boleyn there had been a trial, farcical as it was. Culpepper and Derham had been taken to Guildhall before the Lord Mayor but on either side of the Lord Mayor had sat Suffolk and Audley. Sentence had been quickly pronounced, and the two were judged guilty and condemned to die the horrible lingering death assigned to traitors.

The Dowager Duchess thought of these matters as she lay abed, staring up in terror when she heard the least sound from below. She knew inventories had been made of her goods, and she knew they could not fail to arouse the covetousness of the King, for they were great in value.

What hope had she of escaping death? Even the Duke, old soldier that he was, had shown that he thought the only safe thing for a Howard to do was retreat. He had gone into voluntary retirement, hoping that the King would forget him awhile, until the fortunes of the Howard family were in a happier state.

And as she lay there, that which she dreaded came to

pass. Wriothesley, accompanied by the Earl of Southampton, had come to see her.

Her face was yellow when they entered; they thought she was not malingering but really suffering from some terrible disease. They dared not approach too near the bed, the fear of plague being ever in their minds.

'We but called to see how Your Grace does,' said Wriothesley artfully, never taking his eyes from her face. 'Do not distress yourself, this is but a visit; we would condole with you on the sad happenings which have befallen your family.'

The colour returned slightly to her face. The men could see hope springing up. They exchanged glances. Their little ruse had succeeded, for she had always been a foolish woman ready to believe what she wished rather than what she should have known to be the truth; and she could not hide the wonderful feeling that after all she might be safe. The Dowager Duchess, these two men knew, suffered from no plague, but only from the qualms of a guilty conscience.

They questioned her. She wept and talked incoherently.

She knew nothing . . . nothing! she assured them. She had thought the attraction between Derham and her granddaughter but an affection between two who were united by the bonds of kinship. She had not thought to look for wickedness in that. But had she not found them together, in arms kissing? Had she thought that meet and proper in her whom the King had chosen to honour? Oh, but Catherine had been such a child, and there had been no harm. . . no harm that she had known of. But had she not been told of these things? Had she not beaten the girl, and had not Derham fled for his life?

'I knew it not! I knew it not!' she sobbed.

Wriothesley's cunning eyes took in each rich detail of the room.

'Methinks,' he said, 'Your Grace is well enough to be transported to the Tower.'

* * *

At Tyburn a crowd had gathered to see the death of the Queen's lovers. Culpepper first. How could the Queen have loved such a man? His face was emaciated; his lips drawn down; his skin like bad cheese; his eyes had sunk into black hollows. The people shuddered, knowing that they saw not the Queen's lover, but what the tormentors had made of him. Lucky Culpepper, because he was of noble birth, and was to be but beheaded!

Derham could say Lucky Culpepper! He was of not such noble birth, and although he begged the King for mercy, which meant that he asked to die by the axe or the rope, the King was in no mood for mercy. He saw no reason why sentence should not be carried out as ordained by the judges.

Derham's eyes were dazed with pain; he had suffered much since his arrest; he had not known there could be such cruelty in men; truly, he had known of those grim chambers below the fortress of the Tower of London, but to know by hearsay and to know by experience were two very different matters. He did not wish to live, for if he did he would never forget the gloomy dampness of grey stone walls, the terrible shrieks of agony, pain and the smell of blood and vinegar, and those awful great instruments, like monsters without thought, grimly obedient to the evil will of men.

This he had suffered and he had to suffer yet; he had been submerged in pain, but mayhap he had not yet tested its depth. Nature was more merciful than men, providing for those who suffered great pain such blessedness as fainting; but men were cruel and brought their victims out of faints that the pain might start again.

He clung to the glorious memory of unconsciousness which must inevitably follow an excess of pain. There was another joy he knew, and it was this: He had not betrayed Catherine. They might kill Catherine, but not a drop of her blood should stain his hands. He had loved her; his intentions towards her had been ever honest. In the depth of his passion he had been unable to resist her; but that was natural; that was no sin. He had called her wife and she had called him husband, and it had been the dearest wish of his life that he should marry her. Now, here at Tyburn with the most miserable ordeal yet before him, he could feel lightness of spirit, for his end could not be far off, however they would revive him that he might suffer more. These men, whose cruel eyes were indifferent to his suffering, these monsters who were but hirelings of that spiteful murderer who stood astride all England and subdued her with torture and death, were to be pitied, as was Henry himself. For one day they must die, and they would not die as Derham died; they would not know his agony of body, but neither would they know his peace of mind.

The noose was about his neck; he swung in mid-air. There was a brief jolting pain, and the next he knew was that he was lying on hard wood and he could not breathe; he was choking; but they were tending him solicitously, that he might return to life and suffer more pain.

Now he was sufficiently recovered to smell the Tyburn crowd, to hear a faint hum of voices, to feel a man's hands on his body, to see a flash of steel, to be aware of agony. He felt the knife cold against his flesh. A searing hot pain ran through him. He writhed and screamed, but he seemed to hear a voice close to his ear murmur: 'Soon now, Derham. Not long now, Derham. It cannot last. Remember they are helping you out of this wicked world.'

He could smell the smoke. 'Oh, God!' he moaned, and twisted and groaned afresh in his agony. He could smell his burning entrails. A thousand white hot knives were surely being plunged into him. He tried to raise himself. He tried to sob out to them to have pity. He could not speak. He could do nothing but endure, but give his tortured body up to a million gnawing devils. He had touched pain's depth, for there was never agony such as that endured by men who were hanged by the neck, and then revived that they might feel the knife that ripped their bodies, that they might feel the agony of their burning entrails.

Blessed blackness closed in on him, and the stroke of the axe which severed his head was like a gentle caress.

* * *

Jane Rochford was back in the Tower. She had been

533

calm enough when they took her there, but now her eyes were wild, her hair hung loose about her face; she did not know why she was there; she talked to those who were not there.

'George! You here, George!' She went into shrieks of crazy laughter. 'So we meet here, George. It is so just that we should . . . so just.'

She paused as though listening to the conversation of another; then she went into wild laughter that was followed by deep sobbing. Lady Rochford had gone mad.

She looked from her window and saw the Thames.

She said: 'Why should you come in your pomp and I be here a prisoner? You have everything; I have nothing. The King loves you. George loves you. Oh, George, do not stand there in the shadows. Where is your head, George? Oh, yes, I remember. They took it off.'

There was none who dared stay with her. It was uncanny to hear her talking to those who were not there. It was eerie to watch her eyes as she looked into space.

'Is it the ghost of George Boleyn she talks to?' it was whispered. 'Is he really there and we see him not? Is he haunting her because she sent him to his death?'

Her shrieks terrified all those who heard them, but after a while a calmness settled on her, though the madness was still in her eyes.

She said quietly: 'He has come to mock me now. He says that all my wickedness has but led me to the block. He puts his hands to his head and lifts it off to show me that he is not really George but George's ghost. He says the axe that killed him was wielded by me and it was called vindictiveness. And he says that the axe that will kill me will be wielded by me also and it is called folly. He says I am twice a murderess because I killed him and now I kill myself.'

She flung herself against the window seat, her hands held up in supplication to an empty space.

Her attendants watched her fearfully; they were frightened by the uncanny ways of the mad.

* * *

534

Out of Sion House and down the river to the Tower passed the Queen's barge. She was composed now and looked very beautiful in her gown of black velvet. She thanked God that darkness had fallen and that she might not see the decomposing, fly-pestered heads of the men who had loved her. The suspense was over. Thomas was dead; Francis was dead; there but remained that Catherine should die. She thought with deep compassion of her poor old grandmother who was suffering imprisonment in the Tower. She thought of Manox and Damport and Lord William, who, with members of her family and her grandmother's household had come under suspicion through her. She had heard that Mary Lassells had been commended for her honesty in bringing the case against the Queen to light; she had heard that the King, whose grief and rage had been great, was now recovering, and that he was allowing himself to be amused with entertainments devised by the most beautiful ladies of the court.

Catherine felt calm now, resenting none except perhaps her uncle Norfolk, who now, to save himself, was boasting that it was due to him that the old Dowager Duchess had been brought to her present state. For him, Catherine could feel little but contempt; she remembered her grandmother's telling her how cruel he had been to Anne Boleyn.

Lady Rochford was with Catherine; her madness had left her for awhile though it would keep returning, and it was never known when she would think she saw visions. But there was some comfort for Catherine in having Jane Rochford with her, for she had been a witness of, and participator in, Anne's tragedy. She would talk of that sad time which was but six years ago, and Catherine gained courage in hearing how Anne had nobly conducted herself even to the block.

Sir John Gage, who had taken the place of Sir William Kingston as Constable of the Tower, came to her on the second day in the fortress.

'I come to ask that you prepare yourself for death,' he told her solemnly.

She tried to be brave but she could not. She was not quite

535

twenty years old, so young, so beautiful and in love with life; she was overtaken with hysteria, and wept continually and with such violence as was verging on madness.

In the streets people were murmuring against the King.

'What means this? Another Queen – and this time little more than a child – to go to the block!'

'It is whispered that she has never done aught against even her enemies.'

'Is it not strange that a man should be so cursed in his wives?'

Gage returned to her and told her she would die the next day.

She said: 'I am ready!' And she asked that they should bring the block to her that she might practise laying her head upon it.

'My cousin died most bravely I hear. I would follow her example. But she was a great lady and I fear I am not, nor ever were. What she could do naturally, I must practise.'

It was a strange request but he could not deny it, and the block was brought to her room, where she had them place it in the centre thereof, and graciously she walked to it, looking so young and innocent that it was as though she played some child's game of executions. She laid her head upon it, and kept it there a long time so that the wood was wet with her tears.

She said she was tired and would sleep awhile, and she fell into a deep, peaceful sleep almost as soon as she lay down. In sleep, her auburn hair fell into disorder, her brow was smooth and untroubled; her mouth smiling.

She dreamed she saw her cousin Anne who caressed her as she had done when she was a baby, and bid her be of good cheer for the death was easy. A sharp subtle pain and then peace. But Catherine could not be reassured, for it seemed to her that though she was innocent of adultery, she was in some measure to blame because of what had happened before her marriage. But her cousin continued to soothe her, saying: 'Nay, I was more guilty than you, for I was ambitious and proud, and hurt many, while you never hurt any but yourself.'

She was comforted, and clung to her dream. She knew now that she, like Anne, was innocent of any crime deserving of death. Anne had been murdered; she was about to be. But the death was quick and there was nothing to fear.

In the early morning, when they aroused her, she said almost calmly: 'I had forgotten what the day was. Now I know. Today I am to die.'

*   *   *

She walked with that slow dignity, which she had rehearsed last evening in her room, to the spot before the church where, six years before, Anne had died. She was dressed in black velvet, and was very pale. Her eyes were wide, and she tried to believe she saw her cousin, smiling at her from beyond the haze through which she herself must step. She thought as she walked, I must die like a queen, as Anne died.

She was accompanied by Jane Rochford who was to die with her. Jane's dignity was as complete as that of the Queen. Her eyes were calm, and all the madness had passed from her now; she could face death gladly, for it seemed to her that only by dying could she expiate the sin she had committed against her husband.

The early morning February air was cold and river-damp; the scene was ghostly. Catherine looked for her uncle's face among those of the people gathered there to see her die, and felt a rush of gratitude to know she would be spared seeing him there.

She muttered a little prayer for her grandmother. She would not pray for Thomas and Francis for they were now at peace. Had Anne felt this strange lightening of the heart when her death had been but a moment away; had she felt this queer feeling which had a touch of exultation in it?

She said she would speak a few words. Tears were in the eyes of many who beheld her, for she had none of that haughtiness which had characterized her tragic cousin. In her black velvet gown she looked what she was, a very young girl, innocent of any crime, whose tragedy was that she had had the misfortune to be desired by a ruthless man whose power was absolute. Some remembered that though Anne had been found guilty by a picked jury, she had had an opportunity of defending herself, and this she had done with a clarity, dignity and obvious truthfulness so that all unprejudiced posterity must believe in her innocence; but little Catherine Howard had had no such opportunity; contrary to English law she would be executed without an open trial, and there was but one word for such an execution, and that the ugly one of murder. Some must ask themselves what manner of man was this King of theirs, who twice in six years had sent a young wife to the block! They remembered that this Henry was the first King of England to shed women's blood on the block and burn them at the stake. Was the King's life so moral, they must ask themselves, that he dared express such horror at the frailty of this child?

But she was speaking, and her voice was so low that it was difficult to hear her, and as she spoke tears started from her eyes and ran down her smooth cheeks, for she was speaking of her lover Culpepper, the grisly spectacle of whose head all might see when crossing London Bridge.

She was trying to make these people understand her love for that young man, but she could not tell them how she had met and loved him when at Hollingbourne he had first come into her lonely life.

'I loved Culpepper,' she said, and she tried to tell them how he had urged her not to marry the King. 'I would rather have him for husband than be mistress of the world. . . . And since the fault is mine, mine also is the suffering, and my great sorrow is that Culpepper should have to die through me.'

Her voice faltered; now her words grew fainter and the headsman looked about him, stricken with sorrow at what he must do, for she was so young, but a child, and hardened as he was, it moved him deeply that his should be the hand to strike off her head.

She turned her brimming eyes to him and begged he would not delay. She cried: 'I die a queen, but I would rather die the wife of Culpepper. God have mercy on my soul. Good people . . . I beg you pray for me. . . .'

She fell to her knees and laid her head on the block not so neatly as she had done it in her room, but in such a way as to make many turn away and wipe their eyes.

She was praying when the headsman, with a swift stroke, let fall the axe.

Her attendants, their eyes blinded with tears, rushed forward to cover the mutilated little body with a black cloth, and to carry it away where it might be buried in the chapel, close to that spot where lay Anne Boleyn.

There was none to feel much pity for Lady Rochford. This gaunt woman was a striking contrast to the lovely young Queen. Jane mounted the scaffold like a pilgrim who has, after much tribulation, reached the end of a journey.

She spoke to the watching crowd and said that she was guiltless of the crime for which she was paying this doleful penalty; but she deserved to die, and she believed she was dying as a punishment for having contributed to the death of her husband by her false accusation of Queen Anne Boleyn. Almost with exultation she laid her head on the block.

'She is mad,' said the watchers. 'None but the insane could die so joyfully.'

Jane was smiling after the axe had fallen and her blood gushed forth to mingle with that of the murdered Queen.

* * *

In his palace at Greenwich, the King stood looking over the river. He felt himself to be alone and unloved. He had lost Catherine. Her mutilated body was now buried beside that of another woman whom he had loved and whom he had killed as he had now killed Catherine.

He was afraid. He would always be afraid. Ghosts would haunt his life . . . myriads of ghosts, all the men and women whose blood he had caused to be shed. There were so many that he could not remember them all, although among their number there were a few he would never forget. Buckingham. Wolsey. More. Fisher. Montague. Exeter and the old Countess of Salisbury. Cromwell. These, he could tell his conscience he had destroyed for England's sake. But there were others he had tried harder to forget. Weston. Brereton. Norris. Smeaton. Derham. Culpepper. George Boleyn. Catherine . . . and Anne.

He thought of Anne whom he had once loved so passionately; never had he loved one as he had her; nor ever would he; for his love for Catherine had been an old man's selfish love, the love of a man who is done with roving; but his love for Anne had had all the excitement of the chase, all the urgency of passionate desire; all the tenderness, romance and dreams of an idyll.

A movement beside him startled him and the hair was damp on his forehead, for it seemed to him that Anne was standing beside him. A second glance told him that it was but an image conjured up by the guilty mind of a murderer, for it was not Anne who stood beside him, but Anne's daughter. There were often times when she reminded him of her mother. Of all his children he loved her best because she was the most like him; she was also like her mother. There were times when she angered him; but then, her mother had angered him, and he had loved her. He loved Elizabeth, Elizabeth of the fiery hair and the spirited nature and the quick temper. She would never be the dark-browed beauty that her mother had been; she was tawny-red like her father. He felt sudden anger sweep over him. Why, oh, why had she not been born a boy!

She did not speak to him, but stood quite still beside him, her attention caught and held, for a great ship – his greatest ship – was sailing towards the mouth of the river, and she was watching it, her eyes round with appreciation. He glowed with pride and warmed further towards her because she so admired the ships he had caused to be built.

To contemplate that ship lifted his spirits. He needed to lift his spirits, for he had been troubled, and to think one sees a ghost is unnerving to a man of deep-rooted superstitions. He found himself wondering about this man who was Henry of England, who to him had always seemed such a mighty figure, so right in all that he did.

He was a great king; he had done much for England, for he *was* England. He was a murderer; he knew this now and then; he knew it as he stood looking over the river, Anne's daughter beside him. He had murdered Anne whom he had loved best, and he had murdered Catherine whom he had also loved; but England he had begun to lift to greatness, because he and England were one.

He thought of this land which he loved, of April sunshine and soft, scented rain; of green fields and banks of wild flowers; and the river winding past his palaces to the sea. It was no longer just an island off the coast of Europe; it was a country becoming mighty, promising to be mightier yet; and through him had this begun to happen, for he would let nothing stand in the way of his aggrandisement, and he was England.

He thought backwards over bloodstained years. Wales subdued; but a few weeks ago he had assumed the title of King of Ireland; he planned to marry his son Edward to a Scottish princess. As he reached out for treasure so should England. He would unite these islands under England and then . . .

He wanted greatness for England. He wanted people, in years to come, when they looked back on his reign, not to think of the blood of martyrs but of England's glory.

There were dreams in his eyes. He saw his fine ships. He had made that great Navy into the finest ever known. He had thought of conquering France, but he had never done so. France was powerful, and too much of England's best blood had been shed in France already. But there were new lands as yet undiscovered on the globe. Men sailed the seas from Spain and Portugal and found new lands. The Pope had drawn a line down the globe from pole to pole and declared that all lands discoverable on the east side of that line belonged to Portugal and west of it to Spain. But England had the finest ships in the world. Why not to England? War? He cared not for the shedding of England's blood, for that would weaken her and weaken Henry, for never since Wolsey had left him to govern England did he forget that England was Henry.

No bloodshed for England, for that was not the way to greatness. What if in generations to come England took the place of Spain! He had ever hated Spain as heartily as he loved England. What if English ships carried trade to the new lands, instead of war and pillage, instead of fanaticism and the Inquisition! He had the ships. . . . If Spain were weak. . . . What a future for England!

He thought of his pale, puny son, Jane's son. No! It should have been Anne's son who carried England through these hazy dreams of his to their reality. He looked at Anne's girl – eager, vital, with so much of himself and so much of Anne in her.

Oh, Anne, why did you not give me a son! he thought. Oh, had this girl but been a boy!

What would scholarly Edward do for England? Would he be able to do what this girl might have done, had she been a boy? He looked at her flushed face, at her eyes sparkling as she watched the last of the ship, at her strong profile. A useless girl!

He was trembling with the magnitude of his thoughts, but his moment of clarity was gone. He was an old and peevish man; his leg pained him sorely, and he was very lonely, for he had just killed his wife whose youth and beauty were to have been the warm and glowing fire at which he would have warmed his old body.

He reminded his conscience – better preserved than his body – that Anne had been an adulteress, a traitress, that her death was not murder, only justice.

He scowled at Elizabeth; she was too haughty, too like her mother. He wished he could shut from his mind the sound of screaming, mingling with the chanting voices in the chapel. Catherine was a wanton, a traitress, an adulteress, no less than Anne.

The ship was passing out of sight, and he was no longer thinking of ships, but of women. He pictured one, beautiful and desirable as Anne, demure and obedient as Jane, young and vivacious as Catherine. His hot tongue licked his lips, and he was smiling.

He thought, I must look for a new wife . . . for the sake of England.

I wish to acknowledge most gratefully the help I have had from the following:

Froude's *History of England, Henry VIII,* and *The Divorce of Katharine of Aragon.*
Strickland's *Lives of the Queens of England.*
Trevélyan's *History of England.*
MacDonald's *History of France.*
Salzman's *England in Tudor Times.*
The Quennells' *History of Everyday Things in England.*
Sergeant's *Life of Anne Boleyn.*
Cavendish's *Life of Wolsey.*
Hackett's *Henry VIII.*
Pollard's *Henry VIII.*
Collected Letters of Henry VIII.
Miss Manning's *Household of Sir Thomas More.*
Etc.
Where the authorities differ on various points I have used my own discretion, endeavouring to keep as near to the truth as possible.

J.P.

Jean Plaidy
The other books in her Tudor series

The Sixth Wife 75p

Katharine Parr was haunted by memories of her predecessors in
Henry's bed, but she survived her royal husband.

St Thomas's Eve 70p

A beautifully conceived story of Thomas More, who was snatched from
the peaceful life of his family home to die on the scaffold.

The Spanish Bridegroom 70p

A powerful novel that traces the story of Philip II – and of the women
who came to know him not as a cold-blooded monster, but as a
devoted father and sensual lover.

Gay Lord Robert 70p

Having captured the heart of Elizabeth I, Robert Dudley has to choose
between his monarch and the attendant wealth, and his own sweet
wife Amy Robsart. 'Consistently high standard'
JOHN O' LONDON'S WEEKLY

The Thistle and the Rose 70p

After James IV bled to death on Flodden Field, Margaret Tudor ignored
the dangers of a hasty marriage, and clashed with the power of the
Scottish court.